DESCRIPTIONARY

Also by Marc McCutcheon

The Compass in Your Nose and Other Astonishing Facts About Humans

Experts: The Media Contacts Directory

The Writer's Guide to Everyday Life in the 1800s

DESCRIPTIONARY

■

A THEMATIC DICTIONARY

When you know what it is, but not what it's called

Marc McCutcheon

Ballantine Books · New York

 Published in the United States by Ballantine Books, a division of Random House, Inc., New York, and distributed in Canada by Random House of Canada Limited, Toronto.

This edition published by arrangement with Facts On File.

Library of Congress Catalog Card Number: 92-73731

ISBN: 0-345-38256-0

Cover design by Susan Grube

Manufactured in the United States of America
First Ballantine Books Edition: March 1993
10 9 8 7 6 5 4 3 2 1

To Deanna and Kara

CONTENTS

Introduction

Descriptionary provides indispensable glossaries of terms to help you define and describe whatever subject you're writing about, be it cathedrals or castles, the stock market or stock cars. Consult *Descriptionary* whenever you're tempted to use words like *whatchamacallit, thingamajig* or *doohickey* or whenever you're at a loss for a precise word.

Let's say, for example, you need the word for a sharp, steeply descending peak, but you just can't seem to bring that word to mind. Consult the standard dictionary and you'll confront the age-old problem of how to look up a word when you don't know what that word is. The answer is, you can't. Not with a standard dictionary, anyway. Nor will a thesaurus offer much help. A thesaurus lists the synonyms of mountains, not the components of mountains.

Enter *Descriptionary* to find the word you are looking for—*matterhorn.* This book lists not only definitions and synonyms, but also all the technically accurate words used in *describing* a mountain. Words like *cairn, cordillera, couloir, Krummholz zone, ridgeback, saddle, scree* and *sierra,* to name just a few.

Through a *Descriptionary* listing you'll discover that there *is* a phrase for the leeward side of a mountain *(rain shadow)*, and there *is* a name for the beautiful light that bathes a peak at sunset *(alpenglow)*, and there *is* a word for the lateral ridge that projects from the side *(spur)* of a mountain. And unlike a dictionary, you need only look under MOUNTAINS to find them all.

The value of having related words all in one place will become obvious the more you use *Descriptionary.* For example, you may discover words that you never dreamed existed (Do you know where the *murder holes* are in a castle?), but that you might find useful in giving your work added authority or pizzazz.

Unlike most dictionaries, *Descriptionary* can be picked up and read for sheer entertainment value alone, or for inspiration or ideas.

DESCRIPTIONARY

ENVIRONMENT

GEOLOGY AND LANDFORMS

A-horizon the zone of soil, rich in organic matter, immediately below the surface.

alluvial fan deposits of alluvial material, such as rock and silt, that fan out and form an apron at a mountain's base or lower slope; the land counterpart of a river delta.

anticline a strata or mass of rock bent into an arch, the reverse of a syncline.

aquifer an underground pocket of rocks, gravel, or other permeable material through which groundwater flows.

arroyo a dried-up stream channel often found in desert areas. Also known as a wadi or wash.

asthenosphere the zone between 50 and 250 kilometers below the surface of the Earth where rock is heated and pressurized sufficiently to flow; responsible for many of the Earth's vertical and horizontal movements.

astrogeology geology of celestial bodies.

Atlantic Ridge a mountain range under the mid-Atlantic Ocean extending from Iceland to Antarctica.

badland a desert area of eroded ridges, peaks, and mesas.

bajada a series of coalescing alluvial fans at the base of a mountain or mountains.

batholith a huge igneous mass with a surface area of at least 100 square kilometers and increasing in size as it extends downward, intruded into other rock and found under or within mountain ranges. Also known as a pluton.

bedding the layers in sedimentary rock.

bedding plane the surface area separating one deposit of sedimentary rock from another of different character.

B-horizon zone of soil below the A-horizon.

bolson a flat desert valley surrounded by mountains that drains into a shallow central lake.

butte a mesa that has eroded so that its width and length are less than its height. Also known as a monument.

carbon 14 a radioactive isotope of carbon that has a half-life of 5,730 years. Used to date objects or events up to 50,000 years ago.

cast a fossilized replica of an organic object, formed when sediment fills a mold of the object.

continental drift the drifting of the continents due to spreading of the sea floor.

continental shelf a sloping shelf of a continent that extends into the ocean then descends sharply.

craton the large, generally immobile center portion of a continent.

creep the gradual sliding or slipping of soil and surface material down a slope.

crust the outermost shell of the Earth, extending about 35 kilometers down.

deflation wind erosion of unconsolidated material.

delta the large, delta-shaped deposit of silt found at the mouth of rivers.

dike a long formation of igneous rock intruded into the fissure of another rock.

dome an upfold of rock forming the shape of an inverted cup.

drumlin an elongated hill, 8 to 60 meters high and 0.5 to 1 kilometer in length, consisting of rocks and gravel deposited by a glacier.

eon the longest division of geological time, sometimes denoting two or more eras. Sometimes used to denote a span of 1 billion years.

epoch a subdivision of geological time denoting a portion of a period.

era a major division of geological time comprising one or more periods.

esker a winding ridge of stratified glacial deposits, stretching from a few meters to as long as 160 kilometers.

eustatic change worldwide change of sea level produced by an increase or decrease in amount of ocean water.

extrusive rock rock solidified from magma that has flowed out of the earth and onto the surface.

fault a fracture in strata or, on a larger scale, the Earth's crust.

floodplain an area bordering a stream that periodically floods.

fold bend or wrinkle in rock formed when rock was in a plastic state.

fold mountains mountains consisting of sedimentary rocks that have been folded over and elevated.

frost action erosional process caused by the expansion of water through repeated cycles of freezing and thawing.

geocentric pertaining to the center of the earth.

geochronology the history of the Earth as marked by geological events.

geodesy the science of the measuring of Earth's size, shape, and weight.

geomorphology the study of land forms.

geosyncline a basin in which thousands of meters of sediments have accumulated and which may ultimately become compressed into a mountain system.

Gondwanaland southern hemisphere continent thought to have broken up in the Mesozoic era and now the jumbled continents of South Africa, India, Australia, Africa-Arabia, and Antarctica.

guyot flat-topped mountain under the sea.

igneous rock rock formed from the cooling and solidification of magma.

inselberg a vestigial mountain reduced by erosion to a rocky nubbin or isolated "island," found in ancient desert areas.

intrusive rock rock that has solidified from magma after intruding into or between other rocks.

island-arc deeps deep sea trenches bordering some continents; some reach depths of 9,000 meters.

kame a steep hill of stratified glacial drift.

karst topography an area characterized by numerous sinkholes and caverns, due to limestone erosion.

Kerguelen-Gaussberg Ridge a mountain range under the Indian Ocean between India and Antarctica.

kettle a depression in a large accumulation of glacial drift caused by the melting of an ice block and later forming a lake.

koppies piles of boulders formed by the weathering and breakdown of inselbergs.

lithosphere the outermost layer of the Earth, comprising the crust and the upper mantle.

magnetic reversal a complete shift of Earth's magnetic field which, if occurring today, would make a compass needle point south instead of north. Such reversals have taken place several times throughout the Earth's history.

magnetostratigraphy determining magnetic reversals in the Earth's past by the study of magnetized rocks.

mantle the layer of earth between the crust and the core.

PRECAMBRIAN TIME			
ERA	PERIOD	EPOCH	MILLION YEARS AGO
		Recent	
	Quaternary	Pleistocene	2.5
		Pliocene	7
		Miocene	26
Cenozoic			
	Tertiary	Oligocene	40
		Eocene	
		Paleocene	65
	Cretaceous		135
Mesozoic	Jurassic		190
	Triassic		225
	Permian		270
	Pennsylvanian (Upper carboniferous)		310
	Mississippian (Lower carboniferous)		350
Paleozoic			
	Silurian		430
	Ordovician		500
	Cambrian		500

metamorphic rock rock that has changed or "metamorphosed" into other rock through heat, pressure, or chemical processes.

Mohorovicic discontinuity (Moho) the base of the Earth's crust, ranging from 8 miles under the oceans to 25 miles under the continents.

monolith slender, eroded butte that eventually topples over.

monument another name for a butte.

moraine a large accumulation of glacial till or drift.

orogeny the process by which mountains are formed

paleogeography the geography of a land as it was in the geologic past.

paleomagnetism Earth's magnetic field as it was in the geologic past.

Pangaea the huge ancient supercontinent from which all of today's continents are thought to have split off.

Panthalassa the huge, universal ocean surrounding the supercontinent of Pangaea before it divided.

peneplain a flat, or nearly flat land surface resulting from an advanced stage of erosion.

pingo a mound or hill, sometimes more than 100 meters high, formed by expanding permafrost, found frequently in arctic regions.

plate any one of the seven major lithospheric plates, consisting of either heavy basaltic ocean crust or lighter granitic continental crust, that cover the Earth and float on the plastic upper mantle.

plate tectonics the interaction and subsequent effects of the Earth's lithospheric plates colliding and scraping against one another.

pluton any mass of igneous rock formed beneath the Earth by the hardening of magma.

rift valley a valley formed by faulting.

salt dome a dome formed in sedimentary rock by the upward flow of a large mass of salt.

sea floor spreading the expanding of the sea floor along mid-ocean ridges, forming new crust.

seamount a mountain under the sea.

sedimentary rock rock formed by the accumulation and bedding of silt, gravel, rocks, and organic matter, easily identified by its distinctive layering or strata.

seismic prospecting a technique of determining the nature of an underground rock structure by setting off explosive charges and measuring the time the shock waves take to travel varying underground paths.

seismograph an instrument that records vibrations of the Earth, particularly during an earthquake.

seismology the study of earthquakes.

sinkhole an area of ground, usually consisting of limestone or some other soluble material, that collapses due to water erosion.

stratification the layering of sedimentary rock, with changes of color or texture from one bed to the next.

subduction the descending of one lithospheric plate under another.

subduction zone the area where one lithospheric plate descends beneath another, known by a high frequency of earthquakes.

syncline strata bent downward in an upside-down arch; the reverse of an anticline.

thermal plume in the upper mantle, a huge column of upwelling magma located in a fixed position and therefore known as a "hot spot." Thought to be responsible for volcanic activity.

tor a large rock or pile of rocks rising 20 to 30 feet—actually a mass of granite eroded to give the appearance of individual stones. Seen frequently in England.

DESERTS

alluvial fan the deposits of alluvial material, such as rocks and silt, that fan out at a mountain base or slope.

alluvium deposits of sand, silt, gravel, or rocks transported by water and laid down near stream or lake beds or around the base of mountains.

arroyo a dried-up stream or river bed.

badlands a barren area where soft rocks or clays become eroded, creating ridges, mesas, channels, and gulleys.

bajada the overlapping area of two or more alluvial fans, creating a wide expanse of deposited debris.

barchan a crescent-shaped sand dune, created by a one-directional wind.

Bedouin one of the groups of nomadic Arabs that roam the deserts of Syria and Arabia.

desert pavement a sand-free area of rocks and pebbles fitted together and highly polished by abrasion, forming a colorful mosaic bed. Known as gibber plain in Australia, serir in Libya, and reg in the Sahara.

erg the vast area where sand accumulates in the Sahara, opposed to the sand-free areas of desert known as reg.

gypsum the white mineral making up many of the sand dunes at White Sands National Monument in New Mexico.

inselberg a vestigial mountain reduced by erosion to a rocky nubbin or isolated "island," found in the most ancient desert areas.

mesa an eroded mountain with a flattened top and sheer rock walls; a smaller version of a mesa is known as a butte.

mirage an optical illusion caused by the refraction of light, sometimes causing the illusion of water in the desert, which in reality is only a mirror image of a shimmering blue sky.

oasis an isolated fertile area in the desert, fed by groundwater or irrigation and surrounded by lush vegetation.

phantom rain rain that passes through hot, dry desert air and evaporates before hitting the ground.

playa a level plain that can become a temporary lake after a rain.

pyramid a pryamid-shaped dune.

rain shadow the leeward side of a mountain, where little or no rain falls.

seif a sand dune elongated in the prevailing wind direction, known to grow up to 300 feet high and 1,500 feet long. Also known as a sword or longitudinal dune.

star sand dune formed by winds from several different directions, creating a stationary series of hummocks in the shape of a star.

steppe a semidesert plain devoid of trees.

transverse type of dunes characterized by ridges, giving the appearance of a series of ocean waves.

whaleback a giant sand dune that may stretch as far as 100 miles, sometimes seen in the Sahara.

DESERT VEGETATION

barrel cactus succulent of the U.S. Southwest, known for its stout, branchless barrel shape.

century plant a succulent of the amaryllis family, flowering in about 25 years but popularly thought to bloom after a century; tequila and mescal are derived from it.

cereus a night-blooming succulent that stores water in an underground container.

cholla a cactus with detachable joints that sticks to anything that brushes it, popularly known as a "jumping" cholla or "teddybear cactus."

creosote bush shrub of the American Southwest whose name is derived from the acrid odor it gives off after a rain.

elephant tree tree found in Baja, California, having a pulpy trunk serving as a water reservoir.

hedgehog cactus ground-hugging succulent producing brilliant blooms and red fruit.

ironwood a desert tree known for its unusually hard wood.

Joshua tree a member of the yucca family that grows up to 25 feet high and may live for hundreds of years, commonly found in the Mojave.

mesquite a spiny tree yielding pods and particularly dense wood.

ocotillo barbed shrub with small leaves.

paloverde desert plant with minute leaves, whose stems and branches contain chlorophyll, allowing photosynthesis even after the leaves have dropped.

prickly pear cactus a cactus growing in clumps of spiny paddles.

sagebrush an aromatic shrub commonly found throughout the U.S. Southwest.

saguaro a giant cactus known to grow as tall as 50 feet.

MOUNTAINS

adret French term referring to the side of a mountain that receives the most sunlight and warmth, used in the Alps. See also UBAC.

aiguille a needlelike peak or pinnacle.

alpenglow a peak's rosy glow before sunrise or just after sunset.

alpenhorn a very long, wooden horn used to convey signals in the Alps or other mountainous regions.

alpine any lofty or towering mountain comparable to an Alp. Also used to describe the elevation above 4,800 feet, where vegetation grows in a stunted fashion or not at all.

alpinist a mountain climber.

avalanche a dangerous fall or slide of a large mass of snow, ice, or rocks down the side of a mountain.

avalanche wind a powerful and sometimes dangerous wind generated by an avalanche.

banner cloud a stationary cloud seen frequently over the lee side of some mountains, such as the Matterhorn.

basin a U-shaped bowl created by a glacier.

butte a steep-sided mountain usually having a level top.

cairn a trail marker built of piles of rock, often used near summits.

cirque a large bowl-like or amphitheater-like hollow in the side of a mountain, carved out by snow, ice, and glacier activity.

col a saddle or low pass between two summits.

cordillera a group of parallel mountain ranges.

cornice an overhanging mass of snow or ice; it resembles an ocean wave and is known to collapse and cause avalanches.

couloir a deep, wide gully that acts as a funnel for falling snow, ice, or rocks. Also known as a coulee.

crag a steep and weathered mass of rock.

dome a type of mountain formed by the upwelling of molten rock through a crack in the earth, causing surface mounding or bulging; when the surface crust is eventually eroded away, a dome of hardened lava remains.

escarpment a sheer cliff. A scarp.

faulted block mountain a mountain formed by a massive uplifting of the earth.

folded mountain a geological term describing a mountain formed by corrugation and compression of the earth.

glacial erratics boulders left by glaciers that differ from native rocks, frequently seen near mountainous areas.

flank the side of a mountain.

hogback any sharp ridge or ridges with steeply sloping sides.

inselberg a vestigial mountain reduced by erosion to a rocky nubbin or isolated "island," found in ancient desert areas.

Krumholz "crooked wood"; the stunted vegetation caused by severe cold and wind at high elevations. The Krumholz zone is found wherever alpine vegetation has been twisted and dwarfed by the elements, usually above 4,800 feet.

massif a mountain that forms a mass of peaks.

matterhorn a sharp, steeply descending peak, usually formed by glacial erosion.

monadnock a massive rock that has resisted erosion better than surrounding rock and therefore remains standing as a large hill or small mountain.

mountain sickness an illness brought on by oxygen deprivation at high altitudes; the symptoms include headaches, nausea, and general weakness.

nunatak a mountain surrounded by glacial ice.

oread in Greek mythology, a mountain nymph.

orography the study of mountains.

piedmont pertaining to the foot of a mountain, as a piedmont glacier.

pinnacle the top or peak.

piton French term for a pointed peak.

plateau an elevation with a broad, flat top; mesa; tableland.

rain shadow the leeward side of a mountain, which receives far less rain than the windward side.

rarefied describing the thinner air supply at high elevations.

ridgeback the lengthwise crest of any ridge.

rime ice a freezing fog found at high altitudes that settles on rocks and vegetation. Also known as verglas.

saddle the lowest point between two summits.

scree loose slopes of rock fragments and boulders.

seamount a mountain under the sea.

shoulder a humpback or false ridge.

sierra a mountain range or chain.

skirt the skirting of trees around the mountain below the alpine line.

spectre of the brocken greatly enlarged shadow of a climber seen projected on a cloud or mist near a summit; named after a peak in Germany.

spur a lateral ridge projecting from a mountain.

table mountain same as mesa, plateau.

talus collective term for the boulders, rocks, and gravel fragments often found at the base of cliffs and steep slopes.

tarn a mountain lake, often occupying a cirque.

tundra the barren area where little vegetation grows, above 4,800 feet.

ubac French term for the side of a mountain that is coldest because it receives the least amount of sunlight.

VALLEYS

dale a broad, open valley, especially those found in England and Scotland.

dell a small, forested valley.

drowned valley a valley that has been submerged under water.

glen long, narrow, steep-sided valley, usually having a river or stream in the bottom.

rift valley land that has sunk between two faults, forming a long, relatively narrow valley.

vale a valley, usually with a river.

BEACHES AND SHORES

barchan a crescent-shaped sand dune.

barrier beach a large, low-lying sand bar surrounded by the sea.

barrier reef a long, narrow ridge of rock or coral running parallel to the shore and separated from the beach by deep water.

berm a large terracelike ledge or shelf of sand deposited on a beach over time.

bluff a steep embankment or headland cut or eroded by the sea.

bore a dangerous, often high wave caused by an incoming tide surging upstream in a narrowing estuary; can also be caused by the collision of tidal currents. Also known as an eagre.

crest the top of a wave.

cusps curving mounds of sand several feet long set at regular intervals, caused by the sea breaking at right angles to the beach.

detritus eroded particles of plants, sea creatures, and rocks littering the beach.

eagre high, dangerous wave caused by an incoming, surging tide upstream in a narrowing estuary.

ebb tide a receding tide.

eel grass a type of seaweed.

embayment a small bay or cove.

feldspar common mineral particle found in beach sand.

fetch the distance wind travels from one point on the sea to another and its relation to the size of waves created; the longer the fetch or distance, the bigger the waves.

flotsam and jetsam debris, goods or cargo cast or washed from an imperiled or wrecked ship.

foredune the dune or dunes immediately facing the sea; the closest dune to the shore.

foreshore the shore uncovered by a receding tide.

garnet a common mineral component found in beach sand.

graybeards any frothy or gray-crested waves.

groin a short jetty of stone or other material built at right angles to the shore to catch sand and help combat beach erosion.

headland a high point of land extending out into the water; a promontory.

isthmus a narrow strip of land extending into the water and joinging two land masses, such as a mainland beach and an island.

jetty a structure of rocks or other material extending out into the water to protect a harbor.

lee shore a shore protected from the wind, a safe haven for vessels because of its calmer sea.

littoral pertaining to the shore area.

longshore current a narrow current caused by diagonally breaking waves, known to move large quantities of sand and to build up new or existing beaches.

mermaid's purse a brown, pillowlike object with a tendril extending from each corner; the leathery egg case of a skate, commonly found on many beaches.

neap tide the minimal or low-moving tide occurring after the first and third quarters of the moon, when the sun's tidal force acts at right angles to that of the moon.

parabolic dune a U-shaped beach dune with the open end toward the sea.

plunger a wave with a convex back and a crest that falls suddenly and violently, the most common type of beach wave.

pocket beach a small sand beach contained within an embayment between two cliffed headlands.

promontory headland.

quartz the most common component of beach sand.

red tide a bloom of phytoplankton that colors the water red and releases powerful toxins that kill large populations of fish and taint clams and mussels, making them hazardous for humans to eat.

rill a small water channel formed when a beach is saturated.

riptide a cross or conflicting current making for dangerous swimming conditions.

rockweed a rock-clinging seaweed.

sandbar a ridge of sand formed along beaches.

seaboard the coastline.

shingle beach a beach consisting of small, flat stones and a steep slope descending into deep water with little or no surf, commonly seen in England.

shoal a shallow area formed by a reef or sandbar, hazardous to boating.

spiller a wave with a concave back and a crest that breaks gradually and continuously, most often seen offshore.

spindrift sea spray.

spit a narrow point of land extending into the water.

spring tides the highest and lowest tides occurring at new and full moons and reinforced by the alignment with the sun.

stack a small island of rock isolated from land and set apart from the head of a promontory.

swash a wave's shallow sweep up a beach; a receding swash is also known as backwash.

swash marks long, interlacing ripples and strands of marine debris left by a receding swash.

tombolo a sand bar connecting an island to the mainland or two islands together.

train a series of waves of the same or nearly the same size.

trough the depression or hollow between waves.

wrack any marine vegetation washed to shore; also, the wreckage of a ship cast ashore.

Types of Seashells

abalone, angel wings, baby bonnet, cask, clam, cockle, conch, cone, cowrie, horn, horse conch, limpet, mottled Venus, mussel, nautilus, oyster, periwinkle, razor, scallop, sea pen, slipper, triton, wentletrap.

SEAS AND OCEANS (*Also see* BEACHES AND SHORES)

abyssal pertaining to the depths of the oceans; the abyss.

abyssal hills submarine hills reaching 700 meters in height, smaller than seamounts.

abyssal hills province any area of sea floor completely occupied by abyssal hills.

abyssal plains extensive flat areas of the sea floor.

abyssal zone a term originally denoting any depth of ocean beyond the reach of fisherman but now generally recognized as at least 1,000 meters and extending to about 6,000 meters, the beginning of the hadal zone. Contrast with the bathyal zone.

Antarctic Circumpolar Current the world's largest ocean current, it circles the globe and feeds cold water into the Atlantic, Pacific, and Indian Oceans.

bathometer an instrument used to measure the depth of ocean water.

bathyal zone an upper layer of ocean water, extending from 100 meters to about 1,000 meters down (the actual depth varies with local light penetration), marked by a more varied and richer fauna and higher water temperature.

bathymetry the measurement of ocean depths.

bathyscaph a free-diving, deep-sea research vessel or miniature submarine with a manned observation compartment attached to its underside.

bathysphere a manned, spherical diving chamber lowered by cables.

Beaufort scale a scale in which wind speeds are assigned the code numbers 0 to 12, corresponding to "calm" to "hurricane." At sea, estimates of wind force are often taken from the appearance of the sea by the use of the Douglass sea and swell scale (*see*) in conjunction with the Beaufort scale.

benthic realm the sea bottom and all the creatures that live on it or within it.

benthic storm a muddying of water extending for hundreds of feet in all directions, caused by powerful eddies swirling over the ocean bottom and stirring up sediments, the underwater equivalent of a sand storm.

benthos the ocean floor and the organisms living on it.

bioluminescence the glow or light emitted from several different types of sea organisms, including some fish at deep levels.

caldron a large, steep-sided, pot-shaped depression in the sea floor.

cold wall the northern boundary of the Gulf Stream, where temperature of the water drops by as much as 18 degrees F outside the Stream itself.

continental shelf the submerged shelf of a continent, at its end descending sharply to the sea floor.

Coriolis effect the deflective or curving force explaining the clockwise movements of currents in the Northern Hemisphere and the counterclockwise movements in the Southern Hemisphere.

cross seas occurs when two opposing waves meet head-on and form a towering crest.

dead water a body of water, particularly common in the fjords and seas of Scandinavia, which mysteriously slows or nearly stops the forward progress of ships; thought to be caused by a thin layer of fresh water floating above a layer of denser, salty water that, when mixed, creates a train of slow-moving, submerged waves that exert a powerful drag on vessels passing over it.

deep a deep-sea plain within a large basin.

deep-scattering layer a large body of free-swimming sea organisms, such as fish or squid, that confuses sonar readings by creating a "false bottom" or false sea floor.

doldrums equatorial ocean regions characterized by flat, calm seas and little or no wind.

Douglass sea and swell scale a scale of numbers assigned to descriptive terms (0 = calm, 8 = precipitous, 9 = confused, etc.) to denote the sea's state with a second scale of numbers (0 to 99) to denote low to heavy swells.

eddy a swirling current running contrary to the main current; may be caused by two currents meeting head-on or sidelong.

El Niño a colloquial Spanish term for the Christ child given to a warm current of ocean water that moves into the coastal waters of Peru around Christmas time; the warm waters smother an upwelling of cold water normally in place here with disastrous effects on sea life and worldwide wind and weather patterns.

Emperor Seamounts the largest chain of submarine mountains in the Pacific; links with the Hawaiian Seamounts.

eustatic change a worldwide change of sea level produced by an increase or decrease in the amount of seawater.

fathom a measurement of sea depth; 1 unit or fathom equals 6 feet.

Fathometer a sonic depth finder.

fetch the distance wind travels from one point on the sea to another and its relation to the size of waves created; the longer the fetch, the bigger the waves.

fracture zones areas of submarine fractures in the Earth's crust, marked by troughs, ridges, and mountains.

Graveyard of the Atlantic approximately 220 miles southeast of Cape Hatteras, North Carolina, a site of strong local currents and storms with a powerful undercurrent running underneath the Gulf Stream, the combined causes of thousands of shipwrecks here.

graybeards choppy, frothy waves.

Gulf Stream a warm ocean current originating from the Gulf of Mexico and flowing east around Florida, up the southeast coast of the United States, then east again to the North Atlantic Current.

guyot a flat-topped mountain under the sea.

gyres the circular paths followed by oceanwide currents.

hadal zone the deepest layer of ocean water and all its fauna, starting from 6,000 meters down; usually within a trench. Also known as the ultra-abyssal zone.

hole a sinkhole or vertical chimney in the sea floor.

hydrography the study of the sea to determine its use for navigation.

ichthyology the study of fish.

internal waves submerged or underwater waves, often invisible from the surface.

island-arc deeps deep-sea trenches bordering some continents; some reach depths of 9,000 meters.

meander a bend or bulge in an ocean current that breaks off, forms an eddy, and moves off independently of the current that spawned it.

mid-Atlantic Ridge originally called the Dolphin Rise, after the ship that discovered it, a long chain of mountains under the mid-Atlantic stretching from Iceland to Antarctica.

nautical mile 6,080.2 feet.

neap tide the minimal or low-moving tide occurring after the first and third quarters of the moon, when the sun's tidal force acts at right angles to that of the moon.

nekton collective term for all free-swimming sea creatures, such as fish, squid, or whales.

North Atlantic gyre the large, rotating current of the North Atlantic. Contrast with South Atlantic gyre.

North Pacific gyre the large, rotating current of the North Pacific. Contrast with the South Pacific gyre.

ocean acoustic tomography the scientific technique of using sound transmitters and receivers to map such underwater properties as currents and eddies.

oceanography the study of the oceans.

Panthalassa the huge, universal ocean surrounding the supercontinent of Pangaea before it divided. Also known as the Tethys Sea.

pelagic region referring to the open ocean water, as opposed to the ocean floor.

phytoplankton the microscopic ocean plants living on or near the surface, the bottom of the sea's food chain.

plunger a wave with a convex back and a crest that falls suddenly and violently, usually found on or near shore.

province any region of the sea floor united by a common feature.

Puerto Rico Trough the deepest spot in the Atlantic and the second deepest in all the oceans, 30,246 feet or 9,219 meters.

red tide a bloom of phytoplankton that colors the water red and releases powerful toxins that kill large masses of fish and other sea life; the toxin released by some phytoplankton accumulates in mussels and clams and often proves fatal to humans who eat these shellfish.

ring a meander that has broken off from the main current.

sapropel black organic ooze or sludge, the source material for petroleum and natural gas, found in great accumulations under the ocean.

Sargasso Sea not actually a sea in itself but a section of the North Atlantic (a section the size of the continental U.S.) between the West Indies and the Azores, noted for its small, floating meadows of seaweed.

Sargasso weed the free-floating seaweed, known for its centuries-long life span, that occupies the Sargasso Sea.

sea elements the elements that make up the sea, primarily (96.5%) oxygen and hydrogen, followed in order of prevalence by chlorine, sodium, magnesium, sulfur, calcium, potassium, bromine, carbon, strontium, boron, silicon, and others.

sea floor spreading the expanding of the sea floor along mid-ocean ridges, forming new crust.

sea high an abyssal hill.

seamount a submarine mountain over 700 meters in elevation.

seamount chain a series of seamounts.

seascarp a long, high cliff or wall, often part of a fracture zone.

seaway a sea route taken by vessels.

seiche a wave that oscillates from a few minutes to a few hours, due to either seismic or atmospheric disturbances.

shoal a shallow area, a hazard to navigation.

sill the ridge or saddle between two basins, troughs, or trenches.

slick a patch of smooth surface water surrounded by rippled water, the result of internal wave flow but often mistaken for an effect of wind action.

sounding measurement of the depth of water.

spiller a wave with a concave back and a crest that breaks gradually and continuously, usually found offshore.

spindrift sea spray.

spring tide the very high tides occurring at new and full moons and reinforced by the gravitational pull of the sun.

submarine bar an underwater sandbar.

submarine fan a large, offshore deposit of sediment, sometimes stretching for hundreds of miles and fanning out into the shape of a cone or apron and originating from the mouth of a large river. Also known as a submarine delta or submarine apron.

submarine spring a freshwater spring upwelling from the sea floor.

terrace a steplike section of the sea floor.

Tethys Sea one of the names for the huge, universal sea that surrounded the supercontinent of Pangaea before it divided. Also known as Panthalassa.

thalassic pertaining to the oceans.

thalassophobia the fear of the ocean.

tidal bore a high, dangerous wave caused by a surging incoming tide upstream in a narrowing estuary or by the collision of tidal currents. Also known as an eagre.

trench a steep-sided, narrow depression in the sea floor.

trough same as a trench but gently sided.

tsunami a seismic sea wave, caused by an earthquake, frequently large and dangerous. Erroneously referred to as a tidal wave.

turbidity current an avalanche of sediment-laden water, moving as fast as 50 miles per hour down a continental slope into deeper water and stirring up silt; known to gouge out channels in the sea floor.

upwelling an upwelling of cold, deep water into upper, warmer water layers.

vent an opening on the sea floor releasing heat or volcanic debris.

zooplankton drifting sea worms, jellyfish, and crustaceans.

RIVERS AND STREAMS

Acheron in Greek and Roman mythology, the river of woe, one of the five rivers surrounding Hades.

alluvial fan the debris consisting of silt, gravel, and rocks deposited by rivers along the foot of mountains, creating a fanlike series of ridges.

alluvium any debris eroded by or deposited by a river, such as silt, gravel, rocks, and boulders.

aquifer groundwater, or any natural underground reservoir of water.

bar a ridgelike deposit or accumulation of sand or silt in or along a river.

benthos plants and animals inhabiting the bottom of a river.

boil a water current that "boils" or upwells into a convex mound.

braided river a river divided into several intertwining branches or "braids" created by a series of built-up sandbars or banks.

cataract a waterfall.

chute a descending and steep and narrow passage of water.

delta a triangular-shaped island of deposited sediment forming downstream at a river's mouth.

detritus particles of decaying plants and animals used as a source of food by many aquatic animals.

eddy the backward-rotating current found behind rocks or other obstructions above the surface.

estuary the body of water affected by tides, where the mouth of a river meets the sea.

fiord a long arm or river of ocean water running between high cliffs or banks.

floodplain any flat area flooded by a river that has overflowed its banks.

fluvial referring to rivers, or things found in or formed by rivers.

gradient the rate of descent over a section of river, usually measured in feet per mile.

haystacks the large, standing waves that form at the bottom of rapids wherever the current is decelerating.

hummock a flow of current forming a hump over a rock.

hydraulics the science of water in motion.

hydrologist one who studies the dynamics of water.

hydrophobia the fear of water.

levee an embankment built along the shore of a river to protect from flooding.

meander winding or wandering aimlessly, as in a river.

milldam a dam constructed across a river to raise its water level and pressure in order to turn a mill wheel.

millrace the river or channel of water used to turn a mill wheel.

moraine a huge deposit of boulders, gravel, and silt left behind by a receding glacier and responsible for damming up some rivers to form lakes.

oxbow a noose-shaped loop of water forming along the side of a river, sometimes separating from the river entirely to form a pond.

pitch a section of rapids that is steeper than surrounding sections.

pool slow-moving deep water.

riffles a shallow stream with small ripples caused by a bed of cobbles, rocks, and gravel.

rill a tiny stream or brook.

riparian referring to a riverbank area.

rooster a standing wave with a crest that turns back on itself, sometimes known to swamp canoes or rafts.

runnel a tiny brook or stream.

shoal a shallow area surrounded by deeper water.

sluice an artificial channel for conducting water.

souse hole a foamy, violently turbulent eddy; also known as a white eddy.

Styx the river of hate, one of the five rivers in Greek mythology surrounding Hades.

tongue a smooth passage of black water flowing between two rocks or obstructions, often leading into a chute.

tributary a stream or river that "contributes" its water to a larger river or body of water.

watershed the area from which a river receives its water.

LAKES, PONDS, AND SWAMPS

alkali lake a lake with a high content of sodium carbonate.

battery a large island of decayed vegetation and bottom material floated to the surface of a swamp by swamp gas; the island then floats, grows new vegetation, and gradually roots itself to the bottom.

bayou a marshy inlet or outlet of a lake or river.

benthos the plants and animals that inhabit the bottom of a pond, lake, or other body of water.

bitter lake a lake with a high content of sodium sulfate.

blowup the act of swamp gas blowing bottom material to the surface of a swamp.

boatman an aquatic insect that skims the surface of water.

bog a spongy wetland characterized by peat deposits, floating sedge or sphagnum mats, heath shrubs, and coniferous trees.

brackish describing a mixture of salt water and freshwater, such as found in coastal marshes.

caldera a crater lake formed by volcanic activity.

cirque a small circular basin lake found on the side of mountains.

detritus particles of decaying plants and animals used as a source of food by many aquatic animals.

dimictic a lake whose waters overturn twice a year, due to temperature mixing, most commonly found in temperate regions.

eutrophic a body of water with its oxygen depleted by lush vegetation.

eutrophication the gradual filling-in of a lake by the growth of vegetation and rising sediment so that it gradually becomes a pond, then a marsh, then a swamp, and then finally dries up, the natural aging process of all lakes.

eyes small areas of open water in mat-covered bogs.

fen a marsh or bog.

floaters floating plants, such as water lilies and duckweed.

foxfire luminescence caused by the decaying of wood by certain fungi, seen in swampy areas at night.

hammocks tree islands found in swampy areas.

ice scour a relatively shallow lake formed by glaciers making a shallow depression over a level area.

kettle a natural lake formed in a depression in a glacial moraine.

lacustrine like a lake or pertaining to a lake.

lagoon the pond or body of water within a coral atoll, or any small body of water connecting with a river, lake, or sea.

limnologist one who studies lakes.

limnology the study of lakes.

littoral the shore area from the waterline to the plant line.

loch Scottish word for a lake.

marsh the shallow body of water partially filled-in with vegetation, evolving from a pond.

methane marsh or swamp gas formed by decaying plants.

mire swampy ground or deep mud.

monomictic a lake whose water overturns once a year, due to temperature mixing.

moraine lake formed when rocks and debris dumped by a glacier dam a river.

morass soft, wet ground, as in a marsh or bog.

muskeg a mossy bog found in northern, coniferous forest regions.

oligotrophic a body of water with a high oxygen content and largely devoid of plants and animals.

oxbow lake a lake formed when a bend or meander in a river is cut off from the main flow and isolated.

paternoster lakes a series of glacier-carved basins filled with water and resembling a string of beads.

peat decayed and partially carbonized vegetable matter found in bogs and used for fuel.

plankton tiny plants and animals that float or swim near the surface of water.

playa lake a shallow, temporary lake that forms in a desert playa or basin.

Pleistocene the epoch of glacial activity beginning 2½ million years ago when many of Earth's lakes were formed.

pluvial lake a lake that formed during a period of increased rainfall and decreased evaporation, most notably in nonglaciated southern regions of North America during the time of the last ice age.

quaggy yielding under foot, such as boggy ground.

quagmire marshy or boggy ground.

quaking bog a bog with a floating mat of vegetation, which trembles or "quakes" when disturbed.

seiche lake oscillations, or the tilting back and forth of lake water.

slough a slow, meandering stream that drains a swamp, or a place of deep mud or mire.

sphagnum a common bog moss.

succession the natural evolution of a body of water from a lake to a pond to a marsh and to a swamp, or the gradual filling-in of vegetation and sediment that causes a body of water ultimately to dry up.

swamp a wetland characterized by moss, shrubs, and trees such as cypress and gums; a marsh with trees.

swamp gas methane produced by decaying vegetation.

tannin the chemical released from peat or tree bark that colors water brown or tealike.

tarn a mountain lake formed in a cirque.

Wisconsin ice sheet the glacial ice sheet responsible for the formation of the U.S. Great Lakes.

TREES, FORESTS, AND JUNGLES

aerial roots tiny roots that allow jungle vines to cling to host trees.

alameda a tree-bordered walk.

arborculture cultivation of trees and shrubs.

arborculturist one who practices arborculture.

arboreal pertaining to trees, or living on or among trees.

arboretum a tree garden, usually featuring several varieties.

A-story botanist's term for the crowns or top story of the tallest trees in a jungle.

bast the soft-tissued inner bark, often used in making thread and rope.

beard the bristlelike hairs sometimes found growing out of petals or leaves.

bole the trunk, especially of a large tree.

bonsai a Japanese art form of dwarfing or miniaturizing trees or shrubs by pruning.

bosky thickly treed or shrubbed.

bower a shaded recess created by boughs or twining plants.

bromeliad member of the pineapple family, a common flowering plant found growing from cracks or crevices in the trunks or branches of jungle trees.

B-story the jungle trees and plants growing below the A-story, from 30 to 110 feet up.

burl a warty protuberance found on some tree trunks.

bush rope slang for jungle vines.

buttresses the large, radiating, aboveground root systems supporting many jungle or swamp trees.

cambium the thin layer beneath a tree's bark that produces new wood cells.

canopy the uppermost story of a forest or jungle.

cauliflorous jungle plants that blossom from the side of a tree trunk or branch, commonly found in jungles.

chaparral a thicket of shrubby trees.

chlorosis a yellowing of leaves, a symptom of nutritional deficiency.

cloud forest a wet, mountain forest or jungle frequently shrouded in mist.

conifer any evergreen tree or shrub.

conk the wood-eating tree fungus found projecting from the trunks of some trees.

copse a thicket of small trees or shrubs.

crown the leaf canopy or top portion of a tree.

C-story the tree and plant growth extending from 20 to 30 feet above ground in a forest or jungle.

deciduous any type of tree that sheds its leaves seasonally.

dendrochronology the study of a tree's growth rings to estimate dates of past events, such as forest fires and droughts.

dendrologist one who studies trees.

dendrology the study of trees.

D-story in a jungle or forest, the plants growing from 10 to 20 feet high.

duct a pit or gland, usually filled with sap or resin.

Dutch elm disease a fungus that attacks elms, blocks the flow of sap, and kills the trees.

epiphytes plants that root and grow from the cracks and crevices of a tree's trunk or branches, such as bromeliads and orchids.

E-story in a jungle or forest, the undergrowth of small herbaceous plants and trees.

gall a tumor or nub appearing on the trunk or on a branch, produced and lived in by an insect.

glade a grassy, open space in a forest.

gland a secreting pore or duct exuding resin or sap.

gnarl twisted or knotty, as in an old branch.

growth rings darkened rings within a trunk, used to define the tree's age and stages of growth.

heartwood the center of a tree trunk, containing dead wood and acting as a receptacle for waste.

knot a tough, ringed section of wood marking the past location of a branch or limb.

lateral root a root that extends horizontally from the base or taproot of a tree.

liana a great, woody jungle vine, sometimes growing as thick as a man's waist, found in most jungles.

litter rotting leaves, stems, and debris of a forest or jungle floor.

midrib the central vein or nerve of a leaf.

mor a thick, acidic humus blanket consisting of decayed fir and spruce needles found on a forest floor.

nerve the principal vein of a leaf.

phloem the spongy layer of inner bark.

pitch pocket a concentration or pocket of resin in the wood of a conifer.

pollard a tree with its top cut to stimulate new root growth.

prop roots roots that curve out from a trunk above ground, giving the appearance of stilts, and commonly found in jungle areas where root systems are shallow.

ramose having many branches.

resin secretions, hard or liquid, from small chambers or passages within a tree.

sapling a young tree approximately 2 to 4 inches around.

sapwood the wood between the bark and the heartwood, paler and lighter than heartwood.

second growth growth that replaces that removed by cutting or by fire.

scurf flaky bark, as a birch.

shelterbelt in a field, a strip of trees or shrubs providing shelter from the elements.

stoma a breathing pore of a leaf.

strangler a jungle plant (figs or banyans) starting life as a vine on the branch of a host tree, then working its way down to ground level to root; in time it grows woodier and thicker and may fully encompass the host tree, sometimes killing it.

sunscald localized injury to bark or cambium caused by high heat and sunlight.

sylva collective term for the forest trees of a region.

taiga subarctic coniferous forests consisting of small trees.

taproot the first and strongest central root of a tree, usually growing straight down.

topiary trees or shrubs sculpted into fantastic shapes through pruning.

virgin forest a forest untouched by man.

windfall branches and leaves knocked off by the wind.

windthrow trees knocked over by the wind.

FIELDS AND MEADOWS

heath a large field or plain covered with small shrubs, such as heather.

moor a frequently elevated field covered with heather, bracken, and marshy areas.

pampas the grassy plains lying from the Andes in South America to the Atlantic Ocean. The equivalent of the North American prairie.

prairie grassy plains of midwest North America.

steppes grasslands of Eurasia.

tundra treeless plains with marshy areas, in Siberia and arctic North America.

veld elevated, treeless grassland of South Africa.

GLACIERS AND ICE

ablation the melting and evaporation of ice from a glacier.

arete a steep-sided, serrated mountain ridge formed by glacial erosion.

bergschrund the crevasse or group of crevasses where the head of a glacier is pulling away from a mountain wall.

calving the breaking away of large chunks of ice from the end of a glacier; in tidewater glaciers the fallen chunks become icebergs.

cirque a bowllike or amphitheater-like depression in the side of a mountain, formed by glacial movement.

cold glacier a glacier with no surface melting during summer months; its temperature is always below freezing. *Also see* WARM GLACIER.

crevasse a crack or fracture in a glacier.

dendrochronology the study of a tree's growth rings to determine past climatic changes and fluctuations in glacial movement and growth.

drift rocks and gravel carried by glaciers and eventually deposited. Also known as till.

drumlin an elongated hill consisting of compacted drift or till left by a glacier.

dust well a hole in the surface of a glacier, formed by a clump of dirt or dust that absorbs more sunlight and melts surrounding ice.

erratic a glacially deposited rock that differs from native rocks.

esker a long, winding ridge of till deposited by water flowing through a glacial tunnel.

fiord a glacier-carved valley inundated by the sea to form a long, narrow inlet. Also spelled fjord.

firn granular snow a year old or more at the accumulation zone or head of a glacier.

floe a large slab of sea ice sometimes measuring several miles across and usually consisting of many small ice chunks frozen together.

glacial lakes lake basins carved out by glacial activity. These include (1) rock basin lake: a depression ground out of bedrock; (2) cirque lake: a lake in the side of a mountain, also known as a tarn; (3) moraine lake: formed when glacially dumped drift dams a river or stream; (4) kettle lake: formed within depression in the moraines themselves. (5) ice-dammed lake: formed when the glacier itself dams a stream.

glacial pavement bedrock paved over by glaciers, leaving telltale scrapes, scars, gouges, or a polished appearance.

glaciation the covering and altering of the land by glacial ice.

glacier a mass of accumulated, compacted snow consolidating into ice. A glacier forms when more snow falls than melts over several successive seasons. Types of glaciers include (1) ice sheet: a large sheetlike glacier spreading out in all directions; (2) continental glacier: an ice sheet that covers a large portion or all of a continent, such as the Antarctic ice sheet; (3) valley glacier: a glacier confined to a valley; (4) cirque glacier: a glacier confined to a cirque; (5) piedmont glacier: the glacial portion that emerges from the mouth of a valley and surrounds the foot of a mountain.

glaciere a cave in a glacier.

glaciologist one who studies ice in all its forms.

glaciology the study of ice in all its forms.

glaciospeleology the study of glacier caves.

hanging glacier a glacier that has positioned itself on a high shelf and hangs over a valley, posing a major avalanche danger.

hanging valley a secondary valley whose floor is much higher than the larger valley into which it leads; originally formed by a small, tributary glacier leading to a larger one.

horn a sharp, steeply descending peak formed by the headwalls of three or more cirques.

ice age any cold periods in Earth's history marked by extensive glaciation and alternated with periods of warmth. The most recent ice age, extending from approximately 2,000,000 years to 10,000 years ago and consisting of at least four large-scale glacial advances, was the Pleistocene epoch.

iceblink a yellowish glare in the sky over an ice field.

icefall an avalanche of ice.

indicator a glacially transported rock which can be traced back to its original bedding ground.

kame mounds of stratified sand and gravel deposited along the edge of a glacier by glacial streams.

kettles depressions in moraines, often filling with water and creating lakes anywhere from 10 meters to 10 kilometers in diameter.

loess wind-transported silt and clay, ground fine and deposited by glaciers, and responsible for creating the rich, loamy soils and billowing topography of the Midwest.

moraine a large accumulation of glacially deposited rocks and boulders (till).

moulin a whirlpool of melted water and rocks that falls through a crevasse and carves out a shaft through a glacier to the ground. Also known as a glacier mill.

neve glacial or mountain snow that becomes ice. Also known as firn.

nunatak a hill or mountain peak surrounded by a glacier.

pack ice a large slab of sea ice consisting of chunks and floes held closely together.

permafrost permanently frozen ground.

Pleistocene epoch a period from approximately 2,000,000 years to 10,000 years ago, marked by alternating cold and warm climates and increased glacial activity. Four major glacial advances—when ice covered as much as two-thirds of North America in depths reaching 3,000 meters—are recognized during the Pleistocene epoch. From oldest to youngest, these are known as the Nebraskan, the Kansan, the Illinoian, and the Wisconsin, collectively referred to as the Ice Age.

pressure ridge a ridge of sea ice uplifted by horizontal pressure.

regional snow line the altitude in which more snow accumulates than melts in the summer season, thus eventually forming a glacier.

rock flour rock pulverized by a glacier and carried off by running water.

serac a pinnacle of ice upraised on the surface of a glacier by the intersection of two or more crevasses.

snow bridge an arch of snow formed over a crevasse.

striations scratches and grooves left on rocks and bedrock by passing glaciers.

surge a sudden or rapid advancement of a glacier, sometimes having catastrophic consequences.

till a mixture of powdered rock, gravel, and rocks carried and deposited by a glacier.

trimline the boundary between old, larger trees untouched by glacial movement and younger, smaller trees that sprouted after ice receded.

warm glacier one that reaches melting temperature during summer.

CAVES

angel's hair term for the delicate needles of gypsum found growing in some caves.

breakdown a pile of rocks in a passage resulting from the collapse of a wall or ceiling.

breathing cave a cave passage in which airstreams can be felt moving in two different directions, as in respiration.

calcite calcium carbonate mineral, frequently white and mixing with water and other minerals to form stalactites, stalagmites, and other cave encrustations.

canyon any cave passage that is at least twice as high as it is wide.

cave pearl a flowerlike mineral formation made largely of calcite; also known as a pisolith.

caver a spelunker.

ceiling pocket a small dome formation on the ceiling of a cave.

chimney a narrow, vertical shaft. Also, the term used to describe the method of climbing a vertical shaft.

claustrophobia the fear of enclosed places.

column formation created by the joining of a stalactite with a stalagmite.

conduit a subterranean passage through which water flows or has flowed in the past.

crawl speleological term for any crawl space.

crouchway any passage that can be gotten through only by crouching or stooping.

dome a large, oval opening in the ceiling of a cave passage, closed at the top.

domepit a circular shaft in the floor of a cave, usually consisting of limestone or other soluble rock that has worn away.

dripstone collective term for any stalactite, stalagmite, or other formation created by dripping water, minerals, or lava.

flowstone calcium carbonate deposit forming sheets, drapery, and coatings over rocks.

fluting vertical striations in cave walls.

gallery a large chamber or hall.

glaciere a cave in a glacier.

glaciospeleology the study of glacier caves.

gour a small basin or pool of clear water edged with calcite encrustations.

grape a calcium carbonate deposit with the appearance of a grape or pea, encrusted on a cave wall.

gypsum a white or colorless mineral deposited in caves as calcium sulfate and forming flowers, needles, cotton balls, and other shapes.

karst an area of land characterized by numerous sinkholes and caves, formed by eroded limestone.

knee crawlers knee pads used by spelunkers in crawl spaces.

lava tube cave a conduit or passage through which lava once flowed.

limestone sedimentary rock consisting largely of calcium carbonate. Most caves are limestone formations carved out by water.

master cave the main or largest cave in a group.

moon milk a white, puttylike form of flowstone.

pinched out a narrowing passage that becomes impenetrable. Also known as a pinch.

pitch a vertical shaft.

ponor the point where a stream disappears under a shelf of rock.

pothole any cave system where vertical shafts predominate.

sink a rounded depression often containing water.

sinkhole a hole, depression, or basin formed on the surface of karst land through which water drains underground.

sinkhole entrance access to a cave through a sinkhole.

soda straw a tiny stalactite in the shape of a soda straw.

speleology the study of caves.

spelunker one who studies or explores caves.

stalactite a long, tapering formation hanging from the roof of caves, formed by dripping water, calcium carbonate, and other minerals.

stalagmite conical calcium carbonate formation standing on the floor of caves; the counterpart of a stalactite.

sump an underwater passage in a cave; also known as a syphon.

troglobite any animal specially adapted to live in caves.

troglodyte a caveman.

troglophile any animal who inhabits a cave but may not be specially adapted to live there, such as a bat.

EARTHQUAKES

aftershock an earthquake that follows a larger earthquake.

dendrochronology the study of forest trees' growth rings to determine the location of past earthquakes; the rings reveal when a tree has been partially toppled over—evidence of an earthquake.

earthquake lights mysterious flickering glow seen over the ground during an earthquake, thought to be a natural reaction of rocks when stressed to the breaking point.

epicenter the area directly above the center of an earthquake, where the largest vibrations are usually felt.

fault a fracture in rock strata or, on a larger scale, in the Earth's crust.

foreshock a small earthquake that precedes a larger one by several days or weeks.

Love waves earthquake waves causing side-to-side shaking, similar to the motion of a snake.

Mercalli intensity scale a scale of earthquake intensity based on observed structural damage and people's responses in questionnaires after a local quake, unrelated to the Richter scale, which measures magnitude.

microearthquakes earthquakes with magnitudes of 2.0 or less as measured by the Richter scale, generally not felt by people.

plate tectonics the interaction and subsequent effects of the Earth's continental plates colliding and scraping up against each other, as seen most notably in the San Andreas Fault in California.

precursor a geological event that immediately precedes an earthquake, including a change in seismic velocities, groundwater levels, and a tilting of ground surface.

primary wave the fastest traveling earthquake wave, also known as a P wave or compressional wave. The roar often heard at the start of an earthquake is actually a burst of P waves reaching the Earth's surface and agitating air molecules.

Richter scale a scale determining the magnitude of an earthquake as recorded by seismographs. Due to the logarithmic basis of the scale, each whole number increase in magnitude represents a 10-fold increase in magnitude. For example, an earthquake measuring 6.7 on the Richter scale would be considered 10 times worse than one measuring 5.7.

right-lateral fault faulted ground that moves or has moved to the right as you face it.

secondary wave an earthquake wave, slower than a P wave, but more powerful. However, it cannot move through water. Also known as an S wave or shake wave.

seismic prospecting a technique of determining the nature of an underground rock structure by setting off explosive charges and measuring the time it takes the shock waves to travel varying paths; a seismic profile is attained this way.

seismograph an instrument that records vibrations of the earth.

seismology the study of earthquakes and other vibrations of the Earth.

tsunami a large ocean wave. Also known as a seismic sea wave, because most are caused by earthquake activity.

VOLCANOES

aa Hawaiian term for a rough, crumbly type of hardened lava.

basalt a dark, igneous rock produced by volcanos.

basal wreck the truncated cone left after the eruption and collapse of a volcano.

base surge the explosive reaction of lava when it meets with water.

blowhole a secondary crater or vent through which hot gas is discharged.

bomb a solidified blob of molten rock ejected from a volcano.

caldera a large crater formed by a volcanic eruption, often evolving into a lake.

cataclysm any violent upheaval, inundation, or deluge.

cinder cone a cone-like mound formed by escaping volcanic gas and ash.

clastic any broken or fragmented ejaculate; sand is a clastic material.

crater the mouth of a volcano.

dormant describing an inactive or "sleeping" volcano.

eruption volcanic explosion and release of superheated mass under pressure.

fumarole a gas or steam vent frequently found in volcanic areas.

lahar a hot mud or ash flow down a slope.

lava molten rock *after* it flows out of a volcano. *See* MAGMA.

lava tree the hollow impression of a tree that has been engulfed and destroyed by lava.

lava tube a subterranean passage or cavern where lava once flowed.

magma underground molten rock. Magma technically becomes lava when it flows *out* of a volcano.

monticule a secondary volcanic cone of a volcano.

nuée ardente French term for a fiery cloud or superheated mass of gas and clastic material, considered to be the most devastating weapon in a volcano's arsenal. The cloud fries flesh and carbonizes wood on contact and literally sterilizes the landscape. Often hot enough to melt iron and moving as fast as 100 miles per hour, it has been described as a napalm explosion and gas attack rolled into one.

obsidian volcanic glass.

pahoehoe Hawaiian term for smooth-textured lava with the appearance of congealed molasses.

paroxysm an eruption of extreme violence and magnitude.

plug the solidified lava that fills the throat of a volcano. Highly resistant to erosion, the plug may remain standing as a solitary pinnacle after the outer shell of the mountain or volcano has worn away.

pumice a light, porous stone frequently ejected by volcanoes and known for its ability to float on water.

pyroclastic flow an avalanche of hot gas and ash.

pyrotechnics sometimes used to describe the "fireworks" caused by a volcano.

seismograph a device that senses and records vibrations of the Earth.

shield volcano the largest type of volcano (such as those found in Hawaii) but the least explosive due to a low silica content.

tephra collective term for all clastic material ejected, from sand-sized particles to chunks of rock 200 feet wide.

tiltmeter a vulcanist's tool for measuring the growth rate of a bulge in the side of a volcano.

vulcanist volcanologist; an expert on volcanoes.

Vulcanus the Roman god of fire.

ROCKS AND GEMS

agglomerate a pyroclastic rock consisting mostly of volcanic bombs.

alluvium sand, mud, gravel, and rocks carried and deposited by rivers.

amber yellowish, translucent resin from coniferous trees and fossilized.

amygdule a cavity in igneous rock filled with secondary minerals, such as calcite or quartz.

anthracite a hard, lustrous, jet-black coal formed from prehistoric plant material.

anticline a folded mass of rock with strata sloping down on both sides from a common peak.

aquifer fractured rocks or unconsolidated sand or gravel pockets containing large amounts of groundwater.

basalt dark, igneous rock formed by volcanoes.

batholith a huge igneous mass—with a surface area of at least 100 square kilometers (40 square miles) and increasing in size as it extends downward—intruded into other rock and found under or within mountain ranges. Also known as a pluton.

bedrock the continuous solid rock exposed at the surface or just beneath the soil or overburden.

bituminous a soft coal formed from prehistoric plant material.

boulder train a line of boulders following the historical path of a glacier.

breccia broken pieces of rock cemented or bonded together with other types of rock.

carat unit of weight used in weighing precious gems; 1 carat equals 0.2 gram. Also the measure of the purity of gold; 24 carats equals pure, 100% gold; 18 carat gold is 75% gold and 25% alloy and so forth.

carbonaceous sedimentary rock containing dark organic matter.

chemical weathering the erosion of rocks through oxidation and hydration.

chert fine-grained quartz, once used by the Indians for spearheads, arrowheads, and knives.

conglomerate a mixture of clay, sand, pebbles, and rocks cemented together.

country rock rock into which magma has been intruded.

drift sand, gravel, and rocks deposited by a glacier.

drumlin an elongated hill of compacted rocks and gravel deposited by a glacier.

druse a crust of minute crystals lining a rock cavity.

erratics rocks or boulders transported by glaciers that differ from native rocks.

esker a long, winding ridge of sand and gravel deposited by a glacial stream.

extrusive magma ejected out onto the Earth's surface.

fault a break or large crack in a continuous rock formation.

flint fine-grained quartz.

fold a bend in rock strata.

fool's gold popular name for pyrite, a bright metallic, brassy yellow rock often mistaken for gold.

gastrolith any stone ingested by an animal to aid in digestion.

geode a globular rock with a cavity lined with minerals.

glacial pavement rock paved over by glaciers, leaving telltale scrapes, scars, and gouges, or a polished appearance.

granite a hard igneous rock composed of quartz, feldspar, and mica; a popular building material.

humus the dark, organic matter found in soil.

igneous a class of rocks formed from cooled magma or lava.

intrusive igneous rock or magma that forces its way into or between other rocks and solidifies before reaching the Earth's surface.

karst a topography of limestone consisting of numerous sinkholes or caverns.

lapidary one who cuts and polishes gemstones.

lapilli small volcanic fragments from pebble to cobble size.

limestone sedimentary rock composed of calcium carbonate.

loess deposits of windblown silt.

marble metamorphosed limestone.

matrix the natural rock in which a gemstone is embedded.

metamorphic rock rock that has been "metamorphosed" or altered by heat, steam, or pressure to form other types of rocks.

obsidian volcanic glass.

oil shale a shale rich in organic material, suitable for energy conversion.

oolites tiny round grains or pellets made of calcium carbonate or quartz found in limestones and dolomites.

ore any earth material from which useful commodities can be extracted.

outcrop a jutting out or other natural exposure of bedrock.

overburden loose rock material lying on top of bedrock.

Pele's hair threadlike strands of volcanic glass.

petrify to turn wood or any other organic material into stone by the intrusion of dissolved minerals.

petroglyph a line drawing or carving on a rock face.

petrology the study of rocks and minerals.

petrous pertaining to or resembling a rock.

placer deposit an alluvial or glacial deposit of sand and gravel that contains valuable minerals.

pumice a volcanic rock of a "frothy" appearance, often light enough to float on water.

pyroclastic consolidated volcanic fragments.

riprap a layer of broken stones applied to an embankment of a river, lake, or ocean to help prevent erosion.

sandstone rock made of sand grains bonded together.

sedimentary rock rock made by settled mud, silt, sand, cobbles, pebbles, and organic matter, forming layers or "strata."

silica the main component of sand, gravel, and silica gems.

strata layers or beds of rock.

stratification the layering of sedimentary rock.

striation a scratch or gouge on a rock caused by a passing glacier.

till rocks and gravel deposited by a glacier. A large accumulation of till is known as a moraine.

tuff rock composed of compacted volcanic ash, usually no larger than coarse gravel.

vein a rock fracture filled with minerals.

ventifact a rock that has been shaped or polished by windblown materials.

SOIL

acidic soil soil with a high hydrogen-ion content, sometimes referred to as sour.

agrology soil science.

alkaline soil soil with a high hydroxyl-ion content, sometimes referred to as sweet.

alluvium soil deposited by water such as a flowing river.

duff on a forest floor, leaf litter and other organic debris in various stages of decay.

edaphic pertaining to the soil.

eluvium soil and mineral particles blown and deposited by the wind.

frost heaving bumps and mounds produced at ground level due to the expansion of ice in soil.

gumbo fine, silty soil, found frequently in southern and western United States, and known for the sticky mud it produces when wet.

hummock a low area with deep, rich soil.

humus decomposing plant and animal tissue in and on the surface of the soil.

loam a mixture of soil consisting of sand, clay, silt, and organic matter in proportions conducive to healthy plant growth.

mesic soils that are moist but well drained.

mulch collective term for any material such as straw, leaves, or sawdust spread on soil to cut down water loss and weed growth.

mull an upper mineral layer mixed with organic matter.

peat partially decomposed plant material having little inorganic matter and accumulated in wet areas such as bogs.

pedology the study of soil.

permeability pertaining to the rate of penetration through the soil by water or other material.

pores any spaces between solid particles in soil.

stratification individual layers or beds of soils.

GARDENS

allée in a French garden, a tree-lined walk or avenue.

arbor a shaded shelter, usually made of latticework intertwined with vines, roses, or other flowers. A bower.

arboretum a type of museum where plants and trees, especially rare ones, are grown, studied, and displayed.

bedding the planting of established plants together in a group.

berceau an arched trellis over a walkway.

bonsai the Japanese art of dwarf tree and shrub cultivation. Also, the dwarf plants themselves.

bosquet a grove of trees in a park. Also known as a bosco.

bower a recess shaded with leafy plants.

boxwood evergreen shrubs trimmed to form hedges, borders, or mazes. Also known as box.

broderie plants trimmed with embroiderylike designs. Also known as ricami.

chaniwa a Japanese tea garden.

clairvoyee a windowlike hole cut into a hedge.

compost decomposing organic matter used for fertilizer.

espalier a shrub or tree trained to grow in a flat, symmetrical plane up along a wall. Also, the trellis or frame used to train a plant to grow in this manner.

greenhouse a glass or plastic-enclosed shelter for growing plants.

ha-ha a sunken fence or moat to keep out animals and to provide a clear view of a garden area.

hothouse a heated shelter for plants.

humus decomposed plant material used as fertile soil.

ikebana Japanese flower arranging.

knot garden shrubs interlaced or "knotted" together by clever trimming.

lattice an open framework used to encourage the growth of vines or other climbing plants.

mulch shredded or chipped material, often organic, placed around plants to help control weeds and to prevent roots from freezing.

parterre a French garden laid out in a pattern.

patté d'ole three avenues branching out from a central location.

pergola an arched walkway covered with vines.

piscina a fish pool in a garden, especially Roman.

pleached alley a sheltered walk formed by the interlacing tree branches of two rows of trees.

prune to trim.

rockery a rock garden.

sen-tei a Japanese water garden.

terrarium a glass or plastic box or bottle for growing small plants.

tokonoma a flowered alcove in a Japanese garden.

topiary hedges, shrubs, or trees pruned into fantastic or animallike shapes.

trellis a lattice frame for climbing plants.

FLOWERS AND PLANTS

achene a small, hard, dry, one-seeded fruit that doesn't split open or yawn when ripe, typically found with buttercups and dandelions.

aerial rootlets small rootlike branches growing out of the stems of some climbing vines.

ananthous flowerless.

annual living and growing only one year or season.

anther at the top of a stamen, the tiny organ that secretes and discharges pollen.

armed describing any plants with prickles, spines, or thorns.

aromatic spicy or sweet-smelling.

axis the main stem or center around which plant parts or branches grow.

beard a group of bristles or hairs on a plant.

biennial a plant with the cycle of two years, producing leaves the first year, and fruit or flowers the second.

blade the flat, green expanse prortion of a leaf, as opposed to the stalk.

bloom a white, powdery coating found on some fruits, such as plums, and the leaves and stems of various plants.

bract a small leaf beneath a flower or on the stalk of a flower cluster.

bud a leafy stem or flower unopened and undeveloped.

bulb an underground root or stem with fleshy scales and a food store for the undeveloped plant within.

calyx a collective term for the sepals of a flower; the leaf like green segments forming the outer circle in a flower.

catkin small flower cluster, drooping, and resembling a kitten's tail; commonly found on willow and birch trees.

chaff husks of grain separated from the seed.

chlorophyl the green pigments found in plants.

claw: the stalklike base of a petal.

corm a scaleless bulb or stem base.

corolla the collective term for the petals of a flower, separate or joined.

corymb a flat-topped flower cluster in which the outer flowers open first.

cyme: a flat-topped flower cluster in which the middle or central flowers open first.

disk flower the tubular flowers that project from the center of the heads of daisies, sunflowers, and asters.

downy a coating of short, fine, soft hairs.

drupe any fruit, such as a peach, plum, or cherry, that has a hard pit or stone.

effloresce to blossom, bloom.

elliptic shaped like an ellipse, wide in the middle, tapered at both ends, as a leaf or petal.

evergreen a plant whose leaves remain green all year.

eye a mark or spot in the middle of the flower, prominent and of a different color from the rest of the flower.

filament the stalk of a stamen.

flora the native plants of a region.

floret any small flower, also known as a floweret.

gland any secreting organ of a plant.

head a dense cluster of stalkless flowers.

heliotropic any of the various plants that turn toward or follow the sun's path across the sky; also known as the phototropic response.

horticulture the art and science of cultivating plants, particularly ornamentals.

hortus siccus a collection of dried plants; a herbarium.

humus decomposed, dead vegetation.

hydroponics a soil-less growing method in which plant roots are bathed in dissolved nutrients.

lip an irregularly sized petal on an unequally divided corolla.

midrib the main or central vein of a leaf.

nosegay a small bouquet of flowers.

ornamental a plant grown for the purpose of decoration; a beautiful plant.

palmate a plant with lobes or leaves that spread out as the extended fingers of a hand.

perennial describing a plant with a life span of more than two years; a plant that lives on season after season.

photosynthesis the process through which plants convert sunlight to energy and synthesize organic compounds from inorganic ones.

phototropism the growth or movement of a plant in response to sunlight.

pistil the female organ of a flower, which develops into a fruit.

pollen tiny grains containing the male germ cells, released by the anthers of flowering plants.

pollen count the average number of ragweed pollen grains in a specific volume of air over a 24-hour period, used as a scale to estimate the severity of hay-fever attacks.

pollen tube the thin tube emitted by a grain of pollen that infiltrates an ovule and fertilizes it.

pollinate to transfer pollen from an anther to a stigma for the purpose of fertilization.

pome any fruit with a papery, inner chamber containing the seeds, such as an apple.

pubescent leaves or stems that are covered with fine hairs.

raceme a cluster of flowers in which each flower blooms on a short stalk arising at different points on a common stem.

ray flower any of the flat, strap-shaped flowers crowning the heads of composite flowers, such as daisies. Also known as a ray floret.

rosette a circle of leaves lying nearly flat on the ground.

saprophytic living on dead organic matter, as a plant.

scurfy covered with small scales.

sepal the leaflike green segments forming under the corolla.

slip a cutting from a plant used for grafting or planting; also known as a scion.

spadix a dense spike of flowers.

spathe a large bract surrounding or enclosing a flower cluster.

spatulate leaves that are spoon-shaped with a rounded tip tapering to a stalk tip.

spike a spike-shaped cluster of flowers.

stamen the male element of a flower, consisting of a filament and pollen-bearing anther.

stigma the top of the pistil where pollen is received.

throat the opening into the tube of a corolla or calyx.

tropophyte a plant adapted to extreme weather changes.

umbel a flower cluster in which each flower stalk rises from the same or nearly the same point.

woolly covered with tangled hairs.

GENERAL METEOROLOGY

advection the horizontal movement of air, moisture, or heat.

air mass large mass of air with nearly uniform temperature and moisture.

atmospheric pressure weight of a given area of air; also known as barometric pressure.

condensation the change of a substance from a vapor to a liquid; the opposite of evaporation.

convection the transfer of heat by the vertical motion of air.

depression an area of low pressure.

dew point the temperature at which air becomes saturated; a further drop in temperature causes condensation followed by precipitation.

eye of the storm circular area of light winds and fair weather in the center of tropical storms.

front the line of divergence between air masses of different characteristics.

high a high-pressure system, usually associated with fair weather.

ridge an elongated area of high barometric pressure.

storm surge the raising of shoreline water level by storm winds; also known as storm tide or storm wave.

trough an elongated area of low pressure.

ATMOSPHERE AND SKY

air the mixture of Earth's atmospheric gasses, consisting of approximately 78% nitrogen, 21% oxygen, and small amounts of argon, carbon dioxide, neon, helium, methane, krypton, nitrous oxide, hydrogen, ozone, xenon, nitric oxide, and radon.

airglow the distinct glow or luminescence emanating from the ionosphere, caused by complex electrochemical reactions.

atmospheric layers the series of distinctive layers that make up the Earth's atmosphere; the lowest is the troposphere, followed by the stratosphere, the mesosphere, the ionosphere, the thermosphere, and the exosphere.

chlorofluorocarbon the compound, otherwise known as Freon, in aerosol cans that, when released into the atmosphere, rises to the stratosphere and depletes or destroys the Earth's protective ozone layer.

exosphere the uppermost strata of the Earth's atmosphere, starting about 300 miles up, and eventually giving way to the radiation belts and magnetic fields of space.

fata morgana complex multiple mirages seen along the Atlantic and Pacific coasts, where cliffs and rock formations may appear suspended in the sky or take on the appearance of castles and towers, caused by refraction of light in atmospheric zones of varying densities, named for the legendary castles of Morgan le Fay.

glory a bull's-eye-like rainbow or aura caused by diffraction of sunlight through a thin cloud of water vapor, most frequently seen surrounding an airplane's shadow. Also known as a corona.

green flash a light-refracting phenomenon in which the last portion or bead of the setting sun and surrounding sky flash out in a brilliant green, usually lasting only an instant and rarely seen.

greenhouse effect the trapping of heat and solar radiation in the atmosphere by excess carbon dioxide released by the increased burning of wood and fossil fuels, with the projected long-range effect of warming the Earth's overall climate and raising sea level by melting the polar ice caps.

hydrocarbon pollution pollution of the Earth's atmosphere by unburned or partially burned gasoline vapors.

hydrologic cycle the natural cycle in which water evaporates, forms clouds, and returns water back to Earth in the form of precipitation.

ionosphere the ion-rich layer of Earth's atmosphere found within the thermosphere between 50 and 180 miles up, used for reflecting radio beams in long-distance radio communication.

jet streams rivers of high-speed winds, usually traveling from west to east, from 30,000 to 45,000 feet up.

magnetosphere the huge magnetic envelope that protects the Earth from the Sun's constant blast of ions, found above the atmosphere as part of space.

mesosphere the strata of Earth's atmosphere from 30 to 50 miles up where extremely dry air drops to temperatures as low as −225°F.

mock sun a false image of the sun, often watery in appearance, formed by the refraction or bending of light by hexagonal crystals of ice in the air. Also known as a sun dog.

ozone layer the layer of ozone gas (an explosive form of oxygen) that extends from 10 to 30 miles up in the stratosphere, and protects the Earth by absorbing hazardous ultraviolet radiation from the Sun.

stratosphere the strata of the Earth's atmosphere from 10 to 30 miles up that contains the ozone layer.

thermal a rising column of warm air.

thermosphere the strata of Earth's atmosphere from 50 to 300 miles up that contains ionized bands, collectively known as the ionosphere.

troposphere the strata of Earth's atmosphere from 0 to 10 miles, where most weather systems occur.

untraviolet radiation a form of radiation from the Sun, most of which is absorbed or blocked by the Earth's ozone layer.

X rays a form of the Sun's radiation, which is filtered or absorbed by the Earth's thermosphere.

PRECIPITATION

condensation the change of a substance from a vapor to a liquid; the opposite of evaporation.

corn snow that has melted and refrozen to form a rough, granulated surface.

dew point temperature at which air becomes saturated; a further drop in temperature causes condensation followed by precipitation.

evaporation the dispersal of moisture from surface water into the atmosphere.

firn old, compacted and hardened snow; with further compacting it becomes glacial ice.

graupel falling pellets of snow; also known as soft hail.

humidity moisture content of the air.

hydrologic cycle the process of maintaining a constant water vapor content in the atmosphere by surface evaporation of oceans, lakes, rivers, and moist soil, and by transforming such moisture into a precipitable form. The three phases of the hydrologic cycle are evaporation, condensation, and precipitation.

hydrometeors collective term for all types of precipitation.

hyetography the study of rainfall.

hygrometer a device for measuring the amount of humidity in the air.

precipitation classification drizzle—fine droplets barely reaching the ground before evaporation; mist—fine droplets that usually evaporate before reaching the ground; hail—frozen droplets produced from violent convection in thunderstorms; sleet—frozen rain; rime—freezing fog.

rain gauge a device for measuring the amount of precipitation in a given time period.

saturation 100% humidity, the maximum amount of moisture the air can hold.

snow-blind temporary blindness caused by bright sunlight reflecting off snow.

snowblink a yellowish or whitish glow over a snowfield.

snowflake classification the seven basic types of snowflake are star, hexagonal plate, needle, column, capped column, spatial dendrite, and irregular.

whiteout zero visibility caused by blizzard conditions.

CLOUDS

altocumulus elliptical globular masses, forming individually, in groups, or in bands between 6,500 and 23,000 feet; also known as sheep or woolpack clouds.

altostratus bluish or grayish white sheets covering most or all of the sky between 6,500 and 23,000 feet.

cirrocumulus rippled or banded clouds, often referred to as a "mackerel sky," forming between 16,000 and 45,000 feet.

cirrostratus high, thin, white veils covering all or most of the sky between 16,000 and 45,000 feet.

cirrus detached, feathery or tufted clouds forming between 16,000 and 45,000 feet; also known as mares' tails.

clinometer device used to measure the height of clouds.

contrails vapor trails left by aircraft.

cumulonimbus arise from cumulus into towering clouds 2 to 5 miles in height, yielding rain and sometimes thunderstorms. The thunderstorm cloud itself is called a thunderhead.

cumulus individual cloud masses vertically domed with a cauliflower-like appearance; associated with fair weather.

halo apparent circle around the sun or moon, caused by the refraction of sunlight by ice crystals in high, thin cirrus or cirrostratus clouds.

incus the anvil-shaped top of a thunderhead.

mammatocumulus cloud with extreme billowing or boiling appearance, accompanying severe thunderstorms and tornado conditions.

nephology the study of clouds.

nimbostratus thick, dark gray, and shapeless cloud sheets associated with steady precipitation, forming between 6,500 and 23,000 feet.

noctilucent cloud clouds that appear to "glow" at night, caused by reflected sunlight below the horizon.

scud ragged patch broken off from main cloud by the wind.

stratocumulus heavy rolls or globular masses arranged in bands covering most of the sky, forming between 0 and 6500 feet.

stratus continuous, layerlike cloud deck, with no individual units, forming between 0 and 6500 feet.

virga wisps or trails suspended from clouds, often composed of rain that evaporates before reaching the ground.

FOG

advection fog results from air being cooled by horizontal movement; the passing cool air over warm waters cause the advection fog known as steam fog or sea smoke to form. Most maritime fogs, however, are caused by warm, humid air passing over cooler water.

dew point the temperature at which air becomes saturated; further cooling beyond the dew point causes condensation and fog.

pogonip fog containing ice crystals.

rime freezing fog that deposits frost.

WIND

Aeolus the Greek god of wind.

anemometer three-cupped device that rotates with the wind to measure its velocity.

backing wind a wind that gradually shifts counterclockwise through the compass; the opposite of a veering wind.

breeze classification light—4 to 7 mph; moderate—13 to 18 mph; fresh—19 to 24 mph; strong—25 to 31 mph; gale—39 to 46 mph; strong gale—47 to 54 mph; storm wind—55 to 63 mph; violent storm wind—64 to 72 mph; hurricane—73 mph and up (mph = miles per hour).

cat's paw any slight breeze that lightly ripples the sea's surface.

chinook any warm dry wind descending the leeward slope of a mountain; known as a foehn in Europe.

chubasco a violent squall on the west coast of tropical and subtropical North America.

cordonazo hurricane-borne wind blowing from the south on the west coast of Mexico.

Coriolis force force resulting from the Earth's rotation, which causes wind deflection.

cyclone a massive rotating storm measuring hundreds or thousands of miles across, turning counterclockwise above the equator and clockwise below, generally less violent than a hurricane.

doldrums steamy equatorial regions with dead-calm winds and flat seas.

eolian pertaining to or caused by the wind.

etecians any wind that recurs each year, or the recurring northerly summer winds over the eastern Mediterranean.

harmattan a dry, dusty wind of the west coast of Africa, blowing from the deserts.

jet stream strong winds beginning at 20,000 feet and increasing in velocity (up to 200 miles per hour or more) at 35,000 to 40,000 feet.

khamsin hot, dry southerly wind in Egypt in spring.

mistral stormy, cold northerly wind that blows down from the mountains along the Mediterranean coast.

monsoon seasonal wind that blows along the Asian coast of the Pacific from the Indian Ocean; the summer monsoon is characterized by heavy rains.

shamal a northeast wind of Mesopotamia and the Persian Gulf.

simoon scorching hot, dry wind of Asiatic and African deserts.

sirocco warm winds blowing from northern Africa to the Mediterranean area.

squall a sudden violent burst of wind, usually accompanied by rain.

tehuantepecer powerful northerly wind of the Pacific off southern Mexico and northern Central America, occurring during the cold season.

tornado extremely powerful and violent whirling funnel of air, usually less than 300 yards in width, generating winds exceeding 200 miles per hour.

trade wind a consistent wind of 10 to 15 miles per hour.

veering wind a wind that gradually shifts clockwise through the compass; the opposite of a backing wind.

windfall timber, fruit, or any debris knocked down by the wind.

wind shear the shearing force of a sudden powerful burst of wind, a noted hazard to aircraft.

wind sock cone-shaped bag hung at airports for detecting wind direction.

zephyr a west wind, or any gentle wind.

SUN

acronical occurring at sunset.

aurora the huge curtains of colored light seen shimmering in extreme northern or southern skies at night, the visible manifestation of increased solar wind particles entering Earth's magnetosphere and discharging electricity.

bright spots x-ray and ultraviolet flashes on the sun's surface closely associated with intense magnetic fields.

corona the tenuous outer atmosphere of the sun extending into space for millions of miles but generally only visible during an eclipse.

coronal holes holes in the sun's corona created by openings in the sun's magnetic fields through which are emitted high-speed solar wind particles; largely responsible for the magnetic storms on Earth.

helio referring to the sun.

heliocentric the sun as a center; relative to the sun.

heliolatry worship of the sun.

Helios in Greek mythology, the sun god who drove his chariot across the sky from east to west each day.

heliotaxis the movement of an organism in response to sunlight.

heliotherapy sunlight therapy.

heliotrope any plant that bends or turns to follow the daily path of the sun.

Horus the ancient Egyptian god of the sun, depicted as having the head of a hawk.

mock sun a false image of the sun, often watery in appearance, formed by the refraction or bending of light by hexagonal crystals of ice in the air. Also known as a sun dog.

neutrinos produced by thermonuclear fusion in the sun's core, the massless particles that have the bizarre ability to pass through physical objects such as the Earth.

penumbra the outer, lighter-colored border of a sunspot.

Ra same as Horus.

Sol the Latin name for the sun.

solar constant the total radiant energy put out by the sun on a continuing basis, specifically 1,369 watts per square meter as measured above Earth's atmosphere.

solar cycle the 11-year cycle of sunspot and solar flare activity, known to cause at its peak increased magnetic storm effects on Earth.

solar eclipse the obscuring of the sun caused by the moon passing in front of it.

solar flare a huge tongue of gasses and particles extending suddenly from a catastrophic explosion on the sun's surface to millions of miles out into space.

solar oscillations pulsations of the sun.

solar wind particles and gasses spewed from the sun at speeds exceeding 1 million miles per hour.

sunspots dark spots on the sun's surface having a lower temperature than surrounding areas and strongly associated with intense magnetic fields.

sunspot cycle *see* SOLAR CYCLE.

umbra the dark, central region of a sunspot.

variable star a star with varying luminosity that includes our sun but to only a slight degree.

MOON

albedo the percentage of received sunlight that is reflected off the moon's surface; approximately 7%. (Earth: 40%)

Apennines a 600-mile-long mountain range with summits rising to 15,000 feet (one mountain, Mt. Huygens, rises nearly 20,000 feet) located in the moon's northeast quadrant.

apogee point of the Moon's orbit farthest from the Earth.

Clavius a large, walled plain 145 miles across in the moon's southeast quadrant; from its depressed interior, walls rise 17,000 feet.

Copernicus one of the most famous of the moon's craters, 56 miles in diameter.

crater an impact hole or depression caused by a meteor.

craterlet a small crater.

cusp a horn of the crescent moon.

domes mound structures resembling pingoes on earth.

gibbous moon phase between half and full.

harvest moon full moon that rises early in the evening nearest the time of the autumnal equinox, September 23, providing illumination for the fall harvest.

hunter's moon the first full moon phase following the harvest moon, providing illumination for hunters.

Luna in Roman mythology, the goddess of the moon.

lunacy a form of insanity once thought to be caused or influenced by the moon.

lunar eclipse darkening of the Moon caused by the Earth coming between it and the Sun.

lunar month period between successive new moons, 29 days, 12 hours, 44 minutes.

mare a large dark plain on the moon, once thought to be seas in ancient times. Collective term: maria.

Mare Imbrium the "sea of showers," a circular plain or mare 700 miles in diameter in the northeast quadrant of the moon.

nimbus moon moon with apparent halo or nimbus, caused by the refraction of light by ice crystals in high, thin cirrus or cirrostratus clouds of Earth.

Oceanus Procellarum the "ocean of storms," largest of all lunar mares, with an area of 2 million square miles.

perigee point of Moon's orbit nearest the Earth.

phases dark side facing Earth—new moon (more accurately defined as a "black" moon because it is invisible from Earth); first sliver of moon—crescent; thickened crescent—first quarter; between half and full—gibbous, followed by full and a reversal of phases.

ray an impact line or crack radiating out from some craters.

selenian pertaining to the moon.

selenography the study of the moon's surface.

selenology the study of the moon.

Tranquillitatis, Mare the "sea of tranquility," sight of moon landings, in northwest quadrant.

Tycho the famous rayed crater, 54 miles in diameter, in the southeast quadrant.

wane shrinking phase of moon.

wax growing phase of moon.

SPACE

aphelion a planet or comet's point of orbit farthest from the sun.

apogee point of the moon's orbit farthest from the Earth.

asterism a group of stars not belonging to any of the 88 recognized constellations.

asteroid a minor planet.

astronomical unit mean distance of the Earth from the sun, 92,900,000 miles, used to express the distances of other celestial bodies.

big bang the massive explosion theorized as the birth of the universe, about 18 billion years ago.

binary a double star, each revolving around the other.

black hole a star that has exploded and collapsed to infinity, leaving behind a gravity force so powerful that nothing can escape it, including light.

bolide a bright meteor or fireball.

comet a celestial body composed of ice and rock.

constellation a group of stars, named for an object, animal, or mythical figure.

cosmic ray a stream of ionizing radiation from space, largely of protons, alpha particles, and other atomic nuclei.

culmination when a celestial object reaches its greatest possible altitude above Earth's horizon.

curvature of space according to Einstein's theory of gravitation, massive objects in space, such as a stars cause space to curve and light to bend.

declination the position of a star as located through the combination of two coordinates, east-west (right ascension) and north-south of the celestial equator.

Doppler effect the shift of spectral lines due to a body's motion toward or away from an observer; astronomers can tell by the Doppler effect if a distant star is moving toward or away from us.

eclipse the obscuring of one celestial body by another, most notably when the moon passes in front of the sun.

ephemeris a chart or table providing the future positions of celestial bodies.

evolved star an older star that has converted most or all of its store of hydrogen into helium.

flare star a star whose brightness can increase by as much as 2 to 100 times in a matter of minutes, then return to normal.

galaxy a large grouping of stars, sometimes consisting of billions of stars; also known as an island universe.

light year an astronomical unit of measurement, specifically the distance light travels in a year, 5,880,000,000,000 miles.

magnitude a scale for measuring the apparent brightness of celestial bodies, the brightest being negative, zero or first magnitude, the dimmest visible to the naked eye being sixth magnitude.

meridian the great circle passing through the sky's zenith and touching the north and south horizons.

meteor a rock or metal fragment entering Earth's atmosphere and burning up, popularly known as a shooting star.

meteorite a meteor that isn't completely burned away by the atmosphere and strikes the Earth.

Milky Way the galaxy of stars we live among.

nebula a huge cloud of dust and gas in space.

neutron star the superdense core of a collapsed star, also known as a pulsar.

northern lights popular term for the aurora borealis, the shimmering curtains of colored light seen in the far north and thought to be caused by sunspot activity.

nova an erupting star that temporarily brightens.

occultation the obscuring of a small or distant celestial body by a larger or closer body, such as the moon passing in front of a star or planet.

opposition a planet reaches opposition when it is 180 degrees away from the sun.

orbit the path followed through space by a celestial body.

parsec astronomical unit of measurement equaling 3.26 light years.

perigee point in the orbit of the moon closest to Earth.

perihelion point of a body's orbit nearest the sun.

proper motion the motion of the stars not related to the Earth's rotation.

pulsar a neutron star that emits X rays or other types of radiation.

quasar the most distant objects in the universe, irregular in brightness and highly mysterious.

radiant point where meteor showers appear to originate in the sky.

red giant a cool, red star many times larger than our sun.

satellite object or moon in orbit around a planet.

scintillation twinkling of stars caused by heat in Earth's atmosphere.

shooting star a meteor.

solar wind a stream of gas continually blown out from the sun at hundreds of kilometers per second.

solstice position of the sun when farthest north (summer solstice) or farthest south (winter solstice) in the sky.

star a fiery sphere of gas; a sun.

sunspot cooler area visible as a dark spot in the surface of the sun.

supernova an exploding star that increases its brightness thousands of times, dimming only after a period of months.

supernova remnant a nebula surrounding the site of an earlier supernova explosion.

symbiotic stars two stars so close together they exchange gases and mass.

terminator dividing line between the illuminated and dark portions of the moon or planets in crescent phase.

variable star a star with a varying magnitude or brightness.

white dwarf a tiny star comparable to the size of the Earth but with a mass equal to the Sun's and a density a million times that of water.

zenith the point in the sky directly overhead.

zodiac the 12 constellations aligned along the ecliptic through which the sun, moon, and most of the planets travel.

zodiacal light a hazy band of light consisting of dust illiminated by the sun and sometimes seen from Earth.

CONSTELLATIONS

The Constellations of the Northern Hemisphere

Latin Name	English Equivalent
Andromeda	Andromeda
Aquila	Eagle
Auriga	Charioteer
Boötes	Herdsmen
Camelopardalis	Giraffe
Canes Venacti	Hunting Dogs
Cassiopeia	Cassiopeia
Cepheus	Cepheus
Coma Berenices	Berenice's Hair

Corona Borealis	Northern Crown
Cygnus	Swan
Delphinus	Dolphin
Draco	Dragon
Equuleus	Filly
Hercules	Hercules
Hydra	Sea Serpent
Lacerta	Lizard
Leo Minor	Little Lion
Lynx	Lynx
Lyra	Lyre
Ophiuchus	Serpent Bearer
Pegasus	Pegasus
Perseus	Perseus
Sagitta	Arrow
Scutum	Shield
Serpens	Serpent
Triangulum	Triangle
Ursa Major	Great Bear (Big Dipper)
Ursa Minor	Little Bear (Little Dipper)
Vulpecula	Fox

Constellations of the Southern Hemisphere

Latin Name	English Equivalent
Antlia	Air pump
Apus	Bird of Paradise
Ara	Altar
Caelum	Sculptor's Tool
Canis Major	Greater Dog
Canis Minor	Lesser Dog
Carina	Keel
Centaurus	Centaur
Cetus	Whale
Chameleon	Chameleon
Circinus	Compasses
Columba	Dove
Corona Australis	Southern Crown
Corvus	Crow
Crater	Cup
Crux	Southern Cross
Dorado	Swordfish
Eridanus	River
Fornax	Furnace
Grus	Crane
Horologium	Clock
Hydrus	Water Snake
Indus	Indian
Lepus	Hare
Lupus	Wolf
Mensa	Table
Microscopium	Microscope
Monoceros	Unicorn
Musca	Southern Fly
Norma	Square
Octans	Octant
Orion	Orion (the Hunter)
Pavo	Peacock
Phoenix	Phoenix
Pictor	Painter
Piscis Austrinus	Southern Fish
Puppis	Poop (deck of Argo)
Pyxis	Mariner's compass
Reticulum	Net
Sculptor	Sculptor
Sextans	Sextant
Telescopium	Telescope
Triangulum Australe	Southern Triangle
Tucana	Toucan
Vela	Sail
Volans	Flying Fish

Constellations of the Zodiac

Latin Name	English Equivalent
Aquarius	Water Bearer
Aries	Ram
Cancer	Crab
Capricornus	Goat
Gemini	Twins
Leo	Lion
Libra	Scales
Pisces	Fishes
Sagittarius	Archer
Scorpius	Scorpion
Taurus	Bull
Virgo	Virgin

COMETS

aphelion the point of a comet's orbit farthest from the sun.

coma the cloud of diffuse gas and fine particles that surrounds and obscures a comet's nucleus.

dust tail a relatively short, curving tail that has a high silica content that, reflected by sunlight, gives off a yellowish hue. Also known as a type II comet. See ION TAIL.

elliptical orbit an orbit that traces the path of an ellipse.

exotic ice small components of comet ice made from methane, ammonia, carbon dioxide, or other nonwater source.

fireballs fiery meteors that crash to Earth and are frequently mistaken for comets.

fluorescence the radiating of blue fluorescent light from electrically charged carbon monoxide molecules in a comet's coma.

gegenschein "counterglow"; the faint, eerie glow seen in the sky exactly opposite from where the sun has set, caused by reflected light from a huge ring of cometal debris enveloping the sun. Same as the zodiacal light, but seen in the opposite side of the sky.

hyperbolic comet a distant comet that follows a hyperbolic orbit.

ion tail a long, straight tail colored blue by electrically charged molecules absorbing blue light from the sun and reradiating it to Earth. Also known as a type I comet.

long-period comet a comet that takes centuries to complete its orbit.

nucleus the ball of dirty ice at the center of a comet.

Oort Cloud a vast, unseen repository of over 1 trillion comets surrounding the sun at a distance of 50,000 astronomical units.

perihelion the nearest point to the sun in a comet's orbit.

perturbation a disturbance in the orbit of a comet by the gravity force from a nearby planet or other large body.

rocket effect the melting and vaporizing of comet ice, forming jets of gas and a rocketing effect that disturbs the orbital path of the comet.

short-period comet a comet that completes its orbit every few years.

zodiacal light same as gegenschein, but seen in the opposite side of the sky, above where the sun has set.

ANIMALS

DOGS

apple head a rounded or domed skull, as in the English toy spaniel.

apron the longer hairs found on the chest of many breeds.

badger-marked a coat consisting of gray or black markings on white.

bat ear an erect ear that is rounded at the top, as in a bat.

bay a deep bark.

beard the tuft or long hairs under the chin.

belton a coat consisting of blue or orange and white hair.

bitch female dog.

blaze a white or light-colored streak running along the center of the head.

blond a coat of light yellow or yellowish tan.

bobtail a tail cut short; also known as a docked tail.

brindle a streaked or spotted coat.

brisket part of the chest between and slightly behind the forelegs.

brush a bushy tail.

bullbaiting the long-banned English sport of dogs tormenting bulls.

butterfly nose a nose with two or more different colors.

buttocks the rump.

button ear an ear that folds forward toward the eye, as in a fox terrier.

canine of the dog family, or like a dog.

chops the lower cheeks, especially in a bulldog.

cloddy thickset and low to the ground, as a Scottish terrier.

cobby short-bodied.

crest the ridge of the neck.

crop trimming the ears to make them pointed.

cynology dogs and their history.

cynophobia fear of dogs.

dam mother.

dewclaw one of the short vestigial claws or digits, the remnant of a first toe, now useless.

dewlap the loose fold of skin hanging from the neck of many breeds, such as the bulldog and the bloodhound.

dingo wild dog of the Australian outback.

distemper an infectious disease of puppies and young dogs, caused by a virus.

docking the surgical removal or shortening of the tail.

eyeteeth the two projecting canine teeth in the upper jaw.

fawn a pale, yellowish brown coat.

feather the fringe of hair along the tail and back of the legs.

feral a domesticated dog living in the wild.

fiddle front forelegs that are bowlegged.

frill a fringe of hair around the neck.

grizzle a coat that is gray or streaked with gray.

gun dog any of the sport hunting dogs, such as a setter, pointer, spaniel, or retriever.

hackles neck and back hairs that bristle when a dog is angry or fearful.

harlequin a white coat with black spots of various sizes.

haw the red membrane inside the lower eyelid.

heartworm a worm parasite living in the bloodstream of infected dogs.

hock the backward-bending joint in the hindleg, corresponding to the ankle in humans.

leather the external part of the ear.

litter the puppies brought forth at one birth.

liver a reddish brown or purplish brown coat.

lop-eared loose, dangling ears.

lupine of the wolf family, or like a wolf.

mane the long hair growing from the top or sides of the neck, as in a collie.

mange skin disease caused by parasitic mites, causing hair loss.

mask the dark shading found on the muzzle of several breeds.

mongrel a mixed breed.

muzzle the mouth, nose, and jaws. Or a leather device harnessed around the jaws to prevent biting.

overshot a jaw in which the top extends over the bottom.

pack a group of dogs.

pads the cushioned padding of the feet.

parti-colored a multicolored coat.

pastern the foreleg part between the knee joint and the foot.

pedigree a dog known to have descended from parents of the same breed for at least three generations.

philocynic one who loves dogs.

pied a coat covered with patches or spots of two or more colors.

pit fighting the outlawed gambling sport of dogfighting in a small pit or arena.

plume a feathery tail.

pompon the sculpted tufts of hair left on a dog's tail or body when artistically clipped, especially in poodles.

prick ear an ear carried stiffly erect, as in a German Shepherd.

quarter to range over a field in search of game, especially of pointers, setters, and spaniels.

rabies an infectious viral disease affecting the central nervous system, characterized by convulsions, choking, and an inability to swallow.

racy long-legged and slight of build, as a greyhound.

ringtail a tail that is carried in a tight curl or ring.

ruff a collar of thick hair around the neck.

sable a black or dark brown coat.

screwtail a short, kinky, twisted tail, as in a Boston terrier.

sire father.

snipy a sharply pointed muzzle.

spay removing the ovaries of the female.

swayback a sagging back.

tie a male and female locked together in intercourse for up to 30 minutes, allowing for adequate ejaculation of sperm.

tulip ears erect ears with a slight forward curve.

undershot a jaw in which the bottom extends further out than the top.

walleye a blue eye.

whelp to give birth to pups; also, one of the young of a dog.

whip a stiff, straight tail, as in a pointer.

withers part of the back between the shoulder blades.

CATS

Abyssinian a long, lean breed of cat known for its athleticism and playful personality.

ailurophile one who loves and admires cats.

ailurophobe one who fears cats.

allogrooming the grooming of one cat by another.

Angora Turkish breed of cat with long, silky hair.

blaze a white marking running from a cat's forehead to its nose.

blue coloring from blue gray to slate gray.

brush a bushy or plumelike tail.

Burmese breed related to the Siamese, having short, usually sable-colored hair.

calico coloring combination of tortoiseshell and white.

calling the cries of a sexually receptive female.

caterwaul the cry of cats at mating time.

catnip plant member of the mint family, known for its intoxicating effect on cats.

catus a tabbylike wildcat from North Africa, thought to be the primary ancestor of all domestic cats.

chinchilla coloring in which the tips of the hairs are black or another color, with the under hairs being white or pale.

cobby a low-lying body on short legs.

dam mother.

FAIDS Feline Acquired Immune Deficiency Syndrome, a weakened immune system often brought on by feline leukemia.

feline relating to or resembling a cat.

feral a domestic cat living in the wild.

flehmen response the trancelike sneer often seen on the face of a male as it smells the urine of a sexually receptive female.

frill the hairs framing the head in longhaired breeds, also known as the ruff.

fur ball hair swallowed by a cat and forming a mass or "ball" in the stomach.

ghost markings faint markings on solid-colored cats, revealing a slight trait of another breed.

gloves white patches on the feet, also known as mittens.

haw the third eyelid, or nictitating membrane.

heat the sexually receptive period of a female.

laces white markings on the back of the rear legs of some cats.

lilac coloring of pale pinkish gray, also known as lavender.

litter a group of newborn kittens.

locket a white or other-colored patch under the neck.

lordosis the crouched position of a sexually receptive female inviting entry by the male.

Manx breed of cat without a tail, thought to have originated in the Orient.

milk-treading the "kneading" motion of a kitten's paws in an attempt to stimulate the flow of its mother's milk, the behavior often seen in adult cats kneading the bellies of their human owners.

moggie a mongrel cat.

muzzle the jaws and nose of a cat.

pads the soles of the paws.

Persian breed originating from Asia, known for its flattened or pushed-in face and thick, luxuriant fur.

pheromones chemical substance released in urine and from certain areas of the skin to mark territories or attract the opposite sex.

piebald black-and-white coloring.

pricked ears that point high and erect.

purebred a cat descended from a long line of its own kind.

queen female cat used for breeding.

rangy long-limbed and long-bodied.

Rex breed of cat known for its curly hair and higher body temperature than other cats.

sheath the protective covering over retracted claws.

Siamese angular, elongated breed known for its noisy personality.

sire father

spaying the neutering of a female cat.

spraying the male's act of marking with urine.

tabby a striped cat.

tapetum the light-reflecting layer at the back of a cat's eyes, aiding nocturnal vision, and causing the "glowing" effect at night.

tom a male cat.

Tonkinese a crossbreed of the Burmese and Siamese.

vibrissae the highly sensitive whiskers and hairs found on the cheeks, on the chin, over the eyes, and at the back of the front legs, thought capable of detecting subtle air currents and the movement of prey in the dark.

whip long, thin, tapering tail, typically found on a Siamese.

BIRDS

aerie the lofty nest of a predatory bird, such as an eagle.

altricial chicks born blind and helpless.

alula the group of feathers on the leading edge of a wing, used to keep airflow smooth as the wing is tilted; also known as a false wing.

Anseriformes the order of ducks, geese, and swans.

anting the practice of some birds of placing live ants within their feathers, thought to help rid them of parasites.

apterous without wings, wingless.

aquiline a curved or hooked beak, as an eagle's.

Archaeopteryx the earliest known bird, semireptilian in nature, and living about 150 million years ago.

avian referring to birds.

aviary an enclosure or large cage for birds.

barbs the filaments emanating from the shaft of a feather.

bevy a group or flock of quail.

brood to sit on eggs; also, a group or flock of chickens.

brood spots bare patches on a bird's underbody that are rich in blood vessels and used for warming or incubating eggs.

Charadriiformes birds that live in ravines or cliffs, such as gulls, terns, and plovers.

charm a group or flock of finches.

chattering a group or flock of starlings.

clutch a group of eggs.

cob a male swan.

colony a group or flock of gulls.

Columbiformes the order of doves and pigeons.

comb the fleshy crest on the head of a fowl.

contour feathers the feathers involved in flying and regulating body temperature.

convocation a group of eagles.

covey a group of grouse.

craw the crop or enlargement of the gullet, aiding in digestion.

cygnet a young swan or swan chick.

dancing grounds a mating area where ritualistic displays are performed, especially of grouse and prairie chickens.

down the soft, fluffy plumage beneath the feathers and on the breasts of many birds.

drake male adult duck.

egg tooth a small tooth or nubbin in the upper jaw, used by newborn chicks to chip their way out of an egg, it disappears soon after birth.

exaltation a group or flock of larks.

falconer one who trains hawks or falcons to hunt for them.

Falconiformes the order of vultures, falcons, hawks, and eagles.

falconry the sport of hunting game with trained falcons or other birds of prey.

fall a group of woodcock.

fledgling a young bird with new feathers.

flight a group of doves or swallows.

flyway a migratory route.

gaggle a group or flock of geese.

Galliformes the order of grouse, quail, and turkeys.

gander a made adult goose.

gizzard the second stomach in which food is finely ground, thought to compensate for a bird's lack of teeth.

herd a group or flock of swans.

host a group or flock of sparrows.

keel the breastbone ridge in which most of the flight muscles are attached.

molt to shed the feathers.

murder a group or flock of crows.

murmuration a group or flock of starlings.

muster a group or flock of peacocks.

nye a group or flock of pheasants.

ocellus one of the eyelike spots in the tail of a peacock.

ornithologist one who studies birds.

ornithology the study of birds.

parliament a group of owls.

Passeriformes birds that perch, such as larks, swallows, wrens, sparrows, and warblers, the largest order of birds.

pecking order the order of dominance and submission among a bird group, where a dominant bird may peck a weaker or lower status bird, but not vice versa; once established there is little fighting among the group.

pen a female adult swan.

Phoenix the bird of legend that rises from the ashes.

pigeon milk a thick, cheesy secretion of pigeons and some parrots, fed to the young.

pinnate like a feather or having the shape of a feather.

precocial chicks who are born mature and become active almost immediately.

Procellariiformes the order of albatrosses, fulmars, and petrels.

Psittaciformes the order of parrots, parakeets, cockatoos, macaws, and lovebirds.

quill one of the large, strong flight feathers in the wings or tail.

raptor a bird of prey, such as a falcon, hawk, or eagle.

roc the giant elephant-carrying bird of Arabian legend.

rook a crow

rookery a nesting or breeding colony of sea birds.

ruff a projecting collar of hair or feathers around the neck.

siege a group or flock of herons.

skein a group of flying geese.

static soaring floating on a warm thermal of air.

Strigiformes the order of owls.

syrinx the throat component producing a bird's voice, located at the lower end of the trachea.

talon a claw of a bird.

team a group or flock of ducks.

thermal a rising current of warm air, used by birds to carry them aloft.

wattle the naked, fleshy component hanging from the neck, as in a turkey.

HORSES

appointments equipment and clothing used in a specific riding event.

bag the breast of a mare.

barrel between the fore and hindquarters, the trunk of a horse.

bloom term for describing a healthy-looking coat.

breastplate leather section strapped across a horse's chest that attaches to the saddle to prevent the saddle from sliding back.

bridle head harness used to control a horse, which includes a bit, cheek straps, crownpiece, throatlatch, headband, and reins. Also, a quick or violent upjerk of the horse's head.

bridlewise an experienced horse who can be signaled to change direction by laying the bridle reins on the side of the neck the rider wishes to turn.

broodmare a mare used for breeding.

broomtail a long, bushy tail.

cannon the leg portion between the hock and the fetlock.

canter a three-beat gait or slow gallop.

cantle the rear of an English saddle.

capriole an upward leap with no forward motion, as made by a trained horse.

caracole a half-turn.

caste the condition in which a horse lying down in its stall is unable to get up again without assistance.

cavesson the noseband and headpiece of an English bridle.

cayuse an Indian pony.

cheek strap bridle straps that run down the side of the cheeks to hold the bit or noseband.

cinch the girth of a Western saddle.

cob a stocky, thickset, short-legged horse.

cold back term describing a horse who bolts or bucks when a saddle is placed on its back, due to inexperience or improper training or treatment.

colt a male under age 4.

conformation a horse's overall physique or build.

conformation fault any one of several faults found in a horse's build.

coronet the upper portion of a horse's hoof.

cow-hocked a conformation fault in which the hocks are too close together.

crest the top of a horse's neck.

crop a short, looped whip used in horseback riding.

croup the rump of a horse.

crownpiece the bridle leather fitted over a horse's head and attached to the cheekpieces.

currycomb a horse comb.

cutting horse a horse trained to cut cattle out of a herd.

dam the mother of any horse.

dishing a movement in which the horse's feet swing sideways at a trot, usually a fault of pigeon-toed animals.

dobbin a gentle farm horse.

draft horse a powerful horse bred for farm work, such as plowing.

draft horse a powerful horse bred for farm work, such as plowing.

dressage a refined riding style in which the horse's gait is smooth, flat, and graceful.

driving horse a horse trained or bred to pull wagons or sulkies.

equerry one who acts as a stableman or supervisor of horses in a royal or other household.

equestrian pertaining to horses or horse riding; one who rides horses.

equine pertaining to or resembling a horse.

fetlock the projection and accompanying tuft of hair growing above and behind the hoof, or the joint marked by this projection.

filly a female under the age of 4.

foal a newborn horse of either sex.

forehand the front portion of a horse, including the head, neck, shoulders, and front legs.

forelock bangs or hair of the horse's mane that hangs down over its forehead between its ears.

forging when the rear hoof strikes the toe of the front hoof during a trot, caused by overextending.

fox trot walking with the front legs and trotting with the rear.

gait the speed and sequence of a horse's walk or run; gaits include, walk, trot, canter, gallop, and rack.

gallop a full run.

gambado a low, four-legged leap, as when frolicking.

gaskin part of the hind leg between the stifle and the hock.

gee a traditional horse command meaning to "turn right." Opposite of haw.

gelding a castrated or gelded male.

girth the band of leather that goes around the trunk of a horse for fastening the saddle to its back.

grade a horse of unknown ancestry.

green horse an untrained horse.

green jumper a horse that has been taught to jump.

gymkhana a riding meet or competition.

hack a horse used for pleasure riding.

hackney a horse of English origin, characterized by its flexed knee gait.

halter a rope used for leading or tying a horse.

hand a unit of measurement in which 1 hand equals 4 inches, used to estimate the size of a horse.

haw traditional horse command meaning to "turn left."

headband part of the bridle over the horse's forehead to prevent the bridle from slipping back.

heat the breeding period of a mare, occurring at three-week intervals and lasting about five days.

hock the joint located in the lower leg corresponding to the ankle in humans.

hogback a horse having a rounded back, opposite of a swayback.

hunter a horse bred or trained for hunting, usually a fast runner and strong jumper.

jib a nervous or fidgety movement sideways or backwards.

jodhpurs horse-riding pants made of heavy cloth, fitting tightly at the knees and ankles, and typically worn with ankle-height leather boots, also known as jodhpurs.

jog a slow trot.

lather sweat.

lope canter.

lunge a long rope or rein used for breaking or training a horse by leading it around in a circle.

manger a horse's wooden feeding trough, attached to a stall wall.

mare an adult female.

mudder a horse that runs well on muddy ground, as on a wet racetrack.

muzzle collective term for the nose, nostrils, lips, and chin of a horse.

neigh the cry of a horse.

noseband a strap fitted over the nose as part of Western bridle.

offside the right side of a horse when viewed from behind; also known as the far side.

paddock a fenced-in area adjoining a barn where horses may play.

palfrey a post-horse, or a small horse fit for ladies.

passade a backward movement.

pastern part of the foot between the fetlock and the hoof.

Pegasus the great steed of Greek mythology, known for its wings.

piaffe a test of horsemanship, in which the horse trots slowly in place.

pigeon-toed a horse that stands with its toes pointed inward.

pillion a pad used for an extra rider behind the saddle.

poll the top of a horse's neck behind the ears.

pommel the front portion of the English saddle, fitting over the withers.

posting in English riding, the rising and falling of the rider with the rythmn of the trot.

rack a difficult four-beat gait or gallop used by a trained horse.

rear to stand up on its hind legs.

rip a wornout or useless horse.

sire father of a horse.

span horses in a matched pair.

splayfoot a horse who stands with its toes pointed outward.

staggers a cerebrospinal disease characterized by loss of coordination, staggering, and falling down.

stallion adult male used for breeding.

steed a spirited horse, or a horse ridden in combat.

stifle the joint corresponding to the knee in humans.

swayback an old horse with a swayed back.

volt a partially sideways gait or step.

whinny a low and gentle neigh.

withers highest part of the back, between the shoulder blades.

Horse Breeds

American Albino a Nebraska-bred, snow-white horse having pinkish skin and blue, brown, or hazel eyes.

Andalusian an elegant, good-natured Spanish horse, usually gray or bay and standing about 15 hands high.

Appaloosa bred for endurance by the North American Plains Indians, a horse widely recognized by its spotted rump.

Arab greatly admired, highly prized desert horse, known for its distinctive forehead bump shaped like a shield. Since it has fewer ribs and lumbar bones than other breeds, it has a distinctively short back. The Arab is said to "float" when it runs.

Boulonnais French breed; heavy but elegant, bred today mostly for its meat.

Camargue the ancient breed of southern France; thought to be that depicted in prehistoric cave paintings at Niaux and Lascaux.

Cleveland bay a popular coach-pulling or harness horse in the 19th century. Noted for its stamina and strength, it is now used as a hunter or as a show jumper.

Clydesdale a strong, heavy draught horse of Scottish breed; the Budweiser beer mascot.

cob not a breed, but a stocky short-legged horse noted for its jumping ability.

Connemara intelligent Irish breed known for its sure-footedness and jumping ability.

Criollo Argentine, dun-colored horse having great endurance and toughness, ridden by the gauchos of the pampas.

Dale hardy, calm Yorkshire breed, usually black, and used for riding or as pack horses.

Dartmoor a small, European riding horse having a kind, quiet nature.

Dutch Draught massive, strong horse with a docile temperament, originally bred for farm work.

Exmoor British pony breed, thought to have pulled Roman chariots, now used as fox hunters and children's riding pony.

Fell European breed similar to a Dale but smaller, used as a hunter and as a riding horse.

French Trotter Normandy-bred harness-racing horse, known for its stamina.

Friesian Holland-bred work and harness horse.

Hack a refined, well-mannered and elegant show horse having a trot that appears to "float." The term *hack* is also used to denote any type of riding horse.

Hackney a high-stepping, trotting horse of English breed. It was once a popular carriage horse.

Hannoverian German breed renowned for its show-jumping ability.

Highland Scottish pony breed used for hunting, jumping, and everyday riding.

Holstein a tall (16 to 17 hands high) German carriage horse noted for its intelligence, today used in show jumping.

Hunter European breed ridden in England and Ireland for hunting purposes. It is noted for its agility, stamina, and jumping ability.

Icelandic a small, muscular horse known for its toughness and agility.

Irish Draught a large horse bred for farm work and riding.

Knabstrup ancient Denmark breed having a distinctive spotted coat (like a dalmation), widely used as a circus horse.

Lipizzaner world famous leaping white horse breed of Vienna.

Lusitano courageous and agile Portuguese horse ridden by Portuguese bullfighters.

Missouri Fox-Trotting Horse Missouri breed that is able to walk with its front legs while trotting with its rear legs, thus producing a smoother ride that can be maintained over long distances.

Morgan American breed, strong and muscular, and noted for its versatility.

Norwegian Fjord Norwegian breed once ridden by the Vikings, noted for its sure-footedness and straight-cut mane.

Palomino a golden horse having a cream-colored mane and tail.

Percheron strong, massive draught horse of French breed; it usually has a dark, dappled coat.

pinto not a breed but a color type—brown and white or black and white. A popular horse with Indians. Also known as paint.

Quarter Horse widely popular American racing breed, famous for its ability to gallop at high speed over short distances. Its speed, agility, and intelligence has also made it a favorite cutting horse among cowboys.

Saddlebred Kentucky-bred, all purpose ranch and show horse, noted for its superior rack gait.

Selle Français French, all-purpose horse, often bred for its jumping ability.

Shetland thick-set, short-legged, small (40 inches high; Shetlands are not measured with hands) horse having great strength and a shaggy mane.

Shire very strong, heavy draught horse of English breed.

Standardbred an American harness-racing horse.

Suffolk a strong, heavy draught horse having especially powerful shoulders; an English breed usually chestnut in color.

Tarpan ancient Russian breed thought to be nearly extinct.

Tennessee walking horse an American, all-purpose breed.

Thoroughbred a long-distance racer, usually a cross of an Arabian stallion and an English mare.

Welsh Mountain Pony small breed (no bigger than 12 hands) resembling an Arab and noted for its hardiness and intelligence.

Welsh Pony larger version (13 hands) of the Welsh Mountain Pony.

Horse Colors and Markings

albino white with pinkish skin and blue or hazel eyes.

appaloosa a distinct breed noted for its spotted rump.

bald a white streak on a horse's face and covering one of its eyes. See blaze.

bars black stripes on the legs of some breeds; also known as zebra striping.

bay a reddish brown with a black mane and tail.

blaze a broad, white streak running from between the eyes to the muzzle.

blood bay a deep red bay.

buckskin beige with a black mane and tail; may or may not have an eel stripe.

buttermilk another name for a palomino.

calico a spotted or piebald color; a pinto.

California sorrel reddish gold.

chestnut chestnut, bronze, or coppery. Also known as sorrel.

claybank yellowish cross of a sorrel and a dun.

cremello cream albino with pink skin and blue eyes.

dappled spotted or mottled.

dun beige with a beige or brown mane and tail.

eel stripe a dark stripe extending from the withers to the tail.

flaxen chestnut-colored with a white or cream-colored mane and tail.

grulla bluish gray or mouse-colored. Also known as smokey.

medicine hat black speckles found on mustangs, considered good luck by the Indians.

moros bluish.

paint patterned irregular white with colored areas. Same as pinto.

palomilla milk white with white mane and tail.

palomino light tan or golden with an ivory or cream-colored mane and tail.

piebald black and white.

pinto a piebald; a spotted or irregularly marked horse. Also known as paint or Indian pony.

race a crooked blaze on the forehead.

roan bay, chestnut, or sorrel sprinkled with gray and white.

sabino light red or roan with a white belly.

skewbald patches of white over any color except black. Sometimes humorously referred to as a stewball.

snip a white marking along the nostril.

sock white on leg below the fetlock.

sorrel chestnut or brown.

star small white marking between eyes.

stocking any white extending above the fetlock. See sock.

zebra dun dun-colored with a dorsal stripe and stripes on its legs.

LIVESTOCK

abomasum the fourth or true stomach of a ruminant, where most digestion takes place.

anthrax a frequently fatal blood poisoning disease of cattle, sheep and goats (pigs to a lesser degree) that is highly contagious and characterized by dark, bloody discharges from mouth, nose, and rectum.

barn itch see mange.

boar a male hog or pig.

buck a male goat.

bummer an orphaned lamb.

cloven-footed having feet that are divided by clefts.

crossbreed a cross between two different breeds; a hybrid.

crutching trimming the wool around a ewe's udder and flanks.

cud regurgitated food chewed a second time and then reswallowed, part of the natural digestive process of ruminants.

cull to remove an undesirable animal from a herd.

dam the mother of a pig, cow, sheep, or goat.

dewlap a loose fold of skin hanging from the neck of some breeds of cattle.

disbud to dehorn. Also known as polling.

dock to bob or cut off the end of a tail, usually of lambs for health reasons.

double-muscled said of some breeds of cattle having bulging muscles and a rounded rump, supplying greater meat than other breeds.

elastration livestock castration method in which a rubber band is wound tightly around the scrotum to cut off blood supply, ultimately resulting in the death, drying up, and falling off of testicles.

estrus the period when the female is sexually receptive to the male; in heat.

ewe a female sheep.

facing trimming the wool around a ewe's face.

farrow a litter of pigs; to give birth to such a litter.

flock book a register of purebred sheep.

flushing a method of increasing fertility in animals by increasing their feed a few weeks prior to breeding.

fodder various coarse foods for livestock, including cornstalks, hay, and straw.

foot-and-mouth disease a long-lasting, highly contagious disease of cloven-footed animals, characterized by fever and blisters in the mouth and around the hooves and teats.

gilt a young pig who has not yet produced a litter.

grade an animal with one purebred parent and one grade or scrub.

heat the period of sexual arousal in animals, especially the estrus of females.

heifer a young cow yet to produce young.

herdbook a register of cattle or hog breeds.

hircine like a goat; pertaining to goats.

kid a young goat.

listeriosis a brain inflammation disease in cattle, sheep, and goats associated with corn silage feeding and characterized by facial paralysis, a "depressed," look, and aimless wandering or walking in tight circles. Also known as circling disease.

mange dermatitis caused by mite infestation, characterized by itching and wrinkling of the skin. Also known as barn itch.

mastitis a common disease of sows, dairy goats, and dairy cattle, characterized by reduced milk flow, fever, lack of appetite, and a hot, swollen udder.

omasum the third stomach of a ruminant.

ovine like a sheep; pertaining to sheep.

pedigree a written record or registry of the ancestry of an animal. Also, the registration certificate itself.

poll to cut off or cut short the horns.

pollard an animal with its horns removed.

porcine like a pig; pertaining to a pig or hog.

purebred an animal from two registered parents or from unmixed descent.

ram a male sheep.

reticulum the second stomach of a ruminant.

rumen the first stomach of a ruminant.

ruminant any of the cud-chewing animals, including cattle, sheep, and goats.

ruminate to chew the cud.

rutting sexual excitement of the male.

scours severe diarrhea suffered by livestock animals.

scrub an animal of unknown or unimproved ancestry.

service to stud.

silage green fodder stored in a silo.

sire to father an animal; the father of an animal.

sow an adult female pig.

stud a male used for breeding.

swine collective term for pigs or hogs.

switch the hairy part of a tail.

taurine like a bull; pertaining to bulls.

tribe closely related families within a breed.

ungulate any animal with hooves.

yearling a newly born sheep or goat.

Beef Cattle Breeds

Angus originated in Scotland, black, polled head.

Barzona originated in Arizona, red, specially adapted to arid ranges.

Beefalo a crossbreed of a buffalo, a Charolais, and a Hereford, cold-tolerant, lean, flavorful meat, originating in the United States.

Beef Friesian bred in the United States, black and white, broad-muzzled and strong-jawed.

Beefmaster bred in Texas, red or varied colors, horned or polled, good milk producer.

Belted Galloway originally bred in Galloway, Scotland, black with brown tinge or dun-colored with white belt encircling the body, polled head.

Brahman originating in India, gray, red, or spotted, long face with drooping ears, hump over shoulders, pendulous dewlap, heat- and insect-tolerant.

Brangus bred in Oklahoma, cross between Brahman and Angus, black, polled, sleek coat, crest on neck.

Charbray Texas bred, creamy white, horned, slight vestigial dewlap.

Charolais French bred, creamy white, horned, large size.

Chianina Italian origin, white, horned, black tongue, the largest cattle in the world, with some bulls weighing in at 4,000 pounds.

Devon English breed, red, horns with black tips.

Dexter Irish breed, black or red, horned, small with short legs.

Fleckvieh German breed, red and white-spotted, horned.

Galloway Scottish breed, black or black with brown or red tint, or dun; polled, long, curly hair, cold-tolerant.

Gelbvieh German breed, golden red or rust, horned, large, long, and muscular.

Hays Converter Canadian breed, black with white face, white feet and white tail, good milk producers.

Hereford English breed, red with white markings and white face, horned, thick hair.

Indu Brazil Brazilian breed, light gray silver, dun or red; long, drooping ears, horns pointing up to the rear, hump on shoulders, pendulous dewlap.

Limousin French breed, wheat or rust, horned, long and large, abundant meat.

Lincoln Red English breed, cherry red, horned or polled, long, fast-growing, good milk producer.

Maine-Anjou French breed, dark red with white, long, large, fast-growing.

Marchigiana Italian breed, grayish white, small horns, large-bodied.

Normande French breed, dark red and white, spectaclelike patches over eyes, large-bodied.

Norwegian Red Norwegian breed, red or red and white, horned, good milk producer.

Piedmont Italian breed, white or pale gray, double-muscled, excellent meat producer.

Polled Hereford Iowa breed, red with white markings, white face, polled, thick coat of hair.

Polled Shorthorn U.S. breed, red or white, or red and white, polled.

Ranger U.S. breed of the western range, all colors, hardy, medium-sized.

Red Angus Scottish breed, red, polled, similar to black Angus.

Red Brangus U.S. breed, cross of a Brahman and Angus, broad head, sleek coat.

Salers French breed, deep cherry red, horned or polled, hardy, fast-growing, and large.

Scotch Highland Scottish breed, red, yellow, silver, white, dun, black, or brindle; long, shaggy hair, cold-tolerant.

Shorthorn English breed, red, white, or red and white; short horns curving inward.

Simmental Swiss breed, red and white-spotted, white face, horned, fast-growing, excellent meat and milk producer.

Sussex English breed, mahogany red, mostly polled, high yield of lean meat.

Tarentaise French breed, wheat-colored or light cherry or dark blond, small-bodied.

Texas Longhorn Texas breed, all colors; long, spreading horns, long head, long legs.

Welsh Black Wales breed, black, mostly horned, good milk producer.

Dairy Cattle Breeds

Ayrshire Scottish breed, cherry red, mahogany, brown, or a mixture of these colors; mostly horned.

Brown Swiss Alps breed, solid brown, black nose and tongue, horned, strong and muscular, placid.

Dutch Belted Dutch breed, black and white with white belt extending around the body, horned.

Guernsey originating on the Isle of Guernsey, fawn with white marks; horned, yellow milk.

Holstein-Friesian Netherlands breed, black and white or red and white; broad-muzzled, strong-jawed.

Illawarra Australian breed, red or red and white, horned.

Jersey originating on the Island of Jersey, usually fawn-colored with or without white marks; large, bright eyes.

Milking Shorthorn English breed, red, white, or red and white, horned.

Sheep Breeds

American Merino Spanish breed, white, strong flocking instinct, produces fine wool.

Black-faced Highland Scottish breed, black or mottled, horned, produces carpet wool.

Cheviot Scottish breed, white with black nose, polled, no wool on head or legs.

Columbia Wyoming and Idaho breed, white, polled, face free of wool.

Corriedale New Zealand breed, white with or without black marks, polled.

Cotswold English breed, white or white with gray specks, polled, wavy ringlets and curls, long wool.

Debouillet New Mexico breed, white, horned or polled, produces fine wool.

Delaine Merino Spanish breed, white, rams with horns, strong flocking instinct, produces fine wool.

Dorset English breed, white, horned or polled.

Finnsheep Finnish breed, white, head free of wool, usually polled; medium wool.

Hampshire English breed, deep brown, polled, large, produces medium wool.

Leicester English, white with or without bluish tinge, polled.

Lincoln English breed, white with or without black spots, polled, the largest of all sheep breeds with rams weighing in as much as 375 pounds; produces heavy fleece.

Montadale U.S. breed, white, polled, head free of wool, produces medium wool.

Oxford English breed, gray to brown, polled, large.

Panama U.S. breed, white, polled, long wool.

Shropshire English breed, dark-faced, polled, dense wool on head.

Southdown English breed, light or dark brown, polled, produces medium wool.

Suffolk English breed, black head and legs, polled, no wool around head or ears, produces medium wool.

Targhee U.S. bread, white, polled, open-faced.

Tunis North African breed, reddish brown to light tan, polled, long drooping ears, no wool on head, produces medium wool.

Goat Breeds

American La Mancha U.S. breed, all colors, short or no ears, hornless, milk producer.

Angora Turkish breed, white face, legs and mohair, horned or polled, long locks of mohair.

French Alpine French Alps breed, multicolored, horned or polled, large and deerlike, milk producer.

Nubian a cross of Indian and Egyptian breeds, multicolors, horned or polled, long and droopy ears, Roman nose, milk producer.

Rock Alpine U.S. breed, multicolored, horned or polled, milk producer.

Saanen Swiss breed, white or creamy, horned or polled, large, milk producer.

Swiss Alpine Swiss breed, chamoise or solid brown, polled, erect ears, milk producer.

Toggenburg Swiss breed, fawn to dark brown with white stripes on face and white on legs, polled, milk producer.

Pig Breeds

American Landrace Danish breed, white with small black spots.

Berkshire English breed, black with white feet.

Chester White U.S. breed, white with or without small bluish spots.

Conner Prairie U.S. breed, all colors, large litters.

Duroc U.S. breed, red, medium size.

Hampshire Kentucky breed, black with white belt encircling body; white face.

Hereford U.S. breed, red with white face, similar coloring to that of Hereford cattle.

Lacombe Canadian breed, white, floppy ears.

Managra Canadian breed, white, lop-eared, large litters.

Poland China U.S. breed, black with or without white spots; droopy ears.

Spotted U.S. U.S. breed, spotted black and white.

Tamworth English breed, red with or without black spots.

Wessex Saddleback English breed, black with white belt encircling body.

Yorkshire English breed, white with or without black freckles; long-bodied.

WHALES

ambergris a waxy substance formed in the intestines of sperm whales and used in the manufacture of perfumes.

baleen in baleen whales, the comblike plates hanging from the palate that strain out small fish and crustaceans.

baleen whale a toothless whale that eats plankton.

blowhole the nostril(s) on top of the head.

breaching jumping out of the water.

calf a juvenile whale.

cetacean the order of fishlike aquatic mammals, including whales, dolphins, and porpoises.

cetology the study of whales, porpoises, and dolphins.

dorsal fin the stabilizing fin on the top of the back of many species.

finning said of a whale on its side slapping the water with its fin.

flukes the horizontal tail fins.

Jonah Biblical character who survived three days in the belly of a whale.

lobtailing raising the flukes high out of the water then slapping them down hard on the water.

mysticeti "mustached whales"; the suborder of baleen whales, with 10 species known.

odontoceti the suborder of toothed whales, with more than 66 species known.

orca the species of killer whales.

pod a school of whales.

right whale once considered by whalers as the "right" whale to catch because it is slow and floats when dead.

scrimshaw the decorating and carving of whale bones and teeth.

sonar the use of sound by some whales to locate objects obscured in dark or murky water; echolocation.

sounding diving.

spermaceti a waxy, fatty substance taken from the heads of sperm whales and used for making candles, ointments, and cosmetics.

spy-hop sticking the head upright out of the water.

stranding stranding or beaching in shallow waters.

zeuglodon a prehistoric forerunner of the whale from the Eocene epoch, 50 million years ago.

INSECTS AND SPIDERS

abdomen the posterior segment of an insect's body.

antennae sensory appendages used for probing or smelling.

arachnid the class of insects with four pairs of legs, including spiders, scorpions, mites, and ticks.

arachnoid resembling a spider's web, or pertaining to arachnids.

bristle any stiff hair arising from the body.

carapace a hard covering of the body of some insects, for protection from predators.

caste system a social system in which each insect in a colony has a clearly defined role. Termites, for example, have four castes: workers, soldiers, kings, and queens.

cephalothorax the first segment of a spider's body, including the head and thorax.

cercus a sensory appendage on the abdomen.

chitin the main component in an insect's outer structure or exoskeleton.

claspers part of the male sex organs in some insects, two clasping appendages used to hold the female during mating.

colony a community of insects that work together for each other's benefit.

compound eye multifaceted eyes consisting of several individual lenses.

cryptic coloration coloration that provides camouflage to help an insect blend into its surroundings without detection by predators.

diapause a period of suspended growth or development during the life cycle.

dimorphism having two different forms within the same species.

elytra the hard wing covers of beetles.

entomology the study of insects.

exoskeleton the exterior supporting structure of the insect body.

fang similar to a sharp tooth, the chelicera of a venomous spider.

formic acid the acid injected or sprayed by some ants as a defense.

fritiniency insect noises.

gallmakers insects that cause plants or trees to grow warty protuberances or "galls" around them.

herbivores insects that feed exclusively on plants.

histamine one of the main components of the poison injected by the sting of a wasp.

honeydew the sugary excretion of aphids and some other insects.

insectivore any animal or insect that eats insects.

instar any single stage of insect development in which the insect is transformed from one form to another; some insects have more than a half dozen such instars or stages.

larva the wormlike form of a newly hatched insect before metamorphosis.

leg segments from top to bottom these are the coxa, the trochanter, the femur, the tibia, and the footlike tarsus.

mandible the upper jaw of an insect, used in chewing.

mesothorax the middle segment of the thorax from which are attached the second pair of legs.

metamorphosis the transformation process that changes one form of an insect into another, such as a caterpillar becoming a butterfly.

metathorax the third or last segment of the thorax from which the third pair of legs are attached.

mimicry imitation of shape, colorization, or size of an insect (usually poisonous) by an insect of another species for the purpose of deceiving predators. (For example, a nonpoisonous insect with the exact appearance of a poisonous insect.)

mine a shaft dug by ants or caterpillars.

molt the shedding of skin to allow for metamorphosis or growth.

mouthparts a vast array of tiny mouth instruments, depending on the species, from a sucking proboscis to tools for boring, sawing, cutting, clamping, injecting, and piercing.

nymph the young of insects that undergo incomplete metamorphosis.

ocelli tiny simple eyes (usually three) between the compound eyes.

omnivores an animal or insect that eats plants and animals.

ovipositor a long, tubelike organ on the abdomen of females for depositing eggs.

palp an elongated sensory organ associated with the mouthparts.

parthenogenesis reproduction by unfertilized females with the unfertilized eggs usually developing into one-sex young.

pedipalp on the cephalothorax of a spider, a leglike appendage used for guiding food to the mouth, but also used by the male to transfer sperm.

pheromones scents discharged by some insects to attract members of the opposite sex.

prehensile adapted for grabbing and holding, as the legs of a praying mantis.

proboscis a slender, tubular feeding instrument.

prothorax the first of the three thoracic segments, from which the head and first set of legs are attached.

pupa the inactive stage of metamorphosis following the larval stage and preceding the adult stage.

pupate to become a pupa.

pulvillus the adhesive foot lobe moistened by secretion that allows insects to cling to smooth surfaces.

spinneret one of the two to four pairs of nozzlelike outgrowths in the rear of a spider through which silk is extruded for the construction of webs.

spiracles respiratory holes in the sides of the abdomen and thorax. Also known as stigmata.

stridulation insect chirping sounds, especially that of crickets and grasshoppers.

thorax the segment of the body between the head and abdomen, which in itself consists of three subdivisions (prothorax, mesothorax, metathorax).

untrasounds whistles, tones, and other insect noises pitched too high for humans to hear.

venation the arrangement of veins in the wings that help distinguish orders, families, and genera of insects.

warning coloration conspicuous colorization of some insects that warn predators of the presence of poison or other hazard.

MOTHS AND BUTTERFLIES

abdomen the hind body portion; consisting of 10 segments.

androconia special scales on the abdomen, legs, or wings of males that release sex pheremones.

antenna the sensory appendages on the head.

bird wings the largest of all butterflies, with wingspans as long as 12 inches in some species.

chorion the shell of an insect egg.

chrysalis the pupa of a butterfly, the form reached between the larval or caterpillar stage and the winged butterfly stage.

cocoon the silky protective casing made by a caterpillar while in the chrysalis stage.

cocoon cutter a ridgelike growth on the head of some species that enables them to cut their way out of a coccoon when they're ready to emerge.

compound eye similar to other insects, each eye consisting of several individual units or facets.

cremaster at the tip of the abdomen of a pupa, an extension used to attach the pupa to the place of pupation.

crepuscular active or flying during the twilight, as some species of moths and butterflies.

dagger moths a family of moths recognized by black daggers or dashes on their gray brown forewings.

dash a sharp, short black line on the forewing of many species; also known as a dagger.

diapause a period of suspended growth or development during the life cycle.

diurnal flying or active during the day, as most butterflies.

epiphysis the leaflike appendage on the foreleg, thought to be used for cleaning mouthparts and antennae.

eyespots the eyelike spots found on the wings of some species, thought to frighten birds away. Also known as ocelli and the orbicular spot.

forewing the front wing, attached to the mesothorax.

frass the excrement pellets of caterpillars.

frons the front of the head, between the eyes and above the mouthparts.

geometers evolving from inchworms, the second largest family of moths, recognized by their slender bodies and small to medium overall size.

gossamer wings a family of butterflies not belonging to the skipper family but recognized for their small size and bright wings with metallic or iridescent hues.

hawk moths a family of medium to very large moths with robust bodies, narrow wings without ocelli, long probosci, and a hovering flight similar to a bird. Also known as Sphinx moths or hummingbird moths.

Hesperiidae the butterfly family of skippers.

hind wing the back wing, attached to the metathorax.

instar in the larval stage, the period between molts.

larva the caterpillar stage.

Lepidoptera the order of moths and butterflies.

lepidopterist an entomologist specializing in moths and butterflies.

Lycaenidae the butterfly family of gossamer wings.

mandible the chewing mouthpart of a caterpillar.

Megathymidae the butterfly family of giant skippers.

mesothorax the midportion of a thorax on which the forewings and middle legs are attached.

metamorphosis a transformation of the structure or nature of an organism resulting in a radically different organism; the transformation of a caterpillar to a butterfly, for example; the transformation of Lepidoptera from an egg to a larva to a pupa to a butterfly.

Microlepidoptera a family of medium to small moths recognized by long, slender legs and T-shaped appearance when at rest (its rolled wings are kept folded at right angles to the body.)

nectaring the act of gathering nectar by butterflies.

nocturnal active or flying at night, as most moths.

Nymphalidae the large family of brush-footed butterflies, with forelegs reduced to useless brushes.

ocelli collective term for all eyelike spots found on a wing.

orbicular spot a round or elliptical spot resembling an eye in the middle of a forewing in some species.

Owlet (Noctuid) moths the largest family of moths, with some 20,000 species worldwide, recognized by gray brown coloring with a complex pattern of lines and spots and obscured orbicular spots.

Papilionidae the butterfly family of swallowtails, recognized by their spectacular colors, usually yellow and black, and with wings shaped like a swallow's.

pheromones a sex attractant released by male and female.

Pieridae the butterfly family of whites, sulfurs, and marbles, each resembling its namesake.

proboscis the double-coiled tongue, which is extended to suck up nectar or water.

prothorax the first or frontmost of the three thoracic segments to which the forelegs are attached.

pupa the quiet, metamorphic stage that grows into a butterfly or moth.

reniform spot a kidney-shaped spot on the forewing, similar to an orbicular spot.

skippers once thought to be a link between butterflies and moths, actually a small, quick-flying, short-winged butterfly.

sphragis a device deposited by a male moth on the abdomen of a female to prevent her from mating with another male.

spinneret the silk-spinning organ near the mouth of a caterpillar.

thorax the middle of the three body sections consisting of the prothorax, the mesothorax, and the metathorax.

underwings a large family of moths, recognized by their hind wings, which are all black or brightly colored with black bands; the forewings resemble the bark of trees.

venation the pattern formed by branching veins in wings, helpful in identification.

TERMS FOR ANIMAL GROUPS

Animal	Group	Male	Female	Young
Ant	colony			
Antelope	herd	buck	doe	kid
Ass	herd/drove	jack	jenny	colt/foal
Badger	cete	boar	sow	cub
Bear	sloth	boar	sow	cub
Bee	swarm/hive	drone	queen	
Buffalo	herd	bull	cow	calf
Camel	herd/flock	bull	cow	foal/calf
Cattle	herd/drove	bull	cow	calf/heifer
Deer	herd	buck/stag	doe	fawn
Dog	pack	hound	bitch	puppy/whelp
Elephant	herd	bull	cow	calf
Elk	gang	bull	cow	calf
Ferret	business	dog	bitch	
Fish	shoal/school			
Fox	earth/skulk	vix	vixen	cub
Frog	army			tadpole
Goat	herd/tribe	billy	nanny	kid
Horse	herd/stable	stallion	mare	colt/foal/filly
Kangaroo	troop			joey
Leopard	leap	leopard	leopardess	cub
Lion	pride/troop	lion	lioness	cub
Monkey	troop/tribe			
Moose		bull	cow	calf
Mouse	nest			
Mule	span/barren/rake			
Otter		dog	bitch	
Ox	herd/drove/yoke			
Pig	litter/herd	boar	sow	piglet/farrow/shote
Polecat		hob	jill	
Rabbit	nest	buck	doe	bunny
Rhino	crash			
Seal	herd/pod			cub
Sheep	drove/flock	ram	ewe	lamb

Animal	Group	Male	Female	Young
Squirrel	dray			
Tiger		tiger	tigress	cub
Toad	knot			
Turtle	bale			
Whale	gam/pod	bull	cow	calf
Wolf	pack/rout	dog	bitch	cub/pup/whelp

Human Body and Mind

SKELETAL SYSTEM

Bones, Names of

astragalus the anklebone that connects with the heel bone.

atlas the first vertebrae of the neck.

axis the second vertebrae (below atlas) of the neck.

calcaneus heel bone.

caluarium the top of the skull.

capitate the large center wrist bone.

carpal eight small bones of the wrist: greater multangular, lesser multangular, capitate, hamate, lunate, navicular, triquetrum, pisiform.

clavicle the curved shoulder or collarbone above the first rib.

coccyx the vestigial tailbone.

concha a small, scroll-shaped bone of the outer side of the nasal cavity.

coxae hipbone.

cranium the skull, consisting of the occipital bone, two parietal bones, two temporal bones, a sphenoid bone and an ethmoid bone.

cuboid a small, cubelike bone in the foot.

cuneiform the small bones of the foot.

ethmoid the T-shaped nasal bone at the front of the skull.

femur the thighbone, the longest and heaviest bone in the body.

fibula the outer leg bone extending from the knee to the ankle.

frontal the flat bones forming the front of the skull and parts of the orbit and nose.

humerus the long arm bone between the shoulder and elbow.

hyoid the U-shaped bone in front of the neck above the larynx.

ilium the upper part of the hipbone.

incus in the middle ear, the anvil.

ischium part of the hipbone.

lacrimal the smallest bone of the face.

malar cheekbone.

malleus in the middle ear, the hammer.

mandible the lower jawbone.

maxilla the upper jawbone.

metacarpal the five slender bones of the hand.

metatarsal the five bones of the foot.

nasal the bridge of the nose.

navicular the small, boat-shaped bones of the hands and feet.

occipital the lower back of the skull.

palatine one of two bones making up the hard palate, nose and orbit.

parietal the two bones making up the sides and roof of the skull.

patella kneecap.

pelvis the hipbones, sacrum, and coccyx collectively.

phalanges fingers and toes.

pubis the front lower part of the pelvis.

radius the long bone of the forearm, from the elbow to the wrist.

ribs 12 on each side.

sacrum the five fused vertebrae of the lower back, part of the pelvis.

scapula shoulder blade.

sesamoid the small bones embedded in some tendons, especially in the hands and feet.

skull occipital, sphenoid, ethmoid, two frontal, two parietal, two temporal.

sphenoid the front of the base of the skull and part of the nasal and orbital cavities.

stapes in the middle ear, the stirrup.

sternum the breastbone where the ribs and collarbone are attached.

talus same as astragalus.

temporal the sides of the base of the skull.

tibia the large leg bone extending from knee to ankle.

tympanic collectively, the three small bones of the middle ear, the incus, malleus, and stapes.

ulna the inner forearm bone, from the elbow to the wrist.

vertebrae the spinal column, consisting of 33 vertebrae.

vomer the bone forming the back of the nasal septum.

zygoma same as cheekbone.

Bone Diseases, Disorders, and Breaks

cartilage elastic or fibrous connective tissue that sometimes transforms into bone; gristle.

Colles' fracture the most common type of wrist fracture, involving the radius and ulna bones.

comminuted fracture a bone splintered into many pieces.

compound fracture a fracture accompanied by a flesh wound through which the bone may protrude.

countertraction used in traction to pull bones together and realign them after a break.

crepitation the sound of broken bones when they rub together. Also the cracking of joints.

fatigue fracture a fracture of the metatarsal shaft, usually caused by prolonged marching or walking. Also known as a march fracture.

Kirschner wires the wires threaded through broken bones to help pull them back together.

marble bone a disease in which bones become extremely dense. Also known as Albers-Schönberg disease.

marrow the tissue inside of certain bones that manufacture new blood cells.

ossification the transformation of connective tissue or cartilage into bone.

osteoarthritis a disease characterized by a wasting away of bone and cartilage.

osteochondritis inflammation of bone.

osteoclasis intentionally rebreaking a bone in order to reset it in a more accurate alignment.

osteofibrosis degeneration of bone marrow.

osteogenic sarcoma a malignant bone tumor.

osteology the study of bones.

osteoporosis a condition frequently found in elderly women in which the bones become brittle and easily broken, due to a calcium deficiency.

pathologic fracture a fracture due to a disease process rather than an injury.

Pott's fracture the most common type of lower leg fracture, involving the tibia and fibula.

scoliosis curvature of the spine.

spur a small, projecting growth of bone.

traction the pulling together and alignment of bones by a system of ropes and pulleys.

TEETH

alveolus the socket of a tooth.

bicuspid premolar teeth, between the molars and canines.

bruxism gnashing or grinding the teeth, especially during sleep.

canine teeth the sharp, pointy front teeth. Also known as cuspids.

caries cavities.

cementum the bonelike tissue covering the roots of the teeth.

cusp the pointed part of a tooth.

cuspid canine tooth.

deciduous teeth temporary teeth; first teeth, or baby teeth. Also known as milk teeth.

dedentition loss of teeth.

dentalgia toothache.

dentition the eruption of the teeth through the gums.

denture false teeth; artificial teeth.

enamel the hard, smooth substance covering the crown of a tooth.

gingivitis inflammation of gums; early form of gum disease.

gumboil an abcess found in the root of a rotting tooth.

impacted a condition in which one tooth lies nearly on its side and is wedged tightly against another tooth, usually involving wisdom teeth.

incisor teeth the eight front cutting teeth.

macrodontia abnormally large teeth.

malocclusion a condition in which the top and bottom teeth fail to meet or clench together properly, causing problems with biting and chewing.

masticate to chew.

milk teeth same as deciduous teeth.

molar the large teeth at the back of the mouth used for grinding and chewing.

odontectomy removal of teeth.

odontology dentistry.

odontoma a tumor formed from the tissue involved in tooth growth.

periodontal surrounding a tooth.

periodontal disease any disease of the tissues surrounding the teeth.

periodontitis inflammation of the gums, loss of bone tissue and the formation of pockets around the teeth. Also known as pyorrhea.

plaque a sticky film made of mucous, food particles, and bacteria; it forms on teeth after eating.

premolar the teeth between the canines and the molars.

pyorrhea same as periodontitis.

tartar a yellowish concretion on the teeth composed of calcium phosphate.

wisdom teeth the last or rearmost molar on each side; they erupt last during late adolescence.

MUSCULAR SYSTEM

Muscles, Names of

abductor, fifth finger and toe the small muscles on the back of the hand and foot that pulls the little finger and little toe away from the other digits.

abductor hallucis extending from the base of the big toe to the heel, the muscle that pulls the big toe away from the other toes.

abductor pollicis brevis extending from the base of the thumb to the hand, the muscle that bends the thumb and pulls it away from the fingers.

abductor pollicis longus from the base of the thumb to the forearm, the muscle that straightens the thumb.

adductor brevis extending from the pubic bone to the femur, it adducts (moves inward), flexes, and rotates the thigh.

adductor hallucis from the foot to the base of the big toe, the muscle that flexes and pulls the big toe inward.

adductor magnus from the pubic bone to the femur, the muscle that flexes, rotates, and pulls the thigh inward.

adductor pollicis from the hand to the thumb, the muscle that pulls the thumb into a grasping position.

anconeus extending from the upper arm to the forearm, the muscle that straightens the elbow.

aryepiglottic the muscle that closes the entrance to the larynx.

auricularis in some people, a vestigial muscle that moves or wiggles the outer ear.

biceps brachil the string upper arm muscle.

biceps femoris extending from the femur to the fibula, the muscle that flexes the knee and straightens the hip.

brachialis from upper arm to forearm, the muscle involved in bending the elbow.

buccinator the jaw muscles involved in retracting the angle of the mouth.

chondroglossus on the sides of the tongue, it depresses the tongue.

ciliary the eye muscle that makes the eye more convex to aid in focusing.

constrictor of pharynx constricts the throat muscles when swallowing.

coracobrachial from the shoulder blade to the upper arm, the muscle that flexes and pulls the arm inward.

corrugator forehead muscle that wrinkles the forehead and pulls the eyebrows together.

cremaster from the lower abdomen to the pubis, the muscle that elevates the testicles.

cricothyroid the group of muscles that work the vocal cords.

deltoid from the collarbone to the upper arm, the muscle that lifts, flexes, and extends the upper arm.

depressor a group of muscles that pull the corner of the mouth and bottom lip down.

depressor, nasal septum muscle that constricts the nostrils.

diaphragm between the chest and the abdomen, the muscle involved in inhalation.

dilator of nose muscle that widens nostril.

dilator of pupil eye muscle that widens the pupil.

epicranial the scalp muscle involved in raising the eyebrows.

erector clitoris a sexual muscle, it causes the clitoris to become erect.

erector penis a sexual muscle, it causes the penis to become erect.

erector pili on the skin, the tiny muscles that makes body hair stand on end; goose bumps.

extensor carpi radialis from the humerus to the wrist bones, the muscle involved in straightening the wrist.

extensor carpi ulnaris from the humerus to the wrist bones, the muscle involved in straightening the wrist.

extensor digitorum, feet from the heel to toes, the muscle that straightens the toes.

extensor digitorum, hands from the upper arm to the back of the hand, the muscle that straightens the fingers.

extensor hallucis from the fibula to the heel bone, the muscle that straightens the big toe and helps turn the ankle up.

extensor pollicis from the forearm to the thumb, the muscle that straightens the thumb and pulls it away from the fingers.

flexor carpi radialis from the humerus to the wrist, the muscle that bends the wrist.

flexor carpi ulnaris from the humerus to the wrist, the muscle that bends the wrist.

flexor digitorum, feet from heel bone to toes, the muscle involved in bending toes.

flexor digitorum, hands from forearm to fingers, the muscle involved in flexing or bending the fingers.

flexor hallucis from fibula to foot, the muscle that flexes the big toe.

flexor pollicis from forearm and wrist to thumb, the muscle that flexes the thumb.

gastrocnemius extending from the femur to the heel, the muscle that bends the ankle down.

gemellus from pelvis to thigh, the muscle that rotates femur outward.

genioglossus from the lower jaw to the tongue, the muscle involved in sticking out and returning the tongue.

glossopalatine in the soft palate, the muscle that lifts the tongue.

gluteus maximus, medius, and minimus from the pelvis to the upper thigh, the muscles that straighten the hip and pull the leg away from the body.

gracilis from pubic bone to tibia, the muscle that pulls the leg inward or toward the other leg.

hamstring running down the back of the thigh, the three muscles that flex the knee.

hiacus from pelvis to femur, the muscle that flexes the hip joint.

iliocostal extending from the ribs to the spine, the muscle that straightens the spine and aids in sideways movement of the trunk.

infraspinatus from shoulder blade to upper arm, the muscle that rotates the arm sideways.

intercostal in the rib area, muscles that draw ribs together and aid in breathing.

interossei in the hands and feet, muscles that pull the digits toward one another.

latissimus dorsi from the spine to the upper arm, the muscle involved in extending, rotating, and pulling the arm in toward the body.

levator ani forming a sling in the pelvic region, the muscle that supports the pelvic organs.

levator scapulae from the neck to the shoulder blade, the muscle that lifts the shoulder.

levator of upper eyelid raises upper eyelid.

levator of upper lip raises upper lip and dilates nostril.

lingual a muscle running the length of the tongue and involved in changing its shape.

longissimus the back muscle involved in straightening the spine.

longus capitus from the neck to the base of the skull, the muscle involved in bending the head.

lumbrical in the hands, the muscles that flex the fingers.

masseter from the cheekbone to the mandible, the muscle involved in chewing, especially in closing the mouth and clenching the teeth.

mylohyoid from the lower jaw to the neck, the muscle that elevates the floor of the mouth.

nasalis in the nose area, a muscle involved in some facial expressions.

oblique, abdominal extending from the ribs to the middle of the abdomen down to the pubic area, the muscle that flexes and rotates the vertebral column and supports the abdominal wall.

oblique, eyeball in the orbital cavity, a muscle involved in the eye's rotation.

oblique, head extending from the neck to the base of the skull, a muscle involved in rotating the head.

obturator from the pubis to the thigh, a muscle that rotates the thigh outward.

orbicularis oculi from the orbit to surrounding skin, muscles that close the eyelids.

orbicularis oris in the mouth area, the muscle involved in closing the mouth and pursing or puckering the lips.

palmaris from the forearm to the palm of the hand, a muscle that deepens the "hollow" of the palm.

pectineal extending from the pelvis to the thigh, a muscle that pulls the thigh in toward the other leg and flexes the hip.

pectoral extending from the clavicle, sternum, and ribs to the shoulder blade and upper arm, the muscle that flexes, rotates, and pulls the arm in toward the body.

peroneus from the leg to the foot, the muscle that helps flex and extend the ankle.

piriformis from the pelvis to the thigh, a muscle that aids in turning the thigh outward.

plantaris from the lower thigh to the heel, a muscle that bends the ankle down.

popliteus in the knee area, a muscle that rotates the knee inward.

pronator extending from the upper arm to the forearm, a muscle that rotates the forearm.

psoas from the lower back to the thigh, a muscle involved in bending the trunk and hip.

quadratis femoris in the pelvic and thigh area, a muscle involved in rotating the thigh.

quadratis lumborum from the last rib to the hipbone area, a muscle involved in bending the spine sideways.

rectus abdominus extending from the sternum to the pubis, the muscle that bends the spine forward.

rectus capitis extending from the neck to the skull, the muscle involved in bending the head forward and back.

rectus femoris from the upper thigh to the knee area, a muscle that straightens the knee.

rectus oculi in the orbital area, a muscle involved in rotating the eyes.

rhomboid from the neck to the shoulder blades, the muscle that draws the shoulders backward.

risorius in the mouth area, muscle that pulls the corners of the mouth down.

sartorius from the hip to the tibia, a muscle involved in flexing the thigh and knee.

scalene from the neck to the first ribs, muscle that inclines the neck to either side.

semispinalis from the upper chest to the base of the skull, a muscle that inclines the head back.

serratus extending from the lower back, ribs, and chest, muscle that elevates ribs to aid in breathing.

soleus from the upper leg to the heel, a muscle that flexes the foot and aids in balance.

sphincter ani a muscle that closes the anus.

sphincter pupilae a muscle that contracts the pupil of the eye.

sphincter urethrae in the pubic area, a muscle that tightens the passage of the bladder.

sphincter vaginae in the pubic area, a muscle that constricts the vaginal opening.

spinalis extending from the neck, chest, and back, muscles that straighten the head and spine.

stapedius the middle ear muscle that moves the stapes.

sternothyroid from the sternum to the Adam's apple, the muscle that draws the larynx downward.

styloglossus the muscle that lifts and retracts the tongue.

supinator extending from the upper arm to the lower arm, a muscle that rotates the forearm so that the palm of the hand faces up.

supraspinatus from the scapula to the humerus, a muscle that pulls the arm away from the body.

temporal from the temple to the mandible, a muscle that closes the mouth.

teres major from the scapula to the upper arm, a muscle that rotates the arm inward.

teres minor from the scapula to the upper arm, a muscle that rotates the arm outward.

thyroepiglottis the Adam's apple muscle that closes the larynx and trachea.

tibialis anterior from the lower leg to the foot, a muscle that flexes the foot up and in.

tibialis posterior from the back of the leg to the foot, a muscle that flexes the foot down and in.

transversus abdominus from the lower ribs across the abdomen, a muscle involved in bending the spine forward and supporting the abdominal wall.

trapezius from the top of the neck to the shoulder blade and shoulder, a muscle that raises shoulder and pulls it back.

triceps brachii from the upper arm to the forearm, a muscle that straightens the elbow.

vastus from the thigh to the lower leg, a muscle that straightens the knee.

Muscle Diseases and Disorders

abductor a muscle that pulls a body part away or out from center. Opposite of adductor.

adductor a muscle that pulls a body part in toward center. Opposite of abductor.

Aran-Duchenne disease a disease characterized by a progressive wasting away of muscles.

ataxia lack of muscle coordination.

atrophy withering of muscle when not used for long periods.

bursa a fluid-filled sac composed of connective tissue often present over bony projections, between tendons, and between movable areas or joints to ease friction.

bursitis inflammation of bursa.

contracture a shortening and immobilizing of a muscle; a permanent contraction.

epicondylitis inflammation of the forearm extensor tendons causing elbow and forearm pain and a weak grasp. Also known as tennis elbow.

muscular dystrophy a disease characterized by a progressive wasting of muscles, usually beginning in childhood.

myalgia muscle pain.

myasthenia gravis a disease characterized by a wasting of muscles, particularly those used in swallowing.

myokymia muscle twitching.

myopathy disease of muscle.

myosarcoma malignant tumor of muscle.

myositis an inflamed muscle.

tendinitis inflammation of a tendon.

ORGANS AND GLANDS

adenoids organs of unknown function in the back of the throat behind the nose.

adrenal glands resting above the kidneys, the glands that secrete a wide array of hormones, including adrenalin and cortisone. Also known as the suprarenal.

anus the end portion of the gastrointestinal tract whose muscular action eliminates feces.

apocrine glands sweat glands.

appendix near the large intestine, a vestigial organ whose function is unknown.

bladder in the lower abdomen, a storage sac for urine secreted by the kidneys.

bone marrow the soft tissue in the middle of bones that manufactures new blood cells.

brain the organ of mental and nerve processes, divided into two hemispheres and several suborgans.

A. cerebrum: outer and uppermost portion of the brain responsible for higher brain functions, such as conscious thought.

B. cerebellum: behind and beneath the cerebrum at the back of the skull, the portion of the brain responsible for muscle reflexes, coordination, and equilibrium.

C. medulla oblongata: the lowest portion—oblong in shape—of the brain below the pons and extending to the spinal cord; it transmits nerve impulses.

D. pons: located below the cerebellum, it receives and transmits nerve impulses.

bronchial tubes extending from the trachea to the lungs, the tiny tubes that process air in and out of the lungs.

breasts the outer chest organs that secrete milk.

colon part of the large intestine extending from the cecum to the rectum, it absorbs water and pushes wastes toward the rectum.

Cowper's glands in men, two pea-shaped glands that secrete lubricant for the epithelium during sexual stimulation.

duodenal glands in the duodenum, tubular glands that secrete an alkaline substance to neutralize digestive acids.

duodenum the first portion of the small intestine, it receives bile from the liver and gallbladder and digestive juices from the pancreas.

esophagus the food tube extending from the throat to the stomach.

fallopian tubes two tubes extending laterally from either side of the uterus to the ovaries; the eggs from the ovaries pass through the fallopian tubes and are fertilized there.

gallbladder located on the underside of the liver, it stores bile manufactured by the liver.

gastric glands tubular glands of the stomach that secrete hydrochloric acid and pepsin.

greater vestibular glands on either side of the vagina, glands that secrete mucus for sexual lubrication.

heart the organ that pumps the blood throughout the body.

ileum portion of the small intestine extending from the jejunem to the cecum.

intestinal glands intestinal glands that secrete digestive hormones.

jejunum portion of the small intestine extending from the duodenum to the ileum.

kidneys two bean-shaped organs located in the lower back below the ribs; they regulate blood constituents and water balance throughout the body and discharge urine into the bladder.

lacrimal glands located in the upper portion of the orbit, glands that secrete tears.

larynx the upper part of the respiratory tract containing the vocal cords.

liver the large gland beneath the diaphragm that produces bile and metabolizes fats, carbohydrates, proteins, minerals, and vitamins.

lungs in the chest, five air-processing lobes that oxygenate and remove carbon dioxide from blood.

mammary glands the breast glands that produce milk.

ovaries on either side of the uterus, the female sex glands that produce progesterone, estrogen, and eggs.

pancreas near the duodenum, the organ that manufactures insulin and digestive juices.

parathyroid glands behind the thyroid in the neck, four small glands that produce parathyroid hormone for the regulation of calcium and phosphate metabolism.

parotid glands in front of each ear, the salivary glands.

penis the male sexual organ that conveys urine from the bladder and sperm from the testicles.

pharynx the passage for air and food; the throat.

pituitary gland important gland at the base of the skull, it secretes hormones that control metabolism and growth and the regulation of other glands.

prostate gland in men, a chestnut-shaped gland surrounding the urethra, it secretes the fluid in which sperm are transported in an ejaculation.

pylorus the outlet of the stomach that regulates the flow of food into the small intestine.

seminal vesicles located above the prostate gland in men, they store and discharge semen.

spinal cord from the base of the brain to the lower back, a cord containing nerves that send nerve impulses to and from the brain.

spleen beneath the diaphragm, an organ that destroys old blood cells.

stomach in the upper left portion of the abdomen, the organ that breaks down food through churning and acid action and then sends it on to the small intestine for digestion into the body.

testicles two small, ball-like organs in the scrotal sac that produce sperm and secrete male hormones.

thymus gland located beneath the sternum, it is thought to be useful in development up to the age of 2, after which it degenerates.

thyroid gland on either side of the trachea, it manufactures thyroxin, which regulates body metabolism.

tongue the organ of taste; aids in chewing, swallowing, and speech.

tonsils the lymph glands located at the back of the mouth, which frequently become infected and swollen; their function is unknown.

trachea the windpipe leading to the lungs.

ureters the two urine-conveying tubes leading from the kidneys to the bladder.

uterus in women, the pelvic organ in which an embryo and fetus develops.

vagina the female sexual organ through which sperm is passed and through which a newborn is delivered.

HEART AND CIRCULATORY SYSTEM

aneurysm a ballooning-out of the wall of a vein, an artery or the heart due to weakening of the wall by disease, injury or congenital defect.

angina pectoris chest pain caused by insufficient blood to the heart muscle.

angiocardiography an X ray of the blood vessels or chambers of the heart using a contrasting dye. The X-ray pictures resulting from the procedure are called angiograms.

angioplasty a procedure used to widen narrowed arteries by passing a balloon-tipped catheter into the diseased vessels and inflating the balloon.

aorta the large artery that receives blood from the heart's left ventricle and distributes it to the body.

aortic valve the heart valve between the left ventricle and aorta.

arrhythmia an abnormal rhythm of the heart. Also known as dysrhymnia.

arterioles muscular branches of arteries that when contracted slow blood flow and increase blood pressure.

arteriosclerosis a thickening and loss of elasticity of artery walls, also known as hardening of the arteries.

artery any vessel that carries blood from the heart to the body.

atherosclerosis a form of arteriosclerosis in which the linings of artery walls become thickened with deposits of fats, cholesterol, and other substances collectively known as plaque.

athletic heart syndrome an enlargement of the heart and slowing of heart rate in response to strenuous exercise; may also be accompanied by arrhythmias.

atria the two upper, holding chambers of the heart.

atrioventricular node special conducting tissue of the right atrium through which electrical impulses pass to reach the ventricles.

atrium either of the two upper chambers of the heart in which blood collects before being passed to the ventricles.

balloon angioplasty see angioplasty.

blood clot a clotted mass of blood cells that normally stop the flow of blood at an injury site but can also form inside an artery wall narrowed by disease and cause a heart attack.

blood pressure the force exerted by the heart in pumping blood; the pressure of blood in the arteries.

blue babies infants having bluish skin, a sign of insufficient oxygen in arterial blood and indicating a heart defect.

capillaries tiny blood vessels that distribute blood between the veins and arteries.

cardiac pertaining to the heart.

cardiac arrest when the heart stops beating.

cardiology the study of heart function and heart disease.

cardiopulmonary resuscitation (CPR) the emergency procedure of chest compression and mouth-to-mouth breathing to help keep oxygenated blood flowing to the heart and brain in a cardiac arrest victim.

carotid artery either of the two major arteries in the neck that carries blood to the head.

catheterization an examination of the heart by passing of a thin tube (catheter) into a vein or artery and pushing it into the heart area.

cerebral thrombosis formation of a blood clot in an artery that supplies the brain.

cerebrovascular accident also known as stroke or apoplexy, an impeded flow of blood to the brain and its result.

cholesterol a fatty substance present in some foods and also manufactured by the liver; known to clog arteries over time.

cineangiography a motion picture taken of an opaque dye passing through blood vessels.

collateral circulation smaller "standby" arteries normally closed, but that may open to carry blood to the heart when a coronary artery becomes clogged.

congenital heart defect a heart defect present at birth.

congestive heart failure the inability of the heart to efficiently pump all the blood returned to it, causing blood to back up in the veins and fluid to accumulate in body tissues.

coronary arteries the two arteries arising from the aorta that provide blood to the heart muscle.

coronary artery disease narrowing of the coronary arteries that results in reduced blood flow to the heart muscle.

coronary bypass surgery surgery to improve blood flow to the heart muscle.

coronary occlusion an obstruction in one of the coronary arteries that slows or reduces blood flow to part of the heart muscle. Also known as coronary thrombosis.

cyanosis blueness of the skin, a sign of insufficient oxygen in the blood.

diastolic blood pressure the lowest blood pressure in the arteries, measured between beats of the heart.

digitalis a drug that strengthens the contraction of the heart muscle, helping to eliminate the accumulation of fluids in body parts related to congestive heart failure.

dysrhythmia same as arrhythmia.

echocardiography a diagnostic technique using sound pulses and echoes to explore electronically the surfaces of the heart.

edema the accumulation of fluid in body tissues, caused by congestive heart failure.

electrocardiogram (ECG or EKG): a readout of electrical impulses produced by the heart.

embolus a blood clot that forms in a blood vessel in one part of the body and then is carried to another part of the body.

endarterectomy surgical removal of plaque deposits in arteries.

fibrillation rapid, out-of-control contraction of individual heart muscle fibers, resulting in a partial or complete loss of pumping power in the chamber affected.

heart attack death of or damage to part of the heart muscle due to insufficient blood supply.

heart murmur extra "whishing" sound heard with heartbeat, caused by turbulence in bloodstream; a possible symptom of disease.

hypertension high blood pressure.

ischemia decreased blood flow to an organ due to a restriction or obstruction of an artery.

ischemic heart disease coronary artery disease and coronary heart disease.

lipid a fatty substance insoluble in blood and partially responsible for clogging arteries.

mitral valve the heart valve between the left atrium and left ventricle.

myocardial infarction heart attack.

myocardial ischemia insufficient blood flow to part of the heart muscle.

myocardium the muscular wall of the heart that contracts and relaxes as it pumps blood.

nitroglycerin a drug that causes blood vessels to widen and therefore increase blood flow, used in the treatment of angina pectoris.

open heart surgery surgery performed on the opened heart while blood flow is diverted through a heart-lung machine.

pericarditis inflammation of the outer membrane surrounding the heart.

pericardium the outer membrane that surrounds the heart.

peripheral vascular disease diseased or clogged arteries and veins in the arms and legs.

plaque deposits of fat, cholesterol, and other substances in the linings of arteries.

pulmonary pertaining to the lungs.

pulmonary valve the heart valve between the right ventricle and the pulmonary artery.

rheumatic heart disease damage to the heart caused by bouts of rheumatic fever.

silent ischemia episodes of ischemia without accompanying pain.

sinoatrial node a mass of cells in the top of the right atrium that produces electrical impulses that cause the heart to contract.

sphygmomanometer an instrument used for measuring blood pressure.

stenosis the narrowing or constriction of an opening such as a blood vessel.

systolic blood pressure the highest blood pressure in the arteries, measured when the heart contracts or beats.

tachycardia excessively rapid heartbeat.

thrombolysis the breaking up of a blood clot.

thrombosis the formation or presence of a blood clot in a blood vessel or cavity of the heart.

thrombus a blood clot that forms in a blood vessel or cavity of the heart.

transient ischemic attack a strokelike attack caused by a temporarily blocked blood vessel.

varicose veins veins that have been stretched due to pooling of blood.

vascular pertaining to the blood vessels.

veins the blood vessels that carry blood from body tissues back to the heart; contrast with arteries.

ventricle either one of the two lower chambers of the heart.

ARTERIES

(Arteries carry blood from the heart; veins carry blood back.)

Name	Area Supplied
acetabular	hip joint, top of thighbone

acromial	shoulder and upper back
alveolar	gums, teeth, and chewing muscles
angular	muscles that open and close eyelids; muscles controlling some facial expressions
aorta, abdominal	abdominal wall, diaphragm, abdominal organs, legs
aorta, arch	head, neck, arms
aorta, thoracic	chest, lungs, esophagus, diaphragm
appendicular	first portion of large intestine; appendix
auditory	inner ear
auricular	middle and outer ear, muscles of the lower skull and neck, scalp; salivary gland
axillary	pectoral muscles of chest; shoulder and upper arm muscles
basilar	cerebellum, pons (base of brain), inner ear
brachial	muscles of shoulder, arm, forearm, hand
bronchial	lungs and esophagus
buccal	gums, skin and cheek; some chewing muscles
carotid, common	neck and head
carotid, external	front of face and neck, skull, back of scalp, dura mater
carotid, internal	forehead, front of brain, middle ear, eye, nose
celiac	esophagus and abdominal organs

cerebellar	base of brain, cerebellum
cerebral	brain
cervical	muscles of neck, shoulder, head
choroid	base of brain, optic tract
ciliary	iris and eye membrane
circumflex, femoral	muscles of the thigh and hip
circumflex, humeral	muscles of upper arm, shoulders
circumflex, iliac	muscles of lower back, lower abdominal wall, thigh
circumflex, scapular	muscles of upper back, back of upper arm, joint of shoulder
colic	group of arteries serving the colon
coronary	one of a pair serving the left or right atrium and ventricle of heart
cystic	gallbladder
dental	teeth and gums
digital	fingers or toes
dorsalis pedis	front of foot
epigastric, deep	lower abdomen
epigastric, superior	upper abdomen, diaphragm
esophageal	esophagus
facial	face, chewing muscles, tonsils, throat, lymph glands
femoral	lower abdomen, genitals, muscles and bones of thigh
frontal	forehead
gastric	lower end of esophagus, stomach
gastroduodenal	pylorus of stomach, duodenum, pancreas, bile duct

genicular	muscles of lower thigh; knee joint
gluteal	upper thigh, buttocks, prostrate gland, bladder
hallucis	big toe, second toe
hemorrrhoidal	rectum and anus, lower portion of descending colon
hepatic	liver, gallbladder, stomach, pancreas
ileocolic	appendix, cecum, ascending colon, last portion of small intestine
iliac, common	pelvic organs, genitals, lower abdominal wall
iliac, external	thigh and leg muscles
iliac, internal	pelvic organs, genitals, anal region
iliolumbar	greater psoas muscle, gluteal and abdominal muscles
infraorbital	eyeball muscles, tear gland, upper teeth, cheek, nasal area
innominate	right sides of neck and head, right shoulder, right arm
intercostal of aorta	chest wall, rib cage, muscles of upper back, spine
interosseus	forearm
intestinal	small intestine
labial	lips of the mouth
laryngeal	larynx
lingual	mouth and tongue
lumbar	back muscles, lumbar vertebrae, abdominal wall
malleolar	ankle area
mammary	breast, chest area
maxillary	ear, teeth, eye muscles, lacrimal gland, skin and muscles of face, tonsils, jaws
meningeal	skull, dura mater
mental	chin, lower lip
mesenteric, inferior	colon
mesenteric, superior	duodenum, small intestine, appendix
metacarpal	thumb, fingers
metatarsal	toes
musculophrenic	muscles of upper abdomen, diaphragm, lower ribs
nasal	nose, sinuses
nutrient	term for any artery serving a bone or bone marrow
obturator	bladder, pelvic muscles, hip joint
occipital	posterior neck muscles, back of ears and scalp
ophthalmic	orbit area, eye, sinuses
ovarian	ovary, fallopian tube, uterus
palatine	soft and hard palates, gums, tonsils, upper throat area
palpebral	eyelids, tear sac, eye membrane
pancreaticoduodenal	pancreas, duodenum, bile duct
penis	penis
perineal	base of penis
peroneal	back of leg, ankle joint, portion of foot
pharyngeal	throat, neck muscles, tonsil, ear, soft palate
phrenic	esophagus, spleen, diaphragm, adrenal glands

plantar	bottom of foot
popliteal	thigh
profunda femoris	thigh, hip joint
pudendal	genitals, anal canal, muscles of inner thigh
pulmonary	lungs
radial	forearm and hand
renal	kidney, adrenal glands
sacral	rectum, sacrum, coccyx
scapular	shoulder, scapular, collarbone
sciatic	buttocks, hip area, anus
scrotal	scrotum
sigmoidal	sigmoid colon
spermatic	ureters of kidneys, spermatic cord, uterus
spinal	spinal cord
splenic	spleen, pancreas, portion of stomach
subclavian	muscles of neck and arms, shoulder, thoracic wall, spinal cord, brain
sublingual	sublingual gland, mucus membrane of mouth and gums
submental	skin of chin, muscles beneath chin
subscapular	shoulder joint, back of arm, back
supraorbital	orbit, eyelid, sinuses, forehead
suprascapular	neck, collarbone, shoulder blade, back
tarsal	toe muscles, portion of skin of foot
temporal	facial skin and muscles, eye and temple area, salivary gland
testicular	testicle
thoracic, lateral	front and back muscles of chest
thoracodorsal	side and back muscles of the chest
thymic	thymus gland
thyroid	neck, trachea, esophagus, larynx, thyroid gland
tibial, anterior	front of leg and ankle
tibial, posterior	back of leg and foot; knee area
tympanic	middle ear
ulnar	forearm, portion of hand
uterine	uterus, fallopian tubes
vaginal	vagina, bladder, rectum
vesical	prostrate gland, bladder, ureters
volar arches	hand, fingers
zygomatico orbital	orbit

Blood

anemia a disease causing weakness and fatigue, due to a shortage of red blood cells or a deficiency of their hemoglobin content.

antibodies produced by the white blood cells, various proteins that fight and neutralize invading disease-causing organisms.

blood clot a jellylike mass of blood tissue formed by clotting factors to stop the flow of blood at the site of an injury.

blood count the number of red and white blood cells in a given volume of blood.

bloodletting the outmoded practice of intentionally bleeding a vein to let out supposed toxins.

blood pressure the pressure of the blood in the arteries.

bone marrow the soft material inside bones where most blood cells are manufactured.

coagulation the clotting of blood.

corpuscles blood cells.

cyanosis blue skin tone caused by a deficiency of oxygen in the blood.

embolus a blood clot formed in a vessel in one part of the body that travels to another part of the body.

erythrocytes red blood cells.
See RED BLOOD CELLS.

fibrin a factor in the blood that enmeshes blood cells and helps form a clot.

hemal pertaining to blood or blood vessels.

hematology the study of blood and its diseases.

hematoma a local swelling filled with blood.

hematopoiesis the process of blood cell manufacture in bone marrow.

hemoglobin the respiratory pigment in red blood cells.

hemophilia a disorder caused by a deficiency or absence of clotting factors in the blood, and characterized by uncontrollable bleeding, even from minor injuries.

hemorrhage copious or uncontrollable bleeding.

hemostasis the body's collective methods of controlling bleeding, including vasoconstriction and platelet clumping.

leukemia a disease of the blood and blood-manufacturing tissues, characterized by an increase in leukocytes or white blood cells and producing exhaustion and anemia.

leukocytes white blood cells.
See WHITE BLOOD CELLS.

pernicious anemia a severe form of anemia characterized by an abnormal development of red blood cells and accompanied by gastrointestinal disturbances and lesions of the spinal cord.

plasma a yellowish or straw-colored liquid made of protein and water in which blood cells float and circulate throughout the body.

plasma lipid the fat carried in blood.

platelets the blood component responsible for the clotting of blood.

red blood cells the blood cells that pick up oxygen in the lungs and distribute it throughout the body.

septicemia a blood infection.

sickle-cell anemia a hereditary disorder characterized by sickle-shaped or crescentlike blood cells that help protect against malaria but impede circulation and frequently cause premature deaths among blacks.

thrombocytes same as platelets.

thrombocytopenia the most common cause of bleeding disorders, characterized by a deficient number of circulating platelets.

thrombolysis the breaking up of a blood clot.

thrombus a blood clot.

white blood cells blood cells that manufacture antibodies for fighting and neutralizing disease-causing organisms.

VEINS

(Does not include veins that travel with arteries of the same name.)

Name	Area drained
anterior jugular	front of neck
azygos	right side of chest wall
basilar	posterior base of brain
cavernous sinus	back of eye
cephalic	inner side of hand and forearm
common facial	side of face
coronary sinus	heart
coronary of stomach	stomach

diploic	skull
emissary	skull
external jugular	side of neck
great cardiac	heart ventricles
great cerebral	brain
great saphenous	inner side of leg and thigh
hemiazygos	left side of back and chest
hemorrhoidal	rectum, end of colon
hepatic	liver
inferior petrosal sinus	skull
inferior sagittal sinus	cerebrum of brain
inferior vena cava	abdomen, thighs, legs
innominate	head and neck
intercavernous sinus	one of a pair of large channels containing venous blood in the skull
internal cerebral	inner cerebrum
internal jugular	very large vein draining the brain, face, and neck
internal vertebral veins	spinal cord and spine
middle cardiac	back of heart
occipital sinus	cerebellum of brain near posterior base of skull
parambilical	navel area
plexus	any conglomeration of network of veins
portal	abdominal organs and intestines
posterior left ventricle	left ventricle of heart
prostatic	prostate gland
pudendal plexus	penis
pyloric	stomach
sinus	any large channel of venous blood
small saphenous	back of leg and foot
superior ophthalmic	eye area
superior petrosal sinus	brain
superior sagittal sinus	outer cerebrum
superior vena cava	head, neck, arms, chest well
transverse sinus	brain
vesical plexus	bladder, prostate gland
vorticose	eyeball

LUNGS AND BREATHING

alveolus a tiny air sac in which oxygen is transferred from the lungs to the blood.

apnea a temporary cessation of breathing, usually caused by too much oxygen or too little carbon dioxide in the brain.

asphyxia suffocation.

aspirate to inhale food or fluid into the lungs.

asthma a disease characterized by constriction of breathing passages and shortness of breath.

bronchiole one of the tiny tubes leading to an alveolus.

bronchitis inflammation of the bronchial tubes.

bronchodilator any medication prescribed to dilate the bronchial tubes.

bronchopneumonia inflammation of the bronchial tubes and the lungs; a common type of pneumonia.

byssinosis a lung disease caused by the inhalation of cotton particles.

carbon dioxide the waste gas expelled by the lungs in an exhale.

Cheyne-Stokes breathing in patients suffering from congestive heart failure, breathing characterized by long periods of apnea followed by several deep breaths.

COLD chronic obstructive lung disease; a breakdown of the lungs resulting from long-term bronchitis and emphysema.

cystic fibrosis an inherited childhood disease characterized by the overproduction of mucus that obstructs the normal functioning of the lungs; accompanied by a susceptibility to infections.

devil's grip extreme and sudden pain in the chest that lasts two days or less; it is caused by inflammation of the chest cavity lining. Also known as acute pleurodynia.

diaphragm muscle that separates the abdominal and chest cavities; it is the main breathing muscle.

dyspnea shortness of breath.

emphysema a lung disease characterized by enlargement of the alveoli, causing breathing difficulties and possible damage to the heart.

farmer's lung lung condition caused by the inhalation of particles from moldy hay.

goblet cells lung cells that produce mucus.

hyperventilation excessive breathing with an intake of too much oxygen and exhalation of too much carbon dioxide, which may cause light-headedness, buzzing in the head, tingling of the lips, and a sensation of suffocation. Often brought on by anxiety, it may cause panic and fainting, but is usually relieved by breathing into a paper bag.

hypoxia inadequate oxygen in the lungs and blood.

intercostal muscles between the ribs, the muscles that aid in breathing.

larynx the upper portion of the respiratory tract; the voice box.

lobe one of five divisions that make up the lungs.

orthopnea having to sit up in bed in order to breathe adequately, a sign of abnormal heart function.

pharynx the throat.

pleura the membrance that envelops the lungs and lines the chest cavity.

pleurisy inflammation of the pleura, causing chest pain, especially when breathing deeply or coughing.

pneumonia a viral or bacterial infection of the lungs.

pulmonary pertaining to the lungs.

pulmonary edema excess fluid in the lungs.

respiratory centers portions of the brain that regulate breathing by monitoring levels of oxygen and carbon dioxide in the body.

spirometer a device that measures the amount of air inhaled.

stertorous breathing loud breathing, as in snoring.

stridor loud breathing caused by partial closure of the larynx.

trachea the windpipe leading to the lungs.

tuberculosis a communicable disease characterized by lesions in the tissues of the lungs.

wheeze raspy breathing due to mucus in the trachea or bronchial tubes.

DIGESTIVE SYSTEM

alimentary canal collective term for the digestive parts extending from the mouth to the anus, including the mouth, the pharynx, the esophagus, the stomach, and the small and large intestines. Also known as the gastronintestinal tract.

amylase a digestive enzyme found in saliva and pancreatic juices.

anus the outlet for excrement at the end of the alimentary canal.

appendicitis inflammation of the appendix.

appendix a wormlike sack attached to the cecum of the colon and whose function is unknown.

bile a substance produced by the liver that aids digestion through emulsification of fats.

bolus a clump of chewed food ready to be swallowed.

carbohydrate sugars, starches, and cellulose.

cholesterol a waxy, fatty substance produced by the liver or ingested in the form of saturated fat.

chyme a soupy mixture of fragmented food particles and stomach chemicals resting in the stomach after a meal and waiting to be moved into the duodenum.

cirrhosis a chronic disease of the liver characterized by hardening of connective tissue and increased blockage of circulation, usually caused by chronic alcoholism.

colitis inflammation of the colon.

colon the principal portion of the large intestine.

Crohn's disease an inflammation of any part of the GI tract or alimentary canal (usually the ileum) that extends through all the layers of the intestinal wall.

diabetes sometimes called diabetes mellitus or sugar diabetes, a disease characterized by the body's inability to properly process carbohydrates (sugars and starches), resulting in an excess of sugar in the bloodstream; the main cause is the insufficient production of insulin by the pancreas, which reduces sugar in the blood.

diverticulitis inflammation of the sacs or pouches (diverticula) that have ballooned out through the walls of the colon (usually the sigmoid colon), sometimes causing fatal obstruction, infection, or hemorrhage.

duodenum approximately the first 10 inches of the small intestine.

dysphagia difficulty in swallowing.

emulsify the separation of fat in the form of tiny globules from surrounding fluid food mass.

endoscope an instrument used for examining the alimentary canal.

esophagus the food tube leading from the pharynx to the stomach.

fundus the large curvature of the stomach, bordering the esophagus.

gallbladder a small, pear-shaped sac under the liver that receives and stores bile made by the liver.

gallstones hardened masses of cholesterol forming in the gallbladder.

gastrectomy the surgical removal of part or all of the stomach.

gastrin a digestive hormone.

gastritis inflammation of the stomach.

gastroenteritis inflammation of the stomach lining.

glucose a simple sugar.

glycogen the form of sugar stored in the liver.

hematemesis vomiting of blood.

hemorrhoids enlarged veins inside or outside the anal canal.

hepatitis a viral infection of the liver causing inflammation, characterized by jaundice and fever.

hiatal hernia a disorder in which the lower end of the stomach or esophagus protrudes through the diaphragm.

hydrochloric acid a powerful stomach acid that aids in the digestion of food.

ileocecal valve where the small intestine meets the large intestine.

ileostomy the surgical removal of the colon.

ileum between the jejunum and large intestine, the last portion of the small intestine.

inguinal hernia a disorder in which a loop of intestine protrudes into the groin, often the result of strain from heavy lifting, coughing, or accidents.

insulin a hormone secreted by the pancreas that regulates carbohydrate metabolism by controlling blood sugar levels.

jaundice the yellowing of the skin and whites of the eyes due to the presence of bile pigments, a symptom of an abnormality in bile processing.

jejunum the part of the small intestine between the duodenum and the ileum.

large intestine the last and largest section of the alimentary canal.

lipase a pancreatic enzyme that speeds the hydrolysis of emulsified fats.

lipid fats that are insoluble in water but soluble in certain organic solvents.

liver the largest gland in the body, it aids digestion by producing bile.

lower esophageal sphincter (les) just above the stomach, the musculature that prevents gastric contents from backing up (reflux) into the esophagus.

pancreas a large gland behind the stomach that secretes insulin to help regulate blood sugar levels.

pancreatic juice an alkaline secretion of the pancreas aiding in the digestion of proteins, carbohydrates, and fats.

pancreatitis inflammation of the pancreas, usually caused by biliary tract disease or alcoholism.

parotid gland a saliva-producing gland in the back of the mouth.

pepsin a digestive enzyme secreted by the stomach.

peptic ulcer lesion in the gastric mucosal membrane, caused by the excess production and contact with hydrochloric acid and pepsin.

peristalsis the rhythmic muscular contractions that push food through the alimentary canal.

peritoneum the membrane that lines the abdominal cavity and covers the abdominal organs.

peritonitis acute or chronic inflammation of the peritoneum.

portal vein the vein connecting the liver and the small intestine.

ptyalin a salivary enzyme that breaks down starches.

pylorus the part of the stomach connecting with the duodenum.

reflux the backing up of stomach contents into the esophagus, causing heartburn.

serotonin a common body compound found in the blood and having several functions, one of which is to inhibit gastric secretion.

small intestine between the stomach and the colon, the part of the alimentary canal that absorbs most of the nutrients from food for distribution to other organs and other parts of the body.

solar plexus a large network of nerves located behind the stomach and supplying nerves to the abdominal organs.

sphincter a muscle that opens and closes a body opening, such as the rectum.

trypsin an enzyme that helps digest proteins.

villi fingerlike projections lining the small intestine.

NERVOUS SYSTEM

BRAIN

alexia the inability to understand the written word, a symptom of a brain condition.

amusia loss of the ability to play a musical instrument, due to a brain condition.

anomia the inability to remember names, due to a brain disorder.

aphasia the inability to speak or articulate clearly, usually caused by a stroke.

apoplexy a stroke.

appestat the portion of the brain that regulates appetite.

apraxia the loss of muscle coordination, due to a brain condition.

asemia an inability to comprehend speech or the written word, due to a brain condition.

astroblastoma a malignant brain tumor.

beta rhythm the low-voltage electrical brain wave that predominates when someone is awake and alert.

brain stem a thickening at the top of the spinal cord, the lowest part of the brain.

Broca's area an egg-shaped patch in the left frontal cortex; it controls muscle coordination of the face, tongue, throat, and jaw.

cerebellum the portion of the brain in the back of the skull and beneath the cerebrum; it is responsible for muscular coordination.

cerebrum the large portion of brain extending around the top of the skull; it is responsible for higher thought processes, such as perception, memory, and reasoning.

concussion unconsciousness and brain swelling caused by the brain striking the skull, due to a blow.

convolution one of several deep folds in the cerebrum.

corpus callosum the structure made of strands of fibers that connects the right hemisphere of the brain with the left.

cortex the outer surface and folds of the cerebrum.

delta waves the high-voltage brain waves that predominate when someone is asleep.

dura mater the outer covering of the brain.

dysphasia difficulty in speaking or understanding speech, due to a brain condition.

encephalitis inflammation of the brain.

encephalomeningitis infection of the brain and dura mater.

encephalon the brain.

encephalo sclerosis hardening of the brain.

epilepsy a brain condition characterized by electrical disturbances that cause seizures and loss of consciousness.

gyrus any one of the elevated convolutions at the surface of the cerebrum.

hemisphere the left or right division of the cerebrum.

hydrocephalus a postbirth condition characterized by fluid buildup around the brain, causing enlargement of the skull.

hypothalamus located below the cerebrum, the part of the brain that regulates body temperature and blood pressure.

idiot savant syndrome injury to the left hemisphere of the brain before, during, or after birth, causing the right hemisphere to enlarge and overcompensate. The sufferer has below-average left-brain function while having superhuman right-brain functioning.

limbic system in the upper brain stem, the old or reptilian brain that regulates hunger, thirst, sex, fighting, and basic emotion.

lobe one of four separate sections in each hemisphere of the brain, including frontal, parietal, occipital, and temporal.

medulla oblongata the base of the brain; it regulates respiration and circulation.

meningitis inflammation of the covering of the brain.

microencephalon an abnormally small brain.

neglect a bizarre brain condition in which one hemisphere of the brain is damaged, causing the sufferer to perceive only one side of his environment.

neuron one of millions of specialized nerve cells that carry electrochemical impulses in the brain.

paragraphia confused or distorted handwriting, caused by a brain condition.

Parkinson's disease a disease characterized by a shuffling gait, muscular rigidity, and uncontrollable tremors, thought to be due to a chemical imbalance in the brain.

pituitary attached to the hypothalamus, the gland that controls most of the hormones in the body.

prosopagnosia the inability to recognize faces, including those of close family members, due to a brain condition. The sufferer mây recognize the faces, however, as soon as he hears them speak.

reticular formation the part of the brain stem that regulates wakefulness and attention; it is the part of the brain that is shut off by anesthesia.

sinistrality the right-brain dominance over the left brain that produces left-handedness.

stereoanesthesia the inability to identify objects by touch, due to a brain condition.

synesthesia the confusion of senses (seeing sounds, hearing sights, etc.), a mysterious brain condition.

thalamus at the top of the brain stem, the structure known as the "great relay station" because it conveys signals between the brain stem and the rest of the brain. It is also the origination of the sensations of heat, cold, pain, and pressure.

water on the brain same as hydrocephalus.

wet brain a disease of chronic alcoholism, characterized by fluid buildup and mental deterioration.

NERVES

Name	Function and Location
abducens	supplies eye muscles
accessory	supplies neck muscles, voice box, shoulders
acoustic	supplies the inner ear; deafness results when damaged. Also known as the auditory nerve
alveolar	supplies muscles of the mandible and sensation to teeth
ampullary	supplies inner ear and affects balance
auricular	sensation to the outer ear
axillary	muscles of the shoulders and surrounding skin

buccal	sensation to cheek, mucus membranes of mouth and gums. Also known as buccinator
cardiac	supplies the heart
carotid	in the neck, it serves the cranial blood vessels and glands of the head
cervical	muscle and skin of the neck, shoulders, and arms
chorda tympani	taste sensations in tongue; salivary glands
ciliary	contracts and dilates the pupil of the eye
cranial	12 pairs of nerves atttached to the base of the brain: olfactory, optic, oculomotor, trochlear, trigeminal, abducens, facial, acoustic, glossopharyngeal, vagus, accessory, hypoglossal
cutaneous	sensation to all skin areas of the body
digital facial	skin sensation to fingers and toes; also, muscles of the face
femoral	muscles and skin of hip and thigh
frontal	skin of forehead and upper eyelid, frontal sinus
genitofemoral	sensation to skin of thigh, testicles, and the lips of the vagina
glossopharyngeal	supplies tongue, palate, and pharynx
gluteal	muscles of the buttocks
hemorrhoidal	muscles and skin of the rectum area
hypogastric	pelvic organs
hypoglossal	muscles of the tongue
iliohypogastric	muscles and skin of abdomen and buttocks
ilioinguinal	muscles of the abdominal wall, skin of thigh, scrotum, and labia
infraorbital	supplies upper teeth, nasal floor, facial skin beneath the eyes
interosseous	forearm muscles
labial	sensation to the lips
lacrimal	lacrimal gland and skin of upper eyelid
laryngeal	muscles of the larynx, esophagus, trachea, and tongue
lingual	floor of mouth and a portion of the tongue
lumbar	muscles and skin of the lower back and pelvic organs, sensation to the skin of lower abdomen and legs
mandibular	supplies chewing muscles; sensation to the lower teeth
maxillary	sensation to the skin of the upper face, palate, and upper teeth
median	muscles of the forearm; sensation to the wrist and hand

mental	sensation to the skin of the lower lip and chin
nasal	sensation to the skin of the nose
nasociliary	sensation to the eye and the eyelids
nasopalatine	sensation to the nasal septum and mucus membrane of the hard palate
obturator	hip and knee joints, inner side muscles of the thigh; sensation to the skin of all these regions
occipital	sensation to the scalp over the top and back of head; sensation to the back of the ear and back of the neck
oculomotor	eyeball muscles
olfactory	supplies the olfactory bulb and is responsible for the sense of smell
ophthalmic	sensation to the forehead, eyeball, and sinus area
optic	supplies the retina of the eye; vision is impossible without it
palatine	sensation to the gums, mucus membranes of hard palate, soft palate, and tonsils
palpebral	sensation to the eyelids
peroneal	supplies the knee joint; sensation to the skin of the leg, ankle, and foot
petrosal	serves parts of the palate and salivary glands
phrenic	diaphragm
plantar	toe muscles
plexus	collective term for any group or conglomeration of nerves
popliteal	muscles around the knee
pterygoid	jaw muscles and joints
pudendal	penis and clitoris; skin of the anus
radial	muscles of the upper arm and forearm; also supplies sensation to the skin of the arm and hand
recurrent laryngeal	larynx
sacral	pelvic organs, thigh muscles; also, sensation to these areas
saphenous	sensation to the skin of the inner side of the leg and foot
scapular	muscles that move the shoulder blade
sciatic	large nerve extending from the lower back down the back of the thigh, it supplies the skin and muscles of the thigh and leg
scrotal	sensation to the skin of the scrotum
splanchnic	groups of nerves serving the stomach, gallbladder, liver, pancreas, intestines, and other organs

supraclavicular	sensation to the skin of the neck, shoulders, and chest
supraorbital	sensation to the forehead and upper eyelid
thoracic	12 pairs of spinal nerves supplying skin and muscles of the back, arms, and abdominal wall
thoracic, lateral anterior	pectoral muscles of the chest
thoracodorsal	supplies latissimus dorsi muscle
tibial	skin and muscles of leg and foot
trigeminal	skin and muscles of face and jaw
trochlear	eyeball muscle
ulnar	muscles of the forearm, hand; sensation to the skin in little and ring fingers; responsible for painful "funny bone" sensation when struck
vagus	muscles of the throat, larynx, heart, lungs, abdominal organs
zygomatic	skin of cheek and temple

EYES (*Also see* EYE SURGERY IN SURGICAL PROCEDURES)

aqueous humor the nutrient-rich fluid that fills the chamber between the cornea and the lens.

astigmatism distorted vision—usually affecting peripheral vision—due to abnormal curvature of the eye.

blind spot there are no photoreceptors where the optic nerve passes through the retina; thus the eye is literally blind to any images that fall there.

cataract a clouding of the lens, obscuring vision.

choroid membrane the layer of the eyeball containing blood vessels that nourish the eye.

color blindness an inability to identify color, usually red or green; it rarely affects females.

cones light-reactive nerve cells in the retina that are responsible for detecting color.

conjunctiva the mucus membrane lining the inner eyelid and the outer surface of the eyeball.

conjunctivitis inflammation of the conjuctiva.

cornea the transparent outer membrane of the eyeball.

crocodile tear syndrome shedding tears instead of salivating in anticipation of food, a rare disorder caused by the crossing of the nerves leading to and from the salivary and lacrimal glands, usually due to injury.

detached retina loss or deterioration of vision due to the retina becoming separated from the other layers of the eyeball.

diplopia seeing double.

dry eye syndrome inadequate functioning of the tear glands, producing dry eyes.

ectropion the turning-out of an eyelid so that it lies away from the eyeball.

entropion the turning-in of an eyelid, so that it scratches the eyeball.

epicanthus an extra skin fold covering the inner angle of the eye, normal in

Orientals and children with Down's syndrome.

esotropia a form of strabismus in which one eye is turned or crossed inward.

exophthalmos bulging of the eyeballs, caused by overactivity of the thyroid gland.

exotropia a form of strabismus in which one eye is turned or crossed outward.

floaters floating specks sometimes seen before the eyes; they're usually harmless, dead blood cells.

glaucoma increased intraocular pressure due to overproduction of aqueous humor or an obstruction of its normal flow; it causes visual defects or blindness.

grayout a blurring or temporary loss of vision of airplane pilots due to an oxygen deficiency.

helerochroma iridis having one blue eye and one brown eye, present in two out of every 1,000 people.

hyperopia farsightedness; the ability to see things far away but not close up.

keratitis acute or chronic inflammation of the cornea caused by an infection by herpes simplex type 1 virus.

lacrimal glands tear glands; they keep the eyes constantly moist.

lazy eye a loss or lack of vision in one eye due to misalignment of the eyes.

lens behind the iris, the transparent body that changes shape to focus on objects at various distances.

muscae volitantes seeing floating specks before the eyes.

myopia nearsightedness; the ability to see close up but not far away.

nystagmus jerking, involuntary movements of the eyes due to brain lesions or inflammation, alcohol or drug toxicity, or a congenital disorder.

ocular involving the eyes or vision.

oculomotor pertaining to movements of the eyes.

optic nerve the main nerve leading from the retina that transmits images in the form of electrical impulses to the brain.

orbit an eye socket.

photophobia extreme sensitivity to light, a symptom of an eye disease.

photopsia seeing flashes of light before the eyes, a symptom of an eye disease. Also known as scintillation.

pinkeye inflammation of the conjunctiva marked by redness of the eyeball.

pupil the dark spot surrounded by the iris; the iris makes it enlarge or shrink in response to light or strong emotion.

radial keratotomy a series of surgical incisions made in the cornea to cure nearsightedness, a procedure pioneered in the Soviet Union. For other eye surgeries, *see* SURGICAL PROCEDURES.

retina the innermost layer of the eyeball on which light rays are focused and converted to electrical signals to be sent to the brain.

retinitis pigmentosa a hereditary disorder characterized by progressive destruction of the retina's rods, resulting ultimately in blindness.

retinoblastoma a maligant tumor of the retina.

retinology study of the retina and its diseases and disorders.

sclera the white of the eye.

strabismus group of eye disorders including crosseyes, walleyes, squinting, and general uncoordinated eye movement.

stye a staph infection of the eye producing a painful abcess at the margin of an eyelid.

trachoma a common form of blindness in the Third World.

20-20 vision normal vision at 20 feet.

vascular retinopathies a group of disorders caused by diminished blood flow to the eyes, causing visual defects.

vitreous humor the clear jelly in the large chamber behind the lens.

walleyed strabismus with one or both eyes pointing outward. Also, an eye with a light-colored iris.

EARS

aero-otitis middle ear inflammation produced by changes in altitude.

anvil the middle of the three tiny bones that transmit vibrations in the middle ear. Also known as the incus.

auditory nerve the nerve that carries electrical impulses from the ear to the brain.

auricle the external portion of the ear. Also known as the pinna.

cauliflower ear deformed ear caused by repeated trauma, mainly seen in boxers.

cerumen ear wax.

cochlea the spiral cavity of the inner ear containing the organ of Corti.

conductive deafness deafness caused by any defect of the external or middle ear.

Corti, organ of in the cochlea, it contains sensory cells that code sound waves into electrical signals, which are then sent to the brain.

Darwin's tubercle a point of cartilage in the upper part of the outer ear thought to be a vestige of a pointed ear by Charles Darwin.

eardrum the tympanic membrane.

equilibrium balance of the body, as maintained by the semicircular canal of the inner ear.

eustachian tube the canal leading from the back of the throat to the ear; it allows air pressure in the middle ear to equalize with air pressure outside in order to protect the eardrum from bursting.

hammer one of the three tiny bones that transmit vibrations in the middle ear. Also known as the malleus.

incus same as anvil.

inner ear the interior portion of the ear that contains the cochlear and auditory nerve.

labyrinth the semicircular canal of the inner ear: the organ of balance.

labyrinthitis inflammation of the labyrinth, causing vertigo and dizziness.

malleus same as hammer.

middle ear on the inside of the eardrum, the portion of the ear containing the hammer, anvil, and stirrup as well as the eustachian tube.

ossicles the three bones of the middle ear.

otalgia earache.

otitis externa painful inflammation of the external ear canal and auricle caused by bacteria. Known as swimmer's ear because it is often contracted by swimming in contaminated water.

otitis media inflammation of the middle ear that sometimes causes severe, throbbing pain, usually in children.

otocleisis obstruction of the eustachian tube.

otology the study of ear diseases.

otoplasty plastic surgery on the ears, usually to repair cauliflower ears or lop ears.

otosclerosis a hereditary disorder characterized by the development of spongy bone over the stirrup, disrupting vibrations and causing progressive deafness. It is the most common form of conductive deafness.

pinna the external ear.

semicircular canals same as labyrinth.

sensorineural deafness deafness caused by damage to the inner ear, to the auditory nerve or to the auditory cortex of the brain. Also known as nerve deafness.

stapes same as stirrup.

stirrup one of the three tiny bones that transmit vibrations in the middle ear. Also known as stapes.

tinnitus ringing in the ears.

tympanic membrane the eardrum.

vertigo a sense that one is spinning or whirling around, a symptom of inner ear impairment.

NOSE

anosmesia/anosmia inability to smell.

barosinusitis a sinus inflammation caused by a difference in atmospheric pressure inside and outside the nose.

columella the lower, front portion of the septum.

deviated septum a septum that has become crooked due to surgery, trauma, or abnormal growth; it often causes headaches or sinusitis; or it may block breathing through one nostril.

epistaxis a nosebleed.

nasal polyps benign nasal growths or tumors.

nasopharynx the nose and throat.

olfactory pertaining to the sense of smell.

olfactory bulbs extensions of the brain that relay odor signals to the brain.

olfactory epithelium in the roof of the nose, two yellow brown patches of membrane that trap odor molecules and act as smell receptors.

olfactory nerves transmit smell signals to the olfactory bulbs and to the brain.

osmology the study of the sense of smell.

parosima a distorted sense of smell, occurring in some cases of schizophrenia.

phantosmia odor hallucinations, suffered by some mentally ill patients.

philtrum the divot just below the nose and above the upper lip. Also known as the rhinarium.

postnasal drip mucus from the back of the nose that discharges down the throat.

rhinencephalon the portion of the brain concerned with smell.

rhinitis inflammation of the lining of the nose.

rhinology the study of the nose and its diseases and disorders.

rhinophyma a condition causing enlargement and redness of the nose. Also known as rummy nose, whiskey nose.

rhinoplasty plastic surgery on the nose; a nose job.

rhinorrhea a runny nose.

septum the thin wall of cartilage separating the two nasal passages.

sinuses the four groups of air-filled, mucus-lined chambers in the facial bones: frontal, ethmoidal, sphenoidal, and maxillary.

sinusitis an inflammation of the sinuses, often resulting from the common cold.

vibrissa hair in the nose.

SKIN

achromasia lacking in skin pigmentation, as an albino. Also known as leukoderma.

acne common skin condition, characterized by pustules and cysts, particular on the face; caused by hormonal changes during puberty.

acrogeria premature wrinkling.

alopecia hair loss; balding.

blackhead a plugged sweat gland.

boil a painful, contagious skin swelling caused by bacteria.

carbuncle a group of interconnected boils forming a large, painful mass that discharges pus from several locations.

chloasma brown patches frequently seen on the skin of pregnant women, due to hormonal changes.

collagen skin's network of connective fibers.

contact dermatitis any skin inflammation caused by contact with an irritant, such as poison ivy.

corn a horny, thickening of the skin around the toes, usually formed by friction.

cradle cap an infant scalp condition characterized by greasy, scaly, yellow patches.

cutaneous relating to the skin.

cuticle the hardened skin around the base of fingernails and toenails.

derma skin.

dermabrasion a method of removing scars by scraping off the top layers of skin.

dermatitis inflammation of the skin.

dermatologist a skin specialist.

dermatology the study of skin.

dermis the second layer of skin, below the epidermis.

eczema an acute or chronic inflammatory skin disorder characterized by redness, thickening, crusting, and the formation of papules and vesicles.

epidermis the outermost layer of skin.

erysipelas a streptococcus skin infection characterized by sharply defined red areas and accompanied by high fever. Also known as St. Anthony's fire.

exfoliation the constant process of skin peeling or skin cell shedding.

hives an allergic skin condition characterized by the eruption of itchy welts or blotches.

impetigo a contagious skin disease seen in children and the elderly and characterized by the eruption of itchy, crusting blisters.

keratin produced by the epidermis, the tough skin substance that nails and hair are made from.

keratinization the process by which the epidermis creates new keratin for use in nails and hair.

keratosis an overgrowth and thickening of the skin.

lentigo a brownish spot on the skin unrelated to a freckle.

leukoderma same as achromasia.

lichen any skin eruption.

lichen planus a common skin disease characterized by the eruption of itchy, reddish purple spots on the skin.

lupus erythematosus an acute or chronic skin disease marked by a scaly rash and often forming a butterfly pattern over the nose and cheeks.

lupus vulgaris tuberculosis of the skin, usually affecting the face.

melanin the dark pigment produced by skin.

melanoma cancer originating from skin pigment cells; a malignant mole. *See* CANCER.

melanosis the pigmentation or darkening of the skin after prolonged exposure to sunlight.

mole a congenital growth on the skin composed of a pigmented cluster of cells.

nevus any mark or growth present on the skin since birth.

panniculus a layer of fat beneath the skin.

papule a pimple.

piebald skin patchy areas of skin lacking in pigment, a mysterious condition. Also known as vitiligo.

port-wine stain a wine-colored birthmark.

pruritus itching of the skin.

psoriasis a chronic, noncontagious skin disease characterized by reddish patches covered with silvery scales.

pustule a small, pus-filled abcess.

rosacea an inflammatory skin disorder characterized by the eruption of papules and pustules and the dilation of facial capillaries.

St. Anthony's fire same as erysipelas.

scabies a skin infestation of mites (commonly known as itch mites) causing the formation of itchy lesions.

scleroderma pathologic thickening and hardening of the skin, sometimes with color changes.

sebaceous cyst a cyst containing smelly, fatty material.

sebaceous gland a skin gland that produces and secretes oil (sebum) to help keep the skin moist.

strawberry birthmark birthmark resembling a strawberry, caused by dilated blood vessels.

subcutaneous the layer of fat tissue beneath the dermis. Also, a general term for beneath the skin.

tag a skin polyp or small outgrowth of skin.

vesicle a blister.

vitiligo same as piebald skin.

wheal a hive; a skin swelling.

Zeiss gland an oil-secreting skin gland.

HAIR

achromotrichia lack of color in the hair; graying.

depilate to remove hair.

depilatory any substance that removes hair.

electrolysis removing hair with an electric needle.

hirsute hairy.

hirsutism abnormal hairiness on face and chest, especially in women. Also known as hypertrichosis.

male pattern baldness progressive balding thought to be caused by hormones.

melanocytes cells in the roots that give color to hair.

paratrichosis growth of hair in abnormal or odd places.

poliosis premature graying of the hair.

trichology the study of hair diseases.

HAIRSTYLES

abstract a geometrical haircut in which one side is cut shorter than another.

Afro kinky, puffed out hair, popular in the 1960s.

Afro puffs puffs of Afro-styled hair over each ear.

American Indian a style worn very long and straight and parted in the middle, sometimes worn in ponytails or braids.

bangs a fringe of hair worn over the forehead.

Beatle cut a bowllike cut with sideburns, popularized by the Beatles in the early 1960s.

beehive a woman's high domelike hair, reminiscent of a beehive, popular from late 1950s to mid-1960s.

bob a woman's short haircut, worn with or without bangs.

bouffant a style that is full and puffed out in an exaggerated fashion and held in place by lots of hairspray.

boyish bob a woman's very short haircut shingled in the back.

braids plaited hair worn down the back, over the shoulder or wound around the head.

bun a tight roll of hair held neatly at the crown of the head or the nape of the neck.

chignon a knot or roll of hair twisted into a circle or figure eight at the back of the head.

china doll short, straight hair having bangs in the front, a traditional Chinese cut.

classic pull-back long hair pulled back and tied with a ribbon or worn with a barrette.

Cleopatra hair worn long and straight down the sides, inspired by Cleopatra.

coif another word for a hairstyle.

corkscrew curls elongated curls resembling corkscrews, worn dangling at the sides.

cornrows hair braided into neat rows close to the head, a primarily black hairstyle.

crew cut a flat top; buzzcut.

dreadlocks *See* RASTAFARIAN DREADLOCKS.

ducktail a 1950s haircut in which the hair at the back of the head is combed to a point to resemble a duck's tail, worn by both sexes.

earmuffs a style parted in the middle with braids wound in circles about the ears.

elflocks matted or tangled hair.

empire cone a style in which the hair is pulled back smoothly through a conelike ornament and worn as a ponytail from the top of the head. The cone can also be wound with braids.

feather cut a woman's layered, slightly curled bob, popular in the 1960s and early 1970s.

fishbone braid a braid worn down the center of the back and resembling the spine of a fish. Also known as a French braid.

flat top crew cut.

flip a woman's style with ends forming a curl, worn with bangs.

French braid see fishbone braid.

French roll/twist a style in which the hair is pulled back and twisted into a roll or knot

garconne a woman's bob, worn by flappers in the 1920s.

Gibson girl a woman's puffy pompadour, popular early in the 20th century.

layered cut any style in which the hair is cut in graduated lengths around the head.

lion's tail a long piece of hair allowed to grow long down the back and tied with a cord to resemble a switch.

Mandinko the combination Mohawk, beard, mustache, and sideburns worn by Mr. T. on television.

mohawk a punk style in which all of the head is shaved except an upstanding brush 2 to 6 inches in height down the center of the head from front to back, inspired by the Mohawk Indians.

page boy straight shoulder length or shorter hair having ends that are turned up, worn with bangs.

pigtails braids worn dangling on both sides of the head, popular with little girls.

pixie a short, layered style cut and combed to points around the face and forehead.

pompadour a woman's style in which the hair is swept up high from the forehead. Also, a man's style (popular in the 1950s) in which the hair is swept up high with no part from the forehead.

poodle cut short, curly hair, reminiscent of a poodle's coat.

porcupine a punk haircut characterized by long strands made to stiffen and stand up on the center of the head by mousse or gel.

punk any mohawk, porcupine, dyed, shaved, sculpted, or spiked hair.

queue one long braid extending down the back, as a Chinaman.

Rastafarian dreadlocks a Jamacian style in which the head is covered with tight, dangling braids, shoulder length, or longer.

Sassoon a woman's short, straight, skullcap-like cut with bangs and angled sides whose ends are turned under.

sculptured hair moussed or gelled and arranged in various designs. Also, hair having shaved-in designs, logos, and such like.

shag a long, shaggy bob with bangs.

shingle a tapering of the hair at the back of the head or neck.

spikes moussed or gelled hair formed into long spikes and often dyed.

topknot hair tied into a knot at the crown of the head.

Veronica Lake a woman's style with long hair parted to one side and partially covering one eye, popularized by actress Veronica Lake in the 1940s and revived in the 1960s.

wedge a style in which the front and sides are of equal length while the back is tapered close to the head, worn with short bangs; popularized by Olympic skater Dorothy Hamill in the 1970s.

Hairstyles of the 19th Century

à la Concierge a woman's style in which long hair is pulled to the top of the head and pinned in a knot, popular from the late 19th to the early 20th century.

Apollo knot false hair coiled, looped, or plaited, and wired to stand up on the head, from 1826 on.

barley-sugar curl children's style comprised of long drop curls.

beaver tail a broad, flat loop of hair hung over the nape of the neck, from 1865. Also known as a banging chignon.

blinkers a woman's style in which the hair was allowed to hang down the sides of the face.

caracalla cut a woman's short style having flattened, sausage-shaped curls.

chignon a knot or roll of hair worn at the back of the head by women.

curlicue a curl of a hair worn over the forehead by men.

giraffe mid-century woman's style in which hair is piled high in rolls, supported by a tall comb and dressed with flowers.

gooseberry wig a man's large, frizzled wig, worn in England.

Julian a woman's short hairstyle of the early 1800s.

Marcel wave woman's style in which waves were arranged around the head with a curling iron, popular in the 1890s.

neck coiffure a style in which the hair was pulled up in back and in front and gathered in curls on the crown of the head, popular in the 1890s.

HAIRSTYLES OF THE 18TH CENTURY

Adonis wig a flowing, white-powdered wig popularly worn by young European men from 1734 to 1775.

à la Belle Poule a woman's wig style crowned by a model of a three-masted ship.

à la Charmes de la Liberté a woman's late-century style noted for its dressings of feathers, ribbons, and grasses.

à la Cybelle a woman's foot-high, towerlike style, as that worn by the goddess Cybele.

à la Grecque a man's style in which the hair is curled on each side and drawn into a horseshoelike fashion in back, popular in the 1780s.

à la Victime a French style popular in 1795; the hair was pulled up and away from the neck, as if in preparation for a decapitaion by guillotine, and worn with a blood-red ribbon about the neck, inspired by the French Revolution.

à la Zodiaque a woman's high hairstyle dressed with stars, the moon and sun.

bag a wig of any type. Also a bag wig.

bag wig a man's wig in which the tail was enclosed in a black satin bag, from 1737 on. Also known as a purse wig. See buorse.

bourse the bag in which the tail of a bag wig was enclosed. Also known as a crapaud.

brigadier wig a wig having a double corkscrew tail tied with a bow at the nape of the neck, worn in the second half of the century.

cadogan wig a wig having a broad, straight tail foled back on itself and tied, popular in the 1760s. Also known as a club wig.

cauliflower wig a short, tightly curled, white bob wig worn by doctors and clergy in London.

gorgone a woman's style in which the hair was pulled high with loose, writhing curls, reminiscent of Medusa's serpent head.

lappet curl a corkscrew curl.

macaroni a huge, high, elaborate wig worn by dandies in the 1770s.

morning coiffure a woman's style in which hair at the back is pulled up and plaited, crossed at the crown, and then allowed to hang back to form a thick loop.

periwig a wig.

Picadilly fringe a roll of hair near the forehead, worn by Englishmen in the first half of the century.

pigeon's wing periwig a man's wig having two horizontal rolls above the ears on either side of the head, from the 1750s to 1760s.

pigtail wig a man's wig with a long tail twirled and tied with a ribbon.

pincurls an artificial curl or curls pinned to the hair by a hairpin.

queue the tail of a wig.

snood a band or ribbon used to tie up a woman's hair.

spit curl a curl fashioned and secured to the forehead by spit.

washerwoman's style a woman's style in which hair is pulled up to form a bun at the top of the head, primarily English.

BEARDS

à la Souvaroff a style in which the mustache joins with the sideburns, the chin left clean-shaven.

alfalfa early American slang for a beard.

anchor a short, pointy beard worn at the edge of the chin with a fringe extending up to the center of the bottom lip.

Assyrian a long beard having plaits or spiral curls

aureole a rounded beard.

barbiche a small tuft of hair under the bottom lip. Also known as a barbula.

beaver early 20th-century slang for a beard or a man with a beard.

Belgrave a medium-length, neatly trimmed beard that may be square-cut, rounded, rounded with a point, or pointed.

burnside a mustache joined with sideburns with the chin left clean-shaven, named after General Ambrose Burnside in the 19th century.

cadiz a Spanish-style, pointed beard of medium length.

cathedral beard a long, flowing beard that broadens at the bottom like a fishtail, worn by clergy members in mid-16th to 17th century.

ducktail a neatly trimmed, long slender beard resembling the tail of a duck.

Dundreary whiskers whiskers grown long and hanging off the sides of the face while the chin is left clean-shaven.

forked a beard either combed or cut into two different branches or wisps. *See* SWALLOW-TAIL.

goatee a small, pointed beard, resembling that of a goat.

Imperial a long tuft of hair extending down from beneath the lower lip, named after that worn by Napoleon III in 1839.

Jewish a long, bushy, untrimmed beard, as that prescribed in the book of Leviticus in the Old Testament.

Lincolnesque a medium-length beard and sideburns worn without a mustache.

muttonchops side whiskers or sideburns trimmed to resemble mutton chops.

Old Dutch beard a short, square-cut beard with a clean-shaven upper and lower lip.

Olympian beard a very long, thick beard. Also known as a patriarchal beard.

pencil beard a thin ridge of beard extending from the bottom lip to the chin.

Raleigh a pointed beard, with the facial portion being closely trimmed, named after Sir Walter Raleigh.

Roman T a small, rectangular tuft hanging below the lower lip and accompanied with a straight or rectangular mustache to form the letter T.

Satyric tuft a chin tuft, as that worn by Satyr, the half-goat, half-man creature from Greek mythology.

screw beard a short, slender beard that is twisted or twined, popular in the 17th century. Any twisted beard.

Shenandoah a spade beard.

spade a pointy or rounded beard resembling a spade.

stiletto a long, slender, pointed beard.

swallow-tail a thickly forked beard resembling the tail of a swallow.

tile a long, square-cut beard.

Trojan a thick, square-cut, curly beard of medium length.

Uncle Sam a beard as that worn by the cartoon figure Uncle Sam.

Vandyke a short, pointed beard usually worn without sideburns.

MUSTACHES

à la Souvaroff a style in which the mustache joins with the sideburns, the chin left clean-shaven.

boxcar a rectangle with squared ends.

chevron like a chevron, broad in the center and narrowing toward ends that extend beyond the lips.

Clark Gable a neat thin line.

handlebar short or long, usually thick, with ends turned up like bicycle handlebars.

Hindenburg a very long, thick mustache with turned-up ends.

horseshoe a long mustache that droops down over the chin.

Kaiser a mustache having turned up ends, as worn by Germany's Kaiser in 1914.

mistletoe narrow mustache comprised of two crescents, reminiscent of mistletoe leaves.

pencil line a very narrow mustache, sometimes divided in two at the center lip. Also a line drawn on the upper lip.

pyramid a pyramid-shaped or triangular mustache.

regent a neat mustache resembling a rounded letter M or the twin peaks of round-top mountains.

Roman T a rectangular mustache worn with a narrow tuft hanging from below the lower lip, to form the letter T.

soupstrainer *See* WALRUS.

square button *See* TOOTHBRUSH.

toothbrush a short rectangle or square, as that worn by Charlie Chaplin and Hitler.

walrus a thick, broad mustache allowed to grow and droop over the upper and sometimes even the lower lip. Also known as a soupstrainer.

waxed a mustache in which the ends are waxed to create points or curves.

wings neatly trimmed mustache resembling bird wings.

CONCEPTION, PREGNANCY, AND CHILDBIRTH

abortion the spontaneous or medically induced termination of a pregnancy.

abruptio placentae separation of the placenta from the uterine wall.

active phase during the first stage of labor, the phase characterized by contractions lasting about 60 seconds and occurring every 2 to 5 minutes.

afterpains postbirth pain and cramping caused by contractions of the uterus as it returns to its normal size.

alpha fetoprotein (AFP) a protein produced in the liver of a fetus and passed through the placenta into the mother's bloodstream; a high amount of AFP in the mother's blood indicates a neural tube defect.

amniocentesis the taking of a small ample of amniotic fluid in order to determine the presence of genetic or other disorders in the fetus.

amnion the innermost bag containing the fetus and amniotic fluid; one of two layers making up the amniotic sac.

amniotic fluid waters, urine, and other fluids in which the fetus floats in the uterus.

amniotomy the medically induced rupturing of the amniotic sac to speed up labor.

anencephaly a congenital defect in which only a small part of the brain develops.

antepartum before labor or before childbirth.

anterior position the head position most frequently assumed by an infant during birth, specifically head first and face down.

Apgar score a system for rating a baby's general health at birth, specifically a number score from 0–2 covering heart rate, respiration, muscle tone, reflexes, and color.

artificial insemination the depositing of semen into the cervix through a plastic tube.

blastocyst the earliest form or stage of embryonic development.

bloody show a discharge of blood and mucuous, a symptom of impending labor.

bonding the emotional attachment that grows between parents and child before and after birth.

Bradley method childbirth techniques involving the husband as labor coach and the use of slow, rhythmic breathing and relaxation to control pain.

Braxton-Hicks contractions often mistaken for true labor contractions, actually mild and intermitttent prelabor contractions that go away within a few hours.

breech presentation the delivering baby presenting itself feet first or buttocks first.

caul the fetal membranes covering the head during delivery.

cephalic disproportion the condition of a woman's pelvis being too small for the baby's head to pass through.

cephalic presentation a head-first presentation.

cerclage the temporary closing of the cervix through suturing to prevent premature delivery.

cervical os the opening between the uterus and the vagina.

cervix the neck of uterus.

cesarean section the surgical removal of a baby through the abdominal wall of the mother.

chloasma brown patches or pigmentation that appear on the skin and face of some pregnant woman, known as the "mask of pregnancy."

chorion the outermost or second of two membranes containing the fetus.

chorionic villus sampling removal and evaluation of a small portion of the placenta to determine the presence of genetic abnormalities in the fetus.

chromosomes the rod-shaped bodies in a cell on which the genes are located.

circumcision surgical removal of the foreskin of a male infant's penis.

colostrum the yellowish or whitish fluid secreted from a mother's breast during the last weeks of pregnancy and prior to the production of breast milk.

congenital existing before or at birth, usually used to describe medical conditions.

contraction the uterine muscular action that dilates the cervix during labor.

cordocentesis the taking of a blood sample from the umbilical cord to test for genetic blood disorders.

couvade referring to the sympathetic symptoms of pregnancy developed by the father.

crib death *See* SUDDEN INFANT DEATH SYNDROME.

crowning when the full diameter of the baby's head appears from the vaginal opening.

deoxyribonucleic acid (DNA) the protein containing genetic information.

differentiation the splitting and specializing of cells to become individual body parts.

dihydrotestosterone the hormone responsible for the development of fetal genitalia.

dilation and evacuation an abortion performed by suction.

dystocia a problematic or difficult labor.

ectoderm the outermost layer of embryoblast cells that become the skin, hair, nails and nervous system.

ectopic pregnancy the development of the fertilized egg outside the uterus, in the fallopian tubes.

edema fluid build up in the body tissues during pregnancy, causing swelling.

embryoblast the innermost cells of a blastocyst, from which the embryo develops.

embryo transfer the transferring of a donor embryo into another woman's uterus for development.

endoderm the innermost layer of embryoblast cells that develop into the gastrointestinal tract, the liver and the lungs.

endometritis inflammation of the lining of the uterus.

endometrium the uterine lining where the fertilized ovum is attached.

endoscopy the employment of a lighted instrument to examine an inner body cavity.

epididymis the passage through which sperm travel from the testicles to the vas deferens.

epidural a local anesthesia administered to block pain from the lower part of the body during labor.

episiotomy during labor, an incision made from the vagina down toward the anus to create more room for the passage of the baby's had.

external cephalic version manipulation of the uterus to position the fetus head down.

fallopian tubes the tubes extending laterally from either side of the uterus through which the egg passes each month.

fetal alcohol syndrome various mental and physical defects found in a newborn infant due to a mother's consumption of alcohol.

fetal monitor an instrument that measures fetal heart rate and uterine contractions during labor.

fetoscopy the introduction of a fetoscope (an optical device) through the mother's abdominal wall to visually examine a fetus, take skin and blood samples, or perform surgery.

fontanel one of the two soft spots in a baby's skull to allow molding through the birth canal and to allow for new brain growth in the first 18 months of life.

fraternal twims twins developed from two fertilized ova.

funic souffle sound of fetal blood rushing through umbilical vessels.

gene the part of a chromosome controlling hereditary traits.

gynecology the branch of medicine that deals with a woman's reproductive organs.

human chorionic gonadotrophin the placental hormone whose presence signals that a woman is pregnant.

hysteroscopy an examination of the uterus through an endoscope.

iatrogenic prematurity delivery of an infant earlier than expected due to an inaccurate estimate of gestational age given by a physician.

implantation the attaching of the fertilized egg to the uterine wall, occurring one to nine days after fertilization.

incompetent cervix the inability of the cervix to remain closed during pregnancy, resulting in premature birth.

instillation abortion an abortion induced by an injection of saline or prostaglandin into the amniotic sac.

inversion of the uterus when the uterus is turned inside-out during birth, occurring when the umbilical cord is pulled before the placenta is detached.

in vitro fertilization a method of conception employed in women with damaged fallopian tubes, characterized by the gathering and mixing of ova and sperm, and the implanation of any fertilized eggs in the uterus.

Kegel exercises exercises to strengthen the muscles surrounding the vagina.

labor the regular and powerful contractions of the uterus during childbirth.

lactation the production and secretion of breast milk.

lactogenic hormone the pituitary hormone that stimulates lactation and the growth of breasts.

Lamaze method childbirth method developed by Dr. Fernand Lamaze, consisting of exercises and breathing techniques to help women pass through each stage of labor with a minimum of trauma.

lanugo the fine coat of downy hair covering the fetus from 20 weeks until birth.

latent phase the first phase of the first stage of labor, characterized by moderate contractions occurring at 5- to 15-minute intervals and lasting 30 to 60 seconds each.

Leboyer delivery a natural childbirth method in which the child is delivered in a peaceful atmosphere and with the smallest amount of pain and mental trauma as possible.

Leopold's maneuvers the examination of a woman's abdomen to determine the position of the fetus.

letdown reflex the release of milk from the alveoli of the breasts to the milk ducts, a reflex caused by the hormone oxytocin.

linea nigra a dark line or streak running from the belly button to the public area, seen on many pregnant women.

lochia vaginal discharge of blood, mucus, and tissue after birth.

luteal phase the ovulation phase of the menstrual cycle.

mastitis an infection of breast tissue.

meconium the greenish black, odorless stools passed by the fetus soon after birth.

menarche the onset of the first menstruation.

mesoderm the central layer of the embryolast cells from which muscles, bone, blood, and connective tissue develop.

miscarriage a spontaneous abortion.

midwife a person who delivers or assists in delivering babies.

molding the process by which the infant's head changes shape or "molds" to facilitate delivery through the birth canal.

monozygotic twins twins that develop from a single ovum. Also known as identical twins.

morning sickness nausea and vomiting during pregnancy, now referred to as pregnancy sickness.

neonatal referring to an infant from birth to 28 days.

neonatologist a physicial specializing in newborns.

nurse midwife a registered nurse who has graduated from a midwifery program.

obstetrics the branch of medicine that deals with pregnancy and childbirth.

ovary the gland that produces estrogen and progesterone and that contains eggs in various stages of development.

ovulation the discharge of an egg for possible fertilization by sperm.

ovum an egg or reproductive cell.

oxytocin the pituitary hormone that stimulates uterine contractions and the letdown reflex during lactation.

parturition the process of giving birth; labor.

perineum the area between the anus and the vulva.

periodic breathing common to most preterm infants, episodes of apnea or cessations of breathing.

pica the craving or eating of bizarre substances, such as starch or clay, during pregnancy.

placenta the temporary organ through which the fetus receives nutrients and exchanges oxygen and carbon dioxide from the mother.

polydactyly having an extra finger or toe.

posterior position presentation in which the head emerges face up.

postpartum after childbirth.

postpartum depression depression suffered by some mothers after childbirth, possibly related to hormone fluctuations.

premature labor any labor that begins before the 38th week of gestation.

presentation the part of the baby that emerges first from the vaginal opening; the position of the baby at birth.

preterm infant an infant with a gestational age less than 38 weeks.

progesterone the female hormone responsible for the thickening of the uterine lining before conception.

prostaglandins a group of compounds responsible for uterine contractions.

pseudocyesis when a woman is convinced she is pregnant but is not; false pregnancy.

pudendal block a local anesthetic administered through injection into the vaginal area to numb the pelvic area.

puerperal psychosis severe postpartum depression requiring hospitalization.

quickening a mother's first perception of fetal movement.

recessive inheritance inheritance trait requiring genes from both parents.

sonogram an ultrasound picture of the uterus and fetus.

stillbirth birth of a dead fetus.

striae gravidarum stretch marks.

sudden infant death syndrome (SIDS) the mysterious death of an infant thought to be healthy; also known as crib death.

teratogen any substance or factor that harms the fetus.

transition the last phase of the first stage of labor, characterized by full dilation of the cervix and contractions arriving every 1 to 3 minutes and lasting 60 to 90 seconds each.

trimester any one of the three-month divisions in the nine months of pregnancy.

ultrasound high-frequency sound waves beamed into and reflected off the body to create pictures.

umbilical cord the cord connecting the placental and the fetus.

umbilicus the navel.

vernix caseosa a white, fatty substance coating the skin of the fetus up until birth.

zygote the fertilized egg before it divides.

CANCER AND TUMORS (*Also see* SURGICAL PROCEDURES)

adenocarcinoma a common form of cancer originating in a gland.

Adriamycin a cancer-fighting chemical used in chemotherapy and frequently causing hair loss.

angioblastoma a cancerous tumor consisting of tissue from blood vessels.

arrhenoblastoma an ovarian tumor known for its masculinizing effects.

astroblastoma: a malignant brain tumor.

basal cell tumor a small, common skin cancer frequently found around the nose or under the eyes, usually treatable with surgery or x-rays.

benign not cancerous; not malignant.

biopsy taking a tissue sample from a tumor to help make a diagnosis.

carcinogen any substance that causes cancer.

carcinoma any cancer formed from the cells lining organs.

carcinoma in situ a localized cancer that has not spread and is therefore easier to treat.

carcinomatosis cancer that has spread to or invaded other parts of the body.

carcinosarcoma a malignant tumor of the lining and muscles of the uterus.

chemotherapy the treatment of cancer with drugs or chemicals.

chondrofibroma a benign tumor consisting of cartilage and fibrous tissue.

chondrosarcoma a malignant tumor composed of cartilage.

choriocarcinoma malignant cancer formed in the sexual organs.

cystadenoma a benign tumor containing cysts.

dermatofibroma a benign tumor of the skin.

eosinophilic tumor a tumor of the pituitary gland that in children sometimes causes extreme growth spurts (gigantism).

ependymoma a type of brain tumor.

feminizing tumor an ovarian tumor that in children may cause premature menstruation and precocious breast development; in older women, it may cause new breast growth and a return of vaginal bleeding.

fibroadenoma a common benign tumor made of fibrous and glandular tissue found in the breast.

fibroid tissue benign uterine tumor made of muscle and fibrous tissue.

gamma ray a type of radiation used in treating malignancies.

germinoma a tumor of the testicle.

leukemia collective term for a family of malignant diseases of white blood cells and blood-forming marrow; some cause death within weeks, whereas others may last 20 years or more.

Leukeran an anticancer medication used in treating leukemia.

lipoma common benign tumor made of fat and found beneath the skin.

liposarcoma a malignant tumor copmosed of fat tissue.

lumpectomy surgial removal of a tumor or mass.

lymphoblastoma a malignant tumor of the lymph glands.

malignant deadly, potentially fatal, cancerous.

masculinizing tumor of the ovary ovarian tumor that may produce such masculine traits as a deepening voice and facial hair in women.

mastectomy the surgical removal of a breast as a treatment for cancer.

melanoblastoma malignant skin tumor arising from pigment cells.

melanoma a skin mole that has become cancerous.

metastasis the spread of cancer from one body part to another.

monoclonal antibodies cloned antibodies used as a treatment to resist cancer growth.

myclocytic leukemia a fatal form of leukemia.

myeloma a malignant tumor of bone marrow.

myofibroma a benign tumor made of muscle and fibrous tissue.

myoma a benign tumor of muscle.

myosarcoma a malignant tumor of muscle.

neoplasm a tumor; a growth.

nephroma a kidney tumor.

oncogenic same as carcinogenic.

oncology the branch of medicine concerned with tumors and tumor growth.

osteogenic sarcoma a malignant bone tumor.

papilloma a benign growth of mucus membranes.

photochemotherapy cancer treatment consisting of drugs or chemicals exposed to ultraviolet radiation, which has been shown to increase effectiveness.

polyp a benign growth or tumor arising on a stalk from mucus membranes.

radioresistant a term describing a tumor that is unaffected by radiation therapy.

radiotherapy radiation therapy.

resectable a tumor that can be surgically removed.

sarcoma a malignant tumor composed of bone, muscle, or fat.

thermography measuring the amount of heat given off by different body areas, concerous growths give off slightly higher heat.

Warthin's tumor a benign tumor of the parotid gland.

Wilm's tumor a malignant tumor of the kidney found in young children.

PSYCHOLOGY AND PSYCHIATRY

abreaction the psychoanalytic process of reducing anxiety by reliving through speech or action the experiences that cause anxiety.

accident prone a neurotic desire for attention manifesting itself by an unusual number of accidents or injuries.

achiria a hysterical state in which a person feels he or she has lost one or both of his hands.

aeroneurosis airplane pilot's neurosis characterized by restless anxiety.

alethia dwelling excessively on past events.

ambivert term describing a person with a combination of extroverted and introverted personality traits.

amnesia the total loss of memory of past events.

anaclasis the psychologic attachment to a person who reminds one of his mother or father during childhood.

anomie feelings of not being a part of society; alienation.

anorexia nervosa a psychiatric disorder characterized by extreme dieting to the point of emaciation.

antisocial personality a personality characterized by impulsiveness, absence of conscience, and a complete disregard for others. Formerly known as a sociopath or psychopath.

anxiety hierarchy a list of situations given by an individual that are ranked for how much anxiety they produce, from slight to extreme.

aphagia inability to eat.

aphasia loss of speech or the ability to comprehend speech, often a symptom of brain disease.

asocial lack of interest in other people.

astasia-abasia hysterical state in which the person believes he or she has lost the ability to stand or walk.

atavism the reverting to a primitive behavior or state of mind.

attention deficit disorder in some children, a disorder characterized by an inability to pay attention accompanied by impulsiveness.

autism a misunderstood brain disorder characterized by withdrawal from reality and absorption in inner fantasies.

aversive conditioning changing someone's behavior by punishing them.

behaviorism a school of psychology that holds that valid data can come only from objective observation and experimentation.

biofeedback with the help of a feedback machine, the self-regulating of heart rate, blood pressure, and brain waves to achieve desired results such as deep relaxation.

bipolar disorder mental illness characterized by alternating periods of elation and depression. Also known as manic depression. *See* MANIC DEPRESSIVE PSYCHOSIS.

borderline personality disorder a disorder characterized by persistent instability, impulsivity, and unpredictability accompanied by a chronic sense of emptiness and suicidal impulses.

bulimia an eating disorder characterized by binging followed by intentional vomiting.

cardioneurosis a neurotic manifestation of anxiety characterized by pain in the heart, palpitations, and a sensation of suffocation.

cataphasia frequent repetition of the same word or phrase.

catatonic stupor in which the person becomes motionless and mute.

catharsis the reduction of a negative emotion or impulse by the verbal expression or acting out of that emotion or impulse.

classical conditioning the teaching of an individual to relate one stimulus, such as a bell, to another stimulus, such as food, as in Pavlov's dogs.

classical paranoia an isolated paranoia revolving around a single subject in one's life in which the person may otherwise be normal.

cognitive reprogramming replacing negative thoughts with positive thinking to change a person's perception of himself or the world around him.

compensation an ego defense in which a person compensates for deficiencies by striving for superiority in other areas.

compulsion any ritualistic behavior, often senseless, that a person feels must be carried out.

compulsive personality a personality characterized by tenseness, rigidity, overconscientiousness, and an obsession for trivial details.

consensual validation determining if one person's perception of reality matches with another's.

conversion the unconscious process through which stress is converted into a physical, physiologic, or psychologic symptom.

conversion reaction a neurotic reaction in which overwhelming anxiety manifests itself in a physical way through bodily paralysis or through uncontrollable emotional outburst.

coprophilia abnormal interest in feces.

dacnomania *See* MANIAS.

decompensation the process of psychologic deterioration as a result of severe or long-term stress.

defense mechanism any thought or belief system employed to protect the ego from a lowering of esteem.

deindividuation the loss of social inhibitions and acting out of aggressions and impulses due to anonymity in a crowd or anonymity behind a mask or costume.

delirium tremens alcohol poisoning characterized by hallucinations, trembling and paranoia.

delusion a false belief about oneself or the world held despite evidence to the contrary.

dementia loss of intellectual faculties with accompanying emotional distrubances due to organic brain disorder.

demonomania *See* MANIAS.

dependent personality disorder a disorder characterized by passivity, helplessness, indecisiveness, and an overdependency on other people.

depersonalization a dissociative reaction characterized by feelings of unrealness, separation, isolation, and a loss of identity.

desensitization the cure of a fear or phobia by gradual, step-by-step exposure to the source of the fear.

diffusion of responsibility the tendency for people in groups to fail to take action in an emergency due to the belief that "someone else" will act.

displacement a defense mechanism involving the transfer of feelings or actions from an unacceptable to acceptable form.

dissociation a collective term for the various symptoms that occur when anxiety is handled by a splitting off of part of the personality and the breaking up of the sense of self, with symptoms ranging from a sense of unrealness and loss of identity to fainting.

dissonance inconsistency between one's actions and one's attitudes.

dominance high social rank.

doraphobia *See* PHOBIAS.

double blind an experiment in which neither the investigator nor the subjects know which group is receiving a real treatment or a placebo.

echolalia a disorder in which the person repeats the last words heard.

electroconvulsive therapy electric shock therapy administered to the brain.

electroencephalograph (EEG) a device that measures the electrical activity of the brain.

enuresis bedwetting.

ethnocentricity believing your own beliefs and values are the only right ones; cultural biases.

exhibitionism the compulsive desire to reveal one's genitals.

explosive disorder a disorder characterized by periodic explosive outbursts followed by remorse.

explosive personality a person prone to explosive outbursts.

existentialism the philosophical belief that people have the freedom to make choices, decide the meaning of reality, and to take responsibility for their existence.

fetishism a sexual deviation characterized by an attraction to inanimate objects, such as shoes, or on things like hands and feet, instead of to people.

fight-or-flight response a mental and physical alarm stage that releases adrenalin and other hormones into the bloodstream to prepare the body for fighting or fleeing.

fixation the failure to complete the maturation process in a particular stage of development.

free association the psychoanalytical method of revealing the unconscious by asking a patient to say whatever word pops into his mind first in response to a stimulus word.

free-floating anxiety vague feelings of fear or anxiety without any observable cause or source.

frustration-aggression theory a theory that holds that aggression occurs in response to frustration of goals.

fugue state a dissociative reaction to anxiety in which a person runs away and has no memory of his actions over a period of time.

galvanic skin response changes in the electrical conductivity of skin as detected by a galvanometer and used as an emotional indicator.

Gestalt therapy group therapy featuring one person in the "hot seat" to role-play, explore feelings, fantasies, and dreams, and so forth.

hallucination a false perception; seeing, hearing, feeling, or smelling something that isn't there.

hallucinogen any substance or drug known to cause hallucinations.

hallucinosis symptoms of disordered perception—including auditory, visual, and tactile hallucinations—occurring in people withdrawing from severe alcohol abuse.

hebephrenia a rare form of schizophrenia characterized by regressive behavior and a constant silly grin.

hedonism the theory that man seeks pleasure and avoids pain and that happiness represents the greatest good.

histrionic personality a personality characterized by dramatic atttention seeking, excitability, egocentricity, and overdependency.

hyperactivity a childhood disorder characterized by excessive activity and a failure to inhibit motion or complete tasks.

hypermnesia increased memory through hypnosis.

hyperphagia pathologic overeating.

hyperventilation a common reaction to anxiety, rapid breathing that reduces carbon dioxide in the blood, causing lightheadedness, incoordination, palpitations, and a sensation of needing more air—generally resolved by breathing into a paper bag.

hypnotic trance a dreamlike state of increased suggestibility.

hypochondriasis an excessive anxiety over aches and pains and overall physical health.

hysteria a neurotic state characterized by episodes of hallucinations, amnesia, and other mental aberrations.

id in psychoanalytic theory, the component of personality concerned with such instinctual urges as hunger, thirst, sex, and aggression.

implosive therapy a therapy technique in which a patient is harmlessly frightened as much as possible until anxiety is alleviated.

imprinting the learning of behavior patterns during sensitive periods of growth early in life.

inadequate personality a personality that is inept socially, emotionally, and intellectually.

insight therapy a therapy technique that attempts to reveal a patient's hidden motives behind a specific behavior.

James-Lange theory proposes that physiologic reactions to an outer stimulus produces the experience of emotion.

Korsakoff's psychosis alcoholic psychosis characterized by distorted thinking and loss of memory.

lability an unstable state characterized by rapidly changing moods or behaviors.

lapsus linguae a slip of the tongue.

latency in psychoanalytic theory, the development period between age 6 and puberty, wherein little occurs in the way of psychosexual development.

latent content in Freudian theory, the underlying or hidden meaning of dreams.

logomania nonstop talking.

logorrhea excessive and irrational talking.

malingerer someone who pretends to be ill.

mania elation or euphoria accompanied by irrational behavior, often alternating with deep depression, as in manic-depressive illness.

mania an obsession or crazed desire for something.

Mania	Types
alcohol	dipsomania
animals	zoomania
books	bibliomania
cats	ailuromania
children	pedomania
Christ, delusion that one is	theomania
dancing	choreomania
death	necromania
demons, devil, delusion that one is possessed by	demonomania
dogs	cynomania
eating	sitomania
fire	pyromania
flowers	anthomania
food	phagomania
genius, delusion that one is	sophomania
horses	hippomania
kill, desire to	dacnomania
money	chrematomania
nakedness	gymnomania
night	noctimania
open places, living out in	agoromania
pleasure	hedonomania
sex	aphrodisiomania, nymphomania
sleep	hypnomania
solitude	automania
stealing	kleptomania
sun	heliomania
talking	logomania
travel	hodomania
washing	ablutomania
wealth	plutomania
women	gynemania
woods	hylomania

manic excited.

manic-depressive psychosis a condition characterized by extreme mood swings, from normal to elated, or from normal to depressed, or a combination of all of the above.

marasmus the deterioration and emaciation of an infant due to prolonged maternal separation and deprivation of affection.

masochism deriving sexual pleasure from being hurt by oneself or by another.

Minnesota Multiphasic Personality Inventory a widely used test given by psychologists and psychiatrists to measure personality traits and psychopathology.

misanthropy an aversion to people.

misogyny an aversion to women.

morbid anxiety extreme, incapaciting anxiety.

multiple personality a rare dissociative disorder in which the person develops or displays more than one distinct personality.

narcissism excessive self-love, selfishness, and self-centeredness.

narcohypnosis hypnotizing a person who is under the influence of drugs.

necrophilism sexual attraction to or sexual intercourse with a corpse. Also, a death wish.

nihilistic delusions delusions concerning annihilation of self or body organs.

obsessive-compulsive disorder a mental disorder characterized by thoughts, actions, or rituals repeated again and again, such as checking 10 times to make sure the iron is unplugged before leaving the house.

Oedipus complex the sexual feelings of a child, usuallly male, for a parent of the opposite sex, and accompanied by feelings of hostility to the parent of the same sex.

organic behavior disorder a disorder caused by physical damage to the brain or nervous system.

organic psychiatry emphasizing the physical causes of behavior disorders.

paradoxical psychology reverse psychology.

paranoid schizophrenia a schizophrenic disorder in which the person suffers from delusions of persecution.

paraphrenia a late-life schizophrenia with paranoid ideation.

passive-aggressive personality a chronically discontented, petulant, fault-finding personality that reveals inner hostility by such passive actions as "forgetting" promises or by vacillating between passive dependency on others and stubborn independence.

pedophilia sex act between an adult and child.

phantosmia odor hallucinations.

phobia an irrational fear of a person, place, or thing. Phobias include the following:

animals	zoophobia
animal skin or fur, touching	doraphobia
blood	hemophobia
blushing	erythrophobia
bridges	gephyrophobia
burial alive	taphephobia
cancer	cancerphobia
cats	ailurophobia
children	pedophobia
cold	psychrophobia
confinement in enclosed space	claustrophobia
crowds	demophobia
dark	nyctophobia
dead bodies, death	necrophobia
death	thanatophobia, necrophobia
defecation	rhypophobia
depths	bahtophobia
dirt	mysophobia
dogs	cynophobia
eating	phagophobia
failure	kakorrhaphiophobia
fire	pyrophobia
flood	antlophobia
foreigners or strangers	xenophobia
ghosts	phasmophobia
heights	acrophobia
infinity	apeirophobia
insects	acarophobia, entomophobia
knives	aichmophobia
lice	pediculophobia
marriage	gamophobia
medicine	pharmacophobia

men	androphobia
mice	musophobia
missiles	ballistophobia
money	chrematophobia
night	nyctophobia
noise	phonophobia, acousticophobia
number 13	triskaidekaphobia
ocean	thalassophobia
old age	gerontophobia
open spaces	agoraphobia
pain	algophobia
poison	toxicophobia
precipices	cremnophobia
responsibility	hypengyophobia
ridicule	catagelophobia
robbers	harpaxophobia
sex	coitophobia, genophobia
sharp objects	aichmophobia
sin, committing	peccatiphobia
sleep	hypnophobia
snakes	ophidiophobia
snow	chionophobia
solitude	autophobia
speaking	lalophoia
spiders	arachnophobia
stars	astrophobia
strangers	xenophobia
sunlight	heliophobia
thunderstorms	astraphobia, brontophobia
touched, being	haptephobia
venereal disease	cypridophobia
women	gynophobia
work	ergophobia

posthypnotic suggestion a suggestion given to a hypnotized person that is performed after coming out of the trance.

post traumatic stress disorder extreme symptoms of stress manifesting themselves weeks, months, or years after experiencing a traumatic event.

prefrontal lobotomy partial surgical removal of the frontal brain lobes from the thalamus, a procedure used to treat psychiatric conditions in the 1930s and 1940s.

projection an ego defense mechanism in which an awareness of one's undesirable traits or thoughts are repressed and attributed to someone else.

proxemics the study of such nonverbal expression as physical distance maintained between two or more people in a social situation and their body orientation toward one another.

pseudocyesis false pregnancy, a symptom of conversion hysteria.

psychoanalysis the Freudian school of thought emphasizing the study of the unconscious mind and the accompanying therapy which strives to bring unconscious desires into consciousness and to resolve conflicts dating back to childhood.

psychodrama role-playing psychotherapy in which personal conflicts and fantasies are acted out in front of a group.

psychogenic amnesia the loss of memory of portions of the past that are threatening or painful.

psychogenic pain disorder chronic or severe pain without any identifiable source.

psychopharmacology the study of the effects of drugs on behavior.

psychophysiological disorder any physical pain or illness having a psychological cause. Also known as psychosomatic disorder.

psychotherapy talk therapy

psychotropic drugs mood-altering drugs.

regression returning to a state of immature or primitive behavior.

repression the blocking out of unpleasant or anxiety-provoking thoughts.

retrograde amnesia forgetting events immediately prior to a traumatic event but remembering everything earlier.

Rorschach test a test in which a person gives his interpretation or tells what he sees in special cards marked by distinctive inkblots, a means of revealing the unconscious.

sadism deriving sexual pleasure from inflicting pain on someone.

schizoid personality a personalilty characterized by extreme shyness or aloofness.

schizophrenia a severe psychotic illness affecting the regulation of emotion, thought processes, moods, and personality, with a wide range of symptoms ranging from delusions to hallucinations.

shell shock combat neurosis characterized by jumpiness, fear of noise, inability to sleep, or relax.

social facilitation the enhancement of an individual's performance due solely to the presence of other people.

somatization all ego defense mechanisms causing physical pain or illness as a means of expressing psychological pain.

sublimation the modification of an instinctual impulse into a socially accepted one.

subliminal information received by the brain on an unconscious level, as in subliminal advertising.

superego in psychoanalytic theory, the personality component involving morals, ideals, and conscience.

superiority complex a personality disorder in which one acts superior but actually feels inferior.

tachylogia rapid and excessive talking; manic speech.

transcendental meditation a relaxation technique involving intense concentration on a specially chosen word or "mantra."

traumatic learning associating a frightening event with a neutral event so that the neutral event causes fear or anxiety.

voyeurism sexual pleasure from secretely observing the naked bodies or sex acts of others.

zoosadism deriving sexual pleasure from harming animals.

Architecture

ARCHITECTURE TERMS

abutment the mass of masonry that receives the thrust of an arch or vault.

acanthus Mediterranean plant whose leaves are represented as decoration on the capitals of Corinthian and composite columns.

allegory any symbolic sculpture.

amphiprostyle having columns only at the front and back of a temple or a templelike building.

amphistylar having columns along both sides of a temple or a templelike building.

anteroom a room next to a larger, more important room. Also known as an antechamber.

arabesque decorative acanthus scrolls, swags, candelabrum shafts, and animal and human figures appearing on the pilasters and panels of Roman and Renaissance architecture. Also, decorative geometric designs appearing on same.

arcade a series of arches on raised columns; also, a covered walk with such arches.

arcading a line of columned arches represented as decorative relief against a wall.

arcature arcading or miniature arcading.

arch the curved supporting structure of masonry spanning an opening.

arch brick a wedge-shaped brick used in an arch or any circular masonry construction. Also known as compass brick, radial brick, and voussoir brick.

architrave in the classical orders, the lowest member of the entablature; the common beam that spans a series of columns.

acuated having arches.

ashlar any type of squared building stone.

astylar without columns; a facade lacking columns or pilasters of any kind.

atlas a figure of a man used in place of a supporting column.

backing brick a lower-quality brick used behind face brick.

balconet a false balcony projecting out slightly from a window and intended only for decoration.

balloon framing in a wooden building, studwork that extends the full height of the frame from floor to roof.

baluster any one of the vertical posts supporting a stair handrail or other railing.

balustrade an entire railing system, including rail, balusters, and other components when present.

banister the handrail of a staircase.

bargeboard a decorative board hanging from the projecting end of a roof and covering the gables; the older versions are elaborately carved. Also known as gableboard, vergeboard.

barrel ceiling a semicylindrical ceiling.

barrel vault a masonry vault with a semicylindrical roof.

bar tracery within the arch of a gothic window, the interlocking stone forming a decorative pattern and filled with glass.

basket weave a checkerboard pattern of bricklaying.

bas-relief low relief or protrusion of a carving, embossing, or casting.

bay window a window set in a protruding bay.

bead molding a strip of metal or wood used around a pane of glass to keep it in place. Also, any convex, decorative molding.

belvedere a rooftop pavillion providing an excellent view.

blindstory a floor level without windows.

blindwall a wall unbroken by doors or windows. Also known as a dead wall.

boss a carved ornament placed at the intersection of beams, ribs, or groins.

bowstring beam a girder or truss having a curved or bowed member and a straight member to tie it together.

bow window a window in a rounded or semicylindrical bay. Also known as a compass window.

brick nogging the laying of bricks in the spaces of a timber frame.

brownstone a brown or reddish brown sandstone used in the facades of many eastern U.S. apartment houses in the 19th century.

buttress an exterior mass of masonry bonded into or angled against a wall to add strength and support.

cable molding decorative molding with the appearance of stranded cable or rope.

camberbeam a beam that curves upward slightly.

camber window an arched window.

campanile a freestanding bell tower.

cantilever a beam or truss that projects beyond its supporting foundation, wall, or column. Also, a bracket supporting a balcony.

capital the uppermost member, often ornately carved, of a column or pilaster.

caryatid the figure of a women used in place of a supporting column, pilaster, or pier.

casement window a hinged window that swings open along its length.

catslide a long, sloping roof, as on a saltbox-style house.

checkerwork in a wall or pavement, masonry laid in a checkerboard pattern.

Christian door a colonial door in which the exterior paneling forms a cross.

cilery the decorative carving around a column's capital.

clapboard overlapping horizontal wood siding used on home and building exteriors. Also known as bevel siding or lap siding.

classicism the correct use of Roman, Greek, and Italian Renaissance architecture.

clerestory the windowed upper story of the nave and choir in a church.

cloister a covered or sheltered walkway surrounding an open courtyard.

cloister garth the courtyard surrounded by a cloister.

clustered column several columns massed together to form one large supporting member.

coffer any one of the decorative sunken panels in a coffered ceiling.

coffered ceiling a highly decorative ceiling characterized by sunken panels.

collar beam a beam or plank that ties together two opposing rafters in a roof.

colonnade a series of columns supporting an entablature.

column a long, vertical, and cylindrical support member that includes a base, a shaft, and a capital.

Composite order in classical architecture, one of the five orders, specifically a composite of Corinthian and Ionic orders.

concourse any open space in a building for accommodating large crowds.

console a decorative bracket, often of wood or stone, projecting from a wall and supporting a cornice, a door head, a bust, or a shelf.

console table a table or large shelf attached to a wall and supported by consoles.

coping the top portion, usually slanting to shed water, of a wall or roof. Also known as copestone or capstone.

corbel a masonry or wood bracket, often decorative, projecting from a wall and supporting a cornice, arch, or other overhanging member.

corbeling a layering of masonry in which each course or row of bricks or stones projects further from the wall than the last row.

corbie steps step or stairlike projections running up the gables of a pitched roof, found on many houses of the 17th century. Also known as catsteps or crowsteps.

Corinthian order the most ornate of the five classical orders, characterized by a voluted, bell-shaped capital with acanthus leaf carvings, and an intricately decorated entablature.

cornerstone an inscribed stone situated near the base of any corner in a building, sometimes ceremoniously laid and hollowed out to store historical documents or objects.

cornice a molded projection that crowns a building or wall. Also, any ornamental molding around the walls just below a ceiling.

cosmati cut-stone mosaic inlay forming geometric patterns.

course one row of bricks or stones in a wall.

cove ceiling a ceiling that curves down to meet the walls.

crocket an ornament, usually in the form of a leaf, found along the sloping or vertical edges of gothically styled spires, pinnacles and gables.

curtail the spiraling or scroll-like termination at the end of a stair railing.

dais a raised platform for speakers.

day one division in a window.

deadlight any window not designed to open.

decastyle a portico with 10 columns or rows of 10 columns.

dentil any of the small, square blocks projecting like teeth beneath an entablature.

cupola a small dome or domelike structure on a roof.

diamond work masonry laid out to form the shape of diamonds in a wall or pavement.

distyle having two columns.

Doric order in classical architecture, the least adorned of the orders, characterized by a heavy, fluted column and a simple capital.

dormer a structure or gable projecting out from a sloping roof and containing a window.

drip the protective molding over the top of a window or door to discharge rainwater.

Dutch door a split door consisting of separate bottom-opening and top-opening segments.

eaves the portion of a lower roof projecting beyond the wall.

embedded column a column that is partially within the face of a wall. Also known as an engaged column.

English bond a bricklaying method characterized by alternating courses of headers (heads of the bricks facing out) and stretchers (laid out horizontally in the direction of the wall.)

entablature in a classical order, the upper section resting on the capital, consisting of the architrave, the frieze, and the cornice.

facade the exterior face of a building.

fanlight a semicircular window with radiating sash bars, usually placed over a door.

fascia a flat trim board around the eaves or gables of roofs.

fenestral a small window.

fenestration the design and arrangement of windows in a building.

finial an ornament at the top of a spire or pinnacle.

Flemish bond brickwork in which every other brick laid is a header.

floriated decorated with floral carvings or patterns.

florid highly ornate, heavily embellished.

fluting grooves or channels, as in the shaft of a column.

flying buttress a bar of masonry rising from a pier or arch and abutting against a roof or vault to receive thrust.

French door a door with glass panes running nearly its full length and usually hung in pairs. Also known as a casement door.

French roof a mansard roof.

fresco a painting on plaster.

fret a banded ornament consisting of geometrical patterns.

frieze the middle horizontal member of an entablature, often decorated with carvings of leaves or human and animal figures.

gable the triangular wall portion at either end of a pitched roof.

gableboard same as bargeboard.

gable roof a roof having one or more gables.

gambrel roof a roof pitched twice on each side, with the lowest pitch being the steepest.

gargoyle a grotesque sculpture projecting from a roof gutter and acting as a spout for waste water or rainwater.

gingerbread highly decorative woodwork of gingerbread style houses of the 19th century.

grotesque sculptured ornamentation representing animal or human forms in bizarre and fanciful ways.

header a brick or stone laid so that its head or short side faces out.

hecatonstylon a building with 100 columns.

herringbone pattern masonry work laid in a zigzagging fashion.

hexastyle having six columns.

hip the angle formed at the junction of two sloping roofs.

hip roof a roof having four sloping sides instead of two.

historiated ornamentation representing a narrative of some historic event, usually in the form of human or animal figures.

horseshoe arch a rounded arch in the distinct shape of a horseshoe. Also known as a Moorish arch.

intercolumniation the system of spacing between a colonnade for varying effects. Roman styles of intercolumniation include pycnostyle—1½ diameters; systyle—2 diameters; eustyle—2¼ diameters; diastyle—3 diameters; araeostyle—4 diameters.

Ionic order the classical order of intercolumniation characterized by elegant detailing, although less ornate than Corinthian and less massive than Doric.

jib door a door with no visible hardware on the room side and that stands flush with the wall so as to blend in neatly.

joist one of any of the parallel beams used to support the load from a floor and ceiling.

keystone the central block, sometimes embellished, of an arch.

lancet window a narrow window with a pointed arch, commonly found in churches.

lantern a decorative, lighted structure crowning a dome, turret, or roof.

lintel a horizontal member forming the upper portion of a door or window frame and that supports the load above it.

lozenge a small window.

mansard roof a roof having two slopes on all four sides, the upper portion being almost flat and the lower portion being nearly vertical. Similar to a gambrel roof.

marigold window a round window with radiating mullions. Also known as a rose window.

marquetry wood inlay work.

mezzanine a partial floor level between two main levels in a building; an extended balcony or gallery.

minaret a tall tower associated with a mosque.

molding trim, usually of wood, providing decorative outline and contouring.

monopteron a Greek circular building surrounded by a single row of columns.

motif any repeated decorative design or pattern.

mullion any one of the vertical members supporting or dividing a window or door.

newel the central supporting column or post around which a winding staircase climbs.

obelisk a four-sided stone tower or monument, tapering to a pyramidal tip.

octastyle having eight columns.

onion dome a Russian bulbous dome ending in a point and resembling an onion.

order in classical architecture, the style of intercolumniation and entablature. The Greek orders are Ionic, Doric, and Corinthian. The Roman orders are Tuscan and Composite.

ornament any carved, sculpted, engraved, or painted architectural decoration.

oversailing course a row of bricks that project beyond the face of a wall.

palmette an ornament representing palm leaves.

parapet a low, safeguarding wall along the edges of a rooftop.

parquet inlaid wood flooring, usually forming a geometric pattern.

pavilion roof a pyramidal roof.

pediment in classical architecture, the triangular gable end of a roof. Also, an ornamental feature, such as found over doors and windows, having this shape.

pentastyle a portico having five columns.

pepperbox turret a turret with a conical or domed roof.

peripteral a building surrounded by a colonnade.

peristyle a colonnade surrounding a building or courtyard.

pier a vertical masonry support.

pilaster a flat, rectangular column having a base and capital and set or engaged into a wall.

pilastrade a line of pilasters.

pinnacle a tower or turret.

plinth the square base for a column or pilaster. Also, a block serving as a base for a statue.

portcullis a large iron or timber grated door that can be raised or lowered, as in the entrance to a castle.

portico a porch consisting of a roof supported by columns.

pyramidion a small pyramid, as a cap on an obelisk.

quadrangle a rectangular courtyard surrounded by buildings.

quarry-faced rough, unfinished ashlar.

quoin the stones used to reinforce an external wall corner, sometimes decoratively distinguished from surrounding masonry. Also known as coin.

random course a row of masonry of unequal sizes.

random work masonry laid in irregular courses, with random sizes of stone.

reinforced concrete concrete reinforced with iron or steel mesh or bars embedded within it.

relief a carving or embossing raised against its background.

rib a slender supporting arch.

rose window a large round window, frequently with stained glass and stone tracery. Also known as a marigold window.

rubblework masonry consisting of rubble.

rusticated stone rough-faced stone that has been beveled, popular during the Renaissance and in modern banks and courthouses because of the impregnable appearance they provide to a facade.

sash any window framework.

scroll an ornament resembling a scroll or spiral.

scrollwork ornately carved wood, cut with a scroll saw.

sill a horizontal timber at the bottom of a door or window frame. Also, the horizontal timber resting on a foundation in a wood house.

skirt roof a small false roof between levels of a building, forming a decorative skirt.

sleeper any horizontal beam laid near the ground or foundation of a building.

soffit the exposed surface underneath an architectural member, such as an arch, beam, or lintel.

splay a large bevel.

stretcher a brick or stone laid lengthwise; opposite of a header.

stringer in a stairway, the cut, inclined board on which the steps rest.

stucco textured plaster or cement used on walls for a decorative effect.

swag a relief ornament resembling garlands and gathered drapery.

terra cotta hard, fired clay, unglazed, glazed, or painted, used for ornamental designs and roof and floor tiles.

tessellated having small squares of stone, marble, or glass set in a mosaic pattern, in a floor or wall.

tetrastyle having four columns or rows of four columns.

tholos in Greek architecture, a round building.

trabeated constructed with horizontal beams and lintels instead of arches and vaults.

tracery ornamental stonework supporting glass in a gothically styled window.

travertine a creamy, banded limestone, used for facing a floor.

turret a miniature tower, corbeled out from a corner of a wall, as in a castle.

vault a masonry roof or ceiling over an arched area.

vaulting vaulted ceilings, roofs, hallways, or other structures.

volute a spiral scroll, as found on Ionic, Corithian, and Composite capitals.

wagon vault a semicylindrical vault, or barrel vault.

wainscot decorative paneling or facing placed on a wall near the floor.

widow's walk a platformed walkway on the roofs of early New England houses.

STYLES OF ARCHITECTURE

Anglo-Saxon architecture prominent in England before the Norman conquest in 1066, characterized by round arches and huge walls.

art deco a decorative, "futuristic" style popular in the 1930s, characterized by zigzags, chevrons, and similar geometrical ornamentation typically found on the skyscrapers of the period.

art nouveau decorative style of the later 19th-century France and Belgium, characterized by curvilinear design and whiplash lines. Known as Jugendstil in Germany and Modernismo in Spain.

Aztec from the 14th-century Indian people of central Mexico, an architecture characterized by pyramids and temples dedicated to the gods.

baroque European style prominent between 1550 and the early 1700s characterized by oval spaces, curved surfaces, elaborate decoration, sculpture, and color.

Byzantine architecture of the eastern Roman empire from the 4th century to the middle ages, largely in Greece, and characterized by large domes, round arches, and elaborate columns.

classical architecture of Hellenic Greece and Imperial Rome, the five orders of which are Corinthian, Doric, Ionic, Tuscan, and Composite.

colonial any architectural style borrowed by an overseas colony from the motherland, such as the transplantation of English Georgian to North America in the 18th century.

Dutch colonial Dutch style of architecture transplanted to America and particularly New York state in the 17th century, characterized by gambrel roofs and overhanging eaves.

Egyptian from the third millennium B.C. to the Roman period, a style characterized by temples, pyramids, and funeral monuments.

flamboyant style in the 15th century, a phase of French Gothic architecture characterized by tracery with the appearance of dancing flames.

Georgian prominent in 18th-century Britain and North America, a style derivative of classical, Renaissance, and baroque forms.

Gothic prominent in western Europe from the 12th to the 15th century, characterized by pointed arches, rib vaulting, and flying buttresses.

Islamic (also known as Muslim architecture): an architectural style originating around the Mediterranean and spreading as far as India and China, characterized by round and horseshoe arches, domes, tunnel vaults, and geometric ornamentation.

Japanese from the fifth century A.D. and borrowing from Chinese style, a largely wood timber architecture characterized by pavilion-like buildings and pagodalike buildings.

Maya dating from approximately A.D. 600 to 900, the architecture of the Indian people of Mexico, Guatemala, and Honduras, characterized by temples, pyramids, plazas, and similar structures, with most buildings raised high on platforms.

Renaissance from the 14th through the 16th centuries and developed in Italy, derivative of the classical orders.

revival any style reviving or deriving from another, earlier style.

rococo developed largely in 18th-century France, the final phase of baroque, characterized by florid or elaborate ornamentation intended to produce a delicate effect.

Romanesque begun in early 11th-century western Europe and borrowing from Roman and Byzantine forms, a style characterized by massive walls, round arches, and powerful vaults.

HOUSE STYLES

adobe a Spanish clay-and-straw brick home.

bothy a small cottage of northern England, Scotland, and Ireland.

brownstone a house or apartment building faced with a brown or reddish brown sandstone.

bungalow a one-story, cottagelike house characterized by overhanging gables forming the front porch. Also, a one-story tiled or thatched house surrounded by a wide verandah in India.

cajun cottage a tin-roofed shack of Louisiana.

Cape Cod a rectangular, 1½-story house with a pitched roof, originating in colonial Cape Cod, Massachusetts.

carpenter gothic a 19th-century American homebuilding technique characterized by the application of elaborate gothic motifs with wood.

catslide house slang for a saltbox house, named for its long, sloping roof in the rear and short roof in front.

chateau a French country estate.

colonial any one of several house styles imported from a mother land. For example, a clapboard colonial saltbox with a massive central chimney; a German colonial with heavy stone walls; a fieldstone Dutch colonial with a broad gambrel roof; a stuccoed adobe Spanish colonial with arcarded veranda and red-tiled roof.

Creole townhouse a New Orleans townhouse characterized by iron balconies, slate or tiled roofs, arched and shuttered windows, and plastered or stuccoed facades with colors that include pink, ochre, and yellow.

Dutch colonial originating in Dutch-settled areas of New York and the Hudson Valley in the 17th century, a house characterized by a gambrel roof (two pitches on each side) and overhanging eaves.

Elizabethan an English country house originating in the late 1500s and characterized by large, mullioned windows and decorative strapwork.

English Magpie a style of house popular in Medieval England.

Federal style classic revival style popular from 1790–1830 in the U.S. Notable features include two or four chimneys flanking either end of the house, elaborate fan doorways (some with porticos), paired or twin front stairways, and brass and iron hardware. Most notable: rooms in Federal houses are often round or oval.

Georgian popular in 18th-century Britain and American colonies, and characterized by a columned or pilaster-flanked front entry, heavy stone sills, brass hardware, and ornate roof balustrades.

gambrel same as Dutch colonial.

gingerbread an ornately decorated American house of the 19th century, reminiscent of the fairytale namesake.

Greek revival a revival of Greek and Roman forms early in 19th-century America and England; characterized by Corinthian, Doric, or Ionic wood-columned porticos creating the famous "temple" look. Door surrounds and eaves are carefully carved in Greek foliate or geometric motifs as well.

Gothic revival popular in 18th- and early 19th-century Europe and America, a house characterized by the revival of Gothic forms of architecture.

hacienda a large Spanish estate.

half-timbered 16th- and 17th-century American and European houses built with large timber foundations, supports, and studs, with walls filled in with bricks or plaster.

Italianate (Italian villa style): popular in United States and England in mid-1800s, characterized by slightly pitched roofs, square towers, and round-arched windows.

octagon an eight-sided Victorian house.

pueblo a stone or adobe community dwelling as high as five stories, originating with Indians of the southwestern United States.

Queen Anne a house style popular in the 1870s and 1880s in England and America, actually based on a combination of Elizabethan, Tudor, Gothic, and English Renaissance forms. Features include polygonal or cylindrical towers, bay windows, balconies, and richly decorative woodwork.

Romanesque an early Victorian style popular from 1840 to 1860, characterized by tall towers, arched windows, and decorative arcading beneath the eaves.

row house any one of an unbroken line or series of houses.

saltbox a New England house characterized by a long, sloping roof in the back and a short, pitched roof in front.

Second Empire popular Victorian style characterized by mansard roofs, tall arched windows and doors, and iron roof pinnacles.

shingle style later 18th-century Victorian style, characterized by the dominant use of unpainted wood shingles on roofs and walls.

stick style a wood exposed-frame style popular in the later 19th century.

Tudor a house style characterized by its exposed beams.

vernacular Victorian an understated Victorian, less ornate than earlier styles and usually adopting local forms.

HOUSE CONSTRUCTION

aggregate sand, stone, or gravel used to make concrete.

anchor bolts bolts set in the top of a concrete foundation to hold structural members in place.

backfill earth mounded up around a foundation's walls to create a slope for water runoff.

balloon framing a form of house construction in which the upright studs extend all the way from the sill to the roof, a technique that has largely grown out of favor.

balusters the spindles or poles that support a stair railing.

balustrade a row of balusters topped with a rail.

baseboard the interior trim that runs around the walls next to the floor.

batten a strip of wood used to cover a joint, especially between siding boards.

bay window any curved, rectangular, or polygonal window that projects out from a wall.

beam a large, supportive structural member, usually running from one foundation wall to another and held up by pillars or poles.

bearing wall any wall that bears the weight of a ceiling, floor, or roof above it. Also known as a load-bearing wall or a bearing partition.

belvedere a small, glass-enclosed room used as a lookout on the roof of a house.

berm a mound or bank of earth formed to shunt drainage away from a house.

bevel to cut at an angle, as in beveled siding; thicker on one end than the other.

bib cock or bib nozzle a faucet on the outside of the house around or above the foundation. Also known as a sill cock.

board-and-batten siding siding of broad boards lined together with narrow boards or battens nailed over their joints.

breezeway a sheltered passageway between a garage and a house.

bricklaying terms:

common bond a bricklaying style characterized by several courses of overlapping stretchers interspersed with an occasional course of headers.

course one row of bricks.

English bond a bricklaying style characterized by alternating courses of headers and stretchers.

Flemish bond a bricklaying style characterized by courses consisting of alternating headers and stretchers forming an overall diamond pattern.

garden wall a bricklaying style characterized by courses in which every fourth brick is a header.

header a brick laid with its short end facing out.

rowlock a header laid on its narrow side.

running bond a bricklaying style characterized by overlapping courses of stretchers and no headers.

shiner a stretcher with its broad side facing out.

soldier a brick laid standing on end.

stacked bond a bricklaying style characterized by nonoverlapping courses of stretchers.

stretcher a brick laid lengthwise.

bridging small pieces of wood crossed between studs to add rigidity and to distribute load.

casement window a hinged window that swings open along one vertical edge.

casing the trim around a door or a window.

caulking sealing material used to waterproof cracks and joints, especially around doors and windows.

clapboard a long, beveled board used for siding.

collar beam a beam that connects rafters. Also known as a rafter tie.

conduit, electrical a pipe or tube through which wiring is run.

corbel a projection of wood or masonry to add structural support to a wall.

counterflashing extra flashing used around a chimney to help prevent rain from entering a house.

cripple stud a stud placed over a wall opening, above a header.

curtain wall a non-load-bearing wall.

doorsill a door framing member that serves as a threshold.

dormer a projecting structure, usually containing one or more windows, on a sloping roof.

double-hung window a window that has two sashes that can be moved up or down independently of one another.

drip cap exterior molding above a window or door to direct rain water away from woodwork.

drop siding tongue-and-groove board siding.

drywall any wallboard or other wall covering not needing a plaster finish; gypsum wallboard.

eaves the lowest or overhanging portion of a roof.

English basement a house or apartment building with its first floor halfway underground.

fascia the horizontal trim board running along the roof line; it is attached to the ends of the rafters.

firestop a block placed between framing studs to slow the spread of fire.

flashing sheet metal, weather stripping, or other material used to prevent the entry of rainwater through the joints in a roof.

floating foundation a foundation without footings, used in swampy or other unstable areas.

footings concrete supports under a foundation.

foundation the large supporting structure below ground, forming a basement or a slab.

gable the portion of a wall between the two slopes of a roof.

gambrel roof a double-sloped roof, with the lower portion being the steepest.

gingerbread any elaborate or excessive ornamentation on a house. Also known as gingerbread work.

glazing installing glass into sashes and doors.

grout a thin mortar used in tile work.

gusset a bracket or board applied to intersections of a frame to add rigidity.

gypsum wallboard wall panels made of gypsum and faced with paper.

header the topmost frame member over a door, window, or other wall opening. Also known as a lintel.

hip roof a roof that rises on all four sides of a house; a roof with no gable ends.

jack rafter a short rafter frame between the wall plate and a hip rafter.

jalousie a window or door comprised of adjustable glass louvers.

joist a large timber laid horizontally to support a floor or ceiling.

lintel same as a header.

live load the variable load a structural member must bear, such as snow on a roof or people walking across a floor, as distinguished from dead load or permanent, nonvariable load.

load the weight a structural member bears or supports.

lookout a structural member running between the lower end of rafters; the underside of a roof overhang.

mansard roof a roof having two slopes on all four sides of a house.

masonry stone, brick, tile, concrete block, and such like.

molding any narrow, usually rounded, trim used decoratively to cover joints.

mullion a vertical bar or strip dividing the panes of a window.

newel the principal post supporting the handrail at the bottom of a staircase.

nogging bricks placed between the timbers of a wall, for a decorative effect or as a firestop.

on center builder's term referring to a measurement taken from the center of one structural member to the center of another.

plaster a mixture of lime, cement, and sand, used on walls.

plate a structural member laid horizontally over the top of studs in a wall. It serves as a support for the attic joists and roof rafters.

platform framing a framing method in which the subfloor extends out into a platform for stud walls; walls are usually prefabricated and tilted into place.

plumb a weight hung from a line to determine if a structural member is perfectly vertical; used to test vertical alignments.

post-and-beam construction a framing method characterized by the use of heavy timbers set further apart than standard framing.

purlins the horizontal members that support rafters.

rabbet joint a recess or groove on the end of a board.

rafter a sloping roof framing member extending from the ridge to the eaves.

rake the slope of a roof or roof rafter.

ridgeboard the uppermost horizontal roof member, to which the top of the top of the rafters are attached.

riser the vertical board rising under a stair tread.

roughing-in the installation of drainage and water pipes for hookup with fixtures and appliances. Also, partial completion of electrical wiring.

R-value a number that signifies the efficiency of an insulating material, such as R-19.

sash the framework that holds the glass in a window.

scuttle a small opening giving access to the attic.

shakes handsplit wood shingles.

sheathing collective term for any covering boards, panels or other materials.

sheathing paper a building paper used in the roof and walls to block the passing of air.

sheetrock commonly used commercial name for gypsum wallboard.

shim a thin wedge of wood used to help level framing members, especially window and door frames.

shiplap siding siding comprised of boards that connect with one another with rabbetted joints.

shoe the lowest framing member laid horizontally on a subfloor and used as a base for a stud wall.

sill the lowest of all horizontal structural members; it lies directly on the foundation.

skylight a roof window.

slab a solid concrete foundation without a basement.

sleeper a sill; any large structural member laid horizontally.

soffit the underside of a structural member, such as a beam, a staircase, a roof overhang.

soil stack the large, vertical pipe that receives waste water from all plumbing fixtures and appliances.

soleplate the lowest horizontal member in a wall frame.

stringer the inclined, precut framing member that serves as one of two supports for stair risers and treads.

stucco a wall covering made of cement or plaster.

stud a vertical framing member, usually made of wood.

subfloor the rough flooring laid directly over the floor joists.

sump in the basement, a hole or depression that collects leaking water.

termite shield sheet metal placed in and around a foundation and its openings to prevent entry by termites.

tie beam same as a collar beam or rafter tie.

toenailing to pound a nail in at an angle in order to make it penetrate a second structural member. Also, to drive a nail so that its head will not be visible on the surface.

transom bar a horizontal bar dividing a window.

truss a large, triangular framing unit, often prefabricated, constructed of beams, bars, and ties, and used to span a large space.

valley rafter a rafter rising where two roof slopes of different angles meet; an inside, corner rafter. Similar to a hip rafter.

vapor barrier any material applied to a wall to block the passage of moisture.

wainscot a decorative wall covering skirting the lower portion of a wall.

wallboard sheetrock, gypsum, waferboard, and similar items.

weephole a small hole cut in masonry to drain moisture.

widow's walk an open, railed walkway around a peaked roof, particularly in some New England seacoast homes.

CASTLES AND MEDIEVAL BUILDINGS (includes castle weaponry, castle staffing, and related subjects)

alcazar a Spanish fortress or castle.

alure a gallery or passage along the parapets of a castle.

arbalest a medieval crossbow used to shoot arrows. Also, a large bow mounted on a stand to launch darts, lances, or metal bolts.

archeria apertures through which archers could shoot arrows. Also known as arrow loops, loopholes, balistraria, arrow slits.

assommoir a gallery built over a doorway from which heavy objects could be dropped down on the heads of intruding enemies.

bailey an open ground or courtyard encircled by walls. Also known as a ward.

balistraria a room in which crossbows were kept. Also, small holes in walls to allow the passage of arrows.

barbican a walled outwork or tower protecting a drawbridge or a gateway.

bartizan a projecting or overhanging turret.

bastille a castle or castle tower used as a prison.

bastion a mass of earth faced with stones or sods projecting out from a rampart.

battlement an indented or notched parapet for observing or shooting.

belfry a tall, mobile tower erected at a siege site and pushed up against an outer wall to allow archers or other military men to advance against or shoot at castle defender. Also known as a bear.

brattice any one of the wooden planks or timbers in a stockade or palisade. Also, any castle tower made of timbers.

butler a castle staff member in charge of drinks and the buttery (bottlery.)

buttery a bottlery, or a room used for stocking or preparing drinks.

castellated like a castle in structure.

castellum a fort surrounded by a village or a fortified town.

catapult one of several types of siege engines used to launch such projectiles as rocks and firebombs onto or over castle walls.

cesspit a pit that receives waste from a garderobe.

chamberlain serving under a monarch or lord, an official in charge of the domestic affairs of a castle, especially in supplying the great hall or chamber, where most of the daily living activities took place.

chandlery a storeroom for candles and lighting supplies.

chaplain in medieval times, the religious head who conducted services in a castle chapel but who also kept castle accounts and conducted correspondence because of his ability to read and write.

château a French castle.

chatelaine the lady or mistress of a castle.

chatelet a small castle.

citadel any fortress near a city and keeping its inhabitants in subjugation.

corbel a projection of stones from the face of a wall to support a roof or parapet.

crenel any one of the gaps at the top of a battlement wall for shooting and observation.

crossbowmen archers.

curtain wall any one of the inner or outer protective walls ringing a castle.

dais a raised platform in a great hall or chamber where a lord and lady sat.

donjon (dungeon) the main tower or keep, usually the central and strongest location where fighters withdrew when the enemy had penetrated, often containing a well, apartments, offices, service rooms, and supplies. In early castles, the living quarters of a lord; in later castles, the dungeon or prison, especially the lower or underground portion.

drawbridge spanning a moat or ditch, a bridge that could be raised or drawn back to prevent an enemy from entering.

dungeon see donjon.

embrasure an opening in a wall, sloped to enlarge its interior portion, for shooting and observation; the low portion of a battlement.

falcon one of the predatory birds (also hawks) often kept as pets in a castle for sport hunting purposes.

falconer one who trained a predatory bird to sport hunt.

farrier a castle staff member in charge of shoeing or caring for horses.

feudal system a political and economic system in medieval Europe in which a servant, a peasant, or tenant was granted land in exchange for military service, often involving the guarding or defending of castles.

finial a slender, ornamental stone sometimes fixed on the tops of merlons.

garderobe a latrine or privy, usually located in an outer wall over a ditch, moat, or cesspit.

gargoyle a grotesque sculpture adorning the upper walls of some castles and often used to discharge dirty water.

gatehouse a tower protecting the drawbridge.

Greek fire a mixture of naphtha, sulfur, and quicklime, which ignited by moistening and burned fiercely, hurled as a firebomb over castle walls.

half timber in many medieval castles, a construction method in which wood frame walls are filled with wattle (a mat of woven sticks) and daub (mud or clay).

hedgehog the equivalent of modern barbed wire, thorn bushes and stakes erected to protect an outer wall from the enemy. Also known as a herrison or zareba.

hoarding a makeshift balconylike structure hung from the tops of walls to provide a platform for archers and other warriors during a battle; hardings were made of wood and were usually only temporary.

inner ward in the center of a castle, an open yard.

jester a court fool or comic.

jousting sport in which a knight on horseback tries to knock off another knight on horseback with the use of lance and shield.

keep the donjon or strongest building in a castle.

list the open area immediately in front of a castle's defenses, kept clear to avoid giving cover to the enemy.

lord in feudal law, the owner of a manor or castle.

machicolation a slit or opening between corbels, allowing projectiles or boiling liquids to be dropped down on an enemy.

maiden tower the keep or main tower.

mangon a catapult with a spoon-shaped end in which large stones, timbers, and firebombs were launched; because of its violent kicking after each throw, the Romans called these siege engines "wild asses;" the 12th-century Normans called them "nags."

merlons the solid sections between a wall's crenels or notches.

mining tunneling under a castle during a siege to bring about the collapse of its walls or foundation.

moat a deep, wide trench, usually filled with water around a castle to keep an enemy from penetrating.

motte a mound of hard-packed earth used as a base for early castles.

motte-and-bailey castle an early type of castle perched on a mound of hard-packed earth and surrounded by an open courtyard or bailey and a palisade.

mouse an iron gouge or bore used to pry away bits of stone on a castle wall during a siege.

murder holes arrow loops and other holes or openings in an upper floor, through which defenders could fire down upon an intruding enemy.

oubliette a secret pit with a trapdoor within the floor of a dungeon through which prisoners could be dropped and left to rot.

outer ward an open yard outside of an inner curtain wall.

palisades a barrier or stockade made of strong timbers, often surrounding early castles.

pantler a castle staff member in charge of the pantry.

parapet a low wall along the edge of a roof to protect soldiers from falling off or from being attacked by enemies.

pas-de-souris steps leading from a moat to the entrance.

pepperbox turret a circular turret with a conical roof. Same as a pinnacle.

pikeman a warrior adept at killing with a pike.

portcullis a large, grated door made of oak and iron that could be wound up or down by a windlass and sometimes acted as a counterweight to a drawbridge.

porter a castle official who made sure no one entered or left a castle without the proper authority.

postern a minor gateway set inside a wall, usually at the rear of a castle.

privy latrine.

quintain a wooden dummy that spun on a post, used for lancing practice in a castle's courtyards by knights.

ram a battering ram, usually a large tree trunk fitted with an iron snout.

rampart a surrounding mound or embankment on which a parapet was frequently raised.

rushlights twisted strands of rush dipped in grease or tallow, ignited, and held in wall brackets for lighting.

sapper during a siege, a warrior specifically assigned to batter down the stonework of a castle wall.

scaling ladder a ladder used in scaling castle walls.

scarp a steep slope to slow the advance of an enemy in front of a castle. Also known as an escarpment.

screw stair a winding staircase.

seneschal a steward or majordomo in charge of such domestic affairs as buying provisions, managing servants, planning feasts, or keeping accounts.

shell keep an early castle consisting of a stone-walled motte.

siege the surrounding and attacking of a fortification to gain possession.

siege engine any one of several catapult or battering devices used in a siege against a castle.

solar a sunny room adjacent to the upper end of a hall, used by a lord, his family, and honored guests.

stable marshal an officer in charge of a castle's stables and horses.

stair turret any turret completely filled by a winding staircase.

tiltyard a list or open courtyard where knights practiced their riding and lancing skills.

tortoise a portable shelter made of hides or metal in which attackers could be protected from the arrows and bombs of castle defenders and sometimes used to get safely across a moat.

trebuchet a large siege engine employing counterweights to thrust rocks, firebombs, and the decayed carcasses of dead horses as far as a quarter mile; also known as a tripgate.

turret a small tower set above a larger structure.

usher a castle doorman.

ward the open ground or bailey between encircling walls.

wattle and daub woven sticks and grass sealed with mud or clay (daub), common construction material of medieval times.

MEDIEVAL VILLAGES *Also See* CASTLE

assize of bread and ale laws that fix the prices and standards of goods.

bailiff an official who manages business (looking after crops, stocking supplies, etc.) and enforces the laws of a lord's manor.

beadle a manorial assistant to a reeve; in charge of preserving and sowing seeds from the previous year's crops.

cellarer a monastery official responsible for food stores.

censuarius a tenant who pays rent in lieu of labor.

charter an official document, such as a deed.

cotter a tenant of a cottage.

croft the garden area of a village house.

curia a courtyard.

demesne the portion of a manor cultivated for the lord's personal use.

distraint an arrest or summons.

eyre royal circuit court.

farm lease.

fief a grant of land made by a lord in exchange for services. Also known as a fee.

feudalism the political and social system of medieval days.

frankpledge the responsibility of each division of a community to carry out police duties and to see to it that the law is upheld.

glebe land cultivated to help support a parish church.

hue and cry a law requiring that all citizens within earshot give chase to a fleeing criminal.

infangenthef the right to confiscate the belongings of a convicted thief.

leirwite a fine given a single woman for sexual indiscretions.

manor a lord's estate, including those portions cultivated by tenants.

merchet a serf's payment for a daughter's marriage.

messuage a house and yard in a village.

mortuary a duty, usually one's second-best beast, paid to the church upon death.

pannage a fee paid to a lord to allow one's pigs to forage for acorns, nuts, and apples on a forest floor.

reeve a manor official who made sure that tenants who owed the lord of the manor labor repaid him promptly.

serf a peasant; a villein.

tallage an annual tax paid by villeins to a lord.

tithe traditional donation of 10% of all crops to the church.

tithing a group of 10 to 12 men, each responsible for the other's behavior in a village.

toft a yard of a house in a village.

villein a serf.

virgate a unit of land from 18 to 32 acres, thought to be sufficient to support a peasant and his family.

woodward a manor official responsible for a lord's woodland.

RELIGIOUS BUILDINGS

abat-voix a sound reflector above the pulpit.

abbey a monastery or convent.

agnus dei any artwork representing a lamb that is emblematic of Christ.

agulla the obelisk or spire of a church tower.

almariol a storage room or niche for ecclesiastical vestments. Also known as an ambry.

almehrabh a niche in an Arabian mosque that marks the direction of Mecca.

almemar in a synagogue, a desk on which the Torah rests while being read from to the congregation.

altar the elevated table or structure used for religious offerings or rites.

altar frontal an ornamental hanging or panel fronting the altar.

altar of repose a repository or niche where the Host is kept from Maundy Thursday to Good Friday in a Roman Catholic church.

altarpiece above and behind the altar, an ornamental painting or screen or sculpture.

altar screen a decorative partition separating the altar from the space behind.

altar slab a stone or slab forming the top of an altar.

ambry a repository or niche for sacraments.

ambulatory an aisle or walkway around the apse of a church.

ambulatory church a church with a dome surrounded on three sides by aisles.

antechapel an entrance, porch, or vestibule in front of a chapel.

antenave a porch leading into the nave of a church.

antepodium behind the dais in a choir, seating for the clergy.

apostolaeum any church dedicated to or named after an apostle.

apse the semicylindrical or semidomed space or room housing the altar.

archiepiscopal cross a cross with two transverse arms, the shorter one on top, the longer one near the center.

ark in a synagogue, an ornamental repository for the scrolls of the Torah.

armariolum in a cathedral or monastic church, a wardrobe for keeping vestments.

aspersorium a font for holy water.

aureole the glory or radiance surrounding the head of a sacred figure.

baptistery a building or portion of a building where baptisms are given.

basilica an elongated church with a central high nave with clerestory, side aisles, and a semicircular apse.

bell canopy a gable roof that shelters a bell.

bell cot a small belfry astride the ridge of a roof.

bell gable a roof-ridge turret holding one or more bells.

bellhouse a tower holding a bell.

belltower any tall structure containing a bell.

benitier a basin for holy water.

bestiary in a medieval church, a group of painted or sculpted creatures.

bethel a chapel for seamen.

box pew a pew enclosed by a high back and sides.

calvary sculptures, often life-size, depicting the Crucifixion.

Calvary Cross a Latin cross set on three steps.

cantoria a choir gallery.

carrel a pew in a monastery.

catacumba the atrium or courtyard of a basilican church.

cathedral the home church of a bishop.

catherine-wheel window a large circular, ornamental window at the front of many cathedrals. Also known as a rose window.

Celtic cross a tall cross with short horizontal arms partially enclosed by a circle.

chatya a Buddhist sanctuary.

chancel the sanctuary of a church, or the space near the altar reserved for the clergy and choir.

chancel arch in some churches, an arch that divides the chancel from the nave.

chancel screen a screen separating the chancel from the nave.

chapel a small church or parish or a room or building set apart for worship within a school, college, hospital, or other institution. Also, an area within a church set aside for private prayer.

chapel royal the chapel of a royal palace or castle.

chevet an apse surrounded by an ambulatory.

choir between the nave and the sanctuary, the area occupied by the clergy and choir.

choir loft a choir in a balcony.

choir stall seating for choir and clergy.

choraula a rehearsal room for the choir.

chrismatory a niche holding the consecrated oil for baptism near the font.

church stile an old term for pulpit.

cimeliarch a treasury where holy objects and other valuables are stored in a church.

clausara the part of a monastery or convent occupied by the monks or nuns.

clerestory the windowed, upper portion of the nave, transepts, and choir; any windowed upper wall for light and ventilation.

cloister a place devoted to religious seclusion, as a monastery or convent. Also, a covered walk surrounding an open courtyard, used as a link between buildings in a monastery.

cloister garth the courtyard surrounded by a cloister.

confessional the private booth where a priest sits and listens to confessions from the penitent.

convent a community of nuns; a nunnery.

credence near the altar, a shelf or stand for holding holy objects, service books, and other objects.

crowde a cellar or crypt of a church.

cruciform in the shape of a cross, as many gothic churches with the intersection of the nave, chancel, and apse with the transepts.

crypt an underground or partially underground level containing separate chapels or, sometimes, tombs.

double monastery a monastery and a convent sharing the same church and authority.

duomo an Italian cathedral.

east end where the main altar is located, a tradition of medieval churches.

ecclesiology the study of the decoration and architecture of churches.

epistle side the south side of a church when the main altar is at the east end, the side the epistle is read from.

esonarthex when present, the second narthex from the entrance.

expiatory chapel a chapel erected to atone for a great crime, such as a murder.

fauwara in the court of a mosque, a fountain.

feretory a space where church relics are kept.

font the stone basin that holds water for baptism.

frater house a common eating hall in a monastery.

galilee a chapel for worship at the west side of a church.

galilee porch a galilee acting as a vestibule to the main church.

garbha-griha the darkened sanctuary where the statue of a deity is placed in a Hindu temple.

glory the halo and radiance surrounding the head of a religious figure in a painting.

Gospel side the north side of the church when the main altar is in the east, where the Gospel is read.

hall church a church without clerestories, having an interior of more or less uniform height, as a hall.

high altar the main altar.

inner sanctum the most sacred of places.

interstitium the crossing of a cruciform church.

jami a mosque specially designed for large congregations.

kubba a dome in a mosque.

Lady chapel at the east end of a church, a chapel dedicated to the Virgin Mary.

lancet window a narrow window with a pointed arch, commonly found in many churches. Also, double lancet.

lectern a stand with a slanting top for convenient reading from the Scriptures.

li pai tien a Christian church in China.

lozenge a small window just above a double-lancet window.

manse a clergyman's dwelling.

mensa the top slab or surface of an altar.

mihrab a niche in any religious Moslem building indicating the direction of Mecca.

minaret a tower in or flanking a mosque from which the faithful are called to prayer.

minbar in a mosque, the pulpit.

minster a monastic church.

minstrel gallery a small balcony over the entrance of a church interior.

mission a church supported by a larger church.

mission architecture 18th-century Spanish church and monastery architecture.

mosque a Moslem house of worship.

musalla a Moslem prayer hall.

narthex a vestibule or portico of early Christian or Byzantine churches; any entrance hall leading to the nave.

nave the central portion of a church, flanked by aisles, and intended for the congregation.

nimbus in any artwork, the halo of light around the head of a holy figure.

nunnery a convent.

oratory a small, private chapel.

organ loft the loft or gallery where the organ is placed.

parlatory in a monastery or convent, a place where visitors are received.

parsonage the parson's house; a rectory.

pede window next to a large window, a smaller window symbolizing one of the feet of Christ.

pew a bench for seating of the congregation.

presbytery the place or sanctuary reserved for clergy beyond the choir.

pulpit an elevated platform or lectern where most of the preaching is done. In some churches, an elevated, enclosed stand.

rectory the residence of a minister, priest, or pastor.

refectory a dining room for monks or nuns.

riddle one of a pair of curtains enclosing an altar on either side.

rood a large cross, sometimes supported on a beam (the rood beam) across the entrance of a chancel.

rood screen an ornamental wood or stone screen surmounted by a cross and separating the nave and the chancel.

rood spire a roof spire rising up over the crossing of the transepts and nave.

rose window a large, circular, stained glass window of gothic or medieval design set in the front entrance of a cathedral. Also known as a Catherine wheel window, a marigold window, or a wheel window.

sacristy near the chancel, a room for storing the altar vessels and vestments.

sanctuary same as presbytery; the immediate area around an altar.

sanctus bell a bell hung in a turret over the chancel to call people to service.

seminary a school for preparing men to be Roman Catholic or Episcopal priests or Protestant ministers.

sepulcher in an altar, a receptacle for sacred relics.

shrine a receptacle or building housing sacred relics, or the tomb of a saint or other revered person.

sounding board a canopy above the pulpit used to reflect the preacher's voice into the congregation.

squint a small opening or window in the outside wall of a church allowing a view inside to the main altar.

steeple the tower and spire of a church.

stupa a Buddhist shrine consisting of a built mound, sometimes in the shape of a beehive or bell.

tabernacle a box on an altar for holding the consecrated host and wine of the Eucharist. Also, an ornamental niche in a wall housing a statue.

transept the crossing or transverse portion of a church, forming the arms of a cruciform layout.

transept chapel a chapel entered from the transept.

triapsidal having three apses, sometimes forming a cloverleaf at the altar end of the church.

triforium a gallery or arches above the nave and below the clerestory, sometimes serving as attic space or as a gallery for spectators.

vestry a room near the altar for storing robes of the clergy and choir.

Cemeteries, Tombs, and Monuments

Bateson's belfry a coffin device consisting of a bell and cord that the interred could ring in case he miraculously revived, popular in Victorian times when people were occasionally pronounced dead prematurely.

bier a stand on which a coffin containing a corpse rests to lie in state.

Boot Hill in the American West, a cemetery for gunfighters.

Calvary a sculptured representation, often life-size, of the crucifixion.

catacombs underground passages with niches or recesses for graves or urns.

catafalque a draped scaffold on which is placed a coffin or effigy of the deceased during a state funeral.

cemetery beacon a graveyard lighthouse and altar used in Europe in the 12th and 13th centuries.

cenotaph a monument erected in memory of one not buried under it or interred within it.

centry-garth a burial ground.

cinerarium a vault for storing urns containing the ashes of the dead.

crematory a building for incinerating the bodies of the deceased.

crypt an underground vault, usually under a church, used for burials.

cubiculum an underground chamber with wall compartments for the reception of the dead.

effigy a painted or sculpted representation of the deceased on a monument.

ghoul a grave robber.

golgotha any burial place, named after the hill of Calvary, where Jesus was crucified.

lanterne des morts in medieval France, a graveyard towerlike structure and turret serving as a lantern.

mausoleum a large tomb or building housing one or more tombs.

monument any stone, pillar, sculpture, structure, or building erected in memory of the deceased.

mortuary where bodies are prepared for burial or cremation.

necropolis a large cemetery or city of the dead associated with an ancient city.

ossuary an urn or vault for holding the bones of the dead.

Potter's field a cemetery for paupers.

sarcophagus a stone coffin.

septum a low wall surrounding a tomb.

sepulcher a burial vault.

shaft tomb a vertical shaft leading to underground burial chambers.

solium an elaborately sculpted sarcophagus made of marble, used for kings and other important people.

weepers mourning statues placed within or around some tombs.

BRIDGES

abutment the support at either end of a bridge.

aqueduct bridge structure designed to convey water over a river or hollow and over long distance to supply communities.

arcade collective term for the series of arches and columns that support some types of bridges.

arch structural member supporting and displacing stress under a span.

balustrade a row of balusters topped by a rail serving as a barrier along the edges of a bridge.

bascule type of drawbridge with span arms that pivot and swing upward to let boat traffic pass.

bridle-chord bridge type of bridge in which the girders are supported by steel cables passing over the tops of towers on the main piers.

caisson a watertight chamber filled with compressed air for use in underwater construction by bridge builders.

cantilever type of bridge in which two beams or trusses project from shore toward each other and are connected.

cofferdam enclosure built in the water and continuously pumped dry to allow construction or repair of bridge piers.

gantry bridge structure supporting the rails of a moving construction crane.

gephyrophobia fear of bridges.

parapet any low wall or barrier that protects—as a railing—the edges of a bridge.

pier support at either end of a span.

pile long timber driven in the earth, used to support piers or abutments, or as a direct support for the bridge itself.

pontoon a flat-bottomed boat, or any float, used in the construction of bridges.

saddles blocks over which the cables of a suspension bridge pass.

suspension bridge similar to a bridle-chord bridge but using more cables to support and relieve stress on the girders.

swing bridge bridge with a span that opens by swinging around horizontally to let boat traffic pass.

trestle open-braced framework for supporting a railroad bridge.

truss assembly of beams, bars or rods forming a rigid framework.

vertical lift bridge bridge with a span section that is lifted at both ends from towers to allow boat traffic to pass.

viaduct an arched masonry bridge that carries a roadway over a valley or ravine.

LIGHTHOUSES

ANTS short for Aid to Navigation Teams; Coast Guard personnel who inspect and maintain automated lighthouses quarterly or annually.

caisson a lighthouse mounted on a caisson.

cupola the domed top of a lighthouse.

diaphone fog signal a two-tone fogsignal, making a sound similar to breeeeeooooooo.

gallery a railed walkway around a lantern.

keeper a person who maintains and/or lives in a lighthouse, all but abolished by 1990.

lamp the light inside the lens.

lamp changer a device that automatically changes a wornout light bulb.

lantern collective term for the lamp, the lens, and their containment.

lens a Fresnel lens used to magnify and concentrate light.

lightship a ship fitted with lanterns and anchored permanently at sea to serve as a floating lighthouse.

range lights paired towers consisting of a short lighthouse at the entrance to a harbor or a channel, and a distant, taller lighthouse; a safe course is followed by keeping the lights one atop the other.

screw pile a lighthouse with legs of huge screws that are twisted into the ground as anchors.

skeleton light a lighthouse with an open framework tower.

walkway on a large lighthouse, a railed walkway above the gallery that gives access for cleaning the outside of the lantern glass.

WINDMILLS

air brakes at the leading edge of a sail, boards that spring open in heavy gusts to slow rotation.

axle the windshaft.

backwind a wind hitting the mill from the opposite direction the sails are facing.

beard a decorative board behind the canister.

beehive cap a domed cap.

brake wheel a large cogged wheel that drives the millstone; it is mounted on the windshaft.

bran the husks of grain.

buck the body of a mill that revolves above the trestle to keep the sails facing into the wind.

canister at the end of a windshaft, the socket that receives the stocks of the sails.

cap a movable top on some windmills; it is turned by a fantail so the sails face into the wind at all times.

cloth sail wood-frame sail covered with cloth. Also, the cloth itself.

common sails cloth sails.

concentrator a device used with a modern wind turbine to concentrate the windstream.

cross trees the heavy horizontal beams that rest on piers and carry the weight of the main structure.

crown wheel the horizontal gear that meshes with the vertical gear.

cut-in speed the speed of wind at which the sails of a windmill begin to turn.

fantail a small, helper windmill that turns the cap to face the wind. Also known as a fly tackle.

fly tackle same as fantail.

furling speed speed at which a windmill or wind turbine should be stopped to prevent structural damage from strong wind gusts.

grain hopper a holding bin for grain to be milled.

heel the inner edge of a sail.

jib sails cloth sails that could be furled by a miller to slow the sails in high winds.

leader boards the boards on the leading edge of a sail.

main post the post on which a postmill is turned.

millstones the two stones that grind grain.

patent sails wood-shuttered sails attached to an opening and closing apparatus.

pepper pot a high, domed cap with a flat top.

post-mill a mill in which the entire body or buck revolves around on a trestle to face the wind.

quarter a mill to turn a mill slightly away from the wind to slow the sails.

reef to furl or take in a cloth sail to slow it down.

roundhouse the enclosed trestle portion of a post-mill, used for a storage space for grain and sometimes used as the miller's quarters.

runner stone the top millstone; the one turned by the mill.

sails the long blades or sweeps blown by the wind that drive the mill.

scoop wheel a cast iron wheel fitted with scoops to convey water to another level.

shroud a structure employed to concentrate or deflect wind.

shutter bar a bar linking shutters together.

shutters movable, spring-loaded boards that open and close according to the wind's power.

smock mill a multisided, wooden mill with a movable cap.

spring sail a sail having wind-activated, spring shutters.

sweeps another name for sails.

tower mill a brick or stone mill having a movable cap.

trestle the supporting members on which a post-mill rests and revolves.

vanes the shutters of patent sails. Also, the sails of a fantail.

wallower the first wheel turned by the windshaft; it meshes with the brake wheel.

winded turned to face the wind.

windshaft the axle that is turned by the rotating sails; it turns the gears that run the mill's machinery.

INTERNATIONAL AND NATIVE AMERICAN TERMS

Russian Architecture

dacha a country home.

dvoine a twin-pyramid-towered church.

izba a log cabin or small wooden cottage.

kokoshniki decorative gables or arches not needed for support and usually found in multiple tiers around the drums supporting onion domes.

kremlin a citadel of a city.

krest a cross.

lukovitsa an onion dome.

nalichniki in older wooden cottages, the carved decorations at the ends of gables and around window frames.

onion dome capping a cupola or tower, a bulbous dome ending in a point and resembling an onion.

shatrovy pyramid-shaped towers, commonly found on older Russian churches.

troine a triple-pyramid-towered church.

Middle Eastern Architecture

apadana a columned audience hall in an Iranian palace.

ataurique a Moorish plasterwork design featuring leaves and flowers.

bagnio a Turkish prison.

bazaar an outdoor marketplace of shops and stalls.

chahr bagh an Islamic garden divided into four parts by water channels symbolizing the four rivers of paradise.

cubit an ancient Egyptian and Biblical measure of length equal to 20.62 inches.

horseshoe arch an Arabic or Moorish arch shaped distinctly like a horseshoe.

hosh an inner court of an Egyptian house.

kasr an Arabian castle or palace.

kiosk a Turkish pavilion or feasting pavilion.

kubbu a domed tomb, a common Islamic burial structure. Also known as a turbe.

mihrab a niche in the wall of a mosque indicating the direction of mecca.

minaret a tower within or alongside a mosque from which the faithful are called to prayer.

muristan Iranian term for hospital.

musall Iranian term for burial ground.

qa'a a reception hall in an Egyptian house.

qibla the wall of a mosque oriented toward Mecca.

serai a Turkish palace.

serefe the balcony of a minaret from which the faithful are called to prayer.

Indian Architecture

alinda a veranda.

aryaka an alignment of five columns symbolizing the five Dhiyana Buddhas.

basadi a Jain temple or monastery.

bhumi a floor or story of a building.

bodhika the capital of a column.

chavada a pavilion.

choultry a public assembly place or hall.

dhvajastambham a high pillar in front of a temple.

ghat a stairway leading to a body of water.

gumpha a monastery.

manastambha a freestanding pillar in front of a temple.

mandapa a hall in a temple.

matha a convent or monastery.

sikhara a tower or spire, tapering on both ends, of an Indian temple.

siras the capital of a column.

sringa in southern India, the dome of a Hindu temple.

stupa a Buddhist memorial mound, shaped like a beehive or a bell.

vihara a Buddhist monastery.

Spanish Architecture

adobe sun-dried, unburned clay and straw, a common building material.

alcazar a Spanish castle.

azothea on the roof of a house, a terrace or platform.

capilla mayor the main chapel in a Spanish church.

hacienda a large estate, plantation, or ranch.

mirador a window or roof pavilion with a commanding or spectacular view.

mission architecture Spanish church and monastery architecture, often characterized by twin bell towers.

mission tile semicylindrical clay roofing tile. Also known as Spanish tile.

posada an inn.

ramada a rustic arbor or an open porch.

Far Eastern Architecture

amado in traditional Japanese architecture, a sliding storm shutter, usually set at night.

byo a Japanese mausoleum.

ch'an t'ang in Chinese architecture, a room set apart for meditation.

chashitsu a small rustic house equipped for the Japanese tea ceremony; also, a room so equipped.

chen h'uan a Chinese triangular arch.

ch'iao a Chinese bridge.

chigai-dana in a Japanese house, steplike shelving placed in an alcove.

chu in Chinese construction, a column.

ch'uan in Chinese construction, an arch.

chuang in Chinese construction, a window of any kind.

daikoku-bashira in the center of a traditional Japanese house, a large post associated with the god of fortune.

fang in traditional Chinese architecture, a building with the appearance of a barge, used as a tavern or restaurant, on the shore of a lake or pond.

feng huo t'ai one of the regularly spaced (1½ miles) rectangular towers along the Great Wall of China.

fusuma in a Japanese house, a decoratively painted, sliding interior partition made of wood lattice covered with heavy paper or cloth.

genkan in traditional Japanese architecture, a vestibule where shoes are set before entering a building.

goju-no-tu a five-story pagoda.

haiden a Japanese hall of worship.

hashira in Japanese construction, a column.

hogyo-yane in traditional Japanese architecture, a pyramidal roof.

kaidan Japanese steps.

mado in Japanese architecture, a window.

men in Chinese architecture, a door.

minka a traditional Japanese farmhouse.

mu a Chinese tomb.

nagare-zukuri a popular style of Japanese shrine, characterized by a gabled roof that extends over and beyond the front stairs.

nagaya in traditional Japanese architecture, an elongated apartment house.

nijiriguchi a tiny guest entrance through which one must kneel to a Japanese tea-ceremony house.

ping feng in a traditional Chinese house, a wood or bamboo partition moved when needed for privacy.

she li t'a a Chinese pagoda made of masonry and used as a shrine.

shikkui in traditional Japanese architecture, plaster, mortar, stucco, or whitewash made from lime and clay.

sorin the uppermost or crowning spire of a Japanese pagoda.

sukiya a Japanese tearoom or teahouse.

tatami one of several thick, 6-foot-long straw floormats used in a Japanese house.

tea garden a Japanese garden next to a teahouse or tearoom.

to a Japanese pagoda of two to seven stories, a shrine for Buddhist relics.

yagura in Japanese architecture, a tower.

zashiki in a Japanese house, a room for entertaining guests.

Ancient Greek and Roman Architecture

acaina in ancient Greece, a measure of length equal to 1,215 inches.

acroaterion in ancient Greece, a hall or place where lectures were given.

acrobaticon the scaffolding used in ancient Greek construction.

acropolis the elevated stronghold or plateau-plaza of a Greek city.

additus maximus a main entrance in an ancient Roman ampitheatre.

aerarium the public treasury of ancient Rome.

aethousa a sunny portico of a Greek dwelling.

agalma any ancient Greek work of art dedicated to a god.

agger an ancient Roman rampart or earthwork.

agora in ancient Greece, an outdoor public assembly place or marketplace.

agyieus an altar or statue of Apollo traditionally placed at a street-facing door of a Greek house.

ahenum a boiler system consisting of three copper vessels and a furnace for providing water to ancient Roman baths.

ala a small room or alcove off the atrium of an ancient Roman house.

albani stone the stone commonly used in the construction of ancient Roman buildings before the introduction of marble.

album in ancient Rome, a section of white plaster on a wall in a public place on which public announcements were written.

aleatorium in ancient Rome, a room where dice games were played.

alipterium a room in which ancient Roman bathers anointed themselves.

alveus a Roman sunken bath.

ambivium an ancient Roman road that circumnavigated a site but did not go through it.

amphitheatre an elliptical, circular, or semicircular auditorium.

anatarium a house and yard for raising ducks in ancient Rome.

andron a room used exclusively by men in ancient Greece.

angiportus a narrow road between rows of houses in ancient Rome.

anserium an ancient Roman porticolike structure used for raising geese.

anthemion a common ornamentation based on the honeysuckle or palmette plants, frequently seen in Greek architecture.

apodyterium a room where Greek or Roman bathers undressed.

apotheca a Greek or Roman storeroom that frequently kept wines.

aqueduct a water channel placed on high arches when crossing valleys or low ground.

arabesque in Roman architecture, a decorative pattern of acanthus scrolls, swags, candelabrum shafts, and animal and human forms appearing on panels and pilasters. (Differs from the arabesque pattern of Moslem countries.)

arca custodiae an ancient Roman prison cell.

archivium a building in which archives were kept in ancient Rome and Greece.

arena the sanded central area in a Roman circus or ampitheatre.

arenarium an ancient Roman cemetary, crypt, or grave.

argurokopeion in ancient Greece, a place where money was coined; a mint.

Athenaeum a Roman temple or place of scientific or literary studies, named after Athene.

atrium in a Roman house, a large inner hall with an opening in the roof for rainwater and a basin on the floor to catch it.

auditorium a place where orators, poets, and critics spoke.

baccha a Roman lighthouse.

baphium a Roman establishment for dyeing cloth.

bestiarium where wild animals were kept before their appearance in an ancient Roman amphitheatre.

bronteum in Greek and Roman theatres, a heavy vase filled with stones and shaken to simulate the sound of thunder.

caldarium one of the three components of an ancient Roman bath, consisting of the hot water bath itself. (See frigidarium, tepidarium.)

capeleion a place where wine and provisions were sold in ancient Greece.

caprile a Roman structure used to house goats.

carnificina a Roman underground dungeon in which criminals were tortured or killed.

cartibulum a supported marble slab serving as a table in a Roman atrium.

catadrome a Roman racecourse used by chariots, horses, or men.

caupona a place where wine and provisions were sold in ancient Rome.

cavaedium an atrium or inner courtroom in a Roman house.

cavea the dens of wild animals under the seats of ancient Roman amphitheaters.

cenatio a formal dining room in a Roman house.

choragic monument a Greek commemorative structure.

choragium in Greek and Roman theaters, a storage and rehearsal space behind the stage.

cinearium a Roman depository for urns holding the ashes of the dead.

circus a Roman stadium for races and gladiator shows.

clavus in ancient Roman construction, a nail.

cloaca in ancient Rome, a sewer.

coenaculum any of the upper eating rooms in Roman houses.

colosseum any large Roman amphitheatre.

Columna Maenia a column erected in the Roman Forum to which criminals and slaves were tied and publicly punished.

compitum any crossroads in ancient Rome where altars and shrines were erected.

compluvium in the atrium of a Roman house, an opening in the roof through which rain fell.

conclavium any rectangular room in a Roman house.

conditorium a Roman underground vault in which a corpse was deposited.

Corinthian a highly elaborate and ornate style of Greek architecture.

crepido on the sides of Roman streets, a raised sidewalk for pedestrians.

crypta associated with a Roman farmhouse or villa, a long, narrow vault, usually underground, for storing grains and fruits.

cubiculum a Roman bed chamber.

culina a Roman kitchen.

cyzicene an apartment in a Greek house.

delubrum an ancient Roman temple or sanctuary.

deversorium a Roman inn for travelers.

Doric the oldest and simplest order of Greek architecture, characterized by plain capitals and heavily fluted columns.

ekklesiasterion in a Greek town, a public hall.

elaeothesium where oil was kept in a Roman bath.

emblemata in Roman construction, a decorative, inlaid flooring.

emporium in Roman towns, a building housing imported merchandise for sale to local retailers.

ergastulum on a Roman farm, a prison where slaves worked.

farrarium a Roman grain barn.

favissa a Roman crypt or cellar.

ferriterion a Roman prison keeping chained slaves.

forica public toilets located throughout ancient Rome.

forum any Roman public square surrounded by important buildings.

frigidarium the third of the three chambers in a Roman bath, consisting of the final cold bath and sometimes a swimming pool.

gymnasium same as a modern gymnasium.

gynaeceum the portion of a Greek church or house set apart for women.

hastarium a Roman public auction room.

hemicyclium a semicircular alcovelike structure providing seating for several persons in Roman pleasure gardens or other public spots.

hippodrome a Greek racecourse for horses and chariots and considerably wider to accommodate more racers than a Roman circus.

hippodromos a Roman promenade or garden area used for equestrian exercises.

horreum a Roman barn or granary.

hortus a Roman garden.

hospitalium a guest room in a Roman house.

hypocaustum a Roman central heating system in which warm air was blown from a furnace through flues within walls and floors.

hypodromus a Roman covered walkway.

ianua the outer door of a Roman house.

imagines memorial busts of deceased family members placed in wooden shrines within the walls of an atrium in a Roman house. The busts were accompanied by descriptive inscriptions.

impluvium the cistern or basin within the floor of an atrium, used to collect the rainwater that fell through the compluvium.

Ionic the Greek style of architecture characterized by ornamental scrolls and elegant detailing, but less elaborate than the Corinthian style.

laconicum a sweat room in a Roman bath.

lalarium a shrine to the household gods in a Roman house.

latifundium a large Roman estate.

latrina a Roman bathroom or washroom.

lesche a Greek public clubhouse where people gathered to talk and receive news.

lithostrotum opus a Greek or Roman ornamental pavement such as mosaic.

logeum the stage in Greek and Roman theaters.

lucullite a type of black marble used in Roman construction.

macellum a Roman meat and produce market.

maenianum a balcony or gallery in a Roman theater.

mesaulos in a Greek house, the passage connecting the men's section (andron) with the women's section (gynaeceum).

milliarium on the side of Roman roads, a column erected at intervals of one Roman mile (0.92 mile) to indicate distance traveled.

moneta a Roman mint.

monopteron any circular Greek building surrounded by a single row of columns.

necropolis any large cemetary of ancient Greece.

nosocomium a Greek or Roman hospital for the poor.

opaion in Greek or Roman architecture, any aperture in a roof for smoke to escape.

oppidum a Roman town. Also, a collective term for the towers, gates and horse stalls at the end of a Roman circus, said to resemble a town.

opus tectorium a type of stucco used in Roman construction.

orchestra in Greek theater, the place occupied by the dancers and chorus. In later Roman theater, a space between the stage and first row of seats reserved for senators and other important people.

order an architectural style, particular of columns and entablatures. The Greek orders are Doric, Ionic, and Corinthian. The Romans later added Tuscan and Composite.

ornithon an ancient Roman poultry house; an aviary.

palaestra an athletic training room, smaller than a gymnasium, used by Greek and Roman athletes.

pandokeion a Greek travelers inn.

pantheon a Roman temple dedicated to the gods.

parastatica a pilaster of a Greek temple.

parathura the back door of a Greek house.

paries in Roman construction, a wall.

paries e lapide quadrato a Roman wall made of cut stone or ashlar.

paries lateritius a Roman brick wall.

passus a Roman measure of length, equal to 58.2 inches.

pastas a Greek vestibule.

pavimentum a Roman pavement formed of crushed stone, flint, and tile rammed and composited in a bed of cement.

pavonazzo in Roman construction, a type of marble characterized by dark red veins.

pes (pl. pedes) a Roman measure of length equal to 11.65 inches.

pharos a Greek or Roman lighthouse.

phyrctorion a Greek watchtower used for military purposes.

pinaculum in Greek or Roman construction, any roof that forms a ridge. Most houses of the day had flat roofs.

piscina in Roman construction, a reservoir. Also a pool or basin of water in a Roman bathroom.

platea any wide Roman street.

plethron an ancient Greek measure of length equal to 101¼ feet.

podium the plateau or platform on which Roman temples were built. Also, in a circus, the first or closest row of seats to the racecourse that was protected from the wild animal acts by a 10-foot trench.

polyandrion an ancient Greek monument or burial place dedicated to men killed in battle.

popina a Roman restaurant or tavern patronized by the lower classes.

porta the gateway to a Roman city.

posticum the back door of a Roman house.

postscenium the dressing rooms and storage rooms of the actors in Greek and Roman theaters.

pretorium the Roman residence of a governor.

propnigeum the sweat room furnace in a Greek gymnasium.

prothyron an entrance vestibule in a Greek house.

puteus in Roman construction, a manhole in an aqueduct. Also, a fountain in a Roman house.

robur a chamber below an underground dungeon where criminals were put to death.

ruderatio in Roman construction a common floor made of pieces of brick, stone, and tile.

sacrarium an in-house family shrine or chapel in Roman residences.

scabellum a Roman, freestanding pedestal.

scaena ductilis in Roman and Greek theater, a mobile screen that served as a scenic backdrop.

scalpturatum an ancient Roman pavement inlaid with patterned, colored marble.

scandula a Roman roof shingle.

scansorium Roman scaffolding.

senaculum a Roman council chamber.

specula a Roman watchtower and signal tower.

sphaeristerium part of a Roman gymnasium, a place for ball playing.

spica testacea in ancient Roman flooring, oblong tiles laid in a herringbone pattern.

spicatum opus Roman masonry set in a herringbone pattern.

spina the lengthwise barrier that divided a circus and around which athletes and charioteers raced.

spoliarium a room where the dead were dragged after being defeated in combat in a Roman amphitheater show.

spoliatorium in a Roman bath, a place for keeping the bathers clothing.

stadium a sports arena, or a Roman measure of length equal to 607 feet.

sudatorium in ancient Rome, a sweat room used by athletes.

synnoecia in ancient Greece, a dwelling shared by several families.

taberna a Roman booth, stall, or shop.

telonium a Roman customhouse.

tepidarium in Roman baths, a warm room.

thesaurus a Greek treasury house.

tholos any round building in Greek architecture.

thymele in the central orchestra section of a Greek theater, an altar dedicated to Bacchus.

tribune a place of high status to the immediate right or left of a stage in a Roman theater, reserved for magistrates, emperors, empresses, and the vestal virgins.

triclinium a Roman dining room with a low table surrounded by couches.

ustrinum where corpses were cremated in ancient Rome.

valetudinarium a Roman infirmary or hospital.

velarium an awning that protected the audience from the elements in a Roman theater or amphitheater.

via any paved Roman road.

Via Appia the first Roman highway, built in 312 B.C., and joining Rome with Capua.

via munita a Roman road paved with polygonal blocks of stone or lava.

villa an elaborate Roman residence with gardens and outbuildings.

villa rustica an agricultural villa with apartments for a steward, bookkeeper, and slaves.

vitrum in Roman construction, glass.

vomitory an entrance or exit in a bank of seats in a Roman theater or amphitheater.

water leaf in Greek or Roman ornamentation, a lotus leaf or ivy motif.

Native American Architecture

adobe a sun-dried blend of clay and straw formed into bricks.

banco a shelf around the interior of a kiva or pit house.

burial mound an elevated earthen grave.

cache a hole or chamber for storing dried food or other items.

chinking grass, mud, or clay sealing material applied between the cracks of a log home.

corbeled roof a roof frame comprised of horizontal tiers that graduate in size from peak to base.

cordage hide or plant fiber used to tie structural members together.

cosmic tree the center pole in some Indian structures, noted for its religious symbolism. Also known as the earth navel.

cribbed logs notched horizontal logs that overlap at the corner of a building.

dew cloth a cloth used by Plains Indians to line and insulate the inside of a tipi.

foot drums hollow log ceremonial drums played with the feet.

hogan an earth-covered dwelling built by Navajos.

horno a pueblo baking oven shaped like a beehive.

italwa Creek Indian word for "town."

kashim a large Eskimo building used for social and religious gatherings.

kiva a chamber, frequently underground, where Pueblo Indians meet, conduct rituals, and weave cloth.

latillas in a pueblo roof, the small, round poles spanning between the vigas.

longhouse an Indian meeting house. Also, a long, multifamily dwelling of the Iroquois.

palisade a fence or wall comprised of upright logs, frequently pointed, protecting a village.

pit house a partially underground, one-room house with an earthen roof.

plaza a public center for large gatherings outside.

puddled adobe a wet clay mixture used to finish a floor or wall.

pueblo a stone or adobe community building up to five stories high, built by southwestern Indians.

puncheon a slablike plank.

ramada a log sunshade.

smoke flaps the adjustable portion of a tipi cover; it opens and closes to keep out wind and rain and to let out smoke.

tipi ring a circle of stones used to hold down tipi coverings.

totem pole a large post carved into faces and fantastic figures by northwestern Indians.

travois the V-shaped frame of tipi poles.

tupik a summer tent used by Eskimos.

viga a log beam used as a frame member on a pueblo roof.

wattle and daub a framing technique employing upright or interwoven saplings to hold mud fill, used by southeastern and southwestern tribes.

wickiup a domed hut covered with bark or brush, used by the Kickapoo and Apache tribes.

wigwam an arched or conical dwelling covered with bark, hide, or mats, used by Indians from the Northeast and Great Lakes region.

Art

GENERAL ART TERMS (*Also see* ART TOOLS, SCULPTURE)

abozzo Italian for "sketch." In painting, the initial outline or drawing.

abstract art art composed of distorted, abstruse, stylized, or unrecognizable forms that may or may not represent a person, place, or object.

abstract expressionism a nonrepresentational painting style characterized by the use of abstract and stylized forms to express inner experience or emotion.

academic any style of art based on traditional standards.

acanthus a popular motif featuring the thistlelike acanthus plant of the Mediterranean, most notably found on Corinthian columns.

achromatic colors the noncolors white, black, and gray.

action painting a style of abstract expressionism in which paint is splattered, hurled, or brushed on the canvas impulsively as a reflection of the artist's moods.

advancing and retreating colors the perceived tendency of warm colors to appear at the forefront of a painting while cool colors (blues, violets) recede into the background, an optical illusion.

alla prima an oil painting executed in one application rather than layer by layer. A painting done in one sitting.

alligatoring on old or damaged paintings, a network of cracks resembling an alligator's hide.

amphora a type of large Greek vase with two handles.

anamorphosis a method of distorted painting or drawing in which the subject is unrecognizable unless viewed from a particular angle or distance. Also refers to a subject that appears to transform into a different subject when viewed from various angles.

anthemion a traditional flower and leaf motif featuring palm leaf and/or honeysuckle.

appliqué a style of decoration characterized by the application of materials over other materials to form a design.

aquarelle a painting composed of transparent watercolors.

arabesque an ornate motif featuring intertwined floral, foliate, and geometric figures.

art nouveau originating in the 1880s, an art form characterized by cursive, flowing lines, interlaced patterns, and whiplash curves.

art rupestre French term for prehistoric cave art.

assemblage a three-dimensional art form characterized by the integration of various objects into a meaningful or decorative whole.

asymmetry the use of nonsymmetry in art to more accurately depict reality, as in a portrait of the human face.

à trois crayons a three-colored chalk drawing.

aureole the radiance surrounding a depiction of a holy or religious figure. Also known as a glory.

automatism spontaneous painting or creation without conscious thought or plan.

avant-garde any art that is experimental, original, nontraditional, new, or untried.

bas-relief low relief. Any sculpture or carving that is raised only slightly (such as coins) from its background.

biomorphic form any nongeometric form, such as that of a plant or animal.

bird's-eye view a painting of a scene as it might be viewed from overhead.

bisque firing the first firing of a ceramic.

bleed the migration of some oil paints into adjoining areas on a canvas.

blending in a painting, the imperceptible fusing or merging of two hues.

blister in a painting, a damaged area characterized by a raised spot, caused by moisture or foreign matter.

bloom on a varnished oil painting, an undesirable cloudy or misty surface effect, caused by moisture.

blush the same as bloom, but on clear lacquer.

bottega an Italian art studio or shop where a master painter and assistants work.

brown coat in a fresco, the second coat of plaster, made of sand and lime putty or marble dust and lime putty.

buckeye term for poor quality, mass market landscape paintings.

cabinet picture a small painting, usually 30 inches wide or less.

cachet a distinctive mark, monogram, or cipher used to authenticate an art work in lieu of a signature.

calendering the process of giving paper a smooth finish by running it under heavy pressure between rollers.

calligraphy artistic, stylized, or elegant handwriting.

camaïeu a painting composed of several shades of the same color.

caricature a drawing of a person that exaggerates the physical characteristics of that person.

ceramics art objects made of clay that have been fired in a kiln.

chalking disintegration of surface paint that turns to powder and eventually falls off.

chasing in sculpture, the ornamenting of a metal surface with indentations.

checking a series of square cracks on a painting.

chromatic colors all colors other than white, black, or gray.

chromaticity the properties of color.

chrysography lettering in gold or silver ink, a practice originating with the ancient Greeks.

cinquefoil decoration in the form of five joined leaves or lobes.

cissing an uneven coat of paint that streaks.

classical any ancient Greek or Roman art form. Also, any historic period that produced exceptional art works in a particular style.

classicism art works borrowing from ancient Greek and Roman styles.

cleavage the separating of paint layers on a painting, due to poor materials or improper application.

collage a composition of paper, fabric, or other materials glued on a panel or canvas.

colorist an artist particularly masterful with the use of color.

commercial artist an artist who works in advertising, publishing, industry, design, and related fields.

concours in art school, a student exhibition of selected works at the end of a semester.

cool colors blues, green, violets; the opposite of warm colors.

crackle a network of cracks in a damaged painting.

crawl same as cissing.

cribbled decorative dots or punctures on wood or metal surfaces.

cubism style of art originating in Paris in the early 20th century and characterized by the reduction of natural forms into geometric patterns.

Dada art movement of World War I era; it rejected tradition and advocated unusual or outlandish art forms. Its credo was "everything the artist spits is art."

découpage a decoration consisting of cut-out paper figures or designs covering a surface.

deep relief a sculpted or carved design that projects high off its background. Also known as high relief.

diorama an illuminated, three-dimensional scene with or without a painted background, a popular museum display.

double image a painting that is cleverly designed to represent two different objects, such as a tree that is also a hand, a cloud that is also a face.

dragging stroke a light stroke that covers only the high areas of rough paper with paint.

drollery a humorous picture featuring animals who dress and act as humans.

drypoint a picture printed from an engraving made by a hard needle.

ébauche in oil painting, the first paint layer.

eclecticism borrowing from other art styles to create a new style.

écorché a drawing or statue of a figure with its skin peeled and its inner musculature revealed; it is used as a study aid.

electroplating to coat with a thin layer of metal through an electrochemical process.

emboss to mold or carve in relief.

encaustic a painting painted with heated, colored beeswax. Also, the method of executing this type of painting.

epigone a second-rate imitator.

etching the process of the partial eating away of a surface to create designs or a relief printing surface.

exploded view in technical drawing, the illustration of separate components and their relationship to each other in a complex object, such as a motor.

expressionism an early 20th-century art movement that emphasized the expression of emotion through distorted forms.

fauvism art movement characterized by the use of colorful expressionist forms.

fecit Latin for "he made it," sometimes inscribed after the artist's name on a painting.

festoon a painting of a garland of leaves, flowers, and ribbons. Also known as a swag.

figurine a statue 10 inches or less in height.

filigree delicate ornamental work made from gold, silver or silver-gilt wire.

film a continuous layer or coating of paint.

fine art any art created for its own sake as opposed to art created for purely commercial reasons.

flat without luster, as in flat paint.

flesh color human flesh tone, a color achieved by mixing white and yellow ochre.

floating signature a signature inscribed after a painting has been varnished, a sign of possible fraud.

foliated ornamented with depictions of foliage.

foreground the part of a painting that appears closest to the viewer.

foreshortening the reduction or diminishing of a subject in order to present an accurate picture of perspective as the subject grows into the distance.

foxing on paintings executed on paper, spotting and splotching caused by molds.

fresco Italian for "fresh." The art of painting on fresh plaster. Also, a mural painted by this method.

frilling the formation of waves in thin paint.

frottage making an impression of the texture of stone, wood, fabric, string, and other materials by placing a piece of paper over the material and rubbing the paper with a pencil or crayon. Similar to a rubbing. Also, the impression made by this method.

fugitive colors pigments that gradually fade when exposed to sunlight.

gallery tone on an old painting, the darkening of varnish and the accumulation of grime creating a brownish haze or tone.

garzone Italian term for studio assistant or apprentice.

geometric abstraction an abstract painting featuring geometric shapes.

gilded covered with gold.

gilding the application of thin, metal leaf to a surface.

glost fire the second firing of ceramics.

glyptic art the art of carving designs on gems and semiprecious stones.

goffer to decorate by embossing.

gouache the technique of painting on paper with opaque watercolors. Also, the picture rendered in this manner.

graphic arts any linear visual art, such as drawings, paintings, engravings, etchings, woodcuts, lithographs.

grisaille a monochrome painting done in shades of gray to simulate sculpture.

grotesque ornamental painting or sculpture featuring a motif of leaves and flowers with imaginary or bizarre animal or human figures.

ground on a painting, the prime coat on which the painting is executed.

guilloche a decorative work consisting of interlaced curved lines.

hatching in drawing or painting, shading created with a series of close-set lines.

hue a color or gradation of a color.

icon a picture, image, or sculpture of a holy person.

idiom the predominant art style of a particular period or person.

illumination any drawings and calligraphy used to decorate a manuscript.

impasto a style of painting in which paint is applied in thick layers or strokes, as in many Rembrandts.

impressionism a French art style originating in the 1870s and characterized by discontinuous brush strokes, vague outlines, and the use of bright colors and light effects, as in the works of Claude Monet.

inherent vice an art conservation term referring to anything present within the materials of an art work that may eventually bring about its deterioration.

inlay to insert decorative pieces of wood, metal, stone, or other material in a depression on a surface.

inpainting an art conservation term referring to the painting over of a damaged area so that it blends in with the rest of the painting.

intaglio an incised design, as used in dies for coins. Also, an etching process in which the printing areas are recessed.

intarsia inlay work of small pieces of wood veneer and sometimes marble or mother-of-pearl.

intonaco in a fresco, the last coat of plaster; the coat that is painted on.

journeyman a craftsman or artist who has served an apprenticeship and is qualified to work under a master.

kickwheel a pedal-operated potter's wheel.

kiln a furnace in which ceramics are fired.

kinetic art any art that moves or which has movable components.

kitsch any cheap, pretentious, or sentimental art work that appeals to the masses.

lacuna Latin for "gap." A portion of an art work that is missing due to damage.

landscape a drawing or painting of natural scenery.

limited edition a replica of an art work produced in a predetermined quantity, after which the plate, mold, or die is destroyed so no further copies can be made.

line drawing a drawing executed by lines only.

lithochromy the art of painting on stone.

lithograph a print made by lithography.

lithography a printmaking process employing a metal plate or stone on which a drawing is made with a crayon or greasy ink from which an impression is pressed onto paper.

local color in painting, the real or actual color of an object as distinguished from that subjected to unusual lighting.

magic realism in painting, a highly realistic rendering of a subject accompanied by an air of surrealism due to the subject being placed in a strange or unexpected place or time. Also, a form of realism rendered with flat paint and an absence of shadows.

marbling a form of decoration imitating the swirling patterns of marble.

marouflage the technique of cementing a painted canvas on a wall with strong adhesives.

marquetry inlay work of small pieces of wood, mother-of-pearl, marble, and such like, set in a floral or decorative pattern.

master an artist recognized as having great skill.

masterpiece one of an artist's best works.

mat a dull, flat finish. Also, a kind of inner painting frame or border made of cardboard or other still material.

mechanical drawing drafting.

medium the type of art form in which an artist works.

mezzo fresco a painting executed on partially dry plaster. Also, the method itself.

mobile a three-dimensional art work hung from a stand or from the ceiling and moved by slight air currents.

moiré effect an optical illusion of a nonexistent pattern created by superimposing a repetitive design over another repetitive design.

monochrome a painting painted in shades of one color. Also, the art of painting in this manner.

montage a picture made up of parts of other pictures or prints that are overlapped.

mosaic an assemblage of small pieces of tile, marble, wood, glass, or stone that forms a picture or decorative pattern in a wall or floor.

motif in an art work, an element with a recurrent theme.

mural a painting executed directly on a wall or ceiling or on a canvas that is cemented directly to a wall.

neoclassical art any art influenced by the art of ancient Greece or Rome.

neutral color any color between warm and cool colors. Brown is a neutral color.

nonobjective art art that does not represent anything recognizable.

nouveau French term for a beginning artist or student.

objective art art that represents a person, place, or thing.

objet d'art a small, valuable artistic article.

op art a style of art popular in the 1960s and characterized by repeating abstract patterns that create optical illusions.

opening a private showing the day before an art exhibition opens for the public.

optical mixing painting small dots or strokes of different colors close together so they create the illusion of a mixed color when viewed from a distance. (For example, blue and red dots painted close together will appear as violet from a distance.)

overpainting in oil and tempera painting, the final coat applied after the underpainting.

painterly highly artistic. Also, like a painting.

palmette a palm leaf ornament or design.

pastel a colored crayon made of pigment and chalk. Also known as a pastille. A work of art executed with pastels.

pastel shades soft, delicate hues.

pastiche an art work executed in different styles.

pâte-sur-pâte low relief decoration on ceramics.

perspective the technique of accurately rendering a three-dimensional object or scene on a two-dimensional surface.

petite nature a painting in which the figures are smaller than life-size but larger than half-size.

pochade a quick color sketch on which details are added at a later time.

polychrome executed in several colors, especially referring to a wood or stone carving.

pop art an art style made famous by Andy Warhol and characterized by larger-than-life replicas of commercial or widely recognized objects, such as food labels, packages, comic strip panels, etc.

portrait any work of art representing someone's face. It can also be used to describe a rendering of a full-body shot.

postiche a fake; an imitation.

pouncing a technique of transferring a drawing on one surface to another by perforating the lines of the original drawing and then passing pounce powder through the holes to the transfer surface.

pricking a test to determine a painting's relative age and possible authenticity, characterized by sticking a pin into a thick area of paint; if the pin can be pushed through easily, it means the paint is soft and relatively new and therefore a possible forgery.

primary colors the colors red, yellow, and blue, from which most other hues can be obtained by mixing with each other or with black or white.

primer a white base layer of paint on which a painting is executed. A ground.

primitive an art style uninfluenced by historical or contemporary forms. Also known as naive art.

profil perdu a profile or sideview showing more of the back of the head (or object) than the front.

psychedelic art U.S. abstract art of the 1960s, characterized by wild, swirling curves inspired by the use of hallucinogenic drugs.

realism an art style characterized by the realistic depictions of people, places, or things without abstraction or distortion.

relief a projection from a flat surface; a raised area.

Renaissance French for "rebirth." A period of western European history (roughly 1300s to 1500s) known for its many advances and innovations in the arts.

repoussé a method of forming a relief design by hammering a metal plate from the back.

retouching adding to or changing a finished painting.

rococo a French art style of the 1700s, characterized by elaborate, florid, and delicate ornamentation, especially in architecture.

rubbing a method of making a rough copy of a relief work by placing paper over the design and rubbing it with crayon, charcoal, pencil, or other writing instrument, as in a tombstone rubbing.

scale drawing a drawing whose dimensions are of the same ratio as those of the object drawn.

scrambled colors superficially blended colors that create swirls of different hues, a deliberate effect.

scrimshaw the art of carving on whalebone. Also, the art work itself.

scroll any spirallike decoration.

scumble a thin layer of semitransparent paint applied over a painting to create a hazy effect.

secco a method of painting on dry lime plaster. Also, a mural painted in this manner.

secondary colors the colors green, orange, and purple, formed by mixing primary colors.

serigraph a print made from the silk screen process.

sfumato the soft blending of outlines in a painting, especially in the works of Leonardo da Vinci.

sgraffito creating a design by cutting lines into pottery, plaster, or stucco to reveal a layer of different color beneath.

shading the subtle blending of one color into another.

silhouette a portrait profile executed in a single color.

silk screen a method of color stenciling in which a squeegee is used to force color through a fine screen on which the designless areas are blocked out.

sketch a quick, rough drawing.

smooch a deliberately made smudge made with the fingers on a drawing to produce shading.

sotto in su severe foreshortening of figures in a ceiling painting, an effect that makes them appear suspended in air. Italian for "from below upwards."

squaring a technique in which a drawing is transferred from one surface to another on a different scale by ruling the drawing and transfer surface into small squares.

stenciling a method of making copies of a design by cutting out a template and painting or spraying over its openings.

still life any drawing or painting of inanimate objects, such as a bowl of fruit.

stipple to apply color in dots.

study a rough, preliminary drawing (but more detailed than a sketch), painting, or sculpture.

surrealism an art style characterized by subjects of a dreamy, fantastic, or irrational nature.

tempera pigment dispersed in an emulsion of egg yolk and water. Also, the method of painting with these colors.

tenebrism painting in dark, shadowy hues.

tertiary colors any hues made from the mixing of secondary colors.

tessellated in the form of a checkered mosaic.

thumbnail sketch a tiny, rough sketch.

tondo a circular painting.

tone the prevailing color in a painting.

topographic landscape an accurate rendering of a landscape.

tormented color in an oil painting, a color that has been overworked and rendered drab or ineffective.

traction fissure in an old painting, a wide crack that reveals the ground layer beneath.

trompe l'oeil a style of painting in which the subject is rendered as realistically as possible; the highest form of realism, as in a photograph.

underpainting on a canvas or panel, a preliminary layer of color over which the overpainting is made.

vanishing point in parallel lines showing perspective, the point of convergence at the horizon line.

veduta a painting or drawing showing all or a large part of a town or city.

vignette a photograph or painting in which the subject gradually fades away and disappears toward the borders.

warm colors red, yellow, and any hues between them.

wash in a watercolor, a broad brushstroke or an area painted with broad brushstrokes.

wash brush a large, camel hair brush used to paint washes with watercolors.

watercolors pigments dispersed in water instead of oils, characterized by a transparent quality.

wedging kneading clay to make it more pliable.

woodcut a technique of printing from relief carved on a block of wood. Also, the print made by this method.

worm's-eye view in a painting, a scene or subject depicted from a ground-level perspective.

ART TOOLS AND MATERIALS

acetone a flammable fluid used as a paint solvent.

acrylic brush any brush made with nylon bristles as opposed to hair.

acrylic colors fast-drying, easily removed plastic paints.

airbrush a small, spray-painting apparatus held like a pen and operated by compressed air or carbonic gas; it is used to delicately smooth out tones and create subtle shading effects in commercial art or in retouching of photographs.

alabaster a white, translucent variety of gypsum that is soft and easily carved.

angular liner a paint brush with a slanted end, used for lining. Also known as a fresco liner.

architect's rendering brush a large brush used by water color painters.

armature the skeletonlike frame upon which plaster, clay or other substance is applied to construct a sculpture.

badger blender a round brush with a square end, made of badger hair, and used to create soft effects.

bamboo pen a Japanese pen made from bamboo and used for drawing and calligraphy.

banding wheel a turntable or wheel on which pottery is turned in order to easily apply decorative stripes or bands.

bisque ceramic ware that has been fired once but is unglazed, as in bisque figurines. Also known as biscuit.

blender brush a badger-haired brush that flares out instead of coming to a point; it is used for blending colors.

bright a flat, thin, square-ended brush used in creating effects similar to that provided by a painting knife.

bristle brush the standard oil painting brush, made from hog bristles.

bulletin cutter a large, flag-tipped brush used by sign painters to outline large letters.

burnisher any tool used to smooth, polish, or remove imperfections, especially in etching or gilding.

camel hair brush a brush made not from camel hair but from squirrel hair, commonly used with watercolors.

camera lucida an optical device comprising a stand, an adjustable arm, and a prism; it projects an image of an object or scene into a plane surface for tracing.

canvas the heavy fabric or linen on which oil paintings are painted after being primed.

charcoal a black marker made of charred wood and used for drawing and creating special effects by smudging.

charcoal paper a paper with a grain that holds charcoal well.

chassis the framework that holds an artist's canvas.

chisel brush a straight-edged brush with a beveled tip, like a chisel, used for sign writing.

compass an adjustable instrument with two hinged legs, used for describing perfect circles or arcs.

crayon any drawing material in stick form.

dagger striper a brush having long hairs that taper to a sharp point, used for striping.

earth colors paint pigments derived from colored clays and rocks. Also known as mineral pigments.

easel a freestanding framework or support that holds an artist's canvas during painting.

ellipse guide a template that aids in the drawing of ovals or ellipses.

enamel a vitreous protective and/or decorative coating baked on metal, glass, or ceramics.

fan brush a flat, fan-shaped brush used for blending and creating wispy effects.

filbert brush an oval-ended bristle brush used in oil painting.

fitch brush a brush made from the hair of a polecat. Also, a chisel brush made of bristle and used in sign painting.

fixative a fluid sprayed over pastels and drawings to help prevent smudging.

flag the free end of a brush; opposite of the root.

fluorescent paint paints with a particularly luminous quality, especially after being exposed to ultraviolet light; Day-Glo.

French curve a scroll-like, plastic template used as a guide for ruling curves.

highliner a long-bristled, square-ended brush used for lettering and striping.

lay figure a jointed mannequin that substitutes for a human model in art study.

lettering brush a wide, square-ended brush made of red sable, camel hair, or ox hair and used for lettering or making clean lines.

mahlstick a short rod used by a painter to steady his hand or brush while executing delicate detail work.

mop a large camel hair brush used with watercolors.

mordant an acid mixture used in producing etchings.

oil colors pigments that have been ground with oil.

painting knives a family of thin, flexible knives used in painting and preferred by some artists over brushes.

palette an oval board or tablet with a hand grip and thumb hole, on which a painter lays out and mixes paints.

palette knife a spatulalike knife used to mix oil paints.

panel a wood or wallboard panel sometimes used instead of a canvas for painting on.

pantograph an adjustable hinged-arm device used to trace, reduce or enlarge a drawing.

papier mache a mixture of paper pulp and glue that can be molded into various shapes and painted when dried.

pastel a colored crayon made of pigment and chalk. Also known as pastille.

pate the clay from which ceramic pottery is formed.

potter's wheel a turntable on which pottery is formed.

pounce a powder made from charcoal or chalk used to transfer a drawing from one surface to another.

rigger a narrow, lettering brush.

single-stroke brush a broad brush used for creating broad washes with watercolors.

spatula a large painting knife used for mixing and stirring.

spotting brush a fine, red sable brush with a small point, used to retouch photos and lithographs.

stenciling brush a short, stiff, flat-ended brush used in stenciling.

striper a brush used for making delicate lines and stripes.

stump a cigar-shaped drawing tool made of rolled chamois or paper, used for making smudges and smoothing out tones.

taboret an artist's cabinent table for tools and materials.

tempera pigment dispersed in an emulsion of egg yolk and water.

tessera a small piece of tile, glass, or stone used in creating a mosaic.

turning tools a family of spatulalike tools used to shape clay on a potter's wheel.

wash brush any broad brush used to paint washes with watercolors.

watercolors pigments dispersed in water instead of oils, characterized by a transparent quality.

SCULPTURE

acrolith a Greek marble statue.

armature the skeletonlike frame upon which plaster, clay, or other substance is applied to construct a sculpture.

bas-relief low relief. Any sculpture or carving that is raised only slightly (such as a coin) from its background.

bushhammer a brick-shaped hammer with teeth on either end, used in stone carving to pulverize rock.

bust a sculpture consisting of the subject's head, neck, and part of the shoulders.

bust peg a post on which a bust is sculpted.

butterfly in a large sculpture, a crosslike piece of wood hung inside the framework or armature to help hold up heavy masses of material; a cross-shaped support.

calipers a tool with two movable arms, used by sculptors to measure diameters.

colossal any sculpture that is more than twice as large as life-size.

contrapposto a sculpture of a figure poised with most of its weight resting on one leg.

damascene the inlaying of a precious metal into a plain metal surface.

deep relief a sculpted or carved design that projects high off its background. Also known as high relief.

direct carving creating a sculpture directly without a clay or wax model.

draperie mouillée wet drapery; in figure sculpture, a thin, clingy, form-revealing drapery.

dress to finish or smooth out stone.

fettle to trim a sculpture of rough edges and any other extraneous matter.

firing the subjecting of a clay body to high heat in order to harden it.

grotesque any sculpture featuring a motif of leaves and flowers with imaginary or bizarre animal or human figures.

heroic a figure sculpture that is larger than life-size but smaller than colossal.

icon a sculpture or picture of a holy person.

isocephaly the arrangement of figures so that the heads are at the same level.

mallet a wooden, churnlike sculptor's mallet.

maquette a small wax or clay model of a potential sculpture and presented to a client for approval.

modeling clay reusable, nonhardening clay used for modeling.

rasp an abrasive tool used in rough-shaping, striating, and wearing down surfaces.

relief any projection from a flat surface, a raised area.

repoussé a method of forming a relief design by hammering a metal plate from the back.

sculpture in the round freestanding figures carved in three dimensions, as distinguished from relief work.

statuary marble any white marble suitable for sculpture.

statuette a statue that is half life-size or less.

stun to split, chip, or splinter stone deliberately or by accident.

terra cotta a fired, brownish red clay, commonly used by sculptors and potters.

Sculpting Marbles

bardiglio capella an Italian marble, gray with gray and black streaks.

benou jaune French marble, mottled gold, yellow, and violet.

brèche rose Italian marble, mottled brown, white, and lavender.

campan griotte French marble, mottled brown.

carrara popular Italian marble, white with few gray streaks.

compage melange vert French marble, green.

escalette French marble, yellowish green, and pink.

French grand antique French marble, mottled black and white.

giallo antico popular with ancient Greeks and Romans, an antique yellow marble.

Languedoc French marble, red or scarlet with occasional white splash.

loredo chiaro Italian marble, mottled brown and yellow.

lumachelle French marble, mottled green.

Napoleon gray New England marble, gray.

pavonazza Italian marble, multicolored with peacocklike markings.

Petworth English marble, multicolored and fossil-bearing.

porto marble Italian marble, black with gold veins.

rance Belgian marble, dull red with blue and white streaks.

Roman brèche French marble, mottled pink and blue.

rosso magnaboschi Italian marble, reddish orange.

royal jersey green eastern U.S. marble, green, serpentine.

saccharoidal marble statuary marble.

Saint-Béat French marble, pure white.

Sainte-Anne marble Belgian marble, blue black with white veins.

Sainte-Baume marble French marble, yellow with brown and red veins.

sienna French marble, deep yellow with white and purple veins.

sienna travertine German marble, mottled brown.

PHOTOGRAPHY

airbrush a lab technique of creating or eliminating tone effects in a photo.

anaglyph a three-dimensional photo effect composed of a slightly contrasting dual image.

aperture the amount of opening in a lens; it controls the amount of light entering the camera.

backlight to illuminate a subject from behind.

barrel distortion an aberration in a camera lens that causes abnormal curvature of square images in a photo.

beam combiner a two-way mirror that reflects light, allowing photos to be taken of the real and reflected image simultaneously.

blowback the reenlargement to the original size of a reduced photo.

blowup an enlargement of a photo.

bounce light a flash pointed at the ceiling or wall to reflect light onto the subject.

bugeye see fisheye.

burn to expose a negative to light to retouch an area or to remove areas.

changing bag a black bag in which 35mm film magazines can be loaded or unloaded in daylight; used when a camera jams.

close down to reduce the opening of the camera lens by increasing the depth of field.

color transparencies another name for color slides.

computer enhancement the use of a computer to bring out fine or hazy details in a photograph.

contre jour to take photos with a light source directly facing the camera.

courtesy line the name of the photographer or other source that appears under a photo published in a newspaper, magazine, or book.

crop to trim a portion of a photo.

depth of field the in-focus portion of an image from the closest object to the furthest; the range of sharp focus through a camera lens.

double exposure a dual-image photo of two subjects.

duotone a photo printed in two colors.

84 Charlie military slang for a combat photographer.

enlarger an apparatus that projects an enlarged image of a negative on light-sensitive paper to produce a larger photo.

enlarging paper paper used for printing enlarged images.

expose to admit light.

f short for focal length; lens aperture. See f-STOP.

film speed film sensitivity to light. Fast film is more sensitive to light and is used in low-light situations; slow film is less sensitive to light and is used in bright, clear weather.

filter one of a variety of special lenses placed over the main lens to produce a number of color, light, or special effects.

fisheye a wide-angle (providing 180-degree view) lens, noted for the distorted circular image it produces. Also known as a bugeye.

fixer the chemical solution used to complete the development of a photo.

flat a photo having dull contrast.

focal length the distance between a point in the lens and the film when the lens is focused at infinity.

focal plane at the back of the camera, the area where the image is focused on the film.

fog filter a special-effects filter used to produce a foggy or hazy effect in a photograph.

f-stop a lens aperture setting; the higher the f-stop number the more the aperture is reduced.

glossy a photo having a glossy or smooth finish.

halftone a photo having varying tones of gray.

high hat a short tripod used for making low-angle shots.

hot shoe the receptacle or holder for a camera flash unit.

infinity through a camera lens, any distance at which the subject is a few hundred feet away or more.

iris diaphragm the opening and closing device that regulates the amount of light entering the lens aperture.

light meter a device that measures light to determine proper camera settings. Also known as an exposure meter.

macro lens a lens used to photograph very small objects closeup.

magic hour the hour at dawn and again at dusk, when the sun produces the most photogenic light.

mask a cardboard cutout placed over a lens to create a variety of effects, such as making a picture appear as if it was taken through binoculars or through a keyhole.

matte a decorative cardboard border around a photo. Also spelled mat.

monochrome a photo in several shades of one color.

paparazzi freelance photographers who follow celebrities around and take their photographs for sale to publications. The singular form is paparazzo.

photoflood a studio light of 275 to 1000 watts.

photogenic photographically attractive.

photomacrography photography of small objects.

photometer a light-exposure meter.

photomicrography photography through a microscope.

red eye in a photograph, the reddish glint that sometimes appears in the eye of a subject when a flashbulb has been used.

reflectors studio light reflectors used to bounce light in the desired direction.

retouch to touch up or alter a photograph, as with an airbrush.

scrim a mesh fabric used to produce diffuse lighting.

shutter speed the speed at which the camera shutter opens and closes. A fast speed is needed to capture moving objects without blur.

sky filter a colored filter used in landscape photography.

slow a film that is less sensitive to light than other (fast) film. Also, a lens that allows less light to enter the camera than others.

SLR single-lens reflex camera, noted for its viewfinder that shows the image exactly as it will be recorded on film.

solarize to overexpose a photograph, sometimes done intentionally for effect.

stop bath a chemical solution used in stopping film from developing further, before the fixing process.

stop down to reduce the size of the camera aperture and amount of light entering it.

telephoto a lens used to focus on distant objects.

time exposure a photograph made with the camera shutter left open for several seconds or minutes to show movement of, for example, clouds and stars, or to gather more light from very dim objects.

tripod a three-legged camera stand.

unretouched photo an unaltered photo.

vaseline sometimes applied on glass to shoot pictures through; it produces a hazy effect.

vignette a photo whose edges blend into the surrounding background.

wide-angle lens a lens that allows a wide field of view.

zoom lens a telephoto lens with a range of different focal lengths.

MUSIC

GENERAL MUSIC TERMS *(See also* MUSIC DIRECTIVES, VOCALS AND SONG, and VARIOUS INSTRUMENTS)

accent emphasis on a particular note or chord.

accent, apogic a tone held for a longer time than others.

accent, dynamic a tone played louder than others.

accent, tonic a tone higher in pitch than others.

acciaccato playing the notes of a chord not quite simultaneously, but in quick succession from bottom to top.

accidentals collective term for the signs that raise or lower a pitch or that cancel these; includes sharp, double sharp, flat, double flat, and natural.

acoustics the science of sound properties.

air a simple melody.

aleatory music musical compositions with elements left to chance or the whims of the individual musician.

alto the second or third highest voice class of instruments—alto clarinet, alto sax, and so on. See VOCALS.

answer repeating an original theme in a lower or higher register.

answer, call and the repeating or nearly repeating of a theme played by one instrument by another instrument, creating a kind of echo effect.

answer, real when the answer (above) is played exactly the same as the original theme, with the exception of a higher or lower key.

answer, tonal when the distances between the notes in an answer is played differently than the original theme.

anthem a hymn or composition set to words from the Bible.

anticipation the playing of a single note before a chord that harmonizes with that chord.

aquarelle a delicate composition.

arabesque the musical counterpart to arabesque architecture, an ornate or florid melody section.

arpeggio a chord in which the notes are played individually in quick succession instead of simultaneously.

arrangement the arrangement of a composition for another medium for which it was intended. Also known as a transcription.

ASCAP American Society of Composers, Authors and Publishers.

aubade French term for early morning music as opposed to a serenade or evening music.

augmentation the lengthening of the time values of notes in a composition, for example, from quarter notes to half notes or from half notes to whole notes. Opposite of diminution.

bagatelle French term for any short composition, usually for piano.

bar a measure; a bar line. Also, a guitar chord made by one finger laid straight across all six strings and pressed down.

bar line the vertical line in a musical staff that separates two measures.

baroque a term borrowed from baroque architecture to describe the musical developments between 1600 and 1750, characterized by growing complexity and the popular use of contrasts.

bass the lowest voice in a family of instruments. See VOCALS.

baton the stick used by the conductor to direct a symphony orchestra's timing, phrasing, volume, and so forth.

battle music any musical composition in which battle sounds are recreated.

bebop jazz style, frequently with a fast tempo, originating in the 1940s and characterized by scat singing (see VOCALS), complex rhythms, and off-time beats. Also known as bop.

berceuse French term for lullaby, usually involving an instrumental composition.

bitonality playing two keys simultaneously.

blues originally a form of jazz songs, characterized by depressing themes, a slow tempo, and having flatted thirds and sevenths.

BMI Broadcast Music Inc., an American performing rights society.

boogie woogie jazz piano style popular in the 1930s and 1940s, characterized by the left hand playing a repeating bass pattern while the right plays a melody.

bowing the employment of a bow over the strings of a violin, cello, or other stringed instrument.

break in jazz, an improvised solo.

brevis a double whole note, the longest note in use.

bridge passage a short musical passage that helps one body of a composition flow smoothly into another body.

broken chord a chord in which notes are played not simultaneously but in quick succession; an arpeggio.

buffa comic, as in comic opera.

cadence rhythmic flow, beat. Also, a progression of chords or notes leading to the close of a composition.

cadence, deceptive a cadence that ends on a note or chord other than what the listener expects or anticipates. Also known as an interrupted cadence.

cadence, imperfect a cadence that gives the impression that more music is to follow and is therefore used in the middle of a composition.

cadence, masculine a cadence that ends on a strong beat as opposed to one that ends on a weak beat, as a feminine cadence.

cadenza a virtuoso solo performance near the end of a composition.

calypso music originating in the West Indies and especially in Trinidad, characterized by high syncopation and repetition, improvised lyrics of a humorous or topical nature.

cantata a vocal or instrumental composition of several movements that include arias, duets, and choruses; a type of opera.

chamber music music in which each part is played by a single instrument as opposed to several instruments in an orchestra; music performed by a trio, quartet, quintet, or other group.

chamber orchestra a small orchestra of 40 players or less.

chord any simultaneous playing or sounding of three or more notes.

chord, chromatic a chord played along with one or more notes that are out of key.

clef the symbol at the beginning of a musical staff indicating the pitch of the notes.

coda the final or closing passage of a movement.

colpo the stroke of a bow.

composition a piece of music.

concertmaster the first violinist and assistant conductor.

concerto a composition for the orchestra and one or more soloists, usually performed in three movements.

concert pitch the pitch to which orchestral instruments are tuned, specifically the A above middle C to a frequency of 440 cycles per second.

conservatory a school of music instruction.

consonance in-tune, harmony; pleasant-sounding. The opposite of dissonance.

consort a small instrumental ensemble.

counterpoint the combining of two or more different melodies to create a richer tapestry of sound. Similar to polyphony (see VOCALS) or the use of multiple voice parts.

cross rhythm the playing of two different rhythms at the same time.

decibel one unit in the measurement of sound volume.

demisemiquaver a thirty-second (1/32) note.

diminution shortening the time values of notes, such as whole notes to half notes, half notes to quarter notes. Opposite of augmentation.

discord a harsh or unpleasant-sounding chord, dissonance.

dissonance harsh; unpleasant-sounding; disharmony.

Dixieland New Orleans jazz combining elements of ragtime and blues, originating in the early 20th century.

dotted note a note with a dot over it is to be played lightly and quickly, or staccato. A dot after a note has half of its time value added to it. That is, a dotted quarter ($\frac{1}{4}$) note equals $\frac{1}{4}$ note plus $\frac{1}{8}$ note, and so on. A double dot after a note adds three-fourths the time value to that note, so a double-dotted $\frac{1}{4}$ note equals $\frac{1}{4}$ note plus $\frac{1}{8}$ note, plus 1/16 note.

double-handed a musician who can play two different instruments well.

downbeat the first beat in a measure, named for the starting downswing of a conductor's baton.

duet a performance by two musicians.

duple meter two beats per measure.

dynamics the graduations of sound volume, from soft to loud.

ear, playing by playing music without notation, either by memory or by improvising.

ear training the teaching of pitch and rhythm recognition.

echo a softly repeated musical passage.

eighth note a note having a time value equal to one-eighth of a whole note.

eighth rest a rest or silence lasting as long as $\frac{1}{8}$ note.

elegy a sad song, vocal or instrumental, lamenting the death of someone or something.

embouchure the placement, shaping, and actions of the mouth, lips, and tongue in achieving proper pitch, tone, and effects in a wind instrument. (*See* TONGUING.) Also, the mouthpiece of a wind instrument.

enharmonics notes, intervals, or chords that sound the same but differ by name. For example, C sharp is the equivalent of D flat, D sharp the equivalent of E flat.

ensemble a small performing group of musicians.

etude French term for "study," referring to an instrumental composition designed to test and improve a player's skills, specifically any difficult piece containing arpeggios, trills, scales, and such like.

expression marks collective term for musical directives, including tempo, volume, technique, phrasing, mood, often expressed in Italian.

fanfare a short piece for trumpets to announce the arrival of royalty or to begin some festivities.

fantasia any musical composition that relies more on the whims of the composer than on any standard form; music of an improvisational or fanciful quality. Also, short mood pieces.

finale the final movement in a composition.

fine Italian word for "end."

flamenco Spanish music with vocals, guitar and percussive accompaniment by castanets and fingernail tapping on the belly of the guitar.

flat the pitch of a note subtracted by half a tone; an accidental that lowers the pitch by this amount. Slightly below the correct pitch.

florid music that is highly ornamented.

frog the part of the violin bow that tightens the horsehair. (See Instruments)

fughetta a short fugue.

fugue a polyphonic composition in which themes are sung sequentially by two or more performers and in imitation of the previous performer; a complex form of a round or canon (see Vocals and Song)

fugue, double a fugue having two themes or subjects.

fugue, triple a fugue having three themes or subjects.

glissando sounding up or down the scale of an instrument very rapidly, as drawing one finger up or down the entire length of a piano keyboard or a fingerboard of a guitar, or moving the slide of a trombone to its full extension and back; the sound this produces.

grand opera any lavish or artistic opera production.

half note a note having a time value equal to half of a whole note.

half rest a rest or silence lasting the same length of time as a half note.

hemidemisemiquaver a sixty-fourth note.

hootenanny a performance by folk singers, usually with singalongs from the audience.

hymn any religious song praising God.

imitation the echoing or repetition of one singer's part by another.

improvisation music that is spontaneously generated, made up, faked, and so on.

incidental music music providing background atmosphere in a play or movie. Also, any music played between the acts of a play.

interlude a short passage within a composition, usually an instrumental section between vocals. Also, any incidental music played between acts of a play.

intermezzo originally, a musical playlet, often comic, inserted between acts of a play from the 16th to the 18th centuries. Today, a short piece of music performed to illustrate the passing of time in a play or opera. Also, an interlude.

interval the distance between the pitches of two notes, the smallest of which is a half-tone. Also, two notes played in unison.

intonation the production of pitch by an instrument. Good intonation is the production of accurate pitch.

jam any informal or unprepared performance by a pop, rock, jazz, or folk group. A jam session.

key signature following the clef on a musical staff, the sharp or flat symbols that indicate which key the music is in.

lament a composition of mourning.

ledger short extension lines appearing above or below the five standard staff lines, used to underscore very high or very low notes.

libretto the text of an opera.

lullaby any gentle song intended to put a baby to sleep.

lyrics the words of a song.

maestoso any stately musical passage or movement.

maestro master, as in master musician.

mariachi a Mexican ensemble consisting of at least one of each of the following: guitar, violin, harp, and bass guitar.

measure the section of music contained between two bar lines; same as a bar.

medley a performance of portions of favorite tunes played one after the other.

melisma one syllable of a lyric carried or sung through several notes.

melismatic pertaining to melisma.

melody a group of notes, catchy or at least memorable in some way, making up part or all of a song. Most songs usually have more than one melody.

meter refers to how many beats per measure are in a particular composition.

minstrel a musician or entertainer of the Middle Ages.

minuet music in moderate triple meter, intended for the dance of the same name.

m.m. Maelzel's metronome, used to sound the precise tempo at which a passage or composition is to be played.

modulation the changing of keys within a single composition.

motif the briefest sequence of notes that can be defined as a melody, such as the opening four notes of Beethoven's Fifth Symphony.

movement a major section within a composition, often having its own key signature, and often set apart from following movements by a brief pause.

musicology the study of music.

mute any muffling device used on an instrument to lower its volume or alter its tone.

natural any note not raised or lowered by a sharp or a flat.

nocturne French term pertaining to the night, specifically music that conjures up images of the night and romance in the night. Also, a piano melody played with the right hand accompanied by soft broken chords played by the left.

noel a French Christmas carol.

notation the writing down of music.

octave all eight notes of a minor or major scale.

octet eight; having eight voices or eight instruments; a composition for eight musicians, and similar groupings.

ode a lyrical poem sometimes set to music.

opera buffa comic opera.

operetta an opera of a lighter or more humorous nature.

opus work; the word *opus* is usually followed by a number to designate the order in which a particular work was produced by a composer; for example, opus 27 would designate a composer's 27th work, although not all compositions are so numbered.

oratorio religious text set to music and involving soloists, chorus and orchestra, usually performed without scenery, costumes, or special effects.

orchestra, symphony an orchestra capable of playing symphonies, usually having at least 90 musicians.

orchestration the writing and dividing of parts of a composition to be played by the individual instruments of an orchestra.

ornaments any notes added to a composition to put extra pizzaz into a piece; embellishments; flourishes.

overblow to blow so hard into a woodwind that it raises its normal pitch one octave higher (slightly higher for clarinets), a technique used in playing many musical compositions.

overture a composition of instrumental music preceding or introducing an opera, oratorio, or play.

paraphrase a theme, melody, or passage in a composition that is repeated in a different way.

passion a musical composition set to the Passion, the week's events leading up to the crucifixion of Christ.

pasticcio any composition created by several composers, or a montage of the works of several composers as assembled by an arranger.

pastoral any music that conjures up images of life in the country.

pedal tone the lowest pitch attainable on a wind instrument.

philharmonic amalgamation of two Greek words, "love-harmony." Another name for an orchestra or musical society.

pitch any note in the range between the lowest and the highest notes.

pitch pipe a small wind instrument used to demonstrate proper pitch.

polyrhythmic music with more than one rhythm played at the same time.

portamento similar to a glissando but with smaller note intervals, thus limiting its execution to the violin, trombone, and voice in which no separation of notes of half notes (as by frets) exist.

program music music that tells a story or depicts a mood or emotion.

quarter note a note with a time value equal to one-quarter of a whole note.

quarter rest a rest or silence equal to the time value of a quarter note.

quartet an ensemble of four musicians or a composition written for four musicians.

quintet an ensemble of five musicians or a composition written for five musicians.

R&B abbreviation for rhythm and blues.

ragtime a highly syncopated piano music performed with a quick tempo, popular in the United States early in the 20th century.

rap music originated by black performers in the United States in the 1980s, characterized by a strong beat and recitative singing style.

refrain a section or verse of a musical composition that is repeated at regular intervals and especially at the end of each stanza.

reggae black Jamaican music characterized by off-time beats and simple, repetitive lyrics.

reprise a repetition of or return to an original theme of a composition.

rest a pause or silence.

retrograde refers to a melody that is reversed, so that the first note becomes the last, and vice versa.

rhapsody a free form or improvised composition depicting a mood or emotion.

rhythm and blues black American music originating after World War II, combining elements of jazz and blues and characterized by loud volume, a driving beat, and usually depressing lyrics; the forerunner of rock and roll.

riff any short melodic phrase played on an instrument, but particularly on jazz or rock guitar.

score the music written for a movie or play; any musical composition for orchestra.

secondo in a piano duet, the lower of two parts.

semiquaver British equivalent of a sixteenth note.

septet an ensemble of seven musicians or a composition written for seven musicians.

serenade an instrumental composition similar to a sonata. Also, a love song sung under one's window.

sextet an ensemble of six musicians or a composition written for six musicians.

sharp an accidental that raises the pitch of a note by one-half.

sightreading the ability to perform music on sight without previous practice.

signature the key and meter signs at the beginning of a composition.

sixteenth note a note equal in time value to one-sixteenth of a whole note.

sixteenth rest a rest or pause equal in time value to one-sixteenth note.

solfa syllables the syllables do, re, me, fa, sol, la, ti, do.

sonata an instrumental composition in three to four movements with each differing in key, mood, and tempo.

sonatina a sonata with shorter or fewer movements.

soul style of 1960s music derivative of blues and gospel and often characterized by lyrics with black themes.

spiritual a type of religious song with complex rhythms, developed by black Americans in the 1800s.

staff the set of horizontal lines upon which notes are written and designated a pitch.

stanza in songs with a poetic text, a verse or set of verses. Also, the introductory passage of a song, followed by the chorus.

steel band an ensemble of musicians playing steel drums.

stereophonic refers to music that is recorded with two or more microphones with the intention of playing it back through two or more speakers.

suite an instrumental composition consisting of several movements usually involving dance music, and each in the same key; a popular form from 1600 to 1750.

symphonic poem program music, or music that depicts a scene or story or emotion, usually performed in one extended movement.

symphony a long orchestral composition in four movements, similar to a sonata but performed by the entire orchestra.

syncopation changing time signatures suddenly, accenting the weak beat instead of the strong; off-time rhythms and beats, used widely in jazz, blues, ragtime, and jazz-rock fusion.

time signature at the opening of a composition, a sign consisting of two numbers, one over the other, the top designating beats per measure, the bottom the time value of the note receiving the beat.

toccata a highly elaborate and difficult keyboard composition featuring arpeggios, scales, ornaments, and other techniques.

tonguing the placement and action of the tongue to produce different pitches and effects in a wind instrument.

tonguing, flutter silently pronouncing the letter *R* repeatedly to produce a tremolo effect in the flute.

transcription same as arrangement.

transpose to change the key of a composition in writing and in performance.

treble a high-pitched instrument.

tremolo a shaking or trembling effect produced by quick changes in volume, as in flutter tonguing on the flute.

trill a commonly used musical ornament produced by very quick alternation of a note with another note one-half or one full tone above it.

troubador a poet/musician of the 12th to 13th century.

vamp to improvise an accompaniment when another musician is playing a solo, especially in a jazz composition.

vaudeville comic songs of the early 18th century French opera. Also, in 20th century United States, a variety show.

virtuoso an exceptionally skilled musician.

whole note note with the longest time value.

whole rest a rest or pause with a time value equal to one whole note.

MUSIC DIRECTIVES (tempos, volume, etc.)

accelerando to accelerate gradually.

adagietto a slow tempo, slightly faster than adagio.

adagio a slow tempo, faster than largo, slower than andante, specifically from 98 to 125 quarter notes per minute.

adagissimo extremely slow tempo.

ad libitum ad-libbing tempo, rhythm, accents, notes, and so on.

affettuoso to perform with tenderness.

affrettando to be performed in a rushed manner.

agilmente to be performed lightly and nimbly.

agitato to be performed in an agitated, restless manner.

allargando to slow down; slowing down and increasing in volume.

allegramante to be performed brightly.

allegretto a fast tempo; faster than andante but slower than allegro.

allegro a fast and lively tempo.

allentando to slow down.

altra volta encore.

ancora repeat.

andante a moderate tempo between adagio and allegro.

ängstlich a German directive to perform in a fearful, tense manner.

animo spirited.

appassionato to perform with passion.

attacca attack. A direction to begin the next movement quickly without a break.

Aufschwung German term for "soaring," "lofty."

ballo in dance tempo.

boca chiusa to be hummed.

bouche fermée French term for "humming."

bravura a directive to sing or play confidently a passage requiring a high degree of skill.

brusco a directive to play in a brusque manner.

burlesco a directive to perform in a comical manner.

calando lowering, softening.

calcando gradualy quickening.

calmando a directive to perform quietly and calmly.

cedez French directive to slow down.

comodo a relaxed, leisurely manner.

crescendo perform with increasing volume.

da capo a directive to repeat from the beginning until you reach the word *fine* (end). Often written as D.C.

decrescendo to decrease in volume; to grow softer.

delicato to perform delicately.

delirio to be performed deliriously, in a frenzied manner.

diminuendo same as decrescendo.

dolce to be performed softly and sweetly.

dolente to be performed slowly and with sorrow.

doppio movimento double the previous speed.

dramatico a directive to perform dramatically.

eilend German directive to perform in a hurried manner.

élargissant French directive to slow down and broaden the music.

elegante with grace and refinement.

encore French directive to repeat.

facile fluently.

fastoso in a dignified manner.

festoso in a joyful, festive manner.

feurig German directive to perform in a fiery manner.

fiero to perform boldly.

forte to play loudly.

fortissimo very loudly.

frettoloso in a rushed manner.

funerale mournfully.

furioso wildly and furiously.

geheimnisvoll German directive to play in a mysterious manner.

Generalpause German term for a "general rest," usually referring to a silence lasting one or more measures and involving all musicians.

grave slowly and solemnly.

heftig German directive to perform lightly and cheerfully.

indeciso tentatively or indecisively.

innig German directive to play with deep sincerity.

inquieto in an agitated manner.

lamentoso mournfully.

larghetto a slow tempo between large and andante, specifically from 69 to 98 quarter notes per minute.

largo a very slow tempo, specifically from 42 to 69 quarter notes per minute.

legato smooth-flowing with no pauses, opposite of staccato.

lettissimo very quickly.

malinconico in a melancholy manner.

mancando progressively softer.

marcato with sharp accents.

mezza voce to sing at half the singer's normal volume.

mezzo forte sing or play with moderate loudness.

mezzo piano to play with moderate softness.

militare, alla with a military air.

ossia referring to an alternative and often easier way of performing a particular passage.

parlato "spoken."

pathetique to express deep feeling.

pianissimo very softly.

prestissimo the fastest tempo possible.

presto a very fast tempo, from 182 to 208 quarter notes per minute.

ravvivando to continuously speed up the music.

ritardando Italian directive to gradually slow the tempo.

ritenuto slow the tempo at once.

schleppend German directive to perform in a dragging manner.

sciolto Italian directive to perform nimbly and lightly.

seconda volta Italian term referring to a second ending or a second time played.

slancio, con Italian directive to play with dash.

sospirando to be performed in a plaintive manner.

sotto voce to perform softly.

spiritoso Italian directive to play with high spirit.

staccato Italian directive to perform with quick, light, broken or detached notes.

strisciando Italian directive to perform a very smooth legato.

tacet Latin directive to remain silent throughout a passage.

teneramente Italian directive to perform with tenderness.

tonante perform very loudly.

tranquillo perform in a tranquil manner.

tre, a Italian directive for three instruments to play the same music at the same time.

vide directive alerting a musician that a particular passage may be omitted if desired.

vigoroso Italian directive to perform with vigor.

vivo lively.

volti subito turn the page quickly so the music will continue flowing without a break.

zoppa, alla perform in a syncopated rhythm.

Directives to Individual Instruments

bois a direction to play with the wood of a bow as opposed to the hair.

chiuso to "close" an instrument by inserting a hand into its bell to muffle or change its pitch.

coperto "covered," referring to a cloth to be placed over a drum to muffle or mute its sound.

deux, à French directive for two instruments to play the same music at the same time.

Frosch, am German directive to play with the part of the bow closest to the hand.

gauche French directive to play a note or passage with the left hand.

gedämpft German directive to mute or muffle a tone.

jèté French directive for a violinist to let the bow bounce several times on the strings. Also known as ricochet.

licenza, con alcuna Italian directive allowing a musician some creative license in performing a particular passage.

martelé French directive for a violinist to bow with brief, short strokes, producing a staccato effect.

martellato Italian directive for a piano player to strike the piano keys very hard, as a hammer.

m.d. mano destra or "right hand." A directive to play a piece or passage with the right hand.

m.s. mano sinistra or "left hand." A directive to play a piece or passage with the left hand.

muta Italian directive for wind instrument players to switch instruments or for timpanists to change the tuning of a drum.

ondeggiando Italian directive to a violinist to "rock" the bow back and forth over the strings to produce a tremolo or undulating effect.

pavillons en l'air French directive to a horn player to play with his horn or bell pointing up to project sound further and more powerfully.

piqué French directive to a violinist to bow in an intermittently detached or bouncing manner to produce a slurring, staccato effect.

pizzicato in music for violin or cello, a directive to pluck the strings with the fingers or thumb instead of or in addition to bowing.

punta play with the point of the bow.

sautillé French directive to a violinist to bounce the upper portion of the bow off the strings.

scordatura Italian directive to change the tuning of a stringed instrument in order to perform a particular composition.

sinistra play with the left hand.

sopra in keyboard music, a directive to cross one hand over the other to play a particular passage.

sordino, con Italian directive to a player of a stringed or wind instrument to use a mute.

sotto in keyboard music, a directive to cross one hand under the other to play a particular passage.

spiccato Italian directive to a violin or cello player to play in staccato style with the portion of the bow between the frog and the midpoint.

talon, au French directive to a violinist or cellist to play with the frog end of the bow.

VOCALS AND SONG

absolute pitch the ability to remember, identify, and sing tones accurately without the aid of hearing another tone. Also known as perfect pitch.

a cappella singing without instrumental accompaniment.

alto high; a low register voice of a female (contralto) or a high register or falsetto voice of a male. A register below soprano.

answer, call and the repeating or nearly repeating of a theme sung by two or more singers in succession.

antiphonal sung by two singers or two groups in a choir alternately.

aria a long, elaborate solo vocal piece with instrumental accompaniment, associated with operas, cantatas, and oratorios.

ariette a short aria.

ballad a simple, narrative song, usually of a sentimental or romantic nature.

barcarolle a type of song sung by Venetian gondoliers.

baritone midrange of a male voice, about halfway between tenor and bass.

bass the lowest male voice.

basso buffo a bass singing voice, most fitting of comic opera.

basso cantante a bass singing voice characterized as light and sweet.

basso profundo a bass singing voice characterized as especially deep and powerful.

canon a musical composition featuring echoing voice parts that overlap, for example, "row, row, row your boat."

canon, double a musical composition with two simultaneous canons or a total of four voices singing the same lines at slightly different times.

canon, free a canon in which the imitation or echoing portion is sung in a slightly different way than the original.

canon, mixed a canon accompanied by independent voice parts and melodies.

canon, retrograde a canon with the imitation/echo portion sung backward from the original.

canticle a chant or hymn other than a psalm with words taken directly from the Bible.

cantillation free-rhythm chanting, as in Jewish liturgies.

cantor in Jewish worship, the chief singer of the liturgy. Also, the leader of a choir.

carol to sing joyfully; a Christmas song, usually with several parts.

castrato a male singer who underwent castration before puberty in order to remain an alto or soprano in the Italian opera of the 17th and 18th centuries.

chant a monophonic, nonrhythmic, unaccompanied form of singing.

chest voice the lowest register of the human voice, said to emanate from the chest. See HEAD VOICE.

choral music sung by a chorus.

choral symphony a symphony with choral music.

compass the complete range of a voice, from the lowest to the highest note that can possibly be attained.

contralto the lowest range of a female voice; the range between soprano and tenor.

croon to sing softly.

diction the clear and proper enunciation of song lyrics.

falsetto a method of attaining an unnaturally high pitch in a male voice, a technique notably used by such pop vocal groups as the Bee Gees and the Four Seasons.

glee club a chorus consisting of males or females or both that perform glees and other types of songs.

glees brief, unaccompanied songs for men's chorus, usually having three to four voice parts, popular in the 1800s.

head voice said of the high-pitched voicing that causes the sensation of vibrations in the singer's head.

homophony a composition with one central voice part, as opposed to polyphony or several voice parts.

lyric a light, sweet voice.

madrigal a vocal composition having two or more movements and five or six voice parts.

mezza voce Italian music notation directing the singer to sing at half his or her normal volume.

mezzo-soprano a female voice with a range halfway between alto and soprano.

parlante Italian music notation directing a singer to approximate the sound of speech.

pathetique French music notation directing the singer to express deep feeling.

patter song a type of comedic opera song sung very quickly and in a speechlike style.

plainsong another name for chanting.

polyphonic musical having several voice parts.

prima donna in opera, the lead female singer.

primo uomo in opera, the lead male singer.

recitative a style of operatic singing similar to speech and with few changes in pitch.

round a simple form of a canon; a song with more than one voice part that echos, imitates, or overlaps one another, such as "Three Blind Mice" or "Row, Row, Row Your Boat."

scat style of jazz singing characterized by nonsensical syllables and other vocalizations other than lyrics.

serenade a love song, especially one sung under a lover's window at night.

shanty a work song sung by sailors to keep time in jobs involving teams. "Blow the Man Down" is a typical shanty.

solfeggio a vocal exercise employing the solfa (do, re, me, fa, sol, la, ti, do) syllables.

soprano the highest range of a female voice; the highest range of a young boy.

syllabic music in which only one note is sung for each syllable of the lyrics.

tenor the highest range of a male voice.

WIND INSTRUMENTS

alpenhorn a long (sometimes as long as 12 feet) wooden horn used in the Alps to convey signals, call cattle, or play simple melodies.

aulos a shrill wind instrument of ancient Greece, characterized by several finger holes and a double reed; played two at a time, one in each hand by a single performer.

Bach trumpet a high-pitched trumpet originating in Bach's day and used in many of his compositions.

bagpipe Scottish instrument producing a haunting, droning sound through the use of several pipes and a windbag pumped with the arm.

bamboo pipe a simple recorderlike instrument made of bamboo.

barrel organ an instrument consisting of a wooden barrel with fixed pins or projections that automatically force air into organ pipes with each rotation, usually capable of playing only one tune.

basset horn a type of alto clarinet invented in the 18th century, characterized by a long, slender body and an up-curving metal bell, used frequently in the operas of Mozart and Richard Strauss.

bassoon a very long (8½ feet doubled over) member of the oboe family producing sounds that are sometimes exceptionally comedic or sad.

block flute a recorder or flageolet.

bombardon a type of bass tuba.

bore the conical or cylindrical tube of a wind instrument.

cor de chasse a brass hunting horn originating in the 17th century.

cornet a small brass instrument similar to a trumpet and used in military bands.

crook a curved piece of tubing connecting to the reed with the body of a woodwind; it makes the instrument easier to hold.

crumhorn a J-shaped woodwind of the 16th and 17th centuries.

double reed a mouthpiece consisting of two pieces of cane bound together and between which air is blown; used in the oboe, English horn, bassoon, and others.

drone on a bagpipe, any one of the pipes producing a continuous unchanging pitch.

English flute another name for a recorder.

English horn an alto oboe.

euphonium a brass tenor tuba rarely used in orchestras but frequently seen in brass and military bands.

fife a small flute with six finger holes and having a lower pitch than a piccolo; usually used in military bands.

fipple flute another name for a recorder or flageolet; any flute blown from one end, as a whistle.

flugelhorn a brass instrument similar to a cornet but having a wider bore.

French horn a coiled brass instrument with a flaring bell 11 to 14 inches in diameter, used in orchestras and noted for its mellow sound.

harmonium a keyboardlike instrument that sounds like a pipe organ but is designed to work as a giant harmonica, specifically with air blown through reeds by pedal-operated bellows, popular in the 1800s.

heckelphone a woodwind similar to an oboe but having a larger bore and a more powerful tone, developed in 1904.

helicon a large bass tuba that coils around the musician's body to facilitate carrying in a marching band.

key any one of the small finger levers that open and close over hard-to-reach holes.

key bugle a bugle having keys to produce a wider range of notes, largely replaced by the valved cornet in 1850. Also known as the Kent bugle.

mellophone an instrument similar to the French horn but easier to play; primarily used in marching bands.

musette a French bagpipe popular in the 17th and 18th centuries.

oboe a double-reeded woodwind shaped like a clarinet and widely used in many orchestral compositions.

oboe, baritone a large oboe with a pitch an octave below its standard counterpart.

ocarina a small, potato-shaped instrument having 10 holes and producing a whistlelike sound.

oliphant a horn made from an elephant tusk.

panpipes an instrument consisting of 4 to 12 small pipes of graduating length banded together and blown into to produce different notes; kown as a syrinx by the ancient Greeks. Also known as the pan flute.

piccolo a small flute having a pitch one octave higher than a flute.

saxhorn a brass instrument similar to a flugelhorn but having a funnel-shaped mouthpiece, used in marching bands.

shakuhachi a Japanese flute, blown like a recorder and made of bamboo.

shofar an ancient instrument made of a ram's horn, used for more than 3,000 years to signal the New Year in Jewish religious services.

sousaphone a large bass tuba or helicon.

uilleann pipes Irish bagpipes.

valve any one of the valves or pistons on a brass instrument (except trombone) engaged to produce a different pitch.

woodwinds collective term for all the wind instruments that were originally made from wood, but now including the saxaphone, flute, piccolo, oboe, English horn, bassoon, clarinet, and basset horn.

STRINGED INSTRUMENTS

aeolian harp named for the Greek god of winds, a stringed boxlike instrument placed in a window and played automatically by the wind, known since Biblical times and popular from the 16th to the 19th centuries.

archlute a large lute with a double neck.

Autoharp a type of zither in which strings are plucked or strummed while chords are produced by depressing keys.

balalaika a triangular shaped guitar with a long neck and three strings, used for accompanying folk songs in Russia and Eastern Europe.

bandurria a flat-backed, 12-string guitar used in Spain and Latin America.

banjolin a short-necked banjo with four strings.

baryton an 18th-century guitarlike instrument consisting of six melody strings played with a bow and from 16 to 40 "resonant" strings that could be plucked in accompaniment or simply left to vibrate in sympathy with the melody strings.

bass guitar low-toned guitar having four strings to play the bass line of a melody.

belly the upper body surface of a stringed instrument over which the strings are stretched.

bissex an 18th-century guitar having six strings that were plucked or strummed and another six strings that vibrated in sympathy.

biwa a Japanese, short-necked lute with four strings.

bow a pliable stick strung with horsehair and used on stringed instruments (violin, viola, etc.) to create sound.

bridge a piece of wood or metal where the strings are attached on the belly of a guitar, lute, or similar instrument.

buzuki a pear-shaped, stringed instrument used in Greece as an accompaniment in folk songs.

capo a device clamped over the strings of a fret to shorten the length of vibrations and to facilitate the playing of certain keys. Also known as a capotasto.

cello a bass violin having four strings and stood on the floor when played.

chitarrone a large lute (up to 6½ feet) having between 11 and 16 strings, used for accompanying baroque music in the 16th and 17th centuries.

chyn a seven-stringed zither of ancient China, still in use.

cittern a flat-backed, pear-shaped guitar having 4 to 12 pairs of strings that were plucked or strummed by a quill plectrum, popular in England in the 16th and 17th centuries.

clarsach a small Celtic harp, still in use in Scotland.

clavichord a stringed keyboard set in a rectangular box and producing soft sounds, popular from the 16th to the 18th centuries.

colascione a European, long-necked lute having 24 movable frets, originating in the 16th century.

course in lutes and guitars, two or more strings that are tuned the same and played at the same time to provide greater volume when needed.

crwth an ancient Welsh lyre played by a bow. Also known as a crowd, crouth, or cruit.

double bass the largest and deepest-sounding member of the violin family.

dulcimer an instrument consisting of a shallow box over which 10 or more courses of strings are stretched and struck with small hammers.

dulcimer, Appalachian a three-stringed member of the zither family, plucked or strummed while resting on one's lap.

esraj an Indian instrument with four melodic strings and 10 to 15 sympathetic understrings, played with a bow.

fingerboard the fretted or unfretted portion of the neck of a stringed instrument; where the chords are made.

frets the wood or metal strips on the fingerboard of a guitar, lute, or similar instrument, that act as guides for locating proper pitch.

frog the part of a violin bow that tightens the horsehair.

gittern an early form of guitar having four pairs of strings, originating in the Middle Ages.

gusle a long-necked, one-stringed instrument having a shape like a pear or a heart and played with a bow by Yugoslavian folk singers.

hardanger fiddle a violinlike instrument of Norway having four regular strings and 4 to 5 understrings that vibrate in sympathy, used in folk music.

Hawaiian guitar a lap-held guitar with metal strings that are stopped with a steel bar that is held or slid along with the left hand while the strings are strummed or plucked with the right hand, notable for its nasal, vibrato effects.

hurdy-gurdy an ancient stringed instrument played with a rosined wheel turned by a crank instead of by a bow, still used in European folk music today.

Irish harp a small harp having 30 to 50 brass strings that are plucked with the fingernails as opposed to using the fingertips, as a standard harp.

kantele a flat soundboard or psaltery having as many as 25 strings that are plucked or strummed while held in the lap.

kithara a widely used, lyre-shaped, harplike instrument of the ancient Greeks.

koto the Japanese national instrument, specifically a 13-stringed (strings made of waxed silk) sound board 6 feet in length and resting on the floor.

lira da braccio an early version of the violin, about 28 inches long and having seven strings; invented in Italy in the 15th century.

lute a guitarlike instrument having a pear-shaped body, a broad, flat neck, a bent-back pegbox, and several pairs or courses of strings, widely used throughout the 16th century.

lyra an ancient Greek stringed instrument with a bowlike body made of tortoiseshell. Also called a hurdy gurdy or rebec.

lyre collective term for a large family of harplike instruments including the lyra, kithara, crwth, and rebec.

mandolin a small member of the lute family, having a pear-shaped body and four pairs of strings; used today in folk and country music.

peg any one of the wood or plastic pins turned to adjust the tension and pitch of a string; a tuning peg.

pick a plectrum; any device used for plucking or strumming.

plectrum a pick.

ponticello the bridge of a violin or other stringed instrument.

sarangi Indian stringed instrument carved from a single block of wood, played by bowing in an upright position.

sarod an Indian, short-necked lute with a twangy sound similar to a banjo.

shamisen a long-necked, fretless lute having three strings that are struck rather than plucked; widely used in Japan.

sitar an East Indian, long-necked lute having 16 to 20 movable frets with 5 to 7 regular or melody strings and 11 to 13 sympathetic strings underneath; made of a single block of wood or gourd.

sound hole any of the holes cut into the belly of a stringed instrument.

sound post in many stringed instruments, the wooden dowel connecting the belly with the back; it helps to carry vibrations.

sympathetic strings in older stringed instruments, a series of strings that are not plucked, strummed, or bowed but are simply left to vibrate when other strings are played.

tambura a long-necked lute of India, characterized by strings that are always played open and capable of producing only four, dronelike sounds.

tanbur a popular long-necked lute played in the Near East and southeastern Europe.

theorbo a bass lute, popular from 1600 to 1800.

ukelele a small, four-stringed guitar of Portuguese and Hawaiian origin, used in folk songs.

vihuela a popular Spanish lute of the 16th century.

vina an Indian zither similar to a sitar.

viola a lower-pitched and slightly larger version of the violin, known for its solemn, husky tones.

zither a folk instrument consisting of a flat, wooden sound box over which as many as 42 strings are stretched.

KEYBOARD INSTRUMENTS

baby grand a small grand piano, usually no more than 5 feet in length.

bandoneon the Argentine equivalent of an accordion, characterized by notes that are produced by buttons instead of a keyboard.

calliope any organ played or activated by steam.

celesta a small, keyboardlike instrument in which keys depress hammers that strike tuned steel bars, creating a haunting bell-like sound; invented in 1886 and used in Tchaikovsky's *Dance of the Sugar Plum Fairy.*

concert grand the largest size of piano, usually about 9 feet in length.

concertina a simple accordion with buttons in place of a keyboard.

damper any device that mutes or stops the sound vibrations of an instrument, as in the small pieces of felt-covered wood used in a piano.

damper pedal on a piano, the right-hand pedal that raises all dampers, allowing all of the strings to vibrate freely.

harpsichord a pianolike instrument having strings that are plucked instead of being struck by hammers; popular from the 16th to the 18th centuries and still in use.

hydraulos a type of pipe organ invented by the Greeks, notable for its regulation of air pressure by the displacement of water in special chambers.

key any of the individual levers on a keyboard.

manual a keyboard played by the hands as opposed to one played by the feet, as an organ pedalboard.

pedal either one of the two or three foot pedals controlling volume and tone on a piano.

pedal organ the section of organ pipes, often of low pitch, operated by an organ's pedal board.

player piano a mechanical piano that plays tunes automatically by means of air pressure and special perforated music roles.

soundboard the resonant board over which strings are strung in a piano or harpsichord.

spinet a small harpsichord, popular from the 16th to the 18th centuries.

stop in organs, a lever or knob that stops air to a particular set of pipes; the set of pipes so affected is also called a stop.

synthesizer a modern keyboard instrument capable of producing or reproducing hundreds of different sounds through electronic means.

virginal a small, rectangular harpsichord popular from the 15th to the 17th centuries.

wind chest the air chamber in some organs.

PERCUSSION INSTRUMENTS

bass drum the largest, deepest-sounding drum. On a drum set, the floor drum that is kicked by a pedal.

bell-lyra a portable glockenspiel.

bongos small Cuban drums played with the fingers, thumbs, and heels of the hands.

campanella a small bell.

carillon a set of tuned bells or chimes originating in the 13th century, usually hung in a church tower and played either automatically or by means of a keyboard and pedals.

castanets small, wooden clappers clicked together rhythmically in the hands, used in Spanish dances.

Chinese crash cymbal a crash cymbal with its edge turned up, providing a distinctive crashing sound when struck.

Chinese wood block a 7- to 8-inch block of slotted wood, making a distinctive "tock" sound when struck by a drumstick, popular with jazz drummers. Also known as a clog box.

choke cymbals two cymbals fixed face-to-face on a pedal and rod device and clapped together or struck with drumsticks to keep time or to add flourishes to the beat. More popularly known as a high-hat.

claves wooden stick approximately 8 to 10 inches long and clacked together to add percussion accompaniment in Latin music.

cowbell an actual cowbell with the clapper removed, used in percussive accompaniment.

crescent a Turkish instrument consisting of an inverted crescent hung with small bells.

cymbal, crash a cymbal designed to be struck powerfully to produce a loud crash.

cymbal, finger a pair of tiny, 2-inch cymbals placed on finger and thumb and rung together, of ancient origin but still in use in Greece and Turkey.

cymbal, ride a pop music cymbal that is played lightly to help keep the rhythm or beat.

cymbal, sizzle a type of crash cymbal embedded with loose rivets that produce a "sizzling" sound when struck.

glockenspiel a xylophonelike instrument having two rows of tuned steel bars arranged like the keyboard of a piano. A portable lyre-shaped version used in marching bands is known as a bell lyre.

gong a large bronze cymbal suspended by a cord and struck with a mallet.

grelots sleigh bells.

guiro a hollow gourd cut with a row of deep lines that are scraped with a metal prong to produce a rasping sound, used as percussive accompaniment in Cuba, Puerto Rico, and the Caribbean.

jingling Johnnie same as a crescent.

kettledrum same as a timpani.

maraca a dried gourd filled with seeds and used as a rattle in Latin American music.

marimba a xylophonelike instrument of Central America. It is distinguished from the xylophone by a row or rows of wooden bars with resonant gourds or tubes projecting underneath.

mridanga a two-headed Indian drum shaped like a barrel and played primarily with the fingertips.

pedal on a timpani, the foot pedal that changes the tension and pitch of a drumhead. Also, the foot or "kick" pedal of a bass drum.

roto toms modern, single-headed tom-toms whose pitch can be altered simply by rotating their heads slightly, used primarily in rock bands.

snare drum a somewhat flat drum fixed with a series of metallic strands or snares and used to carry the main beat in most modern music.

steel drum a Caribbean drum originally made from an oil drum, characterized by a multidented head, with each dent producing a different pitch; noted for its pleasing, tinkling sound, and popularly used in Calypso music.

tablas a pair of Indian drums, one made from a log, the other made of metal.

tampon a double-headed drumstick shaken back and forth by the wrist to produce a roll on a bass drum.

tam-tam same as a gong.

timpani a large, kettle-shaped drum tuned to a specific pitch that can be changed instantly by means of a foot pedal. Also known as a kettle drum.

tom-toms small, supplemental drums used primarily for fills, rolls, and flourishes; usually mounted on the bass drum.

triangle a steel rod bent into the shape of a triangle and "clanged" by a metal stick.

tubular bells same as chimes.

vibraphone an instrument similar to the xylophone and marimba, having two rows of tuned metal bars with resonators fitted with lids that open and close to provide a continuous vibrato effect; a popular jazz instrument.

xylophone an instrument similar to a marimba, characterized by two rows of wooden bars of graduating length and struck by hammers to produce a "rattling skeleton" sound.

The Performing Arts and Broadcasting

STAGE AND THEATER

aboard slang for on stage.

above the back of the stage.

ace a 1,000-watt spotlight.

act one segment of a play.

actor-proof a powerfully written play impervious to poor acting performances.

Actors' Equity Association the 30,000-member actors union; they are issued equity cards and are paid according to equity scale.

apple box a 14″×24″ platform used to elevate a performer on stage.

apron the portion of a stage in front of the arch.

arc follow spot a powerful spotlight used to follow a performer.

arena theater theater in which stage is surrounded by seats.

argentine a shiny sheet of metal that simulates a window on a piece of scenery.

artist's assistant one who assists and escorts a performer from the dressing room to the stage, especially in an opera.

ashcan a 1,000-watt floodlight.

audience dress a rehearsal before an audience, before the show's actual opening.

audit stub the ticket portion retained by the theater for accounting purposes.

a vista scene change made while the curtain is still up.

baby spot a small spotlight, usually 750 watts.

backdrop a painted curtain serving as background scenery.

backing light lighting originating from behind a set or scenery.

backstage the nonperformance area in the wings.

bad laugh laughter from the audience at an inappropriate moment.

balcony a second or third upper floor. A first upper floor is a mezzanine or dress circle. A fourth floor is frequently called a gallery.

balcony box an area reserved for spotlights.

balcony lights lights operated from a balcony box.

balcony operator the person who operates the balcony lights.

band call a musicians' rehearsal.

bandshell an outdoor bandstand having a concave back wall and roof.

barn doors adjustable louvers in front of a spotlight to control the intensity of its beam. Also known as blinders, flippers, shutters.

bastard amber a pink amber gel commonly used to color stagelights.

batten a strip of wood or metal from which scenery or lights are hung.

beam projector a spotlight used to project a sharply defined or narrow beam, to simulate a moonbeam or sunbeam.

bedroom farce a comedy centering around antics in the bedroom.

below the front of the stage.

billboard pass a free ticket given to a local retailer in exchange for displaying theater advertising.

black comedy a comedy based on macabre or morbid subjects.

blackout a complete darkening of stage lights to indicate a passage of time or the end of a scene.

blackout switch a switch that controls all of the stage lights.

blind seat a seat with an obstructed view.

block to indicate performer positioning and movements by marking the stage with chalk or tape.

boffo a box office hit.

bomb crater a depression or pit in a stage floor.

bon-bon a 2,000-watt spotlight directed on the face of a performer.

Dakota a line of dialogue that leads into or cues a song.

dark house a nonperformance night at the theater.

dead pack scenery to be removed from the stage, as distinguished from live pack, or scenery to be placed on stage.

dim the house to turn out the houselights over the audience.

dinner theater a theater that combines a meal with a show.

dog a small town or noncritical location where the bugs are worked out of a show; "to try a show out on the dog."

door list a list of people admitted free to a show. Also known as the house list.

double cast casting two performers for the same role, in case one gets sick. See understudy.

downstage the front of the stage, toward the audience.

dramatis personae a list of characters in a play.

drapery setting scenery composed of painted curtains or backdrops.

dress a stage to furnish a stage with scenery, furniture, props, and so on.

dresser a wardrobe assistant; an assistant to the wardrobe chief.

dress extra an extra who provides his own costume and is consequently paid on a higher scale.

dress-room list a posted list of dressing rooms assigned to performers.

drop any stage curtain that can be raised or lowered.

farce a wacky comedy based on wild or unlikely or ludicrous situations.

first-night list a list of reviewers, sponsors, and other VIPs invited to attend an opening night, as distinguished from the second-night list.

five minutes to curtain the traditional warning call to all performers 5 minutes before the show. Also, "five minutes, please."

flashpot a receptacle that holds flash powder that is ignited to produce smoke, fire, or explosive effects.

flat an upright piece of painted scenery.

flood a floodlight or broad-beamed light.

fly a floor, platform, or loft over the stage, for lights and other equipment. Also, to suspend scenery from above the stage floor.

fly crew the crew who operate the overhead lights and other equipment on the fly.

fly gallery a sidewall platform where scenery lines are sometimes secured.

fly plot a diagram of lighting placement in the fly; a rigging plan.

footlights a row of lights along the foot of the stage, sometimes recessed in a trough, sometimes not.

front of the house the box office, lobby, and business offices at the front of a theater.

full-dress a full dress rehearsal.

gel a colored plastic (formerly made from gelatin) filter placed in front of a light to produce a colored beam.

go to table to rehearse lines while sitting around a table with other performers.

grave a hole in the stage.

green room a performer's waiting room near the stage.

ground row a piece of background scenery that simulates a landscape, skyline, horizon, or other location.

head spot a spotlight directed on a performer's head.

high comedy comedy having witty, intelligent dialogue, as distinguished from low comedy.

hit the boards slang for to go on stage.

horseshoe staging seating that forms a horseshoe configuration around the stage.

hot a live mike.

houselights the lights that illuminate the audience.

icebreaker an opening number in a musical.

intermission bell a bell, chime, or buzzer rung to alert the audience that intermission is nearly over.

keg light a 500-watt spotlight shaped like a beer keg.

kill to turn off the lights or to remove scenery from the stage.

klieg light a large, powerful, wide-angle spotlight.

lap dissolve the fading out of one light and brightening of another, for effect.

legitimate theater serious plays and musicals, as distinguished from burlesque and vaudeville.

light rehearsal a practice run of light changes and lighting cues.

light tower a tower, often of scaffolding, on which lights are hung.

live pack scenery to be placed on the stage, as distinguished from dead pack, or scenery to be taken off or that has already been used and put away.

live stage a stage with scenery.

loge a theater box in the front section of a mezzanine or balcony.

low comedy slapstick or physical comedy, as distinguished from high comedy.

lyric theater a theater specializing in producing musicals.

makeup call the time a performer must report to the makeup department.

marquee at the front of a theater, the projecting, rooflike structure advertising the upcoming show and its top performers.

matinee an afternoon show.

melodrama a play in which the emotions are acted out in an exaggerated fashion.

noises off sound effects made from offstage.

Obie annual award given to those involved with off-Broadway productions.

off Broadway low-budget or experimental productions performed in theaters other than those in the Broadway and Times Square area of New York.

oleo a painted curtain used as background for a brief scene while the set is changed from behind.

open full to start the show with the entire cast on stage.

opening night the first formal performance before an audience and critics.

opry house slang for an old theater.

orchestra pit the space below the stage where the musicians play.

overture a musical lead-in to a musical production number.

page a curtain to pull a curtain together so that the two halves meet at midstage.

pan to slowly sweep a spotlight from left to right, or vice versa.

pancake performers' heavy makeup.

papering the house giving away numerous free tickets in order to fill the theater.

parapet a low wall along a balcony.

parquet a theater's main floor, also known as the orchestra.

pass door a door providing access to backstage from the auditorium.

passion play a play centering around the life of a god or around the suffering of Christ.

peanut gallery slang for a top balcony or gallery, where lower-class patrons ate peanuts.

perch an offstage platform on which a spotlight is sometimes placed.

pigeon a platform or riser, smaller than an apple box, used to elevate a performer.

pin spot a spotlight having a very narrow beam.

pit the orchestra pit.

play to the balcony to direct one's performance to the cheaper seats in the balcony, from which the lower classes are quicker to applaud. Also, to play to the gallery.

pool hall lighting dim, overhead lighting, used for effect in some scenes.

positions! the last second call for performers to take their positions before the curtain rises.

practicals stage props that actually function, as distinguished from replicas.

practical set a set having real walls and props that work, as distinguished from facades and replicas.

production number any extravagant act or musical number involving many or all members of the chorus, dance troupe, or other performers.

program a brochure describing the show and its performers, given or sold to audience members.

prologue an introduction to a play.

prompt corner where the prompter positions himself, usually downstage right. See prompter.

prompt box a hoodline projection or alcove in the center of the stage in which a prompter is positioned out of view of the audience.

prompter one who assists actors in remembering lines while the show is in progress. They keep track of the dialogue by means of a prompt book.

prop any object, from a cigarette lighter to a sofa, used in a show.

property personnel the stage crew responsible for props.

proscenium the front of the stage, from the front curtain to the orchestra; the apron.

quick study a performer particularly adept at learning his role and accompanying lines.

raisonneur in a play, a character who observes the action, comments on it, and serves as a narrator to the audience.

rake the slant or inclination of a stage. A raked stage slopes down from back to front.

revue a musical comprised of sketches and songs.

royal box boxed seating near the stage, reserved for royalty or other VIPs.

rumble pot a receptacle in which boiling water and dry ice is mixed to create fog effects.

score the music written for a show.

set designer one who designs and creates a set.

set dressings set furnishings, decor.

snake a special cable that combines several cables, used with stage lighting.

soliloquy talking to the audience or to oneself on stage.

spot a spotlight.

SRO standing room only; a packed house.

stagehand a helper who assembles, dismantles, and moves scenery; operates the curtain, and performs other tasks.

stagestruck having the sudden desire to become a stage performer, usually occurring while watching a stage show.

strike to take down a set.

theater party a performance given for charity, with the beneficiaries often making up part of the audience.

thrust stage a stage that extends out into the middle of an audience.

tormentor a curtain or piece of scenery that conceals the wings of a stage or backstage.

tragedy a play or drama that ends sadly or in tragedy.

trapdoor a door in the stage floor through which performers may enter or exit.

understudy a performer who rehearses the role of another in case a stand-in is needed.

upstage the portion of the stage furthest from the audience.

wagon stage a mobile set on wheels, used to facilitate the changing of sets.

walk-through a rough rehearsal.

wardrobe mistress one responsible for costumes.

white light district a theatrical district. Also known as a white way.

DANCE

BALLET

arabesque a position in which the dancer balances on one leg, the other leg extended backward with straight knee while the arms hold one of various poses.

assemblé a jump in which the dancer thrusts one leg up and then springs off of the other.

attitude grecque an arm position with one arm curving overhead one way and the other arm curving downward toward the legs in the opposite direction.

attitude à terre a leg position in which one foot is pointed sharply to the side while the other leg is bent at the knee and slanted in back with its foot bent over and toes scraping the floor.

baisse lowering the heel or heels to the floor after standing en pointe.

ballerina a female ballet dancer.

ballerina, prima a ballet's leading female dancer.

ballonné a leap beginning and ending with one foot touching the opposite leg at the knee (Grand ballonné) or at the ankle (petit ballonné.)

barre the bar at hip level that runs along the walls of a ballet dancer's practice room.

barre work classroom practice of balance and movements while the hand rests lightly on the barre.

basque, grand pas de a movement in which the dancer thrusts the front leg forward and springs so that the supporting leg rises as the first leg descends.

battements, grand throwing one leg up high with knee straight and foot pointed while the body is kept as still as possible.

battements, tendus sliding out one leg along the floor until the foot is fully pointed and then returning to the starting position.

beat to strike or slap both calves together.

bourrée, pas de gliding across the floor on the toes with quick, mincing steps.

cabriole a movement in which the dancer with one leg raised, springs from the supporting leg and executes a single, double, or triple beat.

cambre bending from the waist in any direction.

chassé sliding the foot out in any direction while keeping the heel flush on the floor.

chat, pas de a movement in which the dancer brings one foot up to the opposite knee or ankle and leaps sideways.

cheval, pas de scraping the ground like a horse with one foot while hopping on the other foot.

choreographer one who creates dances and steps.

choreography the steps and movements of a ballet.

ciseaux, pas leaping and splitting the legs wide apart to the side or from front to back. Also known as the grand écart.

collé jumping steps in which the legs and feet are clung together in the air.

coryphée the rank below a principal dancer and above those in the corps de ballet.

coupée to put down one foot while lifting the other.

course, pas de a succession of running steps.

danseur a male ballet dancer.

danseur, premier the leading male ballet dancer.

défilé, le grand on closing night of a ballet, an onstage parade of all the members of the ballet company.

deux, pas de any dance performed with two people.

divertissement a ballet that shows off the talents of its dancers but does not tell a story.

enlèvement the act of lifting another dancer into the air, who then strikes a pose.

en pointe on tip toe.

entrechat a jump straight up performed with beats and rapid changes of leg position.

fermé a position in which the feet are closed together in opposite directions.

gargouillade a jump in which the legs are brought underneath the dancer, with the feet describing small circles in midair.

glissade sliding or gliding by the soles of the feet. Also known as glisse.

jêté a leap from one foot to the other.

leotard the form-fitting elastic garment worn in dance practice. Also known as tights.

limbering exercises performed to loosen up the body.

mime stylized gestures used to illustrate a passage in a story.

pas step or dance.

pas couru running steps.

pas marché a stylized walk, with the legs swung wider apart than is natural.

piqué stepping sharply onto one toe while keeping the leg straight. Also known as jêté sur la pointe.

pirouette whirling on the toes of one foot.

pistolet throwing the left leg up, then springing with the right and performing a beat followed by a change in leg position, a second beat, and a final leg change before landing with the left leg in the air.

plié a bending of the knee or knees.

pointe a dancer is en pointe when she is standing on tiptoes. Also, the specially blocked shoes used for performing en pointe.

pose placing an extended foot on the ground.

promenade pivoting on the heel.

révoltade a leap in which the dancer appears to jump over his own raised leg.

rolling standing with body weight centered on either the inside or outside of the feet.

rosin a substance used to prevent slipping on the dance floor.

saute a jump in which the takeoff and landing are in the same position.

sickle foot when the natural line of the leg is curved inward. Also known as serpette.

sissone a jump made with a landing on one foot with the raised foot touching the supporting leg at the knee or ankle.

soubresaut a jump in which the legs are clung together without a change in position.

soutenu to be performed slowly.

spotting when turning or spinning, leaving the head frozen in the same position until the last possible moment. A spin in which the head follows far behind the body's rotation.

taquete small, quick steps on tiptoes.

temps de point steps performed on pointe or tiptoes.

tiroirs, faire les when two lines of dancers cross and recross on the stage while performing the same steps or movements.

toe shoes ballet shoes.

tour en l'air springing straight up and executing a single, double or triple turn in midair.

tutu the traditional ballet skirt.

variation solo.

Square Dancing

Alamo style a circle of dancers join hands, with every other dancer facing outward.

all around your left hand lady a move in which the corners dance around each other right shoulder to right shoulder.

allemande a forearm grasp and a swing through made by the corner dancers.

arky couple either two men or two women.

arm swing grasping another's forearm and swinging around.

around one a designated couple turn their backs to one another and both move behind the nearest person.

bend the line breaking up a line of dancers by having the end dancers move forward and the center dancers move back.

break to release hands.

California twirl a move in which a couple raise joined hands to form an arch, which the lady passes under. Also known as frontier whirl.

call a singing direction for the next dance movement, made by the caller.

caller the person who sings or chants out dance directions.

cast off in a line of couples, the center dancers separate and move forward while the end couples join hands and move back.

centers any dancers inside the square or inside any other formation.

cloverleaf couples in a double line break off from the corners, turn back around, and describe a cloverleaf pattern while trailing couples follow.

courtesy turn a couple joins left hands and wheel counterclockwise.

crisscross one couple divides another couple, who then close and cross trails to exchange places.

curlique while holding an arch, the gent walks around the lady, who then backs under the arch, so they end up facing opposite direction while still holding hands.

dive through two couples form an arch, which another couple passes under.

Dixie chain with couples in a single file line, the ladies pull through from right to left hands, followed by the gents, ending in single file.

docey around facing dancers move forward and pass around each other back to back.

do si do same as docey around.

fold one dancer steps forward and turns to face his or her partner.

frontier whirl same as California twirl.

gents traditionally, how males dancers are addressed.

grand chain four ladies move in a right-hand star to opposite gents, who courtesy turn them.

grand right and left weaving in and out around other dancers in a circle, the ladies pulling by in one direction while the gents pull by in the other until partners meet.

hash calls freestyle calls—none of which necessarily rhyme—made spontaneously by the caller. Also known as patter.

hinge the couple turn to face each other, step forward, and join right hands.

hoedown a square dance; also, music traditionally played at a square dance.

honor a call to bow to your partner.

Indian style single file.

look her in the eye a call to face your partner.

make an arch a call for two dancers to join and raise hands overhead to create an arch.

ocean wave four dancers facing in alternate directions form a line and join hands palm to palm at shoulder height; each dancer then takes a step forward and a step back for an undulating effect.

packsaddle star a star in which four dancers form a hub by grabbing each other's wrists.

pass through facing couples pass through one another and end up back to back.

patter same as hash calls.

peel off each dancer in a couple separates and turns back while the trailing couple squeezes between them, separates, and turns back to end up in a line facing the opposite direction.

pigeonwing clasping hands with the elbows pointed up.

promenade with hands crossed, right to right, left to left, with gents' palms facing up, couples follow each other in a circle counterclockwise.

promenade wrong way a promenade danced clockwise.

pull-by two people lightly clasp hands and swing each other through a line or formation.

rock it taking a short step forward and tapping the other foot then stepping back and tapping the other foot. Also known as balance.

sashay (chassé) a couple standing side by side move out of line and sidestep past one another.

set a square.

singing calls predetermined calls that are sung to the music, as distinguished from hash calls.

skirt work the ladies flaring their skirts to the sides.

spread it wide a call to change a hold around the waist to an outstretched handclasp position.

square the square formed by four couples.

square your sets a call to dancers to come onto the floor and form squares.

star dancers touch hands at shoulder height to form a hub, which they circle around. In singles, to grasp hands at shoulder height and rotate around one another.

swing walking around your partner while holding the waist and hands.

trade a side-by-side couple turn to face each other, then walk around each other and end up side-by-side facing the opposite direction.

trailing following the dancer or dancers in front of you.

wrong way any movement in the opposite direction of normal.

Tap Dancing

bells a click of the heels while in midair.

brush a sweep of one foot forward, diagonally or backward while lightly brushing the floor.

buck a move consisting of a stomp of the right foot followed by a hop left on the left foot, a slap down on the right, a slap down on the left, a step right, and then a repeat of the entire move starting on the left foot.

buffalo a leap and a landing on the right while raising the left foot and shuffling it forward and back, followed by a leap and landing on the left foot and a return to the starting position.

chug sliding forward on the ball of the right foot while simultaneously dropping the heel sharply.

coffee grinder in a squatting position with the hands touching the floor, one extended leg describes the action of a coffee grinder by rotating around in a complete circle.

cossack a difficult Russian folk dance with the body in a squatting position and the arms folded at chest level while the legs kick out alternately.

cramp roll a step forward of one foot while raising the heel, followed by a step forward of the other foot with raised heel, then a drop of both heels in quick succession.

dig a step in which the arms are held aloft gracefully to the sides while each foot crosses the other alternately and taps the floor once.

doll hop a step followed by a hop with one leg, followed by another step and a hop with the other leg.

falling off the log a mixture of shuffles and cross steps that produce the illusion of the dancer losing his balance and falling off a log.

flap a brush with the right foot followed by a step on the right foot, producing two sounds.

hell drops moving the right foot forward with the toe pointed up and heel touching the floor, then moving the foot back and repeating with the left foot while arms are placed one over the other at chest level.

heel plate an optional plate placed on the heel of a shoe for tapping.

hop a hop and landing on the same foot.

nerve taps tapping the floor in quick succession with the toe of one foot, frequently used in practice to develop speed and flexibility.

riff a toe tap and a forward slide of the foot while scuffing the heel.

scuff scuffing or scraping the floor with the heel.

shuffle a brush of one foot forward and then back, producing two sounds.

shuffle leap a shuffle followed by a leap and landing on the same foot, producing three sounds.

soft shoe any slow, soft dance with light tapping and a variety of intricate steps, originally performed with sand on the floor.

stamp a tap made by the entire foot, instead of just the ball.

step a simple raising and lowering of one foot, with the weight of the body shifted to that foot.

step-clap a step followed by a hand clap, then repeated with the other foot.

time step any of various combinations of shuffles, flaps, and steps.

toe heel tapping with the ball then the heel of one foot, producing two sounds.

toe point tap a tap with the tip of the toes.

Jazz Dancing

allegro brisk movements.

arabesque balancing on one leg with the other leg raised high to the rear and the arms upraised.

attitude a balancing on one leg with the other leg extended and upraised to the front.

back bend a standing positioin with the back arched and the arms upraised toward the ceiling.

barre warmup exercises performed in a studio at a horizontal bar.

barrel-leap turn a leaping turn made with arms extended.

barrel turn a turn on one foot with arms extended.

battement a leg kick from the hip forward or back.

body roll a roll or flex of the body from the knees and progressing to the thighs, pelvis, torso, and head.

catch step two steps in any direction timed to one and a half counts of the music.

chaîné quick turn made in two steps.

chest lift from a supine position, the chest is lifted forward to an upright position.

compass turn a turn on one foot with the other leg extended and making a full circle.

contraction a drawing together of the body.

corkscrew turn an ascending or descending turn starting and ending with the legs crossed.

coupé a brisk exchange of foot position.

dégagé lifting and pointing a fully arched foot.

demi-plié bending halfway at the knees.

en crois describing the shape of a cross.

en dedans circling into the body.

en dehors circling away from the body.

fouetté a sharp movement from one direction to another.

frog position a seated position with the legs pulled up, bent at the knees, and the feet touching each other.

glissade a sliding step.

grand plié bending fully at the knees with heels raised off the floor.

hitch kick a scissors kick performed with toes pointed.

hop leaping off and landing on the same foot.

inverted long jazz arm the arms extended out to the sides with palms facing up.

isolation isolating and moving one body part in contrast to the rest of the body.

jazz hand palm out, hand facing forward with fingers extended.

jazz sissonne a leap starting and ending with the feet placed together.

jazz split a slide and split to the floor ending with one leg fully extended and the other bent at the knee.

knee hinge kneeling and arching or "hinging" the torso backward.

knee slide sliding across the floor on one's knees.

knee turn a turn performed on both knees.

leap turn a two-step turn and jêté.

outside turn a turn on one foot.

pas de bourrée a three-step series in any direction.

passe moving the leg or foot from front to back.

pelvis roll a circling motion of the pelvis.

pirouette a spinning turn performed on one foot.

plié bending at the knees.

plié-relevé position a position in which the knees are flexed and the heels are raised off the floor while the arms are outstretched to the sides.

port de bras the placement or movement of the arms.

promenade a pivot on the ball of the foot.

renversé bending while making a turn.

rond de jambe performing a circling movement with the leg.

sauté any jumping or leaping movement.

seat spin spinning on the seat of one's pants.

side jazz walk a sideways walk with the knees in the demi-plié position.

spiral turn a winding turn.

stag leap a leap during which the front foot is lifted to the knee of the back leg.

sundari Oriental head motions.

swastika a seated position in which one leg is flexed forward and the other flexed back, a configuration resembling a swastika.

tabletop a position in which the torso is bent over and laid out flat parallel to the floor to resemble a tabletop.

tombé letting the body fall forward, back or to the side onto a leg in the plié position.

tour to turn the body.

triple three steps taken with two counts of the music.

FILM

adaptation a screenplay adapted from a novel, biography, or other source.

aleatory technique a film technique in which scenes are not specifically planned and are left to chance.

arc light a powerful set light.

art director the designer in charge of sets, costumes, or both.

auteur French term for a movie director who "authors" a film by exercising personal artistic vision.

backlighting lighting that originates behind the subject for a silhouetting effect.

back projection the projection of a still or moving background through a translucent screen behind the actors, now largely outmoded by front projection and other techniques.

barn doors the louvres or blinders that are adjusted on large set lights to increase or decrease illumination.

best boy on a set, the assistant to the chief electrician.

bit player an actor with a small part or role.

blue screen a process employing a blue screen and color filters to produce matte shots. Also known as a traveling matte. In television, it's performed electronically at the touch of a button and is known as chroma-key.

boffo industry slang for box office hit.

boom a long, mobile arm used to suspend a microphone above the action and out of view of the camera.

B picture any second-rate, low-budget movie.

cameo role a role in which only a brief appearance is made by a major actor.

card a type of credit optical in which names and titles fade in and out in the same position.

cell one of thousands of individual drawings on celluloid sheets used in creating animation or cartoons.

changeover cue a dot in the corner of a film's frames to cue the projectionist to start the next reel.

Cinemascope a film process invented by 20th Century Fox in which anamorphic lenses are used to squeeze film scenes onto 35mm film so that they can be unsqueezed and expanded by a theater projector to create an image more than twice as wide as it is high.

cinematographer a motion picture photographer. Also known as the director of photography.

cinematography motion picture photography.

cinematology the study of films.

cinephile one who loves movies.

Cinerama a wide-screen process that employed three synchronized cameras, now outmoded.

clapper a hand-held chalkboard with data describing the next shot; a clapstick sounded on its top signals the start of the next scene. Also known as a slate.

color cards cards showing a scale of colors, used as a guide to correct colors when filming.

colorization the computerized process of transforming black and white film into color.

commissary a movie studio's cafeteria.

cover set an alternative set used when outdoor shooting is spoiled by rain.

crane shot an aerial shot taken from a crane or suspended, mechanical arm.

crawl the rolling credits at the end of a movie.

credits at the beginning and end of a film, the list of all the people in the production crew, including the actors.

crosscutting showing alternating scenes in quick succession to illustrate parallel action.

crosslighting lighting that originates from the sides.

cut to switch from one scene to another. Also known as a cutaway.

dailies prints from a day's shooting, viewed by the director and others to determine if any shots need to be done again.

day-for-night photography filming night scenes in daylight by using dark filters over the camera lenses.

detail shot an extreme closeup.

director the one who directs the action of the actors, sets scenes, coordinates other technicians, and so on.

director of photography the chief cinematographer.

dissolve an optical effect in which one scene gradually fades out and melds into another scene.

docudrama a movie based on a real event.

dolly a rolling platform on which a camera is mounted to gain mobility. Also known as a crab dolly.

dolly shot a shot taken from a rolling dolly. Also known as a tracking shot.

dub to record dialogue, foreign dialogue, or sound effects in a studio after the film has been shot. See foley.

Dutch angle a canted camera angle that produces a tilted image on the movie screen.

editing the cutting, splicing, and final arrangement of scenes in a film.

editor one who cuts, splices, and determines the final arrangement or length of scenes in a film.

effects track the soundtrack containing sound effects, to be mixed with other soundtracks.

epic a heroic movie with a storyline that frequently spans many months or years.

establishing shot a shot that establishes the location of the upcoming scene.

extra one hired to play a nonspeaking part in the background of a scene, frequently as a member of a crowd.

extreme long shot a panoramic shot taken from a great distance.

fade-in an optical effect in which a dark background slowly brightens to reveal the next scene.

fade-out an optical effect in which the picture slowly fades to black.

film noir French term meaning, literally, "black film," used to describe some American movies made in the 1940s that were notable for their low-key or dark lighting effects.

filter a gelatin, glass, or plastic plate placed over a camera lens to produce various light or color effects.

final cut the edited, finished film.

fisheye lens an extreme wide-angle lens that distorts images and makes the horizon appear distinctly curved.

flag a device positioned in front of a light to create shadow.

flashback a scene that departs from the present and shows an event from the past.

flash cutting editing a section of film into brief scenes that quickly succeed each other.

flash frame a scene consisting of few or even one frane that passes so quickly the audience barely perceives it.

flood short for a floodlight.

foley to reproduce the sound of a body movement, such as footsteps or rustling clothes, in a recording studio for dubbing onto film.

foley stage a large room with several different types of floor (brick, wood, tile, etc.) used to dub in the sound of footsteps in a film.

foley studio a recording studio in which the picture and soundtrack are played while sound effects are added to match the action of the actors, e.g., clothes rustling or footsteps.

gobo a wooden screen placed in front of a light to dim it or to cast a shadow.

grip a set assistant or stagehand; one in charge of props.

high-hat shot a shot taken from near floor or ground level looking up.

highlighting using a thin beam of light to illuminate a part of the actor's face.

horse opera a western.

in the can industry slang for a movie that has been shot but is not ready for distribution.

jump cut a scene that jumps abruptly into another scene; the joining of two discontinuous shots.

kenworthy a special crane, sometimes computer-programmed, used to film miniature sets.

klieg light a floodlight.

leader the black strip of film showing countdown numbers at the beginning of the film.

lip-sync to match recorded speech with the actors' lip movements on film. Also known as looping.

looping lip-syncing on short loops of film.

married print the soundtrack and film combined into one unit.

mask a shield placed over a camera lens to give the illusion of peering through binoculars or a keyhole.

master shot a long shot that takes in an entire scene. Also called a cover shot.

matte shot a special effect in which part of one scene is masked and combined with another to produce a realistic depiction of something that is normally too difficult or too expensive to shoot, for example, an astronaut filmed in a studio and melded into an image or photograph of space to produce an illusion of an astronaut floating in space.

method actor one who practices a form of naturalistic acting first popularized in the 1930s.

Mickey Mousing combining whimsical music or musical effects with the actions of the actors, a technique frequently used in cartoons and sometimes comedic movies.

mix the combining of different soundtrack elements, such as dialogue, music, sound effects.

mogul the head of a movie studio.

moviola an editing machine.

nickelodeon an early form of American movie theater, with admission costing a nickel.

novelization a novel adapted from a movie.

on location filming in an actual setting, such as an airport, rather than in a studio mockup or set.

optrack an optical soundtrack on a married print; it comprises of a photo image of sound modulations on the side of the film.

outtake a portion of film deleted by the editor.

overcrank to run the camera at a greater speed than normal to produce slow-motion images.

overlap sound dialogue or sound that continues as the scene fades out. Also, dialogue or sound that begins before the scene fades in.

pan to film from side to side.

Panavision wide-screen process that supplanted Cinemascope.

pancake a makeup used on actors to darken skin.

pixillation stop-action photography effect in which an inanimate object is moved between each frame or a small number of frames so that on film the object appears to move on its own, as if by magic.

point of view shot a shot as seen from a character's perspective.

postsynchronization the recording of the soundtrack after the film has been shot.

pratical set a studio set, such as a bedroom mockup, with parts that actually work, such as doors, windows, and so on. Also, any on location set.

producer the person who secures financing, purchases the script, hires artists and technicians, and oversees a film's production.

prop any object used in a flim, for example, chair, table, inkwell, gun, elephant.

property a film story.

pullback a shot in which the camera is pulled back to reveal a larger portion of the scene.

pushover an optical effect in which a new scene appears to push the preceding scene off the screen. Similar to a wipe.

rack focus a change of focus from a subject in the background to a subject in the foreground, or vice versa, without moving the camera.

reaction shot a shot that shows a character's reaction to the action around her or him.

rear projection same as back projection.

Rembrandt lighting a backlighting method modeled after the techniques of the famous painter, in which a soft light is projected from behind a character for a subtle halolike effect, popularly used in the movies of the 1930s and 1940s.

reverse-angle shot a shot of an opposite view, as when switching from one character to another during alternating dialogue.

ripple dissolve an optical effect in which a wavering image serves as a transition to either a flashback, a flashforward, or a dream sequence.

rough cut the first cutting and splicing of a film by the editor in which scenes are placed in the correct general order according to the script.

rushes same as dailies.

score the music composed for a film.

screenplay a film story, with dialogue and descriptions of action. The script.

scrim a plate placed in front of a light to produce shadow.

script supervisor the person in charge of film continuity, for example, making sure details in one shot (such as which side the actor's hair is parted on or whether a jacket is zipped or unzipped) match those in another shot, even though filmed days or weeks apart. Formerly known as the script girl.

Sensurround a gimmicky movie sound system in which stereo speakers are placed in front, in back, and sometimes on the sides of a theater.

set the location where a film is being shot.

shooting script a script having directions for camera angles, shots, and so on, as well as dialogue.

slate same as clapper.

soft focus slightly out-of-focus, as achieved by placing Vaseline or a special filter over the camera lens; used to soften lines in romatic shots.

sound effects all sounds, other than music or dialogue, added to a film after shooting.

sound stage a building in which sets are built and dismantled for filming.

sound track the optical or magnetic track on the side of a film; it contains the music, dialogue, and sound effects.

spaghetti western a European western, usually made in Italy or Spain, popular in the 1960s.

splice to join two pieces of film.

split screen an optical effect showing two different scenes on one frame.

spotting session a meeting in which the director, composer, and editor decide where the music will play in the film.

squib a tiny explosive charge used to simulate gunshots.

steadicam a special, hand-held, waist-supported camera that provides smooth, shake-free shots on a par with dolly shots.

still a photo or enlarged frame from a film, used for publicity.

stock footage existing film borrowed or purchased from a film library and used in a new film.

stop-motion photography a special effects technique in which objects are filmed one frame at a time, allowing the object to be moved between frames. The resulting moving image is known as pixillation.

storyboard a series of captioned drawings showing planned camera shots.

streamer a long line drawn on a film to cue an actor that a scene to be dubbed with dialogue is coming up. Also used to cue conductors for accurate placement of music.

superimposition a special effect in which one scene is superimposed over another, most notably used in creating scenes with ghosts. Also known as a super.

swish pan a rapid, blurring pan of a scene that serves as a transition into the next scene. Also known as a flick pan, whip pan, zip pan.

take any acceptable shot to be used in the final film.

time-lapse photography a method of compressing real time into a much shorter span of time in film by shooting frames at timed intervals.

track the rails on which the camera rides in a tracking shot

tracking shot a moving camera shot on a dolly, on rails, or on foot.

traveling matte same as blue screen.

treatment a detailed description or outline of a film idea, as given by the author.

trucking shot a rail or dolly shot.

two-shot a shot of two characters simultaneously, as distinguished from a shot cutting back and forth between actors during dialogue.

typecasting the casting of a character type to fit a specific character role.

undercrank to run the camera at a slower speed than normal to produce fast-motion images.

walla a sound effect of a murmuring crowd.

washout a fade to white.

wild shooting shooting a film without simultaneous recording of the sound.

wild sound sound recorded apart from the actual filming.

wild walls on a set, temporary walls that can be assembled and disassembled quickly.

wipe an optical effect in which one scene moves from left to right, or vice versa, to knock out another scene and therefore serve as a transitional device.

zoom a shot which, by means of automatic focus, zooms in close to a distant subject.

TELEVISION (*Also see* FILM)

ABC American Broadcasting Company.

affidavit of performance a notarized list of commercials and public service announcements and their air dates and times, provided to the sponsors.

affiliate a local station, frequently independently owned, that contracts to air the programs of a particular national network.

announcer booth in a studio, a small booth where off-camera voice-overs or announcements are made.

Arbitron the TV ratings company that measures the size of a TV viewing audience by means of an electronic meter placed on TV sets.

arc a curving movement left or right (arc right/left) of a TV pedestal camera, as ordered by the director.

art director a supervisor of the art department.

assemble edit the simultaneous recording of audio, video, cue, and control tracks on a tape.

associate director in the control room, an assistant to the director, whose commands are the ones heard by the camera operators.

atmospheric effects specialist a special-effects person who simulates fog, rain, thunder, lightning, smoke, and so on.

audio operator the audio technician responsible for a program's sound quality.

back lot studio property where outdoor scenes are occasionally shot.

backtiming a method of ending a live program exactly on time by providing a rehearsed final segment that can be made shorter or longer at will. Also, in news programs, the time when the last segment must be aired to match the time deadline.

balop a large slide of art work, used as a background scene.

bat blacks to fade out or to fade to black.

bear trap slang for an alligator-type clamp used to attach lights in a studio. Also known as a gaffer grip.

big head a closeup of a performer's head.

billboard the credits at the opening and closing of a program. Also, an announcement made on behalf of the sponsor, such as "This program brought to you by . . ."

bird a satellite used for TV transmission.

birding slang for television transmission via satellite.

bird, lose the to lose the transmission of a TV signal through a satellite.

black level TV control signals that are blocked out of the picture.

blackout the prohibition of local sports coverage due to contract agreements, intended to draw the maximum audience to the local stadium.

block to provide indications or markings of camera or performer placement and their movement during rehearsal.

blunting airing a program of similar content to that of a competing station at the same time.

boom a long, movable arm, crane, or pole used to hold a microphone.

bump to cancel a guest on a talk show.

bumper a transitional device between program segments, such as a fade-out, or an announcement such as, "We'll return after these messages."

cable puller a studio assistant responsible for power, sound, and picture cables who follows camera movements and pulls cables out of the way to prevent entanglement.

call sheet a schedule sheet showing the dates and times a cast and crew must appear for a production.

camera cue a red warning light indicating when a camera is actually shooting. Also known as a cue light or tally light.

camera mixing mixing shots in succession from two or more studio cameras.

camera rehearsal a full dress rehearsal in which camera placement and movements are planned or blocked.

camera riser a platform that elevates a camera.

canned anything prerecorded, such as canned laughter.

cast to hire a performer for an acting part. Also, the collective term for all of the performers in a show.

casting director the director who casts the performers for a show.

casting file a file of performer bios.

cattle call an open audition, usually mobbed by acting hopefuls, for a bit or minor part in a program.

catwalk a narrow walkway or scaffolding above the studio, from which lights can be hung and accessed.

CBS Columbia Broadcasting System.

cc closed captioned for the hearing-impaired; the superimposing of captions over a TV program, seen only by those viewers with special decoders.

chain break during a program break, a brief spot for station identification. Also, a local commercial up to 20 seconds long.

cherry picker a mobile crane holding a boom and camera for moving, outdoor shots; it has three seats, for the director, the camera operator, and the camera assistant.

cinemobile a large vehicle containing dressing rooms and store rooms, used when taping on location.

circle-in a transitional optical effect in which the picture forms a circle and diminishes, while a new scene enlarges from a small circle. Also known as iris-in.

circle wipe an optical effect in which a scene begins as a dot on the screen and enlarges to wipe out the previous scene.

clean entrance a direction to a performer to enter a scene from off-camera, as distinguished from the camera following the performer into the action.

closed set a set or studio closed to the public.

color bar a vertical strip of graduating colors for color testing of TV transmission. The colors are white, yellow, cyan, green, magenta, red, blue, and black. Also known as a colorburst.

come in a director's command to move the camera in closer on the subject.

control room the technical room where the director and engineers control the audio and video.

cover shot a wide shot revealing location at the start of a scene.

crab shot a shot in which the camera moves left or right on its dolly or truck.

crane same as cherry picker.

crane grip the crane or cherry picker operator.

crawl the moving credits at the end of a TV show. Also, any text seen moving across the bottom of the TV screen, as a weather or news bulletin.

credits the acknowledgements of cast and crew at the start or end of a program.

creeper a small camera dolly.

cue card a large card with a performer's lines printed on it. Also known as a flip card or an idiot card.

cue line on ON THE AIR warning light; also a red camera light to indicate shooting.

cue light a line spoken by one actor that serves as a cue to another actor.

cue sheet a schedule of cues and timings.

cyclorama a curved backdrop or wall used on a stage or studio to give the illusion of sky.

day for night filming a night scene in broad daylight by the use of special dark filters.

dead roll starting a program at its normal time but not broadcasting it until a late sporting or other event is over, at which time the program is "joined already in progress."

deaf aid a small earpiece used by reporters, anchors, and others.

decryption the decoding and unscrambling of pay cable TV signals

defocusing dissolve an optical transition effect in which one camera goes slowly out of focus while another camera shoots a different scene that slowly comes into focus.

delayed broadcast the common practice in the Pacific time zone of airing a TV show later than it originally was transmitted.

delay time the 7 seconds of delay time between broadcast and transmission in which obscenities may be removed on a live call-in talk show.

detail set a set used for closeups, having many props and details. Also known as an insert set.

detail shot an extreme closeup.

diagonal dissolve an optical effect in which two corners of a scene merge on screen.

Digital Video Effects an electronic special effects system.

discovery shot a shot that zooms in on something the viewer had previously overlooked or failed to perceive.

dissolve an optical effect, such as fade-in, fade-out, fade-to-black, serving as a transition to the next scene.

dolly grip one who pushes a camera dolly.

dolly-in a director's command to move the camera closer to the subject.

dolly-out a director's command to move the camera away from the subject.

dolly shot a moving camera shot made on a dolly. Also known as a truck or tracking shot.

dolly tracks rails on which a camera and dolly ride during outdoor shots where the ground is uneven.

dress extra an extra who provides his own costume and is thus paid more.

dressing room a room used for dressing and makeup.

dress plot a list of actors' costumes and the order in which they will be worn throughout a program.

dry block a rehearsal without cameras.

dub a record in sound effects, music, dialogue, or foreign dialogue onto a sound track.

ducker a device that automatically lowers volume of background music to allow a voice-over to be heard.

dupe a copy of a taped TV program.

ear prompter a small audio ear plug through which an actor can listen to other actors' lines and play off of them.

editor the person in charge of cutting and splicing video tape to put scenes in their proper sequence.

electronic character generator a typewriter-like device that produces on-screen lettering and characters for sports scores, weather reports, stock updates, and other reports.

electronic matte the combining electronically of images from two different cameras.

electronic still store an electronic storage unit holding photographic slides and titles.

elephant doors the large doors entering onto a TV studio.

embargo the prohibition of the media to release certain news until a particular date or time.

encryption the process of scrambling TV signals to protect pay TV networks from theft of service.

endcue the last four or five words spoken by a performer, newscaster, anchor, for example, used as a cue for the control room engineer and director to cue the music and credits. Also, outcue.

ESU engineering setup. The projection of an image over the shoulder of a news anchor during a news story.

explosion wipe an optical effect in which an upcoming scene appears to expand from the center of the screen.

explosive a loud, sharp sound produced by speech made too close to a microphone, the bane of audio engineers.

extra an actor in a small nonspeaking role.

eye bounce the technique of looking down and sideways while on TV. Looking down without a sideways glance gives a shifty-eyed or fearful appearance.

facade a fake building having only a front wall and nothing behind it, often used on western programs.

fade an optical effect in which the picture fades in or out.

favor an instruction to the cameraman to focus in on a subject.

feed broadcasts transmitted from a network to local stations or vice versa.

field strength the strength of a local station's broadcast signals.

filter mike a microphone used to simulate the sound of someone's voice over the telephone.

first assistant cameraman one who adjusts a camera's focus to a performer's movements away or toward the camera. Also known as a focus puller.

fishbowl in a studio, an observation booth for sponsors and others involved with the program.

fishpole a long microphone boom.

flashcaster a device used to superimpose news, weather, and other bulletins onto a crawl at the bottom of the TV screen.

flash-pan a superfast pan shot that blurs the picture and serves as a transition to the next scene.

flip wipe an optical effect in which a scene appears to turn over, as a page, to reveal a new scene.

floodlight a broad, bright studio light.

foley a sound effect dubbed in, such as footsteps, clothes rustling, or glasses clinking.

foley artist one who performs sound effects in a recording studio.

foley stage where foley effects are performed.

footage a length of video tape.

freeze frame an optical effect in which tape is frozen at the end of a program to provide a still picture over which credits are run.

futures editor a TV news editor who is responsible for getting coverage of upcoming news events.

gaffer a chief electrician on a set or in a studio.

green room a waiting room for guests who are scheduled to appear on a talk show.

grip a stage or studio hand; a general set assistant.

half shot a camera shot halfway between a long shot and a closeup.

hammers set or stage assistants to the grip, not to be confused with set carpenters.

hammocking scheduling a poor program between two highly rated programs to increase the poor program's ratings.

handbasher an 800-watt, hand-held set light.

hiatus time off between a program's shooting schedule, especially during summer reruns.

high definition TV (HDTV) a new generation of televisions having a higher resolution or sharper image.

honey wagon a trailer with dressing rooms and other facilities, for shooting a program on location.

hot microphone a live microphone.

intercutting taking several shots of the same scene from various angles and splicing them together for a more effective viewpoint.

interstitial programming the airing of short programs between long programs to break up the monotony.

iris-in same as circle-in.

jump a cue to step on another performer's lines; to react too early to a cue.

key to light a set. Also, to superimpose text onto the screen.

key light any main source of light on a set.

klieg light a powerful, wide-angle light used on sets.

lap dissolve an optical transitional effect in which one scene is gradually replaced by another.

late fringe TV ratings term for viewers who watch from 11 P.M. to sign-off.

laugh track prerecorded laughter dubbed over a comedy show at appropriate moments.

lavaliere a microphone worn around the neck, as a necklace.

lead-in an introductory announcement leading in to a program.

legend titles or other text keyed onto the screen.

letterbox format the showing of a movie on TV with its original theater aspect ratio (width to height of picture), in which horizontal bands appear on the top and bottom of the TV screen.

live mike a microphone that is on.

live on tape a program recorded as it actually happened or was performed, but not actually live when transmitted or broadcast.

location a real setting (e.g., an airport) as distinguished from a studio set, where a portion of a program is shot.

location manager a production assistant who plans and arranges for shooting on location.

location scout a production assistant who finds and reserves locations for shooting.

makeup call the time at which a performer must report to the makeup department.

master of ceremonies the host of a TV program; the MC or emcee.

match dissolve an optical transitional effect in which a scene fades and is replaced by a similar or nearly identical scene, but at a later time.

maxi-brute a powerful arc spotlight containing nine 1,000-watt lights in three rows. Also known as a nine-light.

minicam a portable TV camera used when taping on location news.

network collective term for a group of affiliated TV stations that air the same programs.

O/C script directive for "on camera."

one-key one 1,000-watt floodlight. A 1,500-watt light equals one-and-a-half key.

open-ended a portion of a national program or commercial in which a local announcer can add local information.

opening billboard an opening preview or the opening credits of a program. Also, an announcement of sponsors, such as "brought to you by . . ."

opticals optical effects; examples are dissolves, fades, superimpositions, and wipes.

outcue the last four words in an interview, dialogue, or newscast, used as a cue to the engineers and director to roll music and run the credits. Also, endcue.

outtakes unused portions of a program tape, edited out due to flubbed lines or other mistakes.

pan a bad review of a program. Also, a direction to the cameraman to sweep slowly across a scene for a panoramic effect.

pan and scan the method by which a motion picture's widescreen aspect ratio is changed to make it suitable for TV broadcast. See also letterbox format.

pancake the heavy makeup used by performers.

paper cut a written schedule or list of cuts and splices keyed to time cues made before the actual editing takes place.

PAR light a commonly used spotlight having a parabolic aluminized reflector.

people meter an electronic system for tracking TV viewers to establish ratings, adopted by A. C. Nielson in 1987 to replace the diary system.

Pepper's ghost a simple special-effects method of producing a ghost image. A camera shoots through an angled mirror to create a reflection of the subject; invented by scientist John Henry Pepper.

performance royalties payments made by a broadcaster to a songwriter or publisher for the right to play their music.

pod a group of commercials.

poop sheet a trivia information sheet on athletes, used by sports announcers between plays in a game.

preempt to broadcast a special in place of a regularly scheduled program.

preview monitor a monitor from which the director chooses the picture to be used by various cameras.

prime time the time period having the largest viewership, from 8 P.M. to 11 P.M.

producer one in charge of financing and staffing a show. In addition to the business end of a program, a producer may also oversee some creative aspects of a show.

prompter a device that enables an actor or announcer to read off a script while looking into the camera. See PROMPTER SCRIPT, TELEPROMPTER.

prompter script a script transmitted to a monitor on top of or beside a camera, or superimposed on the camera lens itself for reading but not seen by the TV audience.

quad split an optical effect in which four different scenes appear on the screen at the same time.

residual a royalty or payment made to a performer for use of their taped performance beyond the original contract.

ripple dissolve a dissolve or fade in which the scene ripples or wavers into the next scene, as in a dream sequence or flashback.

rostrum camera a camera designed to shoot artwork on a table, for animation.

rotoscope a prism and lamphouse device used on a special effects camera to produce traveling mattes.

rug slang for background music in a commercial.

scale minimum standard fee for a performer or model.

scoop the most frequently used light in TV, specifically a 1,000-watt floodlamp having a shovel-like reflector. Also known as a basher.

set the location of a TV production; the scenery, furnishings, props, lighting, and equipment, of a TV program.

set and light director's order to get the set and lighting ready for shooting.

shaky-cam slang for a hand-held camera.

shooting log a notebook with details of a day's shooting and the camera equipment used. Also known as a camera log.

shooting schedule the schedule of when each shot in a movie or TV show will be made, usually out-of-sequence to the storyline but later edited in order.

shot box on a TV camera, a control panel for zoom and other focus changes.

signature montage a sequence of brief, identifying scenes used as an introduction to a program.

simulation a reenactment of an event, used frequently in news programs.

simulcast a program broadcast simultaneously on radio and TV, as a concert or presidential speech.

sister station a TV station afilliated with the same network as another station.

sitcom situation comedy.

snake a special studio cable that combines several cables.

soundbite a quick clip of a quote made by a politician or other newsworthy person, aired on a newscast.

sound dissolve the fading out of sounds in one scene followed by the fading in of sounds from an upcoming scene, a transitional device.

spider a junction box for several electrical outlets, used in studios.

spider dolly a camera mount comprising projecting legs on wheels.

splice to join two pieces of film or tape together.

splicing charge a fee sometimes charged for splicing a commercial into a program.

split screen an optical effect in which two or more scenes are shown on the screen at the same time.

squib a gunpowder charge held in a gelatin capsule, detonated from a distance to simulate gunfire.

squibbed bag a squib placed in a blood bag (imitation blood) and detonated on or under clothing to simulate gunshot wounds.

stable a group of performers under contract with a single agent or network.

standby guest on a talk show, an "extra" guest used as a stand-in in case another guest doesn't show up.

standing set a permanent or semipermanent set used repeatedly, as on a soap opera.

still store an electronic memory unit that stores graphics and photos for use in news programs.

storyboard a sequence of cartoons and sketches that illustrate a proposed commercial. Also used in movies to plan how scenes will be shot.

strike to tear down a set.

sweeps TV ratings periods in November, February, May, and July, noted for the airing of sensational programming in order to attract a large audience.

syndicate a service that distributes a TV program to subscribing stations.

syndication the distribution of a program to subscribing stations.

systems cue an audio, visual, or spoken signal for local station identification.

tabloid TV a pseudo news program featuring sensational stories.

take a 42 an order to take a 42-minute meal break, as prescribed for crew members by union rules.

talent coordinator on talk shows, one who auditions, interviews, and schedules guests.

tally light a red light illuminated on a camera when shooting.

tape to record a program on videotape.

teaser a brief preview or promo of an upcoming show to attract viewers.

technical director the assistant director who oversees the technical aspects of a studio and studio control room.

teleplay a play written or adapted for TV.

TelePrompTer commercial name for a brand of prompter, now used generically. See PROMPTER.

the trades the trade publications of show business, such as *Variety*, *Hollywood Reporter*.

tight two shot director's order to cameraman for a head shot of two people.

tongue left/right a command to extend a crane-mounted camera out horizontally to follow the action.

topic box a window or visual on the screen above a newscaster's shoulder to identify the topic.

trailer a brief, promotional piece of a coming attraction.

transportation captain the head of a studio's transportation and moving department.

truck shot a moving dolly shot. Also, to move the camera sideways.

tulip crane a crane on which a camera platform can be mounted for aboveground shots.

12-14 unit a mobile, remote news truck capable of transmitting at 12 gigahertz and receiving at 14 gigahertz.

two-shot a closeup of two people.

upcutting the unethical practice of cutting off part of a network program in order to insert more local commercials.

veejay video disk jockey.

video operator the control room engineer who operates the camera control units and monitors and is responsible for the overall picture quality.

videotape magnetic tape on which sound and pictures can be recorded.

voice-over a narrator or announcer's voice heard over a commercial or program.

white coat rule an FCC rule that prohibits actors from wearing white lab coats while pitching a medical product unless it is clearly stated that the actor is not a physician or related professional.

wild shot a camera shot taken without accompanying sound.

wild sound real or natural sounds that are recorded, as distinguished from studio sound effects.

wild track a sound track recorded independently of the visual track.

wild wall a set wall that can be dismantled quickly, usually for the insertion of a TV camera.

wind machine a large fan used to simulate wind.

wipe any optical effect that cleans or wipes off the image on the screen.

RADIO

AM amplitude modulated; a radio signal that travels along the surface and curvature of the Earth and thus has a much larger broadcast area than FM.

audio news release a taped news or publicity piece sent to radio stations by publicists for broadcast.

band a range of radio frequencies.

beeper slang for a recorded interview of a person over the telephone, formerly requiring a series of beeps to indicate to listeners that the interview was not being broadcast live.

booking board a posted calendar listing future programs and interview guests.

B-rate the cheapest commercial rates, for airing late at night or on Sunday morning.

breakers the new records receiving the heaviest air time.

Broadcast Music, Inc. (BMI) a nonprofit organization of music publishers and composers who collect royalties of up to 12 cents each time a performer or member's record is played over a radio station.

call letters the identification letters of a radio station, usually beginning with the letter W if located east of the Mississippi and K if located west of the Mississippi.

Canadian call letters begin with C; Mexican call letters begin with X.

class I station a 50,000-watt AM station having FCC protection of frequency for up to 750 miles. Also known as clear channel station.

class III station a 5,000-watt station operating on an unprotected, regional channel.

clear channel station a maximum-power AM station having frequency-protected range of up to 750 miles. Also known as class I station.

cool out to lower the volume of background music at the end of a commercial.

cough button a switch used by an announcer or DJ to turn off the microphone during a cough or sneeze.

cue burn damage to the beginning of a record, due to heavy cueing.

cue up to set a record on a turntable with the cue in position for immediate play.

dead air silence during a radio broadcast, a taboo.

delay time a 7-second delay between a talk show's broadcast and transmission, within which any obscenities from callers may be deleted.

disk record

disk jockey one who plays records over the radio.

DJ disk jockey.

DJ copy a record with only one side recorded on.

drive time important broadcast hours in the morning and late afternoon, when people listen in their cars on their way to and from work.

explosive a loud, explosionlike noise produced by speaking too close to the microphone.

feed broadcasts sent from a national network to local stations, or vice versa.

field strength the power of a station's broadcasting signal.

FM frequency modulation; straight-line radio signals that cannot be received beyond the horizon and therefore have a much smaller range than AM signals; however, FM signals provide high fidelity reception with little or no static.

ground wave a radio signal that travels along the Earth's surface, as distinguished from one that goes into space as it meets the curvature of the Earth.

high frequency a frequency between 3 and 30 megahertz.

indy slang for an independently owned radio station.

low frequency a frequency between 30 and 300 kilocycles per second.

network a group of affiliated radio stations and their headquarters.

outcue the last four or five words in a song, interview, or newscast, that serve as a cue to the engineer or disk jockey to begin another record, commercial, or program.

performance royalties fees paid by radio stations for the rights to play the songs of music publishers and composers.

picket fencing the fading in and out of an FM station at the fringe of its broadcast range.

playlist a schedule of the day's recordings to be played on the air.

PSA public service announcement.

rolloff the faint edges of a radio signal, when a station hasn't been tuned in properly.

rumble low-frequency vibration.

shock radio talk radio featuring loud, rude, or obnoxious hosts who insult their guests and listeners.

simulcast the simultaneous broadcast of a program on television and radio.

soundbite a brief note from a newsworthy person, aired as part of a newscast.

standby guest an emergency stand-in guest used in case a scheduled guest fails to appear.

tape delay a system used on call-in programs, in which a phone call is taped and delayed before airing, to eliminate obscenities.

trailer a brief, promotional piece on an upcoming program, usually played at the end of another program.

translator a station that does not have its own programming but rebroadcasts that of other stations.

upcutting the unethical cutting of part of a network program in order to create more space for local commercials.

urban contemporary radiospeak for inner-city black music.

voice-over a narrator's voice heard over the background music of a commercial.

Sports

ARCHERY

American round a competitive round in which each contestant shoots 30 arrows at 60 yards, 30 at 50 yards, and 30 at 40 yards.

animal round a competitive round in which each contestant shoots at lifelike animal targets from 10 to 60 yards.

archer's paralysis a psychological problem in which the archer "chokes" under pressure, loses his aim, or becomes incapable of releasing when aligned on target.

arm guard an inner forearm covering made of leather or plastic; it protects the bow arm from the bow string.

barebow shooting without a sighting aid on a bow.

battle clouts a competition in which 36 broadhead arrows are shot 200 yards to a large target.

belly the side of the bow closest to the bow string.

blunt an arrow with a flat tip, used to stun small game.

bow the pliable wood and fiberglass apparatus that holds the bowstring.

bow hand when shooting, the hand that holds the bow.

bowsight a sight or aiming aid on the top half of the bow.

bowstring the synthetic or waxed linen string that is pulled back and released to project an arrow.

bow weight a bow's draw weight.

broadhead a hunting arrow having a broad head or two or more blades.

bullseye the center of a target.

clout a 48-foot target with a 1½-foot center, used for long distance shooting and scored the same as a standard-size target.

clout shooting shooting at a clout from 120 to 180 yards away.

crest a row of colored stripes around an arrow's shaft below the fletching; they are used as an identification aid.

crossbow a bow held sideways and fired by a trigger mechanism from a special stock. Its short arrows are known as bolts.

draw to pull the bowstring back.

drawing hand the string hand.

draw weight the force required to pull a bow back one arrow length.

drift deviation of an arrow's flight due to wind.

feather any of the three stabilizing feathers on the shaft. See FLETCHING.

field archery competition featuring various targets located outside in fields or woods to simulate hunting conditions.

fingerstalls thimblelike, protective covers worn on the string fingers.

fletching the feathers attached to an arrow shaft to stablize its flight. Also known as flights.

flight shooting nontarget, distance shooting competition.

foot bow a bow held with the feet while the string is drawn back with both hands, used in distance shooting competition.

green an outdoor shooting range.

King's round a crossbow competition in which contestants shoot six bolts each at a target 40 yards away.

longbow a straight, medieval-style bow.

loose to release the bowstring to project an arrow.

Mediterranean draw pulling the drawstring with three fingertips of the string hand.

Mongolian draw pulling the drawstring with the thumb and index finger.

nock the groove in the limb of the arrow for inserting the bowstring. To insert the bowstring into this groove.

petticoat the nonscoring, outer fringe of a target.

popinjay shooting a competition in which archers shoot blunt arrows at artificial birds.

quiver a case for holding arrows.

string dampener a rubber fitting that deadens the twang of the bowstring upon release, used when hunting.

wand a long, narrow target, usually 6 feet by 2 inches.

wand shooting a competition in which 36 arrows are shot at a wand from 60 to 100 yards.

AUTO RACING

aerofoil a wedge or wing mounted above the front or tail of a car to produce better adhesion to the road.

apron the low edge of a racetrack, used to get on and off the track.

blown said of a motor when a major part (such as a piston seizing from overheating) breaks and produces smoke.

broadslide making a turn while sliding sideways.

catch tanks special tanks fitted on a race car to help prevent fluids from leaking on and fouling the track.

chicane a tight ess-turn or curve.

chute the fast straightaway section of track in front of the grandstand.

crew chief the chief mechanic of a pit crew.

dogging driving bumper-to-bumper with the car ahead in an attempt to pressure a mistake.

drafting the technique of driving directly behind another car to create a vacuum that allows both cars to go faster and to conserve fuel. Also known as slipstreaming.

drag a straightaway race over a short distance, usually a quarter mile.

drift a four-wheeled, sideways slide.

ess an S-turn.

factory team a racing team sponsored by the manufacturer of the race car.

flags a blue flag held still warns of a competitor on one's tail. When waved it warns of a competitor about to pass. A yellow flag indicates an obstruction or hazard ahead. When waved it indicates extreme danger ahead. A green flag means "go, the track is clear." A black flag held up with a board with the number of an offending car is an instruction for that car to pull over at the pits at once, due to some hazard such as leaking oil. A red flag means stop. A white flag indicates that one is entering the final lap. It may also be used to indicate a caution—for example, an ambulance or service vehicle is on the track ahead. A checkered flag indicates the end of the race.

flying start a running start, as distinguished from a standing start.

formula one car a single-seat race car with a 1500cc turbocharged rear engine producing over 900 horsepower.

formula two car a single-seat race car with a 2000 cc, fuel-injected, nonturbocharged rear engine producing 325 horsepower, discontinued in 1984.

formula three car a single-seat race car with a nonturbocharged 1600cc, fuel-injected rear engine producing 165 horsepower.

funny car a drag racing car having an engine mounted in the middle and the driver's seat located far in the back.

Grand Prix an international race for formula cars.

grid positions the starting positions of a line of cars, with the fastest qualifiers usually up front.

hairpin a very sharp, direction-reversing turn.

hang out the laundry in a drag race, to release the parachute at the end of the race.

heel and toe working the accelerator and brake with the toe and heel of the right foot while working the clutch with the left foot.

Indy car a single-seat race car with a 2650cc rear engine producing 750 horsepower; may be turbo or nonturbo.

infield the area within an oval track.

lap to overtake a competitor who then falls one track length behind.

lap of honor a slow lap taken around the track by the winner.

marshal one of several track officials responsible for lining up the racers, inspecting work in the pits, and similar duties.

NASCAR National Association for Stock Car Auto Racing.

nerf bar a side or front bumper that prevents a competitor's car from striking one's wheels.

NHRA National Hot Rod Association, the sanctioning body for drag racing.

pace car the noncompeting lead car that sets the pace through one or two laps before the race begins.

paddock where the cars are kept and prepared for a racing event.

pit board a message board used by a pit crew to communicate with a driver.

pits areas along the track where a team of mechanics repair and service each car during stops in a race.

pole position the front inside position granted the driver with the best qualifying time. The most coveted starting position.

production car a stockcar.

rail a dragster with the engine mounted in front of the rear wheels.

rally a long-distance race.

retaining wall the outside wall that prevents cars from accidently running off the track or crashing into the grandstand.

reverse start a start in which the fastest qualifying cars are lined up last.

roll bar a hollow steel tube that prevents the roof of a car from collapsing on top of a driver in the event of a rollover.

roll cage a network of roll bars for increased protection of the driver during a crash and rollover.

shoes racing tires.

shutdown to defeat a competitor in a drag race.

shutdown strip the end of the racing strip where dragsters slow down and stop.

slicks smooth, treadless tires.

slingshot a passing method in which the trailing car pulls out of the draft of the leader, which produces a vacuum that pulls the lead car back.

slipstream the vacuum created behind a fast-moving car.

spoiler an aerodynamic device for improving handling of the car at high speed.

sprint car a single-seat race car having a wheelbase of at least 84 inches and a front engine producing 575 horsepower.

stage to align a drag racer at the starting line.

stock car a standard sedan modified for racing. Also known as a production car.

T-bone to crash into another car broadside or to run straight on into a retaining wall.

BASEBALL

AAA the principal minor league from which the major league draws players.

abbreviations box score and scorecard abbreviations include some of the following:

A	assist
AB	at bat
AL	active list, American League
B	bunt
BA	batting average
BB	base on balls/walks
BK	balk
CG	complete game
CS	caught stealing
DH	designated hitter, doubleheader
DL	disabled list
DP	double play
E	error
ER	earned run
ERA	earned run average
F	foul out
FC	fielder's choice
FO	force out
FP	fielding percentage
G	game
GS	games started
H	hit
HB	hit batter
HR	home run
IP	innings pitched
IW	intentional walk
K	strikeout
KC	strikeout, called
KS	strikeout, swinging
LOB	left on base
LP	losing pitcher
OF	outfield
PB	passed ball
PO	put out
R	run
RBI	runs batted in
S	sacrifice
SB	stolen base
SF	sacrifice fly
SHO	shutout
SO	strikeout
SS	shortstop
T	total time of game
2B	double
3B	triple
TP	triple play
WP	wild pitch, winning pitcher

aboard on base; as in "two men aboard."

ace a team's best pitcher.

air it out to hit a ball deep into the outfield or over the wall for a home run.

alive a pitch that appears to rise or move on its own accord.

alleys the open areas between the center fielder and the left fielder and the center fielder and the right fielder.

Annie Oakley a free pass to a game.

apple old slang term for the baseball.

around the horn describing a double play in which the ball is fielded by the third baseman, thrown to the second baseman for one out, and then thrown to the first baseman for the second out.

artillery a team's best batters.

Astroturf brand name of a type of artificial grass.

back-door slide intentionally sliding wide of the bag to avoid being tagged-out then quickly grabbing the bag with the hand.

backstop the screen behind home plate that protects the spectators from being hit by foul balls.

bad-ball hitter a batter who tends to swing indiscriminately at pitches outside the strike zone and who either strikes out a lot or produces a lot of fly balls.

bad hop a hit or thrown ball that takes an unexpected hop, making it difficult to field.

bag commonly used term for either first, second, or third base.

balk an illegal motion made by a pitcher with the intention of deceiving a base runner into starting a run for the next base.

balloon a slow-pitched ball that, to the batter, appears big and easy to hit.

baptism the roughing up of a smooth, new baseball with special mud, performed by the umpire prior to a game.

barrel the heavy, top, or hitting portion of a bat.

base on balls a walk. A batter's pass to first base after the pitcher pitches four balls out of the strike zone, at which the batter doesn't swing.

bases loaded runners on every base.

basket catch catching a flyball at belt level with cupped hand and glove, a risky technique.

batfest an inning or game with an unusually high number of hits.

batter's box either one of the 6-foot by 4-foot rectangles a player must stand in while at bat.

battery collective term for the pitcher and catcher.

batting average a percentage determined by dividing the number of hits a player has by the number of times he has been up to bat. 1.000, would be perfect. More realistically, however, .300 is excellent and .400 or above is extraordinary and rarely achieved.

bazooka a powerful throwing arm.

bean to hit a batter in the head with a pitched ball.

beanball a ball intentionally pitched at the batter's head to intimidate or to move him back away from the plate.

beanball war retaliatory pitches at a batter's head by both teams.

behind in the count referring to a batter who has more strikes than balls or a pitcher who has pitched more balls than strikes.

bellywhopper a head-first, diving slide into a base.

benchwarmer a player who rarely plays and can usually be seen sitting on the bench.

big guns same as artillery.

bleachers the cheap seats or benches located around the outfield.

bloop to hit a short flyball that lands between the infielders and outfielders for a hit. Also known as a Texas Leaguer.

blooper a short flyball that lands between the infielders and outfielders for a hit.

blow it by to pitch a ball so fast that the batter can't possibly hit it.

blow smoke to throw fastballs; also throw smoke.

bobble commonly used term for a hit ball that is mishandled or dropped.

box score in newspaper sports sections, a statistical rundown of a game.

box seats the best and most expensive seats in a ballpark located around first base, third base, and home plate.

boys of summer originally a name for the Brooklyn Dodgers of the 1950s but now connoting all baseball players.

bread-and-butter pitch a pitcher's most effective pitch.

breaking said of a curve ball as it "breaks" high, low, fast, or slow.

breaking ball any pitch that alters its trajectory by rising, dipping, or curving.

break the wrists the determining factor in whether a batter has taken a full swing at the ball, missed, and produced a strike; to swing the arms and turn the wrists far enough to be considered a strike.

break-up slide an intentional sliding collision with a defensive player to break up a double or triple play.

brushback pitch a ball pitched deliberately close to the batter's body in order to move him back away from the plate. This is a method of regaining some of the strike zone the batter had crowded out.

bug on the rug a ball bouncing elusively on artificial turf.

bullpen located beyond the outfield, one of two practice or warmup areas for relief pitchers.

bullpen ace a team's most effective relief pitcher.

bunt a lightly hit ball that rolls only a few feet from home plate, used as a sacrifice hit to advance a base runner. If executed well, it can also serve as a hit to get the batter to first.

bush slang for unprofessional or unsportsmanlike play, named after lesser minor leagues such as A or AA, otherwise known as the bush leagues.

bush league the A or AA minor leagues or lower leagues.

buzzer a ball pitched so fast that it literally "buzzes."

cannon a powerful throwing arm.

caught leaning a base runner who has taken too much of a lead from the base and is picked off for an out.

caught looking a batter called out on strikes.

cellar commonly used term for last place.

chalk the white powder used to mark lines and boxes in the playing field. Lime is also used.

change-up a ball thrown to resemble a fastball but that actually moves slowly, used to throw off a batter's timing. Also, any slow ball thrown after a number of successive fastballs, to damage a batter's timing.

check swing a half swing; a partial swing not counted as a strike because the wrists weren't broken.

cheese slang for a fastball. Also known as cheddar.

choke to perform badly in a critical situation. Also, to choke in the clutch.

choke up on the bat to place the hands high up on the handle of the bat to achieve greater control of the swing.

chop a quick, downward swing that usually results in a grounder.

chopper a hit ball that strikes the ground then bounces high.

circus catch a spectacular or acrobatic catch.

clean the bases to get a hit that drives all men on base safely home.

cleanup position in a batting lineup, the fourth batter, who is usually the best batter. The fourth batting position is the one most likely to produce runs.

closer the closing relieving pitcher; the pitcher intended to end the game.

clothesline a line drive to the outfield.

clubhouse collective term for a team's locker room, showers, lounge, and manager's office.

clutch a critical situation.

clutch hitter a player who can be counted on for producing a hit in clutch situations. A player who doesn't choke.

coaches' boxes the 5-foot by 20-foot rectangles where the coaches stand, to the right of first base and to the left of third base.

corked bat a bat whose barrel has been illegally hollowed out and filled with cork or rubber to facilitate hitting the ball further.

curveball a ball pitched with a high degree of spin, causing it to drop or curve suddenly as it nears the plate.

cut ball a ball that has been deeply scratched or nicked, giving it unusual dynamics when pitched.

daisy clipper/daisy cutter a sharply hit ground ball that skims over the grass.

deer slang term for a fast base runner.

designated hitter a 10th player designated to hit in place of the pitcher, but only in the American League. In the National League, the pitchers hit for themselves.

doctor to alter illegally a baseball with nicks, scratches, abrasions, or moisture or to alter illegally a baseball bat by filling it with cork or rubber.

donut the heavy, donutlike weight slipped over a bat to aid a batter in warming up.

double play occurs when the fielders produce two outs with one play.

down the alley a fastball pitched through the middle of the strike zone.

downtown said of a home run's destination, particularly an out-of-the-park home run.

draft the drawing of players from high schools, colleges, minor leagues, and free agents.

drag bunt a slow-rolling bunt hit down the first-base line.

dribbler a slow-moving ground ball.

dugout the enclosed bench area of either team.

dypsydo slang for a slow curveball.

earned run average the average number of runs a pitcher gives up per nine innings, a statistic of his overall performance.

emery ball a baseball that has been illegally scuffed by an emery board or other abrasive object.

English the spin imparted on some pitched balls.

error a fielding misplay that allows the offensive team to advance to a base.

fan to strike out or to strike someone out.

farm system the network of minor leagues from which the Major League draws players.

fastball a very fast pitched ball with a straight trajectory.

finesse pitcher a pitcher who utilizes a variety of clever pitches rather than speed to strike out batters.

fingering the proper placement of the fingers on the ball (especially in relation to the seams) to execute such pitches as curveballs, knuckleballls, and sliders.

fireballer a pitcher particularly adept at throwing fastballs.

$5 ride in a Yellow Cab slang phrase for a home run, especially one hit out of the ball park.

flat-footed slang term referring to being caught off-guard or unprepared.

fork ball a downward-breaking pitch thrown with the index finger and middle finger spread far apart.

foul ball a ball hit out of play.

four-bagger slang for a home run.

free agent a professional player who is not under contract and is free to negotiate with any team.

fungo bazooka an apparatus that automatically shoots balls into the air for fielding practice.

goat nickname for a player who makes a game-losing mistake.

goat's beard the small, protective flap hanging down from the chin of a catcher's or umpire's mask.

go down looking to strike out on a called third strike.

go down swinging to strike out by swinging the bat and missing.

go downtown to hit a home run.

go signal a signal given from a coach to a player to steal a base, to continue advancing around the bases, or to swing at the next pitch. Also known as the green light.

grand slam a home run hit with the bases loaded.

greaseball a baseball illegally altered with Vaseline, hair tonic, lard, or other substance to change its dynamics when pitched.

ground rule double an automatic two-base hit awarded whenever a hit ball lands in fair territory and then bounces out-of-play into the stands.

gun a powerful throwing arm.

gun down to throw out a base runner.

hesitation pitch a pitch in which the pitcher pauses momentarily after his windup in order to throw off the batter's timing.

home whites the home team's traditional uniforms.

horsehide slang for the baseball.

hot corner said of third base because balls are hit sharply there.

hot stove league whimsical name for any group of men who discuss, debate, and gossip about baseball during the off-season.

hummer slang for a fastball.

infield fly rule an automatic out called by an umpire when an infield pop fly is hit with two or more men on base and less than two outs. The automatic out prevents a fielder from intentionally dropping the ball in order to set up an unfair, double-play force situation.

inning one of nine rounds of play in which each team comes to bat once and is allowed three outs.

intentional walk deliberately throwing four balls outside the strike zone to intentionally walk a feared batter in order to pitch to a less talented batter. Intentional walks are also given in order to set up force plays.

knuckleball a ball held against the knuckles or fingernails and pitched without spin to make it more readily affected by wind and air currents.

laugher a game dominated by a team to a ludicrous degree.

loft one to hit a high fly ball.

lollipop slang for a slow or very easy pitch to hit.

lumber slang for the bat or bats.

minors the minor leagues

moon shot slang for a long home run.

mustard velocity. A good fastball has a lot of mustard on it.

MVP abbreviation for most valuable player.

no-hitter a game in which a pitcher does not give up a hit to the opposing side.

no pepper the stenciled signs found in many ball parks prohibiting pepper games—the infield batting and fielding drill involving several players and frequently damaging the playing field.

nubber a weak infield hit.

off-speed pitch any pitch slower than a fastball; a slow pitch.

on-deck batter the next player scheduled to bat after the batter at the plate.

opposite-field hitter a batter who frequently hits a ball into the field opposite from the side he bats from, indicative of a late swing.

palm ball a ball held between the thumb and palm and thrown offspeed [with a pushing motion].

pennant title of a league championship.

pennant race race for the championship.

perfect game a game in which a pitcher gives up zero hits to the opposing team.

pinch hit to bat in place of another player.

pinch hitter a replacement batter usually a better hitter than the one he replaces.

pinch runner a replacement runner, one who runs considerably faster than the man he replaces.

pine tar pine resin substance used on the batter's hands to improve grip on the bat.

pine tar ball a baseball illegally doctored with pine tar.

pitch around a batter frustrating a batter by pitching the ball outside, inside, low, high, and generally out of comfortable swinging range, a method of giving an intentional walk but with a chance of a strikeout.

pitcher's duel a pitcher-dominated game in which no or few hits are made by either team.

pitchout in a potential base-stealing situation, a pitch purposefully thrown high and outside to put the catcher in perfect position for throwing out a base stealer.

place hitter a hitter adept at hitting the ball in any direction he desires.

pop up a high flyball hit over the infield.

pull the ball to swing at the ball early so that it is hit to the same side of the field batted from.

quail a pop fly that drops in safely for a hit. Also known as a dying quail.

RBI runs batted in.

relief pitcher a pitcher who replaces the starting pitcher or another relief pitcher.

ride the bench/pine sit out play until called in to substitute for another player.

rifle a powerful throwing arm.

rip one to hit the ball hard.

road grays traditionally, the uniforms used when a team is playing an away or road game.

rookie a first-season or first-year player.

rope a line drive.

roster the list of active players on a team.

Rotisserie League Baseball a game of imagination and statistics in which enthusiasts draft players and monitor their statistics throughout the season to determine the best team overall.

rounders one of the old British games that baseball is descended from.

rubber the 6-inch by 24-inch rubber plate set on top of the pitcher's mound that must be toed or touched during an actual pitch.

rubbing mud the commercial mud (Lena Blackburne Rubbing Mud) used to rub the gloss off of new baseballs.

sacrifice any hit that gets the batter out but advances a teammate to the next base or home.

scout a person who scouts schools and minor leagues for up-and-coming players.

scouting report a written evaluation of an up-and-coming player in school or in a minor league.

screwball a pitch that curves inside instead of outside. Also known as a reverse curve.

scuffed ball an illegally doctored ball.

seventh-inning stretch the old custom of stadium fans standing and stretching their legs in the seventh inning.

shag flies to practice catching fly balls.

shake off a sign a pitcher's shake of the head in refusing to deliver a pitch suggested by the catcher's signals.

shoestring catch to catch a fly ball at shoe level.

shortstop the infield player's position between second and third base.

shotgun slang for a powerful throwing arm.

shutout a game in which the losing team fails to score any runs.

sidearm a type of pitch delivered in a manner between underhanded and overhanded.

sign one of several types of secret signals conveyed by catchers and coaches to players on the field or up at bat.

sign stealing deciphering an opposing team's signals and using them to advantage.

sinker a pitch thrown with a roll of the wrist, causing the ball to dip or sink suddenly at the plate.

sinking fastball a fastball that acts like a sinker.

6-4-3 a double play started by the shortstop (6), who throws the ball to the second baseman (4), who completes the play by throwing to the first baseman (3).

600 home run club an exclusive hitter's club with only three members, Hank Aaron, Babe Ruth, and Willie Mays.

six o'clock hitter a term describing a player who bats well in practice but performs poorly in a game.

slider a lightly spinning curveball that breaks suddenly but with less curve than a standard curveball.

slump a period in which a player or team plays poorly.

smoke major velocity, as in a smoking fastball.

smoker a fastball.

southpaw a left-handed player, but usually referring to a pitcher.

speed gun an electronic apparatus used to measure the speed of pitched balls.

spitball a ball illegally altered with spit or moisture in order to change its pitching dynamics.

split-fingered fastball a fastball pitched like a forkball and that sinks suddenly.

squibber a weakly hit ball that passes or drops in for a base hit.

standup double/triple a hit that allows a batter enough time to reach second or third base without having to slide.

steal to advance safely to the next base by a surprise run.

stopper a team's best starting or relief pitcher.

switch hitter a player adept at hitting either left-handed or right-handed.

Texas Leaguer a weakly hit ball that manages to get over the infielders' heads for a base hit.

3-6-3 a doubleplay begun by the first baseman (3), who throws the ball to the shortstop (6), who throws back to the first baseman.

throw smoke to throw a fastball; also blow smoke.

triple play getting three outs in one play, a rarity.

unearned run a run scored but not charged to a pitcher's earned run average due to circumstances beyond his control, such as an error.

vaseline ball a ball illegally doctored with vaseline.

warning track the dirt track skirting the length of the outfield wall or fence; it acts as a warning to help prevent players from accidently colliding with the wall when attempting to field a ball.

whiff to strikeout.

BASKETBALL

air ball a ball so poorly shot it misses hitting either the backboard or the rim.

alley-oop a shot in which the ball is caught in midair and slam-dunked before the player's feet touches the floor.

assist a pass by one player to another that results in a score.

backboard the board or fiberglass structure that holds the hoop and net, today referred to as the "glass."

backcourt the defense's forecourt, a definition that changes with possession of the ball.

backcourt foul a foul committed by an offensive player while in his backcourt.

backcourt violation a violation levied on a team that fails to move the ball out of its backcourt within 10 seconds after gaining possession, resulting in loss of possession.

back-door play when an offensive player under the basket darts behind a defender to receive a pass.

bank shot a shot caromed off the backboard and into the basket.

baseline the short boundary lines at the ends of the court behind the baskets.

blocking foul a defensive player moving illegally into the path of an offensive player.

body fake using body language to fake a defender into moving in the opposite direction you wish to go with the ball.

bomb a shot taken from long range.

box out maneuvering in front of a defender to gain the best position for a rebound.

brick a poor shot, usually an airball.

bucket a scored basket.

center circle the circle at midcourt used for the center jump at the start of a game.

charging a personal foul violation given to an offensive player who runs into a defender who has established position (is standing still when hit).

cold term used to describe a player who has missed several shots in a short period of time.

D popular term for "defense."

crashing the boards slang for aggressive rebounding.

double dribble a violation in which a player with the ball starts a dribble, stops and holds the ball, then starts a dribble again and moves his feet.

double team two defensive players guarding one offensive player.

downtown shooting from long range.

draw a foul a player deliberately positioning himself to be fouled in order to be awarded a free throw.

dribble to stand, walk, or run while bouncing the ball on the floor.

driving the lane driving quickly through the free-throw lane for a closeup shot.

dunk slam-dunking the ball through the hoop. Also known as a stuff or a jam.

fallaway a shot taken while falling or fading back away from a defender to get a clear path to the basket.

fast break getting downcourt at a dead run to score a basket before defenders can get back to cover.

feed passing the ball to a player in shooting position.

field goal percentage ratio of shots taken to shots scored.

forced shot a shot taken in a rush, when in poor position or when off-balance.

forwards the two players who usually cover the corner areas on either side of the pivot man.

foul out for a player to commit more fouls than are allowed and be forced to leave the game.

free throw a free shot taken at the free-throw line, awarded to a player who has been fouled.

free-throw lane 19-foot by 16-foot painted lane running from the free-throw line to the end line, also known as the 3-second area.

free-throw line the line where a fouled player takes a free shot, 15 feet in front of the basket.

free-throw percentage ratio of free throws taken by a player to free throws made or scored.

front court the area closest to the basket of the offensive team.

front-court men the two forwards and center.

full-court press close and aggressive guarding by the defense all over the court from the time the ball is inbounded.

goaltending a defensive player blocking a shot near the basket as the ball in flight is descending a violation in which a basket is automatically scored to the offensive team.

guards the positions played by smaller players skilled in ballhandling and dribbling; they generally cover the perimeter of the offensive and defensive zones.

hack hitting an opponent's arm with the hand, a foul violation.

Hail Mary a shot that requires a prayer and the guidance of God to go in the basket. Also known as "throwing up a prayer."

hang time the time a player making a jump shot "hangs" in the air, related to leaping ability.

hook shot a one-handed, over-the-head arc shot. Also called skyhook.

hot hand said of a player on a hot shooting streak.

intentional foul a foul committed intentionally in order to stop the game clock, usually in the closing seconds of a game.

jump ball at the start of a game or when two opposing players wrestle over the ball, a procedure that determines possession: tossing the ball up and having the opposing players jump for it and tap it to a teammate.

jump shot a shot taken while jumping.

layup the closest and easiest shot, made by a player who has moved under the rim.

offensive foul a foul committed by a member of the team with the ball.

one-and-one in amateur ball, a bonus shot given if the first free throw goes in. In the NBA, the second shot is always taken.

outlet pass a long, downcourt pass.

palming turning the ball over in the palm while dribbling, a violation giving possession to the other team.

penalty situation a situation in which free throws will be awarded to a fouled player because a team has used up its allowable fouls for the quarter.

penetration penetrating through defenders to the basket.

percentage shot a shot, usually at close range, that has a high probability of going in.

personal foul illegal physical contact, including hacking, charging, holding, and fighting.

pick a screen created when an offensive player stands still and intentionally blocks the path of a defender so a teammate can get open for a pass or a shot.

pick and roll moving off a pick and running toward the basket for a pass, a method of eluding a defender.

pivot pivoting on one foot to avoid a traveling violation.

point guard a guard who directs the offense.

post the pivot position: the high post is near the foul line; the low post is near the basket.

power forward a forward particulaly adept at rebounding and defense.

pullup driving toward the basket, stopping suddenly, and taking a jump shot.

pump fake faking a shot to the basket (double-pump fake: pumping the arms twice in faking a shot).

rebound getting possession of the ball off the backboard.

reverse dunk dunking the ball from a backwards position.

run and gun a quick-moving, quick-shooting game strategy.

scoop shot an underhand shot taken while running close to the basket.

screen when a player with the ball "hides" behind a teammate and takes an uncontested shot.

shot clock the clock that displays the time left for the offensive team to take a shot, 24 seconds with each new possession.

sixth man the first substitute player off the bench.

slam dunk same as a dunk.

stutter step a swiftly switching foot movement used to fake an opponent.

swish a perfect shot that enters the net without touching the rim.

team foul a foul charged to a team's allowance (four per period in the NBA).

10-second rule the offensive team must bring the ball up over the midcourt line within 10 seconds or lose possession.

3-second violation when an offensive player stays within the free-throw lane for more than 3 consecutive seconds.

trap double-teaming a player with the ball in an attempt to make a steal.

traveling taking more than two steps without dribbling the ball. Also known as a walk.

24-second rule requires a team to shoot within 24 seconds after gaining possession of the ball.

walking traveling.

zone defense defenders guarding an area or zone instead of man-to-man.

BOWLING

address position the starting stance before the approach and delivery.

anchor the best bowler on a team; he or she usually bowls last.

apple the ball.

approach the runway or prerelease area 15 feet in front of the foul line.

arrows guide marks near the foul line used for aiming the release of a ball.

baby split a 2-7 or 3-10 split.

backswing the movement of the arm behind the back prior to release.

backup a ball that curves in the opposite direction of a hook, specifically right for right-handers and left for left-handers.

balk to cross the foul line without releasing the ball.

ball return track the channel in which balls are rolled back to the rack.

barmaid a pin hidden from sight behind another pin. Also known as one in the dark, sleeper.

bed the surface of the lane from the foul line to the pit.

bedposts the 7-10 split. Also known as goalposts, fenceposts, mule ears.

belly the widest portion of a pin.

bellying releasing a ball far to the right to compensate for a lane that hooks too strongly.

big ears a split leaving the 4, 6, 7, and 10. Also known as the big four, double pinochle.

blank a bowling ball without holes.

blind score a predetermined score given to a team to cover an absent member.

blocking an illegally manufactured oil buildup in the middle of a lane that helps guide balls to the strike zone.

blow a rack to bowl a strike that leaves no deadwood.

bocci an Italian bowling game.

body English the contortionistic body language used by bowlers after a release in a vain attempt to "control" the ball.

bonus in tenpins, the extra points added to a score for making a spare or a strike.

bowling on the green lawn bowling.

bridge the space between holes in a bowling ball.

Brooklyn hitting the opposite pocket from the release hand, specifically the 1-2 pocket for right-handers and the 1-3 pocket for lefties. Also known as a crossover, Jersey.

bucket a 2, 4, 5, 8 spare for right-handers or a 3, 5, 6, 9 spare for lefties. Also known as a basket, bread basket.

bury to deliver the ball into a pocket, usually for a strike.

candlepin a cylindrical wooden pin 15¾ inches high. Also, the bowling game using these pins and small balls without holes, as distinguished from tenpins.

cheesecake a lane that tend to produce higher scores than others. Also known as pie alley.

cherry chopping off the front pin so that it fails to knock down any neighboring pins. Also known as pick a cherry, leave a cherry.

chop same as cherry.

Christmas tree a 3-7-10 split for right-handers or a 2-7-10 split for lefties.

Cincinnati an 8-10 split. Also known as a Cincy.

clean game a game without misses or splits.

conditioner lane oil.

convert to make a spare.

count the pinfall from the first ball of a frame following the frame in which a spare or strike has been made. The bonus points.

crank to impart a ball with rotation to make it hook.

creeper a slow-rolling ball.

curve a wide hook.

deadwood pins that have been knocked down and remain on the pin deck.

deck the portion of the lane the pins rest on; the pin deck.

deuce a score of 200.

dodo an illegally weighted ball.

double two strikes in a row.

double pinochle a 4-6-7-10 split. Same as big ears.

double wood two pins left standing, one behind the other.

dress the lane to oil a lane in preparation for a game.

duckpin a pin similar to a tenpin but shorter and squatter, used in the game of duckpins.

dump to release a ball with the fingers and thumb simultaneously in order to prevent it from hooking or curving.

Dutch 200 a game of 200 made with alternating spares and strikes.

English spin on the ball.

fast lane a lane in which the hooking action of balls is diminished.

fence posts same as bedposts.

field goal a shot that goes between split pins and misses everything.

fill the pinfall of one ball counted after a spare; the bonus.

fill the woodbox to throw a strike with the last ball of the game.

finger to snap the fingers upward when releasing to impart lift or spin on a ball.

foul to step on or over the foul line during delivery, an infraction resulting in the forfeiture of any pins knocked down.

foul line the line marking the end of the approach and beginning of the lane.

four horsemen a 1-2-4-7 or 1-3-6-10 leave.

frame one-tenth of a game; one inning or period of play in a game.

full hit a ball that hits the headpin too high and misses or barely touches the 2 or 3 pin behind.

full roller a spinning ball that hooks sharply into a pocket.

goalposts same as bedposts.

grandma's teeth a 7-8-10 or 7-9-10 split.

graveyard a lane that tends to yield low scores.

Greek church a 4-6-7-8-10 or 4-6-7-9-10 split.

grinder a delivery with a powerful hook or curve.

groove a worn track or rut in a lane caused by the impact of balls over an extended period of time.

gutter the channel on either side of a lane that catches poorly thrown balls.

gutter ball a ball that rolls into the gutter.

gutter shot a delivery down along a gutter that hooks or veers out as it reaches the pins.

half Worcester a 3-9 or 2-8 split.

handicap points added to the score of a player or team to make competition even.

hang a pin to miss knocking down a strike by one pin.

headpin the front or number 1 pin. May be called the kingpin in some usage.

high board a high or raised board in a lane that alters a ball's trajectory.

high hit a ball that hits the headpin straight-on.

high-low-jack a 1-7-10 split.

holding lane a lane that diminishes a ball's hooking action. Same as a fast alley, stiff alley.

hole a strike pocket.

hook a ball thrown with rotation that veers into a strike pocket.

inning a frame.

Jersey same as a Brooklyn.

kegler a bowler.

kegling another name for bowling.

kickbacks the side boards running parallel to the pit.

kingpin the central pin; the number 5 pin. In some usage the headpin may be called the kingpin.

lane the 60-foot alley between the foul line and the pit.

laying out the ball delivering the ball smoothly onto the lane without bounces.

leave the pins left standing after delivering the first ball in a frame.

lift snapping the fingers up when releasing to impart rotation on the ball.

line a 10-frame game.

loft a poor delivery in which the ball flies up out of the hand and bounces harshly onto the lane.

mark a spare or a strike.

mixer a well-thrown ball that produces a violent tumbling action among the pins. Also known as a sweeper.

mother-in-law the 7 pin.

move in to start the approach in a center position.

move out to start the approach from a corner position.

mule ears the 7-10 split. Same as bedposts.

nosedive a ball that hits the headpin straight-on.

one in the dark same as a barmaid.

open frame a frame without a spare or a strike.

PBA Professional Bowlers Association.

picket fence a 1-2-4-7 or 1-3-6-10 leave.

pie alley same as cheesecake.

pin deck same as deck.

pinfall the pins that are knocked down by a ball, or all the pins knocked over in a single frame.

pinsetter the apparatus that sets the pins and resets the pins on the deck.

pit the sunken area below the end of a lane, where balls and knocked-down pins are collected.

pocket the area most likely to yield a strike when hit with the ball; for right-handers, this is between the 1 and 3 pins; for lefties, the 1 and 2; the strike pocket.

power player a player who relies more on powerful deliveries to knock down pins rather than on finesse.

pumpkin a weakly thrown ball with little or no hooking action.

rack a setup of 10 pins.

railroad a split.

read the lane to roll practice balls in order to determine a lane's quirks or imperfections.

ringing 8 the 8 pin left standing alone.

rob the cradle to knock down only one pin in a baby split.

roundhouse a wide curving trajectory.

running lane a lane in which hooks can easily be made into the pocket. Also known as a slow lane.

scratch a player's score without any handicap added in. Also, a nonhandicap game.

setup same as a rack.

short pin a pin that is knocked down but that fails to knock down any of its neighbors.

skittles a British bowling game in which a wooden ball or disk is used to knock down nine pins.

sleeper any pin hidden behind another pin.

slow lane same as running lane.

sour apple the 5-7 split.

spare 10 pins knocked down with two balls in a single frame.

split any combination of pins left standing with a gap or gaps between them.

spread eagle a split leaving the 2, 3, 4, 6, 7, and 10 pins.

strike 10 pins knocked down on the first ball rolled. Also, to carry a rack.

strike out to roll three strikes in a row in the last frame of a game.

strike pocket same as pocket.

string one game; 10 frames.

sweep bar the bar apparatus that collects fallen pins from the deck.

sweeper same as mixer.

tenpins the modern game of bowling, characterized by its large balls with drilled holes and its wide-bottomed pins, as distinguished from candlepin.

300 game a game with 12 consecutive strikes for a score of 300.

wood the pins.

Woolworth a split leaving the 5-10.

Worcester a split leaving everything but the 1 and 5.

BOXING

apron the perimeter of the ring floor extending outside of the ropes.

arm puncher a boxer who does not put the weight of his body behind his punches.

babyweight the weight division below lightweight.

bagged fight a fixed fight.

bantamweight the weight division with a 118-pound limit.

below the belt an illegal punch below the belt; it results in a loss of points.

bob and weave to move the head and upper body up and down and back and forth to elude punches.

bolo punch an exaggerated form of the uppercut, having a swing that begins below the hip.

bout a match.

breadbasket slang for the abdomen.

break to pull away from a clinch.

butt to butt the opponent with the top of the head; a foul if intentional.

canvas the floor of the ring.

cauliflower ear a swollen, deformed ear resembling cauliflower, caused by repeated blows.

clinch to hold or embrace the opponent either from exhaustion or to avoid being hit.

cold cock to knock someone out with one punch.

combination a quick succession of varied punches.

cornerman the assistant or trainer that comes into the ring at the end of a round to advise his fighter. See CUT MAN.

crazy bag a small, leather punching bag strung with elastic cords from floor to ceiling, used to develop timing. Also known as a double-end bag.

cross a punch thrown across the opponent's punch.

cruiserweight weight division with a 190-pound limit; found in the WBC only.

cut man a cornerman responsible for stopping the flow of blood from a fighter's cuts.

dance to use footwork to elude an opponent.

decision a win awarded on the basis of points, as distinguished from a knockout.

double up to throw two punches in quick succession.

draw a bout that ends in a tie.

drop one's guard to momentarily drop one's guard hand, leaving the jaw open and vulnerable to a punch.

featherweight weight division with a 126-pound limit.

feint to fake a move in order to deceive the opponent.

fistic concerning boxing.

flyweight weight division with a 112-pound limit.

footwork moving the feet to elude an opponent's punches.

foul an illegal punch, for example, one behind the head or below the belt.

glass jaw a boxer who is easily knocked unconscious.

go the distance to complete all rounds of a bout without being knocked out.

gouge to stick one's thumb into the eye of the opponent.

granite chin said of a boxer who is not easily knocked out.

guard the hand that guards the facial area.

handler trainer.

haymaker a powerful punch.

heavy bag a large, heavy punching bag suspended from the ceiling and used to develop strength.

heavyweight the weight division over 175 pounds.

heel to strike an opponent with the heel of the hand, a foul.

hook a circular punch thrown from the side.

jab a quick, straight punch.

kidney punch an illegal punch to the lower back or kidneys.

knockdown when a fighter is knocked to the canvas; he must get up within 10 seconds or lose the bout.

knockout when a fighter is knocked unconscious or fails to get up from a knockdown within 10 seconds, thus losing the bout. Also known as a KO.

lead the jabbing hand.

light heavyweight weight division with a 175-pound limit.

lightweight weight division with a 135-pound limit.

low blow same as below the belt.

mandatory eight count a rule in which a knocked-down boxer must wait at least 8 seconds before resuming the fight, a safety factor.

middleweight weight division with a 160-pound limit.

mix it up to exchange punches.

mouse a black eye.

neutral corner either of the two corners not used by the fighters and their cornermen; where a fighter must stand for the count after knocking down an opponent.

one-two punch a short left jab followed by a right cross.

on one's bicycle performing footwork.

over and under a head punch followed by a body punch.

overhand punch a punch that starts high and swings down on the opponent's head or upper body.

peanut bag a very small speed bag, used to develop reflexes and timing.

prizefighter a pro boxer.

pugilism the sport of boxing.

pugilist a boxer.

pull a punch to punch with only a portion of one's strength; to hold back.

punch-drunk dazed; mentally deficient or slow in speech due to blows to the head over an extended period.

put away to knock an opponent out.

rabbit punch an illegal blow to the back of the neck.

referee the official who oversees a match.

roadwork boxer's training term for long-distance running to build stamina.

roll with the punch to move one's head back with the thrust of a punch to lessen impact.

round in a pro bout, one 3-minute period.

roundhouse a broad or wide, sweeping hook.

shadow box to spar with an imaginary opponent.

shake the cobwebs to shake off a daze after being punched in the head.

slugfest an exchange of blows without regard to defense.

south of the border same as below the belt.

spar to practice boxing with a sparring partner.

sparring partner one who serves as a practice opponent.

speed bag a pear-shaped punching bag hung at eye-level that bounces back rapidly with each punch, used to develop speed.

split decision a decision in which one official has a scoring disagreement with the other two officials.

square circle another name for the boxing ring.

standing eight count a count of eight given by the referee to a stunned boxer who has fallen but is able to stand.

stick to jab.

sucker punch a surprise punch.

Sunday punch one's best punch.

take out to knock out an opponent.

tale of the tape the weight and measurements of the two boxers before the bout, and how they match up.

technical draw a bout that ends in a draw due to an accidental injury.

technical knockout the awarding of a win to a fighter when his opponent is injured, or unable, or too stunned to resume fighting. Also known as a TKO.

telegraph a punch to communicate unwittingly by body language to an opponent what the next punch will be.

throw in the towel to concede defeat by literally throwing in a towel from the fighter's corner.

thumb same as gouge.

TKO technical knockout.

under and over a punch to the body followed by a punch to the head.

uppercut a punch starting low and hooking straight up with bent elbow to the opponent's head.

WBA World Boxing Association.

WBC World Boxing Council.

weigh-in the inspection of weight before a bout to assure each opponent falls within the divisional weight limit.

welterweight weight division with a 147-pound limit.

BULLFIGHTING

banderilla a 24-inch-long, barbed dart stuck into the bull's neck or shoulder. Several banderillas are usually driven in to these areas to weaken the bull's neck muscles and therefore make it impossible for it to lift its head.

burladero a wooden shelter located near a wall a matador can run into and hide behind to escape a charging bull.

capework the technique of drawing the bull close by waving the cape.

cuadrilla a team that assists the bullfighter in the ring.

gore to peirce with the horn of the bull.

matador the bullfighter.

muleta the red cloth waved to entice the bull into charging.

pass a passing of the bull past the matador's cape or muleta.

pic a picador's lance.

picador one of the cuadrilla on horseback who prods the bull in the neck with a lance.

veronica a pass in which the matador stands still and waves the bull by him with the cape.

CANOEING (See RIVERS AND STREAMS for additional descriptions.)

amidships the middle of a canoe.

aft toward the back of the canoe.

astern behind the canoe.

bailer a scoop used for bailing water.

beam width of a canoe at its widest point.

blade the paddle end of an oar.

bow front of the canoe.

bowman the paddler or passenger occupying the front.

bow stroke the basic paddle stroke made by the bowman to propel the canoe forward with no effort to steer.

broadside either side of a canoe.

Canadian stroke stroke originated by the Canadian Indians in which the sternman passes the paddle blade through the water at a slight angle and finishes with a quick outward stroke, used to avoid fatigue on long excursions.

draw the depth of water displaced by a canoe when floating, also known as the draft.

duffle the apparel and equipment of a canoeist.

freeboard the distance from the waterline to the gunwales.

grip top end of a paddle.

gunwales pronounced "gunnels;" the upper edges of the sides of a canoe.

haystacks standing waves that form at the bottom of rapids wherever the current is decelerating.

hummock a flow of current that forms a "hump" over a rock.

J stroke a steering stroke with a finishing twist made by the sternman.

jam stroke a stroke that brakes the forward motion of a canoe by plunging the blade straight down into the water and holding it.

keel narrow strip running along the underside of a canoe to prevent sideslipping in wind or current; a wider version is known as a shoe or river keel.

lining an alternative to portaging, where a rope is attached to bow and stern to guide the canoe around hazards and obstructions from the safety of shore.

painter a line used to tie or tow a canoe.

pillow a rounded rock partially or fully concealed beneath black water.

port the left side of a canoe facing forward.

portaging carrying a canoe over land between two bodies of water.

ribs skeletal bracketing running between gunwales.

riffles shallow stream with small ripples caused by numerous submerged rocks or cobbles.

rips river water with waves larger than riffles but smaller than rapids.

rooster a river wave with a crest that turns back on itself, sometimes swamping canoes. Also known as a curler.

souse hole violent foamy turbulence where water plunges over boulders, sucks air along with it, and creates dangerous and unpredictable hydraulic properties. Also known as a white eddy.

sponsons air chambers built into the gunwales running the length of a canoe.

starboard the right side of a canoe facing forward.

sternman the paddler at the rear of the canoe.

stern rudder stroke placing the paddle astern or alongside of a canoe and using it as a rudder, known as the lazy man's way to steer.

tongue a smooth passage of black water between two rocks.

yaw to deviate from course or sway, caused by wind or current.

yoke a frame fitting anchored at the gunwales allowing a canoe to be shouldered while carried upside down.

CURLING

besom the broom used for sweeping the ice clean.

biter a stone just touching the outer ring of the house.

bonspiel a curling tournament.

broom same as a besom.

build a house to align the stones in an advantageous position so that they protect each other.

button the first circle out from the center of the house.

chap and lie the delivery of a stone that knocks out an opponent's stone and takes its place.

close a port to fill a gap between two stones.

curling stone a polished, circular stone about 12 inches in diameter, weighing 42 to 44 pounds, and having a removable handle on top.

heavy ice rough ice that slows the momentum of a thrown stone.

hog a stone that fails to clear the far hog line.

hog line the line 7 yards in front of the tee past which a stone must come to rest or be removed from play.

house a 12-foot circular area at each end of a rink, where the stones are delivered.

pebble to sprinkle hot water on the ice to create bumps and increase friction for better control of the stones.

rink the 138-foot by 14-foot playing area having a series of concentric rings (house) at each end where the stones are delivered.

rock a curling stone.

shot rock the stone lying nearest the center of the house.

skip the captain of a curling team.

sooping sweeping of the ice to clear it from any debris.

sweep sooping.

take-out knocking an opponent's stone out of play.

tee the circular area inside the house.

wick to carom off another stone.

DIVING

armstand dive any dive begun with the diver standing on his or her hands at the edge of the diving board.

backflip a backward somersault.

back header a backwards dive in which the head hits the water first.

back jackknife a board-facing dive in the jackknife position.

backward dive a dive in which the diver faces the board, leaps off, turns backward, and hits the water feet first. Also, a dive in which the diver faces away from the board and enters the water headfirst.

backward somersault a dive started facing the board, followed by a backward somersault.

degree of difficulty in competition, the degree of difficulty of a dive and its factoring in the final score.

diving well the deep end of a pool.

full gainer a reverse dive with a somersault.

half gainer a backflip ending headfirst and facing the board.

jackknife a dive in which the body describes the positioning of a closing and opening jackknife, with the body doubled over and hands touching the ankles followed by an extension straight into the water.

springboard a diving board.

swan dive a dive in which the head is tilted back and the arms extended out to the sides.

tuck a diving position in which the legs are tucked or folded up into the chest.

twist any twisting dive.

FENCING

à droite against the right.

à gauche against the left.

aids the three balancing fingers of the weapon hand.

appel a beat or stamp of the foot used to fake an opponent into action.

balestra a short, forward jump followed by a lunge.

beat a sharp blow to the opponent's blade.

bind to take an opponent's blade from a high line diagonally to a low line, or vice versa.

bout one match or fight.

breaking ground backing up a step; retreating.

break time an intentional pause taken between movements to throw off an opponent's timing.

cadence the rhythm in which movements are made.

ceding a parry a yielding parry characterized by a return to the guard position, used as a defense against a taking of the blade.

change of engagement engaging the opponent's blade in a new line.

circular parry a circular blade movement used to pick up an opponent's blade and move it. Also known as a counter parry.

compound attack an offensive action composed of one or more feints.

corps-à-corps body contact between fencers.

coulé a graze made down the opponent's blade.

coup double a double hit.

coupé "cut-over;" passing over the opponent's blade.

covered position a defensive position taken to protect from a direct line or thrust of attack.

croisé taking of an opponent's blade by using the forte to force the blade down.

cut to hit with the side of a saber blade to score.

derobement evading the opponent's attempt to take the blade.

development an arm extension and lunge.

disengage to pass the blade under an opponent's blade.

electric fencing fencing in which points are registered by an electric apparatus.

engagement when opposing blades are in contact with one another.

épée a short dueling weapon similar to a foil but with a fluted blade and a larger guard. Also, the style of fencing used with an epee.

feint a fake attack or movement made to deceive an opponent.

fencing jacket a lined, protective jacket worn by fencers.

flèche a running attack with arm extended.

foible the outer portion and tip of a fencing weapon, as distinguished from the forte.

foil a fencing sword with a thin blade and cup guard.

forte the inner portion of a blade, nearest the grip, as distinguished from the foible.

froissement a deflecting attack made on an opponent's blade.

gauntlet a protective glove with flaring cuff.

guard the protective cup or disk near the grip of a fencing weapon.

high lines target areas located above the weapon hand.

hit to hit the opponent with the point (or with an edge of a saber) to score.

in quartata a step taken to the side to avoid being hit with the opponent's blade.

invitation opening up a vulnerable area to encourage an opponent to make an attack.

judge the director who, with the assistance of judges, makes rulings on hits and nonhits.

jury the president (director) and judges that officiate a fencing bout.

lunge a thrusting attack forward.

making ground advancing.

measure the distance from which a fencer can make a hit with a full lunge; the measure varies with the fencer's body size.

molinello a saber cut made with a full swing of the forearm instead of a less powerful wrist cut.

on guard a stance of balance and readiness, characterized by the feet set apart at right angles, the hips faced three-fourths to the front, both knees bent, and both arms raised in a defensive position.

orthopaedic grip a sword grip providing greater control than the standard handle or "French" grip.

parry to deflect the opponent's attacking sword.

passata sotto ducking under an attacking sword while simultaneously thrusting one's blade at the opponent.

piste the area in which a bout is held.

prise de fer a taking of the blade.

pronation the hand position with the knuckles facing up.

reassemblement taking a half step back and standing erect.

redoublement a renewal of attack while lunging.

reprise a renewal of attack following an on guard position.

riposte offensive moves taken by a fencer who has successfully parried.

saber a dueling sword similar to a foil but having a wraparound guard and a wider, flatter blade that scores points with the point and with the cutting blade itself. The style of fencing used with sabers.

sabreur a fencer who uses a saber.

stop hit countering offensive action with offensive action; attacking an attack.

straight thrust a straight thrust of the weapon into a target area.

supination hand position with the palm upward.

taking the blade taking possession of an opponent's blade; the engagement, bind, croisé, and envelopment.

touché touched.

trompement deceiving the opponent's parry or defense.

underplastron a protective undergarment worn over the upper sword arm and chest.

FOOTBALL

air it out to throw a long pass.

armchair quarterback a know-it-all fan who criticizes play from the stands or while watching a game on TV.

arm tackle to tackle solely with the arm or arms.

audible a play called verbally at the line of scrimmage, often to change a planned play made in a huddle.

back one who plays in the backfield, either offensively or defensively.

backfield the backs.

backfield in motion illegal motion of one or more players in the backfield prior to the snap.

back judge the downfield judge who watches for clips, pass interference, and out-of-bounds plays.

backpedal to run backward, as a quarterback.

Big Ben same as a Hail Mary.

birdcage the protective face bars on a helmet.

blind side the side unseen by the quarterback when in position to pass and the side from which most quarterback tackles occur. A blind-side tackle.

blitz a surprise rush by more than the usual number of defenders toward the quarterback.

body block to throw oneself sidelong into an opponent to block his path.

bomb a very long pass.

bootleg a play in which the quarterback fakes a handoff then runs in the opposite direction with the ball hidden behind his hip.

box-and-chain crew the sideline crew responsible for marking the line of scrimmage with the down box and 10-yard measuring chain. Also known as the chain gang.

break a tackle to break free from a tackle and continue running.

broken play a play that goes awry, usually due to miscommunication. Also known as a busted play.

bullet a powerfully thrown line-drive pass.

butt block to illegally tackle or block an opponent by driving or butting one's helmet into his body.

carry to run with the ball.

center in the offensive line, the center player who snaps the ball to the quarterback to start play.

chain gang same as box and chain crew.

chicken-fight a series of standing blocks made in quick succession against an opponent to keep him away from the quarterback.

chuck to intentionally bump the receiver as he begins his run from the line of scrimmage.

circle pattern a circular pattern run by a receiver to elude a defender.

circus catch any acrobatic or spectacular catch.

cleats football shoes with projections for traction on the soles. Also, the projections themselves.

clipping illegally hitting an opponent without the ball from behind, a foul resulting in a 15-yard penalty.

clothesline to tackle by swinging an arm stiffly into an opponent's head or neck, a foul resulting in a 15-yard penalty.

color commentator a radio or TV sports announcer who analyzes the plays and discusses and criticizes strategy.

comeback a play in which the receiver runs a straight pattern then turns abruptly back toward the quarterback for a pass.

completion a completed forward pass.

conversion to kick the ball through the goalposts for one extra point after a touchdown.

corner short for cornerback.

cornerback one of two defensive backs positioned at the outside end positions to cover sweep runners and wide receivers for passes.

corner blitz a blitz on the quarterback by one or both cornerbacks.

cross pattern a pass pattern in which two wide receivers run downfield along opposite sidelines then turn and cross paths.

cut to change direction abruptly.

decline a penalty the option of an offended team to refuse a penalty award when it is not advantageous.

defensive back a cornerback, safety, or other player positioned behind the linebackers who defends against passes and running plays.

defensive end one of two defensive players positioned on the end of the line of scrimmage who rushes the quarterback or defends against sweep plays.

defensive tackle one of two players positioned next to, and inside of, a defensive end on the line of scrimmage.

defensive unit players who specialize in defense.

delay of game an infraction resulting in a 5-yard penalty.

dime defense a defense using six backs.

double reverse a play in which a back hands the ball off to a teammate running in the opposite direction who in turn hands off to another teammate running in the original direction.

down the point when play is stopped or the ball is declared dead. Also, one of four chances to advance the ball 10 yards with each possession.

draw play a play in which the quarterback backpedals as if to pass and therefore draw a rush by the defense, but instead hands off to a back who runs through the gap left open by the rushing defenders.

drive a series of plays advancing a team downfield.

duck a slow-floating pass that is easy to intercept. Also known as a dying quail.

eat the ball term referring to a quarterback who decides it is safer to let himself be tackled in a play than risk being intercepted by defenders who are covering the receivers closely.

eligible receivers the six players on the offensive team that are eligible to receive a forward pass, specifically the backs and the two ends.

encroachment having a part of one's body over the line of scrimmage just prior to the snap, an infraction resulting in a 5-yard penalty.

end run a play in which the ballcarrier runs around one end of the line.

ends the two players positioned at either end of the line of scrimmage.

end zone the goal zone at either end of the field.

extra point after a touchdown, one extra point added for successfully kicking the ball through the goalposts.

face mask same as bird cage. Also, an infraction in which an opponent is grabbed or tackled by the face mask, a 5- to 15-yard penalty.

fair catch a signal to the officials that the ball receiver wishes to catch the ball without being tackled and is therefore marking the ball down without advancing it.

field goal 3 points scored by kicking the ball through the goalposts.

first and 10 first down and 10 yards to go to reach another first down.

flag a diagonal pass pattern in which the receiver runs downfield and cuts diagonally toward a corner of the end zone. Also, the flag thrown by an official to signal an infraction.

flak jacket a padded, rib-protecting jacket worn like a vest.

flanker flare a short flip pass to a back still in the backfield and moving toward the sideline.

flea-flicker a lateral or a handoff followed by a surprise pass. Also, a pass followed by a lateral.

fly pattern a pass pattern in which the intended receiver runs at top speed straight downfield.

formation the alignment of the defense or offense at the line of scrimmage.

free safety a defensive back positioned well behind the line of scrimmage who is responsible for covering midfield for running plays or passes but who is "free" to assist other defenders in covering receivers.

front line the players aligned along the line of scrimmage.

fullback an offensive back who plays behind the quarterback and blocks or carries the ball on handoffs. A powerful but relatively slow-moving running back.

fumble to drop the ball.

gang tackle to tackle the ballcarrier with more than one tackler.

goal line the line marking the beginning of the end zone, over which the ball must be carried or passed to a teammate for a touchdown.

goalposts the u-shaped upright standing on either endzone and through which goals are kicked.

gridiron a football field.

ground the ball to intentionally throw the ball to the ground or out of bounds to avoid being tackled for a loss of yardage behind the line of scrimmage, an infraction resulting in a 10-yard penalty and a loss of a down.

guards the two offensive linemen who flank the center and block.

Hail Mary a long pass, usually into the end zone, that requires "divine intervention" to be completed. Also known as "throwing up a prayer."

halfback the offensive player positioned in the backfield who acts as a receiver or ball carrier, more commonly known as a running back.

hang time the elapsed time a kicked or thrown ball is suspended in the air.

hike a command to snap the ball to begin play.

hitch a pass pattern in which the receiver runs downfield, cuts abruptly to the outside for a pass.

hitch and go a pass pattern in which a receiver fakes a hitch, then continues straight downfield for a pass.

huddle the huddling together or meeting of players in which plays are planned between downs.

I formation an offensive formation in which the tailback, halfback, and fullback form a line behind the quarterback.

illegal motion illegal motion of a player set on the line of scrimmage just prior to the snap.

incompletion a pass not caught.

ineligible receiver see eligible receiver.

interception a passed ball intended for an offensive receiver but caught by the defense, resulting in an automatic exchange of possession.

kicking team a team's members who specialize in executing punts, field goals, and extra points.

late hit tackling or running into an opponent after the ball has been whistled dead, an infraction resulting in a 15-yard penalty.

lateral a pass thrown underhanded or overhanded in a backwards or sideways direction.

leg whip to intentionally use one's legs after falling to trip up an opponent.

linebackers the defensive players positioned just behind the line who back up the defensive linemen.

line judge the official who keeps time and watches for encroachment, offsides, and illegal motion at the line of scrimmage.

lineman a player positioned on the line of scrimmage.

line of scrimmage the imaginary line that marks where the ball is down and separates the defensive line from the offensive line.

man-for-man a defensive strategy in which each receiver is guarded by only one man.

middle linebacker the linebacker positioned behind the middle of the defensive line.

Monday morning quarterback a fan who criticizes his team's play by using 20/20 hindsight the day after the game.

naked reverse a play in which a team's blockers all move in one direction to draw the defense while the ballcarrier moves in the opposite direction.

nickel back a back that replaces a linebacker in the nickel defense.

nickel defense a defense that uses five backs, the extra back replacing a linebacker.

nose guard a defensive lineman positioned in the center of the line. Also known as a middle guard or nose tackle.

nutcracker a practice drill in which a team's ballcarriers are subjected to tackles by one or more players.

offside being positioned beyond or over the line of scrimmage prior to the snap.

onside kick a low, tumbling, easily fumbled kick made by a team behind in the score in the last moments of a game in the hope of regaining possession of the ball.

on the numbers a well-placed pass reaching the receiver at chest height or "on the numbers."

outlet man a backup receiver used when the primary receiver is closely guarded or when the quarterback is under pressure to get rid of the ball.

overtime an extra period at the end of a game to determine the winner when the score is tied.

pass rush a rush by the defense to tackle the passer.

personal foul hitting, kicking, clipping, tripping, face-masking, or other unnecessary roughness, a 15-yard penalty.

pick off to intercept a pass.

pigskin nickname for the football.

pitchout a pass toward the sidelines and behind the line of scrimmage.

placekick a kick made from a tee or a teammate's hold on the ground.

play-action pass a play in which a handoff is faked to the running back, who pretends to hold the ball in his arms while the quarterback passes.

playbook a book containing a team's strategies and diagrammed plays.

pocket behind the line of scrimmage, a pocket formed by blockers which the quarterback steps into to evade the pass rush.

point spread in betting, the number of points by which one team is estimated to beat another team in a game.

pop a strong tackle or block.

post pattern a pass pattern in which the receiver runs downfield along the sideline then makes a cut toward the goalposts.

prayer a pass requiring "divine intervention" to be completed. Same as a Hail Mary.

primary receiver the planned receiver in a play, as distinguished from a backup or outlet man.

pump to pump or cock the throwing arm once or twice to fake a pass to deceive the defense.

punt a kickoff in which the ball is dropped in the air and booted before it hits the ground, executed when possession must be relinquished on fourth down.

punt return catching a punted ball and advancing as far downfield as possible before being tackled.

QB quarterback.

quarterback the player who calls signals, takes the snap from the center, and either runs or hands off or passes the ball.

quarterback draw a play in which the quarterback drops back as if to pass then runs straight ahead through a gap left by the defense.

quarterback sneak a play in which the quarterback takes the snap and immediately runs forward with the ball through the defense for short yardage.

quick count an unusually quick count that signals the ball to be snapped much earlier than the defense would normally expect, used to throw off the defense's timing.

quick out a pass pattern in which a receiver crosses the line of scrimmage then cuts abruptly to the outside for a quick, short pass.

quick release refers to some quarterbacks' ability to release the ball quickly when throwing.

receiver any offensive player eligible to receive a pass, specifically the backs and two ends (wide receivers).

red dog a blitz by the linebackers.

referee the leading official in charge of a game; he conducts the coin toss at the start of a game, explains fouls, administers penalties, keeps track of the down, among other things.

reverse a play in which the ballcarrier running in one direction hands off to a teammate running in the opposite direction.

rollout left or right lateral movement made by the quarterback after receiving the snap.

roughing the passer charging into or tackling the passer after the ball has been thrown, 15-yard penalty.

running back the more commonly used name for a halfback or a fullback.

rush to advance the ball downfield by a running play rather than a passing play.

sack to tackle the quarterback.

safety a score of two points awarded to the defensive team when a ballcarrier on offense is downed on or behind his own team's goal line. Also, a defensive back.

scrambler a quarterback adept at scrambling.

scrambling the eluding of tacklers by the quarterback behind the line of scrimmage.

screen pass a pass to the side of the line of scrimmage.

scrimmage a practice game.

secondary the defensive backfield made up of the cornerbacks and safeties. Also, the area where these players are positioned.

shank to kick the ball off the ankle or side of the foot instead of the instep.

shiver to thrust the forearms up sharply to deflect an opponent's block.

shoestring catch a catch made at shoe level.

shotgun offense a spread-out formation in which the quarterback stands several yards behind the center to receive the snap in order to set up a pass play.

signals the quarterback's code used at the line of scrimmage to call the snap.

slant a diagonal pass pattern.

sled a padded steel frame on skids, used in blocking practice.

slot in the offensive line, the space between a tackle and an end.

slot formation a formation in which a running back is positioned in the slot between the tackle and the split end.

snap the center's passing of the ball between the legs to the quarterback to start play at the line of scrimmage.

spike after scoring a touchdown, the ritual of slamming the ball to the ground.

spiral the smooth, nontumbling spin of a well-thrown ball. To throw a spiral.

split end a pass receiver positioned far to the outside of the line of scrimmage. More commonly known as a wide receiver.

split the uprights to kick the ball through the goalposts for a field goal or extra point.

squib kick a low, tumbling kick difficult to field without fumbling.

straight-arm to hold one's arm out stiffly to block a potential tackler.

strip the ball to knock or poke the ball out of the ballcarrier's hands and cause a fumble.

strong safety the safety lined up opposite the strong side of an offensive line.

strong side the side on which the tight end is positioned.

stutter step a faked step in one direction; a short, deceiving step or momentary change in running rhythm to throw off the timing of a pursuer.

submarine to duck below a lineman's block.

sudden death same as overtime.

sweep to run to one side behind a wave of blockers.

tackle to knock or pull the ballcarrier down to the ground to stop play.

tackling dummy a stuffed bag used in tackling practice.

tailback in an I formation, the back positioned farthest behind the quarterback.

TD touchdown.

T formation a formation in which the backs assume the configuration of a T, with the fullback positioned far behind the quarterback and between the two halfbacks.

thread the needle to throw a perfectly placed pass between two or more defenders into the hands of a receiver.

throw for a loss to tackle a passer behind the line of scrimmage for a loss of yardage.

tight end an offensive lineman positioned at the end of the line of scrimmage near the tackle.

touchback an occurrence in which the ball is kicked into the opposite team's end zone and downed; it automatically brings the ball out to the receiving team's 20-yard line.

touchdown a goal or score of 6 points, made by successfully running or passing the ball into the opponent's end zone.

turnover a loss of possession of the ball due to a fumble or an interception.

umpire an official positioned behind the defensive line who assists the referee and is also responsible for inspecting players' equipment before a game.

unnecessary roughness kicking, hitting or butting, or tackling an opponent after the play is dead, all 15-yard penalties.

uprights the goalposts.

weak side the side of the line without the tight end.

wide receiver a pass receiver positioned on the end of the line. Also known as an end, split end, flanker.

wishbone a formation, similar to the T, in which the halfbacks are positioned on either side and slightly behind the fullback.

zebra any of the officials, so nicknamed for their black and white-striped shirts.

zone coverage a strategy in which each defender plays a zone instead of a man, as distinguished from man-to-man coverage.

FRISBEE

arcuate vanes the slightly raised diagonal ribs on a Frisbee.

Bernoulli principle the principle of physics by which air flowing over the top of a Frisbee's curved areas is slowed, producing lift.

cheek the inside face of the rim or lip.

crown see cupola.

cupola the raised center area. Also known as the crown, cabin, or dome.

dancing skips see skip flight.

drop a sudden loss of waft.

flight plate the top portion of the disk from rim to rim.

Frisbee finger separation of the fingernail from the nail bed, caused by an errant catch.

hyperspin a shot imparted with extra torque; it produces a hovering flight with little or no warp.

Hyzer angle the left or right angle or deviation from which the disk is thrown, producing a turning flight.

lift the lift from a wind current that propels a disk from a waft to a higher flight plane.

lip the rim.

Mung angle the upward pitch angle of the disk when released. Also known as the attack angle.

navel the indentation in the center of the cupola.

skip flight a disk thrown with negative Mung that bounces off the ground and rises.

tailskating a poor throw, having an extreme Mung angle which produces a sharply ascending and sharply descending flight with no waft.

thermals rising warm air, used by a veteran disk thrower to create lift.

waft floating cleanly without disturbance.

wane the gradual loss of waft; it evolves into wasting.

warp the sideways turning in the opposite direction of spin, occurring at the end of a disk's flight.

wasting the descent and loss of power in a disk's last stage of flight.

wax the stabilizing period after release, when the Mung angle levels out.

well synonymous with climb.

whelm the release of the disk. Also known as the hatch.

yawing spinning.

GOLF

ace a hole made in one stroke.

addressing the ball preparing for a stroke by setting the body in the proper stance and lining the club up with the ball.

albatross scoring three strokes under par for a particular hole. Also known as a double eagle.

approach a stroke to the putting green or pin, usually a medium-length shot.

apron the grass surrounding the putting area; also known as the fringe.

away the ball furthest from the hole; the golfer with the "away" ball shoots first.

back door the back of the hole. A ball "drops in the back door" when it precariously encircles the hole then miraculously drops in from the rear.

back side in an 18-hole course, the second 9 holes.

backspin a reverse spin put on the ball to stop it from rolling too far on the putting green.

backswing the swing motion from the ground to the back of the head.

baffy a No. 5 wood (club) with a face angle similar to a No. 3 or No. 4 iron.

bail out sinking an extra-long putt to keep from losing a hole.

banana ball an extreme slice sending the ball curving in an arc in the shape of a banana.

barranca a deep ravine.

beach any sand trap on a course.

bend one to hook or slice a ball.

birdie scoring one stroke under par for a particular hole.

bisque a handicap stroke that may be used on any hole on the course.

bite club action of putting backspin on a ball.

blade a type of putter.

bladesman name used to describe a superior putter.

blast launching huge cascades of sand when playing a ball out of a sand trap.

blind hole a putting green that cannot be seen by a player who is about to approach.

bogey scoring one stroke over par at a particular hole.

bold a stroke that is too strong.

borrow sloping a ball to compensate for a slight rise or curve in the putting green.

brassie No. 2 wood, used when long distance strokes are needed (originally named for its brass sole plate).

bunker a depression in bare ground, usually covered with sand; a sand hazard.

bunt a short shot.

bye the unplayed holes left after a match has been won.

caddie the person who carries the player's clubs and assists during a match.

can to make a putt and get the ball in the hole.

cap the top part of a club shaft.

carry the distance between where the ball is struck and where it makes its first bounce on the ground.

casting a poor swing technique in which the hands are used too much to control the start of the downswing. Also known as hitting from the top.

casual water a temporary pool or puddle of water or a bank of snow not considered part of a course's official hazards; a player is allowed to remove his ball from casual water without penalty. Also known as a casual lie.

chipping iron an iron used for making chip shots.

chip shot a short, low shot frequently with overspin taken near the putting green.

choke to move the grip further down on the handle of a club. Also to psychologically collapse under pressure and blow an easy shot.

chop hacking the ball with a club to give it extra spin.

chump an opponent who poses little or no competition.

cleek No. 4 wood with a face angle similar to a No. 1 or No. 2 iron.

closed stance a stance in which the left foot is placed over the line of flight with the right foot back.

clubbing a player advising another player which club to use on a particular shot.

club head the portion of the club that strikes the ball.

clubhouse collective term for lockers, restaurant, bar, and meetings rooms.

clubhouse lawyer a person who knows even the most obscure golf rules and who generally makes a pain of himself by advising everyone.

collar the edge of a sand hazard.

course rating a scale defining the playing difficulty of a particular course in comparison to other courses, expressed in strokes and fractions of a stroke.

cup hole.

cut shot a high, soft shot that stops rolling almost immediately after hitting the green.

dead any ball imparted with so much backspin that it stops dead without rolling after hitting the green.

deuce a hole made in two strokes.

dimples the indentations on a golf ball.

divot a slice of turf hacked out by a club during a stroke.

dogleg a curve in the fairway to the right or left.

dormie a situation in which the opponent must win every remaining hole to tie a match.

double bogey scoring 2 over par at a particular hole.

double eagle a score of 3 under par. Also known as an albatross.

down the number of strokes a player is behind his opponent.

draw an intentional hook shot.

drive to hit the ball from a tee.

driver No. 1 wood, used for the maximum distance shot.

dub a poor shot; a missed shot.

duck hook a severe hook hit low to the ground, sometimes causing people on the sidelines to "duck."

duffer a poor golfer. Also known as a hacker.

dunk hitting a ball into a water hazard.

eagle scoring two strokes under par at a hole.

explode same as blast.

face the hitting surface of a club's head.

fade a ball that "fades" to its left or right at the end of its flight.

fairway the manicured terrain between the tee and the putting green.

fan to swing the club and miss the ball completely. Also known as a whiff.

fat shot a shot in which the club has partially struck the ground before hitting the ball, resulting in a high, low, or weak flight.

feather hitting a long, high shot that curves slightly from left to right and then settles with little roll.

flagstick the flagpole placed in a hole to show its location from a distance.

flash trap a small sand bunker, usually shallow.

flier a ball without spin that travels farther than expected.

floater a ball that is hit high and appears to float lightly across the sky.

fore the word shouted to warn players downfield of the impending flight of a ball.

forecaddie a person whose primary responsibility is to mark the position of a player's ball on the course.

fringe same as apron.

frog hair the short grass around the edge of the green.

front side on an 18-hole course, the first nine holes.

gimme a short putt easily made.

go-to-school learning the lay of a green by watching the roll of a putt from another player.

grain the direction in which the grass on a putting green lies after being cut.

grasscutter a low, line-drive shot that skims the grass.

green the whole golf course. (The putting greens are where the holes are located and are frequently referred to as the "green" as well.)

green's fee the fee paid to play on a golf course.

gross a player's score before a handicap is subtracted.

hacker a poor golfer.

half swing a swing in which the club is brought only halfway back.

halved when each player makes a hole in the same number of strokes that hole is "halved."

handicap a stroke or strokes given to a player of lesser ability than his opponent to help even out a match.

handicap player a player who usually plays above par and is thus given a handicap.

hanging lie a ball that comes to rest on a downhill slope.

hazard a bunker or water trap.

heel to hit the ball from the top of the club head near the shaft, resulting in the ball taking off at right angles to the line of play.

hole-in-one a hole made in one stroke. Also known as an ace.

hook a ball that curves to the left.

iron any club with a metal head.

lateral hazard a water hazard running alongside or parallel the line of play.

lie the place where the ball comes to rest after a shot.

links original name for any seaside golf course but now describing any course.

lip the rim of the hole.

loft the height a ball reaches in the air. Also the angle a club face is set at in order to give a ball more lift or "loft."

marshal a person who keeps spectators in line and orderly in a golf tournament.

mashie No. 5 iron.

mashie iron No. 4 iron.

mashie niblick No. 7 iron.

match a golf game played by holes rather than a course. The player winning the most holes wins the match.

midiron No. 2 iron.

mid-mashie No. 3 iron.

Mulligan a second shot allowed off the first tee in nonprofessional or casual games.

neck the socket where the shaft of a club joins the head.

net a player's score after his handicap has been subtracted.

open a tournament open for both amateurs and professionals.

open stance a stance in which the left foot is placed in back of the ball's flight path, allowing a player to face in the direction he wishes to hit.

out of bounds the ground outside the course.

overclubbing using a bigger club than is necessary for a particular shot so that the ball travels further than desired.

par the theoretical number of strokes considered necessary to get the ball in the hole; hitting below par, or with fewer strokes, is superior; hitting above par, or with more strokes, is considered inferior.

penalty stroke a stroke added to a player's score for breaking a rule.

pin the flagstick.

pitch a short, lofting shot to the putting green, often with backspin.

pitch and run same type of shot as a pitch but without the high arc or backspin, allowing the ball to roll after it hits the putting green.

pitching niblick No. 8 iron.

pitching wedge an iron used for making pitch shots.

playing through when one group of players catches up to another group and is allowed to pass ahead.

plugged lie a ball that has been buried in the sand of a bunker. Also known as a fried egg.

pot bunker a small, deep bunker.

pull a ball hit straight but nonetheless to the left of target.

punch a low shot "punched" into the wind with a short, slamming swing.

push opposite of a pull.

putt stroking the ball lightly, as on a putting green.

putter No. 10 iron.

putting green the short-cropped area around the hole.

quail high a long, low shot.

rabbit a ball that bounces erratically after landing.

referee the person who sees to it that all rules are followed.

rough any areas of relatively long grass on a course.

run the distance a ball rolls after striking the ground.

sand trap a sand hazard; bunker.

sand wedge an iron designed for shots out of sand traps.

scoop a poor swing technique in which the club head dips.

scoring lines the indented lines on the faces of irons.

scratch to play at par.

scruff cutting the turf with a club head.

scuffing hitting the ground behind the ball with a club head.

short game collective term for pitching, chipping, and putting.

skulling hitting a chip or pitch shot too far.

sky hitting the ball too low with the club head, sending it "skyward" in a flight resembling a pop fly in baseball.

skywriting a poor swing technique in which the club head makes a looping motion at the top of the backswing.

slice a shot that curves to the right of target.

slider a low shot that bounces erratically.

snake a very long putt.

snipe a severely hooked ball that dives quickly.

sole the bottom of a club head.

spade mashie No. 6 iron.

spoon No. 3 wood.

spray an extremely poor shot hit far off line.

sudden death when a match is tied at the end of the allotted number of holes, the continuation of play until one opponent wins a hole.

sweet spot the center of the face of a club.

tee a wooden or plastic plug on which the ball is balanced for driving. Also the area of the first shot of each hole.

thread a shot through a narrow opening between two obstacles.

toe the outer part of the club head.

toe job a ball hit too much from the club toe.

top hitting the ball above center, causing it to roll or hop.

turn starting the second nine holes.

underclubbing using a club designed for shorter distances when longer distance is needed.

unplayable lie a ball in a position where it cannot be played.

up the number of holes a player is ahead of his opponent.

waggle flexing the wrists and slightly swinging the club back and forth before hitting the ball.

wedge a club with a heavy flange on the bottom.

whiff to miss the ball completely.

wood a club with a wooden head.

yips shaking that causes a player to miss a short putt.

GYMNASTICS

aerial cartwheel a leaping, midair cartwheel, as performed on the balance beam.

afterflight in a pommel horse or other routine, the finishing flight leading to a landing.

back lever on the rings, a position in which the legs are extended out so that the body describes an L-shape.

back Moore on a pommel horse, making circling movements with hands on one pommel or behind the back.

balance beam a 16½-foot-long by 4-inch-wide raised, padded beam, adjustable to various heights.

barani a half-twisting front somersault.

beat the bar on the uneven bars, to strike the lower bar with the abdomen or hips with a whipping motion.

compulsory in a competition, a required exercise or routine.

crash mat the foam safety mat that serves as a cushion for landings or falls.

cross grip on the horizontal bar, a grip in which one hand is crossed over the other; it is used to turn the performer during a swing.

croupe the rear portion of a pommel horse. When facing the horse from the side, the croupe is always on the left.

Deltchev on the uneven bars, a cross-gripped downswing followed by a half turn and a front somersault.

Diamadov on the parallel bars, a full twisting forward swing to a one-armed handstand.

dismount the finishing exercise and flight of a routine.

double flyaway: a horizontal bar dismount consisting of a giant downswing followed by a release on the upswing and the execution of two somersaults before landing.

elgrip an unusual grip, similar to the hand position used with a swimmer's backstroke.

English position a handstand position in which the hands are held closely together.

flip-flop on the balance beam, a backward flip that stops at a handstand and follows through to a standing position. Also, any somersault.

full-in short for "full in to back somersault out;" more specifically, a backward somersault followed by a second backward somersault with a full twist.

full-out short for "back somersault in to full out;" more specifically, a somersault followed by a second somersault with a full twist.

giant swing on the bar or on the rings, an exercise in which the entire body is swung end over end by the hands.

half in–half out a somersault with a half twist followed by another somersault with a half twist.

handspring a jump through a handstand in tumbling or over the vault horse.

handspring vault running up to a horse and flipping over it by upending oneself with a moving handstand.

hanging event an exercise on the horizontal bar or rings.

Hecht dismount on the horizontal bar, a high-swinging dismount.

horizontal bar the raised gymnastics bar; it stands about 8½ feet high.

horse short for pommel horse.

hurdle to leap or hop over.

iron cross on the rings, a position in which the arms are extended out sideways to describe the shape of a cross. Also known as the cross.

layout a straight-out body posture maintained during certain exercises.

limber similar to a walkover but with the legs kept together.

lunge a starting position for some tumbling exercises, characterized by the arms held outstretched overhead and one leg extended with bent knee forward.

mount the starting exercise of a routine.

neck as viewed from the side, the right position of a pommel horse.

Olympic order the event order in professional competition. In men's competition, the order is floor exercise, pommel horse, still rings, long horse vault, parallel bars, and horizontal bar. In women's, the vault, uneven bars, balance beam, and floor exercise.

one-arm giant a giant swing performed with a one-handed grip.

overgrip the most natural hand grip, with the palms of the hands facing away from the gymnast.

parallel bars two 11-foot rails set parallel to each other about 5 feet, 9 inches from the floor.

pike a position in which the body is bent forward at the hips.

planche a position in which the gymnast balances his body parallel to the floor or apparatus.

pommel horse an upholstered, four-legged support having wooden handles (pommels) on the top.

press a very slow, graceful movement to a handstand.

puck position a cross between a tuck and a pike.

rings the still rings. Once known as the flying rings.

routine a series of exercises.

run a series of tumbles.

Russian Moore performing pivots around both pommels of a pommel horse.

saddle on a pommel horse, the area between the pommels; the middle of the horse.

scissors swinging the body and scissoring the legs back and forth across the pommel horse.

spotting the act of assisting or standing by to catch a gymnast in the event of a fall.

spotting belt a training belt suspended by ropes and worn by a gymnast when learning a new exercise to help prevent injuries.

step-out a landing position in which one leg follows the other instead of hitting at the same time.

still rings the rings, flying rings.

streulli on the parallel bars, a backward roll on the upper arms, followed by an extension to a handstand.

stuck landing a perfect or still landing, as if being "stuck" to the floor.

stutz on the parallel bars, swinging from a handstand downward and forward to upward.

symmetry alignment of body parts during an exercise.

tinsica a walkover executed with one hand placed in front of the other.

tuck a somersaulting position in which the legs are folded tightly into the chest and held by the arms.

uneven bars two raised horizontal bars placed one beneath and out from the other.

vault a leap or a leaping somersault over a vault horse.

vault horse same as a pommel horse but without the pommels. It is vaulted over lengthwise.

walkover wheeling around from feet to hands and back.

whip-up while straddling the balance beam, swinging the legs up and backward.

HOCKEY

assist a pass to a teammate that results in a goal.

attacking zone the offensive zone; the area of the goal being shot at.

backcheck checking an opponent in the defensive zone.

backhand a pass made with the back of the stick blade.

backline the defensemen.

banana blade a stick blade with a special curve built-in to help control the puck.

bench minor a 2-minute penalty assessed to a team whose coach, manager, trainer, or player not currently on the ice commits an infraction, usually unsportsmanlike conduct.

blade the bottom or shooting portion of a stick.

blocking glove the large, protective glove worn by the goaltender to deflect pucks. Also known as a blocker.

blue lines the two wide blue lines that divide the rink into the attacking zone, the defensive zone, and the neutral zone. They are used to determine offside and pass violations.

board check to push or body check an opponent into the wall or fence surrounding the rink.

boarding illegal or excessively violent board checking, resulting in a penalty.

boards the fence or wall that surrounds the rink.

body check to bump an opponent with the upper body in order to gain access to the puck.

breakaway to break away from defenders and move quickly toward the goal with the puck.

butt-ending illegally poking an opponent with the butt of the stick.

catching glove the glove used by the goalie to catch the puck in midair, worn on the opposite hand as the blocking glove.

center the central player on the forward line who takes part in most faceoffs and is frequently the player who takes the puck in for a shot on goal; the position played between the two wings.

center ice the neutral zone between the blue lines at the center of the rink.

change on the fly to send in a substitute player while the puck is still in play.

charge run into an opponent from behind, an illegal play.

charging a foul called on a player who deliberately runs into an opponent from behind.

check same as body check. See also, hook check, poke check.

chippy an excessively rough player, team, period of play, or game.

clear to move the puck into a position of safety away from one's own goal or out of the defensive zone entirely.

crease the 8-foot by 4-foot marked rectangle in front of the goal.

cross check to bump an opponent with the stick held up high across the body, an illegal play.

cut down the angle to move out from the goal to meet an oncoming opponent with the puck to reduce his visual angle to the goal.

defensemen the two players who help the goalie defend the goal.

deke to fake a move and deceive an opponent.

drop pass a pass in which a moving player stops the puck and leaves it in place for a player from behind while continuing to move on.

faceoff a method of restarting play by lining up two opposing players against each other and dropping the puck between them in a designated faceoff circle.

faceoff circle one of five 15-foot circles in which faceoffs are executed at the ends and middle of the rink.

flip pass a pass in which the puck is lifted up off the ice and flicked over an opponent's skate or stick.

forecheck to check an opponent in his defensive zone.

forwards the center and the left and right wings; the forward line.

freeze the goalie to fake a goalie with a deceptive move or shot.

give-and-go to pass the puck to a teammate then skate quickly past a defender to receive a return pass.

goalie the goaltender; the player positioned directly in front of the goal.

goal judge one of two officials who make rulings on goals.

goal light on either side of a rink, the red light turned on behind the goal when a goal is scored.

goals against average the statistic indicating the average number of goals a goalie allows per game.

goaltender same as goalie.

hat trick three goals scored in a single game by the same player. See also pure hat trick.

high stick to strike an opponent with a stick held above the shoulders, an illegal play.

hip check a body check with the hip.

hook check an attempt to steal the puck from an opponent from behind or from the side with the stick blade.

hooking illegally catching and holding an opponent with the crook of the stick.

icing illegally shooting the puck from behind the center red line and across the goal line of the opponent where it is first touched by an opponent, excluding the goalie.

kick save stopping a shot on goal by sticking a foot out to block it.

kill a penalty to avoid being scored against when shorthanded a player due to a penalty.

left wing the largely offensive position played on the left side of the rink.

linesmen two officials who make icing and offside calls, conduct faceoffs, and otherwise control the game.

major penalty a 5-minute penalty, levied on a player for unnecessarily rough play or for fighting.

man advantage the advantage of a full team playing against a shorthanded team.

minor penalty a 2-minute penalty levied on a player for minor infractions.

mucking scrambling and battling for the puck in the corners. Also known as digging.

neutral zone the center area of the rink, between the two blue lines.

NHL National Hockey League.

offside a violation in which a player is present in the attacking zone as the puck crosses the blue line. Receiving an illegal pass in this position.

penalty removing a player from the game for a specified amount of time for committing an infraction or foul.

penalty box where penalized players must sit out their penalty time.

penalty killing percentage statistic that indicates the times a team has avoided being scored against when playing shorthanded.

penalty minutes a statistic of total penalty time served by a player or team in a game, series, or season.

penalty shot a free shot on goal defended only by the goalie.

period one of three 20-minute time periods in a game.

poke check poking the puck away from an opponent with the blade of the stick.

policeman an intimidating player with a reputation for quick retribution against any rough play from the opposing side.

power play any man-advantage situation.

power play goal a goal scored on a power play.

puck a 3-inch rubber disk.

pull the goalie in a catch-up situation in the final moments of a game, a strategic move in which the goalie is removed and an offensive player is substituted to increase the odds of scoring a game-tying goal.

pure hat trick a score of three consecutive goals by the same player with no points scored by others in between.

rag the puck to handle the puck for a lengthy period of time.

red light the red goal light.

red line the wide center line that divides the rink in half.

referee the official who enforces rules of the game.

referee's crease the marked semicircle in front of the penalty timekeeper.

roughing to rough up an opponent excessively, an infraction.

rush to move the puck into the attacking zone toward the goal.

save to prevent a goal.

screen to position oneself between the goalie and a teammate preparing to shoot on goal to block the goalie's view.

shadow to guard an opponent closely.

shorthanded short one or more team members.

slapshot a hard, driving shot made with a high backswing of the stick.

slashing illegally slashing an opponent with the stick.

slot the area extending 10 yards out from the goal, from which most goals are scored.

smother the puck to fall on and cover the puck with one's body in order to stop play.

snap pass a quick pass made with little stick movement.

spearing illegally stabbing or poking an opponent with the stick blade.

split the defense to break through two or more defenders into the attacking zone.

stick check stealing the puck away from an opponent with the stick.

take a penalty to commit an infraction intentionally in order to stop play.

take the body to give or receive a body check.

trailer a teammate who skates behind the puckhandler for a possible drop pass.

wing one of two players who play on the right and left sides of the rink.

Zamboni the vehicle used to resurface or freshen the ice between periods.

HUNTING

area drive a hunting method in which one or more hunters drives or scares out game from woods while another hunter waits in ambush along game trail.

bag to shoot and capture a game animal.

bag limit the maximum number of game animals that may be taken legally by one hunter in a hunting season or period.

baiting a method of attracting game by spreading food along game trails, illegal in many areas.

blind a camouflaged or hidden shelter from which a hunter waits to ambush game. A duck blind.

blood to expose a hunting dog to the scent or blood of its prey.

buck fever a psychological problem in which the hunter chokes up under pressure and is unable to aim or shoot at a sighted deer.

buckshot lead shot in large sizes for shooting deer and other big game.

cast the ranging about by a dog in search of game or in search of the game's scent.

dead set a dog's stance when game is located.

decoy a fake duck used to attract other ducks to a hunting area.

deer rifle commonly, a .30-.30, .30-.06, or .308.

gun dog a hunting dog trained to flush out and retrieve small game. A pointer, setter, or retriever.

spoor collective term for the droppings, tracks, shed hair, or other sings of game on a trail.

spread the width of a set of deer antlers.

stool a bunch of decoys grouped together.

MOUNTAINEERING (*Also see* MOUNTAINS)

arrest to slow and stop the fall of a climber by gripping and squeezing the belaying rope.

avalanche cord a long, brightly colored length of cord allowed to trail behind a climber in an avalanche zone; the rope facilitates the location of a climber if buried under an avalanche.

belay any object, such as a rock, a climber uses to tie himself to for security. Also, holding or securing a rope for a fellow climber. Also, playing out a rope to a climber ahead.

bergschrund a crevasse located where a glacier has broken away from a mountain.

bivouac to make a temporary, makeshift shelter on a mountain side. Also, the shelter itself.

brake bar a short bar that attaches to a carabiner to slow or stop a rope during rappeling.

buttress a projection, usually flanked by a gully on either side, on a mountain side.

carabiner a ring having a spring catch, used to connect ropes to pitons.

chimney a narrow, vertical passageway through which a climber may pass.

chockstone a stone wedged in a crack and used as a handhold.

cliff hanger a hook attached to any small projection or crack and hung with a foot stirrup.

cornice a wavelike overhang of ice and snow, notorious for starting avalanches.

couloir a ravine or gorge up the side of a mountain; it provides an easy ascent route, but it is dangerous because it serves as a channel for falling rocks.

crampon toothed, metal boot attachments to increase traction on ice.

crevasse a crack or fissure in a glacier.

descendeur a waist line device for gripping rope and slowing descent when rappeling.

etrier a short rope ladder.

exposure the state of being dangerously exposed on a precipitous cliff or steep flank with open space below the climber's feet.

freeclimbing climbing without the aid of pitons and bolts or any kind of mechanical assistance.

glacis a rock slope up to 30 degrees.

glissade to slide down a slope by the soles of one's feet.

ice axe a spiked, adzelike tool used for cutting steps in ice or used as a belay anchor.

ice hammer a tool with one end having a hammer and the other a long spike.

ice screw a threaded spike screwed into the ice.

mantel to climb up onto a shelf or ledge by holding onto its edge and swinging one leg up and over, as in climbing out of a pool.

mountain sickness sickness encountered at above 10,000 feet where air is thin; symptoms include headaches and nausea, which disappear during the descent.

pendulum traversing a steep face by swinging sideways on a rope; a horizontal rappel.

piton a metal spike, wedge, or peg driven into rock or ice to secure a climber.

rappel to descend a cliff face by the use of ropes.

serac a high wall or tower of ice, hazardous to climb.

slab to move diagonally up a steep slope to make climbing easier.

stance a rest spot on a cliff climb.

summit pack a small backpack for carrying climbing gear and clothing.

switchback zigzagging to counter steep slopes. Also, a trail that zigzags to facilitate climbing.

traverse to move sideways across a slope or cliff.

RACQUETBALL

ace a serve that scores a point without a return from the opponent.

around-the-wall ball a ball played off high on the sidewall that then strikes the front wall, the opposite sidewall, then the floor.

avoidable hinder interference from an opponent that could have been avoided; a violation resulting in a side-out or a point to the player interfered with.

back court court area between the back wall and the short line.

backhand same as a backhand in tennis, with the racquet hand sweeping forward from the opposite side of the body.

backhand corner the court area on each player's backhand side.

back spin rotation or bottom spin imparted on a ball by angling the sweep of the racket.

back wall shot a ball played after it bounces off the rear wall.

block one player getting in front of the other after a shot.

ceiling ball a ball shot into the ceiling and rebounding off the front wall then bouncing high off the floor toward the back wall, a common defensive shot.

ceiling serve any serve that strikes the ceiling before or after contact with the front wall.

crotch any of the junctures where floor and walls meet or where ceiling and walls meet.

crotch shot a shot played into any juncture between floor and wall or ceiling and wall.

cutthroat a game in which three players compete against each other.

dead ball any ball no longer in play, due to interference or being shot out of the court. Also, any old ball that has lost its bounce.

donut a score of zero.

doubles a game in which two teams, of two players each, compete against one another.

down-the-line pass a shot hit straight along a sidewall that returns straight and close to that sidewall, making it difficult to return.

drive serve a low drive into the front wall that rebounds low and fast into the rear court.

English spin imparted on the ball.

face the hitting surface of a racquet.

fault an illegal serve.

fly ball a ball played directly off a wall without a first bounce on the floor.

forehand a stroke in which the ball is hit on the same side as the racquet hand.

forehand corner the court area where each player hits forehand shots.

front court the part of the court near the front wall.

gun hand the hand that is used to grip the racquet.

half-volley hitting a ball on the short hop or the instant it bounces up from the floor.

hypotenuse shot a low shot played from a rear corner to the opposite front corner.

inning one round of play, in which both players have served.

isolation strategy in doubles play, playing the majority of shots to the weakest or least skilled of the two opponents.

kill shot an extremely low shot off the front wall, which barely bounces and is difficult for an opponent to retrieve.

lob a soft, high-arcing serve that drops into one of the rear corners.

long an illegal serve that bounces off the front wall and flies all the way to the back wall without touching the floor.

mercy ball a dangerous situation in which a player attempting to hit a ball might accidently strike the opponent if by swinging the racquet, so consequently he or she chooses not to and lets the ball go by. In most cases the play is taken over.

offhand the hand that does not grip the racquet.

pinch shot a kill shot played into a sidewall first.

portsider a left-handed player; southpaw.

rally the continuous return of the ball by each player until an error is made.

reverse corner kill a kill shot hit crosscourt into the far front corner.

rollout the ball rolling out from the wall after a kill shot.

service box the serving area, marked by the service line and the short line.

short line the line marking the rear of the service box halfway between the front wall and the back wall.

side-out loss of service due to a missed shot or penalty.

straddleball any shot that passes between the legs of a player.

sweet spot the area of the racquet face providing the most power and control, usually the center.

technical one point substracted from a player's score due to unsportsmanlike behavior, such as swearing or stalling.

tension referring to how tightly a racquet is strung.

thong the loop tethered to the butt of a racquet, used as a safety device to keep the racquet from flying out of the hand during play.

volley to strike the ball off a wall before it bounces on the floor.

wallpaper ball a shot that returns as closely as possible along a sidewall without touching it.

z-ball a shot that bounces high off the front wall corner into a sidewall, across to the opposite sidewall, then onto the floor, tracing a Z pattern.

RODEO

bareback riding the riding of a wild, bucking horse for 8 seconds while hanging on with only one hand.

bulldog to wrestle a steer to the ground by grasping its horns and twisting its head down.

bull riding riding a bucking bull for 8 seconds while holding on with one hand.

calf roping roping a calf from horseback, then wrestling the calf to the ground and tying three of its legs.

chute a narrow stall in which a wild horse or bull is held for mounting and release into the arena.

clown a clown who runs into the arena to distract a bull after a rider has been thrown.

hazer an assistant, noncompeting rider who guides a steer in a straight line to make it easier for a contestant to leap onto the steer and wrestle it down.

pickup man a horseman who rides beside a contestant on a bucking bronc to prevent the rider from being kicked or trampled if he falls off.

saddle bronc riding a competition in which each contestant must ride a saddled, bucking horse for 10 seconds while holding on with one hand and continuously spurring the animal.

steer roping same as calf roping but with a full-grown steer.

steer wrestling an event in which each contestant must wrestle a steer to the ground by grabbing onto its head or horns. Also known as bulldogging.

team roping an event in which two contestants working together try to rope a steer around the neck and two hind legs and immobilize the animal as quickly as possible.

SCUBA AND SKIN DIVING

anoxia oxygen depletion from holding one's breath too long when skin diving; it sometimes results in an underwater blackout.

bends a dangerous body reaction in which gas bubbles lodge in joints and tissues, causing crippling pain; it occurs when breathing compressed air at below 33 feet and failing to decompress on the return ascent. Also known as decompression sickness.

bouyancy compensator an inflatable vest used in addition to a weight belt to help control buoyancy.

buddy breathing the sharing of air from one tank by two divers by passing the mouthpiece back and forth.

buddy line a line tied between two divers to keep them together, especially at night or in murky water.

buddy system a safety system in which each diver is responsible for the well-being of a fellow diver while in the water.

decompress to make a slow ascent or to stop at certain depths for specific times to allow gas bubbles accumulated in tissues to be eliminated by the body to avoid contracting the bends.

decompression the lessening of water pressure on a diver as he ascends.

decompression sickness the bends.

decompression tables U.S. Navy tables indicating how much decompression time is required for various depths and dives.

depth gauge a wrist gauge that measures water pressure or depth.

diver down flag a red flag with a white diagonal bar; it is flown from a boat or floated on the surface of the water to warn boaters of divers nearby.

dolphin kick fishlike motion in which the legs are kicked or flapped up and down in tandem.

nitrogen narcosis the dangerous narcotic effect suffered by a diver breathing compressed air at below 100 feet. Also known as rapture of the deep.

rapture of the deep same as nitrogen narcosis.

regulator the breathing apparatus that regulates the flow of air from the air tanks.

scuba an acronym for self-contained underwater breathing apparatus.

snorkel a J-shaped tube with a mouthpiece on one end and an air hole extending above the surface on the other end.

spear gun an underwater trigger gun that shoots small spears for stalking fish.

stride entry the most common method of entering the water from boatside, specifically by taking a giant stride feet first into the water. Also known as the giant stride entry.

weight belt a belt having attached weights to cancel the body's natural bouyancy underwater.

wet suit a thick, skintight, neoprene rubber suit that draws in water, which is heated by the body and helps protect against the cold.

SKATING

arabian a flying spin in which the body is stretched out parallel to the ice.

axel a jump of 1½ revolutions.

axel, double a jump of 2½ revolutions.

axel, inside an axel in which the takeoff and landing are executed on the same foot.

axel, triple a jump with 3½ revolutions.

Bielmann spin a spin in which one leg is held outstretched high overhead.

camel a spin executed in an arabesque position.

Choctaw a forward to backward turn.

crossfoot spin a spin in which one foot is crossed over the other.

deathdrop an arabian with a landing into a back sit spin.

death spiral a pairs move in which the man holds the woman by the arms and pulls her in a circle with her back arched and her head near the ice.

figures the figure eight and its variations; the figures executed in a patch session.

flying camel a flying spin ending in a back camel.

flying sit spin a flying spin that ends with a sitting spin.

free dance skate-dancing to music.

freestyle jumps, spins, and footwork executed to the sound of music. Also known as free skating.

Grafstrom spiral an arabesque executed with bent knees.

hydrant lift a pairs move in which the man lifts the woman over his head with her legs split.

Lutz a one-revolution jump.

overhead lift a pairs move in which the woman is held high over the man's head with her back arched.

pair sit spin a sit spin in which the skating couple embrace.

patch in competition, a "patch" of ice designated to each skater to lay out figures on. A patch session.

pivot a spin with one toe pointed into the ice.

Russian split a jump split in which the skater touches her toes.

Salchow a one-revolution jump started off a back inside edge and ended on a back inside edge on the opposite foot.

serpentine a figure comprising three circles; a three-lobe figure.

spin a rapid rotation on one spot on the ice.

split a jump in which the legs are split or spread wide apart.

spread eagle a gliding position with one skate facing forward and one skate facing backwards.

stag a split jump executed with the leading leg bent at the knee.

stroking gliding and propelling oneself over the ice.

Zamboni the vehicle or machine that resurfaces the ice on a rink.

SKIING

avalement to "swallow" a mogul, or absorb the shock of skiing over a bump by retracting the knees and feet.

back moebius a jump in which the skier does a backward somersault in a straight-out body position while performing a 360-degree twist of the body.

backscratcher an acrobatic jump in which the tips of the skis point straight down while the tails touch or "scratch" the skier's back.

ballet a kind of dance on skis performed with a series of graceful freestyle maneuvers.

biathlon a competition combining skiing and rifle marksmanship.

christie a parallel turn made by leaning into the turning direction.

compression turn a turn used on bumpy terrain in which the skier absorbs the bump by retracting or relaxing his legs then twisting them at the crest to perform a turn.

corn old, coarse, granulated snow.

cornice an overhanging shelf of ice and snow, hazardous to skiers, and known to collapse and cause an avalanche.

crust snow with a hardened surface.

daffy an acrobatic jump in which the skis are scissored in midair.

edging cutting the edges of the skis into the snow to aid in maneuvering; also, walking sideways up a slope.

fall line the direction of a slope's descent.

freestyle avant-garde, acrobatic, or ballet-style skiing.

gelendesprung any ski jump made in a crouching position.

gondola a covered ski lift.

helicopter an acrobatic jump in which the skier spins around 360 degrees in the air, as a helicopter blade.

herringbone a skier's method of walking uphill in which steps are taken at diagonal or wide angles.

kick turn a stationary turn in which one ski is lifted high in the air and swung around to the desired direction.

killer kick an acrobatic maneuver in which the skier "sits" on the back of one ski and kicks the other high in the air, followed by a quick, slicing turn.

langlauf cross-country running on skis.

mogul a bump, hump, or rise of snow.

mogul field a slope with numerous humps.

mule kick an acrobatic jump performed with the skier's knees bent out sideways at a 90-degree angle.

Nordic skiing cross-country skiing.

peacock's tail an acrobatic maneuver in which the skier makes a complete turn on the uprighted tips of the skis.

powder deep, soft snow.

rambling cross-country walking on skis, a slower and more relaxed form than langlauf.

ramp a slope linking different levels of a mountain.

reverse crossover same as a stepover, only with one ski crossed over the other from behind instead of the front.

royal christie a classical ballet skiing maneuver in which one ski is lifted far behind the skier and brought forward gracefully to make a turn.

royal spin a complete turn with one ski held in the air and turned in pirouette fashion.

schuss to ski straight down a steep slope without turns or traverses.

sideslipping slipping sideways while making a turn.

sidestepping walking sideways up a hill with skis on.

sitzmark the form left in the snow by a skier who has fallen backward.

skijoring skiing while being towed by a horse or vehicle.

slalom a race over a winding course marked with posted flags.

snow cannon a cannonlike device that shoots a spray of water into cold air, forming ice and snow, used by ski resorts.

snowplow bringing the tips of skis together in a "vee" or snowplow formation to slow descent or brake. Also known as a wedge.

somersault a backward or forward somersault in the tucked or untucked position.

spatula the front or curved-up end of a ski.

star turn a stationary turn made by raising and putting down the skis alternatively, creating a radius or "star" in the snow.

stepover a ballet maneuver in which one ski is stepped over the other, followed by a royal christie.

swallowing absorbing the impact of a mogul by relaxing or retracting the legs and feet.

undulation a swell or wave in the snow.

traversing a diagonal run across a slope.

washboard a series of small, bumpy waves in the snow.

wedelns a series of very fast and slight changes in direction made by flexing the body joints.

SKYDIVING

automatic opener a device calibrated to deploy automatically a parachute at 1000 to 1200 feet, used with student jumpers.

auxiliary chute a reserve parachute.

bag deployment the fabric container enclosing the parachute canopy.

batwings rigid or semirigid surfaces attached to the arms and body to facilitate gliding and slow descent, used illegally.

breakaway the jettisoning of the main parachute to deploy the reserve chute; the cutting of suspension lines to release the canopy.

cloth extensions sections of fabric sewn into the armpits and crotch area to facilitate gliding and to slow descent; not the same as batwings.

crabbing directing the descending parachute sideways to the wind.

delta position a freefall position in which the arms are held back at the sides with the head held low, to increase the rate of descent.

deployment the release and unfurling of the parachute from its pack.

deployment device a sleeve or bag that contains the canopy, slows its opening and reduces shock.

docking joining hands (or other body parts) with another diver in midair.

drop altitude the altitude at which a skydiver jumps.

drop zone a specified area where a skydiver plans to land.

exit point the point in the air, often over a landmark on the ground, where a jumper exits the plane.

free fall the portion of the jump in which the parachute is not yet deployed. Also, any jump in which the chute is deployed at the skydiver's discretion, as distinguished from a static line jump.

frog position a freefall position in which the jumper assumes a spread-eagle posture with arms upraised.

glide horizontal movement through the sky.

groundhog any nonjumping spectator on the ground.

hank to pull or yank on a steering line.

harness the webbing and strapping that cradles the jumper and connects with the suspension lines.

holding directing the canopy against the wind to slow ground speed.

hop 'n pop pulling the ripcord immediately after exiting from the plane.

inversion a deployment malfunction in which the canopy becomes turned completely or partially inside-out.

jumpmaster an experienced jumper and jump leader; one who oversees the jumps of students.

line-over a deployment malfunction in which one or more lines get caught up over the top of the canopy. Also known as a Mae West.

opening point the point in the air at which the jumper should pull the ripcord in order to land within the specific jump zone.

opening shock the shock or pull felt by the jumper when the chute opens.

oscillation the swinging back and forth of a jumper under a descending canopy, usually occurring during turns.

pack collective term for the parachute assembly, including the container, canopy, connector links, risers, suspension lines, and reserve chute.

pack tray the container part that holds the lines when stowed.

paraboots special shock-absorbent boots worn by jumpers.

pilot chute a small parachute used to help deploy the main parachute.

PLF parachute landing fall; a method of landing in which impact is distributed across several points of the body instead of to the feet and ankles alone.

poised exit an exit made from an airplane wing or strut.

relative work working with others in midair to create formations or to conduct stunts.

reserve the auxiliary chute.

running directing the parachute to fly with the wind to increase ground speed.

smoke flares used to make the jumper easier to spot from spectators on the ground.

spotting choosing the airplane course and a ground landmark over which to jump in order to land at a desired location.

stall the loss of lift.

static line a line attached from the aircraft to the parachute; it automatically deploys the parachute as soon as the jumper exits the plane.

steering lines short lines connected to the suspension lines, used to steer the canopy. Also known as toggle lines.

streamer a deployment malfunction in which part of the canopy clings together and fails to unfurl.

suspension lines the cords connected to the harness from the canopy.

terminal velocity the fastest speed a body can reach while dropping through the air, approximately 120 miles per hour, reached about 12 seconds after exiting an airplane, depending on body position.

toggle lines same as steering lines.

tracking assuming the best body position for horizontal movement.

wind drift indicator a weighted strip of crepe paper, usually about 20 feet long, dropped out of an airplane to determine the amount of drift a jumper can expect during descent.

SOCCER

back a fullback; a player who plays defense in the backfield.

back heel to kick the ball backward with the heel of the foot.

back pass to pass the ball to a player behind.

banana pass to kick the ball off-center to impart it with spin, which produces a curving or "banana" trajectory. Also known as a banana kick, bending the ball.

bending the ball same as banana pass.

bicycle kick a volley in which the player upends himself and kicks the ball with his legs scissoring overhead. Also known as a hitch kick, overhead volley, reverse kick, scissors kick.

block and tackle to block the ball with one's foot or body to prevent an opponent from stealing it.

blue card in indoor soccer, a blue card help up by the referee to indicate that a player is being cited with a time penalty.

board in an indoor soccer match, to push an opponent into the fence or wall surrounding the field, an illegal play.

book to issue a yellow or other card to a player for a foul or for unsportsmanlike behavior.

boots commonly used name for soccer shoes.

box the penalty area or penalty box.

bully a mad scramble for a loose ball by both sides in front of a goal.

card to issue or show a yellow or other card.

catenaccio Italian term for "big chain," a largely defensive mode of play characterized by close, man-to-man coverage and one free man or sweeper who stand guard behind three or four fullbacks.

caution to issue a caution to a player. Same as card, book. A second offense may result in ejection from the game. See RED CARD.

center back the central defender, usually placed in front of a goal.

center circle at the center of the field, the circle from which kickoffs are taken at the start of each half.

center forward the position played closest to the opponent's goal; the offensive position also known as the central striker.

center halfback a midfield player who plays both offensive and defensive roles.

change on the fly in indoor soccer, to take out a player and send in a substitute while the ball is still in play.

charge to rush the shoulders of an opposing player to push him away from the ball, a legal tactic.

charge, illegal deliberate body contact that is violent or dangerous or in an area other than the shoulders, an infraction resulting in a free kick awarded to the offended team.

chest trap to stop a ball in flight with the chest.

chip to kick a high, lofting shot over the head of a defender. Also known as a lob pass.

clear to kick or throw the ball (by the goalie only) out of the goal area.

collecting the act of catching and gaining control of a passed ball with the feet.

convert a corner to score with an awarded corner kick.

convert a penalty to score with a penalty kick.

corner at each corner of the field, a small, quarter circle from which corner kicks are made.

corner kick a direct free kick from a corner taken by the offense after the ball has been propelled out of bounds past the goal line by the defense.

crease in indoor soccer, the 16-foot by 5-foot rectangular area in front of a goal.

cross pass a pass from one side of the field to the other.

curling the ball same as bending the ball.

cut down the angle the goalie's defensive tactic of running out to meet an opponent with the ball to cut down the opponent's visible shooting area to the goal.

defender a fullback or halfback.

direct free kick a direct free kick awarded to a team that has been seriously fouled by the opposing team.

dribble to propel the ball forward with light taps of the feet.

drop ball in a non penalty stoppage, a method of restarting play in which the referee drops the ball between two opposing players.

dropkick to drop the ball and kick it as it bounces; a kick made by the goalie.

drop pass stopping the ball while on the move and then leaving it or passing it backward to a player moving up from behind.

face off two opposing players facing each other during a drop ball.

feinting faking a move to elude an opponent.

flick to crisply pass or jab the ball with the outside of the foot. Also, to bounce the ball off the head for a pass or an attempted goal.

football another name for soccer. Also, the soccer ball.

forward a front line offensive player, responsible for moving the ball close to an opponent's goal and taking shots.

fullback a defender in the last line of defense in front of a goal.

ghost to fade into the background or play casually in the hope of being left undefended at a later, more critical time.

give-and-go to pass to a player, break away from a defender, and then receive a quick return pass.

goalie the goalkeeper.

goalkeeper the player who guards the goal to prevent shots from entering the net and scoring. The goalie.

goal line the boundary line at either end of the field.

goals against average the statistic indicating the average number of goals a goalie allows per game.

hack to kick an opponent, a foul.

hacker a dirty player who frequently commits fouls against opponents.

halfback one of several midfield players involved in offense and defense.

half-volley kick kicking the ball the instant it bounces up from the ground.

handballing illegally touching the ball with the hands.

hat trick three goals scored by the same player in a single game.

heading propelling the ball with the head.

head trap stopping an in flight ball with the head.

heavy pitch a slow playing field, such as one that is wet or has long grass.

heel pass kicking a pass with the back of the foot.

hitch kick same as bicycle kick.

indoor soccer soccer played on a smaller field with fewer players (6 per team instead of the standard 11) and slightly different rules.

inside left, inside right the inside forwards on the left or right sides of the field.

jockeying maneuvering or shepherding an opponent with the ball into a more tightly defended area.

juggling keeping the ball in the air by bouncing it continuously on the knees, feet, or head.

kill the ball to stop or trap a moving ball.

linesman one of two officials who assist the referee in making calls.

linkman same as a midfielder or halfback.

lob a high, arcing pass or shot.

major penalty a penalty in which the offending team must play short a man for 5 minutes.

marking guarding an opponent.

midfielders the offensive and defensive positions in the middle of the field.

MISL Major Indoor Soccer League.

NASL North American Soccer League.

nutmeg to kick the ball between a defender's legs and continue on down the field.

offside being in an illegal position on the opponent's side of the field, specifically between the goal line and the ball, the instant the ball is played with less than two opponents nearer the goal.

offside trap a strategic play to lure an opponent into an offside position in order to gain possession of the ball.

off-the-ball away from the ball.

outside left, outside right the forwards on the outside right or outside left of the field. Also known as wings, wingers.

penalty arc outside each penalty area in front of the goal, a half radius from which penalty kicks are made.

penalty area in front of and around the goal, the 44-yard by 18-yard, marked rectangular area from within which a goalie may handle the ball. A foul committed in this area results in a penalty kick being awarded to the offended team.

penalty kick a direct free kick taken from the penalty arc or penalty spot.

pitch the traditional name for a soccer field.

placekick to kick a ball that has been set motionless on the ground.

policeman a center back; the central backfield defender.

power play in indoor soccer, the man advantage of one team when the other team has temporarily lost a man due to a time penalty.

power play goal in indoor soccer, a goal scored while the defending team is short one man.

pull the goalkeeper a last-ditch effort to score a goal in the closing minutes of a game by replacing the goalie with a field player, which leaves the net open and vulnerable but provides one extra potential scorer.

punt a goalie's long kick away from his goal.

push pass a short pass made with the inside of the foot.

red card a red card held up by the referee when a player is ejected from a game.

referee the official who oversees a game and who is assisted by two linesmen.

scissors kick same as bicycle kick.

screen while dribbling, to keep the body between the ball and a defender. Also known as shielding.

shadow to guard an opponent closely.

show the ball while dribbling, to make the ball appear easy to steal in order to lure a defender closer to or away from a certain position.

slide tackle an attempt to kick or steal the ball away from a dribbler by sliding into the ball feet-first.

sole trap trapping a moving ball against the sole of the foot and the ground.

striker the center forward. A forward.

sweeper a player who represents the last line of defense before a goalkeeper; he plays in front of or behind the back line.

tackle to use the feet to dislodge or steal the ball away from an opponent.

tackle through the ball to run into an opponent while attempting to tackle the ball; it often results in the assessment of a foul.

targetman the central striker, who receives air balls to shoot on goal or to pass to players close to the goal.

thigh trap to trap or stop a moving ball with the thigh.

throw-in the method in which a ball is returned to play after going out of bounds.

touch the out-of-bounds area along the sidelines.

touchlines the sidelines.

trap to stop a ball in motion with the feet, knees, thighs, chest, or head. Also known as killing the ball.

volley kicking a ball in midair, before a bounce.

wings players positioned on the outside or flanks of a line. Also known as wingers.

yellow card a yellow card held up by the referee to show that a player has been cautioned for an infraction.

SQUASH

ace a shot so well placed that the opposing player cannot even make contact with it with his racquet.

alley shot a shot close to the side walls. Also known as a rail shot.

back wall shot bouncing the ball off the back wall powerfully enough so that it reaches the front wall without touching the floor.

boast bouncing the ball off a sidewall powerfully enough so that it reaches the front wall without touching the floor.

boast nick a boast shot aimed in such a way as to strike the front wall and junction of the floor and sidewall in quick succession so that the ball rolls out and is impossible for the opposing player to hit back.

corner shot a ball played into the sidewall close to the front wall and striking the front just above the tell-tale, from which it drops short to the floor making for a difficult return.

crosscourt shot a shot that crosses the court and sometimes forces the opposing player to use his backhand.

die where the ball is declared dead and fails to bounce.

doubles squash played by four players.

drive a slamming shot taken after the ball bounces.

drop nick a soft shot in which the ball hits the junction of the floor and sidewall and rolls out, making it impossible to return.

drop shot a low, soft shot that bounces only slightly, making it difficult to return.

fault an incorrect serve.

foot fault when the server's foot is in an illegal position when serving.

gallery the bleachers or seated area for spectators.

get getting to and returning a difficult shot.

half-volley a ball played after one bounce.

length a play that results in the ball dying before it reaches the back wall.

let the replaying of a point.

let point a point awarded to a player who has been deliberately interfered with by an opponent during play.

lob a high shot against the front wall.

nick any ball that strikes the juncture of floor and wall and rolls out for an impossible return.

Philadelphia boast a reverse boast.

putaway an irretrievable shot.

rally when two opponents return several shots back and forth before a point is finally scored.

service box the quarter circle in the corner of a service court in which a player must have at least one foot while serving.

telltale the line just above the floor on the front court, below which a shot is illegal.

volley a ball played in the air.

TENNIS

ace a perfectly placed serve that an opponent is unable to return.

ad in short for advantage in.

ad out short for advantage out.

advantage in the server's advantage; the point won by the server after deuce.

advantage out the receiver's advantage; the point won by the receiver after deuce.

alley along either side of the court, the long, additional area used only in doubles play.

approach shot a shot that allows a player to move toward the net.

attack the net to move quickly toward the net for a volley or a kill shot.

Australian grip a grip halfway between the eastern and the continental.

backcourt the rear portion of the court, between the baseline and the service line.

backhand a stroke taken from the left side of a right-handed player's body. (Opposite for a lefty.)

backspin reverse spin on a ball.

baseline the line marking the ends of the court.

baseline judge one of two linesmen who watch the baseline and call balls out of play.

blitz to bombard an opponent with a quick succession of fast, hard shots.

block volley to return a ball without swinging the racket; letting the ball bounce passively off the face of the racket.

break to win a game against the server.

break point the point that will win a game against the server.

butt the end of a racket handle.

cannonball a fast, hard serve.

carry literally to carry or hold the ball in play on one's racket, a penalty situation resulting in the loss of the point.

centerline the line dividing the service boxes.

changeover the switching of courts by the opposing players after every odd game in a set.

chip a soft, backspinning shot that dips and barely clears the net. Also known as a dink.

chop a shot made by a chopping swing of the racket, which imparts the ball with heavy spin.

clay court a court surface made of clay.

closed face refers to the face of the racket when it is tilted down toward the ground or down toward an incoming ball, as distinguished from an open face.

continental grip a popular grip that can be used for either forehand or backhand shots, characterized by the palm facing down and the index finger and thumb forming a V around the left side of the handle.

crosscourt shot a ball hit diagonally across the court.

cross slice a short, slicing motion of an open racket; it gives the ball backspin and sidespin simultaneously. Also known as a cut stroke.

Davis Cup an annual international teams tournament.

dead slang for a ball that has gone out of play.

default to forfeit a game, set, or match by failing to complete it.

defensive lob a very high, deep lob, executed to give a defensive player time to get into better position for the opponent's next shot.

deuce when players reach a tie score of 40 to 40. To win, one player must score two points in a row.

die said of a ball that fails to bounce, such as one imparted with underspin.

dink same as a chip.

double fault the failure to deliver a legal or in-bounds serve within two tries.

double hit to hit the ball twice in the same play, an infraction resulting in the loss of the point.

doubles a game with four players, two to a side.

down-the-line shot a shot hit straight down the sideline.

down-the-T shot a shot hit straight down the middle of the court, along the center service line.

drag volley a volley hit with an open racket, imparting some backspin.

drive a hard groundstroke.

drop shot a soft shot that barely clears the net and is therefore difficult for an opponent in the backcourt to reach.

eastern grip popular forehand grip in which the player "shakes hands" with the racket handle in a natural hand position. Also known as the shake hands grip.

error a failed return.

face the stringed, hitting surface of the racket.

fast court a court in which the ball tends to skid or bounce quickly, as on wood or grass.

fault failure to deliver a legal or in-bounds serve.

fifteen the first scoring unit or point.

flat a serve or shot executed with little or no spin.

follow-through the finishing portion of a swing.

foot fault stepping on or over the baseline while making a serve; two consecutive faults result in the loss of the point.

forecourt the area between the net and the service line.

forehand a shot executed on the right side of the body by a right-handed player. (Opposite for a lefty.)

gallery the spectators seating or area.

gallery play a showoff shot made to stir up a reaction from the spectators.

game point a point that wins a game if made by the player who is ahead.

game set a game-winning point in a set-winning game.

Grand Prix a yearlong, worldwide tournament circuit played by professionals, who earn points and prize money for a year-end championship.

grand slam winning the Australian, U.S., French, and Wimbledon singles championship in the same year.

grass court a court made of grass and known for its fast surface.

groundstroke a stroke made after an incoming ball has bounced, as distinguished from a volley.

gut a racket's string material, made from animal intestines.

half-volley to strike the ball immediately after a bounce.

jam to stroke the ball directly at an opponent's body in order to force an off-balance return.

jump smash a powerful, overhead shot made while jumping in the air.

kick the speed, height, and direction of a ball that has bounced up from the ground.

kill a hard, fast shot that eludes the opponent.

let a serve that nicks the top of the net and must be replayed.

linesman any one of the line judges who makes calls on whether a ball hits in or out of court.

lob a high, arcing shot.

love a score of zero.

match winning the best of three or more sets.

mixed doubles doubles in which each team has one male and one female.

moon ball a very high lob.

net judge a judge who sits on one side of the net and calls any lets on a serve.

open a tournament open to professionals and amateurs.

open face the face of the racket when it is tilted back away from an incoming ball, as distinguished from a closed face.

overhead a stroke hit with the arm over the head, as a serve.

passing shot a shot that passes by an opponent who is close to the net.

poach in a doubles game, to move intentionally into a partner's territory to attempt a surprise kill shot.

point the first point is 15, the second is 30, the third is 40, and the fourth is game. Four points wins a game.

point penalty a subtraction of one point for unsportsmanlike conduct.

power player a player who uses powerful serves and drives to win a game, as distinguished from a touch player.

punch volley a volley made by partially swinging or punching the racket.

put away to execute a kill shot.

rally a long exchange of shots between opponents before someone finally fails to make a return.

serve and volley to serve then quickly rush the net for a return volley.

service same as serve.

service box slang for service court.

service break winning a game against the server.

service court either of the 13½-foot by 21-foot rectangular boxes on both sides of the court in which the ball must land when served.

service line the line marking the boundaries of the service boxes.

set a scoring unit, specifically the first six games won by one player by a margin of 2.

set point a point that will win a set if the leading player scores.

sidespin a sideways spin imparted on the ball by a sideways slice of the racket.

singles court the court area measuring 78 feet by 27 feet.

slam same as a smash.

slice hitting under and across a ball to impart it with underspin and sidespin.

slow court a court surface that produces high, rebounding balls, as in clay.

smash a powerful, overhead stroke.

sphairstike the original name for tennis, as coined by its inventor.

spin ball rotation producing a curved flight path and an unpredictable bounce.

spin it in to serve a ball with spin.

stop volley a soft volley that barely drops over the net, used when the opponent is in the backcourt.

straight sets consecutive wins.

sudden death a tie-breaker game.

sweet spot the middle of the racket face; the optimum hitting surface.

tennis elbow painful condition characterized by inflammation of the tendons around the elbow, caused by twisting and general overuse of elbow in tennis.

throat the neck of the racket handle, just below the head.

topspin forward rotation imparted on a ball by brushing the racket face up and over the ball.

touch player a finesse or control player, as distinguished from a power player.

umpire the official seated in a high chair at one end of the net; he keeps the score and makes rulings.

underspin backward rotation imparted on a ball by brushing the racket face down and under the ball.

volley to hit the ball in the air, before it bounces on the ground.

Wimbledon the tennis championships held in Wimbledon, England.

THOROUGHBRED RACING (*Also see* HORSES)

acey deucy a riding style to facilitate balance during turns in which the right stirrup is shorter than the left.

across the board betting on one horse for win, place, and show.

aged a horse 7 years of age or older.

airing an exercise run. Also, a race in which the horse runs only at exercise speed.

also-ran a horse that did not finish in the money.

alter to castrate.

ankle boot a protective leather or rubber bootie for the fetlock.

ankle cutter a horse that strikes and cuts a fetlock with the opposite hoof while running.

apprentice a student jockey.

armchair ride a victory won without having to prod the horse.

baby a 2-year-old.

baby race a 2- to 4-furlong race for 2-year-olds.

back to slow down.

backstretch the straightaway at the far side of the track.

bangtail a bobbed or shortened trail.

barrel the torso of a horse.

barrier the starting gate.

bear in to move toward the inside rail.

bear out to move to the outside of the track, especially during a turn.

bend a turn in the track.

bit the mouth bar to which the reins are secured.

blanket finish a very close finish.

blind switch the position of being blocked by other horses in front and the decision to either drop back and go around them or wait for an opening.

blinkers the eye pieces that partially block a horse's vision, used to keep concentration focused on the track to the front.

blowout a brief workout to warm up a horse before a race.

boat race a fixed race.

bobble to stumble.

bolt to run off in a panic, as when some horses see the starting gate.

boot to kick the horse to make it run faster.

Boots and Saddles the bugle call accompanying the horses entering the track for post parade.

bottom the horse assigned to the outside post position.

break in the air to leap upward instead of out at the starting bell.

break maiden to win the first race of one's career, pertaining to either jockey or horse.

brittle feet hooves that chip easily.

bucked shins inflamed shins, due to stress.

bull ring a small track.

buzzer an illegal, battery-powered, vibrating device used to scare a horse into running faster.

calculator the clerk who calculates pari-mutuel odds.

cannon the foreleg between the ankle and the knee.

canter a slow gallop.

card a racing program.

carry the target to run last from start to finish.

chalk horse the favorite to bet on.

chalk player one who bets on favorites.

choppy abnormally short strides, due to lameness.

chute an extension of a stretch to provide a long, straight run from starting gate to first turn.

claiming race a race in which a horse is subject to purchase.

clerk of the scales the official who weighs riders and tack before and after a race.

clocker one who times workout runs, used as information for betting.

clothes horse blanket.

clubhouse turn a bend or turn in the track closest to the clubhouse. In races that begin on the homestretch, the first turn.

colors riders' colorful, identifying costumes.

croup the uppermost hindquarters of a horse.

cuppy a track broken into clods and hoofprints.

daily double winning a bet by correctly picking both winners of two races.

dark said of a track's nonracing day or night.

dark horse an underrated horse; a sleeper.

dead heat when at least two horses vie for the finish line nose-to-nose.

dead weight weights added to a saddle to raise the overall weight of rider and tack.

deep referring to a track that has been freshly harrowed.

derby race for 3-year-olds.

disqualify officially to drop back a horse's finishing position due to interference or illegal weight.

dope sheet horseracing information sheet.

drench to give medicinal liquid to a horse.

dwell to break slowly at the gate.

eighth furlong.

eighth pole a colored post marking ⅛ of a mile or 1 furlong from the finish line.

exacta picking the winner and place horses.

fade to tire and fall behind at the homestretch or before.

farrier a horseshoer.

fast track a dry, hard track.

fetlock the ankle of a horse.

field collective term for all the entrants in a race.

film patrol the crew that films the race to monitor for interference or other fouls.

five-eighths pole a post marking 5 furlongs from the finish line.

flash a change of odds shown on the tote board.

flatten out position of an exhausted horse, specifically with its head hung low and even with its body.

footing a track's surface condition.

free lance a jockey who works independently and is not contracted by any one stable.

freshener time allotted for rest to restore a horse's energy.

frog the fleshy cushion on the sole of the foot.

furlong one-eighth of a mile.

futurity a race in which horses are entered before they are born.

gad a jockey's whip.

gallop a horse's fastest gait, in which all four feet are intermittently off the ground at the same time.

gelding a castrated male horse.

gentleman jockey an amateur jockey.

graduate to break maiden.

groom the stable assistant who grooms the horse and escorts it to the paddock for a race.

grunter an out-of-condition horse.

gumbo a heavy mud track.

half-mile pole the pole located 4 furlongs from the finish line.

hand a measure of equine height, specifically 4 inches.

handicap the assigning of weights to equalize competition. Also, to study the records of horses' past performances to help in choosing a future winner.

hand ride to teach a horse to take longer or faster strides by pulling on its head at the beginning of each stride.

hat trick a jockey's winning of three races on a single program.

hayburner a horse that costs more money to maintain than it is worth.

head of the stretch the last portion of the final turn.

heat a race.

herd to turn a horse to block another from gaining a superior position.

homestretch the straightaway in front of the stands.

hop to drug a horse illegally.

hot-walker a stable assistant who walks a horse to cool it off after a race.

impost the weight a horse must carry in a handicap race.

infield the area inside of the track, where the tote board is located.

inquiry an official investigation of a race to determine if it was run fairly.

irons stirrups.

jockey the rider. Also, to jockey for position during a race.

juvenile a 2-year-old.

kiss the eighth pole to finish way behind.

lead pony the horse and rider that lead thoroughbreds to the post.

leather a whip.

length 8 to 9 feet.

maiden a jockey or horse that hasn't won a race yet.

mile pole a colored post marking 1 mile to the finish line.

monkey crouch a riding style characterized by a low crouch over the horse's withers.

muck out to clean out a horse's stall.

mudder a horse that runs especially well on muddy tracks.

nightcap the final race on a card.

objection a jockey's complaint of a foul.

odds board the tote board.

odds on odds of less than even money.

off-the-board to finish out of the money.

off-track betting betting conducted away from the track.

outrider the mounted escort who leads horses to the post.

overland making wide turns.

paddock a saddling enclosure or stall. Also, a pasture.

parimutuels a betting system in which the winners collect all the money bet by the losers, minus house percentage.

pasteboard track a fast track that is thin and hard.

pinched back getting pocketed and pushed back behind a group of horses.

pocket being surrounded by other horses.

pony any nonracing, working horse on a track, such as a lead pony.

pool the total amount bet.

post the starting gate.

pull to hold a horse back intentionally to prevent it from winning.

punter one who plays the horses.

quarter pole the colored post 2 furlongs from the finish line.

quinella betting in which the bettor tries to pick first two finishers.

racing secretary the track handicapper and official who assigns weights in handicap races.

rack up to run into or interfere with several horses at once.

rate to hold back a horse early in a race to help conserve its energy for the home stretch.

roar loud coughlike breathing of a horse.

runner a messenger between the people in the clubhouse boxes and the mutuel window.

run wide to run too far out from the inside rail and waste ground.

saliva test a drug test performed on winning horses.

save ground to hug the inside rail, the most efficient means of saving ground and running the track faster.

scenic route a wide run covering too much ground; an inefficient run.

scratch the withdrawal of an entrant from a race.

scratch sheet a racing tip sheet featuring graded handicaps, scratches, and so on.

seat the rider's posture on a horse.

sex allowance a weight concession granted to female horses running against males.

shed row row of barns near the backstretch.

shoe board a sign listing the types of shoes worn by the entrants.

short an out-of-shape horse that fades in a stretch.

shut off to cut in front of another racer and block him out.

silks the costumes worn by the riders.

sixteenth pole the pole marking half a furlong from the finish line.

skin to roll the surface of a track to make it harder and faster.

sleeper an underrated horse.

sophomore a 3-year-old horse.

spit out the bit said of an exhausted horse who refuses to go any further.

sprint any short race, about 7 furlongs or less.

stake the commission paid to the winning jockey or trainer.

stall gate a starting gate having individual compartments for each horse.

stewards the three officials of racing law who judge races.

stiff to hold back a horse intentionally to prevent it from winning.

string collective term for the horses owned by one stable.

tack collective term for the saddle and other equipment placed on the horse.

three-eighths pole the colored pole marking 3 furlongs from the finishing line.

three-quarters pole the colored pole marking 6 furlongs from the finish line.

tout a trainer, groom, stable boy, jockey, or other person connected to the sport who provides "inside information" on a horse or race for a fee.

trackmaster person in charge of maintaining the track.

Triple Crown winning the Kentucky Derby, the Preakness Stakes, and the Belmont Stakes.

urine test a drug test for horses.

valet one who cares for a jockey's clothing and carries his tack.

walking ring an oval walking area near the paddock where the horses are walked for the purpose of observation by the betting public. Also known as the parade ring.

walkover a race in which every horse is scratched but one, who can win simply by walking in.

washy referring to a sweaty horse.

weigh-in the weighing of jockeys with tack after a race is over.

weigh-out the weighing of jockeys with tack before a race begins.

whoop-de-doo an aggressive riding style in which the horse is frequently whipped and is allowed to run as fast as possible without restraint.

VOLLEYBALL

antennas the vertical rods at either edge of the net; a ball striking the antenna on either side is deemed out of bounds.

attack block an aggressive attempt to stop the ball before it passes over the net.

back set a set made by a setter overhead and back to a spiker.

block a defensive move by one or more players to block passage of the ball over or near the net.

bump pass another name for a forearm pass—a ball played underhand off the pressed-together forearms.

candy cane a hard, sizzling jump serve that hooks.

contacted ball a ball that touches or is touched by an part of a player's clothing.

crosscourt serve a serve made to the opponents right-hand sideline.

dig an underhand save close to the floor, used to retrieve or play off a spike; a spiked ball that is saved and passed.

digging saving and passing a powerfully spiked ball.

digging lips slang term for digging someone's best spike or shot repeatedly.

dink a deceptive variation of the spike in which the ball is not smashed with the hand but flicked over blockers by the fingertips.

dive diving to retrieve a ball before it touches the floor and scores.

double block two defenders rising up at the same time to block a spike or other shot.

English imparting spin on the ball; spin.

facial a ball that is spiked into someone's face. Also known as getting mudpacked.

fault a violation of the rules.

floater a ball struck in such a manner as to avoid giving it spin; the result is a ball that when struck may float left or right, rise or drop, or follow an erratic trajectory.

forearm pass same as a bump pass.

foul a violation of the rules.

line serve a serve made down the opponent's left sideline.

lollipop slang term for a soft serve easily returned by the opposition.

mudpacked same as a facial.

netting touching the net while the ball is in play; the offending team loses possession of the ball or loses a point.

off-speed spike a spike struck deceptively soft to throw the blockers' timing off.

overhand pass the standard pass executed with both hands held at head height or above.

seam the open space between two serve receivers, or any vulnerable area between players.

service area where the ball is served, specifically both right rear corners of the court at end lines and extending 6 feet back.

serving rotation the rotation of servers on each new possession of the ball, the players moving clockwise into their new positions.

set an overhand pass that places the ball into good position for a teammate to spike over the net.

setter the player whose primary function it is to set the ball to the spiker.

side out the transfer of the serve to the defensive team after the offensive team fails to score a point.

sizzling the pits spiking the ball directly into a blocker's armpits.

spike a ball that is struck powerfully into the opponent's court.

spiker the player who executes the spike.

thrown ball any ball that is judged to be thrown instead of struck, a foul violation.

WINDSURFING

abeam at right angles to the board.

aft toward the stern.

apparent wind the wind felt by the windsurfer, not the true wind one would feel if standing still.

backing wind a wind that is changing direction in a counterclockwise manner.

beam reach a wind blowing from abeam at 90 degrees to the board's course.

bearing away sailing away from the wind.

beating sailing a zigzagging course to windward close-hauled.

bow the front or nose of the board.

break the point where a wave breaks.

camber the degree of curve or fullness in a sail.

carve to cut a turn at high speed.

cavitation when the small fin or fins at the back of the board fail to grip the water, causing the stern to slip and slide sideways.

cleat a hook or fitting on which line is secured.

clew the outside corner of a sail; it attaches to the end of the wishbone.

clew-first to sail with the outside corner of the sail pointed into the wind, used in freestyle and as a means of changing course.

close-hauled sailing as close to the wind as possible.

close reach term referring to the wind blowing slightly forward of abeam.

cross seas waves or current that strikes the board from abeam.

daggerboard the large, removable center fin that prevents the board from sliding sideways. See STORM DAGGERBOARD.

donkey kick a method of kicking the back of the board down to facilitate launching or jumping off a wave.

dry suit a neoprene suit to protect oneself from cold water and hypothermia.

duck tack to duck under the rig, as opposed to walking around it, when tacking.

eye of the wind the exact direction from which a wind is blowing.

fin a skeg or daggerboard.

following seas waves or current moving toward the board from behind.

foot the bottom of the sail.

freestyle the performance of stunts on the board. In noncompetition, also known as hot dogging.

freshening wind a wind growing in strength.

fresh wind a wind of 17 to 21 knots.

gybing see JIBING.

harden to bring the sail closer to the body.

head the top of the sail.

head sea current or waves that strike the board head on or from the front.

hull the board itself, minus the rig.

hypothermia dangerous loss of body heat, due to extended exposure to cold water or air.

jibing turning from one tack to another so that the stern passes through the eye of the wind. Also spelled *gybing*.

leech the edge of the sail between the clew and the head.

leeward the side furthest from the wind. Opposite of windward.

leeway sideways movement of the board to leeward.

luff the edge of the sail from the head to the tack.

luff up to change course and sail closer to the wind.

marginal sail a sail used in hard winds.

mast same as a mast in a sailboat.

mast foot the portion of the mast that attaches inside the mast foot well.

offshore wind a wind blowing from the land to the water.

onshore wind a wind blowing from the water to the land.

outhaul the line that pulls the clew out to the end of the wishbone.

pintail a board having a tapered tail for better control in strong winds.

plane to skim lightly across the surface of the water.

port when looking forward, the left side of the board.

pumping pumping the rig back and forth to produce added wind in the sail.

purling surfing the bow straight into a wave and going head over heels.

rail the side of the board.

railing sailing with the board slightly inclined on its side.

regatta a meeting of windsurfers who compete in events or races.

rig all of the rigging above the universal joint; collective term for the mast, sail, and wishbone.

roundboard a board having a rounded belly, faster but less stable than a regular board.

running sailing with the wind coming from directly behind.

scoop curvature at the nose of the board.

skeg a small fin at the stern of the board to prevent the tail from sliding.

slalom to jibe and tack.

starboard when looking forward, the right side of the board.

stern the back of the board.

storm daggerboard a short daggerboard.

tack the corner of the sail by the universal joint.

tacking a method of changing course in which the nose of the board passes through the eye of the wind.

trim to let the sail in or out as wind conditions change.

universal joint at the mast foot, the apparatus that allows the rig to be inclined and to be swung 360 degrees.

uphaul the line used to pull the rig up out of the water.

veering wind a wind that is changing direction in a clockwise manner.

wetted area the portion of board touched by water, producing drag.

windward the side of the board nearest the wind.

wishbone the booms.

WRESTLING

advantage position the on-top position.

amplitude a throw with exceptional height. Exceptional height on a throw scores extra points in some styles of wrestling.

ankle ride manipulating an opponent in a disadvantaged position by lifting his ankle.

arm throw locking the opponent's arm and executing a throw by rotating the body.

back-arching a throwing method in which the wrestler grasps his opponent and literally bends over backward, causing the opponent to flip over and be pinned.

bear hug a body lock made with the arms around the torso.

body lock same as a bear hug.

breakdown flattening an opponent on the mat on his belly or side.

chicken wing wrapping an arm around an opponent's arm and pinning it behind his back.

counter wrestling reacting to an opponent's offensive moves instead of initiating such moves.

crossface a headhold across the jaw to the opponent's far shoulder.

disadvantage position the bottom position.

dump to pull an opponent's leg out from under him in order to flip him onto his back.

escape to get out of a bottom position into a neutral position.

fall same as a pin.

far side cradle a pinning technique in which the opponent's head and knee are held together.

fireman's cradle hooking an arm under an opponent's crotch and flipping him over.

freestyle the style of wrestling used in the Olympics and other international competition.

Greco-Roman wrestling an international and Olympic style of wrestling that limits the use of the legs and feet.

half-nelson a pinning hold in which an arm is thrust under the opponent's arm and locked over his neck or head.

hammerlock a hold in which the opponent's arm is pinned up and behind his back.

headlock a hold in which an arm is wrapped around the opponent's head.

key to react to an opponent's reactions and adjust an attack accordingly.

lookaway a method of raising and turning the head to counter a half-nelson.

nearfall a vulnerable position in which the shoulders are exposed to the mat but are not touching.

pin to hold both of an opponent's shoulder blades to the mat for a set amount of time to win the bout. Also known as a fall.

pommeling battling with the arms and hands to gain upper body position.

reversal when a wrestler in the bottom position breaks out and gains control of the man on top.

riding manipulating an opponent from the top position.

roll an attempt at an escape and reversal by rolling out from under an opponent.

scrimmage to practice wrestling maneuvers.

setups false movements or changes of stance that trick an opponent into a vulnerable position.

sit-out escaping from a disadvantaged position by sitting up abruptly.

slam an excessively powerful throw to the mat, resulting in a penalty.

snapdown a takedown in which the opponent's head is snapped back into the mat.

snatch attacking the opponent's leg at the knee. Also known as a high single.

souplesse a body throw made with the back-arch.

standup escaping an opponent's hold by standing up abruptly.

takedown throwing an opponent down on the mat from a neutral position.

turk lifting one leg of an opponent, then tripping the other leg out from under him for a takedown to the mat.

Transportation

HORSE-DRAWN CARRIAGES AND COACHES OF THE 19TH CENTURY

barouche a four-wheeled vehicle having facing seats to accommodate six people, popular with families. The barouche's collapsible top quickly converted it into an open vehicle, which made it the popular choice as a parade carriage for presidents and other dignitaries.

brougham an English-designed, boxlike carriage enclosing two to four passengers, pulled by one horse.

buggy see top buggy.

cabriolet a one-horse, two-wheeled carriage having two seats and a collapsible top.

chaise a one-horse, two-wheeled open carriage with folding hood. Also called a shay.

coachman the driver of a coach or carriage.

Concord the most popular stagecoach of the period, build in Concord, N.H. It could carry up to nine people inside and as many as a dozen outside, hanging off and around the roof.

Conestoga a dory-shaped wagon having a hooped canvas roof, used for long-distance traveling and pulled by a team of six horses.

covered wagon a smaller, lighter version of a conestoga.

curricle an English, two-wheeled open carriage, pulled by two horses.

dormeuse a French traveling carriage.

draft horse a large, strong horse capable of pulling a carriage. Also called a dray.

dray horse a draft horse.

drummer's wagon a merchandise wagon used by salesmen (drummers) serving storekeepers. They were noted for their painted scenes and gilt scrolls decorating the sides.

freight wagon a huge wagon having 6-foot wheels with inch-thick iron tires, noted for making permanent ruts in roads all over the country.

gee driver's traditional command to horses to turn right. See HAW.

gig a one-horse, two-wheeled, American-designed open carriage.

governess cart an open cart for pulling children, for fun.

grocer's wagon a large, open-top wagon.

gurney a rear-entry cab that seated four passengers, popularly used in New York.

hack a one-horse cab. Also, a driving horse.

hansom a one-horse cab or cabriolet. Noted for having its driver's seat located high in the back of the vehicle instead of at the front.

haw a driver's traditional command to horses to turn left. See GEE.

landau a German-designed, four-wheeled, closed carriage having two passenger seats and a roof made in two sections, the rear of which could be folded down.

omnibus a horse-pulled bus.

phaeton a two-horse carriage having a collapsible top, the vehicle of choice among physicians and women.

prairie schooner same as a conestoga but having a flat, boxy body rather than a boatlike one.

road coach an English-designed traveling carriage similar to a stage coach.

rockaway a multipassenger carriage with a roof extending over the driver to protect him from the elements. The rockaway was noted for its front window through which the driver and passengers could converse.

shay a chaise.

Studebaker an open farm wagon pulled by two horses.

surrey a family vehicle having two long seats facing forward and, frequently, a fringed, canopy top.

top buggy a one-horse buggy accommodating one or two people, used for errands and short excursions.

Victoria an elegant wagon resembling a giant slipper on wheels. It had plush upholstery and a collapsible top and was used by the upper class

SHIPS AND BOATS

abeam at right angles to the keel.

aft at, near, or toward the rear of the ship.

air port porthole, for light and ventilation.

aloft in the upper rigging above decks.

amidships at or near the middle of a ship.

anchor, bower the main or largest anchor on a ship, carried in the bow.

anchor, kedge small anchor used for kedging or warping, freeing a vessel from shoals.

anchor, sea conical cloth bag dragged behind a vessel to reduce drift; also known as a drogue.

anchor, stream anchor about one-third the weight of a bower, used when mooring in narrow channels or in a harbor to prevent the vessel's stern from swinging.

argosy large merchant ship, or any fleet of merchant ships.

astern in the rear of a vessel.

auxiliaries collective term for the various motors, winches, pumps, and similar equipment on a vessel.

ballast any portable or fixed weight carried to make a vessel more stable or seaworthy. Types of ballast include sand, concrete, lead, scrap, pig iron, and seawater.

ballast tanks water tanks that are filled or emptied to aid in a vessel's stability; also used in subs for submerging.

batten strip of wood or steel used in securing tarpaulins.

beam the extreme width of a vessel.

berth bed, bunk, or sleeping compartment. Also, any place where a ship is moored.

bilges the rounded portions of a ship's bottom or shell.

bilge pump pump that removes water from the bilges.

binnacle a stand that houses a compass for easy viewing.

block a pulley or system of pulleys.

boiler steam generator.

booby hatch access hatch on the weather deck with a hood and sliding cover to keep water out.

bollard iron or wooden fixture on a vessel or dock to which mooring lines are attached.

boss the curved or swollen portion of the ship's underwater hull around the propellor shaft.

bosun boatswain—petty officer in charge of rigging, sail maintenance, anchors, and deck operations.

bosun's chair a seat for hoisting a person aloft for repairs.

bow front of a ship. Also known as a prow.

bowsprit spar that projects over the bow, used to hold the lower ends of head sails, or used for observation.

bridge an observation platform, often forming the top of a bridge house or pilot house, giving a clear view of the weather deck.

bulkhead any one of the partition walls which divide the interior of a ship into compartments or rooms.

cabin the living quarters for officers and passengers

cabin boy one who waits on the passengers and officers of a ship.

cabin class ship accommodations above tourist class but below first-class.

capstan drum or barrel-shaped apparatus operated by hand or by motor for hauling in heavy anchor chains.

cargo hatch the large opening in the deck to permit loading of cargo below.

cargo net net used to haul cargo aboard.

cargo port an opening with a watertight door in the side of a ship to allow the loading and unloading of cargo.

chafing gear rubber hoses, sheathes, and other materials used to protect ropes from wearing where they rub on sharp edges.

chart house small room adjacent to the bridge for charts and navigating instruments.

cleats piece of wood or metal having two projecting arms or horns on which to belay ropes.

clinometer instrument that indicates the angle of roll or pitch of a vessel.

companionway a hatchway in a deck with a set of steps or ladders leading from one deck to another.

cordage collective term for all of the ropes on a vessel.

cradle wooden frame where boats are stowed on shore.

cross tree athwartship pieces fitted over the trees on a mast.

crow's nest lookout perch attached to or near the head of a mast.

cuddy a small cabin.

davit small crane on a ship's side for hoisting boats or supplies.

deadlight a porthole lid or cover.

deep waterline the depth of a vessel in the water when carrying the maximum amount of allowable weight or cargo.

derrick a type of crane used for hoisting and swinging heavy weights.

door, airtight a door constructed to prevent the passage of air.

door, watertight a door constructed to prevent the passage of water.

draft, draught the depth of a vessel below the waterline.

draft marks numbers on a vessel's bow or stern indicating the draft or depth of the vessel below the waterline.

dry dock a hollow floating structure designed to submerge in order to float a vessel into it, and then to lift the vessel out of the water for repairs or construction.

fantail the overhanging stern section on some vessels.

fathom nautical unit of measurement, in the United States, 6 feet or 1.829 meters.

fender protective plate, bundles of rope, old tires, or other material running along the side of a ship to prevent scratches and dents from rubbing against other vessels or piers.

fetch the distance from a wind's point of origin over the sea to a vessel, affecting the height of waves. Also, to swing around or veer.

fin a projecting keel.

flotilla fleet of small vessels.

flotsam and jetsam debris, goods, or cargo cast or washed from an imperiled or wrecked ship.

flukes the hooks or holding claws of an anchor.

fore the front of a ship or bow area.

fore and aft lengthwise of a ship.

forecastle structure on the upper deck of a ship toward the fore; the crew quarters on a merchant ship.

foul the sea growth or foreign matter covering the underwater portion of a ship's shell.

founder to sink after filling with water.

galley kitchen.

gangplank board or platform used for boarding passengers or cargo.

gangway an opening in a ship's side for the passage of freight or passengers.

grapnel similar to a small anchor, used for recovering small items dropped overboard or to hook onto lines from a distance.

graybeards choppy, frothy waves.

gunwale the upper edge of a side of a vessel.

guys wires, ropes, or chains used to support booms, davits, and such like.

halyards light lines used in hoisting signals or flags; also, the ropes used in hoisting gaffs, sails, or yards.

hatchway accessway or opening in a deck.

hawse hole through which the anchor chain is hoisted or released; any hole through which a chain or cable is passed.

hawser rope or cable used in mooring or towing.

head toilet.

heave to to stop the forward motion of a vessel and lie dead in the water.

heel the leaning of a vessel to one side, caused by wind, waves, or shifting cargo.

helm the steering apparatus, including the tiller, the rudder, and the wheel.

hog scrub broom used for scraping a ship's bottom underwater.

hold space below decks for cargo.

jack ladder ladder with wooden steps and side ropes.

jury temporary structures, such as makeshift masts or rudders, used in an emergency. Also, juryrigging.

keel the main structural member running fore and aft along the bottom of a vessel, also known as the backbone.

keelson a beam running above the keel of a vessel.

knot unit of speed, one nautical mile (6,080 feet) an hour.

lanyard rope having one free end and one attached to any object for the purpose of remote control; or any rope used for fastening riggings.

lee the side of a vessel sheltered from the wind, or leeward; opposite of the windward side.

list deviation of a vessel from an upright position, caused by waves, wind, bilging, or shifting cargo.

magazine storage compartment for the stowage of ammunition.

mast upright pole on the center line of a ship's deck, used for carrying sails or for supporting rigging, cargo, and boat-handling gear.

messroom compartment where crew members eat their meals. An officer's meal compartment is sometimes called a wardroom messroom.

mooring the operation of anchoring a vessel or securing it to a mooring buoy, wharf, or dock.

mooring lines chains, ropes, or cables used to tie a ship to a wharf or dock.

nautical mile 6,080 feet.

panting the pulsations of the bow and stern bottoms as the vessel rises and plunges in rough seas.

pea jacket short, heavy woolen seaman's coat.

pelorus navigational instrument similar to a compass, used in taking bearings. Also known as a dumb compass.

pilot house navigational center near the front of a vessel, providing an unobstructed view in all directions except directly aft.

pitching rising and falling of a vessel's bow as it rides other waves.

pitchpoling the flipping over of a vessel in rough seas, from front to back.

plunger wave with a distinctly convex back with a crest that fails suddenly and violently, usually found near shore. See SPILLER.

poop the structure or raised deck at the aft of a vessel.

port the left side of a vessel when looking from aft forward.

pudding fender material constructed of ropes, canvas, leather, or old tires to prevent chafing or denting from piers or other vessels.

regatta a boat race or series of boat races.

rigging collective term for all ropes, chains, or cables used to support masts, yards, booms, and similar equipment.

roll motion of a vessel from side to side in rough seas.

rudder flat slab of metal or wood used in steering a vessel.

scuppers deck drains or gutters for carrying off rain or seawater.

scuttlebutt drinking fountain.

shellback veteran sailor or old salt.

shroud set of ropes stretched from the masthead to a vessel's side, used for support or to ascend the mast.

sick bay medical service area.

sounding measurement of the depth of water.

spar pole serving as a mast, boom, gaff, yard, bowsprit, and such like.

spiller wave with a concave back with a crest that breaks gradually and continuously, usually found away from shore.

starboard the right side of a vessel when looking aft forward.

stateroom a private room for passengers or officers.

stem the front of a bow.

stern the aft or rear of a vessel.

superstructure any structure built above the uppermost complete deck, such as a pilothouse or bridge.

tack any change of course or veering of a vessel to one side in order to take advantage of a side wind.

tiller an arm attached to the rudder for operation of the rudder.

turn turtle to capsize.

wake wash or churning water left behind a ship's passage.

weather deck uppermost continuous deck exposed to the weather.

windlass a drumlike apparatus used for hoisting heavy anchor chains and hawsers.

yard a spar attached at its middle to a mast and running athwartship as a support for a square sail, halyard, lights, and other equipment.

yardarm outer end of a yard.

SAILING (*Also see* SHIPS AND BOATS)

abeam at right angles to the vessel.

ADF automatic direction finder, a radio direction finder.

aft near or at the stern.

aground hung up on the bottom or on shore.

ahull when a vessel is hove-to with all of its sails lowered.

alee on the side of the boat opposite of the wind direction.

all standing all sails flying.

aloft anything overhead.

anchorage a safe place to lay anchor, preferably protected from wind and current.

anchors aweigh a directive to raise the anchor.

anchor light a white light illuminated on the forestay at night.

anemometer a device for measuring wind speed.

antifoulant a chemical agent, such as copper, used in boat paint to retard the growth of algae and barnacles on the bottom of the boat.

aport to the port or left side of the vessel.

apparent wind the wind strength and direction as perceived on a moving vessel; not the actual wind.

ashore on shore.

aspect ratio the ratio of sail height to sail length, for example, a tall, narrow sail is said to have a high aspect ratio.

astern toward or at the stern.

athwartship same as abeam.

autopilot a device used in tandem with a compass on a boat's steering apparatus to automatically maintain a constant course.

auxiliary an engine used on a sailboat when the wind fails.

back a sail to fill a sail with wind from an opposing direction in order to slow the vessel.

backing wind a wind direction that is changing in a counterclockwise fashion.

backstay a wire rigged to control the amount of bend in a mast.

ballast any heavy objects or substance, such as sand, stones, water, laid in the bottom of a vessel to help stabilize it, especially in heavy seas.

barber hauler an adjustment for a jib sheet to change the sheeting angle.

bare poles said of a vessel sailing with all sails furled, when the wind is powerful enough to move the boat without sails.

barnacles marine animals that attach themselves to a boat's bottom.

barometer an instrument that measures atmospheric pressure.

batten a strip of wood, plastic, or metal fitted into a sail's pockets to help maintain the sail's correct shape.

beach to sail a vessel onto the shore.

beam the width of a vessel at its widest point.

bear away to alter course away from the wind. Also known as bearing off, falling off.

bearing position or direction in relation to something else.

beat to sail to windward close-hauled while tacking; to make a series of tacks on an upwind course.

Beaufort wind scale a wind and sea classification scale, from 0 (flat calm) to 12 (hurricane winds with waves reaching 14 meters).

becalmed unable to move due to wind failure.

belay to wrap or secure a line around a cleat or belaying pin.

belaying pin a wood or metal pin around which line is secured.

bend a sail to attach a sail to the boom and mast.

berth a docking space. Also, a sleeping compartment.

bilge the area beneath the cabin floor, where water (bilge water) tends to collect.

binnacle an encased compass mounted on a pedestal.

bitt a short post on a deck or dock, used for belaying mooring lines.

bitter end the last link of an anchor chain as it is let out. Also, the end of any line.

blanket the loss of wind when one boat positions itself directly upwind of a downwind boat.

block a pulley.

blooper an L-shaped sail.

board to get on or walk on a boat.

boat hook a pole used to aid in mooring or for securing another boat.

boom the spar on which the bottom or foot of a sail is secured.

boom vang a tackle attached to the boom to keep it from rising.

bosun's chair a seat in which a crew member is hoisted to conduct work aloft.

bow the front of a vessel.

bowline a mooring line at the bow. Also known as a painter.

bowsprit a spar projecting beyond the bow, for attaching a headsail.

break ground to break an anchor free from the sea bottom.

breakwater a barrier to protect a harbor from heavy seas.

brightwork collective term for all metal fittings and varnished woodwork.

broach to lose control of the boat, which swings about sideways.

bulkhead a partition.

bulwarks the raised sides of a vessel, above the upper deck.

buoy a flotation device, sometimes having bells and lights, for marking banks, channels, and hazards.

burgee a yacht club pennant.

cabin living space below deck.

camber the curvature of a sail.

cast off to release mooring lines and set sail.

catamaran a twin-hulled sailboat.

centerboard the large center fin or plate, used in place of a keel; it helps prevent rolling. See daggerboard, keel.

chock a deck fitting through which lines are passed.

cleat a one or two-pronged fixture around which line is belayed.

clew the lower aft corner of a fore-and-aft sail.

clinometer an instrument that measures a vessel's sideways inclination or heel.

close-hauled sailing as close to the oncoming wind direction as possible without luffing.

clove hitch a temporary mooring knot that comes untied with sideways tension.

cockpit where the steering wheel or the tiller is located.

come about altering a boat's course from one tack to another.

companionway a stairway or ladder descending to the cabin.

cordage commonly used term for any thick line or rope.

course heading; direction.

crabbing moving sideways through the water; making leeway.

cradle the framed support upon which a vessel rests on shore.

cringle a ring through which rope is threaded in a sail. Also known as a grommet.

daggerboard a small, daggerlike centerboard, commonly found on small boats.

dead ahead directly ahead.

dead reckoning to navigate by deduction through knowledge of current position, speed, and heading.

deep six to throw something overboard.

doldrums equatorial region of the ocean, notorious for its dead calms, the bane of sailors.

downhaul the tackle used to increase tension on the luff of a sail.

draft the portion of a vessel that is submerged. Also known as the draw.

drifter a headsail used in faint winds.

drogue a conelike sea anchor.

earing a short line used to secure a reefed sail to the boom.

ensign a national flag.

fall off same as bear off.

fender any kind of cushioning hung over the hull of a boat to protect it from contact with a dock or another boat.

fend off to push off with the feet, hands, or a boat hook to avoid contact with another boat or a dock.

fetch to sail close-hauled without the need to tack.

fittings hardware and fixtures on a vessel.

fix an exact position, as deduced by navigational skills.

flemish to coil a line flat on a deck in order to dry it uniformly.

following sea current that is traveling in the same direction as the vessel.

foot the bottom edge of a sail.

fore near or at the bow.

fore and aft from the bow to the stern.

foredeck the deck portion forward of the mast.

foresail a triangular sail attached forward of the mast and pronounced for-'s'l.

forestay rigging extending from the top of the mast to the bow to keep the mast from moving backwards.

foul to entangle.

founder the sinking of a boat as it fills with water.

freeboard the portion of the hull that is not under water.

furl to roll up a sail on its boom or spar.

galley a kitchen.

gangplank a bridge walk set as a ramp between a vessel and the dock, to facilitate boarding.

Genoa a large headsail or jib.

ghosting sailing in a calm when the wind is apparently absent.

gimbals fixtures that allow objects, such as a lamp, a barometer, a compass, to swivel and remain level in rough seas.

gunkholing sailing in shallow waters.

gunwale the uppermost edge of the hull's sides, pronounced gunnel.

guy a line or wire.

halyard any line used to hoist a sail.

hand one of the crew.

hard alee to come about.

harden up to sail closer to the wind.

hatch a doorway in a deck.

hauser a heavy line used for mooring or towing.

head the top edge of a sail. Also, a toilet.

heading the direction the boat is sailing in.

headsail any sail set forward of the mast, such as a drifter, jib, or Genoa.

head sea current that is running in the opposite direction of the vessel.

heave crew's pulling together.

heave to to stop forward motion by backing the headsail.

heaving line the mooring line with weighted end, tossed to someone on a dock.

heel the lean or angle of a vessel when sailing.

helm the steering wheel or the tiller.

helmsman the person who steers.

hike to lean far out over the side of a boat to help counter extreme heeling.

hiking straps footstraps used to help secure crew members when hiking.

hoist to raise a sail.

hold a storage area below deck.

hove down extreme heeling.

in irons a boat that has stopped while turning against the wind.

jib a triangular headsail.

jib boom extending beyond the bowsprit, a spar to take an extra headsail.

jibe to tack while sailing downwind.

jury rig to construct a makeshift part to replace a damaged part, a required skill of sailors.

kedge a means of freeing a boat that has run aground on a sandbar, specifically by throwing an anchor in front of the boat and then pulling the boat free. Also, the small anchor used for this purpose.

keel the fixed fore-and-aft member or backbone of a vessel's bottom.

kite another name for a spinnaker.

labor to roll and pitch in heavy seas.

landfall the first sighting of land.

lanyard any short piece of line used to secure a loose object, such as a pail or a tool, or for fastening riggings.

lash to secure a loose object with line.

launch a small boat used to carry people from land to a moored vessel, or vice versa.

lay up to store a boat during winter.

lazarette a small storage compartment in the stern.

leading edge the front portion of a sail.

lee to leeward; on the side of the boat protected from the wind.

leech the unattached edge of a triangular sail.

leeward the direction the wind is blowing, pronounced loo'ard.

leeway sideways motion of a boat, pushed by the wind or current.

line rope.

list leaning of a vessel caused not by wind or current but by unbalanced weight on board.

log an instrument fixed to a vessel's keel for measuring speed. Also, a journal of daily courses, distances sailed, weather conditions, and similar entries.

luff the leading edge of a sail.

luff up to sail into the wind, causing the leech of the sail to flap.

mainsail the main or largest sail on a boat, pronounced mains'l.

make fast to secure a line.

Marconi-rigged a triangular sail rigged fore and aft. Also known as Bermuda-rigged.

mast the large, vertical spar to which sails are attached.

masthead the top of the mast.

masthead fly at the masthead, a weathervane or wind indicator.

midships in or near the middle of the ship. Also, amidships.

mizzenmast the aftmost mast on a yawl or a ketch.

moor to tie up a boat.

mooring an anchorage, often marked with a buoy and pennant.

outhaul the line used to increase tension on the foot of the mainsail.

painter same as bowline.

passage a voyage from one place to another.

pay off to turn the bow away from the wind.

pay out to let out line.

piloting navigating.

pinch to sail too close to the wind.

pitch the rocking-horse-like, fore-and-aft motion of a vessel moving over waves.

pitchpole the complete somersaulting of a vessel in very heavy seas.

planing skimming across the water.

plot to draw out a course and bearings.

port the left side of a vessel when one is looking forward; opposite of starboard.

porthole a window.

port tack a tack in which the wind is blowing over a vessel's port side.

pram a small dinghy, used as a tender.

pulpit the safety rail at the bow and the stern.

quarters the living and sleeping space below deck.

raise a light spotting a light on shore.

rake the angle of a ship's mast in relation to the deck.

ratlines rope steps made of small lines tied across the shrouds; the crew can climb aloft on them.

reach sailing with the wind abeam.

"ready about" a directive to stand by to ready for coming about.

reef to reduce the mainsail and secure its unused part, usually in preparation for storm winds.

reeve to pass a line through a hole.

regatta sailing races.

ride to lie at anchor; to ride out a storm while at anchor.

rigging collective term for the lines and wires used to uphold the mast and manipulate the sails.

roll the side-to-side motion of a vessel in heavy seas.

rudder the movable plate at the bottom or rear of a hull, used to steer the boat.

run to sail with the wind directly behind the vessel; sailing with the wind.

running lights the lights that must be illuminated on a vessel at night.

scud to run before the wind in a gale.

sea anchor a floating anchor that helps stabilize a boat during a storm.

scuppers drains or openings along the gunwales to allow the flow of rough seas over the deck.

set to hoist sails.

sheets lines attached to the sails for trimming.

shrouds wires that stabilize the mast and keep it from bending.

slack tide a brief period of no current movement at the turning of the tide.

slip a berth at a dock.

spanker a fore-and-aft rigged sail on the aftermast of some vessels.

spar a mast, boom, bowsprit.

spill the wind to take the wind out of a sail by moving it out of position.

spinnaker a large, three-cornered sail added to increase downwind speed.

square-rigged having four-sided sails set abeam or athwartships.

starboard the right side of the boat when facing forward, opposite of port.

starboard tack a tack in which the wind blows from starboard to port.

staysail a triangular sail set behind the headsail.

steerage way reaching a high enough speed to steer the vessel.

stem the tide to make headway against the current.

stern the rear of the boat.

storm sails small, strong sails used for their ease of control in stormy weather.

strike to lower a sail.

surfing picking up speed by intentionally riding on top of a wave.

swamp to flood with water.

tabernacle the deck housing for the bottom of the mast.

tack the lower front corner of a sail. Also, the side of the boat opposite the side the sails are on. See tacking.

tacking switching tacks by turning the bow into the wind.

tail to pull or haul in a line.

take in to lower a sail.

telltales short strings of yarn attached to the shrouds as indicators of wind direction.

tender a small boat, such as a dinghy, used to go to and from shore or to other vessels.

tight cover to position one's vessel in a race so that the competitor's vessel loses airflow into his sails.

tiller a steering stick attached to the rudder.

topside on deck.

transom the aftmost board at the stern.

trim the angle of a sail in relation to the wind direction. To trim a sail is to adjust its angle.

trimaran a trihulled vessel.

trysail a small, triangular sail used in stormy weather in place of a mainsail.

turn turtle to capsize completely; to go belly up.

under the lee a position protected by the wind, for example, behind a land barrier or downwind of another vessel.

veering wind a wind that is changing direction in a clockwise fashion.

wake the foamy, turbulent water left behind a vessel.

weather the windward side of a vessel.

weigh anchor to raise the anchor.

winch a reel-like apparatus for winding line.

windage the area of sail actually collecting wind.

windward the side of the boat that is taking the wind directly.

yard a spar on which a square sail is hung.

yaw a drifting turn, caused by heavy seas.

SUBMARINES

anechoic covering any covering material used to absorb sonar pulses to help prevent detection by an enemy vessel.

awash a partially submerged state in which only the conning tower can be seen above the surface.

ballast seawater flooded into wraparound or other tanks to allow a submarine to submerge or descend.

ballast tanks wraparound tanks or other tanks used to hold water or compressed air.

bathyscaph a free-floating bathysphere with ballast and depth controls.

bathysphere a spherical diving bell having windows for observation.

blow the tanks to empty the ballast tanks by filling them with compressed air.

bridge the conning tower, specifically where the periscope is located.

cavitation the noise produced by bubbles formed by propellor action, a crucial factor in detecting submerged submarines.

conning tower the tower or superstructure, now called the sail, that contains the bridge and the periscope.

control room the room containing the control panels for diving, planing, steering, and other movements.

depth charge a bomb dropped from a ship to explode at a certain depth or on contact with the submarine.

draft the depth of water required for a submarine to float.

hangar a missile tube.

helm the control area where the submarine is steered.

helmsman one who steers the vessel.

hydrophone a submersible microphone used to detect sounds from ships or submarines.

hydroplanes horizontal rudders or fins located fore and aft that swivel to deflect water flow around the hull to lift or drop the nose, used to ascend or descend. Also known as planes.

mess the crew meal room.

periscope the viewing apparatus that is raised surreptitiously above the surface of the ocean to observe enemy craft or terrain.

ping the sound made by an active sonar system.

planesman crew member who operates the hydroplanes.

powerplant a diesel-electric or nuclear-driven motor.

reactor a nuclear reactor in nuclear submarines.

rudder the adjustable plane used to steer the submarine.

sail same as conning tower. Also known as a fin.

sail plane a fin located on either side of the conning tower.

screws the propellors

snorkel air-intake and exhaust pipes in diesel-electric submarines. Also known as a snort.

snorkeling moving just below the surface with the snorkel raised above the surface for taking in and expelling air.

sonar acronym for SOund NAvigation Ranging, a system that transmits and receives reflected sound waves to detect submarines and submerged objects.

sonobuoy a sonar device used to detect submerged submarines, which, when activated, relays information by radio.

SOSUS SOund SUrveillance System; a system of listening hydrophones on the seabed linked to stations on shore.

subroc a submerged, submarine-launched, surface-to-surface rocket with nuclear depth charge or homing torpedo, primarily intended for use against other submarines.

torpedo an underwater missile ejected from a tube in the submarine by compressed air; it is propelled to its target by two propellors powered by an electric motor.

torpedo defense net a net employed to close an inner harbor to torpedos fired from seaward or to protect a ship at anchor or underway.

U-boat submarine, especially a German one.

wolfpack a group of submarines working together in a line to destroy enemy vessels.

Sailing Terms of the 18th and 19th Centuries

badge an ornamental window or likeness of a window decorated with marine figures near the stern of a sailing vessel.

barbarising swabbing a deck with sand and cleanser.

belay it much-used saying for "stop it" or "shut up."

bilboes iron bars on the deck to which prisoners were shackled on some warships.

blood money money paid to innkeepers or a boarding house for finding men to fill vacancies on a ship's crew.

bluff bowed a vessel having a broad bow that pushes through the water instead of slicing through it.

broken backed a worn out or structurally weakened vessel with a drooping bow and stern.

caboose a chimney housing in the cook's galley on a merchant ship. Also, the galley itself.

close quarters wooden barriers on a deck, behind which crew could fight off and shoot at enemy boarders.

coach on a large man-of-war, a stern compartment used as captain's quarters.

cobbing disciplinary action practiced by the British Navy, specifically tying a man down on deck and spanking him with a board.

cockpit in a man-of-war, an emergency medical compartment under the lower gundeck.

cod's head and mackerel tail slang describing a vessel having a bluff bow and a narrow or tapering stern.

company the crew of a ship.

cuddy a cabin in the fore of a vessel.

cut of his jib sailor slang for the way a person characteristically looks or behaves.

dead door a wooden shutter sealing a window.

dog watch deck watch from 4 p.m. to 8 p.m.

ducking disciplinary action in which a man was dunked repeatedly in the sea while being hung from a yardarm, a practice abandoned at the end of the 17th century.

graveyard watch deck watch from midnight to 4 a.m.

grog rum diluted with water, a ration of the Royal Navy.

hardtack slang for ship's biscuits.

keel hauling disciplinary action in which a man was pulled underneath the keel of a ship by ropes from one side to another, a practice abandoned in the 19th century.

lady's hole a small storage compartment.

lazarette a quarantine room for person with contagious diseases. Also used as a holding room for troublemakers or as a storeroom.

magazine on a man-of-war, a storeroom for gunpowder and other explosives.

marry the gunner's daughter to be flogged on a Royal Navy vessel.

mess deck a deck on which the crew took its meals. Also, mess room.

monkey poop a low poop deck.

mustering calling a crew together for a drill or inspection.

piping the side sounding the boatswain's whistle as a salute to an arriving or departing officer of high rank.

portage seaman's wages for one voyage.

powder room compartment where gunpowder was kept in bulk on a man-of-war.

ram bow on a man-of-war, a bow equipped with an iron or bronze projection used for ramming enemy vessels.

reefer a pea jacket worn by midshipman.

roundhouse a deckhouse aft of the mainmast.

sailroom a compartment where sails were stored.

saloon on a merchant ship, the officers' mess. Also, a main passenger accommodation.

salt horse salt beef, a staple of seamen.

scrollhead ornamental scroll work at the stem of a ship instead of a figurehead.

scuppers channels cut through the sides of a ship to drain off deck water.

scuttle any small hatchway, usually fitted with a lid.

shanghai to kidnap a sailor from one vessel to enlist him to duty on another vessel, a practice in American ports in the 19th century.

shanty song sung by crew to keep work in unison, especially when heaving ropes.

sick bay a medical compartment for injuries or illnesses.

slop room compartment for storing extra clothes for crew.

slops extra clothes kept on board for new sailors too poor to have their own changes of clothes.

steerage accommodations forward of the main cabin.

tabernacle the three-sided square casing in which a mast is stepped and clamped.

ward-robe a fortified room where valuables taken from enemy vessels were stored.

whaleback slang for a vessel whose deck has a steep arching from middle to sides to drain off water.

Crew of a Large 18th- or 19th-Century Sailing Vessel

able seaman a senior deck hand responsible for rigging, manning guns, and occasionally taking the helm.

boatswain warrant officer responsible for supervising crew and the ship's maintenance. He would beat the crew to get them to work harder; he also served as an executioner. Also spelled bosun or bos'n.

boatswain's mate a petty officer who assisted the boatswain.

cabin boy one who waited on and served as a "gopher" for officers.

call boy carried the pipes and whistles of the boatswain and sometimes relayed whistled commands to other parts of the ship.

carpenter ship's carpenter; a petty officer responsible for the upkeep of all woodwork on board.

cockswain the helmsman of a ship's auxilliary boat; the head of this boat's crew.

conder a lookout who gives directions to the helmsman; one who cons or directs a ship from a lookout position.

deck hand in the merchant navy, a rank below chief officer and boatswain.

deck officer in the merchant navy, an officer who keeps watch on the bridge.

efficient deck hand a deck hand over the age of 18 who has passed a competency test and who has served for at least one year.

first mate chief officer ranking just below master on a merchant navy vessel.

foretopman a seaman whose station is the fore topmast.

helmsman the seaman who steers the vessel. Also known as the quartermaster, wheelman, steerman.

lady of the gunroom Royal Navy slang for seaman responsible for the gunner's stores.

lamp trimmer a seaman responsible for maintaining all oil lamps on a vessel.

lee helmsman the assistant to the helmsman who stands at the lee side of the wheel.

master the commander of a merchant navy vessel. Short for master mariner.

master at arms officer in charge of maintaining law and order on board.

mate first rank below the master. The mate is responsible for organization and navigation. Same as first mate.

midshipman the lowest-ranking commissioned officer.

ordinary seaman seaman who has not yet qualified for able seaman status.

petty officer a noncommissioned naval officer.

quartermaster in the merchant navy, the helmsman. In the Royal Navy, a supervisor of the helmsman.

sailmaker a crew member who constructs and repairs sails and other items made of canvas.

steward crew member in charge of catering, provisioning, and maintaining the living quarters.

storekeeper crew member in charge of stores and their issuance to crew.

supercargo short for superintendent of cargo; the owner or representative of the owner of a ship's cargo who travels on board a merchant vessel.

warrant officer in the Royal Navy, a senior ranking, noncommissioned officer.

yeoman In the Royal Navy, an assistant to the navigator. Also, an assistant to a storekeeper.

TRAINS AND RAILROADS

bank grade.

berth bed in a sleeping car.

bogies the wheeled trucks on which railroad cars ride.

boxcar the enclosed, boxlike freight car.

brakeman conductor's assistant who maintains and inspects the brakes.

bumper a small stop barrier at the end of a track.

cab the driving compartment.

caboose a car with sleeping and eating facilities for the crew; it is pulled at the end of the train.

coach a car for carrying passengers.

coaling road a coal track.

coupler the clamping device that allows each car to lock onto another car.

crossbuck the X-like railroad crossing warning sign.

crow the peep of a steam whistle.

dead-end bay a substation.

dining car a car on which meals are served.

downtrain from the home terminal.

driver the engineman.

engineer one who operates the engine.

engine road a track leading to the engine house.

flatcar a riding platform without roof or walls, for hauling large objects.

gauge the width between the two rails of a track.

gondola an open, shallow freight car.

grade the slope or inclination of a track.

grade crossing an intersection of a road and a rail crossing.

highball a railroad signal to go full-speed ahead.

hopper car a freight car having large funnels or hoppers for carrying and dispensing grains.

linear induction motor the electric motor that powers a maglev train.

livestock car a boxcar having open slats for the transport of livestock.

locomotive the electric or diesel-powered engine that pulls the cars.

locomotive shed an engine terminal.

maglev train an unwheeled train that, levitated on a magnetic field, is free from friction and can travel at great speeds.

marshalling classifying and sorting cars in a yard.

marshal yard a freight yard.

monorail a single-railed track.

piggyback car a flatcar designed to haul the trailers of tractor-trailer trucks.

platform a landing for passengers beside the tracks at a station.

platform car same as flatcar.

Pullman trademark name for a parlor or sleeping car, designed by George Pullman.

redcap a porter in a railway station.

refrigerator car a refrigerated car for hauling perishables.

regulator the throttle.

rolling stock collective term for all of a railroad's wheeled vehicles.

roundhouse a facility, often with a turntable, for repairing and switching locomotives.

semaphore a signaling apparatus emloying lights or pivoting arms.

shed master an engine house foreman.

shunting switching tracks.

signal box a signal tower or station.

signal gantry a raised frame spanning one or more tracks and on which are mounted signal lights.

sleeper a railroad tie. Also a sleeping compartment or car.

switch the apparatus that is adjusted to shunt a train onto another track.

tank car a cylindrical car designed to haul fuels and other fluids.

turntable a rail platform that rotates to turn a locomotive in the opposite direction.

wagon slang for a freight car.

wagon-lit a sleeping car.

yard a receiving and holding yard for trains and cars.

AUTOMOBILES

afterburner an exhaust manifold that burns off carbon monoxide and fuel in the exhaust system to produce extra power.

air cleaner above the carburetor, the round receptacle that holds the air filter.

air filter located in the air cleaner, the round filter that removes dirt and dust from the air before it enters the carburetor.

alignment the proper positioning of the front wheels for optimum handling and minimum tire wear.

alternator a generator device that produces alternating current for powering the electrical equipment while the engine is running.

antifreeze a solution that lowers the freezing point and raises the boiling point of water in the cooling system. Also known as coolant.

antilock brakes brakes designed to prevent locking of the wheels during heavy braking.

automatic transmission a transmission in which gear ratios are changed automatically, thus eliminating the need for a stick shift and clutch.

axle the shaft to which the wheels are attached.

backfire an explosion of the air-fuel mixture in the intake or exhaust system.

badge engineering auto manufacturer's term for a car model sold under a variety of names under which only the trim and name badges differ.

ball joint a ball-and-socket joint providing flexibility to the steering linkage and suspension system.

bearings any ball or roller-type bearings that absorb friction between two moving parts.

bleed to remove air from a brake system, fuel-injection system, or cooling system to aid the smooth flow of fluid.

blue books a variety of books that list the current prices paid for used cars.

bore the diameter of the cylinder hole.

brake drum mounted on each wheel, a metal drum whose insides are pressed against by the brake shoes to slow or stop a car.

brake lines the tubes and hoses through which brake fluid flows from the master cylinder to the brakes.

brake lining attached to each brake shoe, the heat-resistant asbestos lining that presses against the brake drum to slow or stop a car.

brake shoes the arc-shaped pieces of metal that, lined with heat-resistant asbestos, are pressed against the brake drums to slow or stop a car.

bushing a protective liner or sleeve that serves as a barrier against noise and friction.

butterfly valve a small, pivoting metal plate or disk that regulates the flow of air into the carburetor.

cam in the camshaft, a lobed disk that activates the opening and closing of valves.

camber wheel alignment term referring to the outward or inward tilt of the top of a wheel that improves handling and lessens tire wear.

camshaft the shaft with lobed cams that operate the valves.

carburetor the device that vaporizes fuel and mixes it with air in appropriate proportions and then delivers the mixture to the intake manifold.

carburetor barrel the part of the carburetor in which air flows and is mixed with fuel.

caster wheel alignment term referring to the wheel positioning that provides the greatest steering stability.

catalytic converter a mufflerlike afterburner in the tailpipe that burns away unburned or harmful gasses.

charging system the system that generates and stores electricity, comprising the fan belt, the alternator (or generator), and the battery.

chassis the frame that supports the body and motor of a car. In some usage, a collective term for all the parts of a car except the body and fenders.

cherry automotive slang for a used car that has been kept in perfect condition.

choke a plate or valve that chokes off the amount of air entering the carburetor to help produce a richer air-fuel mixture for cold starting.

clutch a coupling that engages and disengages the engine from the transmission to facilitate the changing of gears.

clutch disk at the end of the driveshaft, a spinning plate that is forced against the flywheel when the clutch is engaged.

clutch pedal in a manual transmission, the pedal to the left of the brake that disengages the clutch when pressed.

coil in the ignition system, a transformer that amplifies the voltage from the battery and relays it to the distributor and the spark plugs.

coil springs the large, shock-absorbing springs near the front and sometimes the back wheels.

combustion chamber the space between the piston and the cylinder head, where the fuel-air mixture is compressed and ignited.

connecting rod the rod that connects the piston to the crankshaft. (Throwing a rod refers to breaking a connecting rod.)

coolant an ethyl glycol solution. Same as antifreeze.

cooling system the system that prevents the engine from overheating by cooling and circulating a mixture of coolant and water through water jackets in the engine block. The cooling system comprises the fan, radiator, thermostat, water jackets, and water pump.

crankcase the lower portion of the engine that surrounds the crankshaft above the oil pan.

cranking engaging the starter and turning over the engine.

crankshaft the main rotating shaft in the engine, with cranks attached to the connecting rods to convert up-and-down motion into circular motion. The crankshaft transmits power from the pistons to the driveshaft.

crankshaft pulley at the front of the crankshaft, a wheel that drives the fan belts and alternator.

creeper the rolling board a mechanic moves around on while laying underneath a car.

cruise control a device that automatically maintains a car's speed at a preset level and is disengaged by the brake.

cylinder in the engine block, the hollow pipe in which the piston is housed and moves up and down.

cylinder head above the engine block, the part of the engine that encloses the cylinders and contains the combustion chambers and, in most cases, the valves.

dead axle an axle that does not deliver power to a wheel.

detonation same as knocking.

diesel engine an engine without a carburetor that burns diesel oil rather than gasoline.

dieseling a condition (unrelated to diesel engines) in which the engine continues to sputter after the ignition has been turned off. Also known as afterrunning.

differential located between the rear wheels, an arrangement of gears that drives the rear axle and allows each of the wheels to turn at different speeds when cornering.

dipstick a metal stick used to check fluid levels in a fluid reservoir.

disk brakes brakes of padded calipers that grab a disk on the wheel to slow or stop the car.

distributor the device that distributes a proportional amount of electricity to each spark plug, in sequence.

distributor cap an insulated cap with a central terminal for the coil wire and a series of outer terminals for the spark plug wires, with voltage delivered to each by the rotor.

double clutching releasing and depressing the clutch while in neutral to facilitate coupling of the flywheel and the clutch disk, used mostly in truckdriving.

double-overhead-cam engine an engine having two camshafts in each cylinder head to activate the valves.

downshift to shift to a lower gear to help slow the car and help prevent brake wear.

drive shaft the spinning shaft that transmits power from the transmission to the differential.

drive train collective term for the clutch, transmission, driveshaft, differential, and rear axle.

dual carbs having two carburetors on one engine.

ECU short for electronic control unit.

electrical system the system that generates, stores, and distributes current to start the car and to power electrical equipment, comprising the alternator, battery, regulator, wiring, ignition distributor, and ignition coil.

electrolyte the battery's mixture of sulfuric acid and water.

engine block the main framework or block containing the cylinders and other engine parts. Also known as the cylinder block.

engine flywheel in manual transmissions, a spinning, metal plate at the end of the crankshaft that engages and disengages with the clutch disk.

exhaust manifold a device that, through several passages, receives exhaust gasses from the combustion chambers.

exhaust system the system through which exhaust flows, from the exhaust manifold to the catalytic converter to the muffler and out the tailpipe.

fan between the radiator and the engine, a spinning fan that draws cooling air through the radiator.

fan belt the rubber belt that connects the fan with the alternator.

firewall the protective, insulated wall dividing the engine compartment from the passenger interior.

float bowl in the carburetor, the reservoir that holds a small quantity of gasoline to be vaporized.

four-barrel a four-barreled carburetor, with the third and fourth barrels operating only at high speed or when accelerating, as in a large V-8 engine.

four-stroke cycle the four—down, up, down, up—piston strokes that complete the intake, compression, power, and exhaust cycle.

front-wheel drive a car that is powered by its front wheels.

fuel-air mixture the "mist" of gasoline and air that is compressed and ignited in the cylinders.

fuel filter a fuel line device that removes dirt and other contaminants from gasoline flowing through it.

fuel injection a system that replaces the carburetor by using an electronic sensing device to deliver a proportional amount of fuel to the combustion chambers according to engine speed and power needs.

fuel injector nozzles in fuel-injection systems, the nozzles that inject fuel into the combustion chambers. Also known as fuel injector valves.

fuel lines the hoses through which gasoline flows from the gas tank to the carburetor.

fuel pump the pump that draws gasoline from the gas tank into the fuel lines and on to the carburetor or fuel-injection nozzles.

fuel system collective term for the fuel tank, fuel lines, fuel pump, fuel filter, and the carburetor or the fuel injection system.

gasket a rubber, cork, paper, or metal plate seated between two parts to seal out fluids and help prevent premature wear.

generator a device that generates electricity from mechanical energy.

head gasket the seal seated between the cylinder head and the engine block.

horsepower the energy required to lift 550 pounds 1 foot in 1 second. The pulling power of the engine.

idiot lights slang for the dashboard signals that light up to warn of impending oil depletion, overheating, or other malfunctions.

idle engine speed when in neutral or when the car is not moving.

idle speed screw at the outside bottom of a carburetor, a screw that can be turned to adjust idle speed.

ignition system collective term for the coil, battery, distributor, and spark plugs.

independent suspension a suspension system in which all four wheels ride up and down independently.

intake manifold a set of pipes through which the fuel-air mix flows from the carburetor to the cylinders.

internal combustion engine an engine in which fuel is burned internally rather than in an outside source, as in a steam engine.

jack any device used to jack a car up off the ground to facilitate mechanical repair. Types of jacks include hydraulic, scissors, and tripod.

knocking a metal knocking (resembling marbles rattling in a can) sound in the engine caused by a loose bearing, faulty timing, low-octane gas. Also known as ping, detonation.

leaf springs rear wheel springs comprising metal plates of graduated lengths one atop the other, which flex to absorb road shock.

lube grease pastelike oil used to lubricate a number of moving parts, especially in the steering linkage and suspension system.

lubrication system the system that lubricates moving parts in the engine, comprising the oil, oil pan, oil pump, oil filter, and oil gauge.

lug nuts the large nuts that lock the wheel onto a car.

manual transmission a transmission requiring a stick shift and clutch to change gears.

master brake cylinder the cylinder that holds brake fluid and compresses it through the brake lines to the brakes when the brake pedal is engaged.

misfiring a malfunction in which the fuel-air mixture in one or more cylinders fails to combust.

muffler a device in the exhaust system that muffles the noise of escaping exhaust.

octane rating the rating that reflects a gasoline's antiknock properties; the highest octanes produce the least amount of engine knock or ping.

odometer the dashboad mileage meter.

oil filter a filter that removes dirt and other contaminants from oil as it circulates through the lubrication system.

oil pan the pan that stores oil, located below the crankcase.

oil pump a crankcase pump that draws oil from the oil pan through the lubrication system.

overdrive a special gear, such as fifth gear in a five-speed transmission, that allows the drive wheels to turn faster than the engine, to facilitate coasting and fuel saving at high speed.

overhead cam a camshaft situated above the cylinder head instead of below the cylinders, to remove the need for valve-activating push rods.

passing gear in an automatic transmission, a low gear that is automatically engaged to provide a short burst of speed when the accelerator is sharply depressed.

pinging same as knocking.

piston the cylindrical plug that moves up and down inside the cylinder to compress the fuel-air mixture and to force the connecting rods to rotate the crankshaft.

piston rings the metal rings installed in grooves in the pistons to prevent fuel-air leaks into the crankcase.

points the current-regulating, metal terminals in the distributor.

power brakes a brake system that employs hydraulic or vacuum pressure to assist in braking.

power steering a steering system that employs hydraulics to facilitate steering.

power train same as drive train.

pressure cap the radiator cap.

push rods the rods that extend between the camshaft lifters and the rocker arms and are pushed up by the cam lobes.

rack and pinion steering a steering system in which a pinion on the end of the steering shaft meshes with a notched bar or rack, noted in sports cars for its quick response.

radiator at the front of the engine, the squarish receptacle that cools fluid passing through it by means of numerous air ducts.

resonator a small, secondary muffler that further reduces exhaust noise on some car models.

rings same as piston rings.

rocker arms arms that rock or pivot on shafts as the camshaft rotates, opening and closing the valves.

rotor located on top of the distributor shaft, the device that conducts current in sequence to the spark plug terminals.

rpm revolutions per minute.

SAE abbreviation used with oil gradings, meaning Society of Automotive Engineers.

shock absorber a device placed at each wheel to help limit bounce and compression when driving over bumps or when stopping quickly.

slant engine an engine in which the cylinder block is slanted from the vertical.

sludge an engine-fouling conglomeration of oxidized oil, gas, and water that reduces lubricating efficiency.

spark plug a plug that screws into the cylinder head and delivers a spark to the combustion chamber to ignite the fuel-air mixture.

springs any springlike devices, such as coil springs, leaf springs, or torsion bars that absorb road shock.

stabilizer bar a shaft between the lower suspension arms that reduces swaying or lurching of the car on sharp turns or curves.

starter the small electric motor that turns the crankshaft to start the engine.

steering linkage the interconnections between the front wheels and the steering wheel.

stroke the distance of one stroke of a piston from the top to the bottom of a cylinder, or vice versa.

supercharger a device that pressurizes the air-fuel mixture to increase engine power.

suspension system collective term for the springs, shock absorbers, steering linkage, stabilizers, and torsion bars.

synchromesh in a manual transmission, a device that matches the rotating speeds of transmission gears to facilitate smooth meshing.

tachometer the rpm or engine speed guage on the dashboard.

tail pipe the last portion of the exhaust system.

toe in to align the front wheel so that they point inward slightly, for better handling at high speeds.

torsion bar a bar that produces spring by twisting, especially over an uneven road.

transaxle on front-wheel drive or rear-engine cars, a unit that combines the functions of the transmission, differential, and clutch at the drive axle to eliminate the need for a driveshaft.

transmission the gear box that, through various gear ratios, transmits power from the engine to the drive axle.

transverse engine an engine mounted between the drive wheels, as in front-wheel drive cars.

tune-up a maintenance procedure in which parts of the ignition system are adjusted or replaced. A typical tune-up may include an adjustment of the idle speed, the fuel-air mixture and the timing, the gapping and replacement of spark plugs and points, and the replacement of the rotor and condenser.

turbocharger a supercharger powered by hot exhaust gasses.

undercoating a rustproofing material applied underneath a car.

valves the engine devices that open and close to allow or stop the flow of fuel and air or exhaust gasses.

V-8 an eight-cylinder engine, with the cylinders mounted in two rows forming an angle or V.

venturi in the carburetor, the narrowed passageway that creates a vacuum to draw fuel from the float bowl.

water jackets the engine channels through which coolant flows to cool the engine.

water pump the device that pumps coolant and water through the cooling system.

AVIATION

AIRPLANES

aerodynamics the branch of physics concerning the laws of motion of air under the influence of gravity or other forces.

aileron any one of the hinged movable surfaces or flaps on the trailing edge of a wing, used for executing banks or rolls.

airfoil any surface, such as a wing or an aileron, providing lift or aerodynamic control.

air speed indicator the instrument displaying air speed.

altimeter an instrument consisting of an aneroid barometer, used to determine altitude.

altitude the distance or height above land or water.

amphibian a plane equipped to take off or land on either water or land.

angle of attack the set angle of an airfoil as it meets the air, determining the amount of lift or other aerodynamic control.

approach approaching an airport for landing.

artificial horizon a gyro-stabilized instrument displaying the airplane's pitching and rolling.

autopilot a gyroscopically controlled device that automatically keeps an aircraft steady or is programmed for various maneuvers, such as climbing to a desired altitude.

backwash the powerful air current driven behind an aircraft by its propellers; also known as prop wash or the slipstream.

bank to turn right or left by rolling or tilting an airplane laterally in flight.

barnstorming an exhibition of stunt flying.

biplane a plane with two sets of wings.

black box the flight data recorder, actually colored orange and situated in the tail, and impervious to crashes due to its reinforced construction.

bogie a four-, six-, or eight-wheeled truck on a main landing leg.

bogy slang for an unidentified flying object.

cabane the framework and struts that support the wings at the fuselage.

cabin the cockpit.

camber the curve of a wing from its leading edge to its trailing edge.

ceiling the maximum altitude to which an aircraft can climb under specific weather conditions.

chandelle a high-performance 180-degree climbing turn, usually only performed at air shows or in combat.

clean slang term describing an in-flight plane with all landing gears, flaps, or other extendable devices retracted.

cockpit the cabin or compartment accommodating the pilot, the copilot, the controls, and the instruments.

cowling the removable covering protecting the top and sides of an airplane motor.

critical speed the lowest possible speed of an aircraft in which control can be maintained.

crosswind a wind striking a plane broadside, creating a hazard for landing.

delta wing a triangular-shaped wing.

dihedral angle the angle attained when the main wings are inclined up from the center of the fuselage so that the tips are higher than the remaining portion of the wings, for lateral stability.

dive a steep descent.

drag the resistance the surrounding air exerts on a moving airplane.

drone an unmanned, radio-controlled airplane, often used for military reconnaissance missions.

Dutch roll a sudden roll and yaw caused by a wind gust.

elevator a hinged horizontal surface on the tail assembly, controlling the up-and-down direction of an airplane.

fin the fixed vertical stabilizer at the tail helping to control roll and yaw.

flameout loss of combustion in a gas-turbine engine, resulting in a complete loss of power.

flap any one of the movable surfaces on a wing used for producing either lift or drag.

flight path an air course or route.

fuselage the long body portion to which the wings, tail, and landing gear are attached.

glide a slow descent without engine power.

glidepath the descending path a plane follows when approaching for landing.

glider a motorless airplane towed aloft and used for recreational soaring.

hangar an aircraft shelter and workshop.

hydraulics the fluid-based controls used to maneuver flaps, brakes, landing gear, and other apparatus.

hypersonic greater than five times the speed of sound.

hypoxia a medical condition caused by lack of oxygen at or above 12,500 feet, marked by a false sense of euphoria, increasing disorientation, and, eventually, unconsciousness.

Icarus in Greek mythology, the son of Daedalus, who flew so high on artificial wings that the sun melted the wax fastenings and he fell into the sea and drowned.

inertial navigation system a self-contained airborne system that continuously computes and displays navigational data, replacing the need for a navigator on many flights.

jet engine an engine that mixes oxygen and fuel, converting them into a powerful jet of heated gas, which is expelled under high pressure.

jet stream a river of high-speed winds, usually circulating from west to east at high altitudes, used to aid jet flights when traveling in the same direction.

lazy eights alternating 180-degree climbing and descending S-turns, usually executed for show.

lift the aerodynamic forces that lift an aircraft.

longeron a long spar running from the bow of the fuselage to the stern.

loran LOng RAnge Navigation; a system in which the position of an aircraft is plotted by comparing the time intervals between radio signals from a network of ground stations.

marshaller a taxiway crew member who uses bats or batons to direct aircraft ground traffic.

marshalling ground crew signaling with batons to direct aircraft ground traffic.

microwave landing system a radio landing aid guiding aircraft to a runway from several directions by a microwave beam.

payload cargo, baggage, and passengers.

pitching the nose of an airplane forced up or down by wind.

port light the red light situated on the left side of aircraft, an identification and anticollision aid. See STARBOARD LIGHT.

pressurize in an aircraft compartment, to create an air pressure higher than the low atmospheric pressure found at high altitudes.

prop wash the powerful air current driven behind an aircraft by its propellers; also known as the slipstream.

red-eye an overnight or late-night flight.

rib one of the fore-and-aft supporting members in a wing.

roll to roll left or right; or an acrobatic maneuver in which the craft is rotated completely around while maintaining course.

roll-out the distance an aircraft requires to come to a safe stop after touchdown.

rudder the hinged surface on the tail that is used to turn the airplane left or right.

slipstream the airstream behind the propeller.

sonic boom the explosion heard when an aircraft breaks the speed of sound.

sortie an aircraft sent out on a single military mission.

spin an out-of-control, rotating descent, evolving from a stall.

spinner the spinning, cone-shaped covering over the propeller hub.

spiral a tight, descending turn or series of turns.

spoiler one of the special flaps raised on the wings to "spoil" lift by disrupting airflow, used to slow an aircraft or greatly increase the rate of descent.

stabilizer a fixed horizontal surface on the tail to which the elevator is attached, providing longitudinal stability.

stack when landings are delayed, two or more aircraft circling one above the other at 1,000-foot intervals awaiting approach clearance.

stall the loss of lift when airspeed is too slow, resulting in the nose pitching down and the plane fluttering like a falling leaf.

standing waves the currents of air created by a strong wind blowing over a mountain, hazardous to aircraft.

starboard light the green light situated on the right side of aircraft, an identification and anticollision aid.

strobes the bright, white flashing lights situated on the wingtips as an anticollision aid.

supersonic faster than the speed of sound.

taxi to maneuver an airplane on the ground.

thermal a rising column of warm air, adding lift to light aircraft.

thrust the force of the engines that propel the craft forward.

three-point landing a perfect landing.

torque the left-turning twisting motion of an aircraft caused by the right-turning propeller, compensated by special rigging automatically, but corrected only manually in some aircraft above cruise speed.

turboprop a turbojet engine connected with a propeller.

turbulence disturbed air.

wind shear a rapid change of wind direction or speed affecting airflow over the wings, extremely hazardous to aircraft low to the ground.

TYPES OF AIRPLANES

Taxi and Light Aircraft

Beech Aircraft Super King Air (the Cadillac of the air); Cessna (the Volkswagen of the air) Cessna Titan/Conquest/Piper Navajo/Cheyenne/Chieftain

Business Jets

Learjet
Grumman Gulfstream
Cessna Citation
Lockheed Jet Star
Rockwell Sabreliner

Passenger and Cargo Airliners

Concorde
Airbus
Boeing 707/727/737/747/757
Douglas DC-3/DC-4/DC-6/DC-7/DC-8/DC-9/DC-10
Fokker VFW F 27
Lockheed L-188 Electra/L-1011-Tristar
Tupolev Tu-134/Tu-154 (Soviet)
Tupolev Tu-144 (Soviet Concorde-style jet)

Helicopters

autorotation an unpowered descent in which the rotor blades are rotated by air currents alone.

clutch the control used to engage and disengage the rotors from the engine to allow autorotation.

coaxial rotor system a dual-rotor system mounted one atop the other and rotating in opposing directions.

collective pitch lever the pilot's left-hand control, used to change the pitch of the main rotor blades.

compound helicopter a cross between an airplane and a helicopter, having rotary and fixed-wing components.

cyclic pitch stick the pilot control that changes the pitch of the blades individually, affecting the speed and direction of flight.

flight deck the cockpit.

heliport a helicopter landing pad or landing facility.

lateral rotors dual rotors aligned to the left and right of the body.

rotor brake the control that engages and disengages the main rotor system.

skid the landing feet or rails, as distinguished from wheels.

stall loss of lift.

tail rotor a rotor mounted on the tail to counteract the torque produced by the main rotor.

tandem rotor system a dual-rotor system aligned fore and aft.

Airports

approach lights the platformed lights—some raised as high as 200 feet—leading to a runway. See SEQUENCE FLASHERS.

apron the main loading area.

barrette closely spaced approach lights that from the sky appear as a solid bar of light.

blast fences fixed barriers or walls protecting passengers and equipment from jet-engine wake.

cab the glassed-in enclosure atop the control tower.

centerline approach system the runway approach system used as the national standard, characterized by flashing blue lights paired with white centerline bars leading to white crossbars at 1,000 feet, red crossbars at 200 feet, and a green bar at the threshold of the runway.

centerline lights 200-watt, white lights embedded into the runway.

clearway the clear area past the end of the airport, over which aircraft make their ascent.

control tower the airport nerve center manned by controllers who oversee taxiing, takeoffs, and landings, recognized by its tower and glass-enclosed cab.

flight service center the facility that provides pilots with information on weather, local conditions, winds, routes, and other conditions.

hangar an aircraft storage and maintenance building.

holding bay a large waiting area just off the runway where, in peak hours, pilots must wait in line for takeoff.

holding point a marked threshold along the side of a runway where the second aircraft in line stops and waits for the aircraft in front of it to take off.

marshallers airport personnel who direct taxiing aircraft into or out of parking positions by signals made with batons or paddles.

microwave landing system a system that guides aircraft to the runway by a microwave beam that scans a large area of sky.

rollout lanes high-speed turn-off lanes serving the runway.

safeway pneutronic parking system a system of pressure pads embedded in the aircraft parking and docking area that sense the position of aircraft and direct the pilot left or right.

sequence flashers white strobe lights that blink in sequence to help guide pilots toward the centerline of the runway. One component of the approach lights.

snow lights raised lights marking the edges of the runway when others are buried beneath snow.

taxiway the strip an aircraft drives on leading on or off the runway.

touchdown zone lights the white lights marking the touchdown zone of the runway.

visual approach slope indicators adjacent either side of the touchdown zone, a system of lamps projecting aligned, red and white beams indicating a pilot's angle of approach.

wind sock a bright, conical sock indicating wind speed and direction.

BALLOONING

aeronaut balloon pilot or passenger.

aerostation the art of operating a lighter-than-air craft.

altimeter device that measures the altitude of an aircraft by sensing differences in air pressure.

anemometer device that measures wind speed.

apex the top of a balloon.

apex rope rope attached to the top of the balloon used during inflation to control the balloon's movement; also known as a crown line.

appendix sleeve at the bottom of a balloon where the balloon is filled and through which expanding gas escapes.

attitude describing the balloon's position relative to the horizon.

ballast disposable weight, usually in the form of sandbags, used to maintain altitude or to slow a descent.

balloonmeister authority responsible for the safe operation of ground-based balloon activities.

basket also known as a gondola, which carries the aeronauts, controls, and fuel.

blast-off high-speed lift-off used in windy conditions.

blast valve high-pressure fuel valve.

blimp an airship.

burner unit that burns propane gas to heat the envelope of the balloon.

ceiling distance between the ground and cloud cover.

chase crew crew members who assist in the launch and chase the balloon in flight to aid in its landing.

deflation port panel of the upper envelope that detaches to allow hot air to escape to aid in deflation.

dirigible a powered balloon with directional controls.

envelope interior balloon fabric that contains the hot air.

equator area of the balloon's greatest girth.

gondola basket

gore length of balloon fabric tapering at the end to form sections when sewn to other gores.

helium nonflammable lighter-than-air gas.

hydrogen flammable lighter-than-air gas.

mouth the opening at the base of a balloon.

pyrometer instrument that displays the temperature of the hot air near the top of the balloon.

redline temperature the hottest temperature a balloon fabric can withstand without damage.

rip line a line that is pulled to open the deflation port.

sink rate of descent.

sparker device for igniting the burner's pilot light.

telltale heat-sensitive material near the top of a balloon providing a warning of dangerously high temperatures.

tether anchor line.

thermal rising column of warm air.

variometer device that measures vertical airspeed or the rate of climb or descent.

BLIMPS

ballast bags 50-pound bags hung from a ring encircling the car to help maintain proper weight when loads are light.

ballonets fitted within the large gas bag, two smaller bags that are filled with air to add weight or emptied of air to subtract weight.

bite the volume of air a propeller moves, according to the propeller's pitch and speed.

blimp a nonrigid dirigible.

car attached to the underside of the gas bag, the gondola that carries the pilot, passengers, controls, fuel tanks, and other equipment.

Dacron the rubberized fabric a blimp's gas bag is made from.

dirigible any steerable, lighter-than-air craft.

gas bag the large, helium-filled bag that provides lift.

gondola the car.

hangar a large building where a blimp is inspected and maintained.

helium the lighter-than-air gas that fills the gas bag.

mast a large post to which the nose of a blimp is attached when parked or moored on the ground. The mooring mast.

nose lines lines leading from the nose, used by ground crew to stabilize the blimp during takeoffs and landings.

riggers ground crew work on a blimp's fabric and ropes.

rigid a dirigible having a fabric cover stretched over a rigid framework that is filled with individual gas cells.

trim to balance the blimp in flight by adjusting the amount of air in the ballonets.

wind sock the conelike sock erected on a landing field to indicate wind direction.

zeppelin a large, cigar-shaped dirigible having a rigid body.

SPACE FLIGHT

Satellites and Space Probes

attitude a satellite's orientation in orbit, for example, pointed toward Earth or the Sun.

burn the firing of a spacecraft's thrusters.

Canopus a bright star used as a reference point in a space probe's navigation.

cruise a probe's travel time between planets.

decay the gradual loss of a satellite's orbital altitude due to Earth's gravity.

downlink sending radio signals from a spacecraft to Earth.

explosive bolts explosive bolts detonated to separate experimental packages or other subsystems while in orbit.

geosynchronous orbit an orbit synchronized with the turning of Earth, so that the satellite stays above the same area of Earth at all times.

gravity assist the use of a planet's gravity to deflect or slingshot a space probe deeper into space.

horizon sensor on a satellite, an onboard sensor that perceives Earth's horizon as an aid to maintain proper attitude.

hydrazine space probe's onboard fuel used for attitude-adjusting rockets.

hydrogen peroxide a fuel sometimes used to power a satellite's maneuvering rockets.

JPL Jet Propulsion Laboratory. The scientific facility and body of scientists in Pasadena, California, that oversees and maintains a space probe's mission.

launch corridor a flight path.

launch window a span of time within which a satellite or probe must be launched in order to meet economic, trajectory, or orbital location requirements.

modules independent subsystems on a satellite or probe.

photovoltaics See SOLAR CELLS.

reentry a satellite's reentry into Earth's atmosphere from orbit.

scrub to cancel a launch or mission.

solar cells photovoltaic cells aligned on paddles extending out from a satellite or probe to absorb and utilize solar energy to power onboard systems.

station keeping maintaining a satellite's orbital altitude by firing onboard rockets.

subsystems any onboard instruments or modules.

telemetry the science of taking measurements from a distant point.

tracking station a ground station that tracks satellites.

trajectory flight path of a space probe.

uplink sending radio signals from Earth to a spacecraft.

Space Shuttle

abort to stop a mission in progress, usually due to some malfunction.

airlock a chamber between a pressurized and an unpressurized compartment, or between a pressurized compartment and space.

attitude the orientation or position of the shuttle relative to the Earth's horizon or other reference point.

automatic landing mode a computer-controlled guidance system capable of landing a craft without human assistance.

avionics the electronics systems monitoring the control of the flight.

barbecue mode rolling the shuttle slowly along its axis to diffuse external heat.

beta cloth a flameproof spacesuit material made of glass fibers.

blackout a loss of radio signal.

booster See SOLID ROCKET BOOSTER.

bulkhead any wall of a compartment.

Canopus a bright star used in space navigation to help orient a vessel.

capture the capturing of a satellite or other payload by the remote manipulator arm.

cargo bay the unpressurized midsection of the shuttle's fuselage; it has hinged doors that open wide to space.

crawlerway the reinforced roadway over which space vehicles are transported from an assembly building to the launchpad.

crew egress the crew exitway.

crew ingress the crew entryway.

deck any of three decks on the shuttle: the flight deck, the mid-deck, and the lower deck.

delta wing a triangular wing configuration, as found on the shuttle.

deorbit burn the firing of a retro rocket to slow the craft's orbit for either changing orbit or preparing for reentry into Earth's atmosphere.

deployment the deployment of a payload, such as a satellite, into space.

dock to join two vessels together in space.

downlink a radio broadcast from the shuttle to Earth.

entry the reentry of the shuttle into Earth's atmosphere.

EVA extravehicular activity; activities carried out by crew outside a pressurized compartment, where spacesuits are needed.

flame trench the concrete pit located under a launchpad; it directs rocket flame away from the spacecraft.

flare to pitch the spacecraft nose up to reduce speed for landing.

flying brick the nickname for the shuttle.

g the force of gravity; 1 g equals the gravity of earth; 5 g's equal five times the gravity of Earth, and so on.

geosynchronous orbit an orbit that stays in sync with the earth's rotation, 22,300 miles above the equator.

gimbal an apparatus having ball joints to allow movement in several directions, as a rocket nozzle.

glide slope the landing approach.

hypergolic propellants propellants such as nitrogen tetroxide and monomethylhydrazine that ignite on contact with one another.

hypersonic speeds exceeding five times the speed of sound; above Mach 5.

LOX acronym for liquid oxygen.

mach a term denoting the speed of sound; for example, Mach 2 is twice the speed of sound, Mach 3 is three times the speed of sound.

microgravity the near-zero gravity experienced while in orbit above Earth.

micrometeoroids tiny meteor particles the size of sand grains, known to erode the exterior of the shuttle on impact.

mission specialist a specialist or expert on the shuttle's payload or scientific mission.

mission station a station on the aft flight deck, where payload operations are carried out.

payload changeout room a launchpad room where payload is loaded into the shuttle cargo bay.

pilot the second in command of a flight after the commander.

pitch up-and-down rotational movement of the nose.

remote manipulator system in the cargo bay, a large, mechanical arm used to retrieve or deploy satellites.

retro rocket a rocket that fires in the opposite direction of the shuttle's flight, to slow momentum.

roll an inflight rolling motion of the shuttle along its axis.

rudder a movable surface on the tail to control yaw. Also known as the speed brake.

solid rocket boosters the two solid-propellant rockets that lift the shuttle up to an altitude of 25 miles and then are jettisoned.

speed brake a split and spread rudder that increases drag and slows the shuttle during the landing phase.

telemetry shuttle flight mission data transmitted to Earth.

umbilical an electrical and life support cable attached to an astronaut when working outside the shuttle while in orbit.

uplink radio transmission from Earth to the shuttle.

Vernier engine an engine providing slight thrust for small changes in shuttle position.

vertical stabilizer the tail.

window a period of time within which a mission must be launched or concluded.

yaw left-right rotation of the nose.

Shuttle Acronyms

ADI: attitude direction indicator.
A/G: air-to-ground.
AMI: alpha-Mach indicator.
APU: auxiliary power unit.
CSS: control stick steering.
DCM: displays and controls module.
EMU: extravehicular mobility unit.
EVA: extravehicular activity.
HSI: horizontal situation indicator.
IUS: inertial upper stage.
IVA: intravehicular activity.
LCC: launch control center.
LOS: loss of signal.
MCC: Mission Control Center.
MCC-H: Mission Control Center, Houston.
MET: mission elapsed time.
MLP: mobile launcher platform.
MMU: manned maneuvering unit.
OMS: orbital maneuvering system.
OPF: orbiter processing facility.
PAM: payload assist module.
PLSS: portable life support system.
RCS: reaction control system.
RMS: remote manipulator system.
SCAPE: self-contained atmospheric pressure ensemble.

SOMS: shuttle orbiter medical system.
SRB: solid rocket booster.
SSME: space shuttle main engine.
SSUS: spinning solid upper stage.
tacan: tactical air navigation.
TDRS: tracking and data relay satellite.
TPS: thermal protection system.
WCS: waste collection system.

The Law

CRIMINAL LAW (*Also see* CONTRACT LAW, PROBATE LAW, PROPERTY AND REAL ESTATE LAW)

ABA American Bar Association

abscond to skip town or otherwise avoid court action through hiding or concealing oneself.

abuse of process using process for a purpose other than that intended by law.

accessory one who assists or facilitates others in a crime.

accessory after the fact one who knowingly receives or assists a person who is being sought for committing a felony.

accessory before the fact a person who plans a crime, gives advice about a crime, or commands others to commit a crime, but who does not actively commit the crime.

accomplice a partner in the commission of a crime.

accusatory instrument an accusation, an indictment, or information that forms the basis for a criminal charge.

ACLU American Civil Liberties Union.

acquiescence any behavior that implies consent, such as remaining silent and failing to raise an objection when an accusatory statement is made.

acquit to set free one who has been absolved of charges.

action the prosecuting of one party by another for a misdeed or for protection of rights or other reasons.

ad damnum the amount of damages sued for.

additur an increase of the amount of damages, awarded by the court when a jury award is deemed inadequate.

adjourn to break temporarily from a court proceeding through recess.

Admiralty court a court or tribunal having jurisdiction over actions related to the sea, such as maritime contracts or injuries at sea.

admissible evidence evidence acceptable to the court.

affidavit a written statement made by a person under oath before the court or a notary public.

affirmative action taking tangible action to eliminate the abuses of past discrimination, as through racial quotas in schools and the workplace.

against the weight of the evidence a situation through which a new trial may be ordered because a jury has, in the judge's opinion, given a verdict that is unsupported by the evidence.

age of consent age at which one may marry without parental consent. Also, the age at which a person may consent to sexual intercourse without the risk of statutory rape or sexual assault being charged to the other party.

aggrieved party the person who has been hurt or damaged in a lawsuit.

aid and abet to facilitate or assist knowingly another person in the commission of a crime.

alias otherwise or also known as.

alibi a provable accounting of a person's whereabouts at the time a crime was committed.

alienation of affections malicious acts or behavior by a third party—such as a mother, father-in-law, or outside lover—that interferes with a marriage and alienates one spouse from another.

amnesty a pardon excusing a person of a crime, such as draft evasion.

antitrust laws statutes that help to maintain free competition in the marketplace and that punish any acts by a person or corporation that unfairly restrain a competitor.

appeal to take a case to a higher court in the hope that it will deem the lower court's judgment incorrect and either reverse the judgment or order a new trial.

appellant the party who appeals a decision.

appellate court a court that reviews the rulings and judgments of a lower court.

a priori from cause to effect.

arbitration the settling of disagreements between two parties by an agreed-upon third party, most used in disputes involving labor contracts.

arbitrator the impartial, chosen person who arbitrates a dispute.

arraign to accuse of a wrongdoing or to call a person to answer a charge.

arraignment the formal charging of the defendant with an offense.

artifice a fraudulent device used to commit a crime.

assault, aggravated an assault resulting in serious bodily injury to the assaulted, or any assault judged to be particularly atrocious or depraved.

attachment the seizing of a defendant's property for the payment of a plaintiff's judgment award.

attorney-client privilege the privilege of confidential communication between client and attorney, in which information cannot be shared publicly without consent from the client.

attorney general the chief attorney of the federal government or of each state government.

attractive nuisance the tort doctrine that requires a person who keeps any dangerous object or thing on his or her property that might attract children to protect those children from possible injury, such as by removing the door of an abandoned refrigerator or by fencing a swimming pool.

bail a form of security paid to ensure that the defendant will show up for court proceedings.

bail bond the document used in the release of a person in custody.

bailiff a court officer in charge of keeping order and guarding jurors.

bailment the process of providing bail for a defendant. Also, the delivering of goods or personal property to one in trust.

bailsman one who gives bail for another.

bait and switch an unethical practice wherein a retailer advertises a particularly good buy to attract customers and then coerces or persuades the customers into buying a much more expensive model than the one advertised.

barrister the English equivalent of a trial lawyer.

bench the court. The bench where the judge sits.

bench warrant a court order issued to have a person seized and brought into court to take part in proceedings.

Bill of Rights the first 10 amendments to the U.S. Constitution.

blue law state or local Sunday closing law.

bond a written instrument that guarantees performance of obligations—such as the payment of fees—through sureties. Also, an amount paid as bail.

bondsman a person who provides a bond for another for a fee.

burden of proof the burden of substantiating claims, accusations, or allegations, a responsibility falling on the plaintiff in a court action.

bylaws any in-house rules or laws of a corporation, organization, or association.

canon church law.

capital offense an offense punishable by death.

care in a negligence case, the amount of care a custodian must give to a thing in order to avoid a charge of negligence, which, depending on circumstances, may be great care, ordinary care, reasonable care, and slight care.

caveat let him beware. An urging of caution.

caveat emptor let the buyer beware.

chief justice in a court with more than one judge, the presiding judge.

circumstantial evidence indirect, secondary, or incidental evidence from which a judge or jury might make inferences.

civil action an action filed to protect a civil right.

civil penalties fines and money damages.

class action an action filed on behalf of a group.

clean hands the doctrine holding that claimants seeking justice must not themselves have taken part in an illegal or unethical act relating to the claim.

clear and convincing a standard of proof beyond a preponderance of the evidence but less than beyond a reasonable doubt; more than the degree of proof required in civil cases but below that required by criminal cases.

collusion a conspiracy to commit fraud or other illegal activity.

common law law based on court decisions, customs, and usages, as opposed to law based on codified written laws.

common law marriage a marriage not based on any formal ceremony or legal filing but on personal agreement between the two parties to become husband and wife, followed by a substantial period of cohabitation.

compounding a felony refusal of a felony victim to prosecute the felon in exchange for a bribe.

conjecture inferences from incomplete evidence.

conspiracy two or more people conspiring to commit a crime.

contempt of court an act that obstructs the administration of justice or that demonstrates disrespect for the court's authority.

contumacy defiance of the court's orders or authority.

corpus delecti the facts proving a crime.

crime of passion a nonpremeditated crime committed under the influence of heat of passion or extreme sudden rage.

cross-examination the questioning of a witness by the lawyer other than the one who called the witness, concerning information previously given in the initial examination.

D.A. district attorney.

damages monetary award given to the damaged party in a court action.

damages, double an award twice the normal or standard amount given to the injured party as a form of punishment to the wrongdoer.

damages, exemplary any compensation that exceeds actual damages, awarded to punish the wrongdoer.

damnum absque injuria any loss or injury caused without any wrongdoing by a person or persons, such as by an act of nature, or any damage caused by a lawful act; any damage in which the law provides no recourse.

decriminalization the changing of a law so that what was once a criminal act is no longer so and is therefore no longer punishable by law.

defalcation failure of a trustee to pay out money when it becomes due.

default judgment a judgment made against a defendant for failure to appear in court.

defraud to commit fraud.

degree of proof the degree of evidence necessary for the awarding of damages or conviction of a suspect. The degrees of proof include "preponderance of the evidence," "clear and convincing," and "reasonable doubt."

deliberate to consider all the facts of a case after all the evidence has been given.

de minimis acts too trivial or unimportant to be dealt with in a court of law.

demonstrative evidence weapons, stolen goods, photographs, or other objects displayed in court to help clarify or add evidence to a case.

deposition a pretrial statement taken from a witness under oath.

desuetude referring to laws that have become obsolete and are no longer enforced.

dictum a dogmatic or opinionated pronouncement by the judge concerning a case.

diminished capacity a defense that pleads diminished mental capacity of the defendant, which often lessens a sentence in a criminal conviction.

disbar to rescind the license and right of an attorney to practice law due to unethical or illegal conduct.

district attorney the prosecuting attorney of a given district.

divestiture a selling off of property or assets by an offending party as ordered by the court to prevent the offender from enjoying the gains or "spoils" of his crime, usually used in the enforcement of antitrust laws.

docket the list of cases pending on a court's calendar.

double jeopardy a provision in the Fifth Amendment to the Constitution preventing a second prosecution in a criminal case, regardless of the outcome of the first trial.

embracery obstructing justice by trying to bribe or otherwise influence a juror.

entrapment a defense used in criminal law that excuses a defendant if it is proven he or she was lured into a crime by police inducement and that the crime would not have occurred if it had not been for that inducement.

estoppel a restraint to prevent one from contradicting a previous statement.

executive privilege the right of the president to refuse to disclose confidential information that may impair government functioning.

exemplar nontestimony evidence of identification such as fingerprints, blood samples, handwriting samples, and voice recordings.

exigency any emergency occurrence that excuses one from breaking the law, such as speeding to the hospital with a person having a heart attack.

expungement of records the court-ordered annulment and destruction of all records of arrest and court proceedings concerning a defendant arrested but not convicted.

extenuating circumstances circumstances that justify or partially justify an illegal act and that qualify guilt or blame.

extortion the crime of using one's position in business or government to extort or obtain illegally money or property through abuse of power.

facilitation the statutory offense of aiding another to carry out a crime.

fairness doctrine a requirement of broadcasters to air contrasting viewpoints on controversial issues.

famosus libellus a slanderous or libelous letter, handbill, advertisement, written accusation, or indictment.

felony any crime considered more serious than a misdemeanor, such as homicide, robbery, burglary, rape, arson, or larceny.

felony murder a murder committed in the act of another felony, such as a robbery, burglary, or rape.

fiduciary pertaining to one who holds something in trust for another.

first-degree murder any murder that is willful, deliberate, and premeditated.

foreman among a jury, the spokesman and presiding member.

forensic relating to, belonging to, or used in courts of justice.

forensic medicine a branch of medicine employed to assist in legal matters.

fratricide the murder of one's brother.

fraud willful deceit resulting in harm to another.

Freedom of Information Act the federal law requiring that documents and other materials held in federal offices must be released to the public upon request, although with a few exemptions.

fresh pursuit the right of the police to enter another jurisdiction in order to arrest a felon.

fruit of the poisonous tree doctrine the doctrine that prevents the use of evidence originating from illegal conduct on the part of an official on the grounds that such "tainted" evidence cannot be trusted.

gag order a court order restricting outside comments about a case.

garnish to attach wages or other property.

graft profiting dishonestly from public money through one's political connections.

grand jury a jury of 12 to 23 persons employed to evaluate accusations and persons charged with crimes to determine whether a trial is warranted.

gratis given without reward; given freely, for nothing.

gross willful, inexcusable behavior.

habeas corpus the common law writ designed to prevent unjust imprisonment; law enforcement authorities must obtain a judicial determination of the legality of putting a particular person in custody.

hearing a preliminary judicial investigation of evidence to determine issues of fact.

hearsay rule a rule holding that evidence based on the statements of those other than testifying witnesses is inadmissible.

homicide the killing of one person by another.

hostile witness any biased witness whose testimony may be prejudiced against a court opponent.

hung jury an indecisive jury that cannot agree on a verdict.

ignorantia legis non excusat ignorance of the law is no excuse.

immaterial irrelevant.

immunity referring to immunity from prosecution or exemption from a rule or penalty, sometimes granted to witnesses to get them to testify.

impaneling the jury selection process. Also, a list of those serving on a jury.

impeach to charge a public official with malfeasance while in office.

implied consent consent presumed or inferred from someone's action, inaction, or silence.

impound to place something in the custody of the police or other authority.

in articulo mortis in the moment of death.

in camera proceedings held in a judge's chambers or out of public view.

indictment a written statement formally charging one with a crime and submitted to a grand jury.

inferior court any court whose decisions may be judged by a higher court.

in invitum against the will of another.

injunction a court order that prohibits someone from carrying out a particular action.

injuria non excusat injuriam one wrong doesn't justify another wrong.

inquest a judicial inquiry. Also, a coroner's inquiry into a cause of death.

interrogation police questioning of suspects.

journalist's privilege the privilege of the media in some cases to keep sources of information confidential.

J.P. justice of the peace.

jump bail to fail to appear in court after posting bail.

jural pertaining to law and justice.

jurisprudence the science and philosophy of law.

jury of the vicinage a jury selected form the neighborhood where the crime was committed.

justice synonymous with judge.

laches a doctrine providing a defense to the defendant when the opposing party has delayed prosecution for an unusual amount of time.

larceny stealing.

leading question a query by lawyers in which the question to a witness suggests the wanted answer; allowed in court only in cross-examination.

libel malicious publication of falsehoods that defame a person.

lien a claim or hold on the property of another that secures a debt.

litigants the parties involved in a lawsuit.

litigation legal process

loan sharking loaning money with extremely high interest rates.

majority, age of when one legally becomes adult, usually considered to be aged 18.

malfeasance a wrongful act.

malice the desire to harm others; an act performed with the willful disregard for the welfare of others.

malice aforethought a thought-out design, without justification, to harm others; the state of mind that distinguishes murder from manslaughter.

malicious arrest the arrest of a person without probable cause.

malicious prosecution an action to collect damages caused by a previous prosecution without probable cause and with malice.

malum in se referring to an act that is illegal because it is inherently evil as judged by society. See MALUM PROHIBITUM.

malum prohibitum referring to an act that is illegal because it is prohibited by law for the welfare of the public and not necessarily evil.

mandate an order issued from a superior court to a lesser court.

manslaughter the killing of another without malice aforethought.

manslaughter, voluntary killing in the heat of passion.

manslaughter, involuntary killing someone accidently, as through reckless driving.

material relevant, important.

material witness a witness whose testimony is absolutely vital to a case.

matricide the killing of one's mother.

mediation the settling of disputes out of court.

medical examiner coroner.

mens rea the evil intent or state of mind that accompanies a criminal act; in legal terms, the states of mind include "intentionally," "knowingly," "recklessly," and "grossly negligent."

Miranda rule the requirement to read a person his or her rights (right to remain silent, right to a lawyer's presence, etc.) during an arrest and before police interrogation.

miscarriage of justice damages to a party due to court errors during litigation, sometimes requiring a reversal of judgment.

misdemeanors any crimes considered less serious and having less severe punishment than felonies.

misfeasance performing a lawful act in a dangerous or injurious manner.

misjoinder the joining of separate counts in an indictment.

mistrial a trial that is voided and terminated before a verdict is reached, due to a hung jury, court errors, or death of a juror or an attorney.

mitigating circumstances circumstances that lessen a person's guilt in a crime.

modus operandi the manner of operation; the method used by a criminal in accomplishing a crime.

moot court a make-believe court held in law schools to argue a moot case.

moral certainty to be certain beyond a reasonable doubt, but to be less so than absolutely certain.

moral turpitude depravity, dishonesty, vileness.

motion in a court proceeding, a request for a ruling.

negative pregnant a denial that, by being noticeably qualified or modified, implies an affirmation of facts.

negligence the failure to exercise care in a degree that would be expected from a reasonable person.

negligence, criminal reckless negligence resulting in injury or death. Also known as culpable negligence.

nemo est supra legis no one is above the law.

non compos mentis not of sound mind.

non vult contendere he will not contest. A defendant who neither confesses guilt nor contests the charges against him, therefore acquiesing to be treated as guilty by the courts.

nuisance anything indecent, offensive, obstructive, or disturbing to the free use of one's property.

pain and suffering a type of damages that can be recovered when the opposing party's wrongdoing results in harming someone in an emotional or physical way.

palimony support payments similar to alimony but given to the partner in a defunct, nonmarital relationship.

pander to pimp; to serve the sexual desire of others. Also, to promote obscene literature and movies.

panderer a pimp; one who serves the sexual interests of others.

paralegal a legal assistant.

paternity suit an action filed to determine the father of an illegitimate child and to gain financial support for that child.

patricide the killing of one's father.

penal pertaining to punishments or penalties associated with breaking the law.

penal code the body of laws concerning crime and its punishment.

perjury lying while under oath, a criminal offense.

petit jury a trial jury, as opposed to a grand jury. Also known as a petty jury.

physician-patient privilege the privilege of physicians to keep all forms of communication from a patient confidential unless the patient consents otherwise.

plaintiff in a court action, the person who files suit.

plea bargaining the negotiation between the prosecutor and the accused of a mutually satisfactory disposition of a case to expedite proceedings, usually involving a guilty plea in exchange for a lesser sentence.

plead to argue, persuade, or present a case in court.

polling the jury the surveying by the judge of each juror for their individual decisions concerning the verdict, as requested in some cases by a criminal defendant.

polygraph a lie detector.

postmortem after death. Refers to the examination of a body by a coroner to determine cause of death.

power of attorney granting someone in writing the authority to perform specific acts on his behalf.

precedent a past court case decision that is used as an authority or reference for deciding future cases.

prejudice having a bias in favor of one of the parties in a lawsuit. Also, a preconceived notion of guilt or innocence concerning a party without knowing the facts.

premeditation thinking over something beforehand, an element distinguishing murder from manslaughter.

presentment a written accusation made by a grand jury stemming from its own investigation.

presumption a supposition; a strong probability.

presumption of innocence the principle that the accused is presumed innocent until proven guilty.

priest-penitent privilege the privilege granted to a priest, rabbi, or minister to keep confidential any confessions of a church member unless the church member consents otherwise.

probable cause the required element in a legal search and seizure or in an arrest.

pro bono publico for the public welfare. Most often refers to an attorney representing a case without compensation. A pro bono case.

prosecution the carrying out of a suit in court. Also, the party filing the suit.

prosecutor the person or public official who conducts a prosecution.

prurient interest a shameful interest in sex and nudity.

public defender a government-appointed attorney who defends those unable or unwilling to hire their own attorney.

puffing referring to the extravagent claims made by salesmen concerning their wares, generally not acceptable as a representation of fact or as the basis for fraud.

purloin to steal.

psychotherapist-patient privilege the privilege of a psychiatrist or psychologist to keep all forms of communication from a patient confidential unless the patient consents otherwise.

quid pro quo same as consideration; something for something.

racketeering obtaining money through fraud or extortion or through a conspiracy to commit fraud or extortion.

raised check a check whose original amount has been altered.

real evidence any object, such as a murder weapon or photograph, that can be examined and used as evidence in court. Also known as demonstrative evidence.

reasonable doubt in a criminal trial, the doctrine describing the degree of certainty a juror must have concerning evidence in order to return a guilty verdict against the accused. He must be certain beyond a reasonable doubt.

rebuttal evidence any evidence that contradicts or counteracts other evidence.

recidivist a habitual offender.

recusation the disqualification of a judge or jury due to conflict of interest, bias, or prejudice.

rejoinder the defendant's answer in response to the plaintiff's reply or replication.

remittitur a reduction of a jury's excessive verdict, made by the judge. Opposite of additur.

replication the plaintiff's reply to the defendant's answer.

rescue doctrine a doctrine holding that a negligent person causing an injury to someone is also liable for any injury that befalls the rescuer of a victim during a rescue attempt.

respondeat superior let the superior reply. A doctrine holding that an employer is liable for damages caused by an employee in the course of his duties.

restraining order similar to an injunction but issued without a hearing.

retainer an advance payment to an attorney for services.

retreat, duty to in some jurisdictions, the duty to flee a threatening situation as opposed to defending oneself by injuring another, generally not applicable in one's own home, however.

scienter refers to "guilty knowledge" of one's false statements or representations made when committing a fraud.

scintilla speculative evidence.

search warrant an order issued by a judge for an officer of the law to search a place for persons or things and to bring them before the court.

second degree murder unpremeditated murder with malice aforethought.

service to serve notice or to deliver a pleading or other document in a lawsuit to the opposing party.

sham pleading pleading that is unsupported by the facts.

sheriff's sale the sale of a judgment debtor's property by the sheriff to satisfy an unpaid judgment, mortgage, or lien.

shield laws laws protecting the confidentiality between a news reporter and his or her source. Also includes laws protecting rape victims from questioning about past sexual experiences.

show-up similar to a police lineup, but only with one suspect facing a witness.

sidebar the part of a courtroom out of earshot of the jury and used by the judge and attorneys to discuss issues that would be improper for the jury to hear.

slander false words spoken publicly that damage the reputation of another.

standing mute refusing to plead guilty or not guilty.

statute of limitations any statute that puts a time limit on when judicial action can be taken against someone.

statutory rape engaging in sex with a minor.

stay a court-ordered postponement of an event or action.

stay of execution a court order in which a judgment is postponed for a specific amount of time.

strict liability liability for injuries or damages stemming from dangerous activities (such as the use of explosives) even if those activities are carried out lawfully and with extreme care. Liability without fault or negligence.

subornation of perjury the crime of persuading another to lie in court.

subpoena a court order to force a witness to appear at a judicial proceeding; a subpoena to testify.

subrogation one's fulfilling of an obligation on another's behalf.

suit a broad term for any court proceeding undertaken for the pursuit of justice.

suitor a litigant in a court case.

summation the closing arguments made by each party's counsel in a trial.

summons an order or notification served to a defendant to appear in court or risk a default judgment.

sunshine laws laws that require meetings held by government agencies to be open to the public.

superior court any court that reviews the decisions of lower courts.

suppression of evidence preventing the use of illegally seized evidence or any evidence that may unfairly bias a jury.

supreme court the highest appellate court in a jurisdiction or state.

Supreme Court the highest court in the United States, consisting of nine justices and having jurisdiction over all other courts.

surety one who promises to fulfill certain obligations, particularly financial ones, if his principal fails to do so; one who takes on a liability for another's debt; a bondsman.

surety bond a bond issued by a surety guaranteeing the fulfillment of another's obligations.

tacit something implied.

tainted evidence evidence that cannot be relied upon because of its questionable source. Same as fruit of the poisonous tree.

taking the Fifth pleading the Fifth Amendment right not to provide evidence that will incriminate oneself.

testify the giving of statements while under oath in a court proceeding.

testimony statements or evidence given by a witness while under oath.

tort any wrongful act, damage, or injury associated with a breach of lawful social behavior as opposed to a breach of a contract.

tort-feasor one who commits a tort.

transcript a certified, written record of what occurred and what was said in a court proceeding.

trial, bench a trial with a judge but no jury.

unclean hands see CLEAN HANDS.

usury an excessive or illegal rate of interest on a loan.

verdict, false a verdict unsupported by the facts.

vicarious liability refers to the liability of an employer for the actions of an employee while conducting the duties of his job. Same as respondeat superior.

vice crimes immoral indulgences such as gambling, prostitution, and pornography.

vicinage an area of neighborhood where a crime was committed or where jurors are called from.

vis major a greater force. Refers to an act of God or an act of nature.

voice exemplar a tape recording of a person's voice used as identification in a court proceeding.

voir dire examination an evaluation and a qualifying of prospective jurors.

volenti non fit injuria the volunteer suffers no wrong. In tort law, any person willingly engaging in an activity cannot collect damages if that activity causes injury.

wanton grossly negligent.

warrant a court order issued to have someone arrested.

writ a court order issued to compel someone to carry out some activity or to stop them from carrying out some activity.

writ of execution the court's enforcing of a judgment by levying the judgment debtor's property.

CONTRACT LAW

adhesion contract a contract that heavily favors one party over the other, raising suspicions that the agreements in the contract may have been coerced or involuntary on the part of the disfavored party.

bad faith willful failure to follow through on a contractual obligation.

binding obligatory.

boilerplate any universal or formal language used in a standard contract or legal document.

breach of contract the failure to carry out or follow through on a contract agreement.

consideration the giving or promise of money, goods, or services in return for something else of value, the basis for any contract; the inducement offered to enter into a contract.

covenant an agreement to carry out or perform some duty or promise, as in a deed.

covenantee the person a covenant is intended for.

covenantor the person who makes a covenant.

duress any inducement or action by a person that compels another to do something he or she wouldn't ordinarily do, such as making a threat to force someone to sign a contract.

earnest something of value, such as money, given by one party to another to bind a contract.

escalator clause a clause in a contract that provides for a higher price to be paid if certain conditions occur.

escape clause a clause allowing a person to get out of a contract and be free of liability if certain conditions do or do not occur.

in extremis most often refers to the writing of a will when death is impending but it can also refer to any contract written under "extreme circumstances" that could possibly alter the interpretation of the contract.

meeting of the minds mutual understanding and agreement to the terms of a contract between two parties.

mitigation of damages that a damaged party in a contract must not do anything that will increase the amount of damages.

notary public one authorized to administer oaths, to take depositions, and to witness and certify the signing of documents.

postnuptial agreement an agreement entered into by a husband and wife that determines how assets will be distributed in the event of death or divorce.

prenuptial agreement an agreement entered into by a couple intending to marry that determines how assets will be distributed in the even to of divorce or death.

proviso a stipulation or condition.

rider an amendment or addition added to a contract.

severable contract a contract in which the agreements are considered as separate and independent so that a breach of any agreement does not void the contract as a whole.

PROPERTY AND REAL ESTATE LAW

abandonment the relinquishing of rights or property by one person to another.

appurtenant an easement, covenant, or other burden attached to a property.

burden any restriction limiting the use of one's land, such as restrictive zoning or a covenant.

chattel personal property; movable property or belongings, as distinguished from real estate.

clear title a title without encumbrances or limitations that would make legality questionable.

cloud on title any problem with a title to real estate that impairs or defeats clear title.

community property property acquired by the combined efforts of husband and wife during their marriage.

conservator a person appointed by the court to care for property owned by one deemed incapable of managing the property.

covenant a binding agreement to do or not to do something, often incidental to a deed.

covenantee the person a covenant is intended for.

covenantor the person who makes a covenant.

easement the granted right to use another person's land.

eminent domain the right of the state to take private land for public use.

encumbrance any burden, such as an easement, covenant, or lien on the title of a property.

en ventre sa mere the law of property providing that an unborn child or fetus has the same rights as one who has already been born.

postnuptial agreement an agreement entered into by a husband and wife that determines how assets will be distributed in the event of death or divorce.

prenuptial agreement an agreement entered into by a couple intending to marry that determines how assets will be distributed in the event of divorce or death.

property settlement a division of property between a divorcing husband and wife.

real property land, including any buildings thereon.

run with the land refers to covenants and their passing of burdens or benefits on to succeeding owners of the property, even though they didn't originally contract for them.

subdivision a dividing of land into separate parcels.

tenancy-at-will an agreement between landlord and tenant that works as a kind of open-ended lease in which tenancy may be terminated at any time upon 30-day written notice by either party.

title proof of ownership or possession of property.

title search a search through public records to establish ownership of a property and any liens, encumbrances, and so on, on that property.

PROBATE LAW

advancement an advance granted to a child from a living parent's will.

bequeath the giving of a gift of personal property in a will.

bequest a gift of personal property.

causa mortis the law that states that a gift given in anticipation of death is void if the giver survives.

disinherit to cancel or terminate another's inheritance.

forced heirs heirs who cannot be disinherited, such as a spouse and children.

holographic will a will written, dated, and signed by the testator himself.

in extremis most often refers to the writing of a will when death is impending but it can also refer to any contract written under "extreme circumstances" that could possibly alter the interpretation of that contract.

intestate one who has died without drawing up a will.

legacy same as bequest.

nuncupative will a dying declaration or oral will given by an ill person incapable of drawing up a formal will.

probate a proceeding in which the elements of a will are authenticated and found legal.

probate court a court that deals with the probate of wills.

testacy leaving a valid will upon death.

testator one who makes a will.

Medicine

MEDICAL FIELDS AND SPECIALTIES

Phenomenon Studied	Name of Specialty
aging	geriatrics, gerontology
allergies	allergology
anesthesia	anesthesiology
bacteria	bacteriology
birth	obstetrics
blood	hematology
body function	physiology
body movement	kinesiology
bones	osteology, osteopathy
bones, muscles, and tendons	orthopedics
cells	cytology
children	pediatrics
digestive system	gastroenterology
disease, as examined by diseased tissue	pathology
disease causes	etiology
disease classification science	nosology
disease identification	diagnostics
ear, nose, and throat	otolaryngology
ears	otology
epidemic and contagious disease study	epidemiology
eyes	ophthalmology
eyes, visual acuteness testing	optometry
feet	podiatry, chiropody
female reproductive organs	gynecology
glands	adenology
gums	periodontics
hearing	audiology
heart	cardiology
hernias	herniology
hormones and the glands that secrete them	endocrinology
immune system	immunology
internal organs	internal medicine
intestine	entrology
joints	arthrology, rheumatology
kidneys	nephrology
liver	hepatology
lungs and breathing	pulmonary medicine; pulmonology
lymphatic system	lymphology
mental disorders	psychiatry
mental processing behind behavior and consciousness	psychology
mouth	stomatology, oralogy
muscles	myology, orthopedics
nervous system	neurology, neuropathology
newborns	neonatology
nose	rhinology
parasites	parasitology
plastic surgery	plastic surgery, cosmetic surgery
poisons and toxins	toxicology
rectum and anus	proctology
rheumatic disease	rheumatology
serums	serology
sexually transmitted diseases	venereology
skin	dermatology
skull	craniology
spinal manipulation and correction	chiropractic
stomach	gastrology
symptoms	symptomology
teeth	dentistry
teeth straightening	orthodontics
tissue	histology
tumors	oncology
ulcers	helcology

urinary and urogenital tract (kidney, ureter, bladder, prostate, penis, urethra)	urology
veins	phlebology
viruses	virology
X rays, radiation therapy	radiology

GENERAL MEDICAL TERMINOLOGY AND TESTS

Aesculapius in Green mythology, the god of medicine, the son of Apollo.

asymptomatic without symptoms.

auscultation listening for body sounds through a stethoscope to aid in determining normal health.

autopsy an examination of a corpse to determine the exact cause of death.

barium a whitish contrast medium given orally or through an enema to highlight the gastrointestinal tract under an X ray.

b.d. in prescription writing, an abbreviation for the Latin *bis in diem,* meaning twice daily. Also written as b.i.d.

Bence Jones protein test a urine test given to detect the presence of a bone tumor.

Benedict's test a test for detecting sugar in the urine.

bimanual a two-handed examination of a body area.

biopsy the removal and study of tissue to determine a diagnosis, especially of tumors.

bronchoscopy an examination of the trachea and bronchi through the insertion of a bronchoscope.

bruit a murmur heard through the stethoscope over the heart or an artery; an abnormal sound.

caduceus a serpent coiled around a staff, the official insignia of medicine.

certifiable disease any disease that is contagious and therefore must be reported to the board of health.

Cheyne-Stokes breathing in patients suffering from congestive heart failure, breathing characterized by long periods of apnea (no breathing) ending with several deep breaths.

chronic of long duration, as in some diseases.

contusion a bruise.

culture laboratory-grown germs for the purpose of identification and testing.

diaphanography passing a light through the breast to examine shadows, which may reveal signs of disease.

diathermy the application of heat.

Dick test a skin test given to determine susceptibility to scarlet fever.

diuretic an agent prescribed to increase the amount of urine passed.

d.o.a. abbreviation for dead on arrival, a term used by ambulance paramedics, police, emergency room staff.

dosimetry the science of determining the exact dosage of medication.

emetic an agent that stimulates vomiting.

enteral nutrition feeding through a tube passed through the nose and into the stomach.

epidemic a disease affecting a large group of people at the same time in the same community.

epidemiology the study of the occurrence and spread of a disease.

eponym the name of an illness, disorder, or medical tool as named after the person who first described it or invented it.

euthanasia the mercy killing of someone who is terminally ill.

expectorant a medicine that promotes the expulsion of mucous from the lungs.

extremis on the point of dying.

forensic medicine medical technology used to help solve crimes.

gavage feeding through a tube leading directly into the stomach through a hole created surgically in the abdominal wall.

GOMER slang term for a whining, complaining patient; an acronym for "Get out of my emergency room."

guaiac test a test for blood in the stool.

hematocrit test a blood test to determine the ratio of blood cells to plasma, used to diagnose anemia.

Hippocrates Greek physician known as the father of medicine, lived before Christ's time, and is the author of the Hippocratic oath.

Hippocratic oath an oath all physicians take promising to follow a code of ethical, professional conduct.

hypochondriac a person excessively concerned about his health.

incipient early, beginning stage.

informed consent a patient's legal consent to perform a treatment, procedure, or test after being informed of the risks involved.

intravenous within a vein.

Kline test a blood test for syphilis.

lavage washing out of an organ.

Lee-White test a test to determine the time it takes blood to clot or coagulate.

lesion collective term for damage to tissue, including abcesses, herpes, ulcers, tumors, injuries.

locum tenens Latin term for the temporary taking over of a practice of one doctor by another.

Mantoux test a skin test for tuberculosis.

Mazzini test a test for syphilis.

methylene blue test an injection of dye that should appear in the urine within 30 minutes if the kidneys are functioning normally.

nosocomial referring to the hospital, especially a disease or infection acquired while in the hospital.

nostrum a quack medicine.

occult hidden or concealed, as in blood in the stool.

organotherapy the use of hormones and tissue extracts from animals to treat human diseases.

palliative a medicine that soothes symptoms but does not cure the underlying disease.

palpation feeling with the hands the contours of a body part to help make a diagnosis.

panacea a cure-all; a universal remedy.

pandemic an epidemic that has spread across an entire state or country.

Pap smear a test for cancer.

paracentesis drawing off fluids from a body cavity.

paternity test a test to determine the father of a child by matching blood types.

pathogen any bacteria or virus capable of causing disease or infection.

percussion tapping the chest, abdomen, and back and listening for sounds in response, usually used as a method of detecting lung congestion.

per os by mouth, often abbreviated p.o.

per rectum through the rectum, often abbreviated p.r.

pharmacopeia a book listing medicinal drugs and their formulas; the *U.S. Pharmacopeia* was first published in 1820.

placebo a fake medicine given in experiments and sometimes having a positive medicinal affect due to psychological phenomenon.

position, Fowler's a position in which the patient is lying down with head raised about 20 inches to aid in draining pus in cases of peritonitis.

position, knee-chest a position in which the patient rests on elbows and knees with rump up for rectal exam.

position, lithotomy a position in which the patient is lying on back with knees up and legs spread, for a pelvic exam.

position, recumbent lying flat on back.

position, Sims a position in which the patient rests on the left side with the right leg bent and pulled up, for a rectal exam.

position, Trendelenburg a position in which the patient lies with head 1 to 2 feet below knee level, to increase blood flow to the head to prevent shock. Also known as the shock position.

p.r.n. in prescription writing, a term meaning "whenever necessary."

prodromal symptoms the earliest symptoms of a disease.

prognosis the prediction of the outcome of a disease.

prognosticate to make a prediction of the course a disease will take.

prothrombin time test a test to determine the time it takes blood to clot.

protocol the records of a patient's case.

quack a phony doctor.

radionucleotide test the injecting of a radioisotope into the arm to determine heart damage.

rale clicking sound made by a congested lung, as heard through a stethoscope.

reflex, Achilles ankle reflex caused by a blow to the large tendon above the heel.

reflex, Babinski the reflexive rising of the big toe and fanning of the small toes when the sole of the foot is scratched, often a sign of brain disease.

reflex, patellar the knee-jerk reflex.

relapse the return of a disease after apparent recovery.

remission a temporary or permanent halting of a disease.

resonance the sound of the lungs when they are clear and normal.

rhoncus wheezing sound heard through a stethoscope when excess mucous is present in trachea.

Schick test a skin test to determine immunity to diphtheria.

Schultz-Charlton test a skin test to determine immunity to scarlet fever.

Snellen test a vision test in which perfect vision is signified by the number 20/20.

socialized medicine a health care program paid for by the government through taxation.

sonography reflection of sound waves recorded photographically to produce images of the interior of the body. Also known as ultrasound.

s.o.s. in prescription writing, a term meaning "if necessary."

stat a hospital code word meaning "immediately."

systemic referring to a disease affecting the entire body.

terminal refers to a patient who is near death and who will not recover from his disease.

t.i.d. in prescription writing, an abbreviation for the Latin *tres in diem*, meaning "three times daily."

TPN total parenteral nutrition; feeding of all nutrients through the veins.

traction the drawing or pulling together of broken bones in order to promote healing.

triage in disaster medicine, the sorting of patients by the seriousness and type of injury in order to provide treatment first to those who need it most.

two-step test exercise to test the heart under exertion and to determine the presence of angina pectoris.

ultrasound sonography.

vital capacity test a breathing test of lung capacity, an accurate predictor of life span.

EQUIPMENT AND INSTRUMENTS

autoclave an apparatus that sterilizes medical instruments by steam.

biopsy needle a needle used in obtaining biopsy material.

bistoury a slender surgical knife, used most frequently to open an abscess.

bougie a slender, flexible probe made of rubber or silk and used in the diagnosis and measurement of strictures in the esophagus, the urethra, and other organs.

bronchoscope a tubular instrument inserted through the mouth and down the throat to inspect the trachea and bronchi.

caliper a forcepslike instrument used to measure thicknesses, especially body fat.

cannula a tube designed to fit into the various body channels for the withdrawing or delivering of fluids.

capnograph an instrument that monitors the amount of carbon dioxide in exhaled air.

cardiograph an instrument that records the activity of the heart.

catgut suture material made form the intestines of sheep; it is eventually absorbed by the body.

catheter a slender tube inserted into a body channel to extract or deliver fluids.

catheter, cardiac a slender tube passed through a blood vessel in an extremity to the heart to take blood samples and pressure readings.

CAT scanner computerized axial tomography: an x-ray instrument producing three-dimensional images. Also known as a CT scanner.

cautery an electrical instrument used to scar or destroy abnormal tissue.

Cavitron a motorized scalpel that cuts through delicate flesh but leaves blood vessels and ductal tissue intact; used in brain and liver surgery.

centrifuge a machine that separates substances of varying densities by subjecting them to centrifugal (whirling at high speed) force.

clamp an instrument clamped on a cut blood vessel to stop bleeding; a hemostat.

clip a metal clip used to hold tissues together.

colposcope a microscope used to directly examine the vagina and cervix.

coreometer an instrument that measures the size of the pupil of the eye.

costome an instrument used to cut through ribs.

cryoprobe an instrument that freezes malignant tissue in order to destroy it.

Culdoscope a lighted instrument passed through the vagina and into the pelvic cavity to examine the organs there.

curet a spoonlike instrument used to scrape away diseased tissue and growths or to collect tissue samples.

cystoscope a long, metal tube used to inspect the inside of the bladder.

cytoanalyzer an electronic apparatus that analyzes smears thought to contain malignant cells.

cytometer a device that counts and measures blood cells.

defibrillator an apparatus that delivers an electric current to the heart to restore normal heart rhythm.

dilator an inflatable instrument used to enlarge the opening of an organ or internal cavity.

dioptometer an instrument used to measure eye refraction for the purpose of determining eye defects.

drain a tube or wick used to drain fluid from a wound, sometimes assisted by a pump.

EEG see electroencephalography.

EKG electrocardiogram. Same as cardiogram.

electroencephalograph an instrument used to record the brain's electrical waves.

electromyograph an instrument that records the electrical impulses of contracting muscles.

electron microscope an extremely powerful microscope utilizing electrons rather than visible light to produce magnified images of objects too small for an ordinary microscope to resolve.

elevator surgical hand tool used to pry up bone fragments.

endoscope collective term for a family of instruments used to examine hollow organs or body cavities such as gastroscope, proctoscope, cystoscope.

ergograph an instrument that measures the physical output of a muscle.

fetoscope a fetal stethoscope.

file one of a family of instruments used for cutting, smoothing, or grinding.

flowmeter a device used to measure the flow of a liquid as it is dispensed.

fluoroscope an x-ray device in which x-rays are passed through the body to strike a fluorescent screen and render a live picture of the internal organs in motion.

forceps a tongslike instrument used for grasping, clamping, and extracting tissue.

forceps, bulldog forceps used for clamping cut blood vessels.

forceps, capsule forceps used to extract the lens of the eye in cataract surgery.

forceps, hemostatic a locking forceps used for clamping cut blood vessels.

forceps, mosquito a tiny hemostatic forceps.

forceps, obstetrical forceps used to grasp the head of the fetus.

forceps, rongeur forceps for gouging out bone.

forceps, thumb forceps used to hold soft tissue while suturing.

gastroscope an instrument passed through the mouth and into the stomach to examine the stomach lining.

gouge a chisellike instrument for cutting out bits of bone.

guillotine a rib cutter.

Hagedorn needle a surgical needle with cutting edge, used to sew up skin. Also, the finger-pricking needle used to draw blood.

hemocytometer a device that determines the number of red blood cells in a blood sample.

hemodialyzer an apparatus used to purify or eliminate wastes from the blood, an artificial substitute for a diseased kidney.

hemostat an instrument used to stop bleeding by clamping a cut vein or artery.

kangaroo tendon suture material derived from the tails of kangaroos.

keratome a knife used to cut into the cornea of the eye.

lancet a surgical knife used for puncturing.

laryngoscope a lighted hollow tube used for examining the larynx.

linear accelerator an x-ray machine used for delivering radiation for the treatment of malignancies.

mecometer an instrument used to measure a newborn.

micrometer an instrument used to measure microscopic objects.

microsyringe a syringe designed to measure out precisely tiny portions of fluid.

microtome a lab device for slicing thin sections of tissue for examination with a microscope.

MRI magnetic resonance imaging; a noninvasive internal imaging technique employing magnetic properties instead of x-rays.

ophthalmometer an instrument used to determine problems with vision.

ophthalmoscope an instrument used to inspect the retina or rear lining of the eye.

osteotome a surgical bone chisel.

otoscope a lighted instrument for examining the ear.

panendoscope a cystoscope that provides a panoramic view of the interior of the bladder.

pelvimeter a caliperlike instrument for measuring the size of the pelvis or birth canal.

Penrose drain a rubber tube with a gauze center inserted into a wound to drain fluids. Also known as a cigarette drain.

plexor a rubber-headed hammer used in percussion.

Politzer bag a device used to inflate the middle ear.

proctoscope an instrument used to examine the anus and rectum.

protractor an instrument for removing shrapnel or bullets from a deep wound.

retractor an instrument used in surgery to pull an organ or body part out of the way of work being performed.

rhinoscope an instrument for examining the nasal passages.

rongeur plierslike instrument with sharp edges for cutting bone.

scalpel a thin surgical knife.

serrefine a small clamp used for clamping blood vessels.

sigmoidoscope a lighted tube used to inspect the rectum and sigmoid portion of the large intestine.

snare an instrument fitted with a wire loop used for snaring and severing a tumor or polyp.

speculum an instrument used to enlarge a body cavity.

spirometer a device for measuring the rate and volume of air inhaled and exhaled by the lungs.

splint a support for an injured area or broken bone.

splint, airplane a large support that holds the arm up and to the side of the body.

splint, banjo a support and traction splint made of wire and rubber and resembling a banjo, for a broken finger.

splint, T a T-shaped support for the upper back, used in cases of broken collarbones.

sponge a surgical pad used to absorb fluids.

stethoscope a listening instrument used to amplify internal body sounds.

suture a stitching material used to sew up tissue and wounds. Surgical thread.

suture, catgut suture made from sheep intestine; it is gradually absorbed by the body.

suture, button stitches in which the ends are passed through buttons and tied off.

suture, cobbler a suture with a needle attached to each end.

swab an absorbent material wrapped around a stick or a wire for cleaning wounds or administering medication.

syringe the device used for injecting and withdrawing fluids.

tenaculum tongslike instrument used to hold a body part.

urethroscope a lighted instrument used for inspecting the urethra.

SURGICAL PROCEDURES AND RELATED TERMS

adenectomy removal of a gland.

adenoidectomy removal of the adenoids.

adenotonsillectomy removal of the tonsils and adenoids.

adrenalectomy removal of the adrenal glands.

anesthesia, caudal injection of an anesthetic agent into the lower spinal canal.

anesthesia, endotracheal an anesthetic agent administered through a tube placed into the mouth or nose and down into the trachea or windpipe for inhalation.

anesthesia, epidural injection of an anesthetic agent just outside the spinal canal.

anesthesia, general the administration of a full-body anesthesia involving loss of consciousness.

anesthesia, intravenous injection of an anesthetic agent into a vein.

anesthesia, local an anesthetic agent used in a limited or confined area of the body.

anesthesia, spinal an anesthetic agent injected directly into the spinal fluid of the spinal canal.

anesthesia, topical a local anesthetic applied to a body surface.

appendectomy removal of the appendix.

approach surgical term referring to the method used and route taken to reach a particular organ.

arthroscopy examining the inside of a joint with a lighted instrument.

biopsy removal of tissue samples for the purpose of diagnosis, especially of tumors.

Brunschwig's operation removal of all of the pelvic organs in order to stop a massive spread of cancer.

bypass a blood vessel graft supplied to an area with inadequate blood supply due to clogging of an artery. Also, an operation to shunt intestinal contents from one section of an intestine to another.

canthoplasty plastic surgery on the upper eyelid.

catheterization the passing of a slender tube into a body channel to extract or deliver fluids.

catheterization, cardiac passing a tube through a blood vessel in an extremity and threading it to the vessels of the heart for taking blood samples and pressure readings.

cauterization the burning away of abnormal tissue by electric current, heat, or caustic material.

celiotomy any surgery that opens up the abdomen.

cephalotrypesis cutting a hole through the skull to diagnose or treat a brain disease.

chemonucleolysis injecting a herniated disk with an enzyme in order to dissolve it.

chemotherapy the employment of chemicals to treat infections and tumors.

cholecystectomy removal of the gallbladder.

cholecystogastronomy surgically joining the gallbladder to the stomach.

choledocholithotomy removal of stones from the common bile duct leading from the gall bladder.

closed-chest massage an emergency method of restarting a heart that has stopped beating, specifically by pressing down rhythmically on the breastbone with the palm of the hand 80 times per minute.

closure the suturing of a wound; closing a wound.

colectomy removal of all or part of the large intestine.

colostomy a procedure to bring the large intestine to the abdominal wall, where an opening is made.

craniotomy a skull surgery that exposes the brain.

cryogenics the science of using cold as a medical treatment.

cryosurgery surgery employing extreme cold to destroy diseased tissue.

cryothalectomy the application of extreme cold to the thalamus of the brain; it destroys the area responsible for producing the palsy of Parkinson's disease.

curettage the scraping of tissue to obtain samples or to remove diseased tissue and growths.

cystectomy the removal of a cyst.

denervate to purposely cut a nerve in a body area in order to relieve pain.

divinyl ether an inhaled anesthetic agent.

electrocoagulation the coagulation of tissue through the use of an electric current.

embolectomy surgical removal of a blood clot in an artery to restore normal circulation.

encephalography an x-ray technique revealing parts of the brain.

endoscopic retrograde lithotripsy the passing of an instrument through the bladder and into the ureter to remove stones.

endoscopic shock wave lithotripsy disintegrating and eliminating kidney stones by the use of shock waves instead of surgery.

enterectomy removal of part of the intestine.

esophagectomy removal of the esophagus.

esophagoscopy the passing of an instrument down the throat to inspect the esophagus.

ether an inhaled anesthetic agent.

ethyl chloride a local anesthetic agent that freezes any tissue it comes in contact with.

ethylene an anesthetic gas.

eviscerate to open the abdomen and pull out the intestines.

excision the surgical removal of a tissue or organ.

flap a section (graft) of flesh that includes subcutaneous fat, muscles, nerves, arteries, and veins transplanted to another part of the body by microsurgery.

fluoroscopy a technique of producing live x-ray images of the internal organs in motion on a fluorescent screen.

fundal plication a procedure to correct a hiatus hernia by wrapping the upper end of the stomach around the intruding portion of the esophagus.

gastrectomy removal of part or all of the stomach.

gastric lavage prior to surgery, the washing out of all stomach contents.

gastrostomy the surgical creation of an opening into the stomach through the abdominal wall, when feeding through the mouth is not possible.

gingivectomy the surgical removal of part of the gums.

glossectomy removal of the tongue.

graft the transplanting of tissue from one part of the body to another. Also, the tissue so transplanted.

graft, auto a graft taken from the patient's own body.

graft, fascial a graft consisting of fibrous tissue.

graft, full thickness a graft containing all layers of the skin.

graft, hetero a graft taken from an animal for use on a human.

graft, homo a graft taken from the body of another person.

graft, split thickness a graft consisting of only part of the layers of the skin.

hemostasis the stopping of bleeding, achieved in surgery by clamping and tying off blood vessels.

hernioplasty surgical repair of a hernia.

hypodermic beneath the skin, as a hypodermic injection.

hysterectomy removal of the uterus.

incise to cut surgically.

incision a surgical cut.

intubation the passage of a tube into a body channel.

keratectomy removal of the cornea of the eye.

Kraske's operation removal of the rectum, coccyx, and part of the sacrum.

laryngectomy removal of the larynx (voice box).

Lidocaine a local anesthetic agent.

lipectomy the removal of excess body fat.

lobectomy removal of one of the five lobes of the lungs.

lobotomy removal of the front portion of the brain as a treatment for severe mental illness.

lumpectomy the removal of a tumor or mass.

mammography X rays of the breast to determine the presence of a tumor.

mammoplasty plastic surgery to improve the appearance of the breasts.

mastectomy removal of a breast.

mastoplasty plastic surgery to reduce the size of the breasts.

McBurney's incision an angular incision in the lower right abdomen, for removal of the appendix.

myectomy removal of part or all of a muscle.

myringotomy an incision into the eardrum to remove pus.

nephrectomy removal of a kidney.

neurosurgery surgery of the brian, spinal cord, or nerves.

nitrous oxide the anesthetic gas better known as laughing gas.

Ober operations in cases of paralysis, the transplanting of muscles and tendons.

odontectomy removal of the teeth.

oophorectomy removal of an ovary.

osteoclasis the deliberate rebreaking of a bone to more accurately set its alignment.

otoplasty plastic surgery to correct such ear deformities as flop ears and cauliflower ears.

palatoplasty repair of a cleft palate.

pancreatectomy removal of the pancreas.

pentothal an intravenous anesthetic agent.

percutaneous transluminal coronary angioplasty X-ray imaging of the coronary arteries with the aid of catheterization and a contrast medium or dye.

perfusion the injection and permeation of a fluid into a body part.

perineoplasty after childbirth, the repair of torn tissue between the vagina and the rectum.

phantom limb pain after an amputation, a sensation or perceived pain from the limb that was severed, a poorly understood psychological phenomenon.

phlebectomy the removal of a vein.

pneumonectomy removal of a lung.

postoperative after surgery.

procaine a local anesthetic agent.

prolapsed a term describing an organ that has fallen out of its normal position.

prostatectomy removal of the prostate gland.

purse-string operation the closing of the cervix with a purse-string suture in order to prevent premature childbirth or miscarriage.

radial keratotomy surgery originating in the Soviet Union and involving several incisions made in the cornea of the eye to cure nearsightedness.

radiosurgery the use of any source of radiation in surgery.

rejection reaction the body's attack on foreign substances, including organs or tissues donated from another person, which can often be counteracted by special drugs.

rhinoplasty plastic surgery to improve the appearance of the nose.

rhytidectomy plastic surgery to remove skin wrinkles.

salpingectomy removal of a fallopian tube.

salpingoplasty opening a closed passage in a fallopian tube to cure sterility.

septectomy surgery to correct a deviated septum in the nose.

shunt a bypass.

sigmoidectomy removal of the sigmoid portion of the large intestine.

splenectomy removal of a spleen.

staphylorrhaphy repair of a cleft palate.

sternal puncture taking by needle a marrow sample from the breastbone to test for blood disease.

sternotomy cutting the sternum apart in order to gain access to the heart.

suture to stitch or sew up a wound. Also, the thread used for this purpose.

suture, button suturing technique in which the ends of the thread are passed through buttons and tied off.

suture, catgut suture material made from sheep intestine; it is gradually absorbed by the body.

suture, cobbler a suture with a needle attached to each end.

suture, continuous a suture having only two ties, at the beginning and end of a wound.

suture, interrupted a suture having several ties and separate strands.

suture, inverting a suture that turns in tissue on all sides of a wound.

suture, purse-string a continuous, inverting suture forming a circle.

tamponade stopping blood flow by inserting a cotton sponge in a wound.

tapping the removal of body fluids with a needle.

temporal-cortical bypass an artery bypass applied to the surface of the brain to help restore denuded blood flow.

thoracoscopy an examination of the chest cavity by a special instrument.

thyroidectomy removal of the thyroid gland.

tissue typing the matching of compatible tissue or organs in transplant operations to help prevent rejection reaction.

trachelectomy removal of the cervix and the neck of the uterus.

tracheotomy an emergency incision into the trachea to open up the airways and relieve suffocation.

transfusion the infusing of donor blood into a patient's vein.

trans-sex surgery removal or altering of the sexual organs as an aid in changing one's sex from male to female, or vice versa.

trepanning boring a hole through the skull.

tubal ligation surgically closing the fallopian tubes to prevent pregnancy.

ureteroscopic ultrasonic lithotripsy disintegration of stones in the ureter by means of sound waves.

vaginoplasty repair of a torn vagina after childbirth.

vasectomy sterilization technique involving the cutting of the vas deferens, the tube through which sperm is transported.

Wertheim operation removal of the uterus, fallopian tubes, ovaries, and surrounding tissue to cure extensive cancer.

Finance

STOCKS, BONDS, COMMODITIES, AND MARKET TERMS

acquisition the purchase of a controlling interest in one company by another.

across the board stock market activity in which prices move in the same direction.

air pocket stock any stock that plummets sharply, as an aircraft hitting an air pocket.

American Stock Exchange the stock exchange second in trading volume to the New York Stock Exchange. It is located in New York and handles mostly small to medium-size companies. Also known as Amex and the curb.

analyst a person who analyzes companies and their securities and makes buy and sell recommendations.

arbitrage earning a profit by buying a security from one market and selling it back to another market at a higher price. The practice of taking advantage of price discrepancies between two markets. Also, speculating in the stock of a company that is about to be acquired by another company.

arbitrageur one who uses arbitrage to turn a profit. Also known as an arb.

baby bond a bond with a face value of less than $1,000, for small investors.

back-end load a service fee paid by an investor when withdrawing money from an investment, such as a mutual fund.

back off said of a stock that has suddenly dropped in price after rising.

barometer stock a large stock, such as General Motors, whose market activity reflects the market as a whole. Also known as a bellwether.

bear a person who is pessimistic about the stock market and who believes prices will continue to fall. Opposite of a bull.

bear market a pessimistic market with falling prices over an extended period of time. Opposite of a bull market.

bear raid the practice of selling a large quantity of a stock to force its price down and then rebuying it at the depressed price.

belly up said of a company that is going or has gone bankrupt.

bellwether a security, such as IBM stock, whose price activity indicates which direction the rest of the market will go.

bid and asked respectively, the highest price offered for a share of stock at a given time and the lowest price a seller will sell it for. The disparity between the two is known as the spread.

Big Blue knickname for IBM, International Business Machines.

Big Board the New York Stock Exchange.

Black Friday a term that applies to any sharp drop in a financial market. Also known as a Black Monday.

blue chip a common stock of a large corporation, such as IBM, which has had a long history of strong management and profit growth.

blue sky laws laws protecting the public from securities fraud.

boiler room a room or enterprise in which salesmen use high-pressure tactics to sell high-risk or fraudulent securities to investors over the telephone.

bond an interest-bearing certificate of debt, a form of corporate or government security; a formal IOU.

bond ratings a rating system ranging from AAA (very safe; not likely to default) to D (in default) that illustrates a bond issuer's financial health and predicts the probability of default.

bottom fisher an investor who seeks out a stock whose price has dropped to its lowest levels.

boutique a small brokerage house dealing in specialized stocks.

broad tape in brokerage firms, the enlarged, electronic Dow-Jones ticker tape that continuously displays new financial developments.

broker one who buys and sells securities on behalf of another.

bucket shop a brokerage firm that illegally gambles with its clients' holdings without the clients' awareness.

Buck Rogers a security whose price soars or rises sharply in a short period.

bull one who is optimistic about the market and who believes prices will continue an upward trend. Opposite of a bear.

bull market a prolonged period of rising stocks in the market. An optimistic market.

buying on margin buying securities on credit.

buyout the purchase of a controlling interest in a company.

cash cow a company that generates a lot of surplus cash flow.

cats and dogs speculative stocks with unproven track records; high-risk stocks.

churning the unethical frequent trading of a client's holdings in order to generate more commissions.

closely held a corporation's controlling stock held by only a small number of shareholders.

Comex Commodity Exchange; the New York–based exchange which trades in aluminum, copper, gold, and silver.

commodities grains, foods, metals.

common stock in a corporation, shares of ownership granting the holder a vote on important company issues as well as entitling him to dividends or a share of the profits.

contrarian an investor who follows a buying or selling strategy opposite or contrary to what most other investors are doing.

controlling interest owning 51% or more of a corporation's voting shares.

cornering the market buying a security or commodity in a large enough volume to control its price, an illegal practice.

correction a reversal, usually downward, of a stock's price trend.

crash a collapse of the stock market.

cyclical stock a stock that rises or falls in accordance with the strength or weakness of the economy.

day order a purchase or sell order given to a broker that is good for only one day.

debt instrument a collective term for any formal IOU, such as a bond.

dividend earnings distributed to shareholders, usually paid quarterly.

dog a poorly performing stock.

Dow-Jones industrial average the daily price average of 30 selected blue chip stocks, used as a market indicator or barometer.

Dun & Bradstreet a firm that obtains credit information on various companies and publishes same in reports and a ratings directory.

Fannie Mae knickname for the Federal National Mortgage Association, a corporation that buys mortgages from lenders and sells them to investors.

Fed, the the Federal Reserve System and the Federal Reserve Bank.

fill or kill a purchase or sell order that will be canceled unless it is executed immediately to take advantage of brief price changes.

flat market a market in which prices are neither rising nor falling.

floor the trading floor of the New York Stock Exchange.

floor broker a person who executes buy and sell orders on the floor of an exchange.

floor trader a person who executes orders on the floor of an exchange on his or her own behalf.

foreign crowd members of the New York Stock Exchange who trade in foreign bonds.

fourth market institutional investors who trade securities in large volume between one another to save on broker commissions.

Freddie Mac nickname for the Federal Home Loan Mortgage Corporation (FHLMC) and the mortgage-backed securities it packages and sells.

free-riding the buying and selling of securities quickly on margin and without paying any cash, a violation of fair credit use.

friendly takeover a takeover of one company by another that is welcome and unopposed.

front-end load a sales charge paid when mutual fund shares are purchased.

fungibles securities, bearer instruments, or commodities that are interchangeable in value.

futures commodities such as metals, grains, foods.

futures market a commodity exchange, such as the New York Coffee, Sugar and Cocoa Exchange or the Minneapolis Grain Exchange.

gilt-edged security any high-quality stock or bond.

Ginnie Mae nickname for the Government National Mortgage Association (GNMA) and the securities it guarantees.

going public a term referring to a private company when it offers shares to the public and subsequently becomes a publicly held company.

gold bond a bond through which interest is paid according to the price of gold.

goldbug an analyst or investor who specializes in gold.

graveyard market same as a bear market.

greenmail a payment made by a company takeover candidate to the potential acquiring company to prevent the takeover, a form of legal blackmail.

gun jumping trading securities on information that has not yet reached the public.

hard money strong, secure currency of an economically stable country. Also, gold.

hedge any means of protecting one's investments against losses.

hemline theory the theory that stock prices rise and fall with the hemlines of women's dresses and skirts.

home run a highly profitable gain in a stock in a brief period of time.

hot issue a newly issued stock which proves extremely popular with investors.

hung up being unable to sell without a loss a stock or bond that has dropped below its purchase price.

in-and-out trader a trader who takes advantage of sharp price movements by buying and then reselling a security in the same day.

inside information privileged information concerning a corporation that has not been made public and is therefore illegal to trade on.

insider in a corporation, one who is privy to such information as an impending takeover attempt, a future earnings report, or other development affecting stock prices. Insiders would include top executives, directors, and large shareholders.

institutional investor banks, insurance companies, mutual funds, and others who trade in large blocks of securities.

IPO initial public offering. A company's first sale of stock to the public.

junk bond a high-risk, high-yield bond with a credit rating of BB or less, often used to finance takeovers.

killer bees law firms, PR firms, investment bankers, and others involved in warding off a company takeover attempt.

lamb an inexperienced or naive investor.

leg a long-lasting trend in the market. A trend on its second or third leg is a very long trend.

leveraged buyout the takeover of a company with the use of borrowed money.

leveraged stock a stock bought with credit.

load a mutual fund sales or service charge.

long the investment posture of holding on to securities in the belief they will rise in value.

long bond a bond that takes more than 10 years to mature.

manipulation the buying and selling of large blocks of securities to give the illusion of activity and to influence other investors into buying or selling.

margin the amount of money an investor must have on deposit with a broker in order to purchase securities on credit, specifically at least 50% of the purchase price.

margin account an account held by a broker which allows a client to buy securities on credit.

melon slang for a large dividend.

meltdown the stock market crash of October 1987.

mortgage-backed security a security backed by a large pool of mortgages.

municipal bond a bond issued by a state or local government agency to finance a large project.

municipal revenue bond a bond issued to finance a project that will eventually generate its own revenues, such as a toll bridge.

mutual fund a diversified investment fund trading in many different stocks, bonds, commodities, or money market securities.

NASDAQ National Association of Securities Dealers Automated Quotations system; it provides brokers with price quotations.

new issue a new stock or bond offering.

New York Coffee, Sugar and Cocoa Exchange a commodities exchange trading in futures contracts.

New York Cotton Exchange a commodities exchange trading in futures contracts in cotton, orange juice, and propane.

New York Curb Exchange same as American Stock Exchange or Amex.

New York Mercantile Exchange an exchange trading in oil, gasoline, palladium, platinum, and potatoes.

New York Stock Exchange originating in 1792, the oldest and largest stock exchange in the United States. Also known as the Big Board and The Exchange.

Nifty Fifty the current 50 favorite stocks of institutional investors.

noise stock market movement caused by factors other than general market sentiment.

no-load fund mutual fund shares purchased directly, without a broker, so no sales fee is charged.

nonvoting stock stock, such as preferred stock, that does not give the holder a vote in important corporate affairs.

not rated refers to a security or a company that has not yet been rated by a securities rating company, such as Dun & Bradstreet.

odd lot a purchase or rate of less than 100 shares. See ROUND LOT.

off-board securities not traded on the floor of the New York Stock Exchange, as OTC stocks sold over the phone.

on margin buying securities on credit.

open outcry in a commodity exchange, the shouting out of buy and sell offers by traders looking for buyers and sellers.

opm slang for other people's money, as used when buying securities on credit.

option a right granted to buy or sell a security at a locked-in price by a specific date.

option, call the right (bought by a fee or premium) to purchase shares of a security at a locked-in price by a specific date.

option, put the right (paid for with a premium) to sell a specific number of shares of a stock at a specific price by a specific date.

order ticket a buy or sell order form with all the information needed for a broker to make a transaction on behalf of his client.

OTC over the counter, referring to those securities not traded on an exchange floor but over the telephone by securities dealers.

outstanding a corporate finance term referring to stock held by shareholders.

overbought refers to a security that has risen too far in price and is due for a price decline or correction.

oversold refers to a security that has dropped sharply in price and is due for an increase.

over the counter same as OTC.

overvalued a stock whose price has been driven higher than what is justified by the company's earnings potential.

Pac Man strategy named after the video game in which characters gobble each other up, a defensive strategy of attempting to takeover a company that is trying to take over your company, achieved by buying up the threatening company's common shares.

painting the tape a form of illegal manipulation in which two or more investors buy or sell securities among each other in order to influence other investors into buying or selling.

par the face value of a security.

parking temporarily placing assets in a safe, low-risk investment until market volatility passes.

penny stock a stock that generally sells for under $1 per share.

period of digestion a period of price volatility followed by price stability after the release of a new stock issue.

phantom stock plan a company incentive in which an executive's bonus is paid according to the company's stock growth.

pit where commodities are traded, as distinguished from the floor for stock trading.

plow back a new company's practice of putting earnings back into the business instead of paying it out in dividends.

poison pill a device or strategy of a company that is threatened to be taken over to make its stock appear unattractive to the potential acquiring company.

portfolio an investor's diversified holdings.

portfolio manager a professional who chooses investments and manages the financial portfolios of others.

preferred stock stock in which dividends are paid preferentially over that of common stock. However, it is usually nonvoting stock.

premium bond a bond that sells for a higher price than its face value.

price/earnings ratio a stock price divided by earnings per share for the previous year or projected for the coming year. Also known as the multiple or P/E ratio.

prospectus a circular containing information on a company's history, finances, officers, plans, and so forth, sent to potential investors in a stock offering.

publicly held a company with shares held by the public.

pure play Wall Street term for a company that specializes in only one business, as distinguished from a conglomerate.

quotation a bid and asked price on a security or commodity.

quotation board in a brokerage house, an electronic display of current price quotations.

radar alert the monitoring of unusual trading in a company's stock in order to detect an impending takeover attempt. Also known as shark watching.

raider one who attempts to take over a company by buying up a large portion of its stock.

rally a rise in stock prices after a flat or bear market.

rating a rating of securities and credit risk by rating services such as Standard and Poor's Corporation.

registered competitive trader a New York Stock Exchange member who trades securities on his own behalf.

resistance level the high water mark of a security's price; it is difficult to break through due to market psychology.

return profit on an investment.

rigged market a market being rigged by manipulators.

rollover moving assets from one investment to another.

round lot in stock, 100 shares or a multiple of 100.

round-trip trade a security that is purchased and then resold within a short period of time.

Sallie Mae the National Student Loan Marketing Association.

scalper an investment adviser who purchases a security then recommends it to clients in order to drive up its price and take a quick profit.

scorched earth a strategy of a company threatened to be taken over of making itself less attractive to the potential acquiring company, achieved by selling off the most desirable part of its business. Also known as shark repellent.

scripophily collecting stock and bond certificates for their "collectible" value rather than as securities, as a baseball card collector.

seat a purchased membership on an exchange.

securities stocks, bonds, notes, and similar items.

securities and commodities exchanges where securities, options, and futures contracts are bought and sold.

Securities and Exchange Commission (SEC) a federal agency that regulates and oversees investment companies, over-the-counter brokers and dealers, investment advisers, and the exchanges to protect the public from fraudulent practices.

selling short selling borrowed stocks in anticipation of a drop in price, after which the stocks may be repurchased at a lower price to make a profit.

shakeout a development in the market that scares investors into selling off their stock.

share a unit of ownership in a corporation or mutual fund.

shareholder an owner of stock in a corporation

shark one who attempts a hostile takeover of a company; a corporate raider.

shark repellent collective term for any device or strategy used to ward off a hostile takeover attempt.

shark watcher a firm hired to monitor trading in a company's stock in order to detect an impending takeover attempt.

sideways market same as a flat market.

sleeper a new stock issue with great potential but that is overlooked by investors.

sleeping beauty a corporation rich in assets and ripe for a takeover attempt.

soft currency currency that cannot be interchanged with another country's currency, such as the Russian ruble.

S&P Standard and Poor's.

speculation investing in high-risk securities with the belief they will produce a higher yield.

speculator one who trades in high-risk securities.

split an increase in the number of shares held by corporate shareholders with no change in equity. For example, a two-for-one split would double the number of shares owned but halve their value. A stock split is made to improve the stock's marketability.

spread the difference between a stock's bid and asked price.

stag an investor who regularly purchases then quickly resells securities within a short period of time to make a fast profit.

Standard and Poor's Corp. a company that offers several investment and ratings services.

Standard and Poor's index a measurement of the average up or down movements of 500 widely held common stocks, known as the S&P 500.

stock an equity or ownership interest in a corporation through which earnings are paid out according to the number of shares owned. Stock may also entitle the holder to a vote in important corporate affairs.

stock exchange the marketplace where stocks and bonds are traded.

stock watcher a service that monitors trading on the New York Stock Exchange to prevent unethical or fraudulent trading practices.

stop order an order to a broker to buy or sell a security when it reaches a specific price.

Street short for Wall Street; the Street.

street name securities held in the name of a broker instead of the name of the owner, as required when securities are purchased on margin.

strip to buy stock only for their dividends.

sweetener a bonus feature tacked on to a security to make it more attractive to investors.

swooner any security that is overly sensitive and reacts poorly to bad news in the marketplace.

tailgating a broker's practice of buying or selling for his own account the same security an influential client has just placed an order on, an unethical use of privileged trading information.

take a flyer to invest in a high-risk security; to speculate.

takeover a buying-out of the controlling interest in a corporation and, in hostile instances, the installment of new management.

target company a corporation that is threatened with a takeover.

ticker the electronic display of stock exchange trading activity.

toehold purchase the purchase of 5% of a takeover target's stock, which requires the buyer to file with the Securities and Exchange Commission if a takeover attempt is forthcoming.

tombstone the plain or unadorned advertisement in a newspaper of a new stock offering.

ton bond investor's slang for $100 million.

trader one who buys and sells securities.

triple witching hour refers to the massive trading that occurs when options and futures on stock indexes expire on the last trading hour of the third Friday of March, June, September, and December.

turkey a poorly performing investment.

twisting broker's unethical practice of persuading a client to make frequent trades in order to generate more commissions.

undervalued refers to a security that is selling for less than what analysts believe it is worth.

underwriter the investment banker who insures and distributes a corporation's new issue of securities.

undigested securities new stocks or bonds that have yet to be purchased due to a lack of investor interest.

unlisted security a security traded over the counter as distinguished from one traded on the floor of a stock exchange.

volatile a term commonly used to describe an unstable or rapidly fluctuating stock price or stock market.

volume the number of securities traded in a specific period.

voting stock stock that entitles the holder to a vote in important corporate affairs.

Wall Street in lower Manhattan, the financial district where the New York Stock Exchange, American Stock Exchange, and many investment-oriented firms are located. Also known as the Street.

war babies the stock and bonds of companies involved in defense contracts.

war brides same as war babies.

whipsawed buying a security just before its price drops and then reselling it just before its prices rises.

white knight an acquirer or acquiring company that is welcomed by a takeover target.

white squire a white knight who buys less than a controlling interest in a corporation.

widow and orphan stock any very reliable and safe stock that pays high dividends.

The Military

ARMY, GROUND FORCES, AND GENERAL MILITARY TERMS

Abrams the U.S. forces premier battle tank, having either a 105mm or 120mm gun and a top speed of 40 miles per hour with a four man crew. Also known as the M-1.

all available a request or command for all available fire to be aimed at the same target.

anticrop operation the employment of anticrop agents to destroy an enemy's source of food.

antimaterial agent a chemical or natural substance used to deteriorate or damage enemy equipment.

antipersonnel mine a mine designed to cause casualties to personnel.

antitank mine a mine designed to immobilize or destroy a tank.

armored earthmover a heavy, full-tracked bulldozer used to clear obstructions and fill antitank ditches, used by the engineering unit. Also known as the M-9.

armored personnel carrier a lightly armored, highly mobile, full-tracked vehicle, amphibious and air-droppable, used for transporting personnel.

armored-vehicle-launched bridge a 60-foot folding bridge mounted in place of a turret on an M-60 or M-1 tank; used to span antitank ditches.

army corps a tactical unit larger than a division and smaller than a field army; usually two or more divisions together with auxiliary arms and services.

army group the largest formation of land forces, normally consisting of two or more armies or army corps.

assault echelon a unit scheduled for an initial assault on an area.

back tell the transfer of information from a higher to a lower echelon of command.

ballistics the science of missiles or other vehicles acted upon by propellants, wind, gravity, temperature, or other forces.

banana clip a curved or crescent-shaped ammunition clip holding 30 rounds.

barrage a prearranged barrier of fire designed to protect friendly troops and installations by impeding enemy movements across defensive lines. Also, a protective screen of balloons that are moored to the ground and kept at given heights to hinder operations by enemy aircraft.

basic encyclopedia a compilation of identified installations and physical areas of potential significance as objectives for attack.

basilage the marking of a route by a system of dim beacon lights enabling vehicles to be driven at normal speeds under blackout conditions.

battery left a method of fire in which weapons are discharged from the left one after the other, usually at 5 second intervals.

battery right same as above, but starting from the right.

billet shelter for troops. Or, to quarter troops.

biological agent a microorganism that causes disease in man, plants, or animals or causes the deterioration of materiel.

blister agent a chemical agent that injures the eyes and lungs, and burns or blisters the skin. Also called vessicant agent.

blood agent a chemical compound, including the cyanide group, that affects bodily functions by preventing the normal transfer of oxygen from the blood to body tissues. Also called cyanogen agent.

blood chit a small cloth chart depicting an American flag and a statement in several languages to the effect that anyone assisting the bearer to safety will be rewarded.

blue forces forces used in a friendly role during NATO exercises.

booby trap an explosive or other injuring device deliberately placed to cause casualties when an apparently harmless object is disturbed or a normally safe act is performed.

boot slang for a soldier fresh out of boot camp.

bound a single movement, usually from cover to cover, made by troops under enemy fire.

Bradley infantry fighting vehicle having twin missile launchers to use against enemy tanks and one 22mm cannon firing armor-piercing slugs. Also known as the M-2 and M-3.

breaching securing passage through a minefield.

bridgehead an area of ground held or to be gained on the enemy's side of an obstacle.

brigade a unit smaller than a division to which are attached groups and/or battalions and smaller units.

call for fire a request for fire on a specific target.

camouflage any material used to hide equipment and installations within an environment.

camouflage detection photography infrared photography designed to detect camouflage and what is hidden beneath it.

camouflet the resulting cavity in a deep underground burst when there is no rupture of the surface.

canalize to restrict operations to a narrow zone by use of obstacles or by fire or bombing.

cargo carrier highly mobile, unarmored, full-tracked cargo and logistic carrier capable of traversing inland waterways.

catalytic attack an attack designed to bring about war between two powers through the disguised machinations of a third power.

Chaparral a short-range, low-altitude, surface-to-air, army air defense artillery system.

chemical mine a mine containing a chemical agent designed to kill, injure, or incapacitate personnel.

Cinderella liberty liberty that ends at midnight.

civilian internee a civilian who is interned during armed conflict for security reasons.

civilian internee camp an installation established for the internment of civilians.

click slang for kilometer.

combat engineer vehicle, full-tracked 165mm gun an armored, tracked vehicle that provides engineer support to other combat elements; equipped with a heavy-duty boom and winch, dozer blade, 165mm demolition gun, and a machine gun.

contact mine a mine detonated by physical contact.

continuous illumination fire a type of fire in which illuminating projectiles are fired at specified time intervals to provide lighting over a specified area or target.

counterguerilla warfare operations conducted against guerrillas.

countermining tactics and techniques used to detect, avoid, and/or neutralize enemy mines.

culture any feature of terrain that has been constructed by man, including roads, buildings, canals, and all names and legends on a map.

danger close in artillery support, information in a call for fire to indicate that friendly forces are within 600 meters of the target.

D-day the unnamed day on which a particular operation is to commence.

decontamination station a facility equipped to clean personnel of chemical, biological, or radioactive contaminants.

decoy any phony object, installation, or person intended to deceive the enemy.

DEFCON defense readiness conditions: a system of progressive alert postures for use between the Joint Chiefs of Staff and the commanders of the armed services.

defilade to shield from enemy fire or observation by using natural or artificial obstacles.

defoliant operation the use of defoliating agents on trees, shrubs, and any foliage to make a clearing for military operations.

demilitarized zone a defined area where military installations or military forces are prohibited.

demolition belt an area sown with explosive charges, mines, and other obstacles to deny use of the land to enemy operations and as a protection to friendly troops.

demolition tool kit the tools, materials, and accessories of a nonexplosive nature necessary for preparing demolition charges.

deployment the extension or widening of the front of a military unit to battle formation. Also, the relocation of forces to desired areas of operations.

detachment a part of a unit separated from its main organization for duty elsewhere.

division a tactical unit larger than a regiment or brigade but smaller than a corps.

Dragon a portable antitank weapon consisting of a small missile and launcher.

dump a temporary storage area, usually out in the open, for bombs, ammunition, equipment, and such like.

Duster a self-propelled, twin 40mm antiaircraft weapon for use against low-flying aircraft. Also known as M-42.

echelon any subdivision of a tactical unit.

enfilade sweeping gunfire across the length of a line of troops.

envelopment surrounding the enemy.

flamethrower a weapon that shoots incendiary gas. Nicknamed zippo.

flash blindness temporary or permanent loss of vision caused by intense flash from an explosion.

flash suppressor a device attached to the muzzle of a weapon to diminish its flash upon firing.

glad bag derogatory slang for a body bag.

grunt slang for an infantryman.

guerilla a member of an independent parliamentary raiding band.

gun carriage a mobile or fixed support for a gun.

howitzer a high-trajectory cannon with a barrel longer than a mortar.

hum-vee modern equivalent of the jeep.

igloo space in an earth-sheltered structure, an area designed for the storage of ammunition and explosives.

klick kilometer.

k.p. kitchen police; mess hall duty.

laser rangefinder a device that uses a laser to determine the distance to an object.

litter a basket or frame utilized for the transport of the injured.

logistics the science of carrying out the movement and maintenance of troops.

mark a call for fire on a specific location to indicate targets.

materiel all items, including ships, tanks, aircraft, weapons, repair parts, and equipment, but excluding real property (installations, utilities, etc.) necessary to equip, maintain, and support military activities.

mess dining facility.

military currency currency prepared by a power and declared by its military commander to be legal tender for use by civilian and military personnel in the areas occupied by its forces.

mopping up finishing off the last remnants of enemy resistance in an area.

mortar a muzzle-loading, high-trajectory cannon with a shorter range than a howitzer.

muzzle brake a device attached to the muzzle of a weapon which utilizes escaping gas to reduce recoil.

napalm powdered aluminum soap or similar compound used to gelatinize oil or gasoline for use in napalm bombs or flame throwers. Also, the gelatin substance itself.

nerve agent a potentially lethal chemical agent that interferes with the transmission of nerve impulses.

orange forces those forces used in an enemy role during NATO exercises.

ordnance includes explosives, chemicals, pyrotechnics, guns, ammunition, flares, napalm.

parlimentaire an agent or person sent behind enemy lines to communicate or negotiate openly with the enemy commander.

phonetic alphabet a list of standard words used to identify letters in a message transmitted by radio. The authorized words, in order: Alpha, Bravo, Charlie, Delta, Echo, Foxtrot, Golf, Hotel, India, Juliet, Kilo, Lima, Mike, November, Oscar, Papa, Quebec, Romeo, Sierra, Tango, Uniform, Victor, Whiskey, X-ray, Yankee, and Zulu.

pillbox a small, low fortification that houses machine guns, antitank weapons, and other weapons. It is usually constructed of sandbags or concrete.

pressure mine a mine that responds to pressure.

pull rank to use one's rank to force someone to do something.

purple forces those forces used to oppose both blue and orange forces in NATO exercises.

PX post exchange; a military store.

radar fire gunfire aimed at a target that is tracked by radar.

ratline an organized effort for moving personnel and/or materiel by clandestine means across a denied area or border.

recoilless rifle a weapon capable of being fired from either a ground mount or from a vehicle and capable of destroying tanks.

reconnaissance patrol a patrol used to gain tactical information concerning the enemy.

retrograde movement military doublespeak term for retreat.

rules of engagement directives issued by military authority, which specify the circumstances and limitations under which forces shall engage in combat with the enemy.

sabotage deliberately damaging or destroying an object or facility to interfere with or obstruct the national defense of a country.

safing applying mechanisms, catches, and so on, and similar means to make weapons and ammunition safe to handle.

salvo the simultaneous firing of several weapons aimed at the same target.

scopehead slang for radarman.

sheaf planned lines of fire that produce a desired pattern of bursts with rounds fired by two or more weapons.

sheet explosive plastic explosive in sheet form.

shelling report any report of enemy shelling containing information on caliber, direction, time, density, and area shelled.

sortie a sudden attack made from a defensive position. Also known as a sally. (See under Air Force terms.)

sos chipped beef on toast; favored military meal.

splash in artillery support, the word transmitted to an observer or spotter 5 seconds before the estimated time of the impact of a salvo or round.

spoiling attack a tactical maneuver employed to seriously impair a hostile attack while the enemy is in the process of forming or assembling for an attack.

spotting observing and reporting deviations of artillery fire to aid in homing in on a target.

strafing the firing of aircraft weapons upon ground units.

submunition any munition that is designed to separate from its parent munition to explode independently.

surprise dosage attack a chemical attack carried out too quickly for defending troops to mask or protect themselves.

thermal imagery infrared imagery useful in revealing camouflage and all object and personnel hidden behind camouflage.

tone down a form of camouflage in which surfaces of objects are made to blend in with their surroundings.

tracer bullets treated to create a glowing trajectory.

trench burial a quick burial method employed when casualties are heavy.

triage the evaluation and classification of casualties to determine the order and type of medical attention needed.

vesicant agent same as blister agent.

Vulcan an army air defense artillery gun that provides low-altitude air defense; it is a six-barreled, 20mm rotary-fired weapon.

zulu time Greenwich Mean Time.

AIR FORCE AND AIRCRAFT (includes naval aircraft)

A-4 See SKYHAWK.

A-6 See INTRUDER.

A-7 See CORSAIR II.

A-10 See THUNDERBOLT II.

AC-130 See HERCULES.

aeromedical evacuation the transport of patients to and between hospital facilities by air.

aeromedical evacuation coordinating officer an officer in charge of aeromedical evacuations.

aeromedical staging unit a medical unit operating at an air base or airstrip.

aeronautical chart a map showing features of the Earth to aid in air navigation.

afterburning in the exhaust jet of a turbojet engine, the process of fuel injection and combustion.

afterflight inspection the inspection for defects in an aircraft after a flight; may also include the replenishment of fuel and the securing of the aircraft.

AH-1J See SEA COBRA.

airborne alert a state of aircraft readiness in which aircraft are already in the air and prepared for combat.

airborne assault weapon a full-tracked gun providing antitank capability for airborne troops.

airborne battlefield command and control center an aircraft equipped with communications, data link and display equipment, employed as an airborne command post or as an intelligence relay facility.

air combat fighter an F-16; a single engine, supersonic, turbofan tactical fighter/bomber capable of employing either nuclear or nonnuclear weapons.

air controller one assigned to the control of aircraft by radar, radio, or other means.

air corridor a restricted air route intended for friendly aircraft only.

aircraft arresting barrier a barrier device used to stop the forward motion of an aircraft in an emergency landing or aborted takeoff.

aircraft arresting cable spanning the landing surface or flight deck, a cable used to catch an aircraft's arresting system to stop its forward motion.

aircraft arresting hook a hook device on the bottom of an aircraft to engage arresting gear, especially on the flight deck of an aircraft carrier.

aircraft arresting system a series of components used to catch aircraft and stop their forward progress during landings or aborted takeoffs.

aircraft dispersal area an area on a military installation where aircraft are dispersed or spread apart when parked with the intention of avoiding large-scale destruction in the event of an enemy air raid.

aircraft marshaller one who directs aircraft on the ground by the use of batons.

aircraft marshalling area the area where aircraft line up before takeoff or where aircraft assemble after landing.

aircraft scrambling from a ground alert, the immediate takeoff of aircraft.

aircraft vectoring navigating an aircraft's flight path by the transmission of azimuth headings.

air defense warning conditions air raid codes defined by the following: AIR DEFENSE WARNING YELLOW—attack by hostile aircraft or missiles is probable. AIR DEFENSE WARNING RED—attack by hostile aircraft or missiles is imminent or already in progress. AIR DEFENSE WARNING WHITE—attack by hostile aircraft or missiles is improbable.

airdrop the unloading of cargo or personnel by parachute while in flight.

air-launched ballistic missile a missile launched from an in-flight aircraft.

air picket a "watchdog" aircraft positioned to detect the approach of enemy aircraft or missiles.

air reconnaissance the gathering of intelligence information from aircraft observation.

air strike an attack on a target or targets by aircraft.

airstrip a makeshift landing surface, usually having a minimum of facilities.

air-to-air guided missile a missile launched from an aircraft for use against another in-flight aircraft.

air-to-surface guided missile a missile launched from aircraft for use against a target on the ground or at sea.

ammo minus in an air intercept, a code meaning "I have less than half my ammunition left."

ammo plus in an air intercept, a code meaning "I have more than half my ammunition left."

ammo zero in an air intercept, a code meaning "I have no ammunition left."

anchored in air intercept, a code meaning "am orbiting a visible orbit point."

angels in air intercept and close air support, a code meaning aircraft altitude in thousands of feet.

anti-g suit worn by aircraft crewmen to help protect against extreme gravity or rapid acceleration.

approach clearance authorization for a pilot to approach the airport and land.

apron in an air base or airport, the area for loading, unloading, refueling, parking, and maintenance of aircraft.

area bombing the bombing of a general area instead of a precisely defined target.

attack helicopter a helicopter specifically designed for engaging in combat.

automatic throttle an automatic throttle system activated by flight control computers.

automatic toss a flight control system in which the toss bombing maneuver is carried out automatically.

automatic trim a flight control system that controls the trim (air flaps or foils, etc.) of an aircraft in flight.

aviation medicine the field of medicine that deals with the physical and psychological problems of flight.

AWACS Airborne Early Warning and Control System; air surveillance and control provided by airborne early warning vehicles that are equipped with search and height-finding radar and communications equipment for controlling weapons.

B-52 See STRATOFORTRESS.

beacon a light or electronic signal used to determine bearings or courses.

beacon, double in air intercept, a code meaning "pilot, select double pulse mode on your tracking beacon."

beacon, off in air intercept, a code meaning "turn off your tracking beacon."

beacon, on in air intercept, a code meaning "turn on your tracking beacon."

before-flight inspection a preflight inspection of aircraft safety, disposable loads, fuel, and so forth.

bingo from a pilot, a code meaning "I have reached minimal fuel for safe return to base or to designated alternate." From air control, a code meaning "proceed to alternate field."

bingo field an alternate air field.

bogey an unidentified flying object assumed to be the enemy.

bombing run aircraft bombing including the approach to the target, target aquisition, and the release of the bomb(s).

BQM-34 See FIREBEE.

Bronco an OV-10; a light, twin turboprop observation and support craft with or without machine guns.

buster in air intercept, a code meaning "fly at maximal continuous speed."

C-5A See GALAXY.

C-123 See PROVIDER.

C-130 See HERCULES.

C-140 See JET STAR.

C-141 See STARLIFTER.

call mission an unprepared mission, called for on-the-spot, involving air support.

call sign any combination of words, letters, or numbers identifying by code a facility, an authority, an activity, a unit, and so forth.

Canberra B-57; a twin-jet, electronics intelligence aircraft.

carpet bombing a mass bombing over a wide boundary, inflicting widespread damage.

carrier air group two or more aircraft squadrons formed under one commander on an aircraft carrier.

catapult a device providing auxiliary thrust to launch an aircraft, especially on an aircraft carrier.

CAVU ceiling and visibility unlimited.

central air data computer a computer that determines altitude, vertical speed, air speed, and Mach number from pilot and environmental inputs.

CH-53A See SEA STALLION.

chaff strips of metal foil, wire, or metalized glass fiber dropped from aircraft or expelled from rockets or shells to reflect and confuse radar.

chicks friendly fighter aircraft.

civil reserve air fleet in a national emergency, the allocation of commercial aircraft and crew for military use.

clara in air intercept, a code meaning "radar scope is clear of contacts other than those known to be friendly."

clean aircraft an aircraft in flight configuration, with its landing gear and flaps retracted.

clear weather air defense fighter a fighter aircraft capable of carrying out missions in daylight or at night but only in clear weather.

climb mode the automatic climb mode of a flight control system.

clock code position the position of a target in relation to an aircraft with dead-ahead position designated as 12 o'clock.

close air support air combat conducted close to friendly forces that integrate with the fire and movement of those forces.

cocooning spraying an aircraft with a plastic coating to form a seal against the effects of the atmosphere.

combat air patrol an aircraft patrol around a prescribed area to intercept and destroy enemy aircraft before they reach their target.

combined airspeed indicator an instrument displaying both air speed and Mach number.

compound helicopter a helicopter equipped with an auxiliary propulsion system capable of producing more thrust than the rotors alone.

confused in air intercept, a term meaning "individual contacts not identifiable."

confusion reflector collective term for any kind of object, such as chaff, used to reflect and confuse electromagnetic radiation or radar.

continue port/starboard in air intercept, a term meaning, "continue turning port/starboard at present rate of turn to magnetic heading indicated."

contrail the visible cloud streak left behind by a jet aircraft. Also known as a condensation trail.

Corsair II an A-7; a single-seat, single-turbofan engine, all-weather light attack aircraft designed to operate from aircraft carriers, armed with cannon and capable of carrying a wide assortment of nuclear and nonnuclear missiles.

crash locator beacon an automatic beacon device to aid forces in locating a crashed aircraft.

critical altitude the maximum altitude an aircraft can fly and still function properly.

cruising level the altitude maintained throughout most of a flight.

curve of pursuit the curved path described by a fighter plane making an attack on a moving target while holding the proper aiming allowance.

DADCAP dawn and dusk combat air patrol.

dart a training target towed by a jet and fired upon by a practicing fighter aircraft.

day air defense fighter a fighter aircraft capable of engaging in combat only in daylight and in clear weather.

DC-130 See HERCULES.

Delta Dagger a single-engine turbojet all-weather interceptor with supersonic speed and armed with Falcon missiles. Also known as an F-102A.

Delta Dart a supersonic, single-engine turbojet all-weather interceptor armed with Falcon missiles with nonnuclear warheads and Genie rockets with nuclear warheads. Also known as an F-106.

destroy, beam in air intercept, a code meaning "the interceptor will be vectored to a standard beam attack for interception and destruction of the target."

destroy, cutoff in air intercept, a code meaning "intercept and destroy. Command vectors will produce a cutoff attack."

destroy, frontal in air intercept, a command meaning "the interceptor will be vectored to a standard frontal attack for interception and destruction of the target."

destroy, stern in air intercept, a command meaning "the interceptor will be vectored to a standard stern attack for interception and destruction of the target."

diplomatic authorization authority for a flight over or a landing on foreign soil obtained through diplomatic channels.

dispenser on fighter aircraft, a container used to carry and release submunitions.

ditching a controlled crash-landing in the water.

drone an unmanned, remote-controlled aircraft used primarily for reconaissance.

droop stop a device that helps prevent helicopter rotor blades from drooping excessively after the engine has been shut off.

dropmaster the person in charge of the preparation, inspection, loading, lashing, and ejecting of materials for an airdrop.

drop message a message dropped by air to a ground unit.

duck in air intercept, a code meaning "trouble headed your way."

dummy run a practice bombing run.

E-1B See TRACER.

E-2 See HAWKEYE.

EA-6A See INTRUDER.

EA-6B See PROWLER.

Eagle a twin-engine supersonic, turbofan, all-weather tactical fighter employing a variety of weapons and capable of long range missions through in-flight refueling.

ejection the emergency escape from an in-flight aircraft by means of an independently propelled seat or capsule.

ejection, sequenced a system that ejects crew members one at a time in an emergency situation, to avoid midair collisions.

elevator in air intercept, a code meaning "take altitude indicated."

emergency scramble in air intercept, a code meaning "carrier addressed immediately launch all available fighter aircraft as combat air patrol."

endurance the time an aircraft can continue flying without refueling.

engage to fire upon an enemy aircraft.

escort an aircraft assigned to protect other aircraft.

extraction parachute an auxiliary parachute used to release, extract, and deploy cargo from aircraft in flight.

F-4 See PHANTOM II.

F-5A/B See FREEDOM FIGHTER.

F-14 See TOMCAT.

F-15 See EAGLE.

F-16 See AIR COMBAT FIGHTER.

F-100 See SUPER SABRE.

F-101 See VOODOO.

F-102A See DELTA DAGGER.

F-104 See STARFIGHTER.

F-105 See THUNDERCHIEF.

F-106 See DELTA DART.

F-111 a twin-engine, supersonic turbofan, all-weather tactical fighter armed with nuclear or nonnuclear weapons and capable of taking off from or landing on short runways.

faded in air intercept, a code meaning "contact has disappeared from reporting station's scope, and any position information given is estimated."

faker a friendly aircraft simulating a hostile aircraft in training exercises.

famished in air intercept, a code meaning "have you any instructions for me?"

feet dry in air intercept, a code meaning "I am over land."

feet wet in air intercept, a code meaning "I am over water."

ferret an aircraft especially equipped to detect and analyze electromagnetic radiation.

firebee a remote-controlled, subsonic drone acting as a target in testing to test and evaluate weapon systems employing surface-to-air or air-to-air missiles. Also known as BQM-34.

firepower umbrella the range or distance a naval unit's weaponry can reach, within which is hazardous for enemy aircraft to fly.

flare to change the flight path of an aircraft to decrease the rate of descent for landing.

flight deck in some aircraft, an elevated cockpit.

foam path a path of fire extinguisher foam laid on a runway to help prevent an explosion or fire in an emergency or crash landing.

fox away in air intercept, a code meaning "missile has fired or been released from aircraft."

freddie a controlling unit.

Freedom Fighter a twin-engine supersonic turbojet, multipurpose tactical fighter/bomber. Also known as F-5AB.

free drop the dropping of equipment or supplies from an aircraft without the use of parachutes.

free lance in air intercept, a code meaning "self-control of aircraft is being employed."

Galaxy a large cargo transport aircraft powered by four turbofan engines. Also known as C-5A.

gate in air intercept, a code meaning "fly at maximum possible speed."

glide bomb a bomb fitted with airfoils to provide extra lift.

glide mode a flight control system that automatically positions an aircraft to the center of a glide slope course.

go around mode a flight control system that automatically terminates an approach and initiates a climb mode when needed.

grand slam all enemy aircraft sighted are shot down.

H-2 See SEA SPRITE.

H-3 See SEA KING.

H-46 See SEA KNIGHT.

harassing harassing attacks by air, designed to air ground units in battle.

Harrier a single-engine, turbojet light attack aircraft designed to take off vertically or from short runways. Also known as an AV-8.

Hawkeye a twin turboprop, multicrew airborne early warning and interceptor control aircraft designed to operate from aircraft carriers. It carries a long-range radar and integrated computer system for the detection and tracking of airborne targets. Also known as E-2.

HC-130 See HERCULES.

heading the direction an aircraft is headed expressed in degrees clockwise from north.

heads up in air intercept, a code meaning "enemy got through."

helicopter lane an air corridor reserved for helicopters during operations.

helipad a reserved area used specifically by helicopters when parking, taking off, or landing.

heliport airport facility specifically designed to service helicopters.

Hercules a troop and cargo transport equipped with four turboprop engines.

hypersonic speeds equal to or exceeding five times the speed of sound.

imagery sortie a single reconnaissance flight to obtain photographic and other visual information.

instrument flight a flight controlled by reference to instruments only.

interceptor an aircraft used to identify, intercept, and engage enemy targets.

in the dark a code meaning "not visible on my scope."

Intruder a twin-engine, turbojet, two-place, long-range, all-weather, aircraft carrier–based, low-altitude attack aircraft armed with an assortment of weapons, including Sidewinder, Bullpup, napalm, or all standard Navy rockets. Also known as an A-6.

Iroquois a light, single-rotor helicopter used for cargo and personnel transport and sometimes armed with machine guns or light rockets.

Jet Star a small, fast transport aircraft powered by four turboprop engines. Also known as a C-140.

judy a code meaning "I have contact and am taking over the intercept."

jumpmaster the person who manages or supervises a team of parachutists.

jump speed the airspeed at which parachutists can safely jump from an aircraft.

KA-6 See INTRUDER.

KC-97L See STRATOFREIGHTER.

KC-135 See STRATOTANKER.

landing roll the rollout or deceleration of an aircraft from touchdown to taxi speed.

laydown bombing a low altitude bombing run in which delay fuses or delay devices are used to allow the aircraft time to escape the effects of its own bombs.

liner a code meaning "fly at speed giving maximum cruising range."

LOCAP low combat air patrol.

loft bombing a low altitude bombing run in which the aircraft drops its bombs as it begins to pull up or climb.

machmeter an instrument displaying the Mach number of the aircraft.

mach no a code meaning "I have reached maximum speed and am not closing my target."

mach yes a code meaning "I have reached maximum speed and am closing my target."

mark a term used to designate the exact time of a weapon's release, usually preceded by the word *standby.*

mark mark command from ground controller for an aircraft to release its bombs.

mayday distress call.

merged a code meaning "tracks have come together."

midnight a code meaning "changeover from close to broadcast control."

MIM-14 See NIKE HERCULES.

MIM-23 See HAWK.

MIM-72 See CHAPARRAL.

music in air intercept, a term meaning electronic jamming.

napalm powdered aluminum soap or similar compound used to gelatinize oil or gasoline for use in napalm bombs.

NATO airspace the airspace above any NATO nation and its territorial waters.

near miss a near collision with another aircraft in flight.

negative term meaning "no" in air communications.

night cap night combat air patrol.

no joy a code meaning "I have been unsuccessful," or "I have no information."

notice to airmen a notice containing information on any change in any airport facility, service, procedure, or hazard. Also called NOTAM.

offset bombing any bombing procedure that uses a reference or aiming point other than the actual target.

oranges, sour a code meaning "weather is unsuitable for aircraft mission."

oranges, sweet a code meaning "weather is suitable for aircraft mission."

orbiting a word meaning circling, or circling and searching.

ordnance collective term for pyrotechnic weapons, including bombs, guns and ammunition, flares, smoke, and napalm.

Orion a four-engine, turboprop, all-weather, long-range, land-based antisubmarine aircraft capable of carrying an assortment of search radar, nuclear depth charges, and homing torpedoes. Also known as a P-3.

OV-10 See BRONCO.

overshoot term used to describe a landing that is aborted.

P-3 See ORION.

pan a code meaning the calling station has a very urgent message to transmit concerning the safety of a ship, aircraft, or other vehicle or of some person on board or within sight.

pancake a code meaning "land," or "I wish to land."

pathfinder aircraft an aircraft with a specially trained crew carrying drop zone/landing zone marking teams, target markers, or navigational aids and that precedes the main force to the drop zone or landing zone or target.

pattern bombing the uniform distribution of bombs over a particular area.

payload the cargo and passengers on a flight.

Phantom II a twin-engine, supersonic, multipurpose, all-weather jet fighter/bomber capable of operating from land or from aircraft carriers and armed with either nuclear or nonnuclear weapons.

photoflash bomb a bomb designed to produce a brief and intense illumination for medium-altitude night photography.

pogo a code meaning "switch to communications channel number preceding 'pogo.' If unable to establish communications, switch to channel number following 'pogo.'"

point of no return the point at which an aircraft is incapable of returning to base due to a low fuel supply.

popeye a code meaning "in clouds or area of reduced visibility."

pounce a code meaning "I am in position to engage target."

precision bombing bombing directed at a specific target.

Provider an assault, twin-engine transport that can operate from short, unprepared landing strips to transport troops and equipment. Also known as a C-123.

Prowler a twin turbojet engine, quadruple crew, all-weather, electronic countermeasures aircraft designed to operate from aircraft carriers. Also known as an EA-6B.

prudent limit of endurance the time during which an aircraft can remain airborne and still retain a given safety margin of fuel.

punch a code meaning "you should very soon be obtaining a contact on the aircraft that is being intercepted."

purple a code meaning "the unit indicated is suspected of carrying nuclear weapons."

radar picket radar picket combat air patrol.

radio beacon a radio transmitter that emits a distinctive signal used for the determination of bearings, courses, locations, and so on.

radio fix the location of an aircraft by determining the direction of radio signals coming to the aircraft from two or more sending stations, the locations of which are known.

reconnaissance a mission undertaken to obtain, by visual observation or other detection methods, information about the activities and resources of an enemy; or to secure data concerning the meteorological, hydrographic, or geographic characteristics of a particular area.

reconnaissance by fire disclosing an enemy's position by firing or shooting at its general vicinity and waiting for the flashes of return fire.

reconnaissance in force a mission designed to discover or test an enemy's strength.

RF-4 See PHANTOM II.

RH-53 See SEA STALLION.

roll the rotation of an aircraft in flight.

S-2 See TRACKER.

S-3 See VIKING.

salvo the release or firing of all ordnance of a specific type simultaneously.

saunter a code meaning "fly at best endurance."

scan a code meaning "search sector indicated and report any contacts."

scram a code meaning "am about to open fire. Friendly units keep clear of indicated contact, bogey, or area."

scramble an order directing takeoff of aircraft as quickly as possible.

Sea Cobra a single-rotor, dual crew, light attack helicopter armed with a variety of machine guns, rockets, grenade launchers, and antitank missiles. Also known as an AH-1J.

Sea King a single rotor, medium-lift helicopter utilized for air/sea rescue and personnel and cargo transport in support of aircraft carrier operations. Some may be equipped for antisubmarine operations. Also known as an H-3.

Sea Knight a twin-rotor, medium-lift helicopter utilized for personnel and cargo transport. Also known as an H-46.

Sea Sprite a single-rotor light lift helicopter utilized for air/sea rescue, personnel and cargo transport, and antisubmarine operations from naval vessels. Also known as an H-2.

Sea Stallion a single-rotor heavy-lift helicopter utilized for personnel and cargo transport. Also known as a CH-53.

sick a code meaning "equipment indicated is operating at reduced efficiency."

side-looking airborne radar an airborne radar, viewing at right angles to the axis of the vehicle, which produces a presentation of terrain or moving targets.

skip bombing a method of aerial bombing in which a bomb is released from such a low altitude that it slides or glances along the surface of the water or ground and strikes the target at or above water level or ground level.

skip it a code meaning "cease attack;" "do not attack."

Skyhawk a single-engine, turbojet attack aircraft designed to operate from aircraft carriers, and capable of delivering nuclear or nonnuclear weapons, providing troop support, or conducting reconnaissance missions. It can act as a tanker and can itself be air refueled. Also known as an A-4.

snake mode a control mode in which the pursuing aircraft flies a programmed weaving flight path to allow time to accomplish identification functions.

snow a term meaning sweep jamming.

sortie an operational flight by one aircraft.

spitting in air antisubmarine operations, a code meaning "I am about to lay, or am laying, sonobuoys. I may be out of radio contact for a few minutes."

splashed in air intercept, a code meaning "enemy aircraft shot down."

spoofer a code meaning "a contact employing electronic or tactical deception measures."

Starfighter a supersonic, single-engine, turbojet fighter capable of employing nuclear or nonnuclear weapons. Also known as an F-104.

Starlifter a large cargo transport powered by four turbofan engines, capable of intercontinental range with heavy payloads and airdrops. Also known as a C-141.

state chicken a code meaning "I am at a fuel state requiring recovery, tanker service, or diversion to an airfield."

state lamb a code meaning "I do not have enough fuel for an intercept plus reserve required for carrier recovery."

state tiger a code meaning "I have enough fuel to complete my mission as assigned."

static line a line attached to a parachute pack and to a strop in an aircraft so that when the load is dropped the parachute is automatically deployed.

Stealth Bomber a bomber, otherwise known as the B-2, specially designed in the shape of a flat, flying wing in order to render it invisible to enemy radar.

Stealth Fighter a combat fighter/bomber with stealth (radar-eluding) design. Also known as F-117A.

stern attack an attack by an interceptor that terminates with a heading crossing angle of 45 degrees or less.

stick a number of paratroopers who jump from a door of an aircraft during one run over a drop zone.

stick commander same as jumpmaster.

strafing the delivery of automatic weapons fire by aircraft on ground targets.

strangle a code meaning "switch off equipment indicated."

strangle parrot a code meaning "switch off Identification Friend or Foe equipment."

Stratofortress an all-weather, intercontinental, strategic heavy bomber powered by eight turbojet engines; capable of delivering nuclear and nonnuclear bombs, air-to-surface missiles, and decoys. Also known as a B-52.

Stratofreighter a strategic aerial tanker/freighter powered by four reciprocating engines; it is equipped to refuel bombers and fighters in flight. Also known as a KC-97L.

Stratotanker a multipurpose aerial tanker/transport powered by four turbojet engines; it is equipped for high-speed, high-altitude refueling of bombers and fighters. Also known as KC-135.

stream take off aircraft taking off in column formation.

subsonic speeds less than the speed of sound.

Super Sabre a supersonic, single-engine, turbojet, tactical fighter/bomber. Also known as an F-100.

supersonic speeds greater than the speed of sound.

tally ho a code meaning "target visually sighted."

Thunderbolt II a twin-engine, subsonic, turbofan, tactical fighter/bomber capable of taking off or landing on short fields and of delivering an assortment of weapons; has an internally mounted 30mm cannon and can be refueled in flight. Also known as an A-10.

Thunderchief a supersonic, single-engine, turbojet-powered tactical fighter capable of delivering nuclear weapons as well as nonnuclear bombs and rockets; equipped with a sidewinder weapon and can be refueled in flight. Also known as an F-105.

tied on a code meaning "the aircraft indicated is in formation with me."

Tomcat a twin turbofan, dual crew, supersonic, all-weather, long-range interceptor designed to operate from aircraft carriers. Also known as an F-14.

toss bombing similar to loft bombing but performed at any altitude.

Tracer a twin-reciprocating engine, airborne radar platform designed to operate from aircraft carriers. Its mission is the detection and interception control of airborne targets. Also known as an E-1B.

Tracker a twin-reciprocating-engine, antisubmarine aircraft capable of operating from carriers, and designed primarily for the detection, location, and destruction of submarines. Also known as an S-2.

tracking a code meaning "by my evaluation, target is steering true course indicated."

train bombs dropped in short intervals or sequence.

turbojet a jet engine whose air is supplied by a turbine-driven compressor, the turbine being activated by exhaust gases.

vector a code meaning "alter heading to magnetic heading indicated."

Vigilante a twin turbojet engine, dual-crew, supersonic all-weather reconnaissance aircraft designed to operate from aircraft carriers. It carries a wide assortment of photographic and electronic surveillance systems. Also known as an RA-5.

Viking a twin turbofan engine, multicrew antisubmarine aircraft capable of operating off aircraft carriers. Also known as an S-3.

Voodoo a supersonic, twin-engine turbojet air interceptor with twin cockpits. Also known as an F-101.

Walleye a guided air-to-surface glide bomb; it incorporates a contrast-tracking television system for guidance.

Wild Weasel an aircraft specially modified to identify, locate, and destroy ground-based enemy air defense systems.

wingman an aviator subordinate to, and in support of, the designated section leader; also, the aircraft flown in this role.

zippers target dawn and dusk combat air patrol.

NAVY AND MARINES (*See also* SHIPS, BOATS *in* TRANSPORTATION)

acoustic mine a mine that responds to the sound of a passing ship.

acoustic minehunting the use of sonar to detect mines.

Aegis an integrated shipboard weapon system combining computers, radars, and missiles to provide a defense umbrella for surface shipping.

afloat support logistic support providing fuel, ammunition, and supplies outside the confines of a harbor.

amphibious assault ship a naval ship designed to embark, deploy, and land elements of a landing force in an assault by helicopters, landing craft, amphibious vehicles.

amphibious reconnaissance reconnaissance mission to survey a shore area, usually in secret.

antenna mine a mine fitted with an antenna that, when touched by a ship, explodes the mine.

antirecovery device any device in a mine designed to prevent an enemy from discovering how its exploding mechanism works.

antisubmarine barrier any line of devices or mobile units arranged to detect or deny passage to or destroy hostile submarines.

antisubmarine carrier group a group of ships consisting of one or more antisubmarine carriers and a number of escort vessels whose primary mission is to detect and destroy submarines.

antisubmarine minefield a minefield laid specifically against submarines.

antisubmarine rocket a surface ship-launched, rocket-propelled, nuclear depth charge or homing torpedo.

antisubmarine screen an arrangement of ships that protect or screen another ship or group of ships against submarine attack.

antisubmarine torpedo a submarine-launched, long-range, high-speed, wakeless torpedo capable of carrying a nuclear warhead for use in antisubmarine and antisurface ship operations.

antisweep device any device in the mooring of a mine or in the circuits of a mine to making sweeping of the mine more difficult.

antisweeper mine a mine with a mechanism designed specifically to damage mine countermeasure vehicles.

antiwatching device a device fitted in a moored mine that causes it to sink should it watch, so as to prevent the position of the mine being disclosed.

armed sweep a sweep fitted with cutters or other devices to increase its ability to cut mine moorings.

attack aircraft carrier large ship designed to operate aircraft, engage in attacks on targets afloat or on shore, and engage in sustained operations in support of other forces.

attack cargo ship a transport ship carrying combat cargo.

battery all guns, torpedo tubes, searchlights, or missile launchers of the same size or caliber or used for the same purpose on one ship.

battery left a method of fire in which weapons are discharged from the left, one after the other, at 5-second intervals.

battery right a method of fire in which weapons are discharged from the right, one after the other, at 5-second intervals.

beachhead hostile shore position captured by amphibious units.

beachmaster unit a naval unit supporting the amphibious landing of one division.

beach minefield a shallow water minefield blocking the way to a shoreline or beach.

bottom a mine that remains on the seabed.

bottom sweep a wire or chain sweep close to the bottom.

bouquet mine a mine in which a number of buoyant mine cases are attached to the same sinker, so that when the mooring of one mine case is cut another mine rises from the sinker to its set depth.

clearance diving the use of divers to locate, identify, and dispose of mines.

clock code position the position of a target in relation to a ship with dead-ahead position considered as 12 o'clock.

concentrated fire the fire of the batteries of two or more ships directed against a single target.

convoy a number of ships escorted by other ships or aircraft in passage together.

creeping mine a buoyant mine held below the surface by a chain, which is free to creep along the seabed under the influence of current.

customer ship the ship that receives replenishment supplies from another ship.

cutter a device fitted to a sweep wire to cut or part the moorings of mines.

dan to mark a position or a sea area with dan buoys.

dan buoy a temporary marker buoy used during minesweeping operations to indicate boundaries of swept paths.

dan runner a ship running a line of dan buoys.

datum the last known position of a submarine after contact has been lost.

debarkation the unloading of troops and cargo from a ship.

decoy ship a ship camouflaged with its armament and fighting equipment hidden.

deep minefield an antisubmarine minefield set deep enough so that surface ships can cross it safely.

destroyer a high-speed warship armed with 3-inch and 5-inch dual-purpose guns and various antisubmarine weapons.

dock landing ship a naval ship designed to transport and launch amphibious craft.

drifting mine a mine free to move under the influence of waves, wind, or current.

dummy minefield a minefield containing no live mines.

endurance the amount of time a ship can continue to operate without refueling.

fleet ballistic missile submarine a nuclear-powered submarine designed to deliver ballistic missile attacks from submerged or surface positions.

flight deck the runway on an aircraft carrier.

floating mine a mine visible on the surface of the sea.

flooder a mine that floods after a preset time and sinks to the bottom.

flotilla an administrative or tactical organization consisting of two or more squadrons of destroyers or smaller types together with flagships and tenders.

frigate a warship designed to operate independently, or with strike, antisubmarine warfare, or amphibious forces against submarine, air, and surface threats; its armament includes 3-inch and 5-inch guns and advanced antisubmarine weapons.

general quarters a condition of readiness when naval action is imminent; all battle stations are fully manned and alert and ammunition is ready for instant loading.

guided missile cruiser a warship designed to operate with strike and amphibious forces; armed with 3-inch and 5-inch guns, advanced area-defense antiair-warfare missile system, and antisubmarine weapons.

guided missile destroyer a destroyer equipped with Terrier/Tartar guided missiles, naval gun battery, long-range sonar, and antisubmarine weapons.

guided missile frigate a frigate equipped with Tartar or SM-1 missile launchers and 70mm gun battery.

guinea pig a ship used to determine if an area is free of influence mines. See SHIP INFLUENCE.

heavy-lift ship a ship with a lift capacity of 100 tons.

homing mine a mine fitted with a propulsion system that homes on a target.

hydrofoil patrol craft a fast surface patrol craft.

hydrographic chart a nautical chart showing depths of water, nature of bottom, contours of bottom, and similar information.

lap a section or strip of area assigned to a single minesweeper.

lifeguard submarine a submarine used in rescue operations in enemy territory.

minesweeping the technique of searching for and clearing mines from an area.

net sweep a two-ship sweep using a net-like device designed to collect or scoop up seabed or drifting mines.

obstructor a device laid with the goal of obstructing mechanical minesweeping equipment.

ocean station ship a ship providing a number of services, including search and rescue, meteorological information, navigational aid, and communications facilities.

offshore patrol a patrol operating in coastal waters.

oiler a tanker equipped to replenish other ships at sea.

ordnance collective term for bombs, guns, ammunition, and other pyrotechnic devices.

otter in naval mine warfare, a device that, when towed, displaces itself sideways to a predetermined distance.

Phalanx a close-in weapons system providing automatic, autonomous terminal defense against antiship cruise missiles. The system includes self-contained search and track radars, weapons control, and 20mm M-61 guns.

q-message a classified message relating to navigational dangers, navigational aids, mined areas, and searched or swept channels.

Q-ship same as decoy ship.

rising mine a mine having positive buoyancy that is released from a sinker by a ship influence or by a timing device.

romper a ship that has moved more than 10 miles ahead of its convoy and is unable to rejoin it.

salvo in naval gunfire support, a method of fire in which a number of weapons are fired simultaneously upon the same target.

shadower a maritime unit observing and maintaining contact with an object overtly or covertly.

sheaf in naval gunfire, planned lines of fire that produce a desired pattern of bursts with rounds fired by two or more weapons.

ship influence in naval mine warfare, the magnetic, acoustic, and pressure effects of a ship, or a minesweep simulating a ship, that is detectable by a mine.

sonar a sonic device used primarily for the detection and location of underwater objects.

sonobuoy a sonar device used to detect submerged submarines and to relay its information by radio.

spotter an observer who reports the results of naval gunfire and who may also direct fire on designated targets.

spotting observing and communicating the accuracy or inaccuracy of naval gunfire in order to make necessary adjustments.

squadron an organization of two or more divisions of ships.

sterilizer a built-in device that renders a mine inoperative after a certain amount of time.

submarine havens specified sea areas for submarines in noncombat operations. Also known as submarine sanctuaries.

torpedo defense net a net employed to close an inner harbor to torpedoes fired from seaward or to protect an individual ship at anchor or underway.

tractor group a group of landing ships in an amphibious operation that carries the amphibious vehicles of the landing force.

Trident a nuclear-powered submarine armed with long-range Trident ballistic missiles.

very deep draught ship a ship with a laden draught of 45 feet or more.

ELECTRONIC WARFARE (radar, electronic deception, etc.)

balloon reflector a balloon-supported confusion reflector producing false echoes.

barrage simultaneous electronic jamming over a wide area of frequency spectrum.

burn-through range the distance at which a specific radar can discern targets through the external interference being received.

chaff radar confusion reflectors, which consist of thin, narrow metallic strips of various lengths and frequency responses, used to reflect echoes for confusion purposes.

clutter permanent echoes, clouds, or other atmospheric echo on radar scope.

crystal ball radar scope.

doppler radar a radar system that differentiates between fixed and moving targets by detecting the apparent change in frequency.

electromagnetic intrusion the intentional insertion of electromagnetic energy into transmission paths in any manner, with the objective of deceiving operators.

electronic imitative deception the introduction into the enemy electronic systems of radiations imitating the enemy's own emissions.

electronic jamming the deliberate radiation, reradiation, or reflection of electromagnetic energy for the purpose of disrupting enemy use of electronic devices and systems.

electronic manipulative deception the alteration of friendly electromagnetic emission characteristics, patterns, or procedures to eliminate revealing, or convey misleading indicators that may be used by hostile forces.

gadget radar equipment. May be followed by a color to indicate state of jamming. The color code used is green—clear of jamming; amber—sector partially jammed; red—sector completely jammed; blue—completely jammed.

gull a floating radar reflector used to simulate a surface target at sea for deceptive purposes.

masking the use of additional transmitters to hide a particular electromagnetic radiation as to location of source and/or purpose of the radiation.

meaconing a system of receiving radio beacon signals and rebroadcasting them on the same frequency to confuse navigation.

music in air intercept, a term meaning electronic jamming.

radar beacon a receiver-transmitter that sends out a coded signal when triggered by the proper type of pulse, enabling determination of range and bearing information by the interrogating station or aircraft.

radar camouflage the use of radar absorbent or reflecting materials to change the radar echoing properties of a surface of an object.

radar fire gunfire aimed at a target that is tracked by radar.

radar netting the linking of several radars to a single center to provide integrated target information.

radar picket any ship, aircraft, or vehicle stationed at a distance from the force protected for the purpose of increasing the radar detection range.

radar tracking station a radar facility that tracks moving targets.

radiation intelligence intelligence derived from the electromagnetic emissions of enemy equipment.

radio deception sending false dispatches, using deceptive headings, employing enemy call signs, and so on, over the radio to deceive the enemy.

radio silence a condition in which all or certain radio equipment capable of radiation is kept inoperative.

SIGINT signals intelligence. Personnel and equipment employed in gathering and processing signals intelligence.

MISSILES, NUCLEAR WEAPONS, AND ROCKETS

absolute dud a nuclear weapon that fails to explode.

active material material, such as plutonium and certain isotopes of uranium, that is capable of supporting a fission chain reaction.

acute radiation dose total ionizing radiation dose received at one time and over a period so short that it is fatal.

afterwinds wind currents set up in the vicinity of a nuclear explosion directed toward the burst center, resulting from the updraft accompanying the rise of the fireball.

air-breathing missile a missile with an engine requiring the intake of air for combustion of its fuel, as in a ramjet or turbojet.

airburst an explosion in the air, above ground.

air-to-air guided missile an air-launched guided missile for use against air targets.

ballistic missile any missile that does not rely upon aerodynamic surfaces to provide lift and consequently follows a ballistic trajectory when thrust is terminated.

ballistic missile early warning system an electronic system for providing detection and early warning of attack by enemy intercontinental ballistic missiles.

base surge a cloud that rolls out from the bottom of the column produced by a subsurface burst of a nuclear weapon.

beam rider a missile guided by an electronic beam.

blast wave diffraction the passage around and envelopment of a structure by a nuclear blast wave.

booster an auxiliary or initial propulsion system that travels with a missile and that may or may not separate from the parent craft when its impulse has been delivered.

captive firing a firing test of short duration, conducted with the missile propulsion system operating while secured to a test stand.

chronic radiation dose a dose of ionizing radiation received either continuously or intermittently over a prolonged period of time that may or may not cause radiation sickness and death, depending on the dose rate.

cloud top height the maximum altitude to which a nuclear mushroom cloud rises.

command destruct signal a signal used to operate intentionally the destruction signal in a missile.

condensation cloud a mist or fog of water droplets that temporarily surrounds the fireball following a nuclear detonation in a relatively humid atmosphere.

contamination the deposit and/or absorption of radioactive material on and by structures, areas, personnel, or objects.

controlled effects nuclear weapons nuclear weapons designed to achieve variation of the intensity of specific effects other than normal blast effect.

critical altitude the altitude beyond which an airbreathing guided missile ceases to perform adequately.

critical mass the minimum amount of fissionable material capable of supporting a chain reaction.

cruise missile guided missile, the major portion of whose flight path to its target is conducted at approximately constant velocity.

decay, radioactive the decrease in the radiation intensity of any radioactive material over time.

destruct system a system that, when operated by external command, destroys the missile.

dosimetry the measurement of radiation doses by dosimeters.

dwarf dud a nuclear weapon that, when launched at a target, fails to provide the expected blast yield or destruction.

electromagnetic pulse the electromagnetic radiation from a nuclear explosion caused by Compton-recoil electrons and photoelectrons from photons scattered in the materials of the nuclear device. The resulting electric and magnetic fields may couple with electrical systems to produce damaging current and voltage surges.

fallout the precipitation to Earth of radioactive particles from a nuclear cloud; also applied to the particles themselves.

fallout safe height of burst the height of burst at or above which no militarily significant fallout will be reproduced as a result of a nuclear weapon detonation.

fireball the luminous sphere of hot gases that forms a few millionths of a second after detonation of a nuclear weapon and immediately starts expanding and cooling.

fire storm stationary mass fire within a city which generates strong, inrushing winds from all sides; the winds keep the fires from spreading while adding fresh oxygen to increase their intensity; a side effect of a nuclear blast.

fission the splitting of the nucleus of a heavy element into two nuclei of lighter elements, with the release of substantial amounts of energy.

fission products a general term for the complex mixture of substances produced as a result of nuclear fission.

flare dud a nuclear weapon that detonates with expected yield but at an altitude much higher than intended so that its effects on a target are lessened.

free rocket a rocket not subject to guidance or control in flight.

ground zero the point on the surface of the Earth at, or vertically below or above, the center of a planned or actual nuclear detonation.

guided missile a missile whose flight path is controlled by external or internal mechanisms.

hard missile base a launching base that is protected against a nuclear explosion.

initial radiation the radiation, essentially neutrons and gamma rays, resulting from a nuclear burst and emitted from the fireball within one minute after burst.

intercontinental ballistic missile a ballistic missile with a range from 3,000 to 8,000 miles.

kiloton weapon a nuclear weapon, the yield of which is measured in terms of thousands of tons of trinitrotoluene (TNT) explosive equivalents, producing yields from 1 to 999 kilotons.

launcher a structural device designed to support and hold a missile in position for firing.

megaton weapon a nuclear weapon, the yield of which is measured in terms of millions of tons of trinitrotoluene (TNT) explosive equivalents.

nuclear column a hollow cylinder of water and spray thrown up from an underwater burst of a nuclear weapon, through which the hot, high-pressure gases formed in the explosion are vented to the atmosphere.

nuclear exoatmospheric burst the explosion of a nuclear weapon above the atmosphere, from above 120 kilometers.

operation exposure guide the maximum amount of nuclear radiation a commander of a unit considers safe to be absorbed during an operation.

radiation sickness an illness resulting from excess exposure to ionizing radiation. The earliest symptoms include nausea, vomiting and diarrhea, followed by loss of hair, hemorrhage, inflammation of the mouth and throat, and general fatigue.

rainfall, nuclear the water that falls from base surge clouds after an underwater burst of a nuclear weapon. This rain is radioactive.

rainout radioactive material brought down from the atmosphere by precipitation.

rem roentgen equivalent mammal; One rem is the quantity of ionizing radiation of any type that, when absorbed by man or other mammal, produces a physiologic effect equivalent to that produced by the absorption of 1 roentgen of x-ray or gamma radiation.

roentgen a unit of exposure dose of gamma or x-ray radiation. In field dosimetry, one roentgen is equal to 1 rad.

Safeguard a ballistic missile defense system.

salted weapon a nuclear weapon that has, in addition to its normal components, certain elements that capture neutrons at the time of the explosion and produce radioactive products over and above the usual radioactive weapons debris.

sea skimmer a missile designed to fly at less than 50 feet above the surface of the sea.

short-range ballistic missile a ballistic missile with a range of 600 nautical miles.

soft missile base a launching base not protected against a nuclear explosion.

spray dome the mound of water spray thrown up into the air from the shock wave of an underwater detonation of a nuclear weapon.

stellar guidance a system that refers to certain preselected celestial bodies to guide a missile.

tolerance dose the amount of radiation that may be absorbed by a person over a period of time with negligible health effects.

two-man rule a system designed to prohibit access by an individual to nuclear weapons and related components by requiring the presence at all times of at least two authorized persons each capable of detecting incorrect or unauthorized procedures with respect to the task to be performed.

warhead that part of a missile or rocket that contains the nuclear or thermonuclear system, high-explosive system, or chemical or biologic agents intended to inflict damage.

zero point the center of a burst of a nuclear weapon at the instant of detonation.

Types of Missiles and Rockets

AGM-28A See HOUND DOG.

AGM-45 See SHRIKE.

AGM-53 See CONDOR.

AGM-65 See MAVERICK.

AGM-69 See SHORT-RANGE ATTACK MISSILE.

AGM-78 See STANDARD ARM.

AGM-84A See HARPOON.

AIM-4 See FALCON.

AIM-7 See SPARROW.

AIM-9 See SIDEWINDER.

AIM-54A See PHOENIX.

AIR-2 See GENIE.

Condor an air-to-surface guided missile that provides standoff launch capability for attack aircraft. Also known as AGM-53.

cruise missile highly accurate, computer-guided missile having a land range of up to 1,552 miles. See TOMAHAWK.

Falcon an air-to-air guided missile; optional nuclear warheads.

Genie an air-to-air, unguided rocket equipped with a nuclear warhead. Also known as an AIR-2.

HARM high-speed antiradiation missile; it homes in on radar signals from surface-to-air missile sites and destroys them.

Harpoon an all-weather, antiship cruise missile capable of being employed from ships, submarines, and aircraft. It is turbojet-powered and employs a low-level cruise trajectory.

Hawk a mobile, surface-to-air missile system that provides nonnuclear, low-to-medium altitude air defense coverage for ground forces. Also known as MIM-23.

Hellfire an air-to-surface antitank missile.

Hound Dog a turbojet-propelled, air-to-surface missile designed to be carried externally on the B-52; it is equipped with a nuclear warhead. Also known as AGM-28A.

Lance a mobile, storable, liquid propellant, surface-to-surface guided missile, with nuclear and nonnuclear capability. Also known as XMGM-52.

LGM-25C See TITAN II.

LGM-30 See MINUTEMAN.

Mace a missile guided by a self-contained radar guidance system or by an inertial guidance system and characterized by its long-range, low-level attack capability.

Maverick an air-to-surface missile with launch and leave capability. It is designed for use against stationary or moving small, hard targets such as tanks, armored vehicles, and field fortifications. Also known as AGM-65.

MGM-13 See MACE.

MGM-29A See SERGEANT.

MGM-31A See PERSHING.

MGM-51 See SHILLELAGH.

Minuteman a three-stage, solid-propellant, ballistic missile guided to its target by an all-inertial guidance and control system. It is equipped with a nuclear warhead and is designed for deployment in underground silos. Also known as LGM-30.

MIRV multiple independently targetable reentry; a missile having two or more warheads aimed at different targets.

MX an intercontinental ballistic missile (ICBM) with multiple warheads. Also known as LGM-118A.

Patriot a land-mobile surface-to-air antimissile missile used to protect small areas, such as an airfield.

Pershing a mobile surface-to-surface inertially guided missile of a solid-propellant type; it has a nuclear warhead capability. Also known as MGM-31A.

Phoenix a long-range air-to-air missile with electronic guidance and homing. Also known as AIM-54A.

Polaris an underwater or surface-launched, surface-to-surface, solid-propellant ballistic missile with inertial guidance and nuclear warhead. Also known as UGM-27.

Poseidon a two-stage, solid-propellant ballistic missile capable of being launched from a specially configured submarine operating in either its surface or submerged mode. The missile is equipped with nuclear warheads and a maneuverable bus that has the capability to carry up to 14 weapons that can be directed at 14 separate targets. Also known as UGM-73A.

Quail an air-launched decoy missile carried internally in the B-52 and used to deceive enemy radar, interceptor aircraft, and air defense missiles. Also known as ADM-20.

RGM-66D See STANDARD SSM.

RGM-84 See HARPOON.

RIM-66 See STANDARD MISSILE.

Sam-D an army air defense artillery, surface-to-air missile system.

Sergeant a mobile, inertially guided, solid-propellant, surface-to-surface missile with nuclear warhead capability, designed for short-range targets up to 75 miles. Also known as MGM-29A.

Shillelagh a missile system mounted on the main battle tank and attack reconnaissance vehicle for employment against enemy armor, troops, and field fortifications. Also known as MGM-51.

short-range attack missile an air-to-surface missile, armed with a nuclear warhead, launched from the B-52 and the FB-111 aircraft. Also known as AGM-69.

Shrike an air-launched antiradiation missile designed to home on and destroy radar emitters. Also known as AGM-45.

Sidewinder a solid-propellant, air-to-air missile with nonnuclear warhead and infrared, heat-seeking homer. Also known as AIM-9.

Sparrow an air-to-air solid-propellant missile with nonnuclear warhead and electronic-controlled homing. Also known as AIM-7.

Spartan a nuclear surface-to-air guided missile formerly deployed as part of the Safeguard ballistic missile defense weapon system. It is designed to intercept strategic ballistic reentry vehicle above Earth's atmosphere.

Sprint a high-acceleration, nuclear surface-to-air guided missile designed to intercept strategic ballistic reentry vehicles above Earth's atmosphere.

Standard Arm an air-launched antiradiation missile designed to home on and destroy radar emitters. Also known as AGM-78.

Standard Missile a shipboard, surface-to-surface and surface-to-air missile with solid-propellant rocket engine. Also known as RIM-66.

Standard SSM a surface-to-surface antiradiation missile equipped with a conventional warhead. Also known as RGM-66D.

Stinger a lightweight, portable, shoulder-fired, air defense artillery missile weapon.

Subroc submarine rocket; submerged, submarine-launched, surface-to-surface rocket with nuclear depth charge or homing torpedo payload, primarily antisubmarine. Also known as UUM-44A.

Talos a shipborne, surface-to-air missile with solid-propellant rocket and ramjet engine. It is equipped with nuclear or nonnuclear warhead, and command, beam-rider homing guidance. Also known as RIM-8.

Tartar a shipborne, surface-to-air missile with solid-propellant rocket engine and nonnuclear warhead. Also known as RIM-24.

Terrier a surface-to-air missile with solid-fuel rocket motor. It is equipped with radar beam rider or homing guidance and nuclear or nonnuclear warhead. Also known as RIM-2.

Titan II a liquid-propellant, two-stage, rocket-powered intercontinental ballistic missile guided to its target by an all-inertial guidance and control system. The missile is equipped with a nuclear warhead and designed for deployment in underground silos. Also known as LGM-25C.

Tomahawk an air, land, ship, or submarine-launched cruise missile with conventional or nuclear capability.

Trident II a three-stage, solid-propellant ballistic missile capable of being launched from a Trident submarine. It is equipped with advanced guidance, nuclear warheads, and a maneuverable bus that can deploy warheads to multiple targets; its range is over 4,000 miles. Also known as UGM-96A.

UGM-27 See POLARIS.

UGM-73A See POSEIDON.

UGM-84A See HARPOON.

UGM-96A See TRIDENT.

US Roland a short-range, low altitude, all-weather, army air defense artillery surface-to-air missile system.

MILITARY INSIGNIA AND RANKS (commissioned officers)

ARMY, AIR FORCE, MARINES

General of the Army, Air Force five silver stars, one 2-inch stripe, four ½-inch stripes.

General four silver stars, one 2-inch stripe, three ½-stripes.

Lieutenant General three silver stars, one 2-inch stripe, two ½-inch stripes.

Major General two silver stars, one 2-inch stripe, one ½-inch strip.

Brigadier General one silver star, one 2-inch stripe.

Colonel silver eagle, four ½-inch stripes.

Lieutenant Colonel silver oak leaf, three ½-inch stripes.

Major gold oak leaf, two ½-inch stripes.

Captain: two silver bars, two ½-inch stripes.

First Lieutenant one silver bar, one ½-inch stripe, one ¼-inch stripe.

Second Lieutenant one gold bar, one ½-inch stripe.

Chief Warrant Officer (W-4) silver bar with four enamel bands, one ½-inch stripe.

Chief Warrant Officer (W-3) silver bar with three enamel bands, one ½-inch stripe.

Chief Warrant Officer (W-2) silver bar with two enamel bands, one ½-inch stripe.

Chief Warrant Officer (W-1) silver bar with one enamel band.

NAVY AND COAST GUARD

Fleet Admiral five silver stars, one 2-inch stripe, four ½-inch stripes.

Admiral four silver stars, one 2-inch stripe, three ½-inch stripes.

Vice Admiral three silver stars, one 2-inch stripe, two ½-inch stripes.

Rear Admiral (upper half) two silver stars, one 2-inch stripe, one ½-inch stripe.

Rear Admiral (lower half) one silver star, one 2-inch stripe.

Captain silver eagle, four ½-inch stripes.

Commander silver oak leaf, three ½-inch stripes.

Lieutenant Commander gold oak leaf, two ½-inch stripes, one ¼-inch stripe.

Lieutenant two silver bars, two ½-inch stripes.

Lieutenant (jg) one silver bar, one ½-inch stripe, one ¼-inch stripe.

Ensign one gold bar, one ½-inch stripe.

Chief Warrant Officer (W-4) silver bar with three enamel bands, one ½-inch stripe.

Chief Warrant Officer (W-3) silver bar with two enamel bands, one ½-inch stripe.

Chief Warrant Officer (W-2) gold bar with three enamel bands, one ½-inch stripe.

INTELLIGENCE, ESPIONAGE, DECEPTION, AND PSYCHOLOGICAL WARFARE

acoustic intelligence intelligence derived from the collection and processing of sound.

acoustical surveillance employment of electronic devices, including sound-recording, receiving, or transmitting equipment, for the collection of information.

agent authentication the providing of an agent with personal documents, accoutrements, and equipment that have the appearance of authenticity.

agent net an organization for secret purposes which operates under the direction of a principal agent.

biographical intelligence intelligence collection concerning foreign personalities.

black a term referring to illegal concealment.

black border crossing getting across a border by the use of illegal concealment.

black list a counterintelligence list of enemy collaborators, sympathizers, intelligence suspects, and others.

black, living living under illegal concealment.

black propaganda propaganda that purports to emanate from a source other than the true one.

blow to expose, usually unintentionally, the secret cover of a person, installation, or operation.

bug a concealed microphone or listening device.

bugged a room or object that has been secretly equipped with a microphone or a listening device.

burn to deliberately expose the secret cover of a person, installation, or operation.

burn notice an official statement by one intelligence agency to other agencies that an individual or group is unreliable.

cell a small group of individuals who work together for secret or subversive purposes.

civil censorship censorship of civilian communications, such as messages, printed matter, and films in territories occupied or controlled by armed forces.

classified information information kept secret to protect national interests or national security.

cold war a state of international tension in which political, economic, technological, sociological, psychological, and paramilitary measures short of overt armed conflict are employed to achieve national objectives.

communication deception use of devices, operations, and techniques to confuse the communications link or navigational system of the enemy.

confusion agent an agent dispatched to confound the intelligence or counterintelligence of another nation rather than to collect information.

counterdeception efforts to negate, neutralize, or diminish the effects of a foreign deception operation.

counterespionage the detecting, neutralizing, exploitation, and prevention of espionage activities by another country.

countersabotage action designed to detect and counteract sabotage.

countersubversion action designed to detect and counteract subversion.

covert operations operations conducted by a person whose real identity is concealed.

critical intelligence any information of extreme importance, such as indications of the imminent outbreak of hostilities.

cryptanalysis the converting of encrypted messages into plain text without having knowledge of the encryption key.

cryptology the science of hidden, disguised, or encrypted communications.

cultivation a deliberate and calculated association with a person for the purpose of recruitment, obtaining information, and so forth.

declassify to cancel the security classification of an item of classified matter.

decrypt to convert encrypted text into plain text by deciphering and decoding.

double agent an agent who has infiltrated enemy intelligence and works for them as a "quasi" spy while gathering information for the other side.

dual agent an agent who works for two or more agencies, collecting information for both.

elicitation acquisition of information from a person or group in a manner that does not disclose the intent of the interview or conversation.

encipher to convert plain text into unintelligible form by means of a cipher system.

encrypt to convert plain text into unintelligible form by means of cryptosystem.

escape line a planned route to allow personnel engaged in clandestine activity to depart from a site when the possibility of apprehension exists.

espionage actions directed toward the gathering of information through clandestine operations.

evasion and escape intelligence processed information prepared to assist personnel to escape if captured by the enemy or to evade capture if lost in enemy territory.

evasion and escape net the organization within enemy-held areas that operates to receive and move military personnel to friendly control.

foreign instrumentation signals intelligence (FISINT) intelligence information derived from electromagnetic emissions from enemy hardware, machinery, weapons, and other sources.

gray propaganda propaganda from an unidentified source.

imagery intelligence intelligence gathered from the use of photography, infrared sensors, lasers, electro-optics, and radar sensors.

infiltration the placing of an agent within enemy territory.

infiltration, black crossing a border through illegal concealment.

infiltration, gray crossing a border with the use of false documentation.

infiltration, white legal crossing of a border.

mole a spy, or a double agent who has worked undetected among the enemy for a significant length of time.

overt operation the collection of intelligence openly, without concealment.

padding extraneous text added to a message for the purpose of concealing its beginning, ending, or length.

penetration the recruitment of agents within, or the infiltration of agents or monitoring devices into, an enemy organization.

political intelligence intelligence concerning foreign and domestic policies of governments.

psychological consolidation activities planned psychological activities in peace and war directed at a civilian population in order to achieve desired behavior that supports military objectives.

psychological media all forms of communication media.

psychological operations planned operations designed to influence the emotions and reasoning of a foreign audience. Also known as perception management.

psychological warfare the planned use of propaganda and other psychological tools to influence the opinions, emotions, attitudes, and behavior of hostile foreign groups.

PSYOP psychological operations.

radar intelligence intelligence derived from data collected by radar.

radiation intelligence intelligence derived from the emissions of electromagnetic energy from foreign devices, equipments, and systems but excluding those generated from nuclear weapons.

radio deception deceiving the enemy through the sending of false dispatches, deceptive headings, and enemy call signs over the radio.

receptivity the vulnerability of a target audience to psychological operations.

safe house an innocent-appearing house serving clandestine operations.

signals intelligence (SIGINT) intelligence information comprising all communications, electronics, and telemetry intelligence.

subversion action designed to undermine the military, economic, psychological, political strength, or morale of a regime.

target intelligence intelligence gathered concerning a potential target for destruction.

white propaganda propaganda disseminated and acknowledged by the sponsor.

WORLD WAR II SLANG

ARMY

ack-ack machine gun or antiaircraft gun.

archies antiaircraft guns.

armored cow canned milk.

army banjo shovel.

Aussies soldiers from Australia.

AWOL absent without leave. Also, a wolf on the loose, or after women or liquor.

B-19 a fat woman.

baby food cereal.

barker a large artillery gun.

battery acid coffee.

beans nickname for a commissary officer.

bear grease general-issue soap.

big boot general.

blackout coffee.

blackstrap coffee.

blanket drill sleep.

blitz a bombing.

blow it out of your bag shut up.

bobtail a dishonorable discharge.

bog pocket a cheapskate.

brass hat a staff officer.

brig jail. Also known as the clink, stockade, hoosegow.

brown bombers army laxatives.

bucking trying to get a promotion.

bucking for a section 8 trying to get discharged through any means possible.

bulldog military police.

bunky a buddy, friend, or pal.

Butch nickname for a commanding officer.

cackle jelly eggs.

camel corps infantry.

camp happy a little touched in the head.

canteen an army retail store.

cat beer milk.

cat stabber a bayonet.

CB confined to barracks.

cheese toaster bayonet.

chest hardware medals.

chicken a very young recruit.

chili bowl a military haircut.

civvies civilian clothes.

Clara all clear air raid signal.

corn willie tinned corn beef.

corpuscle corporal.

cowboy a tank driver.

cream on a shingle creamed beef on toast.

croot recruit, rookie, bozo, bucko.

crow chicken.

crowbar hotel any jail.

crumb hunt kitchen inspection.

daisy may a denim fatigue hat.

devil's piano a machine gun.

didie bag bag for keeping valuables in.

dog fat butter.

dog house the guardhouse.

dog tag the metal identification tag worn around the neck.

drive it in the hangar shut up.

duds shells that fail to explode.

elephant trap a large hold dug for refuse.

faint wagon ambulance.

fisheyes tapioca with raisins.

fly one wing low to be drunk.

fox hole a pit dug to protect oneself against enemy fire.

frogskin a dollar bill.

fuzzy-wuzzies winter trousers.

garrison shoes any dress shoes.

general's car a wheelbarrow.

Gertrude a soldier working in an office.

GI general issue.

GI Jesus the chaplain.

goldfish canned salmon.

goof burner one who smokes marijuana.

goofy discharge a discharge given for mental illness.

grandma low gear in a jeep or other vehicle.

grubber lowest ranking.

hay sauerkraut.

hi Jackson a friendly greeting.

hip flask a .45 caliber pistol.

hitch an enlistment.

housewife a sewing kit.

Irish grapes potatoes.

jack money.

Jerries Germans; German planes.

John L's long Johns.

jumping Jesus a chaplain in a paratrooper unit.

Kendall did it an oft-repeated buck-passing line.

kennel rations hash or meat loaf.

k.p. duty assisting the cook in food preparation, serving, and cleanup; kitchen police.

krauts Germans.

lacy said of an effeminate soldier.

laid out for inspection unconscious.

leatherneck a marine.

light chassis a woman with a great figure.

L'il Abners army shoes. Also known as groundhogs.

low on amps and voltage out of ideas.

machine oil pancake syrup.

Mae West a life jacket worn like a vest.

maneuvers putting the make on a woman.

matilda one's blanket roll.

meat wagon ambulance.

mess gear knives, forks, spoons.

nappy nickname for the barber.

noncom noncommissioned officer.

on the beam, are you are you okay?

padre chaplain.

paint remover coffee.

pantywaist a sissy.

pea shooter rifle.

pill rollers medical corps.

pineapple hand grenade.

pipped shot, as in he got pipped.

pocket lettuce dollar bills. Also known as happy cabbage.

police up pick up, clean up.

popeye spinach.

popsicle motorcycle.

post exchange merchandise store; the PX.

prang an avoidable airplane crash.

propeller wash B.S.

ptomaine domain the mess hall.

pull rank to inform another of one's higher rank.

PX post exchange.

Q company a recruit receiving company.

quiff a girl.

rabbit food lettuce, celery, carrots.

Rachel high gear in a jeep or other vehicle.

red nose shrapnel.

rudily doo not worth a damn.

sand and specks salt and pepper.

sawbones an army doctor.

shimmy pudding jello. Also known as shivering Liz.

skirt patrol looking for women.

slingshot pistol.

snafu situation normal all fouled up.

snap snap hurry up, on the double.

squirrel cage the psychoanalyst's office.

stocks and bonds toilet paper.

swampseed rice.

tarheel soldier from the South.

three seventy three square meals and 70 cents, a day's wages.

tin titty canned milk.

tommy Thompson submachine gun.

Waldorf, the mess hall.

NAVY

admiral's watch a good night's sleep.

airedale a naval aviation recruit.

alligator an amphibious tank.

arctic boat refrigerator boat carrying meat. Also known as the beef boat.

armory the gun maintenance shop.

ashcan a submarine depth charge.

AWOL absent without leave.

baffle painting ship camouflage painting.

battlewagon a battleship.

belay stop that or shutup.

bells denotes the time of day. 1 A.M. = 2 bells, 2 A.M. = 4 bells, 3 A.M. = 6 bells, 4 A.M. = 8 bells, 5 A.M. = 2 bells, 6 A.M. = 4 bells, 7 A.M. = 6 bells, 8 A.M. = 8 bells, 9 A.M. = 2 bells, 10 A.M. = 4 bells, 11 A.M. = 6 bells, noon = 8 bells. Same cycle repeated for P.M. hours.

bilge water B.S.

bird boat an aircraft carrier.

blow, a a storm at sea.

boot a newly enlisted sailor.

boot camp a six-week naval training camp on shore.

brass the gold stripes on an officer's sleeve.

brig an onboard jail.

brightwork any metal finishings that need polishing.

brown nose one who kisses an officer's feet; an officer's favorite.

buzzard any eagle insignia.

calk off sleep.

canary a beautiful woman.

canteen on board retail store.

captain of the head one ordered to clean the toilets.

Chicago piano an antiaircraft gun.

cigar box fleet boats carrying landing craft, tanks, and infantry for a shore attack.

coiled up his ropes died.

collision mats waffles.

commissary bullets beans.

crow an ugly woman.

cut of his jib a sailor's appearance or behavior.

EPD extra police duty; cleaning and polishing.

fish a torpedo

flashing his hash throwing up from seasickness.

flying coffin a PBY navy patrol bomber.

foo-foo perfume.

forecastle lawyer one who claims to know all navy regulations.

four-oh 4-0; perfect; okay.

four-striper captain.

French leave to leave a ship without permission.

funnels smokestacks.

furlough any liberty lasting over 72 hours.

galley ship kitchen.

gangway get out of the way.

gig captain's private boat.

gilligen hitch an imaginary knot in a rope.

give it the deep six throw it overboard.

gob sailor.

gone native said of a sailor who has become overly friendly with natives on shore.

gooks natives of the South Seas.

goos goos Philipinos.

hammock what a sailor sleeps in.

heave out and lash up morning greeting to get out of bed and roll up one's hammock.

honey barge the garbage barge.

houligan navy sailor's nickname for the Coast Guard.

katzenjammers the shakes after a night of heavy drinking ashore.

liberty shore leave of 48 hours or less.

limey a British sailor.

mail buoy an imaginary mail box on a buoy; new recruits were told in all seriousness to leave their mail on this buoy for the mailman to pick up.

mast, called to the called in for a reprimanding by the captain.

mess meals; the meal room.

mokers, the the blues.

mosquito boat a light, quick boat equipped with small guns.

muck up clean up.

mud hook anchor.

old man the captain.

one striper an ensign.

ordinary seaman a seaman second class.

pea coat a waist-length, blue wool coat.

pig boats submarines.

pipe him aboard to welcome a high-ranking officer or dignitary aboard by blowing the boatswain's whistle.

plotting room a room where maneuvers were planned over maps and instruments.

pollywog a sailor yet to cross the equator.

scrambled eggs the gold insignia on an officer's cap.

sea gull a loose woman who follows the fleet around from port to port.

sea legs to become accustomed physically and mentally to life at sea.

send a fish fire a torpedo.

shellback an experienced sailor; one who has crossed the equator.

shivering Liz jello.

sick bay on board hospital.

skibbies the Japanese.

slop chute a garbage chute leading to the ocean.

slushy nickname for the cook.

smukes dollars.

sparks a wireless operator.

step off the plank to get married.

straight as a deck seam said of one who can be trusted.

submarine ears hard of hearing.

swab a large mop.

three sheets in the wind drunk.

three striper a commander.

two and a half striper a lieutenant commander.

two striper a lieutenant.

watch a 4-hour watch duty.

watch cap a black, knitted stocking cap.

wicky wicky hurry up; chop chop; on the double.

Marines

belly robber the cook.

boogies Japanese airmen.

boondockers field shoes.

boot a new recruit.

boot camp recruit training camp.

brig rat prisoner.

butcher a medical officer.

canned Willie canned beef.

cattle boat a troop transport boat.

cub one who has not yet crossed the Arctic Circle.

deck ape one who swabs the deck.

ding how okay, derived from the Chinese.

ditty box a small box for personal articles.

dogface soldier.

dragon back one who has crossed the 180th meridian.

FiFi anyone's girlfriend.

flatfoot marine's nickname for a sailor.

48 a two-day leave.

frog sticker a bayonet.

gooks natives.

go-to-hell cap a garrison cap.

gunny a gunnery sergeant.

iron kelly steel helmet. Also known as a tin derby.

Jackson a marine's call to another soldier, "Hey, Jackson."

jamoke coffee.

joe coffee.

Maggie's drawers a red flag waved to indicate a complete miss of the target on a shooting range.

old issue an old marine.

padre chaplain. Also, Holy Joe.

pearl diver a marine assigned to kitchen duty, especially washing dishes.

pollywog a marine who has not yet crossed the equator.

punk bread.

ring tails gunner's nickname for the Japanese.

run aground to get into trouble.

scuttlebut gossip.

shack mammy a native woman of the South Pacific.

sick bay a hospital dispensary.

sinkers doughnuts. Two for a nickel at the time.

slopchute a beer parlor.

swabby nickname for a sailor.

sweetheart one's rifle.

twist a dizzy roll a cigarette.

Australian Soldier Slang

billy a can for boiling tea in.

bloke a man.

bloody an adjective used in a fashion similar to the American, "damned," for example, bloody good, bloody stupid.

bonzer excellent.

boshter great.

bosker fine.

bush the back country. American equivalent of the "boonies."

chivvy back talk.

cliner a woman.

cobber a buddy.

cow bad.

deener a shilling.

dingbats Italians.

dinkie cute.

dinkum the real thing; genuine; real.

Jerries Germans.

knocked up tuckered out; tired; bushed.

larrikin drunk.

Matilda a bundle of personal articles.

nips the Japanese.

Pommies Englishmen.

punting betting.

Sheila a nice-looking woman.

shikkered drunk.

shivoo a party.

squatter a farmer.

station a farm or ranch.

stone a measurement of weight.

stonkered shell-shocked.

tucker food.

zack sixpence.

Nurse's Slang

Annie nickname for a nurse anesthetist.

arthritis of the cerebellum said of a stupid person.

bedpan alley the hospital.

blues the two-tone blue uniforms worn during the war.

brown kitties bronchitis.

dock the hospital.

doctorine a woman doctor.

follow-up man mortician.

gubbins dirty dressings.

idiotorium hospital for the mentally ill.

inkie an incubator baby.

misery hall an emergency room.

scrub nurse a nurse who follows sterile procedures in order to handle operating room instruments.

sick bay ship hospital.

stiffy a paralyzed person.

stink kitchen a chemical laboratory.

temperature, don't run a don't get excited.

WAC Slang

arsenal wear general issue lingerie.

barracks bags bags under the eyes from working a night shift.

blow boy bugler.

boll weevils heavy brown cotton stockings.

book rack bunk bed.

burp class a defense class on gas warfare.

canteen cowboy soldier who hangs out at the canteen to flirt with the women.

cool good.

cut off a scene to leave.

dry ammunition cosmetics.

gigs demerits.

GI Jane an okay person.

gravy he's gravy, a good-looking man.

gruesome twosome regulation shoes.

hair warden the camp hair stylist.

jeep jockeys women auto mechanics in Motor Transport.

jubilee reveille.

monkey suits general issue coveralls.

night maneuvers fooling around with a man.

put a nickel in it hurry up.

scoff to eat.

screwy as a toad a nut case.

square from Delaware a hick girl from a small town.

WAC Woman's Auxiliary Corps, U.S. Army.

WAC shack the barracks. Also known as the Wackery.

wolfing looking for men.

Other Occupations

PUBLISHING AND JOURNALISM

Afghanistanism journalist's term for the avoiding of local controversy by focusing news coverage on distant lands.

allege one of the most frequently used words of journalists who wish to avoid being sued for libel. Known as a hedge word. See also LINDLEY RULE.

angle a story's point of view or perspective.

blacksmith an uninspired but industrious reporter who simply pounds out stories day after day.

blue pencil to edit; to make corrections in a manuscript.

bogus fillers or stock features to be replaced by hard news in a later edition of a daily newspaper.

boil down editor's term meaning to condense a story.

bootjacking the hawking of newspapers on the street.

break where a newspaper story stops on one page to be continued on another page.

bright a brief, light human interest story.

bulldog the early edition of a daily newspaper, usually printed the night before.

bullpup the first edition of a Sunday newspaper, a portion of which may be printed well before Sunday.

bury a story to place a story on an inner page of a newspaper.

byline the reporter's name, which appears above the beginning of a story.

canned copy press releases, publicity releases, features from syndicates—any prewritten material. Also known as A-copy or handouts.

circulation the average number of copies of a newspaper sold in a given period.

city editor the newspaper editor who covers city news; he or she works in the city room.

clean a highly polished manuscript needing little or no editing.

cold dope statistics.

colored story a biased or slanted piece of reporting.

comma chaser slang for a copy editor.

copy any written or illustrated material to be printed.

copy boy/girl one who runs errands; a gopher in a newsroom.

copy editor the editor who checks for style, grammar, and other errors, and makes corrections in manuscripts for the printer.

correspondent a reporter who sends in news stories from remote locations.

crusade a journalist's dedicated effort to expose some wrongdoing, such as government corruption.

cub a new, inexperienced reporter.

date file a file of important anniversaries, holidays, upcoming events to be covered.

dateline at the beginning of a newspaper story, the line indicating the story's point of origin. Formerly, the dateline included the date.

deadline the day or time a story must be submitted for publication.

dirty copy that has been heavily edited and marked.

editorial a personal opinion column. Also, all written copy other than advertising.

editorializing a reporter's insertion of a personal viewpoint in a story.

fair comment the legal right of a reporter to report the facts of a story as he or she understands them to be as long as the facts are presented fairly and without malice.

feature a large article or story, usually of human interest and not necessarily newsworthy.

filler short, stock items, used to fill space in a newspaper or magazine.

five W's the five questions that must be answered in every news story—who, what, where, when, and why?

Fleet Street the London press.

fluff a trite story or article.

free-lance writer a non-staff reporter who submits assigned or unassigned (unsolicited) stories to a newspaper or magazine.

gonzo journalism journalism style given a free reign; wild, outrageous reporting from a personal viewpoint, as in that of Hunter Thompson.

hack any writer or reporter more concerned with making a buck than creating fine writing.

handout a press release.

hedge word any word used by a journalist as protection from a libel suit, as in, "alleged," "reportedly," "reputed."

investigative journalism reporting in which several interviews are conducted along with exhaustive research.

John Garfield still dead story any rehashing of old news.

keyhole journalism unethical journalism that ignores people's right to privacy; gossip news.

kill to cancel a story.

leader a newspaper's lead story.

leg man a reporter who travels to the scene of news and phones in a story to the rewrite editor.

libel any published, false accusation; an untrue, defamatory statement.

Lindley rule a rule to be followed when using nonattributable material, such as sensitive material, by which vague phrases such as "according to official sources" are used. Also known as deep background.

managed news a government-controlled release of news. A government news release in its own interest.

morgue the reference files or reference room of a newspaper.

mouthpiece a publicist or public relations officer; a press secretary.

muckraker a journalist who exposes corruption.

over the transom unsolicited copy received through the mail from freelance writers.

peg the main point or thrust of a story.

photojournalism telling a story with pictures.

press agent a publicity agent.

press gallery a reserved area in a government or other building for use by the press.

press kit publicity material, such as information, photos, handed out or mailed to reporters and newspapers on behalf of a corporation, organization, or movie star.

press pass a card confirming afilliation with a newspaper or magazine and used to gain free admission to a specific event.

press release a handout of a suggested article provided by corporations, universities, and other institutions to gain publicity.

privileged communication the legal right of journalists to keep the names of their sources confidential. See shield law.

puff a trite publicity piece.

put to bed to prepare a newspaper for printing.

rag nickname for a newspaper with a poor reputation.

railroad to hurry a story from typewriter to composing with no editing in between.

retraction a correction noting innaccurate reporting in a previous edition.

rewrite editor an editor who rewrites stories called in over the phone or who rewords press releases.

sacred cow a person or institution favored by members of the press and that they hesitate to criticize or investigate for a story.

scoop to learn of a story and publish it before the competition.

shield law the law that protects reporters from revealing their sources.

silly season a slow news period characterized by trivial news or no news.

skinny inside information.

slant the perspective or point of view of a story.

slush unsolicited manuscripts from freelancers.

spike to kill a story. May also refer to stories held for later use.

spot news current news.

squib a short news item.

staffer a staff reporter, as distinguished from a freelance reporter.

state editor the editor at a large newspaper in charge of state news.

stringer a part-time freelancer who mails in stories from remote locations.

tabloid a half-sized newspaper characterized by sensational stories and photographs.

think piece an editorial or analysis of the news.

UPI United Press International.

vignette a very brief news item.

wire editor the editor in charge of news received form the Associated Press and other wire services.

wire service a news service, for example, the Associated Press, United Press International.

yellow journalism journalism that is irresponsible, sensational, and exploitive.

Types of Headlines

bank a second line of a headline, usually in smaller type.

banner a large headline extending all the way across the top of the front page. Also known as a streamer.

barker similar to a kicker but set in larger type than the headline beneath it.

bikini head a headline illuminating a portion of a story.

binder line an inner page headline stretching over two or more related stories.

bumping heads abutting headlines.

circus makeup a headline using different kinds or sizes of type to draw attention.

crossline the middle line of a three-section headline.

cutline a caption under a picture.

deadhead a vague, abstract, or lackluster headline. Also known as a flathead or a wooden head.

drophead a headline set underneath a banner, and which refers to the same story.

jump head a shortened or abbreviated headline indicating the continuation of a story from a previous page.

kicker a small-type, teaser line set above the headline. Also known as an eyebrow, highline, teaser.

overline a headline set above a picture.

ribbon a one-line headline set in smaller type than a banner but with a width greater than one column.

rocket head a displayed or bold-type quotation set in the middle of a story.

scarehead any alarmist or sensational headline.

screamer a very large banner headline set in bold print.

second coming type the largest and boldest headline type, reserved for stories on a par with the second coming of Christ. Also known as studhorse type.

skyline head a banner headline set above the masthead, at the very top of the front page. Also known as an over-the-roof head.

stock head a standby headline used when another line or story is killed.

subhead a small headline placed within a story.

tombstones two headlines with similar construction that are set beside one another.

Book Publishing

adaptation a novel converted to a screenplay, or vice versa.

advance an amount of money paid to an author up-front for the rights to publish a book.

anthology a book of short stories or other selected writings by one or more authors.

auction the bidding for the purchase of a valuable author's book by several publishers.

authorized biography a biography written with the permission and cooperation of the subject, as distinguished from an unauthorized biography.

backlist a term referring to a publisher's books that have been in print for a significant amount of time yet continue to sell well, such as classics or reference books.

belles lettres literary works appreciated for their aesthetic value rather than their educational content, such as poetry or drama.

blockbuster a hugely successful book.

bodice ripper a form of romance novel in which the courtship gets rough.

brand-name author an author who writes consistently successful and popular books.

chapbook a small booklet or paperback containing poems or ballads.

coffee-table book a large, illustrated book, purchased primarily for its pictures.

commercial fiction popular fiction that can be counted on to generate large sales.

Edgar an award presented by the Mystery Writers of America for best mystery novel of the year.

flap copy description, blurbs, author's capsule biography, or other copy found on a book's flaps.

frontlist a publisher's newest releases.

genre kind, type, or category—western, science fiction, romance, and so on.

ghostwriter a writer who writes a book for someone else, who may or may not give credit to the real author.

Golden Spur an award presented by the Western Writers of America for best western novel of the year.

gothic horror a horror novel that takes place in an old mansion or castle.

gothic romance a romance novel that centers around a naive girl or woman victimized by an evil man and courted by a heroic man, all taking place in or around an old mansion or castle.

hack a writer who churns out books quickly and is more concerned with making a buck than producing fine art.

hard SF hard science fiction; a science fiction novel emphasizing technology.

historical romance a romance novel featuring a story that takes places in the past.

instant book a book published quickly in order to take advantage of some timely event. Also known as a quickie.

interactive book a novel, usually for children, that offers several plot alternatives for the reader to choose.

literary agent a person who sells authors' manuscripts to publishers and negotiates contracts.

literary book an avant-garde, experimental, or highly styled novel that usually has limited sales; a noncommercial book featuring a high degree of writing skill.

managed text a textbook whose writing is supervised by a professor.

mass market paperback a rack-size, commercial paperback sold in magazine outlets as well as bookstores.

midlist books expected to have only moderate sales appeal.

Nebula an award presented by the Science Fiction Writers of America for best science fiction novel or story of the year.

new age collective term for a category of books that includes metaphysical, spiritual, holistic, astrology, mysticism, and faith healing interests.

novelization turning a movie script into a novel.

novella a short novel, from 7,000 to 15,000 words. Also known as a novelette.

o.s.s. obligatory sex scene, as found in many commercial novels.

over the transom an unsolicited manuscript sent to a publisher by a freelance writer or a freelance writer's agent.

pen name a fictitious name used by an author who wishes to remain anonymous. A pseudonym; nom de plume.

police procedural a mystery or crime drama featuring methods of police investigation.

remainder an overstocked book sold at a low price.

reprint a hardcover book republished in a paperback format.

roman à clef a novel featuring real persons given fictitious names.

royalties a percentage of a book's finance paid to the author by the publisher after a certain number of books have been sold and the author's advance has earned out.

SF science fiction.

slush pile stacks of unsolicited manuscripts that pile up at publishing houses.

space opera a science fiction adventure similar to Star Wars.

sword and sorcery a fantasy novel featuring a mythical past with warriors, witches, warlocks, elves, magic, and such like.

trade book a commercial hardcover book intended for a general audience, as distinguished from a college textbook.

trade paperback same as a trade book, but in paperback format.

unauthorized biography a biography written without the cooperation of the subject.

vanity press a publisher who publishes books that are paid for by their authors.

whodunit a mystery.

Additional Book Terms

biblia abiblia worthless books or literature.

bibliobibuli people who read too much and who have little or no other interests.

biblioclasm the burning or destruction of books.

biblioclast one who burns or destroys books.

bibliogony the production of books.

biblioklept one who steals books.

bibliomancy divination by books.

bibliomania a passion for collecting books.

bibliopegy bookbinding as an art.

bibliophagist a devourer of books.

bibliophile one who loves books.

bibliophobia a fear of books.

bibliopoesy the making of books.

bibliopole a bookseller.

bibliotaph one who hides or hoards books.

bibliotheca library.

incunabula books printed before 1500 A.D.

Footnote Abbreviations

abr. abridged.
anon. anonymous.
app. appendix.
ca. (circa) approximately.
cf. (confer) compare.
col. column.
ed. editor.
e.g. for example.
esp. especially.
et al. and others.
etc. (et cetera) and so forth.
et seq. and the following.
f. and the following page.
ff. and the following pages.
fl. flourished.
ibid. in the same place.
id. the same.
i.e. that is.
inf. below.
loc. cit. in the place cited.
ms. manuscript.
mss. manuscripts.
N.B. take special note of.
n.d. no date.
n.s. new series.
op. cit. in the work cited.
o.s. old series.
p. page.
par. paragraph.
pass. throughout.
pl. plate.
pp. pages.
pt. part.
pub. published, publisher.
q.v. which see.
r. reigned.
repr. reprinted.
ser. series.
sup. above.
suppl. supplement.
s.v. under the word.
trans. translation.
v. see.
vide. see.
viz. namely.

POLITICS

act a bill after it passes the House of Representatives or the Senate or both.

activist one who works for a cause.

advance man a publicity person who schedules speeches, conferences, and so on, for a candidate or an incumbent.

advise and consent the power of the Senate to advise the President and consent to proposed appointments or treaties.

amendment a proposal to revise, or an actual revision, of a bill, motion, or act.

armchair strategist one who criticizes or remarks on political events from a comfortable position and particularly with the advantage of hindsight.

back channel the secret or informal circuit of communication used by the CIA and other government agencies.

backer one who supports a political candidate financially.

balance of power the theory that peace is maintained only when nations share equal power.

ballyhoo sensational or exaggerated promotion of a candidate or issue.

bandwagon a popular issue jumped on by politicians in order to be seen as part of the majority.

bargaining chip a negotiating concession.

barnstorm to tour rural areas to make campaign speeches.

bellwether a trendsetter.

bigger bang for the buck in military terms, a weapon or military system that delivers the most for the money.

big stick the deterrent of a large and powerful defense.

bill a proposed law.

bipartisan pertaining to both political parties; the working together of two political parties, despite differences, to achieve a common goal.

black hats political opponents; the bad guys.

bleeding heart liberals extreme liberals—in the view of extreme conservatives. "Bleeding hearts" are suckers for sob stories and are quick to pledge tax money to cure a variety of social ills.

bloc a group of representatives with a common interest.

blue ribbon panel a committee chosen for their expertise to look into a particular matter.

boll weevils nickname for southern conservative Democrats.

boom and bust an economy that follows cycles of prosperity and depression.

boondoggle any government project in which taxes are wasted through poor planning, incompetence, and inefficiency.

brain trust a candidate's group of advisers.

bread-and-butter issue any political issue that affects the voters' pocketbooks.

brouhaha an uproar, as over a controversy.

buck passing passing the burden of responsibility to someone else.

bully pulpit a term referring to the use of the president's high position to moralize and pontificate.

bureaucracy government administration comprised of bureaus headed by nonelected officials. Also, any government office that, through convoluted channels and overly strict adherence to rules, impedes, or slows down action.

cabinet the heads of executive departments who serve as advisers to the president.

cant the vernacular used by a politician; pet words and phrases used by politicians.

canvass to gauge support for a candidate before the vote.

card carrying a member or supporter of a cause or organization, such as a card-carrying member of the ACLU.

caucus a meeting to select candidates and plan a campaign.

chamber the House of Representatives or the Senate.

civil disobedience resisting the law to promote a cause.

cloture in the Senate, the process by which debate time is limited to one hour per senator.

coattail the winning of a congressional seat by party association with a popular presidential candidate.

cold war nonmilitary hostilities between two nations.

Congressional Record the printed daily account of the debates and votes of the House and Senate, published by the Government Printing Office.

conservative one who is generally opposed to change; a supporter of the status quo.

constituency collective term for the citizens of a legislative district. In the case of a senator, a state.

constituent a citizen of a particular legislative district.

consul an official appointed to a foreign city to represent its commercial interests.

consulate the office of a consul.

coup d'état the sudden takeover or overthrow of government.

dark horse a candidate whose chances of winning an election are slight to none.

deep six to throw out or get rid of something, often with the hope that it will never be found or discovered.

delegate a person chosen to represent a constituency at a convention.

delegation a group of representatives from an organization or area.

demagogue a politician who appeals to the greed, fears, and prejudices of the voters; a spellbinding orator who panders to voter selfishness.

Democratic party the political party most noted for its liberal policy positions.

détente the thawing or opening up of relations between two nations previously hostile toward one another.

diplomacy the maintaining of positive relations or negotiations between nations.

diplomat a government official who maintains relationships and carries out negotiations with a foreign nation. Also responsible for protecting the rights of American citizens in a foreign country.

diplomatic corps collective term for all of the diplomatic officials assigned to one nation.

domestic affairs political affairs within a nation's own borders.

dyed-in-the-wool a die-hard partisan through and through.

elder statesman an older, experienced, and highly respected politician.

electoral college collective term for persons elected from each state to cast electoral votes for the president and vice president.

electorate persons eligible to vote.

embassy the residence or office of an ambassador in the capital of another nation.

engrossed bill official copy of a bill after it has been passed.

executive order a presidential order.

executive privilege the right of the president to withold information from Congress.

executive session a meeting closed to the public.

faction a dissenting group within a larger group.

fact-finding trip a trip or junket overseas to gather information on a foreign issue.

fence mending tending to one's local constituency, for example, reestablishing ties with local politicians or media.

fence, on the straddling either side of an issue; being unwilling or unable to decide one way or another.

filibuster a long-winded speech or debate made by a Senator in a minority as a last-ditch attempt to alter the opinion of the majority or to delay a vote. Also made to draw public attention to an issue.

fiscal year the 12-month period for the use of federal funds, beginning October 1.

floor where debating and voting takes place in a legislative chamber.

football, political any issue exploited by a politician for partisan gain.

franking privilege the free use of postal services by senators and representatives.

gag rule a rule that limits the time for debate in a legislative body.

gerrymander the adjusting of representative districts to conform to a voting pattern or favor one party over another.

good soldier a politician willing to put aside his own interests for those of his party.

GOP Grand Old Party; the Republican party.

graft profiting by political corruption.

grass roots deeply rooted, popular support for an issue or a politician.

groundswell popular support for an issue or a politician.

hatchetman a politician's associate who makes vicious attacks against the opposite party.

hat in the ring, to throw one's to announce one's candidacy.

henchman a member of a politician's staff; a right-hand man; used pejoratively.

Hill, the Capitol Hill; the legislative branch of the federal government.

hopper the box where proposed bills are placed in a legislative chamber.

impeach to formally charge a politician with wrongdoing while in office.

imperialism expanding a nation's authority by acquiring new territories, exploiting another land's resources, and so on.

incumbent a politician already in office who is running for reelection against a challenger.

independent a nonpartisan politician. Also, a person who votes for a candidate and not for a candidate's party affiliation.

isolationism the foreign policy of minding one's own business or remaining neutral in international disputes.

Joint Chiefs of Staff the four highest-ranking U.S. military officers: the chiefs of staff of the army, navy, and air force, plus an appointed chairman; they advise the secretary of defense on the nation's military matters.

joint committee a committee of members from both legislative bodies.

joint session a meeting of members of both legislative bodies.

junket a trip taken by a politician at taxpayer expense, ostensibly for research into foreign affairs but often suspected of being more of a free vacation.

kangaroo ticket a ticket in which the candidate for vice president is more popular than the candidate for the President.

keynote the main address designed to rouse emotions or loyalty at a convention.

kitchen cabinet influential close friends and minor officials who advise the president informally.

knee-jerk liberal a liberal intellectual who thinks only superficially about issues.

laissez faire the policy of little or no government intervention into economic issues, with the belief that the private sector will take care of itself.

lame duck a politician whose term is nearly over and whose power is subsequently diminished, especially after being freshly defeated by a challenger in an election.

landslide a huge election victory.

left wing the part of a political organization advocating reform or overthrow of the established order.

legislation laws passed by a legislative body.

liberal one who advocates government action to protect individual liberties and rights; one who is broadminded.

litmus test issue an issue that tests a politician's ideology, whether liberal or conservative or something in between.

lobby the attempt to influence an elected official into voting a certain way on important legislation. Also, an organization that does the influencing.

lobbyist one who tries to influence a politician's decision on an upcoming vote.

logrolling voting for a colleague's issue so they'll return the favor and vote for yours; backscratching among politicians.

majority leader the head of the majority party in the House or Senate.

managed news government news released to the press to serve its own interests.

mandate a demand by the people to an elected official to carry out some action or to take a certain course of action, such as getting tough on environmental issues.

McCarthyism any kind of investigative probe that compromises one's rights and invades one's privacy unjustly.

minority leader the head of the minority party in the House or Senate.

moderate one who takes a middle-of-the-road position on an issue.

mollycoddle to pamper or spoil constituents at taxpayer expense, for example, to vote for every welfare program that is proposed.

mossback one strongly opposed to progress and change.

muckraker a journalist who works to expose government corruption and incompetence.

mudslinging the trading of insults and unsubstantiated charges between politicians; a smear campaign.

mugwump one who frequently votes the opposite of his party's wishes.

nonpartisan neutral; not favoring any one party. An issue in which party ideology is irrelevant.

old guard nickname for conservative Republicans.

oligarchy a government run by a few individuals, such as one run by one family.

ombudsman a government official who investigates citizen complaints against the government and tries to counteract its bureaucracy.

oval office the office of the president.

pairing an agreement between two politicians not to appear at an upcoming vote since their votes would cancel each other out.

palace guard the president's closest circle of advisers and friends; used pejoratively.

paper tiger a nation that flaunts a degree of power it does not have. Also, any danger that has been exaggerated or blown out of proportion.

party line the ideology, policies, and philosophy of a political organization.

pecking order a hierarchy; the chain of command from top to bottom.

Pentagonese abstruse military jargon.

perks the fringe benefits and special privileges accrued to politicians and people in power.

platform a set of promises and things to accomplish adopted by a candidate for office.

playing politics working more for the good of one's party than for the public interest.

play in Peoria the question, "how will it play in Peoria?" refers to the reaction and acceptance of an issue or idea from America's heartland.

plum, political an appointed office or position with good pay for little or no work.

point of order in a legislative meeting, an objection that a rule of order is not being followed correctly.

pork barrel the federal or state treasury from which a share of funds are taken from politicians for local projects.

presidential succession the political officials who move up in power in case something befalls the president in office. Specifically, the line of power is passed from the president to the vice president, followed by the Speaker of the House, the president pro tempore of the Senate, the secretary of state, and the secretary of the treasury.

President of the Senate the vice president serves as the President of the Senate, but rarely presides. See PRESIDENT PRO TEMPORE.

president pro tempore a senator chosen to take the place of the vice president as president of the Senate.

pressure group any organization that seeks to influence politicians through a variety of means.

primary an election of candidates for an upcoming general election.

progressive tax a tax based on a citizen's ability to pay. See regressive tax.

psephology the study of elections and voting patterns.

pump priming using federal money to provide momentum for a sagging economy.

pundit a columnist or broadcaster educated in politics and serving as an analyst or observer.

puppet a politician controlled or manipulated by others.

puppet government a nation controlled by the government of another nation.

purge to eliminate, either through violent or nonviolent means, opposition in a party or government.

quorum the minimum number of members of a legislative body who must be in attendance before official business can be conducted.

radical one who strongly advocates change in government.

reactionary one who favors returning to the politics and policies of the past.

red herring an issue used to distract the public from a more important issue, such as inflation.

referendum a submission to the public of an act, amendment, or statute for a vote.

regressive tax a tax that affects the poor more than the rich.

Republican party the more conservative of the two major parties. The Republican party is generally opposed to such government programs as welfare and favors less regulation for business.

rhetoric persuasive debate, argument, speech, or B.S., widely used by politicians.

right wing conservatives opposed to progress and favoring a return to the politics of the past.

roll call vote a vote in which the name of each member of a legislative body is called out and answered with either a "yea" or a "nay."

rubber chicken circuit election campaign touring and speaking at public luncheons and dinners in which the menu offerings are the least important part of the program.

secretary of state the chief foreign policy adviser to the president.

Security Council the U.S. council responsible for maintaining peace and preventing war.

sedition the inciting of a rebellion against the government.

sergeant at arms the legislative officer who controls access and maintains order in a legislative chamber.

shoo-in a candidate who is a sure winner in an election.

shuttle diplomacy the shuttling back and forth between capital cities of a diplomat involved in negotiations.

sleeper legislation that has more than the expected effect after being passed. Also, an amendment tacked onto a bill to soften or alter its meaning.

smear campaign an election campaign in which politicians slander one another.

sobriquets affectionate nicknames given to politicians, such as the Father of our Country, Rough Rider, the Chief.

sovereignty a nation's authority over its own affairs; self-government; independence.

Speaker of the House the Speaker of the House of Representatives, second in the line of succession after the vice president.

splinter group a dissenting group that splits off from a larger organization.

split ticket a ballot voting for candidates of more than one party.

stemwinder a crowd-rousing speaker or speech.

straw vote a sample or informal vote or poll taken before an election. Also known as a straw poll.

stump to make speeches in an election campaign.

suffrage the right to vote.

swing vote the population of people who vote for a candidate and not necessarily for the candidate's party affiliation.

swing voter one who has the power to decide an election one way or the other.

table a bill a motion to kill a bill or to remove it from consideration.

teller vote a House vote characterized by members passing by tellers who count them as either "for" or "against."

totalitarian an authoritarian government that is highly controlling of its people.

trickle down the economic theory that giving aid to corporations, for example, in the form of tax breaks or other benefits, results in a trickling down of benefits for employees and other citizens, ultimately resulting in stimulating the economy.

two-party system a political system having only two major parties, as the United States.

veto a president's objection to a bill in which the bill is returned unsigned to a legislature.

voice vote a vote in which all in favor say "yea" and all opposed say "no" or "nay."

waffle to hedge; to be wishy-washy and uncommitted to an opinion; to use weasel words.

weasel words ambiguous or unclear language used by politicians.

welfare state a government that provides an economic safety net (welfare) to its citizens.

whip the assistant to the leader of a party in the House or Senate.

witch-hunt an hysterical investigation with rampant finger pointing and blame-casting.

write-in on a ballot, the writing in of a candidate's name by a voter.

POLICE (*Also see* LAW)

A.C.U. anti-crime unit.

A.D.A. assistant district attorney.

A.P.B. all points bulletin; issued to help locate a fleeing suspect.

bag 'em slang; to place a corpse into a body bag.

banker a dealer or other street person who holds cash paid out for drugs.

book, the the rules and regulations of police procedure and law; to go by the book.

bucket the city jail.

bunco-forgery a division in a police department that handles consumer frauds, bribery cases, computer data base crimes, fraudulently printed checks, counterfeit money, forged airline tickets, theft of bank checks and checkwriting equipment, credit card fraud, forged prescriptions, pick-pocketing, and similar crimes. The responsibilities of such a division may vary somewhat from department to department.

C of D chief of detectives.

C of O chief of operations.

chop shop a facility, yard, or garage where stolen cars are stripped of their parts by thieves.

collar slang for arrest.

commissioner the city official who oversees a police chief and police department.

crime lab a laboratory that may work either within or independently of a police department to investigate and process toxics, explosives, narcotics, inflammables, unknown specimens, fingerprints, blood samples, urine, semen, saliva, hairs and fibers, DNA typing, tire impressions, footprints, firearms identification, document analysis, and so forth.

C.S.U. crime scene unit.

D.B. dead body.

division another name for a precinct.

d.o.a. dead on arrival.

frisk to pat a suspect down in search of weapons or contraband.

fugitive section a division within a large department that investigates and captures fugitives.

garden room slang for the morgue.

heist a robbery.

hit man a contracted killer.

holding pen a cell where the newly arrested wait to be booked.

homicide division the division within a department that investigates and processes murders.

hot slang referring to stolen property.

I.A.D. Internal Affairs Division. A division that investigates complaints against police or other department personnel.

john a prostitute's male customer.

jumper a bail jumper.

lead a clue.

mark a victim of a crime; a dupe.

M.E. medical examiner.

M.O. modus operandi; a criminal's method of operating.

narc slang for a narcotics officer.

narcotics division a division that handles crimes dealing with narcotics.

on the take one who is receiving stolen or illegal goods or money.

Organized Crime Intelligence Division a division that investigates and gathers information on members of organized crime.

piece a gun.

precinct a station house or area of a city a station house serves. Also known in some cities as a division.

rap sheet a criminal's record of arrests and convictions.

R.K.C. resident known criminal.

shadow to tail or follow a suspect.

stakeout waiting and observing surreptitiously at a location for a crime to occur.

S.W.A.T. special weapons and tactics or special weapons attack; an elite police force with paramilitary training.

tin slang for a police officer's badge.

vice division a division that processes cases involving gambling, prostitution, and pornography.

warrant a writ authorized by a judge to have an individual arrested.

whip an officer in charge.

wired carrying a concealed recording device.

zapped slang for shot.

FIRE FIGHTING

air tanker a large airplane equipped with a tank for dropping water or chemicals on a forest fire.

borate a saltlike substance used to put out fires.

borate bomber a large airplane equipped with a tank for dropping borate on a fire.

bucket brigade nickname for rural firefighting team comprising people in a line handing down buckets of water.

conflagration a huge, out-of-control fire that extends over a large area or through several buildings.

coop the communication center where calls are received in a fire station.

fire break a strip of land burned or plowed to stop the spread of an oncoming fire.

fire door a heavy door designed to hold back fire for at least 30 minutes.

fire wall a fireproof wall.

fog pattern a broad cloud of water sprayed continuously over an area to keep firemen cool while they work.

gooseneck crane a hinged crane equipped with water nozzles, used for fighting fires high up. Also known as a snorkel.

mars light the red, flashing beacon atop a fire truck.

outrigger a support leg that extends out the side of a ladder truck to help stabilize it.

pack pump a water tank worn on the back, used to carry water to brush fires.

resuscitator apparatus that forces air into the lungs of people suffering from smoke inhalation.

snorkel same as gooseneck crane.

superpumper a huge pump used to draw water from a river, lake, or other body of water.

tillerman one who steers the rear portion of a long, ladder truck.

turnout coat a fireman's waterproof, fireproof coat.

turntable the platform and hydraulic motor that raises a ladder and turns it on a ladder truck.

water cannon a cannon capable of shooting water up to 500 feet. Also known as a deluge gun.

FARMING

baler a machine that compresses and ties hay or straw into rectangles or round bales to facilitate storage.

barn raising the erection of a new barn with the help of neighbors, family, and friends, a popular event in rural America.

bocage farm land divided into fields by hedges and small trees, especially in France.

broadcast to spread seeds in a uniform manner.

bunker silo a horizontal silo built above or below ground.

byre a cow barn.

cash crops any crops intended to be sold for money, as distinguished from crops grown to feed livestock or to be consumed by the farmer's family.

cock a cone-shaped pile of hay or straw. Also known as a haycock.

combine a large harvesting machine that cuts, threshes, cleans, and bags grain.

compost decomposing organic matter used as fertilizer.

contour farming plowing and planting that follows the contours of uneven terrain to help prevent water runoff and soil erosion.

corncrib a storage building having slatted sides for the drying of corn.

cover crop a fast-growing crop sown to prevent erosion of the soil.

cow path a walled or fenced pathway leading from the barn and past crops to pasture for cows.

croft a small subsistence farm—usually comprising no more than 5 acres—in Scotland. The term is sometimes applied to small farms in other countries as well.

crop dusting applying pesticides on crops by airplane, helicopter, or other means.

cultivator an implement that breaks up the soil and uproots weeds around crops.

disk harrow a harrowing implement employing metal disks to break up the soil.

draft animal any animal, such as a large horse or ox, bred or used for pulling.

dry farming collective term for the methods used to raise crops where there is little rainfall and no irrigation. The crops chosen are those well-adapted to near-drought conditions; moisture-stealing weeds are carefully culled, and a mulch is placed over the soil to keep moisture from evaporating too quickly in the sun.

fallow barren; to leave a field unseeded after plowing.

flail chopper a machine used to cut and load standing forage crops.

fodder livestock feed, such as cornstalks, hay, straw.

forage harvester a machine that cuts up forage such as corn.

frost hollow a low area or hollow that tends to draw cold air from higher elevations and thus produces more killing frosts—avoided by farmers.

furrow the long channel or rut cut into soil by a plow.

green manure crop a crop, such as legumes, that restores nitrogen to the soil.

harrow an implement having either spikes or disks for leveling, breaking up clods, and refining plowed soil.

harvester any reaping machine.

haycock same as cock.

hayfork a pitchfork.

hayloft an upper story of a barn, where hay is stored.

headland the unplowed perimeter of a field, where the tractor and equipment can be driven and maneuvered without damaging crops.

husbandry the business of farming.

ley farming sowing an arable plot with grass to be used as pasture for several years.

manure spreader a machine used to spread fertilizer uniformly.

moldboard plow the classic, wedge-shaped plow, used by farmers for centuries.

mower a machine that cuts or mows hay.

pastoral farming the breeding and raising of cattle, sheep, horses, goats, reindeer, or other grass-eating animals.

pasture grass fields for grazing livestock.

planter a seeding machine that meters out and distributes seeds at uniform depths and intervals.

plowshare the cutting edge of a moldboard plow.

rake a tined or toothed implement pulled by a tractor to gather loose hay or to windrow hay for baling.

rotation of crops changing the type of crops grown in a field each year or every few years to help control weeds, pests, and diseases and to help maintain the fertility of the soil.

scythe an old-fashioned implement comprised of a long, curving blade held by a bent handle, used for mowing and reaping.

sickle a small version of a scythe with a straight, one-handed handle.

silage stored and fermented fodder.

silo a cylindrical storage building for fodder.

spreader any machine used to spread manure, lime, or other material in a uniform fashion.

subsistence farming crops and animals raised not to be sold but to be consumed by the farmer's family.

terracing plowing a shelf into a slope to slow water runoff.

thresh to separate grains or seeds from straw by beating the stems and husks.

thresher a machine that threshes.

tiller an implement having rotary tillers or blades for breaking up or plowing soil.

timothy the most commonly grown hay grass on U.S. farms.

truck farming intense farming of vegetable crops and their quick shipment to market by trucks.

windrow a long pile of hay left to dry in a field before being baled or bundled.

Language

WORDS ABOUT WORDS

accidence area of grammar that deals with the inflection of words.

A-copy news reporting term for trite or lazy copy lifted directly from a public relations press release.

acronym a word formed from the initial letters of a name, such as Light Amplification by Stimulated Emission of Radiation (LASER) or Mothers Against Drunk Driving (MADD).

adage a frequently quoted saying or proverb.

addendum something added or that will be added, as a supplement.

ad ignorantium Latin term referring to a statement made by a speaker that is true only to the degree of the listener's ignorance.

ad infinitum to infinity; to go on forever.

ad-lib to make an impromptu, unrehearsed, or improvised remark, speech, and so on.

ad nauseam to the degree of nausea; to continue to a sickening or ridiculous degree.

adnomination punning.

affectation in speech or writing, an unnatural, pretentious, or show-offy style that calls attention to itself.

affix an element of a word that is attached to other elements, such as a prefix or suffix.

agglutination the formation of new words by the combining of other words or word elements, as in dis-figure-ment or broncho-scope.

allegory a story or anecdote that uses metaphor to illustrate a deeper truth.

alliteration in speech or writing, a string of two or more words with the same-sounding initial consonants, as in "the silly sods sunk Sally's ship Sunday."

allonym a pen name that is the borrowed name of another, as distinguished from a pseudonym.

allusion an indirect, incidental, or casual reference that is more meaningful or significant than its presentation would imply.

alphabet soup the extravagant use of initialisms or acronyms, a common practice of the government and the military.

altiloquence any pompous speech or writing.

ambiguity a wording, remark, speech, story, or similar term having more than one meaning.

amphibology an unintentional ambiguity resulting from poor sentence construction, as in "faulty propellers will ground beef lift rescue plan."

anachronism a person, thing, word, saying, and such like placed in the incorrect time in history, as a character in a World War II novel who uses the words, "groovy" or "floppy disk."

anacoluthon in speech or writing, an unexpected change of syntax arriving at midsentence, such as "the flowers were in—but no, they weren't in bloom, come to think of it."

analogy a similarity in comparison between two different things or concepts; making a point by illustrating the similarities between two dissimilar things.

ananym one's name spelled backwards, sometimes used as a pseudonym.

anaphora the repetition of words or phrases for effect, as in "a big, bad man with a big, bad idea for a big, bad world."

anastrophe the reversal of the normal or standard order of words in a sentence construction, for effect, as in "off his rocker he goes."

anecdote a short, interesting account of an incident, often illustrating someone's personality or some historical event.

Anglicize to alter a word or name so that it sounds English, as in Arthur Greenburger to Art Green.

annotation a critical or explanatory note accompanying a literary work.

anonym an anonymous person or an anonymous publication. Also, a concept or idea that has no word to express or describe it.

antiphrasis a form of sarcasm or irony in which the exact opposite of the normal line is used, for effect, as in saying, "Great, wonderful!" in response to your car being stolen, or "it's a tough job, but someone's got to do it," when judging a beauty contest.

antithesis the juxtaposing of sharply contrasting ideas or words, as in "a noisy kind of peace can be found in the camaraderie of war."

antonym a word opposite in meaning to another word. The opposite of a synonym.

aphorism a brief statement that succinctly illustrates a principle or truth.

apocope the omission of a letter at the end of a word, as in "thinkin' " for "thinking."

apocrypha literary works of questionable authenticity or authorship.

aporia admitting to speechlessness; to be at a loss for words.

apostil an annotation in the margin.

archaism in speaking or writing, a word or expression that is out of date or antiquated, as in "forsooth, fair maiden."

argot any special vocabulary or jargon used by a group or class of people.

aside on the stage, a portion of dialogue intended for the ears of the audience only; any confidential dialogue.

assonance a resemblance in sound of words, syllables, or vowels, for effect, as in "winking, blinking, thinking—the robot looked about with alarm."

asyndeton leaving out conjunctions such as "and" between clauses, for effect, as in "we went to the store, walked in quietly, ordered three pounds of ham, left."

a verbis ad verbera from words to blows.

axiom a universally recognized truth or principle.

ballyhoo hype, exaggeration.

barb a sharp-tongued remark; a caustic observation.

barbarism the use of a word that is nonstandard or not accepted by society.

belles lettres literary works appreciated for their aesthetic value rather than their educational content, such as poetry, drama.

bidialectalism the use of two dialects, one informal and one formal or proper, within a language.

bilge b.s., worthless talk.

blarney sweet-talking flattery; b.s.

blather long-winded, stupid talk.

blurb a brief statement of praise or laudatory quote on a book cover.

bon mot a witticism.

brickbat an insult or blunt criticism.

bromide a common and overused remark or observation; a platitude.

cablese an extremely brief or shorthand style of writing, as in that found in a telegram.

cacography poor handwriting. Also, incorrect spelling.

cacology poor or improper pronunciation or diction.

cant whining, pleading, or monotonous speech. Also, any moral, hypocritical language. Also, the jargon of a group or class.

catachresis the incorrect use of a word that has been confused with another word. Also, a paradoxical figure of speech, as in "Latin has always been Greek to me."

catchfools words that are sometimes confused with one another because of their similarity in sound or spelling, for example, masticate and masturbate, deprecate and depreciate. Also known as dangerous pairs.

causerie any conversational or casual piece of writing.

charientism an insult so subtly presented that it is believed by the recipient to be unintended.

chestunt a joke, story, or expression, that has been around and repeated for too long.

cheval de bataille a phrase referring to a person's pet topic or favorite argument; literally, battle horse.

cheville an extraneous word added to the end of a line of poetry to make it flow evenly; literally, a rag.

circumlocution evasive or indirect language achieved by wordiness.

classicism any ancient Greek or Roman word or phrase in English.

chiché any tired, trite, unoriginal, stale, and overused expression.

clinquant a show-off style of writing.

clipped word a word that is clipped of letters or syllables or altered in some way for use in informal speech, such as flu for influenza or fish pole for fishing pole.

coinage the invention of a new word or expression.

colloquial in speech or writing, any natural conversational language; informal diction.

colloquialism an informal expression of everyday speech.

colloquy a formal or mannered conversation.

commoratio the pounding home of a point by repeating its principles in different words.

communique an official communication or announcement.

compendium a short summary.

comprobatio flattering a person in order to win them over in an argument.

connotation the implied or suggestive meaning of a word other than its literal one.

consensus gentium fallacy "common opinion of the nations." Refers to using the erroneous argument that something must be true because so many people believe it to be true.

constructio ad sensum the construction of sentences by sound or instinct rather than by grammatical rules.

contraction the shortening of a word through removal of one or more of its letters, sometimes indicated by an apostrophe, as in isn't for is not.

conundrum a perplexing riddle or problem whose answer involves a pun.

corruption an alternation of a word or term; an improper word usage.

creole a type of language that becomes dominant when two groups having their own languages integrate. Also known as creolized language.

dangler a misplaced modifier that gives a sentence an unintended and often humorous meaning, as in "riffling through my papers, the elephant appeared in front of me."

dead metaphor a metaphor that has become cliched.

decapitable sentence a poorly constructed sentence characterized by overlapping subordinate clauses. Also known as an accordion sentence.

diacritical mark a mark over a character or letter to indicate accent or pronunciation.

dialect a provincial form of a language, characterized by its own idiom, pronunciation, or grammar.

dichaeologia any form of rhetoric used to defend one's failure by blaming it on everything and everybody but oneself.

diction use and choice of words in speech and writing.

digression straying from the main topic.

dilogy any statement that has an unintentional double meaning.

dissertation a treatise; a formal and in-depth investigation or observation of a subject, as a thesis.

double entendre an ambiguous word or statement with an underlying meaning that is risqué or provocative.

double negative the incorrect use of two negatives in one sentence, as in "he doesn't know nobody there."

doublespeak wordy, evasive, or obscure language used to gloss over a subject or hoodwink listeners with circumlocution.

echoic word a word that sounds like the subject it represents, as in tick-tock, crackle, pop,, swish, gong.

elegy a poem or expression of lament, usually for the dead.

eloquence the fluent, persuasive use of language; expressiveness.

embolalia inserting useless words or utterances into speech to stall for time while collecting one's thoughts, such as "uh, you know, like, I mean, you know."

enallage improper use of tense, mood, or gender, for example, calling a herd of cows a herd of cow, or calling a woman a guy.

enunciate to pronounce words clearly and correctly.

epistolary written in the style of a letter or letters, as in some novels.

epithet word or term that characterizes a person or thing. Also, an adjective or descriptive word that forms part of a name, as in Richard the Lion Hearted.

eponym a person from whom a place or thing is named, as in Washington, Addison's disease, Phillips screwdriver.

equivocate to speak ambiguously in order to confuse or mislead.

esprit de l'escalier refers to the witty comment or snappy reply you wish you had said to someone earlier if you had only thought of it, literally, wit from the staircase.

etymology the origin and development of words; the derivation of words.

etymon the root or earliest form of a word, as a foreign word from which an English word is derived. A word's original meaning.

euphemism a substitution of an offensive word or phrase with a more acceptable one, as in "passed on" for "died."

eusystolism the substituting of initials for complete words, as a form of euphemism, as in S.O.B., B.S.

exemplum a short story or anecdote given to illustrate a moral.

exonym the foreign-language spelling of a native geographical name.

exposition a presentation of explanatory information, as distinguished from narrative or description.

expressionist a style of prose characterized by the use of symbolism and surrealism.

extemporaneous performed with little or no preparation, as an impromptu speech.

extrapolate to make an inference beyond the known facts; to surmise.

eyewash flattering or misleading talk; B.S.

facetiae humorous or ribald writings, anecdotes, sayings.

faction nonfiction presented in the style of fiction.

faux pas a socially unacceptable or embarrassing remark; literally, false step.

felicity any apt choice of words.

Freudian slip a slip of the tongue that inadvertently reveals what's on the mind of the speaker.

fused metaphor the incorrect joining of two metaphors; for example, "my monkey to bear" (my cross to bear; a monkey on my back).

fustian pompous or pretentious speech or writing.

Gallicism an English word or phrase derived from French.

glib speaking easily and fluently but superficially, smugly, or insincerely.

grammatism being overly concerned about the proper use of grammar.

hack a writer more concerned with making a buck than creating fine art; one whose writing is trite.

hackneyed writing that is trite, cliched, unoriginal, banal.

heterography inconsistent spelling usage, as in letters that are pronounced differently in different words, as in good and geriatric, car and cite.

heteronym a word having the same spelling as another but with a completely different meaning and pronunciation, as in bass (fish) and bass (drum) or bow (ribbon) and bow (boat).

heterophemy the inadvertent or incorrect use of a word that is similar in spelling or pronunciation to another word, such as cinnamon for synonym. Also, the use of a euphemism with a pregnant pause, as in "the president is . . . indisposed . . . if you know what I mean."

Hispanicism a Spanish word used in English, such as jalapeño, machismo.

hobbyhorse a pet topic or argument.

Hobson-Jobson the alteration of a foreign word into English, for example, compound from the Malay kampong, or grouper from the Portuguese garoupa.

homograph a word identical in spelling with another word but having a different pronunciation, as in bass (fish) and bass (drum).

homonym a word spelled or pronounced the same as another word but having a different meaning, for example, bow (ship) and bow (down).

homonym slip the incorrect writing of one word for another with the same or nearly the same pronunciation, for example, too for two, or then for than.

homophone a word pronounced the same as another but having a different spelling and meaning, such as peace, piece.

hybrid the joining of two words or word elements from two languages to form a new word.

hyperbole an exaggeration used as a figure of speech, such as "I could eat a horse," or "this hangnail is killing me."

hyperurbanism the innaccurate imitation of upper class speech by someone with a lower-class dialect.

hypophora reasoning with oneself out loud.

ideogram a character or symbol, such as $, &, or #. Also, any character used in Chinese writing.

idiolect the unique language of an individual.

idiologism a quirk or characteristic of an individual's speech.

idiom a particular form of speech within a language, as used in a specific community or group. Also, words, phrases, and expressions that cannot be translated literally into a foreign language, such as "life's a bitch," or "join the rat race."

idioticon a dictionary of dialect.

inarticulate unexpressive; the inability to speak fluently or persuasively.

innuendo a subtle implication or allusion, usually of something negative.

inversion the altering or reversal of normal word order, for effect, for example, "through the grass we did run."

irony the use of words to convey the opposite of their literal meaning, especially in a sacrcastic or humorous way, for example, "his wit was as sharp as a wet sponge."

Janus word a word having a double meaning the exact opposite of one another, such as inflammable, cleave.

jargon meaningless gibberish; the special language of a class, profession, or group.

jawbreaker a word that is difficult to pronounce.

je ne sais quoi literally, I don't know what; a certain indescribable something.

King's English normal or proper, understandable English.

laconic terse; reserved.

lallation any noise or utterance typical of a baby.

lapsus calami a slip of the pen.

lapsus linguae a slip of the tongue.

Latinism a Latin word or phrase used in English.

leading question a question designed to prompt a desired answer.

legalese legal jargon.

lethologica the inability to recall a word that is on the tip of one's tongue.

lethonomania forgetting names.

lexicography the compiling and writing of dictionaries and word books.

lexicology the study of word histories, derivations, meanings, and similar pursuits.

lexicon a dictionary, vocabulary book, foreign language word book, or similar publication.

linguistics the study of language and speech.

litotes a form of irony or understatement, achieved by the use of inverted phrasing, for example, "not bad," or "I can't disagree with that."

localism a word or expression unique to a particular community or region.

loganamnosis an obsession to remember a forgotten word.

logomasia an extreme distaste for certain words.

lost positives words whose positive forms are no longer in common use, such as "gruntled" from disgruntled.

lyricism prose executed in a poetically descriptive style.

malapropism the incorrect use of a word that sounds similar to another word, often with humorous results, for example, "I'll sue him for defecation (defamation) of character," or "a pigment (figment) of the imagination."

malonym a metaphor, cliché, or popular expression in which an incorrect word is used, for example, "let's go hole (whole) hog on this," or "you can lead a horse to water but you can't make him think (drink)."

mealymouthed dishonesty, evasiveness; overly euphemistic in speech.

meiosis a form of understatement or underemphasis used to achieve an ironic effect.

melioration the acquisition of a positive meaning by a word that has traditionally had a negative meaning, for example, "bad" is now sometimes used as the equivalent of "cool" or "good."

mendaciloquence artful lying.

metaphor a figure of speech characterized by an implied comparison between two things that are different, for example, "all the world's a stage," or "the evening of life," or "the company is a big ship to turn around."

metastasis in a debate, the mentioning of a subject in a casual manner, as if it were trivial.

metathesis the historical transposing of letters or syllables in a word to create a new, permanent spelling or pronunciation, such as, Old English "brid" to "bird."

metonymy a figure of speech that substitutes a word or phrase with a word or phrase that is closely associated, as in "brass" for military officers, or "the Crown" for British monarchy.

metric prose prose with a poetic rhythm.

mincing word a coyly euphemistic word used to avoid using an undainty word.

misnomer an incorrect word, name, title, belief, and so forth.

mixaprop a fusion of a mixed metaphor and a malapropism, for example, "It took more wind out of his sails than a fish without water."

mixed metaphor the incorrect fusing of two or more metaphors in a single sentence, such as "if he faces the music, it will fall on deaf ears."

neologism a newly created word or expression; an old word given a new meaning. Also, a meaningless or nonsense word coined by a mentally ill person.

nom de plume a pen name; a pseudonym.

non sequitur a remark that is not relevant to the argument at hand; an inference that does not follow from the premise; literally, it does not follow.

nosism the annoying use of "we" to denote oneself in speech or writing.

nudis verbis in naked words.

obfuscation to make unclear or obscure; to use overblown or highly technical language pretentiously.

officialese bureaucratic jargon; government obfuscation; official, formal language.

off-the-cuff spoken casually without preparation; to ad-lib.

onomatopoeia the use of a word that sounds like what it represents, as in chirp, boom, gurgle, swish.

oxymoron a figure of speech characterized by the juxtaposition of words that seem incongruous or contradictory, as in a "cheerful pessimist," "cruel kindness," "eloquent silence."

pabulum insipid writing or ideas; mindless drivel.

padding intentional wordiness, used to lengthen a written work or speech.

palilogy repeating a word in a sentence, for effect.

pan a bad review.

pap same as pabulum.

paradiastole the use of euphemistic language to describe something, as in describing a brothel as a "spirited household."

paradox an apparently contradictory statement that may nevertheless be true, for example, "The man in the time travel story traveled back in time, shot his parents, and then ceased to exist."

paraphrase a restating in different words.

parataxis the use of sentences without conjunctions, especially "and" or "but."

parlance a characteristic manner of speech.

paroemiology the subject of proverbs.

paronym a word having the same derivation or root as another word, as in "beautiful" and "beauteous."

parrot to repeat mindlessly what someone else has said; to imitate without understanding, as a parrot.

pathopoeia agitating or arousing emotion through rhetoric.

pedantry showing off one's education through speech or writing.

personification giving human attributes to abstractions or inanimate objects.

philology the study of historical linguistics.

philophronesis acting submissive and humble in order to mollify someone's anger.

phoneticism a word spelled differently than normal to illustrate its pronunciation, such as the Australian word "mate" spelled "mite."

platform rhetoric the form of oratory most commonly used by politicians.

platitude a trite remark; an obvious or simple observation presented as if it were brilliant.

poetic license breaking the standard rules of form, diction, style, in poetry or prose.

polysyndeton the frequent use of conjunctions, especially *and*, in a sentence with multiple clauses.

pontificate to speak with pompous authority.

prosonomasia a form of pun composed of someone's name, for example, Larry Bird-beak, Katherine Lipburn.

pseudandry the use of a man's pen name by a female writer.

pseudogyny the use of a woman's pen name by a male writer.

psychobabble the jargon used by psychologists and psychiatrists, and especially by those who try to imitate them.

purple prose overblown, overwritten, flowery, or ornate prose; overly poetic prose.

red herring an irrelevant issue designed to draw attention away from the matter at hand, frequently used by politicians and mystery writers.

redundancy unnecessary repetition, as in "merge together," "erupt violently," "gather together," "free gift."

rehash stuff that has been done before; old, reworked material.

rejoinder a reply to a reply.

repartee witty or clever banter.

rhetoric the art of persuasive oratory or writing; the style, content, and structure of speech or writing.

rhetorical question a question that requires no answer; a question with an obvious answer.

satire a literary work that uses irony, wit, and humor to expose evil or folly.

satirist a person who writes satires or who uses wit and humor to expose evil or folly.

saw an old saying often repeated.

semantics the study of the development and change of word meanings throughout history.

simile a figure of speech characterized by the comparison of two unlike things, as in "he hissed like a snake," or "the cliffs rose like cathedral spires."

Socratic irony feigning ignorance in a debate in order to win a point.

soliloquy a dramatic monologue; a speech made aloud to oneself when alone.

spoonerism an inadevertent transposing of word sounds, as in "Hoobert Heever" for Herbert Hoover," or a "White Horse souse" for a "White House source."

staccato a form of speech or writing characterized by the frequent use of short, abrupt sentences, for effect.

stemwinder a crowd-agitating speech.

stream of consciousness in speech or writing, inner dialogue, or the articulation of one's thoughts and emotions.

succinct articulated clearly and to the point with the use of as few words as possible.

suppressio veri suppressing the facts; deliberately ignoring or failing to mention information that may alter someone's decision, as in a court trial.

surrealistic descriptive writing that evokes images of dreams, nightmares, hallucinations, and the unconscious.

synonym a word having the same or similar meaning to another word, such as car and automobile. The opposite of antonym.

syntax the manner in which words, clauses, and sentences are constructed or arranged.

tacenda things that are better off left unsaid.

terse succinct, to the point.

transliteration the altering of letters or words to fit them into another language, as "snap, crackle, pop" translates to "poks, riks, raks" in Finnish.

trite unoriginal, stale, banal.

tu quoque in a debate, accusing a rival of criticizing that which he himself is guilty of.

twaddle foolish, silly talk.

verbatim word for word.

verbiage wordiness.

vernacular native language of a region. Also, trade jargon or idiom.

vogue word a currently hip-to-use word; a word in fashion.

waffle to speak vaguely or evasively.

weasel word any word used to mislead, evade, or whitewash.

whitewash to gloss over a wrong.

GRAMMATICAL TERMS

adjective a word that describes or limits a noun or a pronoun.

adjective, descriptive a word that describes a noun or a pronoun, such as a "beautiful" woman.

adjective, limiting a word that limits a noun or a pronoun, such as "ten" apples, "five fingers," "triple" play.

adjective, proper a descriptive adjective of a proper noun, such as "American" music.

adverb a word or term that modifies a verb, adjective, or another adverb, for example, he ran "quickly," or his pants were "really" strange, or "she walked "very" softly.

agreement in a sentence, the agreement of verbs or other word components in mood, tense, or number.

antecedent a word, phrase, or clause to which a pronoun refers.

antithesis a contrast of ideas within a sentence or paragraph.

apposition a noun or noun phrase placed next to another of the same as a means of explanation, for example, "Boggs, the third baseman . . . ," or "Smith, the house treasurer. . . ."

clause a group of words, including a subject and a predicate, constituting one unit of a compound sentence.

climax in a sentence, the placement of the most important idea last or in the last clause, for strongest impact.

conjugation the inflection of verbs.

conjunction a word that connects clauses or sentence parts, as in "and," "but," "because," "as."

contraction a shortening of a word by the removal of one or more of its letters, replaced by an apostrophe, such as I'll (I will), can't (cannot).

dangler a misplaced modifier that gives a sentence an unintended and sometimes humorous meaning, for example, "Riffling through my papers, the blue jay appeared at the window."

double negative the incorrect use of two negatives in one sentence, such as "He doesn't know nobody there."

gerund the verb form ending in *-ing*, when used as a noun.

infinitive a verb form without limitation of person or number.

inflection the change of a word's form to indicate case, gender, mood, tense, or voice.

interjection an exclamation, especially one that can stand alone, such as "Oh!" or "Heavens!"

modifier a word or clause that limits or qualifies the meaning of another word or words.

noun a name of a person, place, thing, quality.

noun, abstract the name of an idea, quality or other abstraction, such as happiness, knowledge, etc.

noun, collective a name of more than one thing, such as class, club, team.

noun, concrete a name for something that can be perceived through the senses, such as shirt, sky, clouds, smoke, foot.

noun, diminutive a name of something small or young, such as duckling, kitchenette, booklet, ringlet.

noun, gender a noun that indicates sex, such as bachelor, sister, buck, doe, widow, widower.

noun, proper a name of a person or place, or institution, such as Mary, Chicago, *New York Times*.

paradigm a list or table of all the inflectional forms of a word or class of words.

plural a form of a word expressing more than one, such as apples, people, baskets.

predicate in a clause or sentence, a verb and its modifiers.

prefix a form or affix placed at the beginning of a word to alter its meaning, as in *pre*fabricate or *re*run.

preposition a word that indicates the relation of a substantive to a verb, adjective, or other substantive, such as at, by, in, to, from.

pronoun a word that serves as a substitute for a noun to prevent awkward repetition in a sentence.

sentence, complex a sentence having one principal clause and one or more subordinate clauses, for example, "We are going now because it is late."

sentence, compound a sentence having two or more independent clauses, for example, "The fire is out and I am going home."

sentence, declarative a sentence that states, asserts, or affirms, for example, "The dog is mine."

sentence, exclamatory a sentence that expresses sharp emotion, for example, "The dog got away!"

sentence, imperative a sentence that commands, as in "Do not come any closer with that dog."

sentence, interrogative a sentence that questions, as in "Did you see the brown dog?"

singular denoting one of a thing, as distinguished from the plural form of a word.

split infinitive an infinitive in which the word "to" is separated from the verb, as in "to really think."

suffix a form or affix added to the end of a word to alter its meaning, such as sing*ing*, fond*ness*.

tense the verb form denoting past, present, or future, for example, "They were, they are, they will be."

verb a word that expresses action, such as "run," "hit," "sing," "throw," "drive."

verb, auxiliary a helping verb that modifies the meaning of a principal verb; for example, in the sentence "I have eaten," have is auxiliary.

verb, causative a verb causing an action and usually having the suffix "en" added to its end, such as whiten, brighten, shorten, tighten.

verb, copula a linking verb, such as be, become, seem, get.

voice, active refers to the performing of an action by the subject in a sentence, as in "He painted the picture," as distinguished from the passive voice.

voice, passive refers to the subjects of a sentence being acted upon, as in "The picture was painted by him."

WORD GAMES

acrostic a poem, paragraph, or other composition in which initials or other conspicuous letters combined spell out a word or message.

alternade the creation of two words from one by assembling alternate letters, as in "calliopes": CLIPS
ALOE

anagram a word or phrase created by transposing the letters in another word or phrase.

antigram same as an anagram but with an altered word or phrase that is the opposite or reverse in meaning to the original word or phrase.

beheadment the removal of an initial letter of a word to form a new word, as in blather to lather.

charade dividing a word—without changing letter placement—to form multiple words, as in "significant,"—sign if I can't.

charitable word a word in which any of its letters may be removed and still remain a word, as in "seat": eat, sat, set, sea.

curtailment removing the last letter of a word to leave another word, as in "goon" to "goo."

kangaroo word a word that contains within itself another word that is a synonym of itself, as in "evacuate" to "vacate."

letter rebus a rebus comprised of letters only, as in a "B" standing for "abalone" ("a B alone").

linkade joining two words with one overlapping letter to create a new word, as in "pass" and "sing" to form "passing."

lipogram a composition written entirely without the use of a particular letter, such as Ernest Wright's, *Gadsby*, which does not contain the letter *e* anywhere in its text.

metallege transposing two letters in a word to create another word, as in "nuclear" to "unclear."

nonpattern word a word in which each letter is used only once.

palindrome a word spelled the same backwards as forwards, as in "redivider," or a phrase spelled the same each way, as in "A man, a plan, a canal, Panama."

pangram a phrase or sentence containing all the letters of the alphabet, constructed with as few letters as possible.

paronomasia to make a pun out of a popular expression, as in "the rock-hunting nudists left no stone unturned and no stern untoned."

piano word a word in which all of its letters can be played as notes (a, b, c, d, e, f, g) on a musical instrument, as in "cabbage."

rebus a visual puzzle using pictures, symbols, letters, numbers, characters, and so on, that must be deciphered by reading it aloud, as in YYURYYUBICURYY4 me = too wise you are, too wise you be, I see you are to wise for me.

reversal a word that becomes another word when read backwards, as in "live" to "evil."

stinky pinky a noun joined with an adjective that rhymes, such as "fat cat."

Tom Swiftie the creation of a quotation followed by a punning adverb, such as "your eggs are on fire," he said hotly.

transposition creating a new word by rearranging the letters of another word, as in "ocean" from "canoe."

typewriter word a word that can be typed on a single row of a typewriter, such as the word "typewriter."

univocalic a sentence in which only one vowel can be used, as in "it sits in its pit."

VOICE AND PHONETICS

africative a sound or consonant produced by the tongue and hard palate, such as the "ch" sound in chicken, the "tch" sound in match, and the "dge" sound in judge.

alveolar sound a sound produced by the tip of the tongue touching the area of the alveolar ridge, such as *S*, *T*, and *D*.

articulate to speak or pronounce clearly.

brogue an Irish accent; any strong accent.

burr a rough, guttural trilling of the letter *R*, produced by vibrating the uvula against the back of the tongue, as in Scottish pronounciation. To speak with a burr.

cacology improper pronunciation of words.

cadence the measured flow of one's speech; modulation.

consonant the speech sound produced by teeth, tongue, or lips, as distinguished from vowel sounds.

dentiloquist one who speaks with clenched teeth.

dialect the manner of speech, idiom, and pronunciation of a region, as in a southern dialect.

elocution the manner of speaking, especially public speaking.

enunciate to articulate or pronounce words clearly.

fricative a consonant produced by forcing air through a partially closed passage, such as *F, V, S, Z, SH, TH*.

glossolalia nonsensical, incoherent speech, especially that associated with the mentally ill.

inflection a varying of tone or pitch.

intone to chant; to speak in a singing voice, as a prayer; to speak in a monotone.

labial sounds or consonants formed by closing or partially closing the lips, such as *B, M, V, W.*

labialize to round a vowel.

labiodental a sound produced by the lips and teeth.

labionasal a sound produced by the lips and nose together.

labiovelar a sound produced by the lips and the tongue touching the soft palate.

lallation lulling sounds, as with a baby; baby sounds.

linguistics the science of language and speech.

mellifluous a rich, smooth, or resonant tone of voice.

modulation the variation of volume, tone, or pitch; a variation of inflection.

monotone a tone of voice lacking inflection or expression.

morpheme the smallest meaningful unit of language.

orotund forceful and resonant.

paralinguistic all forms of communication that accompany speech, as in tone of voice, speech tempo, gestures, facial expressions.

phoneme the smallest unit of speech.

sibilance suggestive of a hissing sound, as in *S, SH, Z, ZH.*

sibilate to hiss.

singsong a monotonous rising and falling of voice pitch, often used when taunting another.

stentorian a loud, powerful voice.

uvular sound a sound produced by the uvular or by the back of the tongue touching the uvular.

velar a sound produced by the back of the tongue on the soft palate. Also known as a gutteral sound.

vowel a sound or letter produced by the passage of air through the larynx, as distinguished from consonants.

MODERN RELIGIONS

CHRISTIANITY

abbess the female superior of an abbey; the female version of an abbot.

abbey a monastery or convent.

abbot the male superior of an abbey or monastery.

ablutions the washing of the hands before or after certain religious ceremonies, such as before Catholic Mass.

abomination anything repugnant to God.

absolution the forgiveness of sins.

acolyte one who assists a priest or minister at the altar, for example, by lighting or extinguishing candles or handling the offerings.

Acts of the Apostles the new testament book describing Christian history.

Advent the birth of Christ; the Second Coming of Christ. Also, the four weeks preceding Christmas.

Adventists, Second a denomination that believes that the Second Coming will soon arrive and prophesizes the date.

Adventists, Seventh Day a denomination that believes that the Second Coming will soon arrive but does not prophesy a date.

agape in the early Christian Church, a love feast or communal meal of thanksgiving held with the Eucharist.

agnostic one who neither believes nor disbelieves in God due to a lack of evidence or proof.

Agnus Dei the Lamb of God; an icon representing this.

agrapha Greek for "things that are not written," referring to any words of Jesus not included in the Bible's four Gospels but found in other sources.

All Saints' Day observed on November 1, a day commemorating martyrs and saints.

All Souls' Day observed on November 2, a day of prayer commemorating those Christians believed to be in purgatory.

almsgiving giving gifts or money to the poor, a religious practice around the world.

amen Hebrew for, "to trust," denoting faithfulness.

anathema damned; a ban or excommunication.

Angelus a Roman Catholic prayer recited at 6 A.M., noon, and 6 P.M. to commemorate the Annunciation. Also the bell used to announce this prayer.

Annunciation the angel Gabriel's announcement to the Virgin Mary that she would conceive a son.

anoint to apply oil to the body to initiate one into divine service.

Antichrist "he who is against Christ." The great antagonist or "man of lawlessness" posing as a religious leader who will be defeated and banished with Christ's Second Coming. Also known as "the beast."

Apocalypse the last book of the new testament; a revelation of the world to come.

Apocrypha collections of proverbs, sermons, and texts excluded from the Hebrew Bible because they were thought not to be inspired by God. Roman Catholic Bibles include all but two of these texts in the Old Testament. Protestants, however, consider them uncanonical.

apostasy the abandonment of one's religious faith.

apostate one who gives up his faith.

apostle one of the 12 witnesses chosen by Christ to preach the gospel.

Apostles' Creed the oldest statement of Christian faith, sometimes ascribed to the 12 apostles, beginning, "I believe in God the Father Almighty, maker of heaven and earth. . . ."

archangel a chief or high angel, including Michael, Gabriel, and Raphael.

archbishop the highest ranking bishop; he oversees an archdiocese.

archdeacon a priest who oversees a territory and assists a bishop.

archdiocese in the Roman Catholic Church, a diocese under the jurisdication of an archbishop.

Ark of the Covenant the ornate, acacia wood chest containing the Ten Commandments, carried by Hebrews into battle, and responsible for bringing down the walls of Jericho. Sometimes referred to as the footstool of God.

Armageddon "mountain of Megiddo." The location of the final battle between the forces of The Lord Jesus Christ and the Antichrist, as prophesized by the Bible in Revelation 19:16.

Ascension Christ's ascent to heaven on a cloud, commemorated on the 40th day after Easter Sunday, known as Holy Thursday.

Ash Wednesday the first day of Lent, the 40-day period of fasting and repentance preceding Easter. The name is derived from the ash of burned palm branches (from Palm Sunday) dabbed in the configuration of a cross on members of the congregation by a priest.

Assumption in Roman Catholic and Eastern Orthodox Churches, a feast on August 15 to commemorte the resurrection of the Virgin Mary.

atheism the denial of the existence of God.

atonement the making of amends for sins.

avarice greed, one of the seven cardinal or "deadly" sins.

baptism a ceremony through which a young child or an adult becomes a member of the church. In Baptist churches, adults are fully immersed in water. In Eastern Churches and Roman Catholic Churches, young children are sprinkled with or immersed in water three times and sometimes anointed with oil.

Baptist Church the Christian Protestant church that baptizes adults but not infants.

beatification the step prior to canonization, in which the Pope declares a deceased person to be blessed and therefore worthy to be prayed to for help or guidance.

beatific vision seeing God directly.

Beelzebub in the New Testament, the "prince of demons"; synonymous with Satan.

Benedictines nuns or monks who conduct their lives by the Rule of St. Benedict—with emphasis on stability, study, work, worship, and obedience to the abbot.

benediction the act of blessing at the end of a service. In the Roman Catholic Church, the Benediction of the Blessed Sacrament.

benefice any property held by a church.

bishop a high-ranking minister in the Roman Catholic, Anglican, Orthodox, and other churches, who oversees a diocese.

blasphemy to speek evil against God; to curse the name of the Lord.

breviary a books of hymns, prayers, and instructions for reciting daily services in a Roman Catholic Church.

canon ecclesiastical laws, codes, or authoritative writings of a religion. Also, the books of the Bible officially accepted by the Church.

canonical hours the prayers that, according to canonical law, should be recited at specific times of the day. Also, the hours when these prayers are said.

canonize in the Roman Catholic Church, to declare a deceased person a saint after beatification.

canticle a song or chant with words taken from Biblical text; a nonmetrical hymn.

cardinal an official elected by the Pope to advise and assist him in governing the church. Cardinals rank just below the Pope in the Catholic hierarchy; they are responsible for electing a new pope when one dies.

catechism a short book that, in question and answer format, instructs candidates for confirmation in Christian doctrine.

celebrant the presiding priest or minister at the consecration of the bread and wine at Holy Communion or Mass.

celibacy the practice of abstaining from sexual intercourse, a requirement of the Catholic priesthood; the vow of celibacy.

chaplain a rabbi, priest, or minister serving a hospital, prison, school, or military base.

charge a parish.

Charismatics Christians who believe they are blessed with the gift of tongues, healing, or prophesy.

cherubim the second order of angels, below archangels.

chrism in the Roman Catholic and the Orthodox Church, the holy oil used in confirmation rituals.

christening the ceremony of baptizing and giving a name to an infant.

collect a short prayer before the reading of the epistle in the Mass of the Roman Catholic Church.

College of Cardinals the body of cardinals in the Roman Catholic Church.

communion fellowship. See EUCHARIST.

conclave a secret meeting of cardinals to elect a new pope. Also, the location of this meeting.

concupiscence theological term for the desire for the forbidden, especially sex; lust.

confession the admission of sins to a priest in the Roman Catholic Church.

confessor a male saint who did not die a martyr's death, such as most monks, bishops, priests, religious lay persons.

confirmation a service admitting a baptized infant or adolescent into the Church with the gift of the Holy Spirit.

consecrate to bless or make sacred. To change bread and wine into the body and blood of Christ in the Roman Catholic Church.

consistory a meeting of cardinals to conduct business or to appoint bishops.

contrition repentance for having sinned.

convocation an assembling of clergy members to discuss church affairs.

Coptic Church the Christian churches of Egypt and Ethiopia.

corrupt text any Bible passages that have been modified.

covenant a testament or agreement between church members to defend and support the faith.

Dead Sea Scrolls several parchment scrolls dated from about the first century and discovered in caves near the Dead Sea in 1947. The scrolls include hymns, laws, teachings, and the oldest texts of the Old Testament of the Bible.

dean in the Roman Catholic Church, a priest who oversees several parishes. Also, the superior of a cathedral.

defrock to remove the authority from a minister due to unethical behavior.

denomination any branch or sect of the Christian Church.

diocese a district supervised by a bishop. Also known as an eparchy in the Eastern Orthodox Church.

dispensation in the Roman Catholic Church, a bending of the rules in cases of hardship, for example, allowing someone to ignore the fast on Good Friday for health reasons.

district superintendent in the Methodist Church, a supervisor of ministers in a district.

divine office in the Roman Catholic Church, the public prayers, psalms, hymns, readings.

divinity the essence of God and all divine things.

Eastern Orthodox Church the Church of Eastern Europe, the Soviet Union, and the eastern Mediteranean. Also known as the Orthodox Church.

ecclesiastic a priest or minister; a clergyman.

ecumenical pertaining to the unity of the Christian Church around the world.

Epiphany a festival held on January 6 in the Catholic, Orthodox, and Protestant Churches to commemorate the visit of the wise men at Christ's birth.

Episcopal Church the Anglican Church in the United States, Canada, and Scotland. Unlike other Protestant churches, Episcopal churches are governed by bishops.

epistle one of the letters written by the apostles in the New Testament and recited as part of a service.

Eucharist the main sacrament commemorating the Last Supper. The bread and the wine, as the body and blood of Christ, are eaten and drunk by worshippers. Also known as Communion, Holy Communion, and Mass.

evangelism spreading the word of Christ throughout the world through missions.

evangelist one who spreads the word of Christ.

evensong an Anglican evening service similar to Catholic vespers.

ex cathedra "from the chair"; referring to a pronouncement made by the authority of ones office.

excommunication the cutting off from or exclusion from the Catholic church membership or from religious rites, especially that of receiving Holy Communion, due to certain transgressions against the Church.

faith healing the healing of a sick person through prayer and faith in God rather than through medical intervention.

Franciscans the order of Anglican and Roman Catholic friars, founded by St. Francis of Assisi.

friar similar to a monk, but one who is not bound to a single community. A Franciscan, Dominican, or Carmelite.

fundamentalism the 20th-century Protestant movement that holds that the Bible is infallible and should be taken as the literal truth, despite scientific or historical evidence to the contrary.

genuflect to get down on one knee in worship.

glossolalia speaking in tongues, a gift of the Holy Spirit. An unknown language spoken to communicate visions or prophecies, especially in the Pentecostal Church.

Good Friday the day on which Christ's crucifixion is commemorated.

gospels the four accounts of the life and death of Christ by Matthew, Mark, Luke, and John.

hagiarchy a country governed by holy men. Also, a hierarchy of saints.

hands, laying on of healing someone by channeling God's power through touch.

Hebrew Bible the Old Testament.

heresy anything against traditional religious doctrine or dogma.

heretic one who dissents from his religion's doctrine or dogma.

Holy Communion the service of the Eucharist.

Holy Innocents Day a festival held on December 28 commemorating the murder of Bethlehem's male children under 2, as ordered by King Herod.

Holy Land Israel or Palestine.

holy orders the rite of ordination to the priesthood.

Holy Week the last week of Lent.

host the round wafers of unleavened bread used in Holy Communion.

Immaculate Conception in the Roman Catholic Church, the doctrine that holds that the Virgin Mary was free from Original Sin since her conception.

infidel a member of another religion, in regard to Christianity or Islam. Also, one with no religious beliefs.

intercession the Roman Catholic or Orthodox Christian's prayer to a saint requesting that they pray directly to God on their behalf. Prayers made through saints or angels are believed to be more effective.

Isa Arabic for Jesus.

Jesuit a member of the Society of Jesus, a Roman Catholic order.

King James Bible the translation of the Bible into English, as ordered by King James I; it was first published in 1611.

kiss of peace a greeting kiss in the Roman Catholic Mass, the Orthodox Eucharist, and the Lutheran Communion.

laity the nonclergy members of a congregation.

lauds the hour of morning worship in Catholic divine office.

lectionary a book containing lessons from the Bible to be read at services.

Lent the 40-day period, beginning with Ash Wednesday, before Easter Sunday.

litany a prayer of supplications recited by a clergy alternating with replies from the congregation, either sung or spoken.

liturgy the rite of the Eucharist. Also, public worship or any religious ritual. Also, the Book of Common Prayer.

Lutheran Church the Protestant Church that follows the teachings of Martin Luther.

Madonna the Virgin Mary. Also, any depiction, such as a painting, of the Virgin Mary.

martyr one killed for his religious beliefs.

Mass the Roman Catholic term for the Eucharist or Holy Communion.

Maundy Thursday the day of the Last Supper and the day Jesus washed the feet of his disciples.

mendicants friars who take a vow of poverty and live entirely from alms.

Mennonites the Protestant denomination that baptizes adults, stresses nonresistance, and rejects war and violence.

missal in the Roman Catholic Church, a book containing a year of instructions, readings, and prayers for the Mass.

monotheism the belief in only one God.

nones the service that takes place at 3 P.M. at Roman Catholic and Eastern Orthodox Churches.

Original Sin the first sin—that of Adam and Eve eating of the tree of knowledge of good and evil.

Palm Sunday the Sunday before Easter; it commemorates Christ riding into Jerusalem on a donkey, when palms were spread in welcome before him.

papacy the supreme office of the Pope.

papal authority the leadership of the Pope in governing the Roman Catholic Church.

parish a local Catholic community within a specific territorial district.

paschal candle in Roman Catholic and several Anglican Churches, a tall candle lit the night before Easter and kept burning near the altar until the feast of the Ascension or Pentecost Sunday. Also known as the Easter Candle.

Passion the suffering of Christ from the Last Supper to his crucifixion, on our behalf, as recounted from Gospels as a part of Holy Week services.

pastor "shepherd." A minister in the Lutheran, Baptist, and Pentecostal Churches.

patriarch the highest ranking bishop in the Eastern Orthodox Church.

patron saint in the Roman Catholic Church, a saint who has been designated as a special guardian or protector of a nation, community, profession, group, individual, and so forth. Also, any saint for whom an individual is named at baptism.

penance a sacrament comprised of contrition, confession, the imposition of a good work, or the saying of prayers and absolution.

penitent one who has sinned and wishes to repent. Also, a person who confesses his or her wrongdoings to a priest at confession.

Pentecost a festival held on the seventh Sunday after Easter to commemorate the descent of the Holy Spirit after Christ's Ascension. Also known as Whitsunday or Whit Sunday.

Pentecostal Church a multidenominational group of churches stressing the need for believers to receive the Baptism of the Holy Spirit. Most noted for congregation members who spontaneously "speak in tongues" during a service and who claim to have the gift of healing or prophecy.

plainsong a method of chanting psalms or hymns.

polytheism a belief in more than one god.

pontiff the Pope.

Pope the head of the Roman Catholic Church and the bishop of Rome.

Presbyterian Church the Christian Protestant denomination with a doctrine based on the teachings of Calvin. Noted for its lack of elaborate rituals and plain churches.

presbytery a minister's house, often located beside a church.

primate in an Anglican district or group of dioceses, the highest ranking bishop. Also, the highest ranking bishop in a country.

proselyte one who converts from one faith to another.

psalter a book of psalms from the Old Testament.

rector in the Anglican Church, a clergyman in charge of a parish.

rectory the house of a Catholic priest or an Episcopal minister.

requiem a Roman Catholic funeral mass set to music to aid the deceased through purgatory to heaven.

resurrection the restoration of the life of Jesus by God after Christ's crucifixion. Also, the rising of souls from the bodies of the dead.

rosary a circle of beads used as an aid to prayer. Also, a prayer to God directed through the Virgin Mary.

sacrament any one of several rites performed in the Church to receive God's grace. In the Roman Catholic Church, these include baptism, confirmation, the Eucharist, matrimony, orders, penance, and extreme unction. In the Protestant Church, only baptism and the Eucharist are considered sacraments.

sanctus a hymn sung before the prayer of consecration at a Eucharist service.

sanctus bell a bell rung at Roman Catholic Mass to draw attention to the consecration of the bread and wine.

see the center of a bishop's diocese.

seminary a religious training institution for priests and ministers.

seven virtues in Roman Catholic theology, prudence, justice, fortitude, temperance, faith, hope, and charity.

shunning an Amish and Mennonite practice of refusing to socialize with excommunicated members in any way.

synod an ecclesiastical council.

theophany a manifestation of God, as through fire or thunder.

tithe one-tenth; to donate one-tenth of one's income to the church, practiced by some Christians according to Mosaic law.

transfiguration a festival held on August 6 to commemorate Christ's appearance before the Apostles. Known as the Feast of Tabor in the Eastern Orthodox Church.

Trappist a strict order of monks, known for their fasting and extended periods of silence.

Trinity the Holy Trinity; the Father, the Son, and the Holy Ghost.

Unification Church founded by Korean Sun Myung Moon in 1954, the church having a doctrine based on a conglomeration of Christian and Taoist ideas.

Unitarian Church the church noted for its philosophy that all faiths lead to the same truth and for its readings from the sacred texts of various religions, including Christianity, at services.

Vatican the palace home of the Pope in Vatican City.

vestments ecclesiastical garments.

vicar in England, a priest who oversees a parish.

Vicar of Christ the Pope, as representative of Christ on earth.

JUDAISM

Adonai the name of the Lord, pronounced this way whenever the letters YHWH occur in the Torah.

amidah "standing"; the prayer recited at all Jewish services.

anti-Semitism discrimination against Jews.

Bar Mitzvah the initiation rite of a 13-year-old boy, who reads aloud from the Torah and becomes accepted as an adult and as a member of the religious community.

Bat Mitzvah the equivalent of a Bar Mitzvah for 12-year-girls.

cantor the chief singer or prayer leader in a synagogue.

Chanukah a festival commemorating the victory of the Maccabees over the Syrians in 165 B.C. and the rededication of the Temple of Jerusalem. The festival is noted for its ritual of Jewish families lighting a candle every night for eight nights and placing each candle into a menorah (candelabra). Also known as the festival of lights.

Chasidim strict Orthodox Jews, known for their black, widebrim hats, long black coats, and earlocks. Also spelled Hasidim.

dietary laws in Orthodox Judaism, traditional laws pertaining to the consumption and preparation of foods; for example, pork, shellfish, and birds of prey cannot be eaten. Foods fit to be eaten are called kosher.

Elohim Hebrew name of God used in the Torah.

Ezrat Nashim the women's section of a synagogue.

gehenna Greek name for hell; in Hebrew, hinnom.

gentile anyone not a Jew.

Halakah the body of laws in the Torah and the Talmud.

Hanukah see Chanukah.

Hebrew Bible the Old Testament of the Christian Bible; it contains the five books of the Law known collectively as the Torah.

Jehovah name of God.

Jew a believer in Judaism or a person descended from the Hebrew people. By Jewish law, to be a child of a Jewish mother.

kaddish a prayer recited when mourning the loss of a relative to help reaffirm faith.

kaftan the long, black coat worn by Chasidic Jews.

kashrut the code stating which foods are kosher.

kosher food that is fit to eat and unrestricted under Jewish dietary law.

matzah the unleavened bread eaten for eight days by Jewish families over Passover to commemorate the exodus of the Israelites from slavery in Egypt. Also spelled matzoh.

menorah a seven branched candelabra.

messiah the representative of God who will come to earth at the end of the age to establish the Kingdom of God on earth.

mezuzah a scroll with passages from the Hebrew Bible, kept in a box on every doorpost of a Jewish home.

Mishnah Jewish oral law, passed down through the ages.

mitzvah a commandment or duty; a good deed or charitable act.

mohel a Jew who performs circumcisions.

ner tamid in a synagogue, the ever-burning oil lamp in front of the ark.

Orthodox Judaism traditional Judaism, known for its strict adherence to the Law or Torah; for example, no Orthodox Jew shall marry a gentile, no nonkosher foods shall be eaten under any circumstance.

Passover the eight-day festival commemorating the flight of the Jews from slavery in Egypt and their exodus to the Promised Land. Also known as Pesach. Also, the Feast of Unleavened Bread.

rabbi a Jewish minister.

Rosh Hashanah the Jewish New Year, celebrated in late September or early October.

Sabbath Saturday, the seventh day of the week; a day of rest to honor God.

Seder the Passover meal commemorating the Israelites' escape from Egypt. Features of the meal include unleavened bread, four glasses of wine each, a bone of lamb, and green vegetables.

sheitel a wig worn by Orthodox Jewish women in accordance to the rabbinical rule that holds that a woman must keep her hair covered in the presence of any man other than her husband.

Shema a prayer said in the morning and in the evening in Jewish homes. It begins, "Hear O Israel, the Lord Our God, the Lord is one . . ."

siddur a Jewish prayer book.

synagogue a building or church for Jewish worship.

tallith a prayer shawl worn by Jewish men during morning prayers.

Talmud a collection of rabbinical writings forming, along with the Torah, the basis of authority for Judaism. It includes scriptural interpretations, dietary rules, advice for daily living, and sermons, among other writings.

tefillin two small leather boxes containing scrolls from the Torah and strapped to the forehead and left arm of Jewish men during weekday morning services.

Torah the Hebrew Bible; the five books attributed to Moses of the Old Testament.

Weeks, Feast of a summer festival commemorating the receiving of the Ten Commandments by Moses.

Western Wall the Wailing Wall. A vestige of the foundation of the Temple of Jerusalem, where Jews go to pray.

Yahweh the name for God; it is always written as YHWH and never spoken aloud because of its sacredness. See ADONAI, JEHOVAH.

yarmulka the skullcap worn by Jewish men.

Yom Kippur the holiest of all Jewish holidays, devoted to prayer, confession of sins, repentance, and fasting. Also known as the Day of Atonement.

ISLAM

adhan the call to prayers at dawn, midday, midafternoon, sunset, and after dark.

Agni god of fire.

Allah Supreme God; the same God as that pronounced by Moses and Jesus.

al-Rahim one of Islam's 99 Beautiful Names of God, meaning "the compassionate."

al-Rahman one of Islam's 99 Beautiful Names of God, meaning "the merciful."

ayatollah an authority and interpreter of Muslim law.

azan the call to prayer from the minaret of a mosque.

Bismalah a call for Allah's blessing.

Black Stone in the courtyard of the great mosque at Mecca, a sacred stone kissed and touched by pilgrims.

Dome of the Rock in Jerusalem, a domed shrine over the rock from which Muhammad is said to have ascended to heaven.

Fatiha the first chapter of the Qur'an, used as a prayer on many occasions.

five pillars of Islam the five requirements of the Islamic religion: repeating the creed, praying five times per day, giving alms, fasting, and making at least one pilgrimage to Mecca in one's lifetime.

hajj the pilgrimage to Mecca to visit several sacred sites, including the Black Stone.

halal a term similar to kosher in Judaism, meaning food has been judged fit to eat by Islamic dietary law; for example, an animal about to be slaughtered must be facing the direction of Mecca, and its blood must be completely drained before butchering.

imam the leader of prayer in a mosque.

infidel one who belongs to any faith other than Islam.

Jahannam Islamic term for hell.

jihad spreading the faith and fighting against the enemies of Islam. Also, a holy war.

Ka'ba the stone sanctuary in Mecca that contains the Black Stone.

Koran the sacred text that contains the revelations of Allah as made to Muhammad. Also spelled Qur'an.

Lailat-ul-Bara'h the Night of Forgiveness, a Muslim festival devoted to forgiveness.

Lailat-ul-Qadar the Night of Power, a Muslim festival celebrating the giving of the Qur'an to Muhammad.

Mecca in Saudi Arabia, the most sacred city of Islam, where Muhammad, the prophet of God, was born.

minaret the mosque tower from which the faithful are called to prayer.

Moslem see Muslim.

mosque a building for Muslim worship.

muezzin the one who calls the faithful to prayer from the minaret of a mosque.

Muhammad the prophet of God or Allah; he received revelations from God and is the founder of Islam.

mullah a Muslim scholar who interprets Islamic law.

Muslim an adherent of the Islamic religion. Also spelled Moslem.

prayer mat a mat or carpet laid to face Mecca and kneeled on to conduct prayers. Also known as seggadeh.

purdah a term referring to the Qur'an teaching that women must keep their bodies covered and let only their faces and hands show in public to protect their virtue.

Qur'an see Koran.

Ramadan a month of daily fasting between sunrise and sunset accompanied by religious study. It is the ninth month of the lunar calendar.

Salam Alaikum "Peace be upon you," a common Muslim greeting.

Salat the prayers that must be recited five times per day to satisfy one of the five pillars of Islam.

Shi'ites Muslims belonging to the minority Shi'a sect.

shirk the most severe Muslim sin—putting anything on a par with Allah.

Siyam the Muslim requirement to fast during Ramadan.

zakat the giving of alms, one of the five pillars of Islam.

HINDUISM

Agni the god of fire.

ahimsa the doctrine of nonviolence held by many Hindu sects, epitomized by the Hindu leader Mahatma Ghandi.

arti the sacred flame, offered in a lamp to the gods during services.

ashram a communal house where followers or students of a guru live.

avatar the incarnation of a god. Nine avatars are believed to have descended from heaven, including Rama and Krishna, to reestablish law and worship. One remains to come (Kalki), who will destroy the world.

avidya spiritual ignorance, a cause of much suffering.

Bhagavad Gita "the Song of the Lord," a highly influential book of 700 verses featuring the spiritual guidance given Prince Arjuna by his charioteer, Krishna (an incarnation of God), on the battlefield.

Bhagavan "Blessed One" or "Lord," referring to holy men or the god Vishnu.

bhakti knowing God through love and devotion.

Brahma the god of creation and the source of wisdom. Brahma is usually portrayed as having four heads and often seated on a lotus or flying on a swan. He is not widely worshiped by Hindus.

Brahman the Universal Spirit in everyone and everything.

Brahmin the highly revered priestly caste of Hinduism. Brahmins carry out sacrifices and other ceremonies.

chakras places in the body other than the brain where consciousness resides, according to Hindu yoga: the genitals, the naval, behind the lower breastbone, the throat, and between the eyebrows.

chela the student of a guru.

chit Hindu word for consciousness.

Deva "shining being," a god.

dharma caste duties and obligations.

Durga the greatly venerated wife of the god Shiva.

Durga Puja a main festival honoring the goddess Durga.

Ganesha the four-armed, elephant-headed god and son of Shiva, widely worshipped as a "remover of obstacles"; a symbol of luck and prosperity, especially in western India.

guru a spiritual teacher.

Hanuman the Hindu monkey god.

Indra god of rain, thunder, and war.

Janmashtami a festival celebrating the birth of Krishna.

Kalki the last avatar or incarnation of Vishnu; he is due to come in the future and destroy the world to make way for the creation of a new world.

Kamadeva god of love and desire.

karma the central Hindu belief that what goes around comes around; that is, one's fate in life is determined largely by one's behavior earlier in life or in a previous life and that bad karma can be reduced or eliminated by performing good works and living a moral life.

Krishna the widely popular black god and avatar of Vishnu. Many Hindus use Krishna as the name of God.

kshatriyas the warrior caste; the caste second only to the Brahmins.

lingam an erect phallus, the symbol of the god Shiva.

lotus position the yoga position in which the legs are folded tightly together, used in meditation.

mantra a word or phrase repeated continuously in meditation to clear the mind of all intrusive thoughts.

moksha "liberation"; the release from the bondage of endless reincarnation and karma, the highest goal of Hindus; it is achieved by living a good life and creating good karma.

naman three vertical lines worn on the forehead of Vaishnavites.

niyama purifying oneself through discipline, according to Hindu yoga.

Om Sanskrit for "yes" or "so be it," a sacred word uttered before prayers.

puja worship; it is performed three times per day by Orthodox Hindus.

Rama the seventh avatar; an incarnation of Vishnu.

Sacred Thread Ceremony Hindu boy's initiation rite of second birth and passage to maturity.

Sadhu an ascetic holy man.

sannyasin one who abandons all material things except for a pot, a loincloth (dhoti), and alms in an attempt, along with meditation, to achieve moksha; an ascetic.

Shaivism worship of the god Shiva.

Shiva the god of life, death, and rebirth, symbolized by an erect phallus.

shudras the lowest caste of the Hindu caste system, specifically servants and peasants.

Sikhism largely Indian religion, originally guided by Gurus, but now authorized by the Sikh scriptures known as the

Adi Granth. Sikhs believe in a formless God who is beyond human comprehension. Karma and reincarnation are accepted beliefs.

Trimurti the three forces of God: Brahma, the creative force; Vishnu, the preserving force; and Shiva, the destructive force.

Untouchables formerly, those peasants outside the caste system; physical contact with them would "pollute" a caste member and so they were avoided. Such discrimination still exists in rural areas.

Vaishnavism worship of the god Vishnu, thought by some to be the Supreme Being.

Vaishyas the third Hindu caste, ranking below Brahmins and kshyatriyas. Specifically, merchants and businessmen.

vedas Hindu scriptures.

Vishnu the god who preserves life, thought to be the Supreme Being by some followers.

Yama god of the underworld.

yoga a school of Hindu philosophy that combines mental and physical disciplines, noted for its meditation and system of exercises used to achieve spiritual well-being.

yogi one who practices yoga.

BUDDHISM

ahimsa the doctrine of nonviolence and the unwillingness to harm any living creature, including animals for food.

Amida Buddha the Buddha of "immeasurable light."

bhakti the love and devotion a follower feels for someone more spiritually advanced.

bodhi the Buddhist term for enlightenment, the spiritual awakening all Buddhists strive for.

bodhisattva in Mahayana Buddhism, a being or person devoted to attaining enlightenment for all living things.

bodhi-tree the fig tree under which Siddhartha Gautama attained enlightenment while meditating.

Dalai Lama the spiritual leader of Tibetan Buddhism. Every new Dalai Lama is believed to be a reincarnation of the former Dalai Lama.

dharma the path to enlightenment, specifically living a life of generosity, love, and wisdom.

dukkha the Buddhist belief that everything eventually leads to suffering.

enlightenment spiritual awakening; the state of being a Buddha; supreme bliss, perfect wisdom and compassion, and profound insight into the meaning of life. Also known as nirvana or the transcendental.

five precepts a set of rules for moral behavior; in general, don't lie, steal, kill, drink or use drugs, or misconduct oneself sexually.

Four Noble Truths life lessons taught by Buddha: (1) Everything leads to suffering; (2) suffering is caused by desire or greed; (3) eliminating desire and greed eliminates suffering; (4) the pathways of enlightenment are open to anyone who lives morally and meditates.

Gautama, Siddhartha the founder of Buddhism, known as the Buddha.

lama a Vajrayana Buddhist from Tibet who is spiritually learned and developed.

lotus position a seated position in which the legs are folded tightly together, used with meditation.

mantra "instrument of thought"; a word or phrase representing spiritual meaning, recited repeatedly during meditation.

nirvana another term for enlightenment.

prayer wheel a Tibetan Buddhist apparatus consisting of a wheel on which papers inscribed with mantras are attached; the wheel is rotated to release the efficacy of the mantras.

rosary a circle of beads sometimes used when reciting mantras.

satori the sudden achievement of enlightenment.

stupa a Buddhist shrine in the shape of a mound or dome, usually containing a sacred object or marking a sacred place.

Wesak a festival celebrating the enlightenment of Buddha or his birth and death, held in May on the day of the full moon.

zazan meditation in the lotus position.

Zen the Chinese school of Buddhism focusing on the attainment of enlightenment through meditation.

ANCIENT RELIGIONS

GREEK AND ROMAN MYTHOLOGY

(The Romans adopted many of the Greek deities; those that are exclusively Roman are noted as such.)

Acheron the underworld river of woe.

Achilles the Greek warrior who slew Hector and who was himself killed by a wound to his vulnerable heel by Paris.

Adonis the beautiful youth loved by Aphrodite.

Aecus a judge of the dead in Hades; son of Zeus.

Aeetes keeper of the Golden Fleece.

Aegeus he drowned himself after thinking his son had been killed; Aegean Sea named after him.

Aeolus keeper of winds.

aether the pure upper air breathed by the Olympians.

Ajax the Greek warrior who killed himself because the armor of Achilles was given to Odysseus.

Amazons the women warriors who lived near the Black Sea and who supported Troy against the Greeks.

Amphitrite the wife of Poseidon.

Andromeda the daughter of Cepheus and Cassiopeia; she was rescued from a sea monster by her husband Perseus.

Anteros the god who avenged unrequited love.

Aphrodite (Venus) goddess of love and beauty; the daughter of Zeus; mother of Eros.

Apollo the god of the sun, prophecy, music, medicine, and poetry.

Arachne the woman who challened Athena to a weaving contest; she was changed to a spider.

Ares (Mars) god of war; son of Zeus and Hera.

Argo the ship Jason sailed on his quest for the Golden Fleece.

Argus the hundred-eyed monster slain by Hermes; eyes were said to have been placed in the peacock's tail.

Arion the musician saved from drowning by a dolphin.

Artemis (Diana) goddess of the moon, hunting, and chastity.

Asclepius the god of medicine; the son of Apollo.

Astraea the goddess of justice; daughter of Zeus and Themis.

Athena (Minerva) goddess of wisdom and the arts.

Atlas he was condemned to support the world on his shoulders for warring against Zeus.

Bacchus god of wine; son of Zeus and Semele.

Bellona Roman goddess of war.

Briareus the monster with a hundred hands; son of Uranus.

Calliope the goddess of epic poetry.

Calypso a sea nymph who delayed Odysseus on her island for seven years.

Cassandra the prophetess who was never believed; daughter of Priam.

Centaur a half-man, half-horse.

Cepheus the King of Ethiopia; father of Andromeda.

Cerberus the three-headed dog guarding the entrance to Hades.

Charon the ferryman who carried the souls of the dead over the River Styx to Hades; son of Erebus.

Charybdis the personification of a whirlpool off the Sicilian coast opposite a cave.

Chimera a fire-breathing monster with the head of a lion, body of a goat, and tail of a serpent.

Chiron the centaur who taught Achilles and Hercules.

Chronos the personification of time.

Circe the sorceress who transformed the men of Odysseus into swine.

Clio the goddess of history.

Cronus (Saturn) the god of harvests; son of Uranus and Gaea.

Cupid Eros, the god of love.

cyclops a one-eyed giant. See Polyphemus.

Daedalus the builder of the Labyrinth; father of Icarus.

Danae princess of Argos.

Daphne a nymph who was changed to a laurel tree.

Demeter (Ceres) goddess of agriculture.

Diana same as Artemis.

Diomedes the prince of Argos and a hero at Troy.

Dione Titan goddess; mother of Aphrodite.

Dionysus (Bacchus) god of wine; son of Zeus.

Dryads wood nymphs.

Echo a nymph whose unrequited love for Narcissus made her fade away so that only her voice remained.

Eos (Aurora) goddess of dawn.

Erato goddess of lyric and love poetry.

Erebus the dark region that must be passed before reaching Hades; spirit of darkness.

Eros (Amor, Cupid) god of love; son of Aphrodite.

Eurystheus King of Argos who imposed the 12 labors on Hercules.

Euterpe goddess of music.

Flora Roman goddess of flowers.

Fortuna the Roman goddess of fortune.

Furies the avenging spirits.

Gaea the goddess of earth, mother of Titans. Also known as Gaia.

Ganymede the cupbearer of the gods.

Golden Fleece the fleece of the golden ram, quested for by Jason.

Gorgons the three female monsters who had snakes growing out of their heads; gazing upon them turned the beholder to stone. See Medusa.

Graeae the Gorgons' three sentinels; they shared one eye between them.

Hades the abode of the dead.

Hamadryads tree nymphs.

Harpies women with the bodies of birds.

Hecate goddess of sorcery.

Helen fairest woman in the world; her kidnapping caused Trojan War; daughter of Zeus and Leda.

Helios (Sol) god of the sun.

Hephaestus (Vulcan) god of fire; son of Zeus and Hera.

Hera Queen of heaven; wife of Zeus.

Hercules strongman and hero; performed the 12 labors (killing Nemean lion, killing Lernaean Hydra, capturing Erymanthian boar, capturing Cretan bull, etc.) to win immortality.

Hermes (Mercury) the god of physicians and thieves; messenger of the gods; conducted dead to Hades.

Hippolyte the Queen of the Amazons.

Hyacinthus the beautiful youth Apollo loved but accidently killed; Apollo made a hyacinth grow from his blood.

Hydra the nine-headed monster slain by Hercules.

Hyman the god of marriage.

Hyperion the father of Helios.

Hypnos (Somnus) the god of sleep.

Icarus fell into the sea and drowned after wax wings melted when he flew too close to the sun; son of Daedalus.

Iris goddess of rainbow.

Janus the Roman god of gates and doorways, depicted with two opposite faces.

Jason the leader of the Argonauts in the quest for the Golden Fleece.

Lucina the Roman goddess of childbirth.

Mars same as Ares.

Medea the princess sorceress who helped Jason obtain the Golden Fleece.

Medusa the Gorgon whose head was cut off by Perseus.

Melpomene the goddess of tragedy.

Midas the King of Phrysia; all he touched turned to gold.

Minos the King of Crete; after death he became a judge of the dead in Hades; son of Zeus and Europa.

Minotaur the half-man, half-bull kept in the Labyrinth in Crete; slain by Theseus.

Mnemosyne the goddess of memory.

Momus the god of blame and ridicule.

Morpheus the god of sleep and dreams.

Muses the nine goddesses of arts and sciences: Calliope, Clio, Erato, Euterpe, Melpomene, Polymnia, Terpsichore, Thalia, Urani. The daughters of Mnemosyne and Zeus.

Naiads the nymphs who preside over brooks, springs, and fountains.

Narcissus the beautiful youth who fell in love with and pined away for his own reflection in a pool and was transformed into a flower.

Nemesis the goddess of retribution and revenge.

Neptune same as Poseidon.

Nereids the sea nymphs who attended Poseidon.

Nike goddess of victory.

nymph any female spirit of nature.

Nyx goddess of the night.

Oceanus a Titan and god of the sea circling the earth.

Odysseus (Ulysses) King of Ithaca and leader of the Greeks in the Trojan War.

Oedipus King of Thebes; was abandoned at birth; grew up to unwittingly kill his father and marry his mother.

Oreads mountain nymphs.

Orion a great hunter made into a constellation.

Pales Roman goddess of shepherds and herdsmen.

Pan god of woods and fields.

Pandora the woman who opened the box and unwittingly released all the ills of mankind.

Paris he slew Achilles; son of Priam.

Pegasus the winged horse that left Medusa's body after her death.

Pelops his father cooked and served him to the gods.

Penates the gods of Roman households.

Persephone (Proserpine) queen of the underworld; wife of Pluto.

Perseus he killed Medusa and rescued Andromeda from a sea monster; son of Zeus and Danae.

Pleiades the seven daughters of Atlas; they were changed into a constellation.

Pluto god of Hades; brother of Zeus.

Plutus god of wealth.

Polyphemus the cyclops who ate six of Odysseus's men.

Pomona Roman goddess of fruits.

Poseidon god of the sea; brother of Zeus.

Priam king of Troy.

Priapus god of procreation and the guardian of gardens; the personification of an erect phallus.

Procrustes a giant who stretched or shortened victims to make them fit one of his iron beds; slain by Theseus.

Prometheus the Titan who stole fire from heaven and gave it to man; punished by being chained to a rock, where vultures ate from his liver each day.

Proteus a sea god who could change his shape.

Pygmalion King of Cyprus; carved statue of maiden who was brought to life by Aphrodite.

Python the serpent slain by Apollo.

Remus brother of Romulus; was slain by Romulus.

rivers of the underworld Acheron (woe), Cocytus (wailing), Lethe (forgetfulness), Phlegethon (fire), Styx (souls carried across it by Charon).

Romulus son of Mars; raised by a wolf after being abandoned as an infant; he killed his brother Remus; founded Rome in 753 B.C.

Saturn same as Cronus.

Satyrs woodland goatlike gods or demons.

Scylla a rock opposite Charybdis personified as a sea monster who devoured sailors.

Selene goddess of the moon.

Silvanus Roman god of woods and fields.

Sinis the giant who used pines to catapult victims against the side of a mountain; slain by Theseus.

Sirens the deities who entranced sailors to their deaths by their songs.

Sisyphus King of Corinth; condemned to relentlessly roll a heavy stone to the peak of a hill, where it always fell back down again.

Sol Helios.

Sphinx a winged monster having the head of a woman and the body of a lion; killed those who could not answer her riddles; killed herself when Oedipus answered it correctly.

Styx the river on which Charon ferried souls to Hades.

Tantalus the king who, condemned to Hades, underwent the torture of standing in water that always receded when he tried to drink it.

Tartarus the underworld below Hades.

Tellus Roman goddess of earth.

Terminus Roman god of boundaries and landmarks.

Terpsichore goddess of choral dance and song.

Terra Roman goddess of earth.

Thanatos the personification of death.

Theseus son of Aegeus; slew Minotaur, Procrustes, and Sinis.

Titans the original gods before the Olympians.

Triton son of Poseidon.

Uranus personification of the sky; father of the Cyclops and Titans.

Venus Roman goddess of love and beauty.

Zeus (Jupiter) the ruler and father of all the Olympian gods; son of Cronus and Rhea.

ANCIENT EGYPTIAN WORSHIP

Amun the king of the gods.

Anubis the jackal-headed god of the dead and guardian of tombs and cemeteries.

Aten the sun, worshiped exclusively for a time by order of Pharaoh Akhenaten.

Geb earth god.

Hathor cow-headed goddess of the sky and, later, goddess of love, dance, and the underworld.

Horus hawk-headed god of the day and the sun.

Isis queen of gods; goddess of motherhood and fertility.

Khnum ram-headed god of the upper Nile and the creator of mankind.

Maat goddess of justice.

Nepthys goddess of the dead.

Nut goddess of heavens.

Osiris the supreme god of Egypt and the judge of the dead.

Ra (Re) the sun god; the king of the gods and father of humans; portrayed as a lion, cat, or a falcon.

Sebek god of water.

Seth evil god of darkness and storms, often portrayed with the head of a pig.

Thoth originally, the moon god, but later associated with wisdom and magic; portrayed with the head of an ibis.

MONSTERS AND FABULOUS CREATURES (*Also see* GREEK MYTHOLOGY)

Abaia in Melanesian mythology, a great eel who caused floods whenever a fellow fish in his lake was caught.

Aitvaras Lithuanian flying dragon hatched from the egg of a cock, considered a good household spirit.

Alan Philippine half-human, half-bird who lived in gold houses in forests and hung upside-down from trees.

Alicha in Siberian mythology, a beast who lived in the sky and swallowed the sun and moon periodically.

Amarok a giant wolf in the mythology of Eskimos.

Ammut an ancient Egyptian creature part hippo and part lion with the jaws of a crocodile; it ate the hearts of sinners.

Anubis jackal-headed Egyptian god and judge of the dead.

Apop in Egyptian mythology, a sea serpent hiding in darkness.

argopelter a beast of American lore; it lived in the trunks of trees and threw pieces of wood at innocent passersby.

Argus in Greek mythology, a hundred-eyed monster; its eyes were ultimately used to decorate the peacock's tail.

bagwyn heraldic beast with the tail of a horse and the horns of a goat.

baku in Japanese mythology, a tapirlike creature that feeds on the bad dreams of humans.

banshee in Irish and Scottish legend, a spirit having one nostril, a large front tooth, long, streaming hair, webbed feet, and red eyes from continous weeping and wailing. According to legend, she washes the clothes of a man destined to die and, if caught washing by a mortal, must disclose the name of the man and grant three wishes.

baobhan sith a Scottish evil spirit appearing as a beautiful girl in a green dress, which hides her deerlike hooves. She and others seduce young men and suck their blood.

basilisk a 6-inch-long desert serpent described by Pliny and others. A glance from this creature caused death, as did its poisonous breath. It could itself be killed by a weasel, by a cock crowing, or by seeing its own reflection in a mirror.

behemoth in the Apocrypha, a large beast sometimes identified as a hippo. Now taken to mean any large beast.

bergfolk Scandinavian fairies and brownies and the like; the evil outcasts of heaven who live in banks, mounds, and mosses; they could make themselves invisible or change their shape, and were frequently accused of stealing corn and ale.

boggart a mischievous, brownielike spirit.

brollachan a creature or spirit without form, responsible for mysterious occurrences.

brownie a small, shaggy, humanlike creature with shabby clothing. In England and Scotland, they took bread and milk in exchange for household labor; some had the magic ability to settle swarming bees.

bugaboo a small, evil creature that comes down chimneys and snatches naughty children; a favorite of baby-sitters.

bunyip an Australian man-killer who lived in deep pools and streams.

Caecus a cave-dwelling, fire-breathing half-beast, half-man who killed humans and aligned their heads in its lair. The son of Vulcan, slain by Hercules.

calygreyhound heraldic, antelopelike beast having the forelegs and claws of an eagle and the rear legs and feet of an ox.

centaur in Greek mythology, a creature with a human front and the body and hind legs of a horse; known for its benevolence and wisdom.

Cerberus the three-headed dog with serpent manes that guarded the gates of Hades; kidnapped by Hercules.

cetus a sea monster with the head of a greyhound and the body of a dolphin.

ch'i-lin a Chinese unicorn.

chimera Homeric beast having a front like a lion, a middle like a goat, and a rear like a serpent; sometimes depicted with the three heads of these beasts.

cuero a giant octopus of South America having clawed tentacles and ears covered with eyes.

cyclops a cave-dwelling, one-eyed giant described in the *Odyssey*.

devil fish heraldic compound beast of the devil with a fishlike body.

devil's dandy dogs Cornwall legend of fiery-eyed, fire-breathing dogs who followed Satan over the moors on stormy nights.

dobie a brownie guardian of hidden treasure.

dragon a creature taking many forms, sometimes winged, sometimes fire-breathing; usually known for guarding a huge hoard of treasure.

dragon tygre a heraldic compound beast.

dragon wolf a heraldic compound beast.

drake a dragonlike ogre that hunts and travels on horseback; it lives in a palace and eats humans.

dwarf in Scandinavian mythology, a little man with a large head and a long beard, borne from the earth or from mold. It lives in a hollow hill or mound, and sunlight will turn it to stone. Dwarves are usually talented metalsmiths.

elf a little, humanlike creature dwelling underground; noted for its love of music, dancing, mischief, and practical jokes.

enfield heraldic beast having the head of a fox, the body of a lion, the hind quarters of a wolf, and the talons of an eagle.

Erymanthian boar a giant boar driven into a snowdrift and trapped there by Hercules.

fachan an evil Irish spirit known for killing and mutilating travelers; it had one eye in its forehead and one hand protruding from its chest, and it was covered with feathers.

falcon-fish heraldic compound of a fish and a falcon with a hound's ears.

falin Scottish mountain demon.

faun part goat, part man, similar to a nymph.

firedrake a cave-dwelling, fire-breathing dragon who hoarded treasures of the dead.

fuath a Scottish water spirit with webbed feet and yellow hair.

Gabriel Ratchet a ghost hound heard yelping in the sky in the midst of severe storms, believed to be a portent of death.

Ganesha in Indian mythology, a creature having a human body and an elephant head.

gargouille a dragon who made waterspouts in the Seine; the inspiration for gargoyles.

gargoyle a fantastic medieval sculpture having a wide-open mouth for spouting rain or waste water near the roofs of buildings.

Geryon a three-headed, three-bodied man joined at the waist, shot by Hercules.

ghul an evil spirit encountered by travelers in the Arabian desert.

gigelorum a microscopic beast of Scottish folklore; it made its nest in a mite's ear.

Girtablili in the Babylonian epic of creation, a half-man, half-scorpion.

glastig in Scottish folklore, a half-woman, half-goat who wore green and was kind to the old and feeble but who liked to misdirect travelers.

gremlins rabbitlike creatures who sabotaged airplanes and pulled pranks in World War II. Were believed to live in holes around airfields.

griffin in Indian and Arabian folklore, part lion and part eagle.

grylio a medieval, salamanderlike creature said to poison apples in apple trees.

gryphon same as griffin.

harpies vulturelike birds having the head and breasts of women, from Greek legend.

hide behind a mysterious creature known to hide behind trees and sneak up on lumberjacks in North America; they were never seen, however.

hippocampus a half-horse, half-fish with a serpent's tail; it pulled Poseidon's chariot.

hodag a horned, man-eating beast with a spiked back, said to live in the swamps of Wisconsin.

hoop snake a snake said to hold its tail in its mouth and roll about like a wheel, from American lore.

hydra a beast with 7 to 9 heads, one of which is immortal. If any of the heads were cut off the blood would cause a new head to grow back. Hercules killed this beast by burning the heads and burying the immortal head under a rock.

jinshin uwo the giant fish on which Japan was thought to float; the lashing of its tail was the explanation for earthquakes.

kraken a sea creature said to be a mile and a half in length, based on sailor lore of the 1600s and later and probably based on the giant squid.

leprechaun an Irish fairy less than 2 feet in height, believed to haunt wine cellars and to guard huge hoards of treasure.

leviathan the great fish of Hebrew myth.

lindorm a snakelike, heraldic dragon.

Loch Ness monster the elusive lake monster of Scotland.

Medusa the snake-headed gorgon who turned people to stone.

minocane a heraldic beast, half-child, half-spaniel.

Minotaur a bull-headed man kept in a labyrinth and slain by Theseus.

monoceros a howling beast something like a cross between a rhino and a unicorn.

orc according to Pliny, "an enormous mass of flesh armed with teeth," based on the killer whale.

Orthos the two-headed guard dog and brother to Cerberus.

padfoot a devil dog who haunted the area of Leeds.

Pan the Greek god of the woods and fields; a humanlike creature having the belly and legs of a goat.

Peist the Irish dragon whom St. Patrick imprisoned.

phoenix in Egyptian mythology, a brilliantly colored bird who lives more than 500 years, then consumes itself in fire and rises anew from the ashes.

puk a small, household dragon who brings treasure to its master.

roc the giant, eaglelike bird who carried off young elephants and ate them.

rumptifusel a large, vicious beast who slept wrapped around a tree and was often mistaken for a fur coat by passing lumberjacks.

safat a dragon-headed creature that flew so high in the sky it vanished from sight.

salamander a cold-bodied lizard thought to live in fires.

satyre fish a winged, heraldic beast with the head of a satyr and the body of a fish.

satyrs manlike creatures with legs, hindquarters, and horns of a goat; they were the attendants of Bacchus and Pan.

serra a flying sea monster with a lion's head and a fish's tail.

side Irish fairies who lived in barrows.

stringes Greek vampire who sucked the blood of sleeping victims and brought nightmares.

thunderbirds giant Indian bird whose flapping wings were thought to be the cause of thunder.

tritons dolphin-tailed beasts with humanlike faces, the conch-blowing attendants of Neptune.

troll a large, evil fairy or elf who could charm men and who was scared away by church bells. Trolls who roamed at night were turned to stone if caught in daylight. Standing stones are thought to be the petrified bodies of trolls.

were-jaguar South American version of a werewolf.

werewolf a wolf disguised as a human.

wodewoses mute, club-wielding ogres with shaggy green hair who kidnapped women and ate children in medieval times.

wyvern Heraldic flying serpent with a barbed tail and legs like an eagle's.

CLOTHING

COATS

admiral a double-breasted coat with gold buttons, modeled after those worn by U.S. Navy officers.

balmacaan a loose, full overcoat having raglan sleeves and small, turned down collar, usually made of tweed.

car coat a short coat, originally designed to be worn while driving. Also known as a stadium coat, mackinaw.

chesterfield a classic, single- or double-breasted overcoat with black velvet collar and concealed buttons.

clutch a woman's buttonless coat designed to be clutched together with the hand or worn open.

coachman's a double-breasted coat having large lapels and frequently, a cape collar and brass buttons; modeled after a 19th-century British coachman's coat.

cocoon a coat having large shoulders, batwing sleeves; it is cut to wrap about the body then taper to the hem like a cocoon.

coolie a short, square-shaped coat with kimono sleeves and frog fasteners, modeled after those worn by Chinese workers.

duffel coat a short coat closed with toggles, designed after that worn by British navy in World War II.

duster a woman's long, large-shouldered coat having large pockets.

greatcoat a large overcoat, worn by either sex.

Inverness a long coat with a detachable cape.

maxi an ankle-length coat, popular in the early 1970s.

midi any calf-length coat.

pink coat a crimson hunt coat with peaked lapels and black velvet collar, worn by both sexes. Also known as a hunt coat.

raccoon coat a long, large coat made of raccoon fur, popular in the 1920s and revived in the 1960s.

raglan a long, loose coat having extra wide sleeves cut in one piece with the shoulders.

reefer a double-breasted car coat.

Regency a double-breasted coat with wide lapels and high rolled collar.

stadium a long, waterproof coat having two large pockets and a drawstring hood, worn at sporting events.

swallow-tailed a man's formal, open coat with long, scissorlike tails in the back.

tent woman's coat with a sharply flaring hem, like a tent, popular in the 1930s, 1940s, and 1960s.

toggle three-quarter length coat closed by toggles—barrel-shaped buttons passed through loops.

trench coat a long, loose-fitting overcoat or raincoat having several pockets and a belt.

yachting a double-breasted, navy blue wool coat with brass buttons.

Zhivago a long coat trimmed with fur at the neck, cuffs and hem, modeled after that worn in the 1965 film, *Dr. Zhivago.*

JACKETS (*Also see* COATS)

bellhop a waist-length jacket with a standing collar and two rows of brass buttons, sometimes ornamented with gold braid.

blouson a bloused jacket with a knitted or gathered waistband.

bolero a sleeveless, collarless, buttonless, waist-length, vestlike jacket, worn by Spanish bullfighters and adopted for general fashion.

box a woman's straight, unfitted suit or dress jacket.

dinner jacket a man's white jacket worn at semiformal occasions

gendarme a jacket having brass buttons down the front, on the sleeves and on the pockets, fashioned after those worn by French policemen.

Mandarin a Chinese-style jacket with a standing band collar.

Nehru an Indian style jacket with a standing band collar.

smoking jacket a man's velvet jacket tied with a sash.

toreador a woman's waist-length jacket with epaulet shoulders, fashioned after that worn by bullfighters.

SPORT JACKETS

Afghanistan a lambskin jacket with fur left on, worn leather side out with fringe showing around edges, popular in the 1960s.

anorak a short, hooded sealskin jacket worn by Greenland Eskimos.

battle jacket a waist-length army jacket worn in World War II. Also known as an Eisenhower jacket.

blazer a single-breasted suit jacket with patch pockets.

bomber see flight jacket.

buckskin a fringed, deerskin jacket.

bulletproof trade name for a zippered safari-type or flight-type jacket lined with two bullet-proof panels (Kevlar) in front and one in back.

bush same as Safari Jacket.

deck a hooded, zippered, water-resistant jacket with knitted trim around cuffs and neck.

Eisenhower See BATTLE JACKET.

fishing parka a long, waterproof jacket having an attached hood and a large, kangaroo pocket across the chest.

flight jacket a zippered, waist-length jacket, made of nylon or leather, with standing collar, ribbed waistband, and patch or slot pockets.

golf a lightweight, waist-length, zippered jacket made of nylon.

hacking a single-breasted suit jacket with slanting flap pockets and a center vent in back, worn for horseback riding or for general fashion.

lumber jacket a waist-length, plaid wool jacket with ribbed waist and cuffs.

mackinaw a heavy wool, hip-length jacket with blanketlike patterns, and designs.

motorcycle a waist-length black leather jacket, often fastened in front to one side.

Norfolk a hip-length jacket belted at the abdomen and having box pleats from the shoulders to the hem.

parka an insulated jacket with fur-trimmed hood.

pea jacket a straight, double-breasted, navy blue coat, modeled after those worn by U.S. sailors.

racing a lightweight, waterproof, zippered nylon jacket with drawstring hem.

safari jacket a khaki-colored jacket with peaked lapels and four large bellows pockets in front; may also have a belt. Also known as a bush jacket.

shearling a sheepskin and wool jacket, worn leather side out with wool showing around collar, cuffs and hem.

snorkel a hooded parka that zips up over the wearer's chin, giving the hood the appearance of a snorkel.

tweed a man's single-breasted, textured wool sport jacket.

windbreaker trade name for a lightweight, nylon-zippered jacket with fitted waistband.

SWEATERS

Aran Isle a round or V-necked pullover with raised cable knit and diamond-shaped patterns, originating in Ireland.

argyle a jacquard-knit sweater having diamond designs, often worn with matching socks.

bolero a waist-length or shorter sweater with rounded ends and worn open with no fasteners.

cardigan a coatlike sweater, usually with a crew neck, ribbed cuffs and hem.

cashmere any type of sweater made with the hair of a cashmere goat, noted for its softness.

coat sweater a long, cardiganlike sweater, usually having a long V-neck and buttons.

cowl-neck a pullover with a draping, rolled collar.

crew-neck a pullover with a round neck.

dolman a pullover with batwing sleeves.

fanny sweater a long coat sweater pulled over the buttocks.

fisherman's an Irish-designed sweater made of water-repellant wool, known for its bulkiness and natural color.

Icelandic a hand-knit, natural-color sweater made of water-repellant wool, decorated with bands around the neck.

jacquard a sweater having elaborate geometric patterns or a deer on the front or back.

karaca a pullover turtleneck with Turkish embroidered panel down the front.

letter a coat sweater with a school letter on the chest, originally worn by members of a school's sports teams.

shell a sleeveless pullover.

tennis a white, long-sleeved, pullover, cable-knit sweater.

turtleneck a pullover with a soft, folded-over collar covering the neck.

SHIRTS (*Also see* TOPS)

body shirt a shirt that conforms to the curves of the body, popular in the 1960s.

calypso a shirt tied in a knot in front to bare the midriff.

clerical a black or gray shirt with a standing clerical collar, worn by the clergy.

cowboy a western-style shirt, sometimes having pockets and sometimes worn with a string tie or a neckerchief.

C.P.O. a light wool, navy blue shirt with patch pockets, modeled after that worn by chief petty officers in the U.S. Navy.

dandy a shirt with lace or ruffles running down the front center and at the cuffs.

drawstring a shirt having a hem closed with a drawstring to create a bloused effect.

dress shirt traditional dress shirt worn with necktie.

dueling a slip-on shirt with large, full sleeves. Also known as a fencing shirt.

epaulet a long-sleeve, buttoned shirt with patch pockets and epaulet tabs on the shoulders.

fiesta man's white cotton shirt decorated with two bands of embroidery down the front, popular in the 1960s.

flannel a shirt made of flannel, for warmth.

formal a man's white, long-sleeved shirt with pleated front, wing collar, and French cuffs.

Hawaiian man's colorful, floral-print shirt.

hunting shirt a bright, red wool shirt worn by hunters to increase their visibility in the woods.

jockey a colorful woman's shirt fashioned after a jockey's silks, popular in the late 1960s.

medic a white shirt-jacket with standing band collar, worn by some medical professionals. Also known as a Ben Casey shirt.

midriff a woman's shirt cut or tied just below the bustline.

safari a woman's button shirt with lapels and four large pockets in front.

western dress shirt an embroidered cowboy shirt trimmed with fringe, leather, or sequins.

TOPS

bib top a top having a bare back and a front similar to the top of overalls.

bustier a snug-fitting top sometimes laced in corset or camisole fashion.

camisole a top having either thin straps over the shoulders or no straps and held in place by elastic hem, formerly a lingerie piece.

cropped top a half top, frequently comprised of a cutoff T-shirt or sweatshirt, that bares the midriff, popular in the 1980s.

diamante top a top comprised largely of sequins, beads, or paillettes.

flashdance a sweatshirtlike top with large, low-cut neck that leaves one shoulder bare.

halter top a bare-backed top with front supported by a tie around the neck.

smock long-sleeved blouse.

tank top an undershirt with shoulder straps and a low neckline.

tube a snug-fitting, shirred, strapless top.

COLLARS

banded a stand-up collar that buttons.

Bermuda on a woman's blouse, a small, round collar forming right-angled corners and lying flat down the front.

bib any collar that extends over the top of a blouse or dress and drapes down as a child's bib.

bishop a large, rounded collar.

butterfly an oversized collar that hangs down in front in two points nearly to the waist, reminiscent of butterfly wings.

button down a collar folded down and buttoned with tiny buttons to the front of the shirt.

choker a tight, stand-up collar, often made of lace, that rises nearly to the chin and fastens in back. Also known as a Victorian collar.

clerical a stiff, white standing band collar worn by members of the clergy.

cowl a loose draperylike collar that rests around the shoulders.

cowl hood a cowl collar that can be pulled over the head and worn as a hood.

dog's ear a flat collar having rounded ends, reminiscent of a spaniel's ears.

jabot a standing collar with a ruffle hanging from the front.

Mandarin a standing band collar that does not quite meet in the front. Same as a Nehru.

Nehru a standing band collar that does not quite meet in the front, named after that worn by Prime Minister Nehru of India in the early 1960s.

Puritan a large, falling white band that drapes over the shoulders and is tied at the neck.

rolled any collar that extends up the neck and is then folded over.

sailor a large, square collar that drapes over the shoulders, forming a square in back and a V in front.

stand-up a banded collar.

swallow-tail a collar having long, narrow points, reminiscent of a swallow's tail.

turtleneck a soft or knitted, high-band collar extending nearly to the chin and often folded over.

Victorian same as choker.

SKIRTS

accordion-pleated a pleated skirt that flares out from the waistline to the hem.

A-line any flaring skirt, reminiscent of the letter A.

bell a large, full skirt gathered at the waist and flaring like a bell to the hem, sometimes worn with hoops underneath, popular intermittently since mid-1800s.

bias any skirt whose fabric is cut on the diagonal, popular in the 1920s, 1930s, and 1980s.

bouffant any full, gathered skirt.

box pleated a skirt having double pleats formed by two facing folds.

bubble a skirt gathered at the waist then puffing out and tapering—like a bubble; popular in the 1950s. Also known as a tulip skirt.

bustle any skirt with gathered material, ruffles, or a bow at the back.

crinoline an understructure or fabric worn to puff out skirts.

culottes a pair of pants cut with broad, short legs to give the appearance of a skirt. Also known as a pantskirt.

dance skirt a short skirt worn over a dancer's leotard and tights.

dirndl a Tyrolean peasant skirt; a full skirt gathered at the waistline.

Empire a straight skirt having a very high waistline, popular periodically since the early 1800s.

gathered a skirt made of straight panels shirred at the top.

gored a flaring skirt made from 4 to 24 tapering panels or sections. The separate panels are called gores.

granny ankle-length skirt with a ruffled hem.

handkerchief skirt a skirt with a hemline that hangs down in handkerchief-like points.

hip-hugger a 1960s, belted skirt that rode low on the hips.

hoop any skirt puffed out in a bell, cone, or pyramid shape by a crinoline or hoops.

kilt a wraparound, kiltlike skirt, usually plaid, and fastened with a safety pin.

knife-pleated a skirt comprised of 1-inch pleats going all around.

layered skirt a skirt made up of tiered sections.

maxi an ankle-length skirt.

midi a calf-length skirt.

miniskirt a very short, thigh-length skirt.

pant skirt same as culottes.

peasant a full, plain, or embroidered skirt sometimes worn with an apron.

prairie skirt a calico-patterned skirt gathered at the waist and having a ruffled hem.

sarong a floral-print wrap skirt.

sheath a narrow, nonflaring or straight skirt, often with a slit in the back to facilitate walking.

slit a skirt having a slit up both legs, originally worn by Vietnamese women.

square dance a full, puffed-out skirt with ruffled hem.

tiered a skirt layered with flounces.

trumpet skirt a skirt with a sharply flaring flounce at the hem.

tulip skirt same as bubble skirt.

wrap any skirt that wraps around the waist and is fastened with buttons, pins, or ties.

yoke a skirt having a decorative piece attached at the waist.

DRESSES

American Indian a suede or buckskin dress trimmed with beads and fringe.

Andean shift a Peruvian, straight-cut, embroidered dress.

baby doll a smocklike dress having a high neckline and a yoke, designed after doll clothes of the 1930s.

backless a dress having a low or no back.

bare-midriff a tropical, East Indian dress consisting of two pieces that leave the ribs bare.

bathrobe dress a wraparound dress held together by a sash.

blouson a bloused-top dress.

bouffant a dress having a snug-fitting bodice and a full, bell-shaped pleated or ruffled skirt.

bra-shift a sleeveless, figure-conforming shift.

bubble dress a dress having a fitted bodice and a full, bubblelike skirt, popular in the late 1950s.

bustle any dress having gathers of fabric protruding from the rump, popular in the 19th century.

caftan a full-length, robelike dress having embroidery around the neckline, a Moroccan design.

cardigan a dress reminiscent of a cardigan sweater, buttoned down the front and collarless, popular in the 1960s in various lengths, including minis.

chemise a straight-cut dress hanging straight from the shoulders with no waistline. Also known as a sack dress.

cocktail dress a short evening dress with a décolleté neckline.

cutout a dress having holes or cutouts around the arms or midriff, popular in the 1960s.

dashiki an African-inspired, chemiselike dress having bell-shaped sleeves and decorated with an African panel or border print.

diamante a glittery dress consisting of beads, sequins, or paillettes, popular in the mid-1980s.

dinner a formal dress with covered shoulders, worn with a jacket.

dirndl a bell-shaped dress having a gathered waistline and attached to a snug-fitting bodice.

empire any narrow-skirted, high-waistlined dress.

Ethiopian shirtdress a basic shift trimmed with embroidery of Ethiopian design.

evening gown any formal gown or ball gown.

flamenco a dress having a long top and a flounced skirt, reminiscent of Spanish flamenco dancers.

flapper a dress having a long torso and a short skirt, popular in the 1920s and revived in the 1960s.

granny dress an old fashioned, ankle-length dress having a high, tight neckline and long sleeves trimmed with ruffles.

Juliet a medieval-style dress having puffy sleeve tops and a high waistline, inspired by Shakespeare's Juliet.

kabuki a wraparound dress having kimono sleeves and no collar, held together by a sash; inspired by Japanese actors in the kabuki theater.

kiltie dress designed after the Scottish kilt, with wrap skirt closed with a safety pin.

kimono a wraparound dress held together by a sash, inspired by the Japanese kimono robe.

maternity any dress designed with a full front for the comfort of pregnant women.

maxi an ankle-length dress, popular 1969 to 1970.

micro a very short minidress, riding to the top of the thigh, popular in the 1960s.

midi any calf-length dress; first introduced in 1967.

minidress a short-skirted dress popular in the 1960s and reintroduced in the mid-1980s.

monk a cowl-necked dress having bell sleeves and a cord belt, designed after a monk's robe.

muumuu a loose-fitting, ankle-length, Hawaiian, floral-print dress.

patio a light, floral-print shift.

peasant European peasant-style dress having a tight bodice, puffed sleeves, drawstring neckline, and a gathered skirt.

peplum a narrow dress having a short overskirt or ruffle extending below the waistline, popular in the 1930s, 1960s, and again in the 1980s.

pinafore a child's sleeveless dress worn with a separate bib-top apron tied in the back, introduced in 1870.

Pocahontas dress same as American Indian.

prairie an old-fashioned dress having a stand-up neckline, gathered sleeves at the shoulders and bands at the wrist, accompanied by a gored skirt with ruffled hem.

rhumba a dress having a ruffled skirt split up the front, inspired by Carmen Miranda in the 1940s.

sack a chemise.

safari a dress reminiscent of a safari or bush jacket, having multiple pockets on the chest.

sailor a dress having a sailor suit collar, popular from 1890 to 1930.

sari a gold-embroidered silk or cotton dress wrapped about the waist with one loose end draped over the shoulder or covering the head; a Hindu design.

sarong a brightly colored dress wrapped about the waist and draped to one side, an Indonesian design.

seloso a long, flowing African dress.

sheath a snug-fitting dress with a narrow skirt slashed in the back to make walking possible.

shift a chemise.

shirtdress a dress hanging straight from the shoulders and buttoned down the front, as a man's shirt.

shirtwaist dress a classic dress with a shirtlike top, buttoned down to the waist, accompanied by a full or straight skirt, popular in the 1930s, 1940s, and 1980s.

slip dress a dress hanging straight from shoulder straps.

square dancing a dress having puffed sleeves and a full, circular skirt, for square and folk dancing.

step-in a coat-like dress that buttons or zips three-fourths of the way down.

strapless a dress ending at the top of the bosom and held in place by shirring or boning.

sundress a strapless or halter-style dress.

sweater dress a knitted dress.

tent dress a triangular-shaped dress, introduced in the 1960s.

toga an elegant dress that leaves one shoulder uncovered; from the Roman design.

T-shirt dress a T-shirt-like dress.

vintage any classic dress from another era.

wedge a tapering, V-shaped dress having large shoulders and dolman sleeves.

wrap a wraparound dress.

PANTS

bell bottoms jeans or other pants having broadly flaring hems, popular in the late 1960s and early 1970s.

breaker pants having a side zipper that reveals a contrasting lining when opened.

camouflage brown and green military pants.

Capri tight, calf-length pants having short side slits at the hems.

cargo pants having two patch pockets in front and two bellows pockets in back.

chaps seatless leggings worn over pants, originally a cowboy accessory but adopted for women's fashions in the late 1960s.

chinos men's khaki-colored sport pants, made of chino cloth.

choori-dars pants fitting tightly around the thighs and rumpled below the knees, popular in the 1960s and revived in the 1980s.

Clamdiggers trade name for a pair of tight-fitting pants ending at the calf.

continental man's pants with fitted waistband and horizontal, front pockets, popular in the 1960s.

crawlers bib-overall pants for infants.

culottes pants of various length cut with broad legs to give the appearance of a skirt.

deck pants boat pants ending below the knee, popular with both sexes in the 1950s and 1960s.

dhoti Indian pants having a gathered waistline and broad legs tapering to the ankles.

dirndl culottes or pants with a gathered waistline.

drawstring cotton pants cinched around the waist with a drawstring.

fatigues work pants worn by U.S. army personnel. Also known as field pants.

gaucho woman's leather, calf-length pants inspired by South American cowboy pants, popular in the 1960s.

harem pants puffy pants gathered at the waist and ankles, popular in the 1960s.

Harlow pants wide straight pants, inspired by those worn by actress Jean Harlow in the 1930s.

high rise pants that ride high above the waistline.

hip-huggers 1960s pants that rode low on the hips.

hunt breeches riding pants cut wide at the thighs and hips and tight at the knees, usually tan or canary in color.

Ivy League men's narrow-legged pants, popular in the 1950s.

jockey pants breeches having jodhpur-like legs worn tucked into riding boots.

jodhpurs riding pants with flaring thighs and narrow legs below the knee.

luau pants Hawaiian print, calf-length pants, worn by men at Hawaiian luaus.

overalls denim pants and bib top held up by suspenders.

painter's pants having loops on legs to hold brushes, adopted for general fashions in the 1970s and 1980s.

parachute pants having three pockets at the side of the leg and 6-inch zippers at the hems to provide a snug fit around the ankles.

pedal pushers women's straight-cut, below-the-knee pants with cuffs, popular in the 1940s and 1950s for bike-riding, revived in the 1980s.

pleated pants having pleats around the waistband to provide a fuller look in the hip area.

seven-eighth's pants any pants ending just below the calf.

stirrup pants pants having straps or loops hanging from the hems.

stovepipe pants that are straight-cut and snug-fitting from the knee down, intermittently popular.

surfers knee-length pants popular in the 1960s.

toreador pants that are tight-fitting below the knee, made popular by Spanish bullfighters.

FOOTWEAR

SHOES

baby doll shoes having wide, round toes and low heels, similar to MARY JANES.

boat a canvas shoe having a nonskid, rubber sole to prevent slipping on wet decks. Also called deck shoes.

brogan a heavy, ankle-high work shoe.

chain loafer a slip-on, moccasinlike shoe trimmed with metal links.

Chinese a fabric shoe having a crepe sole, a flat heel, and rounded toe, the most common shoe in China.

clog a sandallike shoe having a thick cork or wood sole.

deck a boat shoe.

espadrille a canvas shoe with a rope sole and laced up around the ankle. Most modern versions, however, have no laces.

golf oxford-style shoe with a rubber sole and rubber spikes.

Indian moccasin a heel-less, soft leather shoe, often trimmed with beads or fringe.

kiltie flat a low-heeled shoe with a fringed tongue.

loafer a moccasinlike shoe with a strap attached to the vamp. See penny loafer.

Mary Jane a child's low-heeled shoe with a blunt toe and a strap buttoned or buckled at the center or the side.

Miranda pump a pump with a high, flaring heel, named after Carmen Miranda.

mule a woman's backless shoe or slipper.

open-toed a woman's shoe with an open toe.

oxford a low, strong shoe that laces over the instep; it is made in a variety of styles.

penny loafer a loafer with a strap with a slot over the instep for the insertion of a penny or other coin.

platform a shoe with a raised wood or cork platform, popular with people who wish to appear taller.

pump a woman's low-cut, strapless shoe with a medium to high heel and fitting snugly around the toe and heel.

Ruby Keeler a woman's low-heeled pump tied with a ribbon across the instep.

saddle shoe an oxford made of white buck calf with a brown leather "saddle" extending over the middle of the shoe.

safety shoe a work shoe having a reinforced or steel toe to help prevent injuries.

skimmer a very low cut woman's pump with a flat heel.

slingback any pump or other shoe with an open back and a heel strap.

stocking shoe a soft shoe permanently attached to a heavy stocking.

tuxedo pump a low-heeled pump with a round toe.

wedgies a woman's shoe having a thick wedge-shaped heel that joins with the sole.

white bucks white leather oxfords.

wing-tip an oxford decorated with perforations at the toe and extending along the sides.

Boots

Beatle ankle-high boots with pointed toes, made famous by the Beatles in the 1960s.

chukka ankle-high boot having a rubber sole, laced down the front.

combat a rugged leather, waterproof, laced boot worn by the military.

cowboy high boots having pointed or square toes and ornate, tooled leather.

galoshes a waterproof boot worn over shoes and fastening with a buckle or a zipper.

go-go woman's calf-high, white boots, fashionable with miniskirts in the 1960s.

granny woman's old fashioned high boot laced up the front.

hip thigh-high, rubber fishing boots.

jodhpur ankle-high boot buckled at the side, worn with horseback-riding attire.

mukluk calf-high Eskimo boot made from walrus, seal, or reindeer hide.

pac boot calf-high, insulated or noninsulated, leather or rubber boot having a heavy tread, a popular work and hunting boot.

police high, black leather boot, worn by motorcycle police.

squaw bootie ankle-high buckskin boot fringed around the top and trimmed with beads.

waders waterproof pant-boots extending to the waist or higher and held up by suspenders.

Wellington a boot covering the leg to the knee in front but cut lower in back.

SANDALS

alpargata rope-soled sandals with canvas uppers around the heels, worn in South America and Spain.

clog sandals having a thick wooden or cork sole and either a toe-covering material or straps.

flip-flops See ZORI.

Ganymede a Greek-style sandal with straps that lace up the calf.

geta a Japanese sandal raised on two wooden blocks at the toe and the heel.

gladiator Roman-style sandal with several straps running around the foot from the toes to the lower ankle.

huarache a sling-backed, leather thong with a flat heel, a Mexican design.

platform an open sandal noted for its high-heeled, platformed sole.

thongs flat sandals with leather straps running between the first and second toes.

zori a rubber sandal with straps running between the first and second toes. Also called flip-flops.

PARTS OF A SHOE

aglet the metal tag at the end of a lace. Also known as a tag.

cuff the upper ridge around the back of the shoe.

eyelet a hole through which a lace is thread.

eyelet tab a reinforced leather or fabric in which eyelets are punched.

heel a flat or platformed section corresponding with the heel of the foot.

insole the inner sole of a shoe.

instep the part of the shoe covering the arching portion of the upper foot.

shank the narrow portion of the sole, under the instep. Also the material used to reinforce this area.

sole the bottom supporting member of the shoe.

upper the part of the shoe above the sole.

vamp the part of the shoe covering the instep.

welt the material wedged between the sole and the upper.

CAPS AND HATS

Alpine a fur felt hat with a slightly peaked crown. Also known as a Tyrolean.

bearskin a soft, furry, high domed hat having a chain or strap under the chin, worn by the guards at Buckingham Palace.

bellhop a small, pillbox cap, sometimes having a chinstrap, worn by old-time bellhops.

beret a wool or cloth tam; a visorless, pancakelike hat.

boater a straw hat having a flat, oval crown, previously worn by men, now by women.

bobby a hat having a high, domed crown and a narrow brim, worn by English police (bobbies).

bowler English stiff felt hat having a curving brim and a round crown. Same as the American derby.

bubble beret a brimless, puffed-out beret, worn tilted to one side, popular in the 1960s.

busby a tall, fur or feather hat having an ornamental baglike drapery hanging from the crown to one side of the head, worn by some regiments of the British army.

bush an Australian, cowboylike hat with a large brim turned up on one side.

calotte a beanielike cap made of leather or suede with a stemmed top.

cartwheel a woman's hat having a very broad brim and a low, round crown.

chukka a narrow-brimmed, high-domed hat similar to an English bobby's hat, worn by polo players.

cloche a soft, domelike hat pulled down low over the forehead, worn by women.

coolie a bamboo or straw parasol-like hat worn as protection against the sun by the Chinese.

cossack a high, brimless, Russian fur hat worn by men.

crusher a soft felt hat that can be rolled up and stowed in the pocket for traveling, popular in the early 1900s and again in the 1980s.

Davy Crockett coonskin cap famous for its raccoon fur and tail hanging from the back, popular with boys in the 1950s and early 1960s.

deerstalker a tweed cap having ear flaps and a visor extending from the front and back, made famous by Sherlock Holmes.

derby American name for the English bowler.

Dutch boy a visored wool cap having a soft, broad crown.

eight-point cap a cap having an octagon-shaped crown, worn by policemen.

engineer's a blue-and-white striped cap with a visor, worn by railroad workers.

envoy a man's fur-crowned hat, similar to a cossack, popular in the 1960s.

fatigue cap an army cap similar in cut to an engineer's cap.

fedora a man's soft, felt hat having a medium brim usually worn turned up and a crown that is creased down the middle from front to back.

fez a red felt hat in the shape of a truncated cone; a black tassel hangs from the crown; worn by Turkish men.

French beret See PANCAKE BERET.

French sailor a large cotton tam, usually blue or white with a red pompon on the crown.

garrison cap an olive or khaki-colored cloth dress cap creased lengthwise to facilitate folding, worn by army and air force personnel in World War I and World War II. Also known as an overseas cap.

gaucho a black felt hat having a broad brim and a flat, cylindrical crown, held in place by a chin strap; a South American cowboy hat fashionable with women in the 1960s.

glengarry a creased cloth cap having a regiment badge on the front side and two black ribbons streaming from the back, worn by Scottish Highland Military.

Greek fisherman's a soft denim or wool cap with a braided visor, a popular boating hat worn by both sexes in the 1980s.

homburg a man's felt hat having a creased crown and a narrow, rolled brim.

hunt a riding cap worn with a riding habit, characterized by a round crown with a button on top along with a chin strap and small visor.

hunting a bright orange cap with a visor.

jockey cap a visored cap similar to a baseball cap but with a deeper crown, worn by jockeys.

Juliet a skullcap made of chain, jewels, pearls, or rich fabric, worn with wedding veils or with evening attire.

kepi the French Foreign Legion cap having a flat, cylindrical crown and a visor, sometimes worn with a cloth havelock to protect the back of the neck from sunburn.

leghorn a woman's broad-brimmed, yellow straw hat.

Legionnaire's same as a kepi.

matador a hat reminiscent of the top of a bull's head, having two hornlike projections and a crown made of embroidered velvet.

mod a popular cap of the 1960s, actually an exaggerated form of the newsboy cap of the 1920s.

mortarboard the square, cloth-covered cardboard with tassel and skullcap worn at graduations.

mountie's a broad-brimmed hat with a tall crown creased into four sections, worn by state police and by the Royal Canadian Mounted Police.

newsboy a visored cap with a puffed or bloused crown that could be snapped to the visor; worn by newsboys in the early 1900s and made famous by Jackie Coogan in the films of the 1920s.

opera hat a tall, silk hat having a crown that could be collapsed, similar to a top hat but having a duller finish.

overseas cap same as garrison cap.

painter's cap a visored cap having a round, flat-topped crown, worn by painters.

Panama a man's hand-plaited hat made from the straw of the jipijapa plant.

pancake beret a flat felt tam, sometimes worn tilted to one side by artists. Also called a French beret.

picture hat a large-brimmed hat made of straw, worn by women.

pillbox a small, round, brimless hat worn on the front, side, or back of the head, a popular woman's fashion since the 1920s.

planter's a broad-brimmed, banded straw hat with a dented crown.

porkpie a man's snap-brim hat with a low, flat crown.

profile a woman's hat having a brim turned sharply down on one side, popular in the 1930s.

Puritan a man's tall black hat, adorned with a black band and silver buckle, worn by 17th-century Puritans and revived for women's fashion in the 1970s.

Rex Harrison a man's wool tweed, snap brim hat, popularized by Rex Harrison in *My Fair Lady*.

safari hat a straw or fabric hat with a medium brim and a round, shallow crown.

Scottie a brimless hat having a creased crown ornamented with ribbons or feathers in the back, similar to a glengarry.

shako a tall, cylinderlike hat with a visor and a feather cockade in front, worn by members of a marching band.

skimmer a boater with a wider brim and a shallower crown.

skullcap any cap, such as a swimmer's cap, that fits snugly around the crown of the head.

snap-brim a hat having a brim that can be adjusted at different angles.

sombrero a straw or felt hat having a tall, tapering crown and a broad, upturned brim, worn in Mexico.

sou'wester a rain hat with a domelike crown and a broad brim that is longer in the back, originally a New England fisherman's hat.

Stetson the trademark name for a cowboy or 10-gallon hat.

stocking cap a knitted winter cap with a long tail frequently fitted with a pompon or tassel. Also known as a toboggan cap.

tam short for tam-o-shanter. A flat, Scottish cap having a pompon or tassel in the center, similar to a beret.

top hat a man's tall, stove-pipelike hat with narrow brim and shiny, silk finish; not collapsible like an opera hat.

trooper a fur or pile-lined leather or imitation leather cap having a flap at the sides and back that can be folded down to protect the ears or left up to show the lining, worn by mailman, policemen, and, originally, by state troopers.

turban a head-wrapping; a linen scarf wound around the head.

Tyrolean same as Alpine.

watch cap a close-fitting, knitted cap having a turned-up cuff, originally navy blue and worn by sailors on watch, now a popular winter cap.

yarmulka an embroidered or crocheted fabric skullcap, worn by Orthodox Jewish men and, on religious occasions, by non-Orthodox Jewish men.

zucchetto a skullcap worn by a pope (white), a cardinal (red), or a bishop (purple).

GLASSES AND SUNGLASSES

aviator's sunglasses modeled after the goggles worn by early airplane pilots, characterized by oversized lenses.

Ben Franklins delicate glasses having small, elliptical, octagonal or oblong lenses, worn on the middle of the nose. Also known as granny glasses.

bifocals glasses having lenses divided to aid both closeup and distant vision.

butterfly glasses rimless sunglasses with lenses shaped like butterfly wings.

clip-ons frameless sunglasses that clip on over the lenses of prescription glasses.

Courreges headband-like sunglasses consisting of a strip of opaque plastic wrapping around the face to the ears, with a narrow strip of glass or plastic in the center.

granny same as Ben Franklins.

half-glasses reading glasses having half-lenses to allow the eyes to peer over the rims to focus on a distant object.

harlequin glasses with diamond-shaped lenses.

horn-rimmed glasses having heavy, dark, or mottled brown frames.

Lennon specs sunglasses having circular, metal-rimmed lenses, named after those worn by Beatle John Lennon.

lorgnette glasses having a handle for holding instead of frames, such as opera glasses.

monocle a single lens attached to a ribbon worn around the neck.

owl oversized sunglasses with wide rims and broad lenses.

pince-nez frameless glasses having circular lenses that pinch in place over the bridge of the nose.

planos fake glasses having dark rims to provide a "studious look," worn only for fashion.

tortoiseshell glasses having frames made from authentic or imitation tortoiseshell, usually mottled brown.

wraparound wide sunglasses that wrap around the front of the head like a headband.

FABRICS AND FABRIC DESIGNS

abattre quilted or depressed effects in fabric.

abercrombie Scottish tartan with a blue and black ground and a green and white overcheck.

accordion pleat see pleat.

acrylic a synthetic fiber derived from coal, water, petroleum, and limestone.

alpaca cousin of the llama, from which fleece of variegated color is obtained.

angora the hair of the angora rabbit or angora goat.

antique lace see lace.

appliqué fabric pieces cut out and attached to another fabric for decorative effect.

argyle knit a decorative design pattern in which diamonds are crossed by narrow stripes, found on socks and sweaters.

artificial silk an early name for rayon.

awning stripes See STRIPES, AWNING.

bagheera a crease-resistant, uncut pile velvet.

bargello decorative needlepoint characterized by geometric designs, diamonds, and flames.

batik Indonesian dyeing method using wax to cover areas to be left undyed. It often has a streaked or veined appearance where dye has worked through cracks in the wax.

batiste a light, sheer, combed muslin.

beetling a method of pounding linen to produce a surface with a sheen.

bird's-eye a woven fabric with a bird's-eye or dot in the center of the pattern.

blister any design, such as a flower, that bumps out from the fabric.

bolt a quantity of fabric, usually from 15 to 20 yards.

box pleat see pleat.

braid fabric made by interlacing three or more yarns or fabrics.

broadcloth a lustrous, tightly woven fabric having a fine rib.

brocade a heavy, jacquard-woven fabric having raised floral or other patterns, often made with metallic threads.

brushing a technique in which a fabric is combed by wire bristles to produce a NAP, as in blankets or brushed denim.

buckskin deer or elk leather.

calico any fabric having small, bright, and colorful print designs.

canvas strong, plain-weave fabric, usually made of cotton. Also known as duckcloth or sailcloth.

cashmere a very soft wool that grows underneath the outer hair of the cashmere (Kashmir) goat.

cavalry twill a strong, twilled fabric used in uniforms and riding breeches.

chalk stripe see stripes.

challis a soft, light fabric printed with bright floral patterns or paisley patterns.

chambray a fine, light gingham having a colored warp and a white filling.

chamois a soft, pliable leather from the chamois goat. Also, a cloth woven to imitate this leather.

chantilly See LACE, CHANTILLY.

check any small pattern of squares, woven or printed on a fabric.

check, houndstooth pointed checks.

check, pin very small checks.

chenille a soft, tufted cord used for fringes.

chiffon a sheer silk or rayon fabric, used in women's dresses.

chino a sturdy, twilled cotton fabric having a slight sheen, used in uniforms and men's work or casual pants.

chintz a glazed cotton fabric printed in bright designs, used mostly in drapes and upholstery.

cloque same as blistered fabric.

corded a fabric having lengthwise ribs, as in corduroy.

corduroy corded, cut-pile fabric, usually made from cotton.

crepe a soft fabric having a crinkled surface.

damask a fabric having a heavy jacquard weave, used in tablecloths and in some clothing.

denim a coarse twill-weave fabric, used in jeans.

dobby a fabric with woven geometric figures.

duckcloth another name for canvas.

duffel cloth a thick, heavy fabric used in some coats.

dungaree heavy blue denim.

embroidery decorative stitches made with thread or yarn.

faille a finely ribbed, dressy fabric used in evening clothes and shoes.

fishnet a coarse fabric with holes, used for curtains and for hosiery.

flannel a soft wool or cotton fabric having a brushed surface.

fleece the wool of an animal.

flock waste fibers in near-powder form, applied in decorative patterns (flock printing) on other fabrics.

Fortrel trademark name for a polyester fiber.

foulard a plain or twill-weaved, lightweight, soft fabric used for neckties and scarves.

gabardine a strong, twill-weaved fabric, made from all types of fibers.

georgette a sheer, crepelike fabric, similar to chiffon.

gingham a yarn-dyed fabric woven with checks, plaids, or stripes.

glazed referring to a fabric given a shiny surface. Also known as glace.

gossamer any very sheer, light fabric.

ground the background color on which other colors or designs are made.

harlequin a diamond design, from the original harlequin costume of the 16th century.

Harris tweed hand-woven tweed, derived from yarns spun on islands off the coast of Scotland, including Harris Island.

heather a misty effect on fabric, produced by cross dyeing or by using contrasting warp and filling yarns.

herringbone a twill weave with a V-pattern.

honeycomb a weave that resembles a honeycomb pattern.

houndstooth See CHECK, HOUNDSTOOTH.

Irish tweed a tweed made in Ireland, characterized by a white warp with colored filling threads.

jacquard any fabric with a woven or knitted design.

khaki a fabric having an earth or olive green color, as in military uniforms.

knit, double a fabric made in two layers.

knit, jacquard any design knit into a fabric.

lace, aloe a lace made from aloe plant fibers.

lace, antique a heavy, coarse, open form of darned lace, used in curtains. Also called spider work.

lace, binch a lace of handmade motifs attached to a net ground.

lace, bourdon scroll-patterned lace with heavy thread outline.

lace, chantilly a popular bridal lace characterized by delicate scrolls, branches and flowers.

lace, Irish crochet and needlepoint type laces made in Ireland.

lace, venise needlepoint lace in a floral pattern edged with small, decorative loops.

lamé fabric made from metallic yarns, used in evening dresses.

lawn a sheer, lightweight, plain-weave fabric.

leather the cleaned hide of an animal.

linen one of the oldest fabrics, made from flax.

lisle two-ply cotton or wool yarn used for socks.

Lycra trademark name for spandex fiber.

mackinaw a thick, heavy, coarse fabric, named after blankets made by the Mackinaw Indians, now found in plaid or checked hunting jackets.

macrame a method of knotting and weaving to produce a coarse lacework.

madras a fine-textured cotton cloth from Madras, India, usually having a checked, striped, or plaid pattern whose dyes eventually bleed into one another after several washings.

marl a yarn made from different colored yarns.

matelassé fabric having a quilted or blistered appearance, produced with the use of puckered material.

matte a dull, flat finish on a fabric.

merino a fine, dense wool derived from the merino sheep.

metallic fibers man-made metal or metal-covered fibers.

middy twill a durable twill-weave fabric.

mohair the long, shiny hair of the angora goat.

monk's cloth a heavy, coarse fabric that is loosely woven, used in draperies and in some clothing.

motif a design that is usually repeated in a pattern on a fabric.

muslin a plain weave fabric made of cotton and man-made fibers in various weights; used in sheets and in making prototypes of garments to save cutting into expensive material.

naked wool sheer, lightweight woolen fabric.

nap a hairy, fuzzy, or soft surface, produced by brushing with wire bristles.

napping the brushing process that produces nap on a fabric.

needlepoint decorative needlework or embroidery on open fabric.

nun's veiling a plain-weave, lightweight, sheer fabric used by nuns for veils.

oilskin waterproof raincoat fabric.

organdy a sheer, lightweight fabric used in curtains, blouses, and evening wear.

Orlon trademark name for DuPont acrylic fiber.

ottoman wool, silk, or man-made fabric having wide, horizontal ribs, used in evening wear.

Oxford gray a very dark gray used in men's suits and slacks.

paisley swirling, conelike design woven or printed on fabric. A soft wool fabric having this design.

Panama a lightweight wool worsted used in summer suits.

patchwork combining bits or patches of different materials to create a large piece, as a quilt.

pebble refers to fabric having a bumpy or grainy surface.

percale a blend of combed and carded cotton and man-made fibers, used in sheets; softer and smoother than muslin.

picot an edging consisting of a series of small, decorative loops.

pile a nappy fabric surface comprised of cut or uncut loops of yarn.

pique a fabric having woven, raised geometrical patterns.

plaid, argyle a plaid pattern of diamonds.

pleat a permanently set fold of fabric.

pleats, accordion very narrow, straight pleats.

pleats, box a double pleat made by two facing folds.

pleats, knife narrow, straight pleats running in one direction.

pleats, sunburst pleats that radiate out to the edge of a skirt.

plissé a fabric that has been permanently puckered by a chemical or heat process.

plush thick deep pile.

pointillism printing dots on a fabric to give the illusion of a solid color from a distance.

polyester a strong, wrinkle-resistant, man-made fiber that tends to trap body heat.

poodle cloth looped fabric used in coats.

poplin shiny, durable imitation silk with a fine, horizontal rib, used for dresses.

printing applying a colored pattern or design onto a fabric.

rayon the first man-made fiber, originally known as artificial silk, used in some women's apparel.

rib a cord or ridge running vertically or horizontally.

sailcloth same as canvas.

sateen a strong, shiny satin weave fabric made of cotton.

satin a glossy-faced fabric made of silk, cotton, rayon, or nylon.

satin, crepe-backed fabric having a satin face and a crepe back, used in jacket or coat linings.

satin, duchesse a rich, heavy satin used in formal wear.

scallops decorative edging comprised of semicircular curves.

seersucker a lightweight, puckered fabric that is often striped but may also be plain, plaid, or printed.

sequin a decorative, metallic spangle.

serge a smooth, twill-weave fabric used in suits.

sheer transparent or nearly transparent.

shetland yarn very soft, fluffy, two-ply yarn, as that derived from the wool of sheep on the Shetland Islands off the coast of Scotland.

shirring gathers of fabric used to create fullness, used in women's apparel.

silk material produced by the silk worm, now largely replaced by man-made fibers.

smocking rows of shirring given to a fabric to provide stretch and decoration.

spandex a synthetiz elastic fiber used in stretch pants and other elastic clothing.

stripes, awning any stripe at least 1½ inches wide.

stripes, chalk narrow white stripes on a dark fabric.

stripes, pin very narrow stripes of any color.

stripes, Roman narrow, colored stripes that cover the entire surface of a fabric.

studs small, decorative, rivetlike ornaments attached to fabrics (especially denim jackets) when in style.

suede leather having a soft, napped surface.

taffeta a crisp, plain-weave fabric with a shiny surface, used in women's apparel and noted for its "rustling" noise.

taffeta, antique a stiff taffeta reminiscent of that made in the 18th century.

taffeta paper a very light, crisp taffeta for evening wear.

tartan a pattern of intersecting, colored stripes, associated with a specific Scottish family or clan. A plaid.

tartan, Barclay a yellow background crossed with wide black stripes and narrower white stripes.

tartan, Black Watch a light blue background crossed with green stripes, worn by the 42nd Royal Highland Regiment.

tartan, Campbell a blue background crossed with green stripes and dark blue stripes.

tartan, Cumming dark and light green stripes combined with red and blue stripes.

tartan, Ogilvie a complex pattern of red, yellow, greenish blue, and dark blue stripes.

tartan, Rob Roy red and black check pattern, as that used on hunting jackets.

tartan, Stewart a red or white background spaced widely with narrow stripes of blue, white, and yellow.

terry cloth soft, absorbent cotton or cotton blend fabric having uncut loops on one or both sides, used in robes and towels.

textured yarn yarn that has been crimped, coiled, or curled.

tweed a rough, strong, nubby wool or man-made fabric, used primarily in suits and coats.

twill a fabric woven with diagonal ribs.

velour a soft fabric having a thick, short pile.

velvet rich, soft-textured warp (made from warp threads) pile fabric.

velveteen a soft, cotton fabric with a cut pile thicker than corduroy. Pile is made of filling threads, as distinguished from the warp threads used in velvet.

vicuna type of expensive wool from South American llama.

virgin fibers fibers that have never been processed (as remnant fibers) in a fabric before.

virgin wool same as virgin fibers.

voile a crisp, lightweight, sheer fabric used in blouses and curtains.

wale the lengthwise ribs on corduroy or other fabric.

wale, pin narrow ribbing.

wale, wide wide ribbing.

warp the yarns woven first on a loom when a fabric is made; it forms the length of a fabric, as distinguished from the filling threads that are woven under and over the warp in a crosswise fashion.

wash and wear term describing fabrics needing little or no ironing.

weft another name for the filling threads woven over and under the warp.

wool fleece of a sheep or other animal.

worsted fabric made of yarns that have been combed and carded; it is smoother, cleaner (less fuzzy) than ordinary wool.

FASHION STYLES

Afro native African style characterized by Afro haircuts, and such African garments as bubas, dashikis, and selosos, popular in the late 60s and early 70s.

American Indian style characterized by beads and fringed, deerskin dresses and pants.

androgynous a style combining male and female characteristics, for example, women wearing men's haircuts and suits; men wearing long hair and earrings.

Annie Hall a style characterized by baggy pants, challis skirts, and a general uncoordinated look, inspired by the movie by the same name in the 1970s.

baby doll a style characterized by childlike or doll-like attire, such as baby doll or Mary Jane shoes, gathered or pleated dresses.

Bonnie and Clyde inspired by the movie *Bonnie and Clyde*, an attire that includes pinstripe gangster suits, above-the-knees skirts from the 1930s, and a woman's beret worn to the side.

Brooks Brothers tailored business person's look characterized by button-down collars, tailored skirts, Ivy League suits, trenchcoats, balmacaan coats, and so on.

Carnaby the mod look of the 1960s, featuring miniskirts, polka-dot shirts with large white collars, bell-bottom pants, and newsboy caps, named after Carnaby Street in London where it originated.

cowpunk an amalgamation of punk and western looks, for example, fringed jackets, miniskirts, chains, western belts, punk or dyed hairstyles.

dandy a style characterized by ruffles at the neck and wrists, worn by both sexes in the 1960s and 1970s.

denim jeans and jeans jackets.

Edwardian an early 1900s fashion characterized by regency collars, capes, and neck ruffles.

ethnic any style that borrows from the fashions of other nations; may include Gypsy, harem, and peasant clothes.

flapper look style borrowing from the flappers of the 1920s, featuring long-torso dresses ornamented with beads and ropes of pearls, short bob haircuts, and so on.

funky a 1960s or early 1970s look featuring platform shoes, newsboy hats, or faded dresses.

gaucho Spanish cowboy style featuring calf-length pants, long-sleeved blouses, boleros, and gaucho hats, popular with women in the 1960s and 1970s.

Gibson Girl classic look of the late 1800s to early 1900s and revived many times; it features lace-trim blouses with leg-of-mutton sleeves and high, choker collars, long, gathered skirt, pompadour hairstyle, and so on.

granny look old-fashioned, ankle-length dresses with ruffled neckline and hem.

gypsy a look featuring hoop earrings, head scarves, shawls, boleros, and full skirts.

harem a look typified by ankle-length harem pants, bare midriff, chains, and sandals. Also known as the Arabian Nights Look.

hippie a slack, unkempt look featuring long hair, tie-dyed shirts, tank tops, old jeans, miniskirts, love beads, and peace symbols.

hunt look a riding apparel look featuring jodhpurs, stirrup pants, derby, stock tie, pleated trousers, full-length coat; mid-length, side-slitted skirt worn with boots, velvet jacket.

Japanese any bulky, oversized robelike fashions.

kiltie look Scottish look featuring kiltlike skirts in plaids, knee socks, tam-o-shanter or glengarry caps.

maxi ankle-length skirts, dresses, coats.

midi calf-length skirts, dresses, coats.

military armed forces look featuring camouflage pants, fatigues, combat boots.

peasant old-world fashions featuring full skirts, puffed sleeves, drawstring necklines, aprons.

prairie a midwest style characterized by long, calico dresses with long sleeves and high neckline.

preppy the upper class student look featuring Ivy League shirts, cashmere sweaters, chinos and corduroys, oxfords, loafers, pumps.

punk rebellious teen look of the 1980s, featuring chains, safety pins, torn clothes, heavy lipstick, strange haircuts (mohawk, spikes, shaved, dyed), black leather jackets, slitted skirts.

retro any styles from the past.

Tyrolean an Austrian or Bavarian look featuring dirndl skirts and embroidered vests, Lederhosen, knee socks, and Alpine hats.

vintage classic fashions from the past.

western western cowboy look featuring tight jeans, cowboy shirts, string ties, Stetson hats, tooled-leather belts.

CLOTHING OF THE 19TH CENTURY

adelaide boots women's boots with fur around the tops.

albert a short chain connecting a watch to a buttonhole, popular from 1849 on.

albert overcoat a calf-length overcoat having breast and hip pockets and a half-circle cape resting on the shoulders.

alberts side-lacing half boots with cloth tops and false mother-of-pearl buttons on the front.

ankle jacks half-boots.

Apollo knot two or more wide loops of false hair wired to stand up on top of the head with decorative lace, flowers or jeweled combs, popular with women from 1824 to the 1830s.

banyan a long informal coat with flared skirts, worn around the house in the morning.

batswing a variation of the bowtie having a very small knot, fashionable in the 1890s.

bavolet a frill attached to the back of a bonnet to protect the neck from sun.

Benjamin a loose topcoat worn when traveling.

Benoiton chains long beads of black wood or filigreed gold or silver that hung from each side of the head and draped across the bosom, popular from 1865 to 1870.

beret a crepe or silk evening hat, usually decorated with ribbons, flowers, or feathers. Also, a turban decorated with a plume.

bertha a frilled and ribboned border covering the sleeves and falling over the top of a bodice.

bloomers frilled trousers gathered about the ankles and worn under a short skirt.

boa a scarf of feathers. Also, a scarf of fur made from skunk, opossum, beaver, sable, or fox.

bodice the corsetlike, fitted portion of a dress from the waist to the upper chest, fastened up the back with hooks and eyes and boned in front, often heavily padded at the bosom.

bolero a short jacket joined only at the breast or not at all.

bollinger a hat with a wide brim topped by a domed crown or "hemisphere." Also known as a hemisphere hat.

bosom, artificial any material used to plump out the bosom, most frequently cotton or wax.

bowler a stiff felt hat with a narrow brim and a round crown.

braces suspenders.

breeches tight, high-waisted pants extending nearly to mid-calf.

burnous a small cape or shawl with a hood attached.

bustle a crescent-shaped, wool-stuffed pad, worn in the back of the dress to plump out the behind.

calash a hood that could be folded by means of cane hoops and carried in a bag to an evening function.

capote a puffy bonnet with a stiff brim projecting around the face.

cardigan a short, close-fitting jacket without a collar, made of wool or English worsted.

catagan a chignon brought down to the nape of the neck.

chemise robe a dress or frock buttoning down the front from the neck to the hem.

chemisette white edging around the top of a low-necked bodice. Also known as a tucker.

chesterfield a large overcoat or topcoat with a velvet collar and several pockets, widely popular from the 1840s on.

chignon a mass of coiled or plaited hair, sometimes supplemented with false hair, gathered at the back of the head and often covered with a net.

cloak a long and voluminous overcoat without sleeves and fastened around the body like a cape. In the second half of the century cloaks had sleeves and many had detachable capes.

cornette a generic term for any bonnet tied under the chin.

cossacks loose, voluminous trousers having leg bottoms drawn closed by ribbons, popular from about 1817 to the 1830s.

cravat a light, linen scarf tied around the neck in a knot or bow.

crinoline a dome, funnel, or pyramidal-shaped understructure made of whalebone or spring hoops used to distend or widen skirts to as large as 18 feet in circumference. The skirt itself was often hitched up to show a scarlet petticoat beneath.

cummerbund a wide silk sash worn around the waist with a dress suit, popular with men from the 1890s on.

deerstalker cap a Harris tweed cap with ear flaps.

Dolly Varden dress a variation of the Polonaise, having a short overskirt bunched up severely in the back.

duster a short, summer overcoat.

follow-me-lads popular name for ribbon streamers trailing behind a woman's hat.

frock coat a knee-length, military-style overcoat.

gaiters leather or cloth leggings extended from the knee to the instep. Ankle-length gaiters were known as spats.

Garibaldi shirt a black-buttoned, red merino shirt worn with a belt and a black or other colored skirt.

gibus a top hat capable of being squashed flat and carried under the arm.

great coat a knee or ankle-length overcoat, buttoning to just below the waist.

Grecian bend an odd fad in which a stooped posture was considered fashionable among women; a bustle was worn high on the back of the skirt to enhance this effect, popular from 1815 to 1819 and revived in 1868.

Hessians boots rising to just below the knee and decorated with tassels, worn most frequently with pantaloons.

highlows ankle boots buckled or strapped in front.

indispensable a circular or lozenge-shaped handbag favored by women. Also known as a ridicule.

inexpressibles prudish name given to trousers to avoid being vulgar in speech. Also known as unmentionables and unwhisperables.

Inverness a great coat having a deep cape, popular from 1859 on.

jacket bodice a full-sleeved, form-fitting bodice spreading out over the waist.

knickerbockers a loose form of breeches, but longer and wider; they buckled at the knee and were worn from the 1870s on for shooting, boating, golf, and riding.

mackintosh an overcoat made of rubber bonded over cloth, a source of complaints due to its unpleasant odor.

mantle a long cloak, frequently having a cape.

mob cap a bonnetlike cap with a puffed-out crown and frill and ribbon trim, worn most frequently in the kitchen by women.

muff a handwarmer made of fur or feathers.

paletot a short overcoat for men. Also, a large jacket that spread over a crinoline dress.

pantaloons close-fitting pants, held to the feet by straps. Also known as tights.

pelerine a cape.

pelisse a long, short-waisted, ankle-length overcoat with a broad, turned-down collar.

picadilly a man's stand-up collar.

poke bonnet a bonnet with a forward projecting brim.

Polonaise a very popular dress having an overskirt attached at the bodice and draped up at the rump. It was sometimes left unbuttoned from the waist down. Also known as a Princess Polonaise.

porkpie hat a lady's hat having a low, flat crown, resembling a pie.

princess dress a dress having a bodice extending down to serve as an overskirt. Also known as an Isabeau dress.

pumps dress shoes open at the instep and just covering the toes, tied with ribbons.

rationals bicycle bloomers, popular in the 1890s.

reticule a small, draw-stringed handbag made of silk, satin, or velvet.

ridicule same as INDISPENSABLE.

riding habit skirt a very long skirt worn when riding to hide the legs from view.

sailor suit a popular boy's suit, consisting of a sailor's hat, knickerbockers, and a blouse with a square flat collar and V-neck, worn from the 1860s on.

shawl a garment draped over the shoulders to warm the upper body.

skeleton suit a young boy's suit consisting of high-waisted trousers buttoned up over a fitted jacket having a broad, white collar, from 1800 to 1834.

spats see gaiters.

Spencer a short jacket pulled in at the waist, worn by women.

surtout a short overcoat.

tam-o'-shanter a close-fitting, Scottish cap having a pompon, feather, or tassel sticking up from the center.

tea gown a loose dress without a corset, frequently trimmed with flounces and ruffled sleeves.

three storeys and a basement a woman's high-crowned hat.

tippet a cape.

top coat a great coat or overcoat.

top hat a narrow-brimmed hat with a tall crown, most frequently shiny black in color. Also called a chimney pot hat.

trilby a soft felt hat having a dent along the crown from front to back.

ugly on a bonnet, an extra silk brim tied over the existing brim for extra shading against the sun.

ulster an overcoat worn with a belt and having a detachable hood, introduced in 1869.

unmentionables same as inexpressibles.

unwhisperables same as inexpressibles.

waistcoat a sleeved or sleeveless jacket; a vest.

whangee a popular cane or walking stick.

wide-awake a popular wide-brimmed straw or felt hat having a low crown, worn by men.

CLOTHING OF THE 18TH CENTURY

Artois buckles large, square shoe buckles worn by both sexes in the second half of the century.

bag an ornamental purse of silk tied to men's hair. See BAGWIG.

bagwig a dress wig with the pigtail tucked into a black silk bag in the back of the neck. Also known as a bag.

banyan men's calf-length dressing gown.

beaver a hat made from beaver fur.

bedgown a full-length muslin or silk gown tied with a sash, worn by women.

bob wig a curly or frizzy wig in various lengths, worn by the middle class from the 1720s on.

breeches knee-length pants, buckled below the knee.

Brunswick a type of sack having a false bodice front and long, tight sleeves.

buffon a large handkerchief covering the open area left by a low-neck bodice.

buffskin buff-colored leather, fashionable in breeches and waistcoats.

bustle a gathering of material on the back of a woman's skirt forming a false rump.

cadogan a thick tail of hair, formed into a loop on the back of men's heads, fashionable in the 1770s to 1780s.

chatelaine a clasp or chain worn from the waist for holding perfume bottles, stay hooks, and other cosmetic accessories.

caraco a woman's thigh-length jacket.

cardinal a woman's knee-length, scarlet coat.

chemise a woman's full-length shift with ruffled neck and sleeves.

commode a woman's lace and linen headdress with lappets.

corset a sleeveless bodice laced from the back.

cravat a light, linen scarf tied around the neck.

fantail hat a hat with a broad, turned-up front rim, worn by men.

fly cap a lace and wire cap shaped like a butterfly and sometimes decorated with jewels.

frock a long, loose, informal coat with a turned-down collar, worn by men for sport, riding, or other activities.

frogging looped braid fastenings, derived from military uniforms.

great coat a large, loose, calf-length overcoat with capelike collars for shedding rain, favored by coachmen. Also known as a surtout or a wrap-rascal.

Hessians short riding boots decorated with tassels.

hoop a hooped petticoat used for puffing out skirts.

indispensable a handbag introduced at the end of the century. Also known as a ridicule.

lappet a woman's hat streamer.

lawn a fine linen.

major wig a wig with two short pigtails.

milkmaid hat a round, low-crowned hat having a wide brim, worn at various angles by women. Also known as a bergere.

mob cap a bonnetlike cap with a puffed-out crown and frill and ribbon trim, worn by women.

modesty piece a strip of lace that covered the open area left by a low-necked bodice.

morning gown a gown worn by either sex before formally dressing in the morning.

night gown a loose, indoor coat, not worn to bed.

night rail a long, indoor cape worn by women.

open robe a bodice and skirt, open in the front to reveal an elegant underskirt.

pantaloons introduced in the 1790s, long pants that extended to the ankles; worn by men.

paste glass cut and polished to look like gems.

petenlair a lady's thigh-length jacket with a sack back.

petticoat the name used for a woman's skirt.

physical wig a bushy, long wig worn by doctors and surgeons.

pinner a cap surrounded by a linen frill, worn by women.

polonaise an open gown bunched up in the back of the waist to form three separate bunches or swags.

pompon jeweled feathers or ribbons worn on the hair or on a cap.

riding habit a lady's dress with riding coat and waistcoat.

rollups stockings pulled up over the breeches at the knee.

rump a crescent-shaped bustle.

sack a voluminous gown with a back having box pleats stitched down each side.

shift a woman's linen and lace undergarment.

spencer a waist length jacket having a roll collar and cuffs, worn by both sexes.

stomacher on the front of a bodice, an inverted triangle of stiffened material, usually elaborately embroidered.

tie wig a wig having a pigtail tied with a bow at the nape of the neck.

tippet a short shoulder cape, often white in color, worn by women over the bosom or tucked into the bodice.

tricorne a three-cornered hat with the brim turned up on all sides.

tucker white edging around the top of a low-necked bodice.

waistcoat a sleeved or sleeveless jacket having slit sleeves and worn under a coat.

witch's hat a hat with a pointed crown, worn most often by rural women.

CLOTHING OF THE 17TH CENTURY

aigrette a tuft of feathers held together by gemstones.

basque a wide band that attached below a bodice or doublet. Also, a close-fitting bodice.

beaver a hat made from beaver fur.

black work black embroidery on white linen.

bombast cotton padding used to fill out garments.

boot hose an everyday hose worn over fine hose to protect it from boot wear.

breeches knee-length pants.

canions short, pantlike extensions worn with trunk hose.

cloak a coat, sometimes sleeved, and sometimes having a cape.

clocks embroidery on the sides of stockings.

cornet a woman's cap, having ribbons and streamers, and worn on the back of the head.

doublet a man's sleeved jacket, buttoned down the front.

Dutch breeches breeches ending above the knee.

echelles a row of bows of graduating length running down the front of a stomacher.

falling band a turned-down collar.

farthingale the hooped understructure of a hoop skirt. Also, the skirt itself.

fontange a high, tiered, frilled woman's headdress worn on the back of the head.

frogging ornamental rows of braids, buttons, and loops running down the front of a garment, most often associated with military uniforms.

gaberdine a long, loose coat having wide sleeves.

gauntlet gloves reminiscent of the armored gloves worn by knights but having decorative embroidery and fringes; worn by both sexes.

gorget a steel collar that protected the throat.

jerkin a sleeveless jacket worn over the doublet by men.

kerchief a folded square of material worn around the neck and shoulders.

lappets lace or linen streamers running down from the back of a woman's hat.

mantua a loose gown sashed or belted at the waist.

mules flat shoes with toe caps and no backs.

nightcap an embroidered, informal hat worn by men, not necessarily at night.

panes strips or ribbons of material produced by slashing a garment; fashionable in sleeves, doublets, and bodices.

peascod a padded doublet making the belly appear similar to a pea pod.

periwig a man's wig.

Persian vest a loose coat closed by a sash or a belt, worn by men.

petticoat breeches voluminously wide, pleated pants, reminiscent of a skirt, worn by men.

pickadil a framework used to support a ruff or a standing collar.

pinking a decorative pattern of small holes and slits.

plumpers cork balls placed in each cheek to plump them out, a fashion of women toward the end of the century.

points ribbon, linen, or silk laces tipped with aglets, used most frequently to tie hose to a doublet.

ruching decorative gathers and pleats.

ruff a radiating, pleated, and layered neckband made of lace or linen. A ruff of lace folded in a figure-8 pattern was popular.

shag a thick cloth and fur lining.

shoe rose a ribbon or lace rosette used decorate shoes.

smock a woman's T-shaped undergarment.

spangles decorative metal pieces.

Spanish breeches long breeches ending below the knee.

Steinkerk a loosely tied scarf or cravat worn with its ends drawn through a buttonhole or pinned to a coat.

stomacher an inverted triangle of stiffened material on a bodice.

sugarloaf hat a very high domed hat with a brim turned up on one side, made from block felt and worn by women. Formerly known as a copotain.

tippet a waist-length cape.

tricorne a triangular or three-cornered hat with turned-up brim, worn by men.

trunk hose padded or billowing round breeches.

wings decorative epaulettes on doublets and jerkins.

CLOTHING OF THE 16TH CENTURY

apron an apron made of wool or linen, worn with bibs by working class or rural women, worn without bibs by higher classes.

band a linen collar.

bases a knee-length skirt worn by men over their armor.

beaver a hat. Also, the fur used to make this hat.

biggin a close-fitting cap worn by infants and children.

billiment a decorative and frequently jeweled border on a French hood.

blackwork black embroidery on white linen.

bodyes a bodice.

bonnet a soft hat worn by both men and women.

boothose stockings with decorative tops turned down over boots.

breastplate an armor piece protecting the chest.

breeches pants extending from the waist to the knees and worn with stockings.

carcenet a heavy, bejeweled necklace made of gold and worn like a collar.

caul a decorative hairnet made of gold thread or silk.

chemise a woman's smock or undergarment.

chin-clout a type of light scarf worn over the chin and mouth of rural women.

chopins clogs; shoes with raised platforms made of wood or cork.

cod-piece a projecting pouch or appendage allowing room for the groin area in men's tight-fitting breeches or hose.

coif a linen skullcap, tied on under the chin by straps.

copotain a very high domed hat with a brim turned up on one side, made from block felt. Also known as a sugarloaf hat.

damask rich silk having floral or geometric decoration.

doublet a short, tuniclike garment worn over the shirt.

English hood a woman's hood that drapes over the sides of the face and forms an arch or gable over the forehead. Also known as a gable or pediment headdress.

ermine the most highly prized fur of the time, worn only by the nobility and royalty.

falling band a turned-down collar.

farthingale a hooped understructure employed to widen a woman's skirt from the waist down. Also, the skirt worn over this understructure.

French cloak a long cloak, usually worn draped over one shoulder.

French hood a small hood having a horseshoe-shaped crown, worn far back on the head.

galligaskins baggy breeches.

garters decorative bands used to hold up stockings.

girdle a decorative belt, band, or chain.

gorget a steel collar, an armor piece.

guards bands of material employed to cover seams, usually of contrasting color.

head rail a linen square arranged about the head. In the later portion of the century it was wired into elaborate shapes and trimmed with lace.

hose a man's body stockings, from waist to feet.

jacket same as today's jacket.

jerkin a sleeved or sleeveless waistcoat, worn over the doublet.

kerchief a large square of material worn as a shawl over the shoulders.

kirtle before 1545, a bodice and skirt; after 1545, the skirt alone.

lappet a decorative border on an English hood; it hung down on either side of the face or was turned up and pinned to the crown.

loose gown a garment that hung loosely in folds from the shoulders.

mandilion a loose, hip-length jacket with a standing collar.

mantle a large, diaphanous material worn as a shawl.

Mary Stuart hood a hood wired into a heart shape.

Milan bonnet a cornered hat with a turned-up, slit brim and a soft, pleated crown.

muckminder slang for handkerchief or napkin.

mules flat shoes without backs.

nightcap a men's indoor, linen cap.

nightgown a fur-lined gown worn by men and women either indoors or outdoors.

panes a decorative technique of slashing material vertically, as in a doublet or other outer garment.

pantofles short leather boots with thick cork soles.

pauldrons armor pieces that covered the shoulders.

peascod a form of doublet having a swollen belly, reminiscent of the shape of a peapod.

petticoat an underskirt.

pinking a decorative pattern of small holes or slits.

points ribbon, linen or silk laces tipped with aglets, used most frequently to tie hose to a doublet.

puffs material pulled through slashes in an outer garment. See PANES.

rail a square of material worn around the head or on the shoulders like a shawl.

rebato a wired collar that stands up around the back of the head and fans out in a series of pleats, worn by women.

rerebrace an armor piece that protects the upper arm.

ruching folded gathers used as a form of trim.

ruff the elaborate frill that radiated around standing collars of men and women.

russet a coarse wool worn by rural people.

sable a highly desired fur.

shag thick cloth used in linings.

slashing same as panes.

slops wide breeches.

snoskyn a woman's muff.

Spanish cloak a short, hooded cloak.

Spanish farthingale a bell or funnel-shaped skirt, formed by an understructure of this shape. See FARTHINGALE.

startups loose leather shoes.

stomacher on the front of the bodice, an inverted triangle of stiffened material.

tippet a short cape.

trunk hose hose that swelled out from the waist to the thighs.

trunk sleeve a sleeve swelled out from the upper arm and closing at the wrist.

underpropper a collar wire that supported the ruff.

vambrace an armor piece that protected the forearm.

velvet popular material of the upper classes.

Venetians breeches that stopped at the knee. These were either baggy, close-fitting, or pear-shaped.

waistcoat a type of jacket worn by men or women.

CLOTHING OF MEDIEVAL ENGLAND AND FRANCE (13th, 14th, and 15th Centuries)

agrafe a large metal brooch used to fasten cloaks and robes.

aiglets metal tips at the ends of laces to facilitate lacing of garments.

alb a long white tunic made of linen, a vestment of the clergy.

almoner tied to a girdlelike belt by a cord, a purse used for almsgiving.

almuce a large, fur-lined cape, often edged with fur tails and having a hood, worn by doctors of divinity and canons.

amice a white linen napkin adjusted about the neck, a vestment of the clergy.

anelace a long dagger worn from the belt by civilians.

baguette a lappet of mail.

bainbergs lower leg armor. Also known as bamberges.

balandrana a wide cloak, popularly used in the 13th and 14th centuries when traveling.

balays pink rubies.

baldric a wide, decorative belt, sometimes worn over the shoulder and hung with bells.

barmecloth an apron.

bascinet a domed, pointed helmet of the 14th and 15th centuries.

beavor facial armor.

bliant a garment resembling the surcoat, sometimes fur-lined; worn by both sexes.

bouchette a breastplate fastener.

bourdon a decorative walking staff.

brassarts steel arm plates or armor.

brayette a steel petticoat, similar to a baguette.

buskins high boots popularly worn by rural people and travelers.

bycoket a hat turned down in the front and turned up in the back.

camail the mail encircling the bottom of a bascinet and protecting the wearer's neck and upper chest.

capa a hooded robe.

cappa clausa a closed cape having only a small slit in the center to extend the hands out in an attitude of prayer; worn by the clergy.

cappa nigra a black choir cape, sometimes hooded.

capuchon a hood or cowl. Also known as a chaperon.

caputium a combination hood and cape. In the 15th century the color and lining of the hood denoted academic rank.

casque a helmet.

cassock a very long coat, fur-lined, and having tight sleeves; it fastened down the front and was worn by men.

cendal a material made of woven silk.

chain mail wrought iron rings riveted together and sewn onto a leather foundation for use as protective armor.

chapel de fer an iron hat of war.

chasuble a large, round garment with a center hole, slipped over the head and covering the body in voluminous folds, a clergyman's vestment.

chausses tight hose worn over the legs.

cingulum a waist belt.

cockers high-laced boots worn by rural men.

coif a close-fitting skull cap held on with a chin strap, worn by men.

coif-de-mailles a protective hat of mail.

colobium a plain tunic.

cope a large, full-bodied, decorative cape, frequently hooded and worn by the clergy.

cote an ordinary dress or gownlike garment worn by both sexes.

cotehardie a tight-fitting tunic worn by men. Also, a long, tight-fitting gown worn by women.

coudierès elbow guards, a form of armor.

cowl same as capuchon.

cracowes long-toed boots or shoes.

crespine a woman's headdress of the 14th century, characterized by two jeweled cauls or nets of wires holding hair in on either side of the head.

cuirass breast and back armor.

cuir-bouilli leather that has been boiled to harden it for use as protective armor.

cuissards armor pieces covering the thighs. Also known as cuisses.

dagges ornamental edgings on garments of the 14th century.

dalmatic a vestment similar to but shorter than an alb and having wider sleeves and a slit at the sides.

damask a rich, patterned fabric.

diaper ornamental embroidery.

dorelet a jewel-embroidered hairnet.

doublet a short, padded tunic.

dunster a broadcloth of the 14th century.

enbraude embroidery.

epaulières armor pieces protecting the shoulders.

ermine the most highly desired fur, worn by kings.

fitchets slits in outer garments used to provide access to inner garments or to purses, keys, and so forth.

fret a decorative hair net.

frontlet a cloth, silk, or velvet band worn on the forehead by 15th-century women.

frounce a flounce.

fustian cotton or wool cloth.

gambeson an early form of gipon.

gardcorp an outdoor garment worn by both sexes.

gauntlet a glove with protective metal plates to protect the hand, worn by knights.

gazzatum a fine silk of the 13th century.

genuilliers armor pieces protecting the knees.

gipon a close-fitting, waisted, quilted garment worn over a shirt; it evolved from the tunic. Also known as a doublet.

gipser a purse.

girdle a belt, usually decorative.

gite a gown.

gorget an armor piece protecting the throat. Also, the lower portion of a hood, covering the neck and upper chest.

greaves armor pieces protecting the shins. Also known as jambs, jambarts.

grise a gray fur from the Russian squirrel, popular with the upper middle classes.

hatere attire.

hauberk a coat or shirt of mail.

helm a helmet.

heuke a cloak worn by men or women.

hure a cap.

jambarts same as greaves.

kennel a form of hood forming a gable or pyramid shape over the forehead, popular with women in the 15th century. Also known as a gable or pedimental headdress.

kersche a kerchief.

kirtle a long, loose gown with flowing draperies and trains. Also, a waistcoat.

latchet a shoe or clog fastener.

lettice a pale, gray fur.

liripipe a short or long hanging tail extending from the point of some hoods and hats, sometimes twisting around the head like a turban.

mahoîtres padded shoulders, popular in the late 15th century.

mantle a loose, sleeveless coat.

mentonieres armor pieces protecting the throat and chin.

misericorde a dagger worn by knights on the right hip.

mitre a pointed or horned cap worn by bishops and cardinals during services.

nifles a 15th-century veil.

nouch a jeweled clasp.

pauldrons shoulder guards.

pelicon a long, loose outer garment.

petticoat a small coat worn under a larger one in the late 15th century.

pilche a coat made of skins of fur.

pilion a round hat of the 14th and 15th centuries.

plate steel armor pieces that eventually replaced mail.

points laces or ties with metal tips, used most frequently for attaching hose.

ponge a purse.

poulaines long-pointed shoes.

ray striped cloth.

rerebrace an armor piece protecting the upper arm.

roskyn squirrel fur.

sabbatons very broad, square-toed shoes. Also known as duck-billed shoes.

sable highly prized (but less so than ermine) fur worn by princes.

samite a rich silk interwoven with gold thread.

slops in the 14th century, a jacket. In the 15th century, a shoe or cassock. In the 16th century, wide breeches.

standard of mail a collar of mail for protecting the neck.

sequanie a loose outer frock, worn by rural women.

surcoat a tunic worn over armor.

taces a skirt of protective plate, extending from the waist to the thighs.

tilting helm a large helmet.

tippet a long streamer or cape.

tunic a long or short, sleeved or sleeveless garment, sometimes having slits at the front or sides; eventually replaced by the gipon.

vair black and white squirrel skins arranged in decorative patterns.

vambraces armour pieces protecting the lower arms.

visor a slitted, face shield that pivoted on a knight's helmet.

volupere a nightcap of the 14th century.

wimple a veil worn over the neck and chin in the 13th century.

CLOTHING OF ANCIENT ROME

abolla a man's woolen cloak folded double and fastened with a brooch.

balteus a belt formed from the twisted folds of a toga.

birrus a hooded cape worn in inclement weather.

calceus an untanned leather boot having slits at the ankle, drawn together by leather thongs.

clavus a stripe.

crepida a low, half-boot exposing the toes.

cucullus a hood.

cuirass a metal tunic, hinged front to back and molded to fit the figure, worn by the military.

laena a man's thick, woolen cloak worn in very cold weather.

loincloth worn under the toga before tunics came into vogue.

paenula a poncholike, wool cape, sometimes having a hood, worn by both sexes.

palla long, loose outer garment worn by women; similar to the Greek himation.

paludamentum a purple cloak clasping at the right shoulder, worn by military officers.

pilleus a felt, conical hat, worn by men.

sagum a thick, woolen cloak, usually red, worn by those who were not officers in the military. Similar to the abolla.

sandals the popular footwear of the period.

stola a long tunic reaching to the feet. When it had sleeves, they were attached separately by means of brooches.

toga a circular segment of fabric about 18 feet long and 7 feet wide; it was elaborately wrapped and draped about the body (and sometimes over the head in religious ceremonies) and was made of natural-colored wool.

toga candida a plain, white toga worn by campaigning politicians.

toga cinctus Gabinus a toga worn with the baltaeus passed twice around the waist instead of over the left shoulder.

toga picta a purple toga with gold embroidery, worn by emperors, consuls, and generals.

toga praetexta a white toga having a purple or scarlet band along its straight edge, worn by children under age 16 and by magistrates.

toga pulla a black or dark-colored toga for mourning.

toga pura the natural-colored wool toga for everyday wear.

tunica a wool or linen tunic.

tunica palmata a purple tunic richly embroidered in gold, worn by emperors and consuls.

CLOTHING OF ANCIENT GREECE

ampyx a metal diadem or women's headband, often worn with a hairnet.

cestus an elaborate outer girdle.

chiton a short or long tunic. The short version was sometimes attached to only one shoulder. The long version tended to be worn by older men or men of prestige.

chitoniscus a knitted vest worn over a chiton.

chlamys a man's oblong wrap or cape made of wool; it fastened with a clasp in front or at the right shoulder.

diplax a woman's outdoor wrap, similar to a chlamys.

Greek fillet a braid of hair wound about the head several times, worn by women and by male athletes.

himation a long, loose outer garment wrapped about the body and arranged in folds and sometimes pulled up over the head. It was worn by men and women and its elaborate wrapping was difficult to master.

petasos a flat felt hat with flaps over the front and back and over the ears.

pilos a conical felt or leather hat worn by sailors, fishermen, and artisans.

sakkos a slinglike headdress made of goat's hair, worn by women.

splendone a slinglike headress made of decorated cloth or leather and ending in a tie or band, worn by women.

stephane a metal circlet hair bow.

tribon a small, oblong shawl worn by men.

Weapons

GUNS AND BULLETS

assault rifle any automatic rifle intended to be used for an assault or attack on humans.

automatic any gun that fires continuously while the trigger is pressed.

barrel the metal tube through which bullets are projected after firing.

baton rounds shotgun projectiles that stun but do not kill; used in riot situations.

bayonet a knife mounted on the barrel of a rifle for use in hand-to-hand combat.

bead a small projection on the muzzle of a gun, used for sighting.

bird shot small shotgun pellets used in bird hunting; may also be used to control a crowd in riot situations.

bluing the colored finish on the metal parts of a gun.

bolt a sliding rod that pushes a cartridge into the firing chamber.

bolt-action a gun having a manually operated bolt.

bore the inside portion and diameter of the barrel, extending from the breech to the muzzle. Also known as the gauge.

box magazine a rectangular or square magazine.

brass catcher a firearm attachment that catches spent cartridges ejected from an automatic or semiautomatic rifle.

breech the rear portion of a gun, behind the bore.

buck and ball a cartridge having a round ball and three buckshot.

buckshot large shotgun pellets used for large game.

bullet, cannelured an elongated, grooved bullet.

bullet, elongated a long bullet, as distinguished from a round one.

bullet, flat-point a bullet having a flat nose.

bullet, hollow-point a bullet having a hollow nose; it produces a wider area of damage on impact.

bullet, metal-case a bullet in which a metal jacket covers the nose.

bullet, soft-point a bullet having a lead tip; it produces a wider area of damage on impact.

bullet, wad-cutter a cylindrical, flat-topped bullet noted for making clean holes, used for target practice.

bullpup a firearm in which a magazine is inserted in the buttstock, behind the trigger mechanism.

butt the bottom of the grip on a pistol; the portion of a rifle placed against the shoulder when firing. Also known as the buttstock.

caliber the diameter of the barrel hole.

carbine a rifle having a barrel less than 22 inches in length.

cartridge the container holding the explosive charge.

centerfire cartridge a cartridge having its primer in the center of its base.

chamber the rear portion of the barrel; it receives the shell or cartridge.

choke a device that alters a shotgun muzzle to achieve a desired shot pattern.

clip a receptacle used to hold several cartridges that are loaded simultaneously.

cock same as hammer.

cylinder a revolving cylinder containing several cartridge chambers.

derringer a single-shot, pocket-sized pistol having a short barrel, the ultimate firearm for concealment.

double-action refers to a revolver that can fire successive shots simply by pulling the trigger without having to first cock the hammer.

drift deviation laterally of a bullet's trajectory.

drum a round, spring-loaded magazine.

duckbill choke a muzzle attachment on a combat rifle used to spread shot in a wide line to hit more than one advancing target.

ejector a device that ejects a cartridge case.

firing pin the projection on the firing mechanism that strikes the primer or cap to detonate the powder charge.

flash hider a muzzle attachment used to conceal the flash of firing, especially at night.

fléchette a finned projectile used in a combat shotgun to produce greater wound penetration.

gauge the interior diameter of a shotgun barrel. Also known as the bore.

grip the handle on a pistol.

hair trigger a sensitive trigger requiring only a light pull to release it.

hammer the cock or lock portion that strikes the primer of a cartridge to fire it.

jacket a covering on a bullet.

kick the recoil after firing.

lock the mechanism that detonates a charge. Also, to engage the safety.

machine pistol a compact, automatic, or semiautomatic firearm.

magazine in a repeating firearm, the receptacle or clip that holds and advances the ammunition to the chamber.

muzzle the mouth or front of the barrel, from which the bullets emerge.

muzzle brake a rifle attachment that reduces recoil by diverting internal gases.

muzzle velocity the speed of a bullet as it emerges from the muzzle.

pistol carbine a pistol having a removable shoulder stock to allow it to be fired as a rifle.

recoil the kick of a gun after firing.

revolver any pistol with a rotating, chambered cylinder allowing firing in quick succession.

rimfire cartridge a cartridge with its primer rimming the base, as distinguished from a centerfire cartridge.

riot gun a short shotgun that fires nonlethal projectiles in riot control situations.

safety a lock or mechanism that is set to prevent the unintentional firing of a gun.

shotgun a gun that fires a number of small pellets instead of a single bullet with each shot.

sight any bead or device aligned with the eye to facilitate aiming.

silencer see suppressor.

single-action refers to a firearm that must be manually cocked before each shot.

stock the wooden part of a rifle that rests against the shoulder when firing.

submachine gun a light, hand-held machine gun that fires standard pistol rounds.

suppressor a noise-suppressing, baffled tube attaching to the muzzle of a gun.

tracer bullet a bullet that leaves a glowing trail, allowing its trajectory to be seen at night; used in the military.

trigger pull refers to the pressure necessary to pull and release a trigger; descriptive terms include hair trigger, creeping pull, dragging pull, still pull, hard pull, smooth pull, and fine pull.

Types of Guns

revolvers Browning, Colt, Ruger Bearcat .22, Ruger GP 100-.357, Mauser, Dan Wesson .44 Magnum, Dan Wesson .22 Magnum, Dan Wesson .41 Magnum, Smith and Wesson .44 Magnum, Smith and Wesson .25, Smith and Wesson Police .686.

automatic and semiautomatic handguns Beretta Pistola Automatica 9mm, Beretta Pistola Automatica Brevetto 7.65mm, Charter .38, Colt Police .45, Lugar 7.65, 9mm Parabellum, Mauser C96, Remington, Singer, .357 Magnum (several makers), Walther .38.

machine guns Barrett, British Lancaster, British Sterling, Calico 100, AK 47, Colt AR-15, Harrison and Richards, Plainfield, Ruger Mini 14, Sten, Thompson, Universal, Uzi.

rifles, carbines, shotguns Browning, Calico, Enfield, Harrison and Richards, Martin, Mauser, Plainfield, Remington, Ruger, Shiloh, Winchester.

antique guns blunderbuss, breech-loader, Colt six-shooter, dueling pistols, flintlock, gatling gun, musket, muzzle loader.

SWORDS

baldric a tooled-leather belt worn across the chest to support a sword.

broadsword any sword with a broad blade.

claymore a large, dual-edged broadsword used by the Scottish Highlanders.

cutlass a relatively short sword with a curved blade, used by 18th-century sailors and pirates.

ensiform shaped like a sword.

epee a fencing sword having a cupped handle and a blade with no edge but a blunt point.

Excalibur King Arthur's famous sword.

falchion a short sword with a broad, curving blade.

false edge term used to describe a single-edged sword whose tip has been sharpened on both sides.

foil a thin-bladed fencing sword with a flat guard.

gladiate shaped like a sword.

hand-and-a-half an intermediate or smaller sword than a two-handed sword.

hanger any short sword hung from the side of the body and used as a backup for a larger sword. Also known as a side-arm.

hilt a sword handle.

knuckle-bow a knuckle guard at the hilt.

one-hand sword a very short sword.

pommel the knob at the end of the hilt, sometimes weighted to help balance the sword.

quillons small side projections at the hilt.

rapier a long, slender, dual-edged sword with a cupped hilt, used in the 16th and 17th centuries. An 18th-century version had no cutting edge but a sharp point for thrusting.

saber a heavy sword with a slightly curved blade, used by the cavalry. Also a two-edged sword used in fencing.

scabbard a sword sheath.

scimitar an Oriental sword with a curved blade.

shamshir classic Persian and Indian saber with a curved blade.

sidearm same as a hanger.

smallsword a small sword used as a fashionable costume item in the 17th and 18th centuries.

spear point a symmetrical blade with a sharp point.

two-hand sword a very large sword requiring two hands to swing.

DAGGERS

anlace a dual-edged, medieval dagger.

baselard a dagger having a crosspiece as a guard for the hand at the pommel.

bodkin a medieval dagger or stiletto.

bowie knife U.S. fighting and hunting knife having dual edge at the tip.

dudgeon dagger having a handle made out of wood of the same name. Also, the hilt of any dagger.

fullers grooves in a dagger blade.

grip the handle.

hilt the handle.

jambiya classic Arabian dagger with dual-edged, curved blade.

khanjar Indian and Persian dagger having a jade or ivory, pistollike grip and a forward or backward-curving handle.

knuckle-guard a bar or shield at the hilt to protect the fingers.

kris classic Malay dagger with a wavy blade.

misericord in medieval times, a narrow dagger used to deliver death quickly to an already wounded knight.

pommel the knob at the butt end of some daggers, sometimes highly ornamented.

pugio an ancient Roman military dagger having a very broad blade and a narrow grip.

quillons two side projections at the guard or hilt.

quillon dagger a dagger having quillons.

rondel a medieval dagger having a disk-like pommel and guard and a narrow blade, used from 1320 to 1550.

skean Irish and Scottish dual-edged dagger.

stiletto dagger having a very narrow blade for stabbing or thrusting only.

swordbreaker a dagger having a deeply notched blade for catching and breaking the blade of a sword.

CLUBS AND HAMMERS

chigiriki a heavy ball suspended on a 4- to 6-foot chain, which is attached to a long shaft and swung about to strike or entangle an enemy; of Japanese origin.

horseman's hammer a combination hammer and pick mounted on a shaft, used by horsemen to knock out or kill an enemy.

kusarigama a Japanese pick hammer with a long chain and weighted ball at the end.

mace a club with a weighty or spiked end.

morning star a spiked ball on a chain suspended from a shaft.

truncheon a heavy club.

war-flail one or more heavy weights attached to a short chain or chains on a shaft.

POLE ARMS (halberds, lances, pikes, etc.)

bardiche a Russian poleax used from the 16th to the 18th centuries.

bill a large curving or hooking blade (with the cutting edge on the inside, as a scythe) attached to a long pole.

catchpole a long pole with spring arms, used to catch a man by an arm or leg and pull him off his horse during battle. Also known as a mancatcher. See sleeve-tangler.

glaive a long, broad knifelike blade attached to a long pole.

halberd a weapon head consisting of an ax blade, a sharp spike or point, and a beak, attached to a long pole; used in the 15th and 16th centuries.

half-moon a broad, two-pronged blade in the shape of a crescent moon, a Spanish weapon.

hammer a weapon head consisting of a sharp hammer head on a long shaft, for piercing armor or knocking an enemy out through armor.

lance a sharp metal head on a long shaft, used by soldiers on horseback.

mancatcher same as catchpole.

military fork a two-pronged fork mounted on a long shaft.

partisan a weapon head consisting of a broad spear tip with a crescent base attached to a long shaft.

pike 16-foot shaft with sharp point, used to defend musketeers against attacking cavalry in the 17th century.

poleax a broad ax blade mounted on a long shaft.

quarterstaff a simple wooden staff.

ranseur a weapon head consisting of one long point and two shorter points or blades projecting from its base. Also known as a corseque or spetum.

sleeve tangler a Japanese, multitoothed pole used to catch or snag apparel in order to pull an enemy off a horse.

spontoon a short pike.

thrusting spear a long-shafted spear with a broad, sharp point meant for stabbing instead of slashing.

trident a three-pronged fork on a long shaft.

Food and Drink

BOTTLES AND GLASSES

cocktail glass a broad, tulip-shaped glass holding 3 to 6 ounces.

cooler a tall glass holding 14 to 21 ounces.

cordial a very small, tulip-shaped glass with a narrowed top holding 1 ounce.

delmonico similar to a cocktail glass but having a slightly taller, narrower cup that holds 4½ to 7 ounces.

deep-saucer champagne glass a glass having a tall stem and broad, saucerlike cup and holding 6 ounces or more.

fifth a bottle holding one-fifth of a gallon.

flagon a wine or liquor bottle having a handle and a spout for pouring

highball a tall glass holding 8 to 11 ounces. Also known as a collins glass.

jeroboam a wine bottle holding four-fifths of a gallon.

jigger a small glass holding 1½ ounces, used largely for measuring. Also known as a shot glass.

keg a small cask or barrel holding 5 to 10 gallons of beer.

magnum a bottle holding two-fifths of a gallon of wine or liquor.

old fashioned a standard drink glass, narrow at the bottom and widening at the top and holding 6 to 15 ounces.

schooner a large beer glass.

shot same as jigger.

snifter a gobletlike glass narrowed at the top and usually holding about 6 ounces.

tankard a large, drinking mug with a handle and often a hinged cover.

wine glass a tall, long-stemmed, tulip-shaped glass holding 8 to 11 ounces.

WINES AND WINE TERMS

Asti Spumante Italian sparkling white wine.

astringency the quality of wine that makes the mouth pucker, especially found in red wines.

Bardolino a light red wine produced in northern Italy.

Barolo a rich Italian red wine from Piedmont.

Beaujolais a light and fruity French red wine from southern Burgundy.

Beerenauslese wine made from individually picked grapes rather than bunches.

blanc de blancs French term meaning, "white of whites," referring to the lightest, most delicate white wines made from all white grapes.

body flavor intensity.

Bordeaux a city in France's southwestern wine region.

Botrytis cinerea a beneficial mold that grows on late-harvest grapes that helps to produce a rich, sweet wine.

bouquet the fragrance of a wine.

brut French term referring to the driest of all champagnes.

Burgundy French region renowned for producing fine wines.

Cabernet Sauvignon the red grape used in the making of exceptional red wines, especially those of Bordeaux and California.

Catawba an American, light red grape used in white and sparkling wines.

cave French term for "cellar."

Chablis a town in northern Burgundy region of France, renowned for its dry, white wines.

champagne sparkling white wine.

château any vineyard property in Bordeaux.

chewy wine connoisseur's term to describe great-bodied red wines with a strong taste and aftertaste.

Chianti a dry red wine produced in the Monti Chianti region of Italy.

claret the English term for Bordeaux red wines.

clos French term for a stone-walled vineyard.

coarse wine connoisseur's term describing a wine having a rough flavor with no finesse.

complex wine connoisseur's term describing a wine with multiple flavor overtones.

decant to pour out wine slowly into a decanter to eliminate its sediment.

demi-sec champagne term meaning "half-dry."

Diamond U.S. white grape used to produce tart white wine and champagne.

Dom Perignon the 17th-century cellar-master of France, known as the inventor of champagne.

dry opposite of sweet.

finesse wine connoisseur's term describing a wine whose flavor is distinct and delicate.

finish a wine's aftertaste.

flabby wine connoisseur's term describing a poor quality wine with weak, characterless flavor.

flat wine connoisseur's term for a wine with dull flavor or a sparkling wine whose effervescence has dissipated.

flinty wine connoisseur's term describing a dry white wine with a crisp flavor.

Gallo a giant winery in California.

Gamay a red grape from which French Beaujolais is made.

green young, unaged wines high in acidity.

Grenache a red grape used in dessert wines and rosés.

hard describes the flavor of tannin in wine that has barely aged.

Inglenook California winery known for its Cabernet Sauvignon wines.

Kabinett German term meaning the driest of wines.

Madeira a fortified Portuguese wine, similar to sherry in flavor.

mellow wine connoisseur's term describing a soft wine with full flavor.

Moselle German river and adjacent area where delicate white wines are produced.

must the juice drawn from the grapes in the first step of wine making.

musty wine connoisseur's term describing wine with a flavor similar to old, rotten wood, as a moldy wine cask.

Napa Valley renowned wine-producing region north of San Francisco, California.

nose boquet of a wine.

pétillant French term for a wine with slight sparkle.

Petite-Syrah a grape that produces a deep, red wine.

Pinot Blanc a white grape used mostly for blending.

Pinot Chardonnay a white grape that produces French white Burgundies and California white wines.

piquant wine connoisseur's term describing a lively and not unpleasant acidic flavor.

Port Portuguese blended dessert wine.

Rheingau renowned wine-producing region on the banks of the Rhine in Germany.

Rhine wine German white wine produced on the banks of the Rhine River.

rosé a fruity, pink-colored wine.

rough wine connoisseur's term describing a wine that hasn't aged long enough and has a puckerish or coarse aftertaste.

Sauternes in Bordeaux, a wine district known for its sweet white wines.

sec French term for "dry."

sherry Spanish wine fortified with brandy.

short wine connoisseur's term describing a wine whose taste is only briefly perceived.

Soave Italian dry white wine.

soft wine with a low alcohol content.

sommelier French term for a wine waiter who has keys to and great knowledge of the wine cellar. A wine steward.

spritzer a cold drink made of wine mixed with sparkling water.

tannin a substance in wine known to produce an astringent flavor.

tart a sharp flavor.

Tokay Hungarian white dessert wine.

Trockenbeerenauslese German term for a white wine produced from a very late harvest of grapes that has been infected with botrytis.

varietal wine any wine named after the principal grape it is made from.

vin ordinaire French term for a cheap, red wine.

vintage the year of a grape's harvest, as labeled on a bottle of wine.

vintner a wine merchant.

wine cooler a mixed cold drink of wine, fruit juice, and soda water.

woody wine connoisseur's term describing a wine that tastes woody, as if it were left too long in its cask.

Zinfandel a red grape that produces a fruity red wine when young. When aged, it produces a rich, complex wine.

LIQUEURS

abisante a licorice-flavored liqueur used as a substitute for absinthe.

abricots, crême de a French apricot liqueur.

absinthe a green liqueur having a high alcohol content and a bitter licorice flavor, derived from wormwood and other herbs.

'advokaat eggnog liqueur.

almondrado a blend of almond liqueur and tequila.

amande, crème d' liqueur made from almonds.

amaretto an almond-flavored liqueur made from the pits of apricots.

amer picon a French aperitif made from gentian, oranges, and quinine.

anise a licorice-flavored liqueur made from anise seeds. Also called anisette.

apry a liqueur made from apricot pits.

B and B a blend of brandy and bénédictine.

Benedictine a blend of brandy, sugar, and 27 different herbs, including hyssop, mint, and melissa; developed by French Benedictine monks.

cacao, crème de a blend of chocolate and vanilla beans.

café bénédictine a blend of benedictine and coffee liqueur.

café orange a coffee and orange liqueur.

cassis, crème de liqueur derived from black currants.

cerise, crème de French cherry liqueur.

chartreuse a spicy, French blend of brandy, plants, and more than 100 herbs.

chéri-suisse a cherry and chocolate liqueur.

cherry marnier French cherry liqueur having a slight almond flavor.

cherry rocher French cherry liqueur.

choclair American chocolate and coconut-flavored liqueur.

chococo a chocolate and coconut liqueur from the Virgin Islands.

cocoribe a coconut and rum liqueur.

coffee liqueur a coffee bean liqueur.

coffee sambuca a blend of coffee liqueur and sambuca.

cointreau French liqueur derived from orange peels.

cordial médoc a French blend of brandy, crême de cacao, cherries, and oranges.

curaçao a liqueur derived from curaçao orange peels.

drambuie a blend of scotch, heather, honey, and herbs.

fraises, crème de strawberry liqueur.

framboise French raspberry liqueur.

galliano a liqueur flavored with anise and vanilla.

glayva a blend of scotch, anise, honey, and herbs.

grand marnier French blend of cognac and orange flavor.

Irish mist blend of Irish whiskey, honey, and orange.

kahlua a Mexican coffee liqueur flavored with vanilla.

kümmel a caraway-flavored liqueur.

mandarine cognac with tangerine flavor.

maraschino cherry and almond liqueur.

menthe, crème de a liqueur flavored with mint leaves and menthol.

midori a Japanese liqueur having a honeydew melon flavor.

noyaux, crème de almond-flavored liqueur made from the pits of apricots, cherries, peaches, and plums.

ouzo Greek, anise-flavored liqueur.

parfait a'amour a liqueur flavored with several ingredients, including lemon, coriander, anisette, vanilla, orange, and flowers.

pasha a Turkish coffee liqueur.

peppermint schnapps liqueur flavored with mint.

pernod licorice-flavored liqueur.

prunella a plum-flavored liqueur.

rock and rye a blend of rye, rock candy syrup, and fruit juice.

roiano an Italian liqueur flavored with anise and vanilla.

ron coco liqueur flavored with coconut and rum.

rosé, crème de liqueur made from vanilla and spices.

sabra an Israeli liqueur flavored with chocolate and orange.

sambuca an Italian, licorice-flavored liqueur.

sciarada Italian liqueur flavored with lemon and orange.

sloe gin liqueur made from sloe plums.

Southern Comfort New Orleans peach-flavored whiskey.

tia maria Jamaican liqueur made from coffee beans and spices.

tuaca Italian brandy with citrus and milk.

van der mint chocolate mint.

Wild Turkey bourbon flavored with spices.

Yukon Jack Canadian whiskey flavored with citrus and herbs.

FRENCH COOKING TERMS

accolade an arrangement of two chickens, ducks, or fish back to back on a serving platter.

affriole fresh from the garden.

aillade garlic sauce.

à la bayonnaise in the style of Bayonne—garnished with braised onions and gherkins.

à la béarnaise in the style of Bearn—a thick sauce made from eggs, butter, and mustard.

à la Beauharnais in the style of Beauharnais—garnished with artichokes in tarragon sauce.

à la bigarade in Seville-orange style—served with sour-orange sauce.

à la boulangère in the style of the baker's wife—served with fried onions and potatoes.

à la broche served on a skewer.

à la calédonienne baked in butter, parsley, and lemon juice.

à la carte by the bill of fare—ordering each item separately instead of by set combination.

à la châtelaine in the style of the lady of the castle—garnished with celery, artichoke hearts, baked tomatoes, and sautéed potatoes.

à la Clermont in the style of Clermont—garnished with fried onions and stuffed potatoes.

à la cordon bleu in blue ribbon style—stuffed with ham and cheddar cheese and topped with creamy mushrooms.

à la crapaudine in toad style—chicken broiled and trussed to resemble a toad.

à la créole in creole style—served with onions, peppers, and tomatoes.

à la Croissy in the style of Marquis de Croissy—with carrots and turnips.

à la diable in devil style—deviled or served spicy.

à la duchesse in duchess style—a fish served with oyster sauce; a meat served with braised lettuce and duchesse potatoes; or a soup with asparagus tips and truffles.

à la fermière in the style of the farmer's wife—a roast served with turnips, carrots, celery, and onions.

à la flamande in Flemish style—with braised cabbage, carrots, potatoes, and pork.

à la florentine in the style of Florence—garnished with spinach.

à la forestière in the style of the forester's wife—with mushrooms and potato balls browned in butter.

à la française in French style—with mixed vegetables and hollandaise sauce.

à l'africaine in African style—curried and spiced.

à la genèvoise in Geneva style—with red wine sauce.

à la Godard in the style of Godard—garnished with truffles and mushrooms.

à la grecque in Greek style—with olives, oil, and rice.

à la Hong Kong Hong Kong style—with noodles and rice.

à la hongroise Hungarian style—with paprika and sour cream.

à la julienne in Juliana style—with thin strips of vegetables.

à la king mushrooms in a creamy white sauce with red pimentos.

à l'allemande in German style—garnished with potatoes and sauerkraut.

à la luzonia in Luzon style—with pork and rice.

à la macédoine in Macedonian style—with diced fruits and vegetables.

à la Marengo in Marengo style—served with a sauce comprised of mushrooms, tomatoes, olives, olive oil, and wine.

à la meunière in the style of the miller's wife—a fish sautéed in butter, dipped in flour, and served with a butter and lemon sauce.

à la milanaise in Milan style—dipped in egg, bread crumbs, and parmesan cheese.

à la mode de Caen in the style of Caen—with leeks, vegetables, and wine, prepared with tripe.

à la moscovite in Moscow style—garnished with caviar.

à la napolitaine in Neapolitan style—a meat served with eggplant and tomatoes or spaghetti served with tomato sauce and cheese.

à l'andalouse in Andalusian style—a soup served with eggplant, red peppers, and rice.

à la neige in snowy style—served with egg whites or rice.

à la Normande braised in white wine, in the Norman style.

à la parisienne in Parisian style—garnished with small, sautéed potatoes and braised celery.

à la périgourdine in the style of Périgord—with truffles or truffle-based sauce.

à la portugaise in Portuguese style—with olive oil, garlic, onions, and tomatoes.

à la provençale in Provençale style—with mushrooms, onions, tomatoes, olive oil, and garlic.

à la reine in the queen's style—chicken with truffles and mushrooms.

à l'arménienne in Armenian style—with rice pilaf.

à la Rossini in the style of Rossini—with a sauce of madeira wine, mushrooms, goose liver paste, and truffles.

à la soubise in onion-purée style.

à la tartare minced beef served raw with capers and a raw egg.

à l'indienne in East Indian style—with curried sauce or curried rice.

à l'italienne in Italian style—with artichoke bottoms and macaroni.

à point medium.

assaisonnement seasoning.

au beurre noir with browned butter sauce.

au blanc in white style—with a white sauce.

au bleu in blue style—cooked fish in vinegar.

au brun cooked in brown sauce.

au gras in the fat. Cooked in the broth or gravy.

au gratin with a crust of bread crumbs or grated cheese and browned slightly.

au maigre lean style, without fat.

au naturel food served uncooked, unseasoned, in its natural state.

au vin blanc made in white wine.

aux fines herbes served with finely chopped chives, onions, parsley, shallots, and sorrel.

baton breadstick.

batterie de cuisine all the necessary kitchen utensils and equipment.

beurre butter.

beurre fondu melted butter.

beurre noir browned butter sauce seasoned with parsley and wine vinegar.

bien cuit well done.

blanc d'oeuf egg white.

boeuf épicé spiced beef.

bon appétit good appetite.

bouquet garni herbs tied in a cheesecloth bag and cooked with sauces, soups, stews, and other dishes to flavor them.

buisson a mound of food.

canard à la presse pressed duck.

cannelé fluted; pastry crust or decoratively cut vegetables.

carottes à la flamande Flemish style carrots—cooked in sugar and cream.

carte de vins wine list.

carte du jour menu of the day.

champignons au gratin baked mushrooms with a crust.

chantilly flavored whipped cream.

chapon a breadcrust cooked in soup.

château potatoes parboiled and braised potatoes.

chausson puff pastry.

chef de cuisine the head chef.

civet rabbit stew made with blood and red wine.

consommé clear soup; broth, bouillon.

coq au vin chicken simmered in wine.

coq au vin rouge chicken cooked in red wine.

coquille a pastry shell resembling the shell of a scallop.

Cordon Bleu Blue Ribbon, a Paris cooking school.

crème chantilly vanilla-flavored whipped cream.

crème vichyssoise leek and potato cream soup served cold.

crêpe a thin pancake.

crêpe Suzette orange-flavored crêpe filled with cream and served with flaming brandy.

croissant crescent-shaped roll.

croquette a little ball of minced chicken, meat, seafood, or vegetables coated with egg and bread crumbs.

croustade a crust dish made of bread or a pastry shell fried in deep fat.

croûte au pot crust for the pot; clear soup with floating toast pieces.

du jour of the day; today's.

duxelles sautéed mushroom hash.

entrée entrance; the main dish in the United States.

épigramme a meal having two different kinds of fish or meat. It may also include the same fish or meat cooked in two different ways.

filet mignon dainty fillet; boned steak.

flambé flaming; any food served aflame—a brandy or rum coating set on fire.

flan piecrust with sweet filling.

florentine served on a bed of spinach.

fond de cuisine stocks, broths.

fromage cheese.

garbure bacon and cabbage soup.

garçon boy; waiter.

hollandaise in the Dutch style; a sauce of butter, egg yolks, and lemon juice or vinegar.

hors d'oeuvre appetizer.

limande lemon sole.

macédoine a medley of fruits or vegetables in a dessert, sauce, or salad.

macédoine de fruits fruit salad.

nappé napkined; lightly coated with icing or sauce.

oeuf egg.

oeufs à la coque eggs in shell.

oeufs farcis deviled eggs.

omelette aux fines herbes omelet with herbs.

omelette aux pointes d'asperges omelet with asparagus tips.

pain bread.

paner to coat with bread crumbs.

pâté liver or meat paste.

pâté d'amandes almond paste.

pâté d'anchois anchovy paste.

pâté de foie gras goose liver paste.

paysanne peasant style; meat or poultry braised and served with bacon and buttery vegetables.

persillade chopped parsley garnish.

petit pain a roll.

pièce de résistance piece of resistance; the main dish or main course.

pointes d'asperges asparagus tips.

poivrade peppery sauce.

pomme de terre potato.

potage crême d'orge cream of barley soup.

potage purée à la reine puree soup in the queen's style; cream of chicken soup.

potage purée de marrons chestnut soup.

potage Rossini cream of onion soup with grated cheese.

potage velours velvet soup; a very smooth carrot and tapioca soup.

potpourri rotten pot; hodgepodge; a mixture of things.

poulette a young hen.

printanière springlike; refers to mixed vegetables cut into decorative shapes.

ragoût stew.

ragoût de mouton mutton stew.

ratatouille a stew comprised of eggplant, squash, tomato, onions, and olive oil.

ravigote revive; strongly seasoned white sauce.

remoulade remolded; mayonnaise seasoned with anchovy paste, capers, gherkins, herbs, and mustard.

ribaude baked apple dumpling.

ris de veau sweetbread of a calf.

rissole turnover with savory filling.

riz au lait rice pudding.

roulade rolled up.

roux reddish brown; browned butter and flour mixture, used to thicken sauces and soups.

saignant underdone; bloody.

salade niçoise salad in the style of Nice; a salad of potatoes, string beans, tomatoes, anchovy fillets, capers, and olives.

sauce béarnaise a butter sauce with egg yolks, chopped onions, and vinegar.

sauce béchamel a white cream sauce.

sauce bordelaise Bourdeaux-style sauce; brown sauce with a flavoring of bordeaux wine.

sauce suprême a rich white sauce made from chicken stock and cream.

serviette napkin.

smitane sour cream.

sommelier wine steward.

soufflé puffed up; a light and fluffy baked dish made as a dessert or as a main dish.

soupçon suspicion; a pinch or hint of an ingredient.

soupe à l'oignon onion soup.

talmouse cheesecake.

tourte a round, meat-filled pie.

velouté velvety; a very smooth white sauce made of chicken or veal stock.

vichyssoise soup made of leeks, potatoes, chicken consommé, butter, and cream, and served cold.

vinaigrette salad dressing of olive oil, vinegar, and seasonings.

zéphir anything light and frothy.

HANDTOOLS

WRENCHES

adjustable wrench a common steel wrench with adjustable jaws for loosening or tightening nuts and bolts. Also known as a Crescent™ wrench.

allen wrench an L-shaped, hexagonal rod, used for turning hexagonal screws or bolts. Also known as a hex key.

box wrench a steel wrench with a toothed ring on each end, for loosening or tightening nuts and bolts.

chain wrench a wrench with a chain on one end, used when a powerful torque is needed, as for pipes or pipe fittings.

combination wrench a steel wrench with standard open jaws on one end and a box wrench (toothed ring) on the other.

Crescent™ wrench brand name for an adjustable wrench.

crow's foot wrench a standard, open-jawed wrench with a special hole in its neck in which a socket wrench can be inserted for driving; commonly used in hard-to-reach areas.

deep-throat socket wrench a hollow, steel tube with hexagonal openings on either end, for turning nuts and valves. Also known as a plumber's wrench.

faucet spanner a flat, metal bar having various openings on its ends and down its length, used in several plumbing applications.

monkey wrench a large, heavy adjustable wrench used in plumbing.

nut driver a screwdriverlike wrench with a hex opening at the end of its shaft for turning hex nuts and bolts in tight places.

nut splitter a P-shaped tool used to cut away nuts that are frozen or irretractable.

pipe wrench a large, heavy adjustable wrench with toothed jaws, used by plumbers for turning pipes and pipe fittings.

socket wrench a steel wrench with a head containing a ratcheting mechanism and a square plug on which variably sized sockets are attached, for turning nuts and bolts in limited space.

spanner an English word for a wrench. Also, a plumbing wrench with special notches for loosening faucet nuts.

spud wrench a metal wrench with large open jaws on either end, used to turn oversized nuts, such as those used in plumbing fixtures.

strap wrench a wrench with a fabric strap on one end, used for turning pipe without making scratches.

PLIERS

end nippers metal pliers with wide, beveled jaws, used for pulling out or cutting off nails.

fence pliers multiuse pliers with jaws to pull wire, a hammerlike end for driving staples into posts, and a hook or claw for pulling staples out, used to erect wire fences.

lineman's pliers square-jawed pliers for cutting and manipulating wire. Also known as electrician's pliers or wiring pliers.

locking pliers pliers that can be locked or clamped onto an object; the adjustable jaws are widened or closed by turning a screw in the wrench's handle. Also known as Vise-Grips™.

long-nose pliers needle-nose pliers used to hold and manipulate wire, especially in tight spaces.

slip-joint pliers a metal pliers with jaws that are adjusted for size by means of a pivoting joint in its neck.

tongue-and-groove pliers long, straight-handled pliers with jaws that are adjusted by a pivot and a series of grooves.

wire cutters pliers with curved handles and jaws for cutting wire.

HAMMERS AND NAIL PULLERS

ball peen hammer a standard hammer with a rounded back surface instead of claws. Also known as a machinist's hammer.

brad driver a small, spring-loaded, screwdriverlike tool used to drive brads (tiny nails).

cat's paw a crowbarlike steel bar with a slotted tip for pulling up nails.

claw hammer the standard hammer with nail-pulling claws. Also known as a carpenter's hammer.

deadblow hammer a mallet with a head filled with shot to prevent rebounding.

engineer's hammer a very small sledgehammer.

mallet a wood-handled hammer having a cylindrical or square head made of wood, rubber, or plastic; it is used primarily to pound chisels and to manipulate metal.

maul a sledgehammer.

nail gun a gunlike apparatus that automatically drives nails without hammering.

nail set a thick, naillike shaft with a pointed tip, pounded with a hammer to countersink nails.

rip hammer a hammer having straight claws, used in flooring work.

sledgehammer a hammer with a long or short handle and a very heavy, oblong head for driving chisels, wedges, and spikes, and for demolition.

tack hammer a hammer with a square, narrow head that has been magnetized to hold tiny tacks and nails for driving.

tack puller a screwdriverlike tool with a clawed tip for prying out tacks.

SCREWDRIVERS

offset screwdriver an S-shaped screwdriver that is turned as a crank, used for getting at screws in tight spaces. Also known as a cranked screwdriver.

Phillips head screwdriver a common screwdriver with a cross or crisscross head, for use with Phillips head screws.

return spiral ratchet screwdriver a ratcheting screwdriver with a blade turned by pushing down on the handle.

screw-gripper screwdriver a screwdriver with a split blade for holding screws in place, for one-hand use.

spiral ratchet screwdriver a screwdriver with a ball-like handle and a ratcheting mechanism.

stubby a short screwdriver for use in tight spaces.

CUTTING TOOLS AND KNIVES

glass cutter a toothbrush-shaped metal tool with a notched head and a small cutting wheel, used for scoring and cutting glass.

hawk's bill snips tin snips used for cutting tight circles.

linoleum cutter a short, wood-handled knife with a hooked blade, used for cutting vinyl and linoleum flooring.

oilstone a stone made of aluminum oxide or silicon carbide, used to sharpen blades on. Also known as a whetstone, benchstone, sharpening stone, hone stone.

precision knife a pencillike metal knife with a small, triangular blade, used for cutting paper and other light materials. Also known as an Xacto™ knife.

razor knife a wooden or plastic handle with a slot for holding a razor blade.

tin snips heavy, metal shears used for cutting thin metals. Types of tin snips include aviation, duckbill, hawk's bill, and universal.

utility knife a hollow, metal handle with a retractable blade, used for cutting soft material, such as drywall or roofing products.

SAWS

azebiki a short, thin Japanese saw with a double-edged blade, for starting cuts in the middle of a panel or board.

backsaw a handsaw with a spined, rectangular blade with fine teeth, used for making precise cuts, especially when used with a miter box. Also known as a miter box saw.

band saw a large, stationary power saw with a blade in the configuration of a loop that continuously rotates through a table guide; used for making curving or elaborate cuts.

bayonet saw see RECIPROCATING SAW.

buck saw a large, bow-shaped handsaw with large teeth, used for cutting logs or branches.

circular saw a popular, high-speed power saw with a circular blade, used primarily for making straight cuts.

compass saw a small, fine-toothed hand saw with a curved handle and a long, thin blade (sometimes pointed), used for cutting holes and curves. Also known as a keyhole saw.

coping saw a small hand saw with a very short and narrow blade held in a U-shaped metal frame, used for making fine, precise, or decorative cuts. Also known as a fret saw or a scroll saw.

crosscut saw the most commonly used handsaw; it has a wood or plastic handle with a long, tapering toothed blade and is used for sawing wood across the grain.

dovetail saw a small backsaw with a small hand grip.

dozuki a thin, hatchetlike saw with very fine, sharp teeth, for cabinet work and for cutting joints such as dovetails.

hacksaw a hand saw with a fine-toothed blade, used for cutting metal or plastic.

hole saw a drill bit having a small cuplike saw blade, for making perfect holes.

jig saw See SABERSAW.

keyhole saw same as compass saw.

miter box a boxlike cutting guide having 45-degree and 90-degree cutting slots, for making perfect angle cuts.

pocket saw a flexible wire that has been coated with fine particles of tungsten carbide; it can be carried in a pocket, is used for rough cutting, and is popular with campers.

radial arm saw a circular saw mounted permanently in a stationary table; it is used for a variety of cuts and can be angled 90 degrees.

reciprocating saw an elongated, upright power saw used for cutting in tight spaces or for cutting through walls and nails at the same time, as in renovation work. Also known as a bayonet saw.

rip saw same as a crosscut saw but having teeth designed for cutting wood with or along the grain, such as down the length of a board.

ryoba a Japanese saw resembling a meatcutter's knife; its blade has teeth on both sides—one side for crosscutting and one side for ripping.

saber saw a portable power saw with a short, thin blade that bobs up and down, used for making elaborate cuts. Also known as a jigsaw.

table saw a stationary table in which a circular saw protrudes from a slot; wood is fed into the saw, unlike a radial arm saw.

veneer saw a small saw for cutting veneer or for making shallow cuts.

WEIGHTS AND MEASURES

astronomical unit (A.U.) the average distance of the Sun from the Earth, about 93,000,000 miles, a commonly used measurement of distance in astronomy.

bale a large bundle, such as cotton, weighing approximately 500 pounds.

board foot 144 cubic inches—12 inches by 12 inches by 1 inch.

bolt 40 yards, a measurement for fabric.

Btu British thermal unit. The amount of heat needed to raise the temperature of one pound of water one degree Fahrenheit.

carat 200 milligrams, for weighing precious stones.

chain 66 feet; 80 chains in a mile; a measurement used in surveying. Also known as Gunter's chain.

cubit an ancient unit of measurement, derived from the length of the forearm to the tip of the middle finger, approximately 17 to 22 inches.

decibel a unit of loudness, specifically the softest amount of change the human ear can detect.

freight ton as a measurement for mass cargo, the equivalent of 40 cubic feet of freight.

great gross 12 gross or 1,728.

gross 12 dozen or 144.

hand derived from the width of the hand, specifically 4 inches, as used to measure the height of horses.

hertz a unit of frequency equal to one cycle per second.

hogshead two liquid barrels; 14,653 cubic inches.

horsepower a unit of power equal to 745.7 watts; the power necessary to lift 33,000 pounds for a distance of one foot in one minute.

karat a measurement denoting the purity of gold, for example, 12 karat gold is

50% gold and 50% alloy; 24 karat gold is 100% pure gold.

knot a unit of speed equal to one nautical mile per hour, or about 1.15 statute miles per hour.

league a unit of distance equal to 3 miles.

light-year an astronomical unit of measurement, specifically the distance light travels in a year's time, about 5,880, 000,000,000 miles.

link a surveyor's unit of measurement equal to 0.01 chain or 7.92 inches.

magnum a 2-liter bottle.

nautical mile 6,076 feet or 1,852 meters.

parsec an astronomical unit of measurement equal to 3.26 light-years or 19.2 trillion miles.

pi the ratio of the circumference of a circle to its diameter, approximately 3.14159265.

pipe a unit for measuring liquids, the equivalent of 2 hogsheads.

ream a unit for measuring paper, the equivalent of 500 sheets.

roentgen a unit of radiation exposure produced by x-rays.

score a group of 20 units or items.

sounding a measured depth of water.

sound, speed of approximately 1,088 feet per second when measured at 32 degrees Fahrenheit at sea level; the speed varies according to altitude and temperature.

span a measuring unit derived from an outstretched hand, the equivalent of 9 inches or 22.86 centimeters.

square 100 square feet; used in construction.

stone in Great Britain, the equivalent of 14 pounds avoirdupois.

therm 100,000 Btus.

township a unit of measurement used in surveying, specifically the equivalent of 36 square miles.

tun 252 gallons, as used for measuring wine or other liquids.

ELECTRONICS

GENERAL ELECTRONIC TERMS

ampere a measure of electric current, specifically the number of electrons that flow by a given point each second. Also known as an amp.

brownout a drop in the amount of voltage running through a power line. Brownouts are known to cause damage to some electronic equipment.

capacitance the amount of electric charge a capacitor can store.

capacitor a device that stores an electric charge.

cathode-ray tube a type of vacuum tube in which an electron beam is focused electrostatically or electromagnetically onto a sensitized screen, forming a picture, as in a television set.

chip an integrated circuit.

circuit a closed pathway through which electricity can flow.

conductor any element through which electricity can freely flow.

current electricity; a flow of electrons through a conductive medium.

diode a device that permits electrons to pass in only one direction.

doping adding an impurity, such as phosphorus, to semiconducting silicon, to alter its conducting properties.

electrode any of the elements in a transistor that emits or controls the movement of electrons.

electron a subatomic particle with a negative charge.

farad a unit of capacitance.

germanium a semiconducting material used in making electronic components.

ground a large, conducting body, such as the earth, to which an electrical circuit is connected to prevent cables from picking up noise or emitting radio frequency interference.

henry the unit of inductance in which the variation of current at one ampere per second induces an electromotive force of one volt.

hole an area where no electron is present on the crystal of a P-type semiconductor; it acts as a positive charge.

impedance a measure of the opposition to the flow of current in an alternating-current circuit.

inductance the measure of a magnetic field generated by current passing through an inductor.

inductor a wire coil that stores energy in the form of a magnetic field.

insulator any material through which electricity cannot flow. Opposite of a conductor.

integrated circuit a conglomeration of transistors and other electronic components on a silicon wafer.

junction on a transistor or a diode, the area where opposite types of semiconductor elements meet.

LED an acronym for light-emitting diode, as used in lighted calculator displays.

N-type a region of a semiconductor that has been treated (doped) with an impurity to create free negative charges.

ohm a measurement of electrical resistance, equal to the resistance of a conductor carrying one ampere of current at a potential difference of one volt between the terminals.

P-type a region of a semiconductor that has been treated with an impurity to create holes (an absence of electrons), which act as positive charges.

resistance a measure of how difficult it is for electricity to flow through a component, measured in ohms.

resistor a device used to introduce resistance into an electrical circuit.

semiconductor any element that is both a poor conductor and a poor insulator, such as silicon.

series two or more components connected end to end so that the same current flows through each component.

silicon the most widely used semiconductor material; it goes into the manufacture of transistors, diodes, integrated circuits, and other components.

solid state electronic components with no moving parts.

transistor a miniature electronic component that controls and amplifies electric current; it is composed of a layer of semiconducting material sandwiched between two opposing layers of semiconducting material.

vacuum tube a glass tube from which all air has been removed and containing electrodes between which current may be passed.

volt a unit of electromotive force.

watt a unit of power.

COMPUTERS

acoustic coupler a modem that attaches to a telephone handset to transmit computer information over telephone lines.

address refers to the specific location of a piece of data in a computer's memory.

ALGOL Algorithmic Language. Originating in 1963, a programming language characterized by blocks of statements, now nearly obsolete.

algorithm a set of specific, sequenced directions illustrating how to perform a task or solve a problem; a computer program.

ALU Arithmetic/Logic Unit. In the central processing unit, the component that carries out arithmetic and logic functions.

analog computer a computer in which numerical data is represented by analogous quantities, such as variable voltage. See DIGITAL COMPUTER.

antidote any program designed to protect a computer from being infected with a virus.

archival storage any medium, such as tape cartridges, disks, or diskettes (floppy disks) used to store computer information.

array a collection of related data stored under one name.

artificial intelligence creative computer intelligence, as in solving problems by thinking as the human brain does rather than by mindlessly spitting out numbers and data; the highest form of computer intelligence.

BASIC a simple computer language in which line numbers precede each statement, popularly used by students and microcomputer owners.

baud a measurement, in bits per second, of the time it takes a computer to transfer data.

BBS Bulletin Board Service. A central computer system that can be accessed over the telephone to relay data to a remote computer or to exchange messages with other computer users.

bells and whistles sales jargon for any unnecessary gadgetry or features on a computer.

bidirectional printer a printer that can print with its print head moving backward or forward over a page.

bit short for binary digit, the smallest unit of information, represented by either a 1 or a 0.

blue affectionate nickname for an IBM computer, named after Big Blue.

board a printed circuit board.

boot to start up a computer.

bootstrap a brief program that gets a computer started.

buffer an area of memory that temporarily holds incoming or outgoing data.

bug a mistake in a computer program.

bus the connections or wires through which information is relayed to all of a computer's components.

byte 8 bits of memory space.

cache a data storage area that can be accessed quickly.

CAD acronym for Computer-Aided Design.

CAM acronym for Computer-Aided Manufacturing.

card a printed circuit board.

cartridge a medium for storing programs.

catalog a list of a disk's contents.

CD-Rom Compact Disk Read Only Memory. A compact disk (similar to the audio disk version) that stores huge volumes of computer information coded into it by the manufacturer.

chip an integrated circuit.

chiphead a computer enthusiast.

clone an imitation; it refers to a computer brand that imitates another computer brand or model.

COBOL an easy-to-read program for business data processing.

compatibles any same-brand or competitive-brand computers or components that can work together.

CPU Central Processing Unit. The part of a computer that executes directions and performs arithmetic and logic functions.

crash any condition in which a computer malfunctions or stops operating.

Cray a family of state-of-the-art supercomputers manufactured by Cray Research, Inc.

CRT Cathode Ray Tube; a computer screen or TV screen.

cursor on a computer screen or monitor, the symbol that points out where the next typed-in character will appear.

cyberphobe one who has an aversion to computers.

data base a computer catalog of information.

data communication the passing of data from one computer to another.

DDT a debugging program.

debug to work the bugs out of or remove the mistakes from a computer program.

desktop publishing the use of computer-generated typesetting and graphics to create newsletters, reports, books, and so forth.

digital computer a computer in which quantities are represented by digits electronically, as distinguished from an analog.

computer most modern computers are digital computers.

disk a medium, either built-in or independent, that stores computer information.

disk drive the device that gives a computer the ability to read and write information on disks.

DOS Disk Operating System.

dot matrix printer a printer that prints characters as a pattern of dots.

down refers to a malfunctioning or inoperable computer.

download to transfer information from a main computer to a smaller computer or a remote computer.

DRAM Dynamic Random Access Memory.

editor a program that allows the user to add, delete, or change information in a file or program.

E mail electronic mail. Messages sent between different computer terminals.

ENIAC Electronic Numerical Integrator and Calculator, the first electronic computer, composed of some 18,000 vacuum tubes, and built in the 1940s.

EPROM a memory chip that can be erased by exposing it to ultraviolet light.

expert system a computer program using a form of artificial intelligence drawn from an extensive knowledge base and an inference engine.

floppy disk a small disk of magnetic film used for storing computer data.

flowchart a chart composed of characters and words to help guide a user through an algorithm.

font a group of type characters in one style, such as boldface or italics.

FORTRAN FORmula TRANslation, a programming language developed in the 1950s.

GIGO acronym for Garbage In, Garbage Out, referring to the fact that poor information fed into the computer always results in poor information coming out.

hack to program computers as a pastime. Also, to break into the computers of others without authorization. Also, to commit pranks with a computer.

hacker one who hacks; a computer enthusiast.

hard card a hard disk in the shape of a card.

hard copy a paper printout of computer data.

hard disk an information storage medium in the form of a built-in, nonremovable platter. Also known as a Winchester disk.

hardware the physical components of a computer system, such as the terminal, the monitor, the integrated circuits, as distinguished from software.

hash useless information.

host a master unit in a computer network.

hygiene collective term for measures taken to prevent a computer from being infected with a virus.

ink-jet printer a printer that forms type characters with dots of ink.

integrated circuit a conglomeration of tiny transistors and other components on a silicon wafer less than ¼-inch square. Also known as a chip.

ISDN Integrated Services Digital Network, an all-digital telephone line that transmits digital data and voice without a modem.

K short for kilobyte, the equivalent of approximately 1,024 bytes. Each kilobyte memory unit is capable of storing 1,024 characters.

kilobyte same as K.

laptop a portable, battery-operated computer that can be operated on one's lap while traveling.

laser printer a printer that uses a laser beam to produce characters and images that are transferred to paper electrostatically.

LCD Liquid Crystal Display, as employed on portable computers.

letter quality refers to the high-quality type print produced by some computer printers, as distinguished from poorer-quality dot matrix.

light pen an instrument used to manipulate or change pictures on a computer screen.

LISP List Processor, a programming language characterized by its prolific use of lists and parentheses and used in handling complex data, such as that involved in artificial intelligence.

load to pass information on a disk to a computer.

LOGO a simplified programming language used to familiarize children with computers.

log on to sign in with a computer and identify oneself as an authorized user.

mainframe computer a large computer that can be set up to serve as many as 500 users at one time.

MB megabyte, the equivalent of 1,024 kilobytes or 1,048,576 bytes. As a unit of memory, it can store over 1 million characters.

memory where data is stored in a computer; the core.

memory chips add-on memory in the form of RAM chips.

menu a list of options appearing on screen in a program.

micro a prefix standing for one-millionth, as in one-millionth of a second or microsecond.

microcomputer a small computer intended for one user at a time, as a home computer, and characterized by a central processing unit (CPU) composed of only one integrated circuit called a microprocessor.

microprocessor a computer central processing unit composed of only one chip or integrated circuit.

MIDI Musical Instrument Digital Interface, used to transfer musical data between electronic instruments or between an electronic instrument and a computer.

minicomputer a computer that is smaller than a mainframe but larger than a microcomputer.

modem short for modulator-demodulator, a device that enables computers to communicate with other computers over telephone lines.

monitor the TV-like screen that shows the computer input and output.

mouse a small, external input device connected to a computer by a wire; moving a mouse moves the cursor on a computer screen, useful for selecting commands without having to type them in.

MS-DOS short for Microsoft Disk Operating System.

multitasking running more than one program in the same computer at the same time.

nano a prefix for one-billionth, as in a nanosecond.

network several computers linked together.

nibble half of a byte.

number cruncher slang for any computer used largely for carrying out highly complex numerical calculations. Also, the programmer involved in this work.

PASCAL a popular, general-purpose programming language for use with microcomputers.

password a secret word that must be logged in to the computer in order to authorize use.

PC short for personal computer.

peripheral any device that connects to a computer, such as a terminal, a disk drive, a printer.

plotter a computer-controlled device that draws pictures on paper.

port any connection through which information enters or leaves a computer.

program instructions to a computer.

programmer one who writes instructions for a computer.

PROLOG a programming language used for writing logic programs.

PROM short for Programmable Read Only Memory; computer memory that cannot be erased or reprogrammed.

RAM short for Random Access Memory, a computer's main memory store, from which all information can be located roughly within the same amount of time.

ROM short for read only memory, a chip containing manufacturer-installed information that cannot be erased or changed.

scanner a computer device that reads printed or handwritten pages.

scrolling the downward and/or upward movement of text on a computer screen.

semiconductor a material, such as silicon, that is both a poor conductor and a poor insulator. Semiconductor devices include diodes, transistors, and chips.

silicon the nonmetallic, silica-based element used in the manufacture of semiconductors.

Silicon Valley the area outside of San Francisco where a large number of computer-related firms are located.

software the nonphysical components of a computer system, such as programming information.

spike an abnormal surge of electricity, sometimes caused by a lightning strike, that can damage a computer.

spreadsheet a spreadsheet program, specifically any calculations based on rows and columns of numbers.

store to commit data to a computer's memory.

supercomputer a computer with more power or speed than a typical mainframe computer.

surge protector a device that protects a computer from a spike.

tape magnetic tape, similar to that used in a tape recorder, that can be used to store computer information; it is a cheaper memory storage medium than a disk, but accessing its information usually takes much longer.

tape drive a device that enables data on magnetic tape to be transmitted via signals to a computer.

terminal collective term for the keyboard and CRT or TV screen portion of a computer.

timesharing a method of running multiple programs on a computer at the same time.

tractor feed on a printer, the moving, toothed gears that propel paper forward.

trap door a programming gap inserted intentionally as a means of bypassing security and gaining access to the program at a later date.

turtle in some computer graphics systems, an imaginary turtle that moves about the computer screen and draws patterns on command.

upload to transfer data from a small or remote computer to a large or central computer.

user-friendly refers to any computer program that is easy to use.

vaccine any program designed to protect a computer from being infected with a virus.

virus a prank program that disrupts computer operations by erasing, adding, or altering information and by making copies of itself and infecting other programs.

wallpaper slang for any long printout.

window on a computer screen, a superimposed square or rectangle containing commands or other information

worm a rigged program that makes endless copies of itself and disrupts computer functioning. Similar to a virus.

zap slang term meaning to erase information.

ROBOTICS (*Also see* COMPUTERS)

actuator a servo mechanism.

AGV automated guided vehicle.

algorithm a series of programmable steps used to solve a mathematically based problem.

android a robot having a humanlike form, as distinguished from a boxlike robot or an industrial robot arm.

artificial intelligence any form of computer intelligence, but specifically higher functioning, such as thought, judgment, perception, creativity.

automation a mechanical system that automatically controls its own tasks.

automaton robot

BASIC a computer language popularly used on home computers.

bionics artificial organs or other human parts designed to replace real parts.

bugs errors in software.

CAD computer-aided design.

CAM computer-aided manufacture.

Cartesian coordinates a system that defines an object's position; that is, an X coordinate (left to right) along one dimension, a Y coordinate (front to back) along another, and a Z coordinate indicating up and down. A robot arm capable of moving along these coordinates.

CIAM computerized, integrated, and automated manufacturing.

cybernetics the science of communications and control as they apply to complex machines and living organisms.

cyborg in science fiction, a human equipped with bionic parts.

degrees of freedom the distance or amount a robot arm is capable of moving along any dimension, for example, up, down, left, right, cylindrically.

drive system the power plant and components that enable a robot to move.

droid a robot programmed to cause no harm to humans, a popular device used in science fiction.

end effectors devices or tools, such as drills, saws, screwdrivers, grippers, attached to the end of a robot arm to perform different tasks.

feedback refers to a robot's ability to sense external stimuli and respond to it.

first-generation robot a deaf, dumb, and blind robot; an early model with no sensory ability.

fixed-stop robot a simple robot in which motion is controlled by a series of mechanical stops.

gripper a hand or manipulator used for grasping; an end effector.

hard automation a low-tech form of automation that can be altered only by shutting down the system and changing its physical components. See SOFT AUTOMATION.

hardware the mechanical parts and electronic components of a computer or automation system, as distinguished from software or programming.

humanoid any robot similar to a human in appearance or behavior.

interface a mechanical connection between two components, say a computer and a robot arm.

joystick control a stick moved by an operator to control a robot's motions.

manipulator the arm or hand of an industrial robot.

menu a list of possible motions of a robot, used by an operator in programming tasks.

pick-and-place robot a simple form of robot consisting of an arm that transfers objects from one place to another.

point-to-point control programming a robot's arm movement along a series of points.

program a series of computer commands processed in binary language of 0's and 1's to control a robot's actions.

programmable robot a robot that can be programmed and reprogrammed to perform various tasks.

proximity sensor a device that senses position and distance of objects.

PUMA programmable universal machine for assembly; commercial name for a widely used manufacturing robot arm.

resolution refers to a robot's accuracy at placing its end effectors within the desired parameters.

revolute coordinate robot a robot arm jointed at the shoulder, elbow, and wrist.

second-generation robot a robot equipped with sensory apparatus allowing it to react to visual, auditory, or tactile stimuli.

sensor any detection device used to sense temperature, moisture, radiation, light, distance, motion.

servo mechanism an actuator or motor and a feedback device that conduct accurate movement and correct any deviation in intended movement. Also called a servo motor.

soft automation an automated system that can be altered or modified by software programming. See hard automation.

software a computer program, as distinguished from hardware.

syntaxeur a machine used to teach a robot a series of movements by driving a control device through the same motions.

telechiric device a robot hand or arm manipulated by an operator from a remote location.

teleoperated any machine or robot arm controlled from a remote location by an operator.

telepresence manipulating a mechanical arm or hand and receiving stimulus or feedback from it while in a remote location.

third-generation robot a robot having a high form of artificial intelligence, for example, the ability to make decisions on its own.

work envelope the collective area within which a robot arm can reach and work.

wrist articulation the ability of a robot wrist to bend up and down, turn side-to-side, and rotate.

yaw side-to-side movement of a robot arm.

Index

About the Author

MARC MCCUTCHEON is the author of *The Compass in Your Nose and Other Astonishing Facts About Humans*, *Experts: The Media Contacts Directory*, and *The Writer's Guide to Everyday Life in the 1800s.* He is also a freelance writer and a frequent contributor to magazines such as *Omni*, *Science Digest*, *American Health*, and others. He lives in South Portland, Maine.